Schmick's
    Mahican Dictionary

Schmick, Schmeck, Schmiegg, and partly *Schmieg(e)*, from Wendish *smějk* 'laugh'; with *Schmich*, from Czech *smich* 'laugh'; some possible influence of German *Schmicke* 'whiplash.'

Cover symbols
    Three clans—turtle, bear, wolf
    The four or eight directions, leading to, *arrow,* the following:
    Recent symbols for the four or eight directions and the center from which people and plants grow

Back-cover symbols
    Three clans—bear, wolf, turtle (Ken Mynter, 1967)
    Fish-shaped wooden club with iron blade (Stockbridge, pre-1800, about 56 cm)
    Turtle pendant (Turtle Island = North America)
    Beadwork decorations (recent)
    Thunderbird from facial tattoos on Etow Oh Koam, a Mahican about 1710
    Four-directions shield with feathers

Title letter style
    Arnold Bocklin Berthold Fototype

Schmick's Mahican Dictionary

EDITED

by CARL MASTHAY

―――――――――

with a Mahican historical phonology

MEMOIRS OF THE
AMERICAN PHILOSOPHICAL SOCIETY
Held at Philadelphia
For Promoting Useful Knowledge
Volume 197

© American Philosophical Society 1991

Mahican Historical Phonology, copyright © David H. Pentland, 1991

All rights reserved. No part of this publication may be
reproduced, stored in a retrieval system, or transmitted,
in any form or by any means, electronic, mechanical,
photocopying, recording or otherwise, without
prior written permission from the publisher.

Printed in the United States of America

Library of Congress Catalog Card Number 86-90530
ISBN: 0-87169-197-3
US ISSN: 0065-9738

In Quinnipiac, the extinct language of my homeland (1658):

To all mankind for 500 years . . . . Re wame rènnawawk wutche antseunganak re antsúnganak*

To Shirley Norrie, my buoyantly cheerful sister . . . . Wówerríewunk quah pompawoytammowunk ke-rakque†

☆ my mother, Anna Marie Bartusiewicz Masthay . . . . Attarwejanúnguesóunk wewâuhtâuwunganak-terre‡

☆ the Fields family–Janet, the mother, Terry Birch, Cynthia, Tracy Scott, and especially Michelle Amber Fields, who shaped a different future . . . . M.A.F.: Kowômarrush michéme youh mittâukuk-terre.§

☆ Josephine Palazzo, who also saw Schmick's manuscript with me in 1975 in Philadelphia

☆ Rebecca Burns, in the never-ending expanse illegible

★ 𝕮𝖆𝖗𝖔𝖑𝖊 𝕬𝖓𝖓 𝕭𝖆𝖚𝖊𝖗, *sparkling catalyst*

Schmick útteranjemen ewo útteoitammewunk spe wuskw<u>h</u>oshitten ewo uttuwâwungansh youh wuskwhêgannak-terre, ne ren hom naumen, okkekkenâumen, quah waughtaun.¶

In memoriam
of our former woods
at Pratt's Corner,
Southington,
Connecticut

---

*Quiripi (Quinnipiac): 'To all mankind from age to age.'
†'Happiness and pleasure to you.'
‡Polish: *'Sława w zrozumienie,'* or 'glory in understanding.'
§Or in Mahican: *'Nia ktachwahnan gommáwe nannò ahkēĕk.'*
¶'Schmick reveals his will by causing his words to be written in this book, that man may see, read, and understand.' [*h* for error *k*?] (p. 30 in Pierson, 1658, my adaptation; Pierson's *ewo*, 'he,' for 'his' + unmarked affix may be bad grammar)

ACKNOWLEDGMENTS CHRONOLOGICALLY

I wish to thank

Ives Goddard (Smithsonian Institution, Washington, D.C.)
for some linguistic help and direction

Gordon M. Day (Ottawa, Ontario)
serene and caring, and I patterned my book after his in part

Dorothy Davids (Stoughton, Wisconsin)
for her referral to her sister Bernice and wish for a "grammar"

Bernice Miller Pigeon (Bowler, Wisconsin)
for patience with my initial unending letters and for just being

Nora Thompson Dean (Dewey, Oklahoma)
for her immense help with Delaware and delightful, clear letters (sorrow for her death on November 29, 1984)

Kenneth Mynter (Claverack, New York)
for Mahican culture and letter friendship

Emily Johnson (Thamesville, Ontario)
a cheerful Munsee speaker who helped on untranslated Mahican words (sorrow for her death on February 10, 1985)

Frank T. Siebert, Jr. (Old Town, Maine)
the old pro, scholar of Penobscot, and the one who gave me the most courage for these rigors, Schmick insights, and various warnings

Jane Warne (Montréal, Québec)
for her scholarly initiation into Schmick

Thomas L. Markey (Ann Arbor, Michigan)
for the Germanic feeling and his encouragement

David H. Pentland (Winnipeg, Manitoba)
for his immensely valuable criticism with copious comments and notes, veritable support, and writing of the phonology

Howard Tate (Ferguson, Missouri)
for his genius in repairing my always imperfect IBM "Selectric" Composer machine

Patrick A. Clifford (St. Louis, Missouri)
as president of The C.V. Mosby Company for his encouragement in my project and for his Indian interests

My thanks for comments from
  John Rokusek
  Eugenia Klein
  Alison Miller
  Kathleen Burmann
  Mark Spann
  Gail Hudson
  Susan Lane
  Ginny Douglas

Contents

Two-page copy of Schmick's entire manuscript, x and xi (Frontispiece)
Background and explanatory description, 1
    Description of Schmick's two-volume manuscript, 10
    Pronunciation, 12
    Postscript, 13
Mahican historical phonology
    Condensed key to paragraphs, 14
    Key to help find specific Schmick pronunciations, 14
    Mahican historical phonology, 15
    Footnotes and References, 27
Schmick's Mahican dictionary, 29
    Abbreviations of sources used, 30
    English-Mahican-German section (from *Vocabularium Mahicandicum*), 31
        Long sentences or related texts that were split up for dictionary examples, 154
        No translation given in German, 155
            Original order of words, 155
            Alphabetical order of words with speculative translation, 155
            Untranslated "biblical" exhortative text on ms. p. (366), 156
    Schmick manuscript p. (366) (a copy), 157
    Original manuscript p. (102) with facing comment, 158 and 159
    Original manuscript p. (375) part concerning **pānnäkékäck,** 159
Mahican-English glossary and index, 161
Decorative words, 188

Figures

Fig. 1. Dialect areas of Prussia, 6
Fig. 2. Territory of Mahican and Mahican confederacy, 7
Fig. 3. Algonquian language relationships, 8
Fig. 4. The four Paugussett tribes and their territories about 1630 A.D., 187

Preface

Schmick's Mahican Dictionary, a modern reworking of the manuscript of Johann Jacob Schmick, is in the "Moravian" dialect of Mahican and is divided into an English-Mahican-German section and a Mahican-English section. It includes a Mahican historical phonology and a background and explanatory description.

It was in the American Philosophical Society Library in Philadelphia that I first saw Schmick's bound, two-volume manuscript of the Mahican language, or as he called it *Vocabularium Mahicandicum* (or on its title page *Miscellanea linguae nationis Indicae Mahikan dictae, curā susceptā ā Joh. Jac. Schmick*). This language was once used in the western part of my native Connecticut, western Massachusetts, western Vermont, and eastern New York State. It seemed strange to me that such an important work lay unseen, unused, perhaps unknown, and certainly unpublished. Later I came to understand that indeed it was known to a few Algonquianists, including Frank T. Siebert, Jr., who had handcopied it long ago.

Thus in that library I soon knew what I should do: work on it and publish it. The two-volume manuscript was not on microfilm, another surprise considering again its importance. Since I was not a truly qualified worker in Algonquian linguistics and did not expect the library to respond to my request for microfilming, I asked Bernice Miller Pigeon, the principal "gatherer" for the Stockbridge-Munsee Historical Library Museum, of Bowler, Wisconsin, to request the microfilming of Schmick's manuscript because Mahican was an ancestral language of the Stockbridge-Munsees, and she had it done.

The years passed as I worked up each stage from the illegible hidden script to the splendid, clear printed words—an endeavor of great tedium and some frustration, but during that time I also received comfort and support from scholars and Indians in distant cities in the United States and Canada. Through their enduring lectures, advice, suggestions, and elucidations I came to feel the life that still pulsed in that dead language—new patterns still to be seen or surmised. William Cowan, of Ottawa, was the first to state that I had an obvious interest in Algonquian languages; Gordon Day, also of Ottawa, helped me find Wampanóag materials and from there feel comfortable in the friendships formed at annual Algonquian conferences meeting in city after city; Ives Goddard, of the Smithsonian Institution, who first wanted someone to work up a Mahican dictionary early on helped me feel as though I could be of use in his backyard linguistic turf; fatherly Frank Siebert, of Old Town, Maine, kept me from going off the deep end with uncertainties or too much romanticism or inspired me with a little more independence.

But it was David Pentland, of Winnipeg, an Algonquianist who thoroughly plowed through my work, wrenching out etymological improprieties, and writing up a precise treatise on Mahican historical phonology for this book—a task he agreeably and willingly assumed 4 years before its completion.

Up to the camera-ready acetate-sheet stage I personally completed all steps. The compositing was done on my obsolescent IBM "Selectric" Composer at great expense, including machine breakdowns, fixed by Howard Tate. Thus major typesetting costs for the publisher were avoided, and I could work as I wished, generally once a year for a couple of meticulously spent months, stage by stage.

This dictionary has prevented the loss of another iceberg peak of Algonquian culture from rapidly melting away and is for the scholarly reuse or even resurrection of *our own* ancient and obscure languages. *Schmick's Mahican Dictionary* is useful for Indians of the East Coast who want to know their ancestral languages better, for of course Algonquianists, whether as linguists or ethnohistorians, for Germanists, and for general readers who want some background on Schmick's era in Pennsylvania. The explanatory background can also be used as a study of linguistic influences.

Carl David Masthay
St. Louis, Missouri, 1986

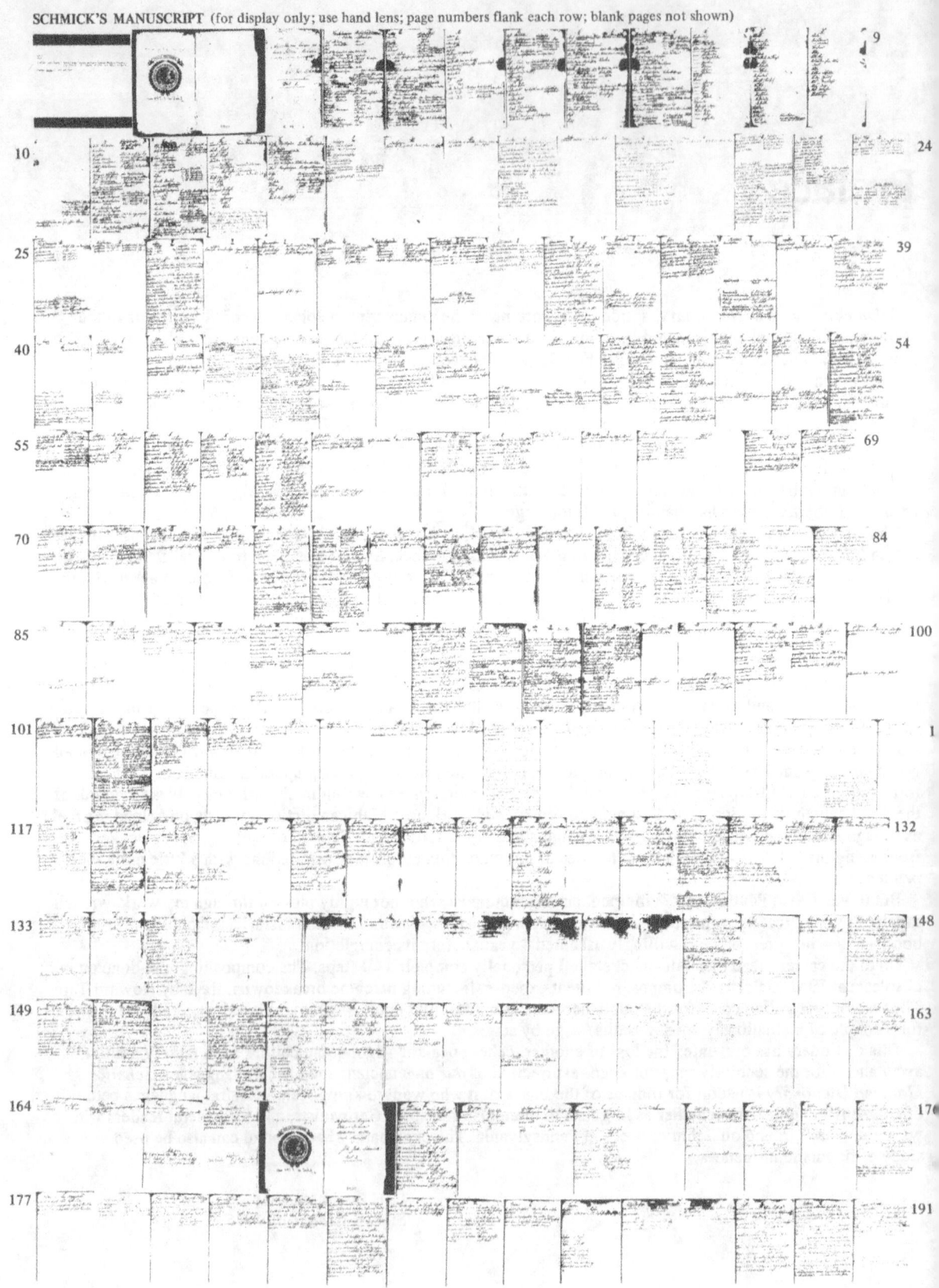

SCHMICK'S MANUSCRIPT (for display only; use hand lens; page numbers flank each row; blank pages not shown)

x

Toonpaooh　　Muchquauh　　Mechchaooh

[túnpau]　　[móhkw^{ah}]　　[mḗəxčáu]

Turtle　　*Bear*　　*Wolf*

(Mahican clans)

BACKGROUND AND EXPLANATORY DESCRIPTION
FOR THIS MAHICAN DICTIONARY

Ramblings in the background

Frozen dead words are all that exist of the corpus of the Mahican (/məˈhēkən/) language. Only two or three words are known by some Stockbridge-Munsees of Bowler, Wisconsin, the descendants of the once-powerful Mahicans of eastern New York (hard by the once ferocious Iroquoian Mohawks) and of western Massachusetts and northwestern Connecticut. This is the language of the Mahicans (*Muhheakunneyuk* [Ruttenber] 'those dwelling on the great tidewater'), the Algonquian people made famous in James Fenimore Cooper's novel *The Last of the Mohicans* (1826), literarily fusing Mahicans and Mohegans.

As Brasser (1974) writes:[1]

Adriaen Block (1614) and later colonial authorities usually referred to the tribe as "Mahicans," "Mahikanders," and similar names. It is possible that these names resulted from the early Dutch use of Delaware or Munsee Indian interpreters from coastal New Netherland, who pronounced the tribe's name as *Mauheekunee, Mahiˈkanak, Mà·hí·kan, Mà·hí·kani·w.*

Following the practice of the Algonquin Indians [in Québec and Ontario], the early French sources refer to the Mahican as "wolves," either in French: "Loups," or in Algonquin: "*Maïngan*," "*Mahingan,*" etc. By 1662 the name "Loups" began to lose its specificity, and was used to refer to several tribes in New England and New York State. The close resemblance of the colonial New York names and the Algonquin appellation appears to be at the root of the common misconception that the Hudson River Mahican referred to themselves as "Wolves" [even though one of their three clans was the Wolf clan]. The Mahican tribe is not to be confused with the Mohegan of coastal Connecticut. These tribes were not related to each other, as was formerly thought, although their tribal names have been subject to the same mistake in translation. [Italics and bracketed words mine.]

¤ The true meaning of the <u>southeastern</u> Connecticut "Mohegan" whether from the Mohegan self-designation *Mahí·ks* (1902) and Pequot *Moheges* (1762; cf. Pequot *mucks*, 'wolf') or from *Mmooyauhegunnewuck* [Mm?] (1786), *Moyanhegunnewog* (1749), and *Mohanhegumewog* [error?] or related to Penobscot (in Maine) *Mauhigaˈnewak*, 'people of the mouth of the river where it opens out into a harbor' (Speck, 1928) is too <u>uncertain</u>, even when the Penobscot word appears to align with that for <u>northwestern</u> Connecticut and New York Mahican (*Muhheakunneyuk; Muhhekaneok,* 1788), 'those of the great tide water.' ¤

---

[1] Brasser, T.J.: *Riding on the frontier's crest: Mahican Indian culture and culture change*, no. 13, Ottawa, 1974, National Museums of Canada.

Here compiled is the first Mahican and English dictionary. It is based on the Moravian variety or dialect of Mahican, *circa* 1755, as opposed to the Stockbridge dialect recorded in Wisconsin as late as 1914 by Michelson and 1935 and 1937 by Siebert.

Although a Mahican-English set of cards (about 6100) written by Swadesh sits in the American Philosophical Society Library in Philadelphia, no dictionary exists.

A plea by Dorothy Davids of Stoughton, Wisconsin, and her sister Bernice Miller Pigeon of the Stockbridge-Munsee Historical Library Museum in Bowler for someone to write a Mahican grammar made me search first for vocabularies and "dictionaries" to provide the necessary foundation for such a grammar.

Mahican was an important language because its speakers were at one time in a relatively dominant leading position in New England and New York. With such an importance, it is a wonder that a work like this was not published earlier as had been done for Massachusett (Natick), Delaware, and Narragansett.

Ives Goddard of the Smithsonian Institution in one of his published works once commented that sufficient Mahican materials existed for the compilation of a dictionary. Of course, this dictionary covers only a part of those materials.

I grew up in Southington, Connecticut, on a picturesque farm with woods through which I would walk and wonder about the speech of the ancient inhabitants there who had been pushed away so long ago by an alien wave of distant peoples, with whom I am bound. Back then, in driving through the vast former Algonquian-speaking region of America and seeing road signs of river and town names with often unmanageable un-European letter patterns, I grew curious as to what they meant and then what their makers saw when they made the names, how they felt when they used their language or languages, and how they felt when they were being overwhelmed. Their remnants are spread up to a thousand miles away from their original homelands, with these rare few still living in New York, Massachusetts, Connecticut, and Wisconsin and traces in Ontario and maybe Kansas.

This dictionary is thus my effort for the Stockbridge-Munsees especially and the Algonquians and other Indians in general. I wanted to be the person (white and of Polish descent) to give a certain group of original Americans something that they are losing steadily and something that I know to be hidden in the depths of libraries, unreachable not only because of the complexity of modern ways and scattered sources but also because the major Mahican word source was hidden in another incomprehensible and illegible medium—German clothed in its old hand-written script based on fraktur. Since I already had such qualifications, I used them to break the moldy shell of German, its difficult hand-written script, and some Latin, all of which explained the old sentences and words in Mahican and left them an obscure, ugly jumble that is simply unworkable and unusable to original-American eyes. Now we may scan smoothly, with the only difficulty being the ready comprehension of the inner working of the language itself, which I have perhaps superficially tried to exhibit by culling together the Mahican word, phrase, or sentence for each similar concept that matches its English equivalent. Although the main section of this book explains little grammar, such patterns may be discernible in a short while because I have followed Schmick's heavy usage of verb paradigms and even some noun groupings and have extended his method to some other parts of speech.

Except for the numerals and bracketed notes, this dictionary is based wholly on *Miscellanea linguae nationis Indicae Mahikan dictae, curā susceptā ā Joh[ann] Jac[ob] Schmick* (translation: 'Miscellaneous [words] of the language of the Indian nation called Mahican, with the work undertaken by Johann Jacob Schmick'), the two volumes of which were probably begun about 1753, compiled until 1755, and then added to for several years, possibly to 1767, by Schmick, who, according to Brinton, "was a Moravian missionary, born in 1714, died 1778" and who "acquired the Mohegan dialect among the converts at Gnadenhütten." Gnadenhütten (German for 'huts or tents of grace') was first "settled in 1746 by Moravian Mahicans from Shecomeco and Scatticook on the north side of Mahoning creek . . . about the present Lehighton, Carbon Co., Pa. In 1754 it was abandoned for a new village, called New Gnadenhütten, on the site of Weissport, Carbon Co., Pa. Delawares and Mahicans occupied the village together. Soon after removing here the old village was burned by hostile Indians in 1755, and the new place was for a time deserted." [2] This village was inhabited until 1772.

Further evidence from the manuscript is that Schmick was in Pennsylvania (rather than northwestern Connecticut) because he mentions on ms. p. (151) the names Nazareth, Bethlehem, and Shekomeko (pronounced /she-ko-mé-ko/, but now often with shifted accent /she-kóm-e-ko/), all villages in the future state of Pennsylvania. Since he wrote on p. (151) the German phrase Da kommen Chekomker, Nazarether, Bethlehem[er?], he had to be in a village other than those three. Thus this passage shows that Schmick compiled his manuscript sometime between 1753 and 1755 (with 1751 and 1752 being too early), when he was in the first and second Gnadenhüttens, since he was only a short while in Wyoming, Pa., in 1755 and took refuge in Bethlehem after January 1, 1756, when Gnadenhütten was burned. (See his life outline later.) He may have completed it in Friedenshütten possibly by 1767. Schmick's Mahican informant was almost certainly Joshua, Sr., a convert.

---

[2] From Hodge, F.W.: *Handbook of the American Indians*, 1907; Totowa, N.J., 1975 reprint, Rowman & Littlefield.

[3] From Donehoo, G.P.: *A history of Indian villages and place names in Pennsylvania*, Harrisburg, Pa., 1928, The Telegraph Press.

Gnadenhütten

Because of the importance of the village of Gnadenhütten to Schmick's work, I include the following more detailed excerpt from Donehoo [3] with my bracketed information and italics:

GNADENHUETTEN. "Tents of Grace." There were five villages of this name, founded by the Moravian Church, and occupied by the Indian converts; *First* the village near the mouth of Mahoning Creek, Carbon County, at the site of Lehighton. This village was commenced in the spring of 1746, and was occupied by the Christian Indians from Shecomeco, who had found a temporary home at Bethlehem. The mission prospered under the influence of Martin Mack and his helpers. Various tracts of land had been purchased by the Moravian Church, until in 1754 there were 1382 acres in the mission tract, on both sides of the Lehigh. In 1747 a grist mill was built on the Mahoning. A saw mill and black-smith shop were added to the settlement. In 1749 Bishop Cammerhoff dedicated the chapel. Various additions were made to the population from Pachgatgoch, Wcchquadnach and Meniolágoméka [meaning 'a rich spot of land surrounded by barren lands'; Heckewelder in Donehoo], from 1747 to 1754. In May 1754 the mission was transferred to the east side of the river, to the site of Weissport. This was the *second* Gnadenhuetten. In Dec. 1754 the mission numbered 137 Mohickon and Delawares, besides the converts living at Wyoming and Nescopeck. The entire village had been invited to remove to Wyoming, through the influence of Tedyuskung. In April 1754, 70 converts removed to Wyoming—fifteen of these afterwards removed to Nescopeck. The chapel at the second Gnadenhuetten was dedicated in 1754. At this time the defeat of Washington at the Great Meadows, and the conflict for the possession of the Ohio, was drawing many of the Delaware and Shawnee to the French influence. The defeat of Braddock in 1755 led to the open hostility of the Delaware and the Shawnee, who then commenced to make raids upon the settlements. The massacre at Penn's Creek and other acts of hostility aroused the white settlers throughout the entire frontier to a bitter hatred of the Indians. The mission at Gnadenhuetten was in [the] charge of Mack, Grube, *Schmick* and Schebosh. These lived on the east side of the Lehigh, with the Indian converts. Many of the buildings were on the Mahoning. Anna Senseman, Gottlieb Anders, Martin Nitschmann and other Moravian helpers lived on the Mahoning. On the 24th. of November Zeisberger reached Gnadenhuetten, on the Lehigh, and was getting ready to go to the Mahoning, when Mack tried to persuade him to remain. But Zeisberger was determined to go on. He was fording the Lehigh when he heard the cry of horror from the mission house. He reached the other shore and then turned back. The Brethren at Gnadenhuetten had been attacked by the Delawares, when at supper. Ten were killed, and one captured. The buildings were destroyed. Zeisberger carried the news to Bethlehem, where he arrived at 3 o'clock on the morning of Nov. 25th. The entire body of Indian converts fled from Gnadenhuetten, on the Lehigh, to Bethlehem. Susanna Nitschmann was the only captive taken. She died some months after at Tioga. The massacre created a great deal of feeling throughout the state. It was found out later that the party which made this attack was made up of Munsee, under Jacheabus. The destruction of this village led to the attempt to build a fort at the site of Gnadenhuetten, on the Lehigh. On Jan. 1st. 1756, the savages made an attack upon the soldiers at this place, drove them away, and burned the village. Benjamin Franklin arrived at the site of Gnadenhuetten and at once commenced the erection of Fort Allen.

The *third* Gnadenhuetten was a settlement of white persons at the site of Gnadenhuetten the Second. The *fourth* Gnadenhuetten was situated on the Tuscarawas River, Clay Township, Ohio, at the site of the present Gnadenhuetten, Ohio. This village was established in 1772, through the efforts of Zeisberger, who had been working on the Beaver River.

The *fifth* Gnadenhuetten was founded after the return of the Christian Indians from Canada . . . June 1st. 1796.

Monocasy Creek

A creek name of note is Monocasy Creek, as in Henry (p. 236; see later) "at the Manockisy, on the road to Gnadenhütten." Schmick on ms. p. (5) has "Creek, wie Manahkse." *Menagachsink* was the name given to the site of Bethlehem by the Delawares. See further note under the entry "Monocasy Creek."

Bethlehem and Spangenberg

"Bethlehem" is named frequently in Schmick's manuscript. Because Schmick may have added to his dictionary (ms. pp. 332 to 378?) while he was in Bethlehem after 1756 and because the town was also an important center of Moravian and Mahican life, some detailed background may be desirable.

Herrnhaag ('Lord's enclosure, Lord's city') was near Büdingen (50.17 N, 9.07 E) in present-day West Germany. It is currently being reconstructed. For 12 years, from 1738 to 1750, it and Marienborn were centers of religious ecstasy and linguistic excesses during the Moravian *Sichtungszeit*, 'sifting time.' This was not a rebellion against church leadership. One of the results was the desertion and final abandonment of Herrnhaag. In the last 2 years of Herrnhaag (1748 to 1750) Johann Jacob Schmick took his First Communion there and served there and later in Marienborn and Hennersdorf, after which he was sent to North America. Many of those who had been in Herrnhaag went away from the more conservative leaders in Herrnhut to the New World, especially to Count Zinzendorf's followers who founded the settlement of Bethlehem in December 1741 about 10 miles above the forks of the Delaware River. (See p. 13 for a postscript about their Saxon patron Count Zinzendorf and his Mahican companions.) Bishop David Nitschmann, who established Herrnhut, came to America to do missionary work among the Indians and Negroes in Georgia, but after the failure of the mission there Nitschmann was assigned to Bethlehem, where he led the congregation.

In that December of 1741, there was a proposal to name the settlement "Bethlechem" for Hebrew *beth*, 'house,' on the *Lecha*, the German short form of Delaware *Lechauwiechink*, 'forks-at' (English *Lehigh*). Because of the similarity of "Bethlechem" to "Bethlehem" (Hebrew 'house of bread,' or 'house of Lahamu' [a deity]) and "as the scenes of Bethlehem, in Judea, on the night of the Saviour's nativity had just been commemorated, it was suggested it should be changed to Bethlehem." [4]

Because of the Herrnhaagian excesses in Bethlehem, August Gottlieb Spangenberg was sent to Bethlehem, replaced John Nitschmann (David's relative), and rooted out those tendencies by 1750. Spangenberg is mentioned twice in Schmick's manuscript, where he is "literally" honored.

During the French and Indian War about 100 Indians took refuge among the Moravians in Bethlehem. Then in 1756, after the burning of Gnadenhütten and other destruction, 600 more took asylum there. The following paragraphs of a hundred years later catch the linguistic and religious spirit of the Moravian times, though a bit haughtily composed by J. Henry (his pp. 233 to 235):

> The red man, who was thus domiciled and domesticated among the Moravians, soon became attached to the new mode of life he had assumed and the new religion he had adopted in exchange for that which he had laid aside. The services for the Indian audience were performed in their own language, translations being provided for them, and every facility was afforded for the proper comprehension of that Divine instruction, which now, for the first time, threw a flood of light upon their souls. In reading these passages of Moravian life, where the Indian group engrosses the picture, we are struck with the unique and marked peculiarity of the people whose history and fame we are thus cursorily dwelling upon.
>
> The period that characterized early Bethlehem was one of the poetical phases in the history of our race, and although the modes and associations of life were rude, the aims were purely spiritual, and every individual was endowed with inner impulses. As the imagination carries us back to that period, we hear a solemn chaunt, the music of the Moravian hymn, in the Mohican tongue. The actors in this scene are in primitive costume, modified by intercourse with the whites; and as the anthem ascends on high, or the Christian prayer is poured out in heathen tones, the spectacle becomes interesting, and significant of the lofty mission of the early Moravians. At that time, as well as at the present, the entire passion and aims of life were directed to reclaim the savage, and to witness the effects, upon the untamed mind, of the doctrine of salvation, couched in the fascinating imagery of Moravianism. If all the transactions of that life could be brought to view, the real history, and not the fiction of the Indian character, might be realized.
>
> The occupation of those Indians consisted in making brooms, weaving baskets and other similar articles; and their attachment to the Brethren lasted through life, few ever forsaking it when once formed, but living, dying, and receiving interment in this place of their adoption. Many of the graves of these early converts are still visible in the cemetery, on its northern side, with their respective names chiseled on the mouldering stones. To these I would have the pilgrim bend his steps, whenever he may feel prompted, by visiting Bethlehem, to recall the thoughts and pictures of an earlier age.

Brother Schmick

The following is an outline of Schmick's life kindly sent to me in 1980 by *Pastorin* Ingeborg Baldauf, the archivist of the Archiv der Brüder-Unität of Herrnhut, German Democratic Republic, and translated from German with my bracketed notes:

SCHMICK, Johann Jacob (also Jakob)

1714, Oct. 9 [Oct. 19 (20?) new style]	Born in Königsberg [now Kaliningrad, USSR: 54.40 N, 20.30 E], in Prussia.
	Parents' names unknown.
–	Received a good education.
–	Studied theology.
1742	Came as Lutheran theologian to Livonia [Latvia and Estonia] for the instruction of the children; became acquainted with the [United] Brethren.

---

[4] On p. 232 of James Henry's *Sketches of Moravian Life and Character*, Philadelphia, 1859, J.B. Lippincott & Co.; much of the preceding information and some later on is paraphrased or quoted from this work.

1748	Came to Herrnhaag [Herrnhag, 'Lord's enclosure or city'; near Büdingen, West Germany; 50.17 N, 9.07 E]
—	Here admitted into the congregation and took his First Communion with the congregation.
—	Served with the children in Marienborn [in Mainz, West Germany].
—	Then in Hennersdorf.
1751	Called to missionary service among the Indians of North America.
1752, May 7	Ordained *diaconus* ['deacon'] in Philadelphia (*Ord. Buch*).
1753, Jan.	Took wedding vows with the unmarried Sister Johanna Ingerheidt.
	They served the Indian congregation in Gnadenhütten on the Mahony [Mahoning, on the Lehigh] until its destruction.
1755	Short while with the Indians at Wajomick [Wyoming, Pa.].
[1756, Jan.]	Then in Bethlehem with the Indian congregation that took refuge there.
1758	In Pachgatgoch [Scat(t)icook, Schaghticook, Conn.], New England
1759	They were called to Berbice [Surinam, South America].
1759, March 4	Ordained *presbyter* ['elder, priest'] in Bethlehem (*Ord. Buch*).
	They had to interrupt the trip to Berbice; they were called back to Bethlehem to replace Brother Martin Mack with the Indian congregation in Nain [in West Bethlehem].
	Brother Schmick mastered the language of the Mahicans and was taken by the Shawnees into their nation.
[1763]	Accompanied the captive Indian congregation in their assigned exile in Philadelphia.
1765	They returned again with the Indian congregation to Wyalusing [a Munsee village called *M'chwihilusing*, 'place of the old man'; after 1763 called Friedenshütten, 'tents of peace,' Pa.].
	Then they served 7 years in newly built Friedenshütten on the Susquehanna.
	Then in Hope, [New] Jersey.
1773	Removed to Gnadenhütten on the Muskingum, Ohio (4 years).
1777, Aug.	He was transferred to Lititz [in Pennsylvania] because of new Indian unrest, was an assistant there to Bishop Hehl, also taking over the duties of helper at married persons' choir [German: *Chor*, 'class of people'] after Sister Hehl returned home; he attended also the wounded soldiers in the hospital.
1778, Jan. 23	Brother Schmick died in Lititz [Pa.] at 64 years of age [of "camp fever"].

The above biographical outline is from the official organ of the United Brethren called *Gemeinnachrichten* [= *GN*], No. 4, pp. 418-423, 1779; the *Archivrubrik* [= *R*], 22.1.c.6.–4 pages; and the *Gottesackerbuch von Lititz*, No. 49, p. 236.

There is also the journal called *Diarium von der Geschwister Schmicks und Br. Antons Ind. Reise und Besuch an der Susquehanna vom 23ten Septbr. bis 4ten Octbr. 1755*, in R 15.1.a.5.20.–16 pages. The Indian words in the *Diarium* (= *D*) are the following:

Only three general Mahican words occur:
(1) *Onéowe*, 'thanks' (*D*. p. 3)
(2, 3) *Kia P'gachganom*, 'your blood' (*D*. p. 10)

Two personal names, probably Mahican: (1) *Paxnouss* (*passim*. Was he a chief?); (2) *Apowachanant* (*D*. p. 14)

Three Munsee or Unami Delaware place names: (1) *dem Mennissinger Town, Lechawachneck*, 'Lackawanna' (*D*. p. 3); (2) *Nescopeke*, 'Nescopeck,' 'black-spring' (*D*. p. 3); (3) *Wajomick*, 'Wyoming,' '(great-)plain-upon' (*passim*)

One Delaware word occurring thrice: *Kéhelle*, 'yes' (*D*. pp. 7, 11, 12)

The following is most of the article by Dr. Lawrence W. Hartzell "Musical Moravian Missionaries, Part III: Johann Jakob Schmick" (*Moravian Music Journal* 30(2):36-37, Fall 1985) with my bracketed comments per Hartzell's communication to me (August 19, 1986):

Schmick's first missionary assignment was at the Gnadenhütten mission in Pennsylvania, where he served as a teacher of reading, writing and singing. A performer on the spinet, he gave keyboard lessons to a young Indian. Although the exact name of the Indian is not known, it was undoubtedly Joshua, Jr., the son of a Mohican native assistant who was a member of the mission personnel [Joshua, Sr.].

As a musician Schmick is variously identified as performing on the spinet, zither, guitar and violin. In addition, his singing ability was obviously such that he could perform vocal solos. In this capacity he sang his first public solo at a lovefeast given at Gnadenhütten on February 26, 1752.

For a short time Schmick was missionary at Meniolágoméka, Pennsylvania. On the day of his first service, November 20, 1753, he attempted to call the congregation by blowing a signal horn. Not being a brass player he was unable to make a sound on the instrument, thereby causing the service to be missed. This incident led one researcher to state that Schmick was probably not a good musician. This unfortunate conclusion is totally refuted by the evidence contained in mission records.

After his work at Meniolagomeka was completed, Schmick and his wife returned to Gnadenhütten, Pennsylvania, where he was elected *Gemein-Jünger*. It was during this period (1754-55) that he and Bernhard Grube shared school-teaching duties. It was also during this period that Schmick seems to have incurred some official displeasure.

Although Schmick had been conducting services in the Indian language for some time, and had made many translations of hymn texts into that language, Nathaniel Seidel, the future bishop, seems to have viewed his progress with some reservation. One of the reservations was the fact that a younger missionary, Gottfried Roesler, noticeably surpassed Schmick in his linguistic studies [but probably in Delaware, not Mahican]. However, after an announcement that Schmick would return to Bethlehem, the Indians made a point of showing their appreciation for him precisely because of his knowledge of their language.

By 1763 conditions between whites and Indians had deteriorated to the point where the governor of Pennsylvania ordered the Moravian Indians to be housed in the army barracks on Providence Island in Philadelphia. Although this was done for the protection of the Indians, the move effectively placed them under house arrest.

During this period Schmick's spinet pupil, Joshua, Jr., demonstrated his keyboard facility by performing for the governor and at the home of Mr. Fox. The latter gentleman was the commissary and a friend to the Moravian Indians during their confinement. Joshua's performances as well as the devout and beautiful singing of the Indians during their religious exercises did much to change the negative attitude toward Indians held by many Philadelphians.

Schmick seems to have been involved in the many negotiations necessary to acquire the release of the Indians on March 20, 1765. After leaving Philadelphia the Indians relocated at a new mission in the Pennsylvania interior called Friedenshütten. David Zeisberger was appointed resident missionary; however, soon after his arrival, Zeisberger became ill and had to return to Bethlehem. This move forced Schmick into the position of resident missionary, and it is to his credit that he proved himself an able administrator.

Schmick began work on his contribution to Indian philology, *Miscellanea Linguae* [etc.], in 1767 [J.W. Jordan in *Penn. Mag. Hist. Biog.* 10:125-157, 1886].

Eventually the westward movement of Indians caused the Moravian Church to decide that the future of its missionary program lay in Ohio. Consequently plans were made for removal of the Pennsylvania missions to Ohio's Tuscarawas Valley. During this period Schmick was reassigned to Bethlehem and was not involved in any of the various travels necessitated by the westward migration.

As early as the mission at Gnadenhütten, Pennsylvania, difficulties had arisen between the Mohican and Delaware Indians. Try as they might, the Moravian missionaries could not completely stamp out the intertribal jealousies and rivalries that were carried over from pre-Christian days. Thus when the Ohio missions were in the planning stages, the Mohican elder, Joshua, Sr., requested a mission station especially for Mohican Indians. In compliance with this request the Moravians established the mission at Gnadenhütten, Ohio, six months after their initial Ohio mission at Schoenbrunn.

Until August 1773 Gnadenhütten, Ohio, had no missionary, being served primarily by David Zeisberger. However, during this month Schmick and his wife arrived as resident missionaries. Thus a large percentage of the Indians from Friedenshütten were reunited with their former missionary family.

. . .

During the summer of 1777 war parties connected with the Revolutionary War began to infiltrate the Tuscarawas missions, and conditions rapidly became very unsafe. For various reasons the Delaware chief requested that Schmick and his wife leave the mission station. Their departure took place on August 10, 1777, with their destination being Lititz, Pennsylvania.

While at Lititz, Schmick served as assistant to Bishop Hehl, and Mrs. Schmick became the spiritual overseer of the Married Sisters. In December of that year a U.S. military hospital was established at Lititz, and Schmick served as chaplain for the wounded soldiers. Through this work he contracted "camp fever" and died January 23, 1778.

Unlike Pyrlaeus and Grube, Schmick's influence on the mission field was quite lengthy. Also, where the majority of their significant musical contributions were in non-mission communities, Schmick's were primarily, if not completely, in the mission field. Additionally, all of the important Indian musicians discovered through the current research project (Joshua, Jr., Marcus and Samuel Nanticoke) were either students of Schmick or were long under his influence. However, undoubtedly the greatest testament to his musical work comes from the diary of the mission station at Fairfield, Canada. Under the date June 22, 1798 (20 years after his death), David Zeisberger recorded that Schmick was still affectionately remembered by some of the Indians as a fine performer on the spinet.

Schmick's death brought to a close an active period in the musical life of the Moravian Indian missions. While there would still be musical missionaries, and while music would still be important within mission life, no future Moravian mission would develop a musical life as multifaceted as Gnadenhütten, Nain, and Friedenshütten in Pennsylvania and Gnadenhütten in Ohio, all of which were served by Schmick.

Schmick's probable language background

Schmick used standard High German, but there were interesting linguistic influences on him. We are not certain about the languages Schmick knew, but since he was born in Königsberg, Prussia, in 1714, we can surmise some things.

Schmick was born into the East Samland variety of the Low Prussian group of Low German dialects of East Prussia (see *map, poem, numerals*, p. 6). Low Prussian was the easternmost extension of Low German. These dialects indeed sound more like Dutch than German; for example, 'water' is *Wasser* ([vásər]) in German but *Woater* ([vǭtəř], with velar [r]) in Samlandic, and compare the Low German numerals with those of Dutch. Although Königsberg is clearly in the East Samland dialect area, the city lies at the mouth of the Pregolya or Pregel River, emptying into the Frisches Haff, which is flanked on the north by the West Samland dialect and on the south by the Natangen-Barten dialect. Königsberg thus lies near the point of three Low Prussian dialects, which were still used up to 1945. Over 60 km south of Königsberg was the High German–speaking area, even in the eighteenth century. French was also widely used in Prussia.

In addition, the Slavic area southward beyond Prussia continues to be Polish, and westward 150 km of Königsberg was and still is Kashubian, one of the Pomeranian Slavic languages. Northeast of Königsberg beyond the Kurisches Haff was the eastern-region variety of Low Prussian up to Memel (now Klaipéda), north of which was Lithuanian, a language of the Baltic branch of the Indo-European family.

It is to the Baltic languages that the district name of Samland is attributed (*sam-* does not mean 'commonality'). Samland is the heartland of Old Prussian, a Baltic language that became extinct in the seventeenth century, only several decades earlier than Schmick's year of birth. Earlier, in the fifteenth century, from the north came immigrants speaking yet another Baltic language called Curonian (*kurisch* or *altkurisch*) who settled on the coast of Samland. They left place names in the form of *Kuhren*. In Schmick's youth even Latvian immigrants, also speaking a Baltic language, came to the Kurische Nehrung (a strip of land separating the sea from the Haff, or lagoon) and to Samland and left a dialect of Latvian in Samland till 1945. Now Kaliningrad is thoroughly Russian speaking (see Bogdan Zaborski's map in *Goode's World Atlas*, 1964, p. 108).

We know that from 1714 to 1742 Schmick "received a good education," and despite having been born into a Low Prussian dialect area, with an overlay of standard High German in Königsberg, Schmick is thus presumed to have used good standard High German of the time, but always with the ever-present influence of underlying linguistic diversity nearby. In his Mahican manuscript there is very little that truly diverges from the German one reads now. It is only a matter of script styles, contractions of words (such as dus for du es and schmeistu for schmeisst du), some shifts of meaning, and occasional rare forms, such as Happel, happeln (not found in Riemann's *Preussisches Wörterbuch*, 1974), kroppen ('seize'), alhier ('here'), Fallter (' "fence" '), and Versel (see under 'sing'). Thus his dictionary German was not influenced by the Low Prussian dialect of Low German.

I assume that Schmick, perhaps feeling the pulse of the earlier Baltic layers of languages of his homeland and its individualistic Prussian dialects and knowing perhaps either Latvian or Estonian of Livonia and certainly Latin and later English, had developed a sense for languages that in America culminated in his compilation of a major living Algonquian language—Mahican. Such may have been the pressures or a curiosity or a sensitivity driving him. After all, at that time there had not been many persons of European descent who methodically recorded Indian languages—the French doing so a little more than others had. Most people in the American colonies were busy dispersing the ancient inhabitants for reasons of greed or promotion of a "superior" culture. Schmick behaved oppositely by being sensitive to that language and nurturing it. Did he learn his language sensitivity back in Livonia and nearby areas with their linguistic vigor?

Provenience of the manuscript and my background

In 1820 the Rev. John (Johann Gottlieb Ernestus) Heckewelder, the famous missionary among the Delaware, donated the two-volume Schmick manuscript to the American Philosophical Society in Philadelphia, where it is now deposited in the society's library. The date for the manuscript given as "*ca.* 1760?" in J.F. Freeman and Murphy Smith's *A Guide to Manuscripts Relating to the*

Examples of Low Prussian dialect

Min Heimatort[5]

In Somland is min Heimatort,
Da steiht min lewe Mähl,
Da klappert se so munter fort,
Vertellt mi ok so vel.

In Somland is min Heimatort,
Ach wie mi da glick ward,
Da kloppt mi jedet pladitsch Wort
So trulich an dat Hart.

Da ruscht min oler Lindebom,
Da singt de Lewark wit;
Dat ruscht on singt manch söte Drom
Mi ut de Kindertid.

Et dröft mi nich no Ost on West,
Priest ju de Welt ok vel,
To Hus is doc am allerbest,
Da steiht min lewe Mähl.

Numbers in West Samland Low Prussian	
1	(e)
2	tvē
3	drē
4	(fīr?)
5	fıf
6	ses
7	zēvə
8	(oxt?)
9	nēįə
10	tijə, tTə

[5] From Tr. Bergmüller: In *S. Ost- und Westpreussen-Almanach 1910*, Königsberg, Samland. In Walther Ziesemer: *Die ostpreussischen Mundarten*, 1924; reprint Wiesbaden, 1970, Dr. Martin Sändig oHG.

Fig. 1. Dialect areas of Prussia. (Translated from Erhard Riemann: *Wörterbuch*, Neumünster, 1974, Karl Wachholtz Verlag.)

American Indian in the Library of the American Philosophical Society, 1966, is much too late or perhaps is a completion date. It was probably begun as early as 1753. Daniel Brinton in 1884 mentioned that the dictionary was unpublished, and until now it has remained so. My studies of four New England Algonquian languages—Massachusett, Narragansett, Quiripi (or Quinnipiac), and Mohegan (southeastern Connecticut) enabled me to begin work on Schmick's manuscript. Further studies included Bloomfield's *The Menomini Language* (Wisconsin: Hockett, 1962); Jones's *Fox Texts* (1907); Day's *The Mots loups of Father Mathevet* (1975: "Nipmuck"?); and several Lenâpé works by both Brinton and Zeisberger.

Thus Schmick, over 200 years ago, left a valuable work. It needed attention so that Algonquianists may better define the standing Mahican has in relation to nearby Algonquian languages such as Munsee, Delaware, and Nipmuck-Pocumtuck.

Original territory and environment of Mahicans

The following initial paragraphs are taken from Brasser's chapter "Mahican" (1978).

The homeland of the Mahican Indians extended from Lake Champlain southward into the western part of Dutchess County, New York, and from the valley of the Schoharie Creek in the west to south-central Vermont in the east (Fig. 2). With increasing unity among the Iroquois tribes in the sixteenth century, relations with the Mohawk appeared to have become markedly hostile, making it impossible for the Mahican to use their domains west of the Hudson

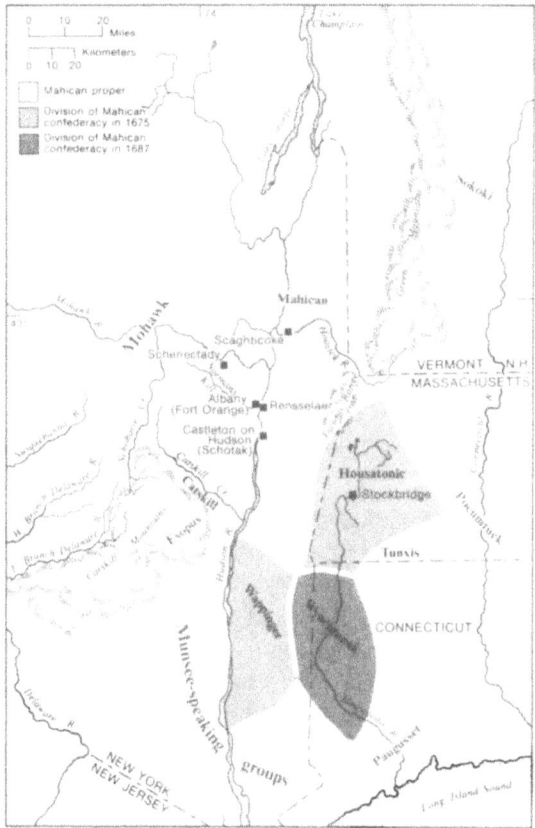

Fig. 2. Territory of Mahican and Mahican confederacy. (From Brasser, T.J.: In Trigger, B.C., ed.: *Northeast*, 15:198, Smithsonian Institution, 1978.) [Per Gordon Day, May 10, 1986; *Ruttenber* gave the "Mahican confederacy" undue importance. For a better map of the Wyachtonok (Weantinock) see p. 187.]

River for purposes other than hunting. On the other hand, the Mohawk did not dare to establish villages east of Schoharie Creek.

Mahican country is part of the coastal uplands through which several rivers have cut north-south valleys. Of these, the valley of the Hudson River forms a lowland passage from Lake Champlain and the Saint Lawrence to the Atlantic coast. North of the Hudson River highlands the valley is rimmed on the west by the glaciated Allegheny plateau, and on the east by the rugged area of the Taconic and Green mountains. Most of the land was forested with a mixture of conifers and broad-leaved hardwoods. The diversified environment offered a habitat for black bears, deer, moose, beaver, otter, bobcat, mink, rabbit, raccoon, turkey and many other birds, while the rivers teemed with fish. In general, animal life as well as the Indian population concentrated in the valleys of the rivers and creeks.

To a large extent, the Mahican way of life [about 1600] was similar to that of their direct neighbors—Mohawk, Esopus, Wappinger, Housatonic, and Sokoki. Particularly in their social organization and intertribal relations, the Mahican were most closely related to the Wappinger, Esopus, and other Munsee-speaking groups along the upper course of the Delaware River.

Background and explanatory description 7

Sources of Mahican history

The following six works are the best sources on Mahican history:

Brasser, T.J.: *Riding on the frontier's crest: Mahican Indian culture and culture change*, no. 13, Ottawa 1974, National Museums of Canada, 91 pp.

Brasser, T.J.: Mahican, pp. 198-212. In Trigger, B.C., editor: *Northeast*, vol. 15 of Sturtevant, W.C., editor: *Handbook of North American Indians*, Washington, D.C., 1978, Smithsonian Institution.

Colee, P.S.: "The Housatonic-Stockbridge Indians: 1734-1749," Albany, 1977, doctoral thesis, State University of New York at Albany; 77-19,939, Xerox University Microfilms, 300 North Zeeb Rd., Ann Arbor, Michigan 48106.

Davidson, J.N.: *Muh-he-ka-ne-ok: a history of the Stockbridge nation*, Milwaukee, 1893, Silas Chapman, xviii, 66 pp.

Hopkins, S.: *Historical memoirs, relating to the Houssatunnuk Indians* (etc.), Boston, 1753, S. Kneeland; imperfect edition, 1911; imperfect reprint, New York, 1972, Johnson Reprint Corp.

Ruttenber, E.M.: *History of the Indian tribes of Hudson's River*, 1872; Port Washington, N.Y., 1971, Kennikat Press (a general history with errors).

Position of Mahican in Eastern Algonquian

The following are initial statements concerning the Eastern Algonquian subgroup of Algonquian languages:[6]

The Eastern Algonquian languages were spoken aboriginally from the Maritimes to North Carolina along the Atlantic coast and immediately inland from it. Since they share a number of innovations that the Algonquian languages farther west do not attest, it must be assumed that they descend from an ancestral Proto-Eastern Algonquian language (PEA) that had had a certain period of independent development after branching off from the common parent of the whole family, Proto-Algonquian (PA). For example, all the Eastern languages have undergone a major restructuring of the verbal paradigm that expresses action on inanimate objects, whereby, among other changes, the singular ending PA *-a·ni* was replaced by PEA *-amən*: Ojibwa *nimikka·n* 'I find it' but Unami *nəmáxkamən*. . . . Consequently, the Eastern Algonquian languages do not differ among themselves as much as the languages of the entire family taken together, and the time depth of the Eastern subgroup is not so great as that of Algonquian as a whole (see Fig. 3). Nevertheless the Eastern languages exhibit an extensive diversity, and (although there is no accurate method of estimation) they must have been diverging from each other for something on the order of 2,000 years.

Each Eastern Algonquian language shares features with each of its immediate neighbors, and the resulting continuum is of a sort that is likely to have resulted from the spread of linguistic innovations among forms of speech that were already differentiated but still similar enough to make partial bilingualism easy.

---

[6] From Goddard, I.: Eastern Algonquian languages, pp. 70-77, in Trigger, B.C., editor: *Northeast*, vol. 15. In Sturtevant, W.C., editor: *Handbook of North American Indians*, Washington, D.C., 1978, Smithsonian Institution.

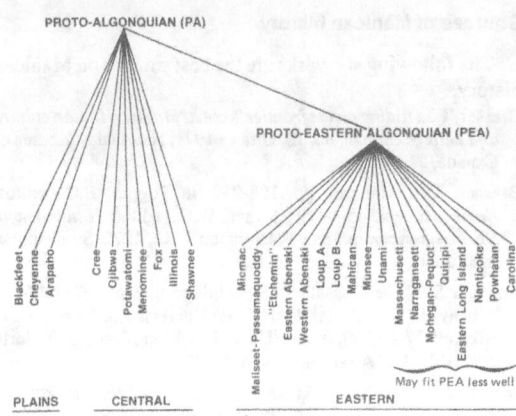

Fig. 3. Algonquian linguistic relationships. (Modification, that is, comment and rearrangement, by C.M. per David Pentland from Trigger, B.G., ed.: *Northeast,* 15:70, Smithsonian Institution, 1978.)

The following outline is Siebert's detailed classification of Eastern Algonquian,[7] with my bracketed comments as modified or approved by Siebert in 1985.

CLASSIFICATION OF EASTERN ALGONQUIAN

I. **Boreal division**
      1. *Micmac*
II. **Subboreal division**
   A. *Etchemin*
      2. *Malecite-Passamaquoddy*
        (a) Malecite
        (b) Passamaquoddy
   B. *Abenaki*
      3. *Eastern Abenaki* (Note: Of these, Penobscot and Caniba, at least, have coastal and inland subdialects with partly differing rules of syncope.)
        (a) Penobscot
        (b) Caniba
        (c) Aroosagunticook
        (d) Sokoki-Pequaket (or Pigwacket)
      4. *Western Abenaki* (modern aggregate, *St. Francis Abenaki*)
        (a) Pennacook
        (b) Pentucket
III. **Medial division**
   A. *Taconic*
      5. *Mahican* (modern aggregate, *Stockbridge*)
        (a) Eastern Mahican [Stockbridge (Mass.), east of Albany, S.W. Vermont]
        (b) Western Mahican ["Moravian" Mahican; N.W. Conn.; Dutchess County, N.Y.]
   B. *Delaware*
      6. *Munsee* (Minsi)
        (a) Northern Munsee [Esopus and Catskill]
        (b) Eastern Munsee [highlands of west Hudson, Hackensack, etc.]
        (c) Western Munsee [Minisinks and east branch of Susquehanna River]
      7. *Unami*
        (a) Northern Unami [Lehigh, Delaware R. forks]
        (b) Eastern Unami [Sankhikans, Raritan, Navasink, central N.J. coast, Pine Barrens of central New Jersey]
        (c) Southern Unami [Rancocas, Camden, Philadelphia area, Arwaymouse in N.J., Brandywine Creek, etc., in Penn. and Del.]
      8. *Unalachtigo*
IV. **Archaic Coastal division** (PEA-A descendants)
   A. *Southern New England (SNE)*
    (I) Eastern SNE (*n*-languages)
      9. *Massachusee* [or Massachusett]
        (a) Northern Massachusee (Saugus and Ipswich Rivers)
        (b) Central Massachusee (Natick) (Charles and Neponset Rivers)
        (c) Southern Massachusee (Martha's Vineyard)
        (d) Nauset (Cape Cod and Nantucket)
     10. *Wampanoag*
     11. *Cowesit* (Northern Narragansett)
    (II) Western SNE (modern aggregate, *Brotherton,* for groups [A] and [B])
     (A) *y*-languages
      12. *Narragansett*
        (a) Southern Narragansett
        (b) Niantic [both Eastern and Western]
      13. *Mohegan-Pequot*
        (a) Pequot
        (b) Mohegan
      14. *Montauk* (or Eastern Long Island)
        (a) Montauk
        (b) Shinnecock
     (B) *r*-languages
      15. *Wampano* (modern aggregate, Scaticook)
        (a) Quinnipiac [Quiripi; "Naugatuck" word list from East Haven and Derby; Paugussett]
        (b) Mattabesec
        (c) Tunxis
        (d) Siwanoy
      16. *Insular Wampano*
        (a) Unquachog (Poosepátuck)
        (b) Setauket
        (c) Matinecoc
        (d) Massapequa
     (C) *l*-languages
      17. *Nipmuck-Pocumtuck* (*Loup* of some French missionaries)
        (a) Nipmuck
        (b) Nashua
        (c) Pocumtuck
   B. *Chesapeake*
     18. *Nanticoke*
     19. *Conoy* (Kanawha)
   C. *Powhatan*
     20. *Chickahominy*
        (a) Chickahominy
        (b) Appomattox
     21. *Pamunkey*

---

[7] From Siebert, F.T., Jr.: Resurrecting Virginia Algonquian From the Dead: classification of Eastern Algonquian (pp. 444-446), reprinted from *Studies in Southeastern Indian languages,* J.M. Crawford, editor, © 1975, University of Georgia Press, Athens, Ga.

              (a) Pamunkey
              (b) Mattapony [Mattaponi]
       22. *Nansemond*
    D. *Windgandcon* [Siebert's term from Wingandacoa, 1584]
       23. *Chowan*
       24. *Pamlico* (Pampticough)

Mahican is an Eastern Algonquian language of the upper Hudson River area. It may have been spoken by the Catskill Indians too. In the eighteenth century, Mahican was spoken in the mission villages of Stockbridge, on the upper Housatonic, and Shecomeco, in northeastern Dutchess County, New York, but its aboriginal extent to the east and south is not known exactly. There is much variation in the spelling systems of Mahican recordings, and a proper description reflecting dialect differences has not been made yet, nor has a systematic orthography been adopted because the language died out by the 1930s (Goddard, 15:72, 1978). Those linguistic data betray the diverse composition of the "Mahican" population, which had incorporated many remnant groups from New England, who were drawn to Stockbridge, Massachusetts, and Scaticook, Connecticut.

The neighboring languages with which Mahican bears some affinity are Munsee to the south, Loup B (appearing in a 14-page mixed-language vocabulary collected by Magnon de Terlaye in 1755 that probably came from the northeast of Mahican and resembles Mahican and Western Abenaki), and "Nipmuck" (Loup A) to the east. By 1687 the Housatonic, Wyachtonok (Wawyachtonoc), and Wappinger to the east and south were confederated with the Mahicans, but since there are no vocabularies extant from these tribes, one can only suppose some linguistic affinity of Housatonic and Wyachtonok to Mahican, as opposed to Wappinger, which may have been a Munsee dialect (Goddard, 15:237, 1978). However, see p. 15, nos. 24 to 26, of *Mahican-Language Hymns* (etc.) (Masthay, 1980) for *r*-dialect hymns.

Two main dialects

After 1740 there were two main focal points of Mahican movements — one at Stockbridge, Massachusetts (1744), and the other at Bethlehem, Pennsylvania (1746). These eventually gave rise to the two main dialects of Mahican — Stockbridge Mahican and Moravian Mahican. The *Stockbridge Mahicans* were composed of New York Mahicans (to the north and west) and Housatonic, Wappinger, Wyachtonok, and some other Connecticut tribes (to the south and east). They were under the care of Reverend John Sergeant and his assistant in translations, John Quinney (Quanakaunt), and were aligned with David Brainerd in nearby Kaunaumeek (near Lebanon or Chatham?, N.Y.), which group also moved to Stockbridge. They had another village at Skatekook, Mass. In 1788, Jonathan Edwards, the younger, wrote a treatise on the Mahican dialect of Stockbridge. These Indians were Reformed Congregationalists (a sect derived from Puritans), and the spelling of their Mahican writings thus follows English conventions. This group of Stockbridge Mahicans from 1783 to 1788 moved to Oneida Creek, New York, near the Brothertons, who were composed of southern New England Indians and some Mahicans. They then moved from 1822 to 1830 through Ohio and Indiana to Wisconsin, first at South Kaukauna near the Menominee and Winnebago and then abortively to Kansas from 1839 to 1846 with the Quapaw (and called "Christian Indians") and finally from 1856 to 1859 back to Wisconsin, where they settled permanently in Shawano County. The last speaker of this variety of Mahican allegedly died in 1933).

The other variety is *"Moravian" Mahican.* It was used when in 1740 Moravian missionaries began work with the Mahican and Wyachtonok of Dutchess County, New York, and Scaticook (Pachgatgoch, Pis[h]gachtigok, Schaghticoke) near Kent, Connecticut. In 1746 these Moravian Indians removed to Bethlehem, Pennsylvania, and joined Munsee converts there. An earlier movement in 1730 brought some Mahicans from Schaghticoke (Scaghticoke), 18 miles north of Albany, New York, to Wyoming, Pennsylvania, where Schmick was a short while in 1755. Did this influence his Mahican? This group was affiliated with Gnadenhütten. A series of moves after the massacre at the second Gnadenhütten in Pennsylvania brought the Moravian Indians to the fourth Gnadenhütten, in Ohio. After 1782 they wandered until settling on the Thames River at Moraviantown, Ontario. In 1783 a second group of Munsee and Mahican moved to Ohsweken, Ontario; there is now no trace of the Mahican element in this group. In 1837 some Moravian Munsee moved from Canada to Stockbridge on Lake Winnebago in Wisconsin. The Indians of this Stockbridge later moved to the Stockbridge Indian Reservations (Moheconnuck) near Bowler and Gresham, Wisconsin. This variety of Mahican thus disappeared in the nineteenth century.

This short sketch separates the two varieties. I drew much from Brasser's *Riding on the Frontier's Crest* (1974).

. . .

There is a peripheral issue that needs discussion. The Indians of Schaghticoke (Skachkook) above Albany were regarded in New York documents as the core of the River Indian association (a "Mahican confederacy") in contrast to the Mahikanders ("River Indians"), who were in a scattered distribution south of Albany. At other times they were regarded as one group. In 1701 the sachem of Schaghticoke, Sacquans (Soquan, Suckwame), "specified that the Mahikanders were the first inhabitants of the Hudson Valley and that the Schaghticoke had come to the Hudson Valley immediately after, and as a direct result of, the war in New England [in 1675]." (See p. 7 for Colee ref., his pp. 88-89.) So the Schaghticoke people were immigrants to Schaghticoke, and according to Gordon Day's reconstruction they were:

a mixed village of refugees from King Phillip's War — perhaps a Mahican substratum but overlain by Sokokis from Squakheag, who were Abenakis, and by Pocumtucs, Nonotucks, Agawams, and others who were not. . . . There seems to have been a slow steady drift northward from Schaghticoke after 1700, and in 1754 the last twelve families abandoned the place and moved to St. Francis [1973:54].

These Schaghticoke, despite their importance, thus may have had little influence on the Stockbridge variety of Mahican. In addition, those Schaghticoke who in 1730 went to Wyoming, Pa., probably had an equally minor influence on the Moravian variety of Mahican. The main body had slowly migrated to Canada.

One should distinguish (1) *Schaghticoke* in New York, (2) *Skatekook* in Massachusetts, and (3) *Scaticook* (later the *Schaghticoke tribe*) in Connecticut, all spelled variously but meaning 'at the river fork,' unless 'little wave (person),' for the tribe's being near a body of water.

DESCRIPTION OF SCHMICK'S TWO-VOLUME MANUSCRIPT

Order of original manuscript (see Frontispiece)

In the original manuscript the order of the pages is as follows:

PAGE NUMBER	LETTER, COMMENT, GLOSS (WITH PAGE)
(No folio):	Title page to vol. 1
(1) to (4):	*Vocabularium Mahicandicum;* German words under *A*
(5) to (13):	Folios *1* to *9* (thereafter Schmick left them unmarked)
(5) to (14):	*B*
(15):	*C*
(16) to (26):	*D*
(27) to (39):	*E*
(40) to (71):	*F* (not very alphabetical)
(72) to (101):	*G*
(102) to (137):	*H;* p. (102) was the hardest to transliterate; happeln, p. (108)
(138) to (144):	*J;* p. (143): *I*
(145) to (167):	*K*
(No folio):	Title page to vol. 2
(168) to (197):	*L*
(198) to (211):	*M;* milk (in English) on p. (206); tired (in English) on p. (211)
(212) to (220):	*N*
(221) and (222):	*O*
(223) to (230):	*P*
(231):	*Q*
(232) to (251):	*R*
(252) to (319):	*S;* Schmick deleted schmecken ('taste good') and its first line, p. (262), but repeated it on p. (272); seyn ('to be'), pp. (297) and (311); somewhat unalphabetical
(320) and (321):	*T*
(322) and (323):	*U*
(324) to (328):	*V*
(329) and (330):	*W*
(331):	*Z*
(332) to (378):	Miscellaneous sentences; more paradigms (isolated ones = *) + repeated paradigms:

afraid *:	(371)
ashamed:	(347) + (258)
born:	(348) + (73)
cook:	(350) to (352) + (152) + (153)
corrupt:	(340) + (325)
do, make:	(340) + (198)
earn:	(341) + (323)
greet:	(338) + (98)
have been:	(349) + (297)
have not:	(339) + (104)
help:	(343) + (117)
hungry:	(338) + (134)
know*:	(371)
light fire:	(347) + (49)
lost*:	(353)
make, do:	see 'do, make' (340) + (198)
obedient:	(343) + (344) + (96)
(is) outside:	(349) + (24)
pray*:	(339)
preach:	(345) + (230)
run:	(346) + (173)
serve:	(350) + (19)
sing:	(342) + (301)
sleep:	(338) + (264)
speak:	(338) + (233)
spring:	(346) + (307)
stay*:	(348)
sweat:	(341) + (285)
thirsty:	(338) + (26)
thought:	(349) + (17)
to warm*:	(332)
Indian names:	(356)
Miscellaneous sentences	(332) to (337), (353) to (355); (357) to (365); (367) to (378)
Untranslated "biblical" text:	(366)
First untranslated sentence:	Bottom of (371)
Untranslated sentences:	(374) + (375)

Order, description, comments

The order of my work is as follows:

Two-page copy of Schmick's entire manuscript
Background and explanatory description
Mahican historical phonology (by David H. Pentland)
Abbreviations of sources used
English-Mahican-German section (from *Vocabularium Mahicandicum*)
    Long sentences or related texts that were split up for dictionary examples
    No translation given in German
        Original order of words
        Alphabetical order of words with speculative translation
        Untranslated "biblical" exhortative text on ms. p. (366)
        Schmick manuscript p. (366) (a copy)
        Original manuscript p. (102) with facing comment
        Original manuscript p. (375) part concerning pānnäkékäck
Mahican-English glossary and index

The English words are in alphabetical order followed by the Mahican word or phrase and by the German translation. If there is any uncertainty as to the correct spelling or limit of the Mahican word or concept, its position is left blank but in the next line or lines it occurs in its original context. I have often used only fragments of sentences so that they may be grouped under similar concepts. Using the "Mahican-English Glossary and Index," one can trace all isolated phrases or words back to their full sentences in the English-Mahican section.

I have split words generally according to their appearance in Schmick's work just as he had separated them. It may be arbitrary on my part, but it may be arbitrary even on Schmick's part to make certain combinations of letters into a word. The prime example is the word **nguttòksenà**, which appears thus on one page (ms. 282) and as **ngutto** ksenà on another (ms. p. 223), the space in it being rather narrow because of his writing style or slight pause in his recording a "word." In addition, his use of accents is an aid. When I deliberately split up a work, I use a hyphen.

Early on I realized that even though pp. (1) to (331) were following the German alphabet there were many nonsequential items under most letters and from pp. (332) to (378) there was no order, just a jumble of miscellaneous words, paradigms, and sentences. The only small sequence at all discernible in the whole manuscript appears on p. (369) and I have specifically separated it by putting it on p. 37 and on p. 155. Other sequences were the verb paradigms, which I have generally kept in their original order or regularized by *I, you, he, we (inclusive, exclusive), you (plural), they, the negative forms, the perfect,* and *the future*—a pattern Schmick generally followed.

From the first time I used the two-volume manuscript in Philadelphia I considered following the German alphabet, but after working all the way through by putting all German words in alphabetical order, I found that method to be cumbersome and unwieldy for those who do not know German. Perhaps 60% of the German entries in the original manuscript are in alphabetical order. Thus the use of English and its alphabetical order was the most useful method. It is clear, direct, and understandable.

For this book I have made a synoptic display of all 378 pages in two pages (from a film base) for those who wish to see the character of the manuscript. Perhaps a hand lens will bring out desired features. The bewildering fraktur penmanship of Schmick's German is remarkably legible, with perhaps only 10 items being uncertain, of which only two or three are beyond hope. These I have indicated by their respective manuscript pages in the dictionary. Thus the readings are trustworthy. I have done all the work in allowing the user to avoid ever having to decipher the "Gothic" script. The Mahican and Latin words are written much like the way English letters are now written. Very few of these letters were unreadable, and where they were I have given second readings, marked by two or more dots under the letter or letters. I have also often used a more colloquial English word in translation, such as *won't, didn't, doesn't,* and *a lot.*

David Pentland offered another valid critical point. Many German words have semantic ranges that do not correspond to their supposed glosses in English. To have a useful tool in English, I had to make some compromise in translation by giving several meanings in English and then referring them all to one entry so that the user will not be lost. There is no sense of "to be" in Mahican, but the German text did have two such entries seyn. I translated geboren ('born') as 'bring forth' and umgehen ('go around with') as 'be present, be with' (even though a Delaware word matches the Mahican word in the 'go around with' sense). The translation of Happel as 'hobble' is a true problem. 'Cat' has an interesting convoluted origin.

Initially I felt insecure with the Mahican meaning that would help define the German gloss, and so I was thrown upon heavy usage of German, and many English words reflect the Germanicized range. For example, ich habe gesehen is not really 'I have seen' but the normal English 'I saw' or 'I did see,' but to prevent a burgeoning of alternative translations and thus the use of more space, I usually put, for example, the gloss 'I have seen,' and it is for the user to select the normal English alternative. This is actually a minor problem, but unfortunately it can be confusing.

I have used solid and dotted underlining. Some of these are from the manuscript, but most are of my doing to allow one to spot the proper gloss and thereby learn easier than without them. They can be ignored. Usually double underlining is originally from the manuscript (see 'rust') probably, for example, to show a digraph such as c̲h̲ being the voiceless velar fricative. Brackets, of course, mean my added parts of words or explanatory notes or variant readings. Since I have rearranged the entries, some readings in brackets may look strange by not being near the entry in the original. Use of the Mahican-English Glossary and Index will allow one to find the base form. My brackets are not meant to signify the "symbol" of a phonetic reading used in linguistics.

There are some alphabetical groups that are of Schmick's making, such as Indian names, ms. p. (356), or of my compiling, such as Delaware (Unami or Lenâpé) words (a bit hard to read!), Loan words, Numerals, Personal pronouns and some affixes, Place names in Schmick, and Pronominal affixes, and at the end the subsections called "Long Sentences or Related Texts that were Split Up For Dictionary Examples" and "No Translation Given in German" (with subordinate materials). The list of Numerals is the only group in which I incorporated almost all available numerals from all periods and dialects of Mahican. Later I added several more numerals after the word "thousands." It is the first such list published and almost complete. It helps show the continuity of the language despite the missing words or noncontemporaneous and dialectal forms.

There was a need to show, first, the only running text from Schmick in its original form on ms. p. (366) to aid in matching my tentative translation (pp. 156 and 157) and to show, second, the full ms. p. (102) in the hope that someone will be able to read the two unknown words (for which I give an unbearably long note discussing possibilities on p. 159).

The Mahican-English Glossary and Index is explained adequately at its beginning under Symbols and Usage, but I need to reiterate that the gloss in single quotes directly follows the Mahican word, and after the virgule the bracketed words are where one can find that Mahican word. It is a key to finding the original full sentence for each Mahican word. The bold-faced brackets around the *whole* entry show that the Mahican word is not from Schmick.

Words from other Algonquian languages mentioned in the notes in the English-Mahican section are neither listed in the Mahican-English section nor compiled in a separate glossary.

I have been uncertain about the meaning of many words. My use of the question mark symbol, though excessive, was necessary. They usually appear in parentheses to separate them from real question words, but because of punctuation problems, I often dropped the question-mark parentheses when the whole combination of glosses was conjectural and

12 Schmick's Mahican dictionary

thus symbolized by being in parentheses. See **áne** for examples.

I have done more splitting of words in this section; see the entries starting with a hyphen, or **-n g-** and **-n t-**, or **-ck opákka**.

When a line runs over to the next column or page, its end is indicated by an upward arrow (↑). The next line is indicated by a downward arrow (↓). Do not confuse the downward arrow as applying to the entry following it.

The z in **zéboos** is probably covered over by an s, since z would be the incorrect ts, which is an unexpected pronunciation probably influenced by English.

The abbreviation **DHld**, or **dHld**, is used so much that I use its full form **der Heiland** ('the Savior, God') unbracketed.

Since I am not a biblical scholar, some biblical phrases or sentences are not translated into English in accord with those of most bibles.

There are a few Mahican words or phrases that were left untranslated by Schmick, and I have placed them at the end of the English-Mahican-German section, p. 155. I have generally not succeeded in getting some clue as to their meaning.

There have been a few words I have been perplexed about as to the meaning of the available German gloss, namely, **Akridges** (see 'grits' and 'potatoes'). **Küfer[baum]** (see note under 'cooper's wood'), **Affe** (see 'monkey'), and **Happel, happeln** (words not in Rieman's *Preussisches Wörterbuch*; see 'hobble').

Schmick used the normal German ligature digraph ß, but I have used the open digraph ss throughout, for example, **issestus** for his **ißestus**, 'you eat it,' and **Hauss** for his **Hauß** (=Haus or Hauss), 'house,' and so on.

Some Latin accompanying words in the manuscript are not used in my final work, for example, *præsens sing., præs. plur., perfectum,* and *imperat.*

The initial letter of one or two words (such as **N-** or **K-**) may have been cut off when the manuscript was bound, but David Pentland has reassured me about the correctness of such words.

PRONUNCIATION

Many Mahican sources use different spelling systems. The pronunciation of Mahican words follows *German* rules in Schmick and Heckewelder and possibly in some of Ruttenber's works, but those authors using *English* rules for Mahican are DeForest, Edwards, Jefferson, Jenks (with Konkapot), and the ones who wrote *The Assembly's [Shorter] Catechism* (Quinney and Aupaumut). Use the "scientific" *phonetic* rules of various forms for these authors: Michelson, Prince, Speck and Moses, and Swadesh.

The Moravian dialect of Mahican ceased to be spoken by anyone before the invention of phonetic alphabets and tape recorders. Schmick's spellings generally follow German rules, but for consonants he had more symbols than he needed whereas for vowels he did not have enough. Pentland's respellings (in italicized sans-serif font in his chapter, Mahican Historical Phonology) are intended to be *phonemic;* that is, they indicate the contrastive sounds of the language, not the phonetic details that Schmick tried to record. The main correspondences between Schmick's orthography and Pentland's phonemicizations are the following (see also p. 14 for a condensed key to sound changes and phonemes):

Vowels

a, aa	a, ā, ã
e	e, ey, ī
ee	ī
i, ii	e, ey
o	e, ew, we, o, ō, ōw, ã
oo	ō
u	e, ew, we
ai	ay
ei	ay, ey
ou	ew
au	aw, āw, ãw

Consecutive vowels are always separated by *w* or *y*, but Schmick sometimes may not indicate the intervening glide.

Consonants

b	p
ch	h, x
chch	x
d	t
g	k
h	h (before a vowel); before a consonant Schmick's **h** indicates that the preceding vowel is phonetically long
j	y
k, ck, kk	k, kw, hk, hkw
m	m, hm
n	n, hn
p, pp	p, hp
q(u), kq(u), ckq(u), kw, kᵘ	kw, hkw
s, ss	s
sch	š
t, tt	t, ht
tsch	č, hč
w	w
x	ks, kws
xx	hks
z	ts (also č?)
chp	hp, xp
cht	ht (*xt* does not exist except as *x*· [dropped vowel]·*t*)
chtsch	hč
chc, chg, chk	hk, hkw, xk, xkw
chkw, chq(u)	hkw, xkw
chx	hks
chm	hm
chn	hn

(See also §70 for the combinations **achp, acht, achtsch, achk, achq,** etc.)

Phonetic details

For practical purposes, the consonants may be pronounced as in English (note the *č* is English *ch*, *š* is English *sh*, and *x* is the final consonant in Scottish *loch* or German *ach*), but *p, t,* and *k* were probably unaspirated and lenis in contrast to their English equivalents.

Some Mahican vowels had rather broad phonetic ranges compared to those of the vowels of English. The approximate phonetic values of the phonemicized forms are as follows:

a   [a ~ ʌ], ranging from the vowel in French *bas* to English *but*

ā	[aˑ], similar to the vowel in American English *cod*
ã	[ã ~ ɑ̃], similar to the vowel in French *dans*
e	[ə ~ e ~ ɪ], ranging from the first vowel of English *about* (or the last vowel of *sofa*) to the vowels of *bet* and *bit*
ī	[iˑ ~ eˑ], ranging between the vowels of English *beat* and *bait*
o	[o ~ ɔ], similar to the vowel in English *caught*
ō	[uˑ ~ oˑ], ranging between the vowels of English *boot* and *boat*

Caution: Pentland uses the symbol *ă* for *a + h*. The symbol *e* is a typographical convenience for a range of vowels.

Marks (all uncertain)

¯ Perhaps lengthening, nasality, or other function
' Sometimes symbol of final unwritten [h], §70
′ Stressed syllable; other uncertain usages
~ ~ Mark of lengthening?
, No punctuation and probably not [ə]
˘ Uncertain and varying functions

In Pentland's phonology there are several points on which I believe there may be further discussion in regard to pronunciation:

1. He may show excessive nasalization of the vowel a in the Moravian variety of Mahican. Even Frank T. Siebert, who has heard the Stockbridge variety in the mid-1930s, states that the Mahican he heard had few nasal a's. Prime example (Pentland/Schmick):

   pãpãhtamawãyakw (păpāchtămăwájaku) 'as we pray'

   Why should the first vowel be nasalized when some Algonquian languages show it to be short and the next vowel long? Schmick himself shows a difference in vowels and later in the word shows similar vowels, which Pentland gives as nonnasalized.

2. *nmačayī* (nmátschai) 'I sin' — Why not *nmačaī*?
3. Why the y glide in *wãhkamāyew* (wachkamáo) 'it is day' and in *mxāyew* (m'cháo) 'it is big'? Even in 1759 wóchcamáo (Masthay, 1980) the word doesn't show j for y, yet other unrelated words do, for example, (n'wénajoom) 'my wife.' Compare Pentland's *pmāwesīt* (p'máoseēt) 'she lives,' where he uses *w*.

Postscript (for p. 3): **A strong opinion to take in context**

From W.C. Reichel: *Memorials of the Moravian Church* (Philadelphia, 1870, J.B. Lippincott & Co., vol. 1, pp. 54-55) there are embarrassing comments about "Mohicans" that should not be avoided.

Count Zinzendorf was a very strong-willed, self-opinionated man. About a year after the Moravians began their work with the New York Indians (and about 12 years before Schmick started his dictionary) we get a pungent opinion about the Mahicans from Zinzendorf on his trip to Shecomeco in August 1742.

Bro. Rauch lodged us in his hut for the night, and on the 17th we occupied the house that had been built for us. I was delighted with it; it was a perfect palace of bark, and furnished with a table and writing materials for my special convenience. My seat was on the ground. Here we lodged eight days, and, although it rained almost continuously, and we underwent numerous internal conflicts, our dear Indians had clear sky overhead, and rejoiced us each day anew. They are Mohicans, a confessedly worthless tribe of Indians. . . .

The Mohicans, although naturally fierce and vindictive, and given to excessive drinking, are tender-hearted, and susceptible of good impressions. When our pale-faced Bro. Rauch first came among them, they regarded him as a fool, and threatened his life. But after his recital of the Saviour's sufferings had made a powerful impression upon the most abandoned of their number (an impression which allowed him peace neither day nor night, until he experienced the preciousness of grace), the work of the Lord proceeded, and others were moved.

All the machinations of his mother-in-law, who sought to perplex him, were unsuccessful, although they proved effectual in causing his wife and daughter to vacillate. This brand snatched from the fire, is no longer Tschoop [alias Wasamapah], but *John,* and is an esteemed teacher among his people. Abraham, Isaac, and Jacob, who, you recollect, were baptized at Oley, were appointed to officers in the mission—Abraham elder, Jacob exhorter, and Isaac sexton.

The four are in all respects incomparable Indians, and men of God. When met in conference on affairs of the mission, they deliberated in a manner which astonished us. I confess that at times I felt pity for these poor people, whose imperfect language is inadequate for the expression of their new experiences, and of their views and wishes, as assistants in the Saviour's work. Our language is divine in comparison with theirs, and yet how unsatisfactorily can we give utterance to the emotions and aspirations of our hearts!

[Footnote modified, p. 55: Their Mohicans were organized into a congregation on August 22, 1742, after the missionary Rauch had baptized the Indians *Kaubus, Kermelok, Harris,* and the wives of *Abraham, Isaac,* and *Harris,* who, in baptism, were called respectively *Timothy, Jonas, Thomas, Sarah, Rebecca,* and *Esther.* These ten constituted the first congregation of Christian Indians for the Brethren.]

On p. 60, from a deposition for August 26, 1742, there is an interesting linguistic comment:

[Near Hurley, New York] . . . on the present occasion [Dominie von Thürstein] confined himself to his writing, appearing disinclined to speak in the presence of the [Mohican] Indians, who all understood Low Dutch [all three Mohican converts, that is].

FOR THE MAHICAN HISTORICAL PHONOLOGY

Condensed key to paragraphs
Symbols
Consonants and consonant clusters
§ 1. *p > p
2. *mp > p
3. p in loanwords
4. *hp/*xp/*čp > hp
5. *θp > xp
6. *šp > sp
7. *t > t
8. *nt > t
9. t in loanwords
10. *ʔt/*ht > ht
11. *[č] > č
12. *[nč] > č
13. č in loanwords
14. *[hč]/*[ʔč] > hč
15. t + s, č
16. final *t
17. diminutive č
18. *k > k; *kʷ/*kw > kw
19. k
20. *nk > k
21. k in loanwords
22. kw
23. *nkʷ/*nkw > kw
24. ks/kws
25. kk- > k-
26. *hk > h; *hkʷ/*hkw > hw
27. *xk(ʷ/w)/*čk(ʷ/w)/*sk(ʷ/w) > hk(w)
28. hks
29. *θk(ʷ/w) > xk(w)
30. *sk(ʷ/w) > sk(w)
31. *s > s
32. *ns/*hs/*ʔs > s
33. *š > š

§34. *nš > š
35. s instead of š
36. š instead of s
37. diminutive s > š
38. *hš/*ʔš > x
39. *h > h
40. *θ/*l > n
41. n in loanwords
42. *l/*nl > h
43. *-ali/*-ili > -an/-īn, -īh
44. *-ali/*-ili > Stockbridge -an/-īn
45. *nθ/*nl/*ʔl > hn
46. *θ/*-l > x
47. *š → *θ (> n)
48. *m > m; *n > n
49. m, n in loanwords
50. nn > n-
51. *ʔm > hm
52. *-ʔmepani > -hep
53. first plural *-ʔm-
54. unusual *-ʔmeC-
Vowels and semivowels
55. *w and *y
56. *w > w
57. w in loanwords
58. *y > y
59. lost *w
60. lost *y
61. noun-stem *y > ey
62. II *-yā-
63. AI *-yā-
64. long vowels
65. *ā > ǟ; *ē > ā̃
66. vowel length
67. *i > ī; *o > ō
68. *a > a

§69. unstressed a- + h/x
70. [ah]
71. some TI -am- > -em-
72. *e > e
73. e- > a-/zero
74. e(+ rounded C) > o
75. some e(+ m, p, hp) > o
76. e(+ x) > a
77. e(+ h) > a
78. we- > o-
79. we = [wə] ∼ [u]
80. *we > *o > ō
81. *ye > ī
82. ī/ō(+ w, y) > e
83. īw, ōw
84. awe > ã(+ C)
85. ewe > ō(+ C)
Stress and syncope
86. long-vowel stress
87. unstressed e > zero
88. "loss" of ne-
89. vowel alternations
90. e ∼ zero
91. o ∼ e
92. a ∼ e
93. a ∼ zero (< *e)
94. a ∼ zero (< *a)
95. e ∼ zero
96. o ∼ a
97. final *i
98. final short-vowel loss
99. final long vowels
100. final *Cw
101. final PA sonorant
102. conclusion

(Both lists compiled by C.M.)

Key to help find specific Schmick pronunciations—examples within paragraphs
(Expanded from pronunciation guide on pp. 12 and 13. *Note:* semicolons separate variants.)

aã, ã̃ã̃, ã̃	§65, 102	n	§40, 41, 48
a	72?	-ñ-	nn?
-a	99	n'n	50
ach	102; /ã̃/, 70	o	/ō/, 70, 71; /o/, 71, 72, 74; /ew/, 70, 77, 79, 81
ai	46, 58, (61)	ŏã̆	82
-an	65	oo	64, 80
-ao	26, 27, 62; 80, 84	ou	70
áŭ	60	p	1
ay	69	p'ch	/p/ + /x/ = /px/, §46; but cf. pĕcháãn
c, k, ck, q	26	p'h	/p/ + /h/ = /ph/, not /f/ as in Philip; see p'hága
ch *alone*	39, 46		
ch + *cons.*	51	q, qᵘ	§22; /ᵘ/ = 'rounded and devoiced'
chk, chq	19, 20, 29; note 11, p. 27	r	41
chs	46	s, ss	31
chtsch	14	sch	34, 35
d	7, 8	sh	Possible error for sch, but may appear for /s/ + /h/, as in weeshécan ('mark, goal')
e	/i/, 19-21, 29-31, 67, 74; /e/, 61, 71, 75		
-ĕ-	46		
-e	67, 78 versus 90	t	§7
-ĕ	88, 97	tsch	11, 12
ee	7, 16, 64, 81	u	[wə] ∼ [u], 79; /e/, 72, 73; /o/, 21, 74, 78, 91
ei	4, 46, 77, 88; 61	-u	62
g	25	-uoch	/wahw/; §94
h + *cons.*	8, 10, 65, 66	uu	/wə/; §68
-i	61	w	§55-57
i + *cons.*	74, 75	x	24; sometimes /kš/?, §35
ia	47, 101; 82 [/nia/ instead of /neya/?]	xx	28
ii	75	y, ÿ, ij	Offglide semiconsonantal [j] or [əi]?
j	58	z	§15
k	22, 79		

MAHICAN HISTORICAL PHONOLOGY

DAVID H. PENTLAND

University of Manitoba

The following sketch of Mahican historical phonology is intended to cover only the main developments in the long period between Proto-Algonquian and eighteenth-century Moravian Mahican. It is not concerned with any of the intermediate stages, with other varieties of Mahican, nor with minor details relevant only to a few words.

Mahican is one of the descendants of Proto-Eastern Algonquian, a subgroup of the Algonquian family first identified by Ives Goddard (1967). Unlike Goddard, however, I do not include all of the eastern languages in the subgroup. Proto-Eastern Algonquian is based, for the most part, on modern Micmac, Malecite-Passamaquoddy, Penobscot (Eastern Abenaki), St. Francis (Western) Abenaki, and Unami and Munsee Delaware: it naturally accounts quite well for the languages from which it was reconstructed. The languages of southern New England (Massachusett, Narragansett, etc.) and the southeast (Powhatan, Nanticoke, etc.) fit less well, and I doubt that they were part of the subgroup—the few innovations they share with Eastern Algonquian may have spread across language boundaries in relatively recent times.

Within Eastern Algonquian, Mahican fits best between the Abenaki dialects and Delaware, as might be expected from its geographic position in the historic period. There are many similarities with Munsee and Unami Delaware, but some appear to be late additions to the grammar of Mahican; at an earlier stage Mahican may have been more like the Abenaki languages.

There were at least two distinct dialects of Mahican (here termed Moravian and Stockbridge), which differ significantly in the features they share with neighboring languages. The most obvious difference is that the obviative inflections in Moravian Mahican agree with Western Abenaki (and more distantly with southern New England languages), while Stockbridge Mahican agrees with Eastern Abenaki and the languages farther north. Stockbridge materials cannot therefore be used as evidence for Moravian Mahican, however tempting it might be to rely on Truman Michelson's accurate phonetic recordings.

There is substantial agreement between Moravian Mahican and Munsee Delaware in the distribution and phonetic realization of allophones: I have therefore followed closely Ives Goddard's description of Munsee historical phonology (1982), which often provides useful clues in interpreting Schmick's spellings. It follows from this that I have rejected the analysis of Mahican phonology put forward by Janet Warne (1980): we agree fairly closely on the consonants (except that she has both *h* and *hk* < *xk*; *xk* < *sk*; *hs* < *hs* and *?s*; and no examples for half a dozen clusters), but she considers that *ē and *a merged as *a* whereas short *i and *o did not merge with their long counterparts. Proulx (1983) adopts Warne's analysis of the consonants and makes *ē and *a merge as short *a* but correctly notes that the short and long high vowels fall together; I cannot agree, however, that the high vowels become short *e* and *o*, since the stress patterns show that they (and the reflex of *ē) are long.

Symbols

A subscript dot indicates an uncertain reading in the Schmick manuscript, an uncertain reconstruction in the Proto-Algonquian form, or a difficulty in phonemicizing the Mahican form (usually because the etymology is not completely clear).

A hyphen after a vowel marks the preverb boundary (between preverbs and verb stems, after reduplicated syllables, and between elements in compound words); after *θ the hyphen indicates that Mahican has reversed the palatalization of *θ to *š.

In the Proto-Algonquian reconstructions *č is replaced by *t (cf. Pentland 1983a); *kʷ is distinguished (where possible) from *kw; and final long vowels are written as such. Other potential revisions, such as a distinction between glottalized and unglottalized sonorants (Pentland 1983b), appear to be irrelevant to the history of Mahican and are therefore ignored. Elements which are not part of the normal Proto-Algonquian reconstruction but which are required to explain the Mahican form are included in parentheses; very rarely parentheses are also used to enclose parts of the Proto-Algonquian word which are not continued in Mahican. All reconstructed forms are preceded by an asterisk.

Long vowels are marked with a macron (¯); nasalized *a* is marked with the tilde (ã); θ is *th* in English *thick*, č is *ch* in *church*, š is *sh* in *she*, *x* is *ch* in German *Bach*, and ? is the glottal stop (as in English [rɪʔn] *written*). Regular sound changes are indicated by > 'becomes' and < 'derives from,' whereas irregular reshapings are marked by → and ←.

Consonants and consonant clusters

1. Proto-Algonquian *p remains in Mahican as *p*, which Schmick writes **p** or **pp**, rarely **b** (usually after *m* or *n*):

papīkw (**papēĕk**) 'flea'	**papikʷa*
pmāwesōp (**p'mawosōŏp**) 'he lived'	**pemāwesiwepani*
kmehtapnāp (**kmēchtapp'nap**) 'you were born'	**kemweʔtapināpani*
ntapsī (**-n dappsè**) 'I warm myself'	**netapeswi*
npōp (**npōp, mbōŏp**) 'he has died'	**nep(e)wepani*
sīpōk (**sébook**) 'to the creek'	**sīpyiwenki* 'to/in the river'
nāphah (**nabhà**) 'string it (wampum)'	**θāpahanlwe*

2. The consonant cluster *mp loses its nasal component, merging with Mahican *p*:

nsīwanạ̄tpā (nsewanadpà, n'sewanà t'pà)   **nesīwaḻātempē*
   'I have a headache'

3. Mahican *p* also represents German, Dutch, and English p, b, and f (but not German w = [v]) in loanwords:[1]

apenes (ápĕnĕs) 'apple'	D. appel (+ dim. *-es*)	
pešop (bishop) 'bishop'	E. bishop	
pnaš (pnàsch) 'bottle'	G. Flasche	
snep (snùp) 'snuff'	E. snuff	
peyŏnhamāw (piŏnhamáu)	D. viool (+ *-aham-ā-*)	
'he plays the violin'		

4. The clusters **hp*, **xp*, and **čp* probably merge as *hp* in Mahican, but there do not appear to be any cognates reflecting **hp* or **čp* (if the latter was really distinct from **xp* in Proto-Algonquian). Schmick usually writes the reflex of **xp* as *chp*, but occasionally he does not indicate the preaspiration:

āhpapīmek (aáchpapémick 'Bank')   **ēxpapi(me)nki*
   'what one sits on'
kohpaka[n] (-ck opákka) 'it is thick'   **kexpakanwi*
kwīhpōmīhnā (kwĕchpōmĕnăn)   **kewīxpōmiʔmenāni*
   'you eat with us'
wahpoxkwanek (wapuchquanek, wapóchquanik)
   'in his side'   **wexpeθkʷanenki*
nahpasay, kahpasay (nachpássei, ghapássei) 'my, your breast'
   *nexpasēwi, *kexpasēwi (final reshaped)[2]

5. The rare consonant cluster **θp* probably becomes *xp* (as in Delaware), but Schmick writes it *chp*, the same as Mahican *hp*:

naxpī (nachpè, nāāchpè) 'with, together'   **naθpyi*

6. Proto-Algonquian **šp* becomes *sp*:

spomek (spommuck) 'up above'   **ešpemenki*
nkīspī (n'kéespe 'bistu satt') 'I am full'   **nekīšpwi*

7. Proto-Algonquian **t* remains as Mahican *t*, which was probably a dental stop rather than alveolar as in English. Schmick writes *t* or *tt*, sometimes *d*:

ntāptōnā (ntáāptonà) 'I speak'   **netāpetonē*
onet (-ŭnit) 'it is good'   **weθetwi*
onetŏwī (ŏnìttówe) 'it is not good'   **weθet(owi)wi*
ntatāwāwī (-n tăttăwāwĕ) 'I don't buy (it)'   **netatāwā(wi)*
tmahīkan (t'mahégan, d'mahégan) 'ax'   **temahikani*
osītan (osétan, osēdan) 'his feet'   **wesitali*
kātmāksīt (kat'maxēĕd 'he who is poor')   **kētemākesita*

8. The Proto-Algonquian cluster **nt* also becomes Mahican *t*, written *t, tt,* and *d*:

otāw (otáu) 'it boils'   **wentēwi*
petawīh (péttăwè) 'hear me'   **pentawilwe*
pīthah (pehdhà) 'fill it up'   **pīntahanlwe*
ăkītah (ăchkĕtă 'lesen') 'read (it)'   **akintanlwe* 'count it'
nt(e)pāntamen (-n t'páäntammèn)   **netepēlentameni*
   'I own it'
nemenātamen (nĕmĕnnátámĕn 'riechen')
   'I smell it'   **nemelāntameni*

9. German, Dutch, and English *t* and *nt* (presumably also *d* and *nd*) are borrowed as Mahican *t*:

kastīnek (Găstênik) 'Albany'   D. kasteel (+ loc. *-ek*)

pōten (póten) 'butter'   D. boter[3]
pnatwīn (p'natt'wĕn) 'brandy'   G. Brandtwein

Schmick's Gemēēnde, Gemēēnde (kemīnte? < G. Gemeinde 'congregation') is not fully assimilated into Mahican, since it still has *nd* instead of *t* (as in *pnatwīn* 'brandy').

10. Proto-Algonquian **ʔt* falls together with **ht* as Mahican *ht*. Schmick usually writes *cht*, but occasionally only *t*, omitting the preaspiration:

kahtemnāw (kahtem'náu, katemnáu)
   'he is lazy'   **kehtemiwa* (final reshaped)
onīhtāw (onechtău) 'he makes it'   **weθ-ihtāwa*
okīsīhtān (okeschechtăn)   **wekīšihtāni*
   'he has done it'
knenōhtānōw (knenóchtànò)   **kenenwehtaweθ(ow)e*
   'I don't understand you'

ahtāw (achtáŭ 'drinne') 'it is there'   **aʔtēwi*
mahtokw (machtòkq) 'wood'   **meʔtekʷi*
nahtaw (nachtàu) 'once'   **neʔtawi*
wīhtōnayah (wechtonajà) 'his facial hairs'   **wīʔtonayahi*

11. Before **i, *ī,* and **y*, Proto-Algonquian **t* was phonetically **[č]*; various changes (especially the loss of postconsonantal **y* or **w*, or both) have made *č* (or a later development from it) phonemic in all the Algonquian languages. In Mahican **[č]* is continued as *č*, which Schmick regularly spells in the German fashion as *tsch*:

čīkhah (tschēĕkhà) 'sweep it out'   **tīkahanlwe*
nmačayī (nmátschai) 'I sin'   **nemati-ayi* 'I am bad'
māčīh (matschè) 'go home'   **mātyīlwe*
onīčānah (onétschănă) 'his daughter'   **wenītyānali*
   'his child'
newīčāwāw (ne wetschawáu) 'I go with him'   **newītyēwāwa*
pāyāčīk (pajatschēĕk) 'they who come'   **pyēyātiki*

12. The consonant cluster **[nč]* (= Proto-Algonquian **nt* before **i, *ī,* or **y*) also becomes *č*:

očī (otschè) 'from there'   **wenti*
kōčayīhemā (-gótschai hamà)   **kewenti-ayiʔmwāwi*
   'you are from there'
apīnčāsīh (appēĕn tschassè)   **apiθentyēswilwe*
   'warm your hands'
menačīw (menatschéu) 'he is left-handed'   **menantīwa*

13. In loanwords Mahican probably had *č* from English and German *č* and *nč*, but no examples were recorded by Schmick.

14. Before **i, *ī,* and **y*, Proto-Algonquian **ht* was phonetically **[hč]* and **ʔt* was **[ʔč]*; there are no Mahican examples reflecting **[hč]*, but **[ʔč]* becomes *hč*, which Schmick writes as *chtsch* (or occasionally just *tsch*):

kahčay (kachtschai) 'old man'   **keʔti-aya*
māhč, māhčī (perfective preverb and particle)
   *mēʔti 'to exhaustion'
[as in *nkīsī-māhč-nmatapī* (nkeschemàchtsch nmattapè) 'I have already sat,' *māhč kenāwī* (machtschkenáwe) 'you have seen me,' *māhčī nā(w)ahkwātā* (machtschè nāāchquatà) 'when it is after noon']
oċehčākwah (ŏtschitschaquà) 'his soul' **weteʔtyākʷali*

15. The combination *t + s* is occasionally spelled z, as in German:
ăptōnătsa (ăăptónāzā) 'when he says' *ăpetonāt(e)sani

It is possible that Schmick also occasionally writes z for *č*, confusing the TI verb *mīčī-* 'eat it' (< **mīty-*) with the AI *mītsī-* 'eat' (< **mītehswi-*):
mītsītā (mezéta) 'when he had eaten' **mītehswitē* (AI)
kmīčīhnā (kmĕtschĕchnă) 'we eat it' **kemītye?menawi* (TI)

kmīčīhnŏk (and kmītsīhnŏk ?) 'we eat (it)'
  *kemītye?menaw(ek)i (and **kemītehswi?menaw(ek)i* ?)
  [in "Gáquaik ĕn kmetschechnŏk" and "Gaquai ene kmezechnŏŏk," both translated 'What do we have to eat?']

16. Like most other Algonquian languages, Mahican has undone the palatalization of **t* to *[č]* in certain morphological environments (the singular of inanimate nouns and the third person singular of conjunct verbs) where the conditioning vowel (**i*) has been lost at the end of a word:
nsīt (nsēēd) 'my foot'   **nesiti*
ăpīt (ápēēd) 'he sits'   **ēpiti*
nāwāt (nawaāt) 'he sees him' **nēwāti*
kwxat (kchàt) 'you fear him' **kwe?θati*

However, *č* remains in the third person injunctive ('let him. . .'), where the palatalization was conditioned by **-yē*, and in the prohibitive ('he must not. . .'), which in Proto-Algonquian had the same suffix as the ordinary conjunct:
pmāwesīč (pmawoseētsch) 'let him live' **pemāwesityē*
  [versus pmāwesīt (p'máosēēt) 'he lives' < **pemāwesiti*]
nt(e)mīkāhīč (-n tmegahēētsch)   **natemwikēhkiti* [4]
  'he must not go in'

17. Mahican freely creates new examples of *č* by an optional rule of diminutive consonant symbolism, which changes *t* to *č* in words with diminutive meaning:
čmahīkanes (tsch'mahéganis) 'little ax' **temahikanehsi*
očōnes (utschunis, Masthay 1980:38) **wetōnehsi*
  'his little mouth'
čahkwăpčōnăkač(š?)ew (tschachquaăptschŏnăchgătschò)
  'it is a short word' **taxkwăpetonakatehsiwi*

18. Proto-Algonquian **k* remains in Mahican as *k*, whereas the combination **kw* and the single consonant[5] **kʷ* both become *kw*. In Mahican *kw* is best treated as a sequence of *k* plus *w*, since the *w* is sometimes absorbed into the following vowel, but at an earlier stage in the language it was probably the unit *kʷ*.

19. Schmick writes Mahican *k* as k, g, ck, and kk:
kīkaxkwāw (kékăchquáu) 'girl, maiden' **kīkeθkwēwa*
kīkāpāw (gegapau) 'unmarried man' **kīkāpēwa*
kōnī-kawī (kōne kawè, góne gawè) **keweθ-i-kawī*
  'you sleep well'
khakay (k'hackei, khakkei) 'yourself' **kahakayi* 'your skin'
kakāhkīmen (gagachgémen) 'I teach you' **kekakyēxkimeθe*

20. The Proto-Algonquian cluster **nk* also becomes *k*:
kīkan (gégan) 'it is sharp'   **kīnkanwi*
wīkan (wĕgan) 'it is sweet'   **wīnkanwi*
osīkīnawāwah (oschegenawáwa) **wesīnkinawāwali*
  'he hates him'

ntenemakan (ntennemágan)   **neteθemankani*
  'my shoulder'
onaxkek (ŏnachgĕk) 'in his hand(s)' **weneθkenki*
amatakā (ămáttakà) 'when he feels it' **amantankē*

21. In loanwords Mahican *k* represents Dutch, German, and English k (and, no doubt, g, nk, and ng):
kīkīpsak (keképsak) 'chickens' D. kip, kiep kiep (+ -es-ak)
komkomšan (kumkumschàn) D. komkommer (+ -eš-an)
  'cucumbers'
kaneš (kánnisch) 'pitcher' E. can (+ -eš)
kōnan (gónan 'Kraut') 'cabbages' G. Kohl (+ -an)
omāmāksemah (ŏmāmāksĭmmà) D. mekker- 'bleat'(?)
  'his sheep'   (+ -es-em-ah)

22. Mahican *kw* is usually spelled kw or qu, but at the end of a word (and occasionally elsewhere) Schmick also writes ku, kq, or often just k (etc.) without indication of the following *w*:
kwaxāw (kwacháu) 'you fear him' **kekwe?θāwa*
kwxat (kchát) 'you fear him' **kwe?θati*
kwīnākw (quenāku) 'he seeks you' **kekwīθawekwa*
nkwečīmōnokw (n'kutschemónuk) **nekwetim(oθ)ekwa*
  'he asks me'
mahtokw (machtòk, machtòkq, **me?tekʷi*
  machtóqk) 'wood'

23. Proto-Algonquian **nkʷ* and **nkw* lose their nasal component, becoming Mahican *kw*:
pekwīw (pùkqũeũ, pùckqueüw) 'ashes' **penkwi(wi)*
pekwesak (pĕkússak) 'mosquitoes, gnats' **penkwehsa*
kakawekwaxīn (gagauuquacheēn) **ka-kawenkwa?ši(n)wa*
  'he is sleepy'
pāpāhtamawāyakw (păpăchtămăwájaku)
  'as we (incl.) pray' **pā-pyā?tamawāyankʷi*

24. Both *ks* and *kws* are sometimes spelled x:
ksī (xè, ksè) 'you say'   **kesi*
kt(e)māksōp (kt'maxōōp) 'he was poor' **ketemākesiwepani*
onāhnayōksemah (hŏnāchnājŏxĕmà, hŏnāchnājŏksĕmà)
  'his horse'   **wenē-nayōnk(ēw)ehsemali*
pnaksak (pnáxak) 'flax (pl.)' E. flax (+ -ak)
nmāmāksemsak (mamaximsàk, D. mekker- (?)
  mamaksimsàk) 'my sheep (pl.)' (+ -es-em-ak)

kōnīnākwsī (konenaxè 'es ist hübsch') **keweθ-inākʷesi*
  'you look nice'
anīnākwsītep (anènããxétip) **eθ-inākʷesit(e)pani*
  'he appeared so'

25. Mahican apparently has the same rule as Munsee, by which initial *kk-* is reduced to *k-*; although Schmick sometimes writes ck or kk, he also has g, clearly indicating a single *k-*:
kakāhkīmen (gagachgémen) 'I teach you' **kekakyēxkimeθe*
katopīhmā (gatopechmà)   **kekatwepwi?mwāwi*
  'you (pl.) are hungry'
kawī (kawè, gawè) 'you sleep' **kekawī*
kīšihokōp (késchehogoōp) 'he made you' **kekīšihekwepani*
kwīnākōnaw (quenacónau) **kekwīθawekwenawi*
  'he is looking for us'

26. Like Munsee and Unami Delaware, Mahican has *h* from Proto-Algonquian **hk* and *hw* from **hkʷ* and **hkw*. Schmick usually writes h, hw, but occasionally ch, chw:
tahāyew (d'háju, tahao) 'it is cold'   **tahkyēwi*
anīhtāhākw (anechtahāku) 'don't lose it'   **wanihtāhkēkʷi*

pahwahah (pahwahà) 'peel it (bark)'   **pahkʷahanlwe*
ătohw (ăchtòh, ăchtóhu) 'deer'   **atehkʷa*
otohōn < otohwan (ŏttŏhòhn) 'branch'   **wetehkwani*
āhwesew (achussò, achwussò) 'he is avaricious'   **āhkwesiwa*

27. The consonant clusters **xk*, **čk* (if it was distinct from **xk* in Proto-Algonquian), and **sk* (no example) fall together as *hk* in Mahican, whereas **xkʷ/*xkw*, **skʷ/*skw* (and **čkʷ/*čkw*) merge as *hkw*. Schmick writes chg, showing that *hk(w)* was a true consonant cluster with *h* followed by lenis *k*, as well as chk, chc, chq, etc.:
pkahkan (p'gachgan) 'blood'   **pakaxkanwi*
wāhkamāyew (wachkamáo) 'it is day'   **wāxkamyēwi*
nahkahkwan (nąchgāchquān) 'my shinbone'   **nexkaxkʷani*
mātehk (matechk) 'that which is bad'   **mētexki*
āhkwī (áchque) 'cease'   **ēxkwi*
osītāhkw (osétòchq 'Axthelm') 'ax handle'   **wesitāxkʷi*
matahkw (matàchą̌) 'cloud'   **mataxkwi*

kahkāyew (kakkajòh)   **kečkyēwa* (= **kexkyēwa*)
'he is old, the oldest'

nōhkwātah (nŭchquātà 'sie sollens lecken')   **nōskwātanlwe*
'lick it'
mahkwīpanāhkwī (?) (măchkwèpánăchkwè 'rothe Stöcke')
'red stick'   **meskʷipanāxkʷi(-)*

Except in the word 'red stick' (which is apparently incomplete, with connective -ī- before some missing final element), Mahican has replaced the root **meskʷ-* 'red' with **meθk-* or **maθk-* (> *maxk-*, as in Munsee and Unami).

28. The combination *hks* is sometimes written chx or even xx:
čahkwahksen (tschachquachxen)   **taxkʷaxkeseni*
   'old(?) shoe'   'short shoe'
nmahksen (máxxen, máksen) 'my shoe'   **nemaxkeseni*

29. As in Munsee and Unami Delaware, Proto-Algonquian **θk* probably becomes *xk* in Mahican, and **θkʷ/*θkw* probably yields Mahican *xkw*, but Schmick writes chk, chq, etc., the same as Mahican *hk(w)*:
naxk (n'nachk) 'my hand'   **neneθki*
waxkan (wachgàn) '(his) bone'   **weθkani*
nmaxkam (n'máchgam) 'I find it'   **nemeθkame*

maxkw (màchq) 'bear'   **maθkʷa*
amoxkw (ămùchq) 'beaver'   **ameθkʷa*
kaxkwākākan (kāchquākachcan)   **keθkʷayikan(kan)i*
   'your neck'
kīkaxkwāw (kékāchquáu) 'girl, maiden'   **kīkeθkwēwa*

30. The consonant clusters **šk* and **škʷ/*škw* become sk and skw respectively:
oskāyew (uskáju) 'it is new'   **weškyēwi*
aseskewahohw (ăsusquahō) 'clay pot'   **ašyeškyiwaxkehkwa*

tmaskhamek (t'māskhămăk)   **temaškahamenki*
   'that one cut the grass'

nīskwan (nisquàn 'Arm') 'my elbow'[6]
   *nīškʷani (← **neškʷani*)
xaskwīmī(n) (chăsquēmē, chasquemen)   **meʔθaškwimini*
   'corn'

31. Proto-Algonquian **s* remains as *s* in Mahican. Schmick writes both s and ss, probably following the spelling conventions of English rather than his native German:
sīpōk (sébook) 'to the creek'   **sīpyiwenki* 'to/in the river'
sōkeneh (sogenè) 'pour it in'   **sōkenanlwe*
kōsāmī-sāsāmčāhāwak (kōsămē sasam'tschaháwak)
   'you whip them too much' **kewesāmi-sā-sāmetyēhāwaki*
ntapsī (-n dappsè) 'I warm myself'   **netapeswi*
apesīh (appessè) 'warm yourself'   **apeswilwe*
apīsītāsīh (appesseęd tassè) 'warm your feet' **apisitēswilwe*

32. The Proto-Algonquian consonant clusters **ns*, **hs*, and **ʔs* also become *s*:
osew (osòh) 'he (kettle) is boiling'   **wenswiwa*
pīspāyan (pēspājàn) 'that you sweat'   **pīnsepyēyani*
anīwīsew (ănēwěsŏ) 'he is named thus'   **eθ-i-wīnswiwa*

nmīs (mēēs) 'my older sister'   **nemyehsa*
mekōs (măkōōs) 'awl'   **mekwehsi*
nmītsī (n'méze) 'I eat'   **nemītehswi*

nsekī-tākwahw (nsĕgĕtăhquòch)   **neʔseki-takwahw(ān)a*
   'brown bread'
wīsakan (wésăkàn) 'it is bitter'   **wīʔsakanwi*
matasen (măttássèn) 'stone pipe'   **mataʔsenya*
namās (namāās) 'fish'   **namēʔsa*
namāsak (nămąąsak, namaássak) 'fish (pl.)' **namēʔsaki*

33. Proto-Algonquian **š* generally remains in Mahican as *š*, which Schmick spells sch, as in German:
šāpnīkan (schāāpnégan) 'needle'   **šāpwenikana*
mešāw (mëschául) 'he shoots him'   **mešwēwa*
nīšewak (néschᵒwak) 'they are two'   **nyīšiwaki*
okīšīhāwah (okeschehάwa)   **wekīšihāwahi*
   'he has made them'
anahkāšīkāwak (annachkaschegáwak)   **eθaxkyēšikēwaki*
   'they plow'
nwīwašī (n'wéwaschè 'kanstu ... tragen')   **newīwaši*
   'I have a pack'

34. The cluster **nš* loses the nasal component, merging with *š*:
kāwīšīmīn (gaweschemen) 'blackberry'**kāwinšyimina*
māmōšmahtamek (machmŏōschmachtámik)
   'razor'   **ma-mōnš...amenki*

In the word for 'eye,' **nš* becomes *č* (written tsch):
oskīčokw (uskétschùk) 'his eye'   **weškīnšekwi*
oskīčkwan (oskétschquan) 'his eyes'   **weškīnšekwali*

This development, also found in Powhatan, Nanticoke, and Munsee (but not Unami), probably occurred before the loss of **n* in the cluster **nš*, when a three-consonant group was created by the loss of unstressed **e* in the plural and other inflected forms, i.e., *nškʷ > *nčkʷ (> Mahican čkw); č was then analogically extended to forms like the singular in which the vowel remains.

35. In a few forms, Schmick's spellings indicate s instead of š:

ăswīn (as'wehhn) 'he swims'	*ášawilwa
aseskewahohw (ăsusquahō) 'clay pot'	*ašyeškyiwaxkehkwa
sašewak (săschuak) 'that which is salty; salt'	*ša-šīwanki
kāstāk (kástâăk) 'that which is warm'	*kešyetēki
[versus kšetāw- (xschittáw-) 'it is warm' < *kešyetēwi]	
ntemesem (n'tummesim) 'I cut it'	*netemešame
[versus ntemšem (ntemmschim) 'I cut it']	
skwešāw (sguscháu) 'he cuts him'	*šekwešēwa
[versus kšekwešā (kschukquaschà) 'you cut him' < *kešekwešwā]	

Schmick also occasionally writes x (= kš) or xsch (= kšš ?) instead of ksch (= kš):

nk(e)šīhnā (nxechnà, nkschechnà)	*nekešyīʔlē
'I jump quickly'	
kšahtāw (xschàchtăŭ) 'it is smoking'	*kešyaʔtēwi (?)

In 'clay pot' Mahican has s instead of š by assimilation to the following s (as in Munsee ắsíˑskəw 'mud,' Goddard 1982: 21); on the other hand, the s in 'salt' must be due to dissimilation unless it is just a spelling error. There is no explanation for the s in 'swim' (four examples), but the other cases of s and ks are probably no more than occasional lapses by Schmick, since he often gives other forms of the same stems with the expected š or kš.

36. There is also one example with š given as an alternative to the historically correct s:

kšīkamīšew, kšīkamīsew (kschēkăméscho, -so)
'he (kettle) is boiling' *kešyikamyeswiwa

37. In diminutives, Mahican s (from all sources—*s, *ns, *hs, and *ʔs) optionally becomes š:

awāšīs (ăwāsches) 'child'	*awās(V̄hs)a
onesīsew (honesséscho)	*weθes(V̄hs)iwa
'he (child) is beautiful'	
čakešīsewah, čakešīsewah (tsackĕschéssĕwa, tsackĕscheschĕwà) 'they (obv.) are small'	*tankes(V̄hs)iwali
šīpōšīs (schébohsches [crossed out by Schmick])	
'little creek'	*sīpyiwehs(V̄hs)i

38. Proto-Algonquian *hš and *ʔš become x (a voiceless velar or uvular fricative), which Schmick writes with the German digraph ch:

kpaxāwak (kpacháwak) 'they are deaf'	*kepehšēwaki
ktaxamāw (ktachamáu) 'you feed him'	*ketahšamāwa
nčīk-anīxīn (tschegănēchēn) 'I lie still'	*netīki-eθ-ihšine
wāxeyā (wăchīă) 'my husband'	*wēʔšiyāna 'he who I have as husband'
maxānī (măchănĕ) 'many'	*meʔšyeθ-i
nkakawekwxīn (n'gāgăŭkcheēn)	*neka-kawenkwaʔši(ne)
'I am sleepy'	

39. Proto-Algonquian *h remains as h in Mahican. Schmick usually writes h but occasionally ch (the same as x, the reflex of *hš, *hθ, etc.):

nhakay (nháckai) 'myself'	*nahakayi 'my skin'
ntāh (ndàh) 'my heart'	*netēhyi
anītāhāw (anètaháu) 'he thinks so'	*eθ-itēhēwa
otahākan (ōtăhágan, otáhacàn) 'canoe (?)'	*wetahākani 'paddle'
tăkwahw (tachquòch) 'bread'	*takwahw(ān)a
omāmāwanah (omàmawănà, omàmāwanàch) 'his eyebrows'	*wemāmāwanahi

40. The two Proto-Algonquian consonants conventionally written *θ and *l have fallen together in most Algonquian languages. In Mahican both become n:

nānāwat (nánawàt) 'it is halfway, in the middle'	*θā-θāwatwi
anāhānsī (anàhaansè) 'throw yourself down'	*eθāhkāθesilwe
kōnamansī (konamansè) 'you feel well'	*keweθamaθesi
nīnem (nénim) 'my (male) brother's wife'	*nīθemwa
ktenen (ktēnnèn) 'I say to you'	*keteθeθe
nīmanāw (némanáu) 'man, male'	*nyīmaθēwa
nākaw (năăgaù, nágaū) 'sand'	*lēkawi
anewīwī (annuwéwe, ánnowéwe) 'more than'	*alyiwi(wi)
anenāpāwak (anenapáwak) 'Indians'	*elenāpēwaki
wanamanah (wanammana) 'vermilion (obv.)'	*walamanali
kmīnen (kménen) 'I give it to you'	*kemīleθe
sōknān (sōk'nàhn) 'it rains'	*sōkelānwi

41. In words borrowed from European languages l and r become n:

apenes (ápĕnĕš) 'apple'	D. appel (+ -es)
pnaš (pnàsch) 'bottle'	G. Flasche
kōnan (gónan 'Kraut') 'cabbages'	G. Kohl (+ -an)
pnaksak (pnáxak) 'flax (pl.)'	E. flax (+ -ak)
pnōmes (p'nōmĭs) 'broom'	E. broom (+ -es)
pīnekesak (pénĕgĕsàk) 'peach trees'	D. pirkes (+ -ak)
pnatwīn (p'nattʼwēn) 'brandy'	G. Brandtwein

42. In the last syllable of inflectional suffixes, *l and the cluster *nl become h in Mahican; Schmick seldom indicates the consonant, usually writing instead a grave accent on the preceding vowel:

wīwah (wĕwa) 'his wife'	*wīwali
okīšīhāwah (okescheháwa) 'he made him'	*wekīšihāwali
kawīh (gawè) 'go to sleep'	*kawīlwe
pīthah (pehdhà) 'fill it up'	*pīntahanlwe
nāteh (năăde) 'fetch it'	*nāt(an)lwe
kīkāhīh (gegahè) 'heal me'	*kīkēhilwe
pāyanīh (pájănĕ) 'whenever you come'	*pyāyanili
wāwāhkamākīh (wáwochkamakè) 'whenever it is day'	*wā-wāxkamyēkili

43. However, the inanimate plural suffix *-ali (apparently homonymous in Proto-Algonquian with the obviative singular) becomes -an (with the normal development of *l to n) instead of -ah. In pronouns inanimate plural *-ili similarly becomes -īn, but in participles it yields -īh:

nīpan (népan) 'my arrows'	*nīpali
kpetōnāwan (kpetonáwan) 'they (inan.) are silent'	*kepetonēwali

nīn (néēn) 'those (inan.)'   *anili
āhtākīh (achtáge) 'those things that are there' *ēʔtēkili

All three forms of the inanimate plural (Op) suffix occur in the following sentence:
ktamătamen nīn āptōnawăkanan ānī-kanaweyanīh ktāhek
(Ktammachtammen néēn aaptonawaganan ănèkănawójannè ktahàk.) 'Do you feel those(Op) words(Op) that you sing(AI participle 2+Op) in your heart?'

44. In the Stockbridge dialect of Mahican, on the other hand, obviative singular *-ali and *-ili become -an and -īn (like the inanimate plural) in nouns, pronouns, and independent-order verbs, but *-ili becomes -īh (as in Moravian Mahican) in conjunct-order verbs, including participles:
neen kausekhoikeh wchehchuhqun 'the Holy Ghost' (lit. 'that soul of his that is holy')(Quinney & Aupaumut 1818[?], 6A)
op·ot·awán pask·owán nemánan 'she heard one man' (Prince 1905, iii)
umáskawăn paᶜpaᶜkōwan 'he found a partridge' (Michelson ms, 1914, ii)

Schmick and the other Moravian missionaries occasionally recorded obviatives with the Stockbridge dialect suffixes:
Jesus ŏtènnahn néēn Petrusasan wăk Johannes[an ?]
'Jesus said to Peter and John' (Masthay 1980:29)

wānsīcīh očehčăkwan (wah'nssetsche otschitschachquan) 'the Holy Ghost' (lit. 'his soul which is beautiful')
                        < *wēθesitili weteʔtyākʷali

The Stockbridge form of the suffix seems to occur most often in the Moravian writings in the phrase 'the Holy Ghost' (the only example noted in Schmick, and three times in the letter from Jonas printed in Masthay 1980:27-28), but even here Schmick also has the Moravian dialect version wānsīcīh očehčăkwah (wáhnsetschè ŏtschitschachquà).

45. The Proto-Algonquian consonant clusters *nθ, *nl, and *ʔl merge as hl in Munsee and Unami Delaware; with the change of *l to n in Mahican the clusters become hn, which Schmick spells chn:
māhnes (?) (machnisk) 'flint'   *mānθehsi

onōhnāwah (onochnáwa) 'she suckles him' *wenōnlāwali

wāhnemōxāhan (wăchnĕmòchāhàn)   *wāʔlemohθēhkani
  'don't go far'
ahnapey (?) (anápe) 'armband of wampum' *aʔlapya 'net'
ksīhnāh (kschechnà) 'jump quickly'   *kešyīʔlēlwe
tpīhnāw (tpechnáu) 'he falls down'   *tapiʔlēwa

46. The other consonant clusters ending in *-θ and *-l— Proto-Algonquian *hθ, *ʔθ, and the unique *hl—fall together as x (as in Munsee and Unami); Schmick writes ch, chch:
xay (chai, chei) 'hide, skin'   *ahθaya
nōx (nŏŏch) 'my father'   *nōhθa
kāxā (kácha, káchcha) 'how many?'   *kēhθē-
ntāxapī (ntachapè) 'I ride (on horseback)' *netēhθapi
otamaxōnewā (otàmmachoonwa) *wet(a)mehθō(e)wāwi
  'their boat'

pxān (p'chan, pĕchāān) 'it snows'   *peʔθānwi
naxa (nacha) 'three'   *neʔθwi (ending reshaped)
kmaxāntamnānaw (kmachāhntamnánau)
  'we think big'   *kemeʔθēlentamenānawi
nkwaxāw (nkwacháu) 'I fear him'   *nekweʔθāwa
kōnīxsīwī (-konechséwe)   *keweliʔθesi(wi)
  'you don't speak correctly'

otāhkwī-nāxān (udàchquènăchāān)   *wetēxkwi-lēhlēni
  'he died'   'he ceased breathing'

47. The merger of *hθ and *ʔθ with *hš and *ʔš (as Mahican x) partially conceals an innovation which Mahican shares with Delaware and the languages of northern New England—the automatic replacement of *θ by *š before *i, *ī, and *y has been levelled out except where the derived status of *š is no longer obvious. Mahican therefore has n (the reflex of *θ) in many words where š (< *š) might be expected; in this study the unpalatalized *θ has been written in the Proto-Algonquian forms, with a following hyphen to indicate that they are not the normal reconstructions:
anī (anè) 'so, thus'   *eθ-i
tanī (tanè 'auf') 'there'   *taθ-i
anīwīsew (ănēwěsŏ) 'he is named thus' *eθ-i-wīnswiwa
onīhtāw (onechtáu) 'he makes it'   *weθ-ihtāwa

anīh (anè) 'say (thou) it to me'   *eθ-ilwe
anīkw (anēku) 'say (ye) it to me'   *eθ-ikwe
āneyan (ánĭăn) 'what you say to me' *ēθ-iyani

48. Proto-Algonquian *m and *n remain as m and n in Mahican:
māwekwāmōtōk (măŏquāmōtōk) *māwenkwāmwetaw(ek)e
  'let's sleep together'
kmāmāwan (kmàmáwàn) 'your eyebrow' *kemāmāwana
tmaskhamek (t'maskhămăk)   *temaškahamenki
  'that one cuts the grass'
omešōtamen (ōmĕschótamen)   *wemešotameni
  'he hits it (target)'
nōm (nŏŏm, nŏm) 'I come from'   *neweme
nmenăčī (n'menachtschè) 'I am left-handed' *nemenantī
onāmen (onámen) 'he sees it'   *wenēmeni
nwīnayom (n'wénajoom) 'my wife' * newīnayema
                        'my old woman'
onīčănah (onétschănă) 'his daughter' *wenītyānali
                        'his child'

49. In loanwords from European languages, m and n remain unchanged except before a homorganic consonant (see §9):
komkomšan (kumkumschàn)   D. komkommer (+ -eš-an)
  'cucumbers'
nōmanīhemīwī (nomanehĕméwe) 'I have no money'
                E. money (+ nō-...emīwī 'I have not')
kaneš (kánnisch) 'pitcher'   E. can (+ -eš)

50. In Munsee, initial nn- is simplified to single n-; Schmick's spellings make it almost impossible to tell whether Mahican had n- or nn- (he sometimes writes n'n-), but the language shares so many other phonetic details with Munsee that it probably had this rule as well:

nep (nep) 'I die'	*nenepe
nāwāw (náwăŭ) 'I see him'	*nenēwāwa
nătamākw (nachtamāku) 'he helps me'	*nenătamawekwa

Schmick sometimes fails to indicate an initial *n*- before other consonants as well, probably in error:

nmatăpīh (matachpè) 'sit down'	*θematapilwe
npenawāw (pennawáu) 'I see him'	*nepenawāwa
nkwīnawāwī (quenawáwe)	*nekwīθawā(wi)
'I'm not looking for him'	
[versus nkwīnawāw (n'quénăwáu) 'I am looking for him' < *nekwīθawāwa]	

51. The regular development of Proto-Algonquian *ˀm in Mahican is *hm*, which Schmick spells *chm*:

wīkewāhm (weēquachm) 'house'	*wīkiwāˀmi

In the second person plural of independent-order verbs, both *-hmā* and *-hemā* occur, apparently in free variation; Schmick writes *-chma* but *-hema* or *-hama*:

kawīhmā (kaweēchma) 'you (pl.) sleep'	*kekawīˀmwāwi
ktāhemā (ktahamà) 'you (pl.) go'	*ketāˀmwāwi
knāwāhmā (knāwochmà), knāwāhemā (knawahemā, knawahamà) 'you (pl.) see him'	*kenēwāˀmwāwi
knāwenohmā (knawunochma) 'we see you'	*kenēweθeˀmwāwi
knāwenōwehemā (knawunowuhamà) 'we don't see you'	*kenēweθ(ow)eˀmwāwi

52. In the independent preterite the combination *-ˀmepani* metathesized to *-hempa(ni)* (> Unami *-həmp*); in Mahican the nasal was subsequently lost as usual before a consonant, yielding *-hep*:

kekīš-anahkāhep (kekéschanachkáhip 'ich bin fertig gewesen') 'you have finished working'	*kekīši-aθoxkyāˀmepani
nmačayīhop (< -hep) (n'matschaihòp) 'I have sinned'	*nemati-ayiˀmepani

53. In the first person plural (exclusive and inclusive) of the independent-order paradigms, *-ˀm-* combines with *-enān-* and *-enaw-* to form *-hnā/-henā* and *-hnaw/-henaw* (also "plural" *-hnōk/-henōk*):

ntāhenā (ntáhănà) 'we (excl.) go'	*netāˀmenāni
ktāhenaw (ktáhanau) 'we (incl.) go'	*ketāˀmenawi
ktāhenōk (ktahanōōk) 'we (incl. pl.) go'	*ketāˀmenaw(ek)i
nāwāhnā (nawochnà 'wir sehen euch'), nāwāhenā (nawahanà, náwăhănà) 'we (excl.) see him'	*nenēwāˀmenāni

54. The unusual developments of *-ˀmeC-* sequences (*-ˀmep-* > *-hemp-*; *-ˀmen-* > *-hemn-* > *-h(e)n-*) are shared with Munsee and Unami Delaware, but Mahican often differs from the neighboring languages in its treatment of the vowels in such forms. To account for the similarities we must either set up a special subdivision of Eastern Algonquian which contains only Mahican and Delaware (cf. Warne 1980:168) or acknowledge the possibility that even reshapings which destroy the basic regularity of a paradigm may be borrowed from one language to another: I prefer the latter solution, since if we must assign Mahican to a subdivision within Eastern Algonquian I would prefer to group it with the Abenaki dialects, not Delaware. There is really no need to set up such subgroups, however, since the Eastern Algonquian languages behave very much like any other dialect chain, freely exchanging innovations up and down the line.

Vowels and semivowels

55. The two Proto-Algonquian semivowels *w and *y may appear anywhere in a word before a vowel, but some environments are rare or were eliminated by later phonological developments. Although *w is very common in initial position, *y seldom or never occurs initially, and neither semivowel seems to have remained before *o or *ō.

56. In Mahican initial and postvocalic *w usually remains as *w*, which Schmick spells the English way:

wāwentōwīn (wawuntoweēn) 'they are not good'	*wā-weθet(owi)wali
wīwah (weēwa) 'his wife'	*wīwali
wīwīn (weweēn) 'horn'	*wīwīθa
nwīwašī (n'wéwaschè 'kanstu... tragen') 'I have a pack'	*newīwaši
newīčāwāw (ne wetschawáu) 'I go with him'	*newītyēwāwa
kawīw (gawéu, gauwéu) 'he sleeps'	*kawīwa

57. In loanwords Mahican *w* replaces German *w* (phonetic [v]) even after a consonant:

pnatwīn (p'natt'wēn) 'brandy'		G. Brandtwein

58. After a vowel *y remains as *y*; Schmick usually writes *j* (as in German) but also uses other spellings in special circumstances:

ayāpāw (ajápăŭ) 'buck'	*ayāpēwa
āpeyāk (ápeak, ápejak) 'where we sit'	*ēpiyānki
mačayew (matschaju) 'he sins'	*mati-ayiwa
xay (chai, cheì) 'hide, skin'	*ahθaya
kākway (gaquai) 'what?'	*kēkʷayi

59. After any consonant except *k* or *h*, *w is lost in Mahican:

npām (n'.pāām) 'my thigh'	*nepwāmi
anaham (ánàham) 'he points at it'	*eθwahamwa
mešāw (meschǎŭ) 'he shoots him'	*mešwēwa
kmōtak (kmōōtăāk) 'they steal'	*kemōtwaki
nmītsī (n'méze) 'I eat'	*nemītehswi
apesīh (appessè) 'warm yourself'	*apeswilwe
nīhenī (nehenè) 'oneself'	*nīhelwi

60. Proto-Algonquian *y is lost after all consonants:

pāw (páŭ) 'he comes'	*pyēwa
māčīmākwat (machtschémăquàt) 'it smells bad'	*matimyākʷatwi
nāspah (nāāspa) 'fetch water'	*nāsepyēlwe
nāwa (náwa) 'four'	*nyēwi (ending reshaped)
nānan (nánan) 'five'	*nyāθanwi
anewīwī (annuwéwe, ánnowéwe) 'more than'	*alyiwi(wi)
māčīh (matschè) 'go away'	*mātyīlwe
kakāhkīmen (gagachgémen) 'I teach you'	*kekakyēxkimeθe

61. At the end of noun stems, however, *y usually be-

comes *ey*, which Schmick spells -i, -e, and -ei:
ahkey (ahhkì, ăhkì) 'earth, land'   **axkyi*
npey (n'pè, mbeì, mpëi) 'water'   **nepyi*
pmey (p'mèh, pòmi) 'fat, grease'   **pemyi*
tpīnaxkắpey, -an (tpenachgápe, pl. tpenachgápean)
    'bracelet'   **tepineθkēpyi, -pyali*
ahnapey (?) (anápe) 'armband of wampum' **aʔlapya* 'net'

The following do not have *-ey*:
matasen (măttássèn) 'stone pipe'   **mataʔsenya*
ntāh (ndàh) 'my heart'   **netēhyi*
okekah (okeckà) 'his mother'   **we(ke)kyali*
ahpanan (ahpánan 'Akridches') 'tubers(?)' **wexpenyali*

62. The inanimate intransitive (II) verb final *-yā- (> *-yē̄-
before *w) has been reshaped in most of the eastern languages. In southern New England *-yā- becomes *-ēyi- before third-person *w (> -āyəw); in Micmac and Malecite-Passamaquoddy *-ēyi- was generalized (> Malecite-Passamaquoddy -eyo, -eyik, Micmac -ēg); the Delaware and Abenaki groups do not participate in the reshaping. Mahican inanimate intransitive verbs appear to follow the southern New England pattern:[7]
wāpāyew (wapáju) 'it is white'   **wāpyēwi*
onāwāyew (onawáju) 'it is blue'   **welāw-yēwi*
tahāyew (taháo, d'háju) 'it is cold'   **tahkyēwi*

mxāyew (m'cháo) 'it is big'   **meʔθ-yēwi*
māxāk (máchaak, machǎǎk) 'that which is big' **mēʔθ-yēki*

wāhkamāyew (wachkamáo, wochkamáo)   **wāxkamyēwi*
    'it is day'
wāwāhkamākīh (wáwochkamakè)   **wā-wāxkamyēkili*
    'whenever it is day'

63. In Mahican the II final has been extended to several animate intransitive (AI) verbs, but here the reshaped form *-ēyi- occurs throughout the paradigm (** indicates the shape it would have had in PA had it existed):
oskāyew (uskáju) 'he is new'   ***weškyēwa*
wāskāyīkīk (wáskǎĭkèck) 'they who are new' ***weškyēkili*

onāyew (onáju) 'he is good'   ***weθ-yēwa*
onāyīh (unáje) 'be good'   ***weθ-yēlwe*
wāwenāyīkīk (wáŭnǎĭkĕĕk)   ***wē-weθ-yēkiki*
    'they who are good'

The inanimate origin of the verb final is no doubt the reason that it takes third person -*k* (plural -*kīk*) instead of -*t* (plural -*čīk*) in the conjunct. Contrast the following AI verb, which already had the final *-yā- in Proto-Algonquian:
kahkāyew (kakkajòh) 'he is old, the oldest'   **kexkyēwa*
kāhkāyīt (gachgajēd) 'he who is old(est)'   **kēxkyēta*

64. The four Proto-Algonquian long vowels (*ā *ē *ī *ō) are kept distinct in Mahican, but with some substantial phonetic changes. The long high vowels—*ī and *ō—remain as ī and ō, for which Schmick uses the English spellings e, ee, and o, oo:
wīwīn (wewēēn) 'horn'   **wīwīθa*
wīkewāhm (wēēquachm) 'house'   **wīkiwāʔmi*
wīkewāhmek (wéquǎchmŭk) 'in the house' **wīkiwāʔmenki*

nmīnekwen (mēnĕkùn) 'he gives it to me'   **nemīlekweni*
kmīnekwen (kmēēnkùn) 'he gives it to you'   **kemīlekweni*
kǎkāpīkwāw (gachgapequáu) 'he is blind' **kakyēpīnkʷēwa*

nkīšī-sōkenemen (nkesche sogenimmen)
    'I have poured it'   **nekīšī-sōkenameni*

nōx (nŏŏch) 'my father'   **nōhθa*
wātōxeyakw (watóchiak)   **wētōhθ-iyankʷa*
    'he who is our father'
kmōt (kmŏŏt) 'he steals'   **kemōtwa*
kmōthan (kmōthèn) '(don't) steal'   **kemōtehkani*
mǎtantōw (machtandò) 'devil'   **matanetōwa*

65. In Mahican the Proto-Algonquian long low vowels—*ē̄ and *ā̄—participate in a push-pull chain shift which spread from the languages of southern New England: *ē̄ is backed to ā̄, but *ā̄ becomes nasalized ā̃ to maintain the contrast. Schmick seldom distinguishes ā̃ from ā̄ or a (the reflex of short *a) but occasionally indicates by a following n the nasalization which is better recorded by other Moravian writers and by those who heard the Stockbridge dialect:
wāpākā (wápachcǎ, wāpǎchgà [Schmick], wohmpachgâh
    [Büttner, Masthay 1980:38]; Stockbridge wâmp·ka [Michelson])   'when it will be morning'   **wāpankē*
anenāpāw, -ak (anenapáwak [Schmick], ann'nnampắu
    [Büttner, Masthay 1980:38]; Stockbridge nenânpāhō
    [Michelson]) 'person(s), Indian(s)' **elenāpēwa, -waki*
nkwetāšī (guttāasch [Schmick]; Stockbridge n-co-taunsh,
    ngut-taasch [Jefferson], ngutəⁿs [Michelson], gúdqus
    [Swadesh])   'six'   **nekʷetwāši*

ktenākōmāk (ktennangomǎǎk)   **keteθānkōmāwaki*
    'you have them as relatives'
npetamehnā (péttǎmēchnōn)   **nepentameʔmenāni*
    'we hear it'
kwīhpōmīhnā (kwěchpōmĕnǎn)   **kewīxpōmiʔmenāni*
    'you eat with us'

Schmick usually writes a or aa (with various accents) for both ā̄ and ā̃:
otāhkwī-nāxān (udàchquènǎchǎǎn)   **wetēxkwi-lēhlēni*
    'he died'   'he ceased breathing'
nākaw (nǎǎgaù, nágaū) 'sand'   **lēkawi*
wāwānāntam (wawanáhntam)   **wā-welēlentamwa*
    'he laughs'
kīkāpāw (gegapau) 'unmarried man'   **kīkāpēwa*
anītāhāw (anètaháu) 'he thinks'   **eθ-itēhēwa*
pxān (p'chǎn, pěchǎǎn) 'it snows'   **peʔθānwi*
nānāwat (nánawàt)   **θā-θāwatwi*
    'it is halfway, in the middle'
kmāmāwan (kmàmáwàn) 'your eyebrow' **kemāmāwana*
māwekwāmōtōk (mǎǒquǎmōtōk)**māwenkwāmwetaw(ek)e*
    'let's sleep together'

66. Although Schmick follows English usage rather than German in writing e for Mahican ī, he indicates vowel length with the German spelling conventions. Both English and German use double letters for long ee and oo, but English does not allow aa for a long low back vowel. Schmick also occasionally writes h before a consonant to indicate that

the preceding vowel is long:
nkawīn (ngawĕ̄hn) 'I sleep' *nekawīni
otōnek (otóhnick) 'in his mouth' *wetōnenki
kmaxāntamnānaw (kmachähntamnánau)
    'we think big' *kemeʔθēlentamenānawi
sōknān (sŏk'nahn, soognahn) 'it rains' *sōkelānwi

67. In most environments the Proto-Algonquian short high vowels *i and *o have merged with their long counterparts, appearing as Mahican ī and ō:
āpīt (ápēēd, ápeed) 'where he sits' *ēpiti
apīsītāsīh (appessḕed tassè) *apisitēswilwe
    'warm your feet'
očī (otschè) 'from there' *wenti
kāwīšīmīn (gaweschemen) 'blackberry' *kāwinšyimina
ntenīwīsī (-n tĕ̆nĕ̄wĕ̆šĕ̆) 'I am named thus' *neteθ-i-wīnswi
xaskwīmī(n) (chäsquĕ̄me, chasquemen) *meʔθaškwimini
    'corn'

wīhtōnayah (wechtonajà) 'his facial hairs' *wīʔtonayahi
mamatōxāw (mamatocháu) 'he is crippled' *ma-matohθēwa
wāhnemōxāhan (wắchnĕ̆mòchāhàn) *wāʔlemohθēhkani
    '(don't) go far'
omešōtamōwī (ōmĕ̆schótamówe) *wemešotam(owi)wa
    'he didn't hit it'
sōkenemōkw (sogenimmṓqu) 'pour it' *sōkenamokwe

68. Proto-Algonquian short *a remains as a; Schmick usually writes a, which is also his most common spelling of ā and ā̆:
amatakā (ămáttakà) 'when he feels it' *amantankē
wanamanah (wanammana) 'vermilion (obv.)' *walamanali
kakawekwaxīn (gagauuquachḕen) *ka-kawenkwaʔši(n)wa
    'he is sleepy'
knayatamen (knajátamen) 'you carry it' *kenayantameni
ktaxamāw (ktachamáu) 'you feed him' *ketahšamāwa
tmahīkan (t'mahégan, d'mahégan) 'ax' *temahikani

69. Unstressed a in open syllables becomes zero before Mahican h and also usually drops before Mahican x:
hapew (hapò) 'he sits' *ahapiwa
nhakay (nháckai, n'hackay) *nahakayi 'my skin'
    'my body, myself'
nāphah (nabhà) 'string it (wampum)' *θāpahanlwe
tmaskhamek (t'mäskhämăk) *temaškahamenki
    'that one cut the grass'

xamāhan (chammáhan) 'don't feed him' *ahšamāhkani
kepxāhemā (kupchahamà) *kekepehšēʔmwāwi
    'you (pl.) are deaf' [cf. kpaxāwak (kpacháwak) 'they are deaf' < *kepehšēwaki]

70. Elsewhere before voiceless consonants unstressed a in open syllables becomes ā̆, phonetically probably [ah] (as in Unami); Schmick usually writes ach before a stop, but before other consonants just a:
ā̆pew (achpóu) 'he sits' *apiwa
nmatā̆pīh (matachpè, mattappè) 'sit down' *θematapilwe
nīmātak (nĕmächtăk) *nīmataki
    'my brother's children' 'my brothers (of male)'
măčīmākwat (machtschémăquàt) *matimyākʷatwi
    'it smells bad'

kaxkwākăkan (kăchquākachcan) *keθkʷayikan(kan)i
    'your neck'

ăšōkew (ăschókò) 'he is poor' *ašōkiwa
măxewī (machowe) 'old' *meHšiwi

Except for the last two examples above, in this study ā̆ is marked only when Schmick writes ach.

71. The transitive inanimate verb suffix -am- becomes -em- after finals in -eC- (-en- 'by hand,' etc.) and in a few other stems:
nsōkenemen (nsogenimmen) 'I pour it in' *nesōkenameni
sōkeneh (sogenè) 'pour it in' *sōkenanlwe
okennemen (okènnĕ̆mèn) 'he carries it' *wekeθenameni
ntemšem (ntemmschim) 'I cut it' *netemešame

knātem (knátim, gnatim) 'you fetch it' *kenāt(am)e
nāteh (nāāde) 'fetch it' *nāt(an)lwe
kpaheh (kpahè) 'close it' *kepahanlwe

72. Proto-Algonquian short *e becomes e in Mahican; when stressed, it probably varied phonetically from [ə] to [e], with allophones as high as [ɪ] in some cases:
ntenemakan (ntenněmágan) 'my shoulder' *neteθemankani
ntemešemen (ntŭmmeschímmen) *netemešameni
    'I cut it off'
nkehtemnā (nkechtem'nà) 'I am lazy' *nekehtemi (final reshaped)
opetamen (opettamen) 'he hears it' *wepentameni
kmešnemen (kmischnimman-) *kemešenameni
    'you touch it'

73. As in the Abenaki dialects, initial e- (which is always unstressed) becomes a-:
awa (awà) 'he says' *ewa
anenāpāwak (anenapáwak) 'Indians' *elenāpēwaki
anāhānsīh (anàhaansè) *eθāhkāθesilwe
    'throw yourself down'

However, in closed syllables (i.e., before a consonant cluster) initial unstressed e- becomes zero:
spomek (spommuck) 'up above' *ešpemenki

74. Before a rounded consonant (Mahican hw and kw, including clusters ending in kw) stressed e is rounded to o:
ătohw (ăchtóhu, ăchtòh) 'deer' *atehkʷa
aseskewahohw (ăsusquahō̆) 'clay pot' *ašyeškyiwaxkehkwa
otohōn < otohwan (ŏttŏ̆hòhn) 'branch' *wetehkwani

mahtokw (machtòkq) 'wood' *meʔtekʷi
nskīčokw (n'skétschok) 'my eye' *neškīnšekwi
kīkāhokw (gegahōk) 'he heals you' *kekīkēhekwa
ntokwen (-n tockun) 'he says to me' *netekweni

amoxkw (ămùchkq) 'beaver' *ameθkʷa
wahpoxkwanek (wapuchquanek, *wexpeθkwanenki
    wapochquanik) 'in his side'

75. In a few forms *e* is also rounded to *o* next to *m*, *p*, or *hp*:

wīnayomah (wenajŏma) 'his wife'	*wīnayemali
tpohkew (t'póchgo) 'it is night'	*tepexkiwi
spomek (spommuck) 'up above'	*ešpemenki
nkatopī (ngattópe) 'I am hungry'	*nekatwepwi
kohpaka[n] (-ck opákka) 'it is thick'	*kexpakanwi

In most cases, however, *e* remains before and after *m* and *p*:

nīnem (nénim) 'my brother's wife (of male)' *nīθemwa
phānem (p'chánim) 'woman' *pehēnemwa

kpenawīwī (kpennawéwe) 'you don't see me' *kepenawi(wi)
kpetawī (kpettāwe) 'you hear me' *kepentawi

nep (nep) 'I die' *nenepe
knep (kniipp) 'you die' *kenepe
nkephamen (nkupphamen, n'k'phammen)
  'I close it' *nekepahameni

76. Elsewhere before *x* (i.e., when unstressed before Mahican *xkw* and both stressed and unstressed before unrounded *x* and *xk*), *e* becomes *a*:

kaxkwākākan (kăchquākachcan) *keθk^wayikan(kan)i
  'your neck'
kīkaxkwāw (kékăchquáu) 'girl, maiden' *kīkeθkwēwa

waxkan (wachgàn) '(his) bone' *weθkani
onaxkek (ŏnàchgĕk, onàchkek) 'in his hand' *weneθkenki
maxkawāw (machgawáu) 'he finds him' *meθkawēwa

maxānī (măchānĕ) 'many' *me?šyēθ-i
kpaxāwak (kpacháwak) 'they are deaf' *kepehšēwaki
nkwaxāw (nkwacháu) 'I fear him' *nekwe?θāwa

77. Unstressed *e* also becomes *a* before Mahican *h*:

nahpasay (nachpássei) 'my breast' *nexpasēwi (final reshaped)
mahtapew (machtáppo) 'he was born' *mwe?tapiwa
kahčay (kachtschaì) 'old man' *ke?ti-aya
nahkīwan (nachkèwan) 'my nose' *nexkiwani

78. Word-initially *we-* becomes *o-*:

onākwīkā (onaquéga) 'when it will be evening' *weθākwikē
osāmī (osáme) 'too much' *wesāmi
otenān (otinnāhn) 'it rains from there' *wentelānwi
osītek (osédik, osédick) 'at his feet' *wesitenki
otenāwah (utenáwa) 'he says to him' *weteθāwali

79. Elsewhere (i.e., after *k* and *h*) *we* appears to vary phonetically from [wə] to [ʊ]; Schmick usually writes u, occasionally wu:

nkwečīmōnokw (n'kutschemónuk) *nekwetim(oθ)ekwa
  'he asks me'
pekwesak (pĕkússak) 'mosquitoes, gnats' *penkwehsa
āhwesew (achussò, achwussò) *āhkwesiwa
  'he is avaricious'
skwesāw (sgucháu) 'he cuts him' *sekwešwēwa
kšekwešā (kschukquaschà) 'you cut him' *kešekwešwā

80. In a few forms *we unpredictably became *o at an early date, developing regularly to Mahican *ō*:

mekōs (măkōōs) 'awl' *mekwehsi
txōkwnakekā (t'chōōknakkekà) *tahθwekwenakenkē
  'when it will be so many days'
knenōhtānōw (knenóchtānò) *kenenwehtaweθ(ow)e
  'I don't understand you'

māšōt (maschōōt) 'one who shoots' *mēšwenta
kīšīhokōp (késchehogoōp) 'he made you' *kekīšihekwepani
kwīnākōnaw (quenacónau) *kekwīθawekwenawi
  'he is looking for us'
māwekwāmōtōk (măŏquāmōtōk) *māwenkwāmwetaw(ek)e
  'let's sleep together'

81. Similarly *ye becomes *i (except after *š), yielding Mahican *ī*:

nmīs (mēēs) 'my older sister' *nemyehsa
kšīkamīšew, -sew (kschĕkăméscho, -so) *kešyikamyeswiwa
  'he (kettle) is boiling'

82. Before *w* and *y*, the Mahican high vowels *ī* and *ō* (< *i/*ī and *o/*ō) usually become *e*:

maxewāyew (machowáju) 'it is old'
  *meHšiwēyiwi ← *meHšiw-yēwi
wīkewāhm (wēēquachm) 'house' *wīkiwā?mi
npāšewā (báschŏă) 'I bring him' *nepyēšiwā
wačew (wachtschù, wachtschò, *watyiwi
  wachtschóu) 'mountain'
osew (osòh) 'he (kettle) is boiling' *wenswiwa
nīšewak (nésch°wak) 'they are two' *nyīšiwaki

sašewak (săschuak) 'that which is salty; salt' *ša-šīwanki

āmewāw (amuáu) 'bee' *āmōw(ēw)a

wāxeyā (wāchīā) 'my husband' *wē?šiyāna 'he who I have
  as husband'
wātōxeyakw (watóchiak) *wētōhθ-iyank^wa
  'he who is our father'
ānī-wīkeyan (áne wékian) 'where you live' *ēθ-i-wīkiyani

neya (nià) 'I, me' *nīyawi 'my body'
weyās (wĕjāās, ojāās, wiās, wojás) 'meat, flesh' *wīyawehsi

83. In a smaller number of forms Mahican *ī* and *ō* retain their usual reflexes before *w*:

nahkīwan (nachkèwan) 'my nose' *nexkiwani
ayīwī (ajéwe) 'he is not there' *ayi(wi)wa

wīwah (wĕwa) 'his wife' *wīwali
kawīw (gawéu) 'he sleeps' *kawīwa
menačīw (menatschéu) 'he is left-handed' *menantīwa
māyāwīwak (majáwewak) 'they assemble' *māwēwīwaki[8]

nmaxkamōwen (n'machgamówun) *nemeθkam(ow)eni
  'I didn't find it'
onetōwī (ŏnìttówe) 'it is not good' *weθet(owi)wi

mătantōw (machtandò) 'devil' *matanetōwa

Munsee and Unami Delaware in general agree with Mahican in the distribution of *e* versus *ī* and *ō* before semivowels (Goddard 1982:39-40).

84. In both derivation and inflection, the sequence *awe* contracts to *ā* before a consonant:
weyās (wějáās, wiās) 'meat, flesh' *wīyawehsi
keyānaw (kiánau) 'we (incl.)' *kīyawenawi 'our body'
kpetān (k'pettāăn, kpettāhn) 'I hear you' *kepentaweθe
kpetākōnaw (kpettacónau) *kepentawekwenawi
    'he hears us'

Although the contraction rule is productive in verb inflection, it fails to apply in the derivation of some stems (which may therefore be relatively new formations):
pmāwesew (pŏmáoso) 'he lives' *pemāwesiwa
npahpenawesī (npachpenawussè) *nepa-penawesi 'I see
    'I look in the mirror'   myself'

In the new first person inclusive "plural" suffixes (which Mahican shares only with Munsee and Unami), *awe* contracts to *ō*:
ktāhenaw (ktáhănāu) 'we (few) are going' *ketāʔmenawi
ktāhenōk (ktahanōōk) 'we (all) are going' *ketāʔmenaw(ek)i

pmātaw (p'mataù) 'let's shoot' *pemwātawe
pmātōk (p'matōōk) 'let's (all) shoot' *pemwātaw(ek)e

85. The sequence *ewe* contracts to *ō* before a consonant; in many examples the first *e* derives from an underlying *ī* (usually from *ʔi) before *w*:
ōp (ōp) 'he said' *ewepani
nōnīhtān (n'onechtān) 'I make it' *neweθ-ihtāweni
kōm (kōōm, kōm) 'you come from' *keweme
npōp (npōp, mbōōp) 'he has died' *nep(e)wepani

sīpōk (sébook) 'to the creek' *sīpyiwenki 'to/in the river'
mačayōp (matschaijōp) 'he has sinned' *mati-ayiwepani

Stress and syncope

86. Mahican for the most part continues the stress rules of Proto-Algonquian. All long vowels are stressed; in Mahican this includes *ī* and *ō* from *i, *o, and *we. A stress also falls on the final syllable and on every even-numbered short vowel (beginning the count anew after each long vowel). No doubt all but one stress in each word was reduced to secondary stress, but I have not tried to guess which of Schmick's many accents indicates the primary stress.

87. Unstressed *e* often drops, even in the environments (before *x* and *h*) where it usually becomes *a*:
ndapsī (-n dappsè) 'I warm myself' *netapeswi
kmaxāntamnāhaw (kmachāhntamnánau) *kemeʔθēlentamenānawi
    'we think big'

pxān (p'chān, pěchāăn) 'it snows'⁹ *peʔθānwi
kwxat (kchàt) 'you fear him' *kweʔθati
xaskwīmī(n) (chăsquěmě, chasquemen) *meʔθaškwimini
    'corn'

Schmick's spellings sometimes suggest that two consecutive *e*'s have been lost, but often there are alternative forms given in which the second (which would have been stressed) remains:
nk(e)mōt (ngmōōt) 'I steal' *nekemōte
np(e)mā (np'mà) 'I shoot him' *nepemwā

nk(e)šīhnā (nkschechnà, nxechnà) 'I jump' *nekešyīʔlē
kt(e)kōnaw (kt'kónāū, kt̯̆cónau) *ketekwenawi
    'he says to us'
nk(e)phamen (n'k'phammen, nkupphammen) *nekepahameni
    'I close it'

88. A few forms appear to have a stress pattern opposite to that described above; in all cases an initial syllable (usually *ne-*) with syncopated vowel has not been written by Schmick (cf. §50):
(n)mahksen (máksen) '(my) shoe' *nemaxkeseni
(n)mehtkwīnōtay (mechtquenótei) *nemeʔtekʷinotayi
    '(my) basket'
(n)matăpīh (matachpè, mattappè) *θematapilweh
    'sit down'
(n)sekanōmī (sěkănōmě) *neʔsekalōmina
    'black corn, buckwheat'

89. The stress and syncope rules create many alternations between the short vowels *e*, *a*, *o*, and zero. The addition of a prefix reverses the stress pattern of the stem (up to the first long vowel), but the boundary between preverbs and stems (conventionally indicated by a hyphen) functions like a full word boundary:
nep (nep) 'I die' *nenepe
newīkā-npehnā (ne wéga npechnà) *newīnkē-nepeʔmenāni
    'we die willingly'

ktenen (ktēnnèn) 'I say to you' *keteθeθe
kataw-kākway-anen (gattaw gáquai anen) 'I want to say
    something to you' *kekatawi-(kēkʷayi-)eθeθe

90. In stem-initial position, underlying *e-* is usually restored when a prefix is added:
anīh (anè) 'say to me' *eθ-ilwe
otenāwah (utenáwa) 'he says to him' *weteθāwali

anītāhāw (anètaháu) 'he thinks' *eθ-itēhēwa
ntenītāhā (ntenètáha) 'I think' *neteθ-itēhē

However, the noun *anahīkan* 'index finger' (< *eθwahikani) retains *a-* in possessed forms:¹⁰
ntanahīkan (ntannahégan) 'my finger' *neteθwahikani

91. Before *hw* and *kw* (including *hkw* and *skw*), stressed *o* alternates with unstressed *e* or zero:
ntokwen (-n tóckun) 'he says to me' *netekweni
ntenokw (ntennùk) 'he says to me' *neteθekwa
ktenkōwī (ktenkówe) *keteθek(owi)wa
    'he doesn't say to you'
ktokōnāw (ktukkonánāū) 'he says to us' *ketekwenānawi
ktenekōnāw (ktenněkōnānaù) *keteθekwenānawi
    'he says to us'

92. Before *h* (not followed by *w*) underlying *e* is realized as unstressed *a* alternating with stressed *e*:
mahtapew (machtáppo) 'he was born' *mweʔtapiwa
nmehtapī (n'mechtappè) 'I was born' *nemweʔtapi
kahtemnāw (kahtem'náu, katemnáu) *kehtemiwa (ending
    'he is lazy'   reshaped)
nkehtemnā (nkechtem'nà) 'I am lazy' *nekehtemi

93. Before unrounded *x*, underlying *e* yields an alternation between stressed *a* and zero:

kpaxāwak (kpacháwak) 'they are deaf'		*kepehšēwaki
kepxāhemā̀ (kupchahamà) 'you are deaf'		*kekepehšē'mwāwi

kwaxāw (kwacháu) 'you fear him'		*kekwe'θāwa
kwxat (kchàt) 'you fear him'		*kwe'θati

94. On the other hand, underlying *a* is realized as *a* (stressed) alternating with zero before both *h* and *x*:

tăkwahw (tachquòch, taquòch) 'bread'		*takwahw(ān)a
otakwhōmah (otacchomàh) 'his bread'		*wetakwahw(ān)ali

ktaxamāw (ktachamáu) 'you feed him'		*ketahšamāwa
xamāhan (chammáhan) 'don't feed him'		*ahšamāhkani

95. The most common alternation is between stressed *e* and zero:

onamanesīt (onammanisséēd) 'he feels well'		*weθamaθesiti
kōnamansī (konamansè) 'you feel well'		*keweθamaθesi

onesew (onessò) 'he is beautiful'		*weθesiwa
nōnsīhenā̀ (non'sehenà) 'we are beautiful'		*neweθesi'menāni

mšenmōkwā̀ (m'schìnmóquà) 'when he doesn't touch it'		*mešenamokwē
kmešnemen (kmischnimman-) 'you touch it'		*kemešenameni

96. No examples have been found of the expected alternation between stressed *o* and unstressed *a* before *xkw*.

97. Most word-final Proto-Algonquian vowels have been lost in Mahican, but some particles retain final *-i (> -ī):

osāmī (osáme) 'too much'		*wesāmi
očī (otschè) 'from there'		*wenti
maxewī (machowe) 'old'		*mehšiwi
maxānī (māchānē̆) 'many'		*me'šyeθ-i
naxpī (nachpè) 'together, with'		*naθpyi

Intransitive verbs also retain stem-final *-i:

ksī (ksè) 'you say'		*kesi
ntahwesī (ntachwussè) 'I am avaricious'		*netāhkwesi
nkīspī (n'kéēspe 'bistu satt') 'I am full'		*nekīspwi
ntenīwīsī (-n tĕnēwĕšĕ́) 'I am named thus'		*neteθ-i-wīnswi

Monosyllabic short-vowel stems retain a one-syllable ending:[11]

awa (awà) 'he says'		*ewa
oma (?) (-óoma, -ōma) 'he comes from'		*wemwa

ewa (uwà) 'this (anim.)'		*awa
na (nà) 'that (anim.)'		*ana
nī (nè, ni) 'that (inan.)'		*ani

98. Most Proto-Algonquian short vowels have been lost in word-final position:

āw (áu) 'he goes'		*ēwa
pāw (páŭ) 'he comes'		*pyēwa
knāwāw (knáwăŭ) 'you see him'		*kenēwāwa

namās (namáās) 'fish'		*namē'sa
awān (awān̄) 'someone; who?'		*awēna

nk(e)mōt (ngmōōt) 'I steal'		*nekemōte
nōm (nōōm, nŏm) 'I come from'		*neweme
nmaxkam (n'máchgam) 'I find it'		*nemeθkame

wīnes (wénes) 'his head'		*wīθehsi
osītan (osétan, osēdan) 'his feet'		*wesitali
osītek (osédick) 'at his feet'		*wesitenki
ahtāw (achtáŭ 'drinne') 'it is there'		*a'tēwi
pnaw (p'naù) 'look at him'		*penawi

99. Proto-Algonquian long vowels are retained (or perhaps, in some cases, restored by analogy with other forms in the paradigm):

npā̀ (npà) 'I come'		*nepyā
knāwā̀ (knáwa) 'you see him'		*kenēwā
nmamatōxā̀ (nmamatócha) 'I am crippled'		*nema-matohθē
nmenăčī (n'menachtschè) 'I am left-handed'		*nemenantī

pāyanā̀ (-ppājanà) 'when you (sg.) come'		*pyāyanē
pā̀mā̀ (páma) 'come (later)'		*pyāmē
kōxā̀ (kócha) 'your father (inaccessible)'		*kōhθā
kākwayā̀ (gaquajà) 'what? (inaccessible)'		*kēkʷayē

The injunctive suffix *-yē was apparently shortened to *-ye at an early date and therefore drops:

pmāwesīč (pmawoseētsch) 'let him live'		*pemāwesityē

100. When the final vowel has been lost, a preceding postconsonantal *w is also dropped except after Mahican *k* and *h*:

nīnem (nénim) 'my brother's wife (of male)'		*nīθemwa
kmōt (kmōōt) 'he steals'		*kemōtwa
mătet (măchtett) 'it is bad'		*matetwi
kpahan (kpahàn) 'it freezes over'		*kepahanwi

matahkw (matàchq̌) 'cloud'		*mataxkwi
ătohw (ăchtóhu, ăchtòh) 'deer'		*atehkʷa

101. Proto-Algonquian apparently dropped many final syllables consisting of a sonorant followed by a short vowel; in most cases the syllable has been analogically restored, but Mahican inherited a few irregularities:

āpeyā̀ (ápea) 'where I sit'		*ēpiyā(ni)
ntayīhenā̀ (ntajehenà) 'we are there'		*netayi'menā(ni)
ktayīhemā̀ (ktajehema) 'you are there'		*ketayi'mwā(wi)

neya (nià) 'I, me'		*nīya(wi) 'my body'
manōmī (manóme) 'wheat'		*malōmi(ni)
mahtapōsa (machtappósa) 'he has been born'		*mwe'tapiwesa(ni)
mahtapōp (machtappōōp) 'he was born'		*mwe'tapiwepa(ni)

It is not clear why the preterite suffix *-pa(ni) loses a secondarily final short vowel when the present suffix *-sa(ni) retains it.

102. Schmick's dictionary is the fullest and best record that we have of the Moravian dialect of Mahican, but it is

far from perfect. Like the other missionaries, Schmick was not a fluent speaker of the language; unlike the others, however, he seldom made up sentences on his own, thus avoiding gross grammatical errors. His ear seems to have been fairly good, and he could draw on the spelling conventions of his native German as well as English to represent the sounds he heard, but these resources were insufficient to deal with some aspects of Mahican phonology.

Schmick's weakest point is in his recording of the Mahican vowels. It is reasonably certain that there were three low vowels—*a*, *ā*, and *ã*—but Schmick usually spells them all the same. In some environments this creates enormous ambiguity: *ach* in the first syllable of a word (before a consonant) may represent *ã*, *ah*, *āh*, *ãh*, *ax*, *āx*, or *ãx*.

There are relatively few complications in identifying the consonants, since all the Mahican consonants would be familiar from German or English, even if some of the combinations are different; Schmick's only difficulty was that he had too many symbols available and tried to use them all.

FOOTNOTES to Mahican Historical Phonology

1 (§3). It is often difficult to determine which European language was the source of the Mahican words (assuming, of course, that only one was involved in each case): *apenes* may derive from D. *appel*, E. *apple*, or G. *Apfel*; *pešop* could come from either E. *bishop* or G. *Bischof*, but Schmick spells it the English way. Mahican *snep* 'snuff,' on the other hand, must be a loan from English for G. *Schnupf(tobak)* would have given *šnop*.

2 (§4). Mahican appears to have reshaped the ending from *-ēwi to *-ayi. Cree *ospasēw* 'his side' agrees with Mahican in requiring *-xpas-, but several other languages (e.g., Shawnee oʔpalēwa 'his chest') demand *-xpaθ- or *-xpal-.

3 (§9). Mahican *pōten* may be a loan from G. Butter instead of D. *boter*, but Nipmuck ("Loup A") "boutel" makes Dutch the more likely source, since the Nipmuck were not in direct contact with German missionaries. Neither Mahican nor Nipmuck can have borrowed English butter, since it would have become *peten* or *peta* in Mahican and *petel* or *peta* in Nipmuck.

4 (§16). The reconstruction is based only on the Mahican forms (nattemegãã(n) 'I go in,' ntemégawe 'he did not go in,' etc.) and a similar Unami word (mattemigeu 'he enters,' Zeisberger 1887:67) with m- rather than n-; the first syllable is therefore not certain.

5 (§18). Proto-Algonquian *kʷ can be distinguished from *kw by at least two criteria: the labial component of *kʷ does not disappear before verb finals (*kenwāxkʷesiwa 'he (wood or solid) is long' versus *kenwāpeθkesiwa 'he (stone or metal) is long,' noun finals *-āxkʷi and *-āpeθkwi respectively), and *kʷa before a consonant does not become *kō (*ameθkʷaki 'beavers' versus *axkehkwaki > *axkehkōki 'kettles'; cf. Goddard 1981a:280-283). Where the evidence for *kʷ is ambiguous or lacking the traditional *kw is written.

6 (§30). It is unlikely that *nešk^wani 'my elbow' came to mean 'my arm' in Mahican, especially since the reflex of *-neθki 'hand, arm' is also glossed "Arm" by Schmick. Zeisberger's Mahican vocabulary has "nisquan, elbow."

7 (§62). There is at least one exception to the reshaping: the reflex of *ma-mānkyēwali 'they (inan.) are big' is *mamākāwan* (mamagáwan) rather than reshaped *mamākāyewan*.

8 (§83). For *māy-* instead of *māw-*, cf. Massachusett /māyā(w)īak/ "miáeog, miyawéog" (which Goddard [1981b:60] reads as /māā-/, contrary to his own explanation of Massachusett "i" as /ay/).

9 (§87). Zeisberger's Mahican vocabulary gives "pachan" with the expected *a* in the first syllable.

10 (§90). The possessed form of *anahīkan* is also irregular in retaining unstressed *a* before *h*.

11 (§97). The only monosyllabic short-vowel noun stem noted—*maxkw* (màchq) 'bear' < *maθk^wa—has lost the final vowel. The form machquà in the sentence "Pajachquenaxò machquà, Ich habe lange keinen Bären gesehen" (lit. 'a bear has not appeared for a long time') is surely inaccessible *maxkwā*.

REFERENCES

Goddard, Ives 1967. The Algonquian independent indicative. *National Museum of Canada Bulletin* 214:66-106.

——— 1979. *Delaware verbal morphology: a descriptive and comparative study*. New York & London: Garland.

——— 1981a. Against the linguistic evidence claimed for some Algonquian dialectal relationships. *Anthropological Linguistics* 23:271-297.

——— 1981b. Massachusett phonology: a preliminary look. In William Cowan, editor, *Papers of the Twelfth Algonquian Conference* (Ottawa: Carleton University), 57-105.

——— 1982. The historical phonology of Munsee. *International Journal of American Linguistics* 48:16-48.

Masthay, Carl 1980. *Mahican Language Hymns, Biblical Prose, and Vocabularies from Moravian Sources, with 11 Mohawk Hymns*. St. Louis, Missouri.

Pentland, David H. 1983a. Proto-Algonquian [č] and [š]. In William Cowan, editor, *Actes du quatorzième Congrès des Algonquinistes* (Ottawa: Carleton University), 379-396.

——— 1983b. Glottalized sonorants in Algonquian. Unpublished paper read at the Linguistic Society of America annual meeting, Minneapolis, December 29, 1983.

Prince, John Dyneley 1905. A tale in the Hudson River Indian language. *American Anthropologist* n.s. 7:74-84.

Proulx, Paul: 1983. Mahican social organization and the Middle Atlantic Algonquian cultural climax. *Anthropological Linguistics* 25:82-100.

Quinney, John, and Capt. Hendrick Aupaumut 1818(?). *The Assembly's [Shorter] Catechism*. Stockbridge, Mass.(?) [Pilling 1891, p. 416].

Warne, Janet L. 1980. Time-depth in Mahican diachronic phonology: evidence from the Schmick manuscript. In William Cowan, editor, *Papers of the Eleventh Algonquian Conference* (Ottawa: Carleton University), 166-182.

Zeisberger, David 1887. *Zeisberger's Indian Dictionary, English, German, Iroquois—the Onondaga and Algonquian—the Delaware*. Cambridge, Mass.: John Wilson & Son.

SCHMICK'S MAHICAN DICTIONARY
TRANSCRIBED, TRANSLATED, AND REARRANGED BY ENGLISH WORD ORDER

by
Carl Masthay

An English-Mahican-German alphabetic wordlist
with a Mahican-English glossary and index
based on
**Miscellanea linguae nationis Indicae Mahikan dictae,
curā susceptā ā Joh. Jac. Schmick**
["Miscellaneous (words) of the language of the Indian Nation called Mahican,
with the work undertaken by Johann Jacob Schmick"]

A post-1754 manuscript originating from the Moravian Archives, but deposited in the American Philosophical Society Library, and consisting of words, phrases, and sentences in Mahican and German largely according to German alphabetization, with the title and a few words (mostly explanatory) in Latin, a few phrases and words in English, and 18 phrases and words in Delaware

American Philosophical Society Library (105 South Fifth Street, Philadelphia, Pennsylvania 19106) card catalog no. 497.3 Sch5 and Freeman Guide nos. 163 and 2079, D. 2 vols. of 131L. and 191L., with vol. 1 (5843) being 167 pages and vol. 2 (5860) being 211 pages; also available in microfilm

ABBREVIATIONS OF SOURCES USED

Baraga   Baraga, R. R. Bishop: *A dictionary of the Otchipwe language*, 1878; Minneapolis, 1973, Ross & Haines, Inc.

Brinton   Brinton, Daniel G., and Anthony, Albert Seqaqkind, editors: *A Lenâpé-English dictionary*, Philadelphia, 1888, The Historical Society of Pennsylvania; New York, 1979, AMS Press, Inc.

D   DeForest, John W.: *History of the Indians of Connecticut from the earliest known period to 1850*, Hartford, Conn., 1851, Hamersley, p. 491.

Day   Day, Gordon M.: *The Mots loups of Father Mathevet*, National Museum of Man, Publications in Ethnology, No. 8, Ottawa, 1975, National Museums of Canada.

E   Edwards, Jonathan: *Observations on the language of the Muhhekaneew Indians*, New Haven, Conn., 1788, Connecticut Society of Arts and Sciences.

H   Heckewelder, John G. E.: *Mahicanni [Mohegan] words taken down from the mouth of one of that nation who had been born in Connecticut*, Philadelphia, (n.d.), American Philosophical Society Library, Freeman Guide 2077.

H1   Heckewelder, John G. E.: Three-page manuscript called "Comparative by Hechewelder" (who as in *H* spells his name with a *ch*, not *ck*), Philadelphia, (n.d.), American Philosophical Society Library, Freeman Guide 350.

Ho   Hodge, Frederick Webb: Handbook of American Indians north of Mexico, Smithsonian Institution, *Bureau of American Ethnology Bulletin* 30:788-789, 1907.

J   Jefferson, Thomas: *A manuscript comparative vocabulary of several Indian languages*, (1802-1808), American Philosophical Society Library, Freeman Guide, 1289.

Jn   Jenks, William: Language of the Moheagans, *Collections of the Massachusetts Historical Society* 9:98-99, 1804.

K   Konkapot, John, informant to Jenks; see *Jn*.

M   Michelson, Truman: *Mahican or Stockbridge linguistic notes, texts, etc.*, Bureau of American Ethnology ms. no. 2734, 1914-1915. (Note the following informants:)

M-?   Informant unknown; Wm. Dick or Lucius Dick?

M-AM   Alfred Miller

M-EM   Edwin Miller

M-Me   Berenice Metoxen [Robinson]

Masthay   Masthay, Carl: *Mahican-language hymns, biblical prose, and vocabularies from Moravian sources, with 11 Mohawk hymns (transcription and translation)*, St. Louis, Mo., 1980, self-published.

NTD   Nora Thompson Dean (Lenâpé: *Weenǰipahkihəléxkwe*, 'Touching Leaves Woman'), a fluent Unami Delaware speaker, 927 Portland Avenue, Dewey, Oklahoma 74029. (She died November 29, 1984.)

P   Prince, J. Dyneley: A tale in the Hudson River Indian language, *American Anthropologist*, n.s. 7:74, 1905.

Proulx   Proulx, Paul: Mahican social organization and the Middle Atlantic Algonquian cultural climax, *Anthropological Linguistics*, pp. 82-100, Spring 1983.

R   Ruttenber, E. M.: *History of the Indian tribes of Hudson's River*, 1872; Port Washington, N. Y., 1971, Kennikat Press, p. 360.

R1   Ruttenber, E. M.: *Footprints of the Red men. Indian geographical names*, 1906, New York State Historical Association.

S&M   Speck, Frank G., and Moses, Jesse: *The celestial bear comes down to earth*, Scientific Publications, no. 7, Reading, Pa., 1945, Reading Public Museum and Art Gallery.

Sc   Schmick, Johann Jacob: *Miscellanea linguae nationis Indicae Mahikan dictae*, post 1754, American Philosophical Society Library, Freeman Guide, 163 and 2079.

Si   Siebert, Frank T.: Personal communication, Old Town, Maine, 1979; for phonemic numeral list taken from several informants in 1935 and 1937, Gresham, Wisconsin.

Sw   Swadesh, Morris: *Mohican lexical file*, 1937, American Philosophical Society Library, Freeman Guide, 2080.

Sw-A   Swadesh, Morris: *Mohican lexical materials*, 1939, American Philosophical Society Library, Freeman Guide, 2081.

Sw-D   Swadesh, Morris: *Mohican field notes*, 1937-1938, American Philosophical Society Library, Freeman Guide, 2083; Hannah Dick, 1935, Wisconsin, as given to Frank Siebert.

Sw-e   Unknown source in *Sw.*, early twentieth century?

Sw-R   See *Sw-D*, but Berenice Robinson, 1935, Gresham, Wisconsin. (She was born Berenice Metoxen; see *M-Me*.)

Trumbull   Trumbull, James Hammond: Natick dictionary, Smithsonian Institution, *Bureau of American Ethnology Bulletin* 25, Washington, D. C., 1903, Government Printing Office.

W   Westminster Assembly of Divines: *The Assembly's [shorter] catechism.* (In the Moheakunnuk, or Stockbridge Indian language) [by John Quinney and Hendrick Aupaumut], Stockbridge, Mass., 1795, printed by Loring Andrews.

Warne   Warne, Janet: Time-depth in Mahican diachronic phonology: evidence from the Schmick manuscript. In Cowan, William, editor: *Papers of the Eleventh Algonquian Conference*, Ottawa, 1980, Carleton University, pp. 166-182.

I have the entire corpus of Mahican-language writings if someone needs such material: Carl Masthay, 838 Larkin Lane, Crève Cœur, (St. Louis), Missouri 63141; (314) 432-4231.

VOCABULARIUM MAHICANDICUM
(MAHICAN VOCABULARY)

Vocabularium Mahicandicum.

English	Mahican	German
a, an [see also one]	ngutte, gútta; na [= that, the?; as?]	
That you were born a man.	Nannoha atane machtappetip na némana.	Dass du geboren bist ein Mensch.
a pair of shoes	nguttò ksenà māh'ksenan	ein Paar Schue
a person, one	pa̧ǎschco, pǟschco	—
One ran.	Pa̧ǎschco nāhà / áū̆.	Einer lief.
(as) long as a finger	nà átān gútta nōo̧ssà	wie ein Finger lang
a sheet of paper	gútta népăchkè	ein Blatt
a little, few	sskéwesche, skéwēschē	Bisgen oder wenig
There is a little inside.	Tschachkewesche nhachtáū̆.	Es ist wenig drinne.
a little thin [cf. thin]	machachū̆quattschischò	ein wenig dünn
a lot [see cost; lot (much)]	muchtsche, macháne	
abashed, confused	—	beschämt
about that	nò wátsche	darüber
I am very glad about that.	Nò wátsche múchtsche ănnămmenājà.	Darüber freue ich mich sehr.
above [see up there]		
accept [see also take, get]	—	annehmen
He will accept you.	Nahk'ma̧atsch gnótenuck.	Er wird dich annehmen.
accompany [see go with]		
accomplished [see happen; do, make]		
accustomed (to be)	—	gewohnt seyn
to pray from habit	săchnēk ŏtĕnìn kătschĕnáū̆	aus Gewohnheit beten
I am accustomed to it.	Ntĕnnikătschĕēn.	Ich bin es gewohnt. Ich habe es gewohnt.
I can do that. I am used to it.	Păchkătschĭn tĕnīntăchtāān.	Das kan ich thun (ich bins gewohnt).
ache [see pain]		
acknowledge [see reveal]		
acquainted with, associated with [see also know, be acquainted with]		hat Umgang, geht ... um
My heart is associated with or is acquainted with his wounds.	Niàn dàh nàn nè mbáp'máin ánepapáquaik.	Mein Herz hat Umgang mit den Wunden oder geht mit s[einen] Wunden um.
affable [see pleasant]		
afraid, fearful, timid		sich fürchten
I am afraid.	Kwachódam, Quachōdam.	Ich fürchte mich.
I am afraid of my Savior.	Nkwacháu npacht[amawa̧ǎs].	Ich fürchte mich vor d[em] H[ei]l[an]d.
You are afraid of your Savior.	Kwacháu [kpachtamawa̧ǎs].	Fürchtestu dich [vor dem Heiland].
Why are you afraid?	Gaqua̧ǎtsch kchàt?	Warum fürchtestu dich?
Don't be afraid.	Tsche kwachaan.	Fürchte dich nicht.
He is afraid of the [your!] Savior.	Okwachawa kpach[tamawaas]nawa.	Er fürchtet sich vor dem Heiland.
We are afraid of our Savior.	Nkwachahanà np[achtamawaas]naù.	Wir fürchten uns for dem Heiland.
You (pl.) are afraid of your Savior.	Kwachawà kp[achtamawaas]naù.	Fürchtet ihr euch [vor dem Heiland].
They are afraid.	Okwacháwa.	Sie fürchten sich.
He is not afraid.	Sta okwacháwe.	Er fürchtet sich nicht.
I am not afraid.	Sta nkwacháwe.	Ich fürchte mich nicht.
Don't (pl.) be afraid.	Tsche kwachanawà.	Fürchtet euch nicht.
Don't (pl.) be afraid.	Tschĕĕk kwachanawà.	Fürchtet euch nicht.
We are not afraid.	Stà nkwachaweunà.	Wir fürchten uns nicht.
They are not afraid.	Sta okwachawewā̆.	Sie fürchten sich nicht.
I am afraid of you.	Kwachōōn kià.	Ich fürchte mich vor dich.
Don't be afraid of me.	Tschĕne kwachĕēn.	Fürchte dich nicht vor mich.
Why are you afraid of me?	Gaqua̧ǎtsch kwacheàn?	Warum fürchtestu dich vor mich?
I am afraid.	N'wéschasè.	Ich bin bange.
Are you afraid?	Kwéschasè[?]	Bistu bange?
I am not afraid.	Niàsch tàn wéschasè.	Ich bin nicht bange.

32 *Schmick's Mahican dictionary*

He is afraid.	Weschasò. Wéschasò.	Er ist bange. Er fürchtet sich.
We are afraid.	N'weschaséhéēnà.	Wir sind bange.
We are not afraid.	Niána astàn wéschasewahannà.	Wir sind nicht bange.
You (*pl.*) are afraid.	Kwĕscháseēchmà.	Ihr seyd bange.
They are afraid.	Nahkma wéschasowàk.	Sie sind bange.
You must not be afraid.	Tscheēn kwéschaseēn.	Du must dich nicht fürchten.
You must not be timid, fearful.	Tscheēn wéschăséhàn.	Du must nicht furchtsam seyn.
You must not be afraid.	[Tscheēn] kcháhan.	Du must nicht bange seyn.
I am so afraid.	[N?]weschasoŏpkà.	Ich bin so furchtsam.
Don't be afraid.	Tscheēn kwaweschaseēn.	Fürchte dich nicht.

after [*see* follow (after); *long note under* hear *(point 5)*]
after you [*see under* thirst *or under* to]

afternoon	pakatschè nawachquega [already], machtschè nāāchquatà	Nachmittag
again	wăk, wak; tschĕwăk; mĕtschēme [= again, back]	abermals, wieder, wider [*Schmick's spelling*]

When **wăk** (also, again) is placed in front, it means 'to come again,' as **Wăk npà**. 'I come again.'
 Wăk vorgesetzt so heissts widerkommen als **Wăk npà**. Ich komme wider.

He is coming back (or again).	Páu tschĕwăk.	Er kommt wider.
to find again	náhapáowe	wieder finden
I have found it again.	Ne māchgămmen. [Ne = it; *word* again *not present*]	Ich habs wider gefunden.
Come again soon. Come back soon.	Mĕtschēme páma. [*see also under* easy]	Komm bald wider.
age	—	Alter

ago [*see* year]

agree, *see* one, become (as) one	—	ein Herz seyn *vid[e]* eins seyn [*i.e.*, eins werden?]
Albany	Găstĕnik	Albanien (*Albanira*)

[*Dutch kasteel* = castle, fort + *Mahican* -ik = at; *other spellings:* Castinek = Orange *(Day, p. 245, Castleton, Mahican loan?); Ga-isch-ti-nic or Kaishtinic for Albany (Schoolcraft) and Gaasch-tinick or Albany (Heckewelder) (both in Beauchamp, 1907); Frank T. Siebert's suggestion that it is Castleton (near Schodac, ancient council fire of the Mahicans, about 12 miles south of Albany on the opposite side of the Hudson River) may be an error because the preceding authors glossed it unambiguously. The problem lies in the Dutch word kasteel, which the Mahicans preserved in Găstĕnik, but the Dutch used the word (from perhaps 1614 on) for successively moved sites that ended at the present Albany.*]

alive [*see* live; living water]

all [*see also* whole; world]	máwe, máowe; awăne [= ?(all) whoever?]	alle
all the people	máowe awăn, mawe awăneek	alle Menschen

all men, all who [*see* everyone]

ally, confederate [*see also* friends, to have]	ktennangómen	Bundsgenosse
almost, nearly	pachŏŏd	beinahe
alone	nquéchtsche	allein
He comes alone.	Nquéchtsche ăht páŭ.	Er kommt allein.
not alone	Tscheèn quechtsche	nicht allein
completely alone	—	allein ganz
already [*see also* just]	pag(g)átsche, păggătschè; pachgatsche [? *see* mix]; apagatschè [? *see* swallow]; păgăchtschē [*see* see]; pákatschè [*see* bloodied]; păkătsche [*see* blow a horn]	schon
I have already eaten.	Paggátsche méze.	Ich habe schon gegessen.
I have already sat. [*see* fill up]	Nkeschemàchtsch nmattapè.	Ich habe schon gesessen.
also, again, and	wăk, wăk, wak, ŏăăk	auch, und
always, ever	gommáo, gommáŏwĕ, gŏmmáwe, g'máo, gòmáo	allezeit, immer
ambles along	—	geht den Pass
The horse is ambling along.	Ounamachnáu [nachnióges].	Das Pferd geht den Pass.
among		
We will share it among us [only?].	Niana kdákkennàmāwăchtēnana psuk.	Wir wollen unter uns vertheilen.
You (*pl.*) must share it among yourselves.	Akkennámawechteèkq.	Ihr solts unter euch vertheilen.
They divided or distributed it among themselves.	Utschatschăăppĕnĕmmànawawà.	Sie vertheilten ihn unter sich.

English-Mahican-German 33

anchor	–	Ancker
and [see also]	wăk, wak	und
anger	nachkessoákan	Zorn
great anger, rage	máchche nachkessoákan	grosser Zorn
another [see other]	ktàk	–
another, another person	ktàk	ein ander
another day, the other day	ktàk wochkamáo	einen andern Tag, den andern Tag
answer	–	Antwort
Is that the way you are answering?	Nooktàhăăchtaaptonamăăk.	Antwortestu so.
ants	ananeges	Ameisen
anvil	–	Ambos
any [see none]		
anyone [see someone]		
ape [see monkey]		
apostle	–	Apostel
appear [see under gloomy; sad; seem]		
appear as		
Do you believe that the one who came, who made everything, appeared as one of us [looked as we looked]?	Kŏnsittamennà nò pájaḳŏp maowe gáquai kescheechtátip ne anenăăxíjàk anènăăxétip. [ḳ = k or t?]	Glaubestu dass der, der alles gemacht[,] ist höher kommen als einer von uns.
apple [see also tree]	ápenes [from Dutch appel + dim. -es]	Apfel
apple drink	–	[Apfel]trank
apple juice	–	[Apfel]blüth
apple skin, rind	ápĕnĕs p'chakschă	[Apfel]schaale
apple tree	ápĕnĕsak, ápĕnĕssáchkq, plur[alis] apenessàchquăăm	[Apfel]baum, Apfel[baum]
apple tree (also)	schèpăăchpenès [schepăăchpene]ssàchq[u-_?], plur[alis]	Apfel[baum] iterum
apple wood	– [cut off in ms.]	[Apfel]holz
Dry apples don't make one sick.	Kàhăăp'néssàk astà mémachpĕŭnăăk.	Trocken Äpfel machen einem nicht kranck.
apportion [see divide]		
approach, draw near to	–	hinzu nahen, n[ahen] sich
These (those, the ones [who?]) draw near to Jesus with believing hearts.	Neĕk onáham Jesu onìstawájaquà ktáhennăăk ŭtschè.	Die [on opposite side of page:] mit gläubigem Herzen sich zu Jesu nahen.
apron-string [see band]		
area [see enclosed place]		
arm (where there is one)	tennemaganégan	Arm, wo er da ist
arm (my arm)	nisquàn [cf. Massachusett meesk and Unquachog keésquan, elbow]	Arm
arm band of sewan	anápe	[Arm-]band von Seewand
bracelet, bangle. Note: The men have only one, but the women have more.	tpenachgápe, plur[alis] tpenachgápean	[Arm]spangen NB. Die Männer haben nur eine, die Weiber aber mehrere.
in the arms, in his arm	onàchkek [in his hands]	in die Arme, in seinen Arm
arrogant [see proud]		
around here, around there [see thereabouts]		
arrows	wépan	Pfeile
many arrows	machănnta wépan [n = n covers h]	viele Pfeile
How many arrows do you have?	Káchcha nà képan? [How many those your arrows?]	Wieviel Pfeile hast du?
Are the (your) arrows good?	Wawuntà képan?	Sind die Pfeile gut?
My arrows are not good. They are not sharp(-pointed).	Stàn népan wawuntoweĕn, stà tschachschippajeweĕn.	Meine Pfeile sind nicht gut, nicht spizig.
artful [see ingenious]		
article, item		Artickel
as	[note construction below:]	als
As (since, when) they came here.	Nohà pājătéta.	Als (Da) sie dahin kamen.
When (as) it became day.	Nàn nèn najàppawè.	Wie es Tag wurde.
As you are crucified.	Neáne schepòchquatahaseàn.	Wie du gecreuzigt bist.
as [see also like (similar to); just as]	ŏtĕnnè . . . ăne . . . [? how . . . that(?)]	wie

English	Mahican	German
A man must love his wife as the Savior [loves] his congregation.	Nemanáu nitschwāk wēwa ŏtĕnnĕ channawehaān Tāpānāmŭkquāk āne channaweēchtaād Gemeēnde.	Ein Mann muss seine Frau lieben, wie der Heiland seine Gemein[d]e.
My son has the same name as I do.	Ntajŏm ntäinewesechnà.	Mein Sohn heist, wie ich.
I am called the same as you.	Ktäinewesehhnaù.	Ich heiss wie du.
You are called the same as I.	Kteneweseen aneweseà.	Du heisst wie ich.
(as) long as a finger	nà átān gútta nŏ͞ossà [= that-in one finger?]	wie ein Finger lang
Do you believe that the one who came, who made everything, appeared as one of us [looked as we looked]?	Kŏnsittamennà nò pájakŏp maowe gáquai kescheechtátip ne anenāāxíjàk anènāāxétip. [k̲ = k or t?]	Glaubestu dass der, der alles gemacht[,] ist höher kommen als einer von uns.
as for, concerns	äijétscheek	betrifft
as long as [see as; because]		
as soon as [see also immediately; sound (verb)]	schawà, schawāhn, scháwa, scháwah	alsbald, [also]bald; gleich
When (as soon as) he said that...	Ne máchtsche ne éta.	Als er das gesagt hatte.
ash [see ashes]		
ashamed (to be) [see also blush under redden]		schämen sich; Roth werden
I am ashamed.	N'mĕchănsè. Mechannsè.	Ich schäme mich.
You are ashamed.	K[mĕchănsè]. Gmechannsè.	Schämstu dich.
He or she is ashamed.	Mechansò. Mechanissò. Mechannsò.	Er oder sie schämt sich.
We are ashamed.	Mechansehenà. Mechannsehenà.	Wir schämen uns.
You (pl.) are ashamed.	K[mechansehe]mà. G[mechannse]hemà.	Ihr [schämt euch].
They are ashamed.	Mechansówak. Mechannesowàk.	Sie [schämen sich].
Don't be ashamed. Aren't you ashamed?	Aschk kmechànséu.	Schämstu dich nicht.
She isn't ashamed.	Sta mechansèwe.	Sie schämt sich nicht.
We aren't ashamed.	Sta mechannsewehanà.	Wir schämen uns nicht.
You (pl.) aren't ashamed.	[Sta] k[mechannsewe]hamà.	Ihr [schämt] euch [nicht].
They aren't ashamed.	[Sta] mechann'sewewàk. [Sta mechan]nesewewàk.	Sie [schämen] sich [nicht].
ashes, punk [from English spunk influenced by Delaware?]	pùkquḗu, pùckqueüw, p'quéi [cf. Delaware pungw = ashes, powder, dust (NTD)]	Asche. Die Pung
hard ashes	wochganépuk	harte [Asche]
hot ashes	xep'quachtáu	heisse [Asche]
ash sifter, cinder sifter	schechtégan	Aschen-sieb
ask (a question) [see also examine]	–	fragen
I ask.	Kutschemónen.	Ich frage.
Go ask the brothers.	Kutschemóna ketachgenanak.	Geh frage die Brüder.
I will ask him.	Nia ēn kutschemonáu.	Ich will ihn fragen.
Ask me.	Kutschemonemà.	Frag mich.
Why are you asking me?	Gaquai wátsche gutschémohn niákq?	Warum fragstu mich [?]
Ask him (Christian).	Kutschemonamà Xstian.	Frage ihn.
Ask us.	Niána kutschemonemāāk.	Frage uns.
He asks me. Without the N it means, 'He asks you.'	N'kutschemónuk.	Er fragt mich: ohne N. heisst es, Er fragt dich.
He asks him.	Okutschemonáwa.	Er fragt ihn.
He asks us.	O[kutsche]mo͞onkónau.	Er fragt uns.
He asks you (pl.).	Kutschemo͞onkówa.	Er fragt euch.
He asks them.	Kutschemonáwa.	[Er fragt] sie.
Ask your heart.	Kutschemóna ktàh.	Frage dein Herz.
I will ask my heart.	Nkutschemonáu éne ntah.	Ich will mein Herz fragen.
Your (pl.) hearts ask.	Kutschemonòchk ktáhawa.	Fragt eure Herz.
ask (request of)		bitten
Now I will ask (request of) you (pl.).	Nià āām nóno machmàtŭămnāhkwà.	Ich bitte euch nun.
I ask, look into your heart.	Kmăchmātŭammĕn náwah nā ktah?	Ich bitte, sieh in dein Herz.
I ask Him that he ...	N'machmátuammàk nahk'ma, nè ...	Ich bitte Ihn, dass er ...
Ask that you may receive.	Machmatuammè kmischnimmantschè.	Bitte so soltu krigen.
Why do they ask that they have to get?	Anè machmatuamnáwak omischnemnáwak. [?what they-ask (is what) they-get?]	Warum sie bitten dass sollen sie krigen.
When they [we, incl.] ask the Lord with believing hearts.	Ŏnìstăwájăquà ktáhĕnnāāk kmàchmātŭămneēchĕnà Tápānmŭkáāk.	Wenn sie mit gläubigen Herzen den Heiland bitten.

English-Mahican-German 35

assemble, come together, meet, gather together [cf. trust (verb)]		kommen zusammen, versammlen [sic for modern versammeln]
We are coming together, assembling.	Majáowenánau.	Wir kommen zusammen.
We are coming together, assembling.	Kmajawéh'naù.	Wir kommen zusammen.
We [both] will meet.	Majahanátau.	Wir wollen zusammen kommen.
The children are assembling.	Majáowenáwa awásches.	Die Kinder kommen zusammen.
And when it sounds (or rings), you (pl.) must come immediately to school; it is not good to come together so late.	Wǎk tschenuáka taūtaū aaschkēēknpĕ kmajáwēēchma, astaù ŏnìttówe meēchkaù kmajáwenáwa.	Wenn gelautet wird, so müsst ihr gleich zur Schule kommen, es ist nicht gut so spät zusammen zu kommen.
It is time to ring for the meeting [for us to assemble].	Tautau nanamaha kmajàwēēchnaù.	Es ist Zeit zur Versammlung zu lauten [for läuten].
Then the (Indian) people gather together...	...nitsch tanè majáwewak anenapaak...	...so versammlen sich die [Indianer]...
associated with [see acquainted with]		
astonishingly, marvelously	mǟschchǎkke	erstaunlich
astray, go astray, get lost, get confused		Irre laufen
He cannot let her (them?) run astray, get lost, get confused.	Sta ǟm késche ǟnētāhāwĕ ǟnaù [a?] pǎpamsēchtēĕtsch.	Er kan sie nicht in der Irre laufen lassen.
asylum [see safe]		
at, at the	átan, nà	an, am
at the visit, with the visit	nè átan ótāwĕchtēet	bei dem Besuch
at once [see immediately; as soon as]		
attack	–	Anfall
attend to [see care for]		
attention [see also observe]		
You are not paying attention.	Astà önēechonǎmówe. [o = o or p?]	Du gibst nicht Achtung.
He is not paying attention.	[Astà] gǎchchǎnnĕwātǎmówe.	Er gibt nicht Achtung.
Pay attention.	Onènchāsè.	Gebt Achtung.
Pay (pl.) attention.	Oneēkchannawatamóŏk.	Gebt Achtung.
attentive, observant	–	aufmerksam
avaricious [see covetous]		
away, onward [see also chase out; tear away; go away]		fort
Run away quickly. [see also run after]	Ánameh kschech'nà.	Lauf hurtig fort.
You must go away.	Nāhǎnĕ àh.	Du must weggehen.
Throw it away, or put it away.	Attàchpannéwe.	Wirf es weg, oder leg es weg.
awl, shoemaker's awl	mǎkoŏs	Schu-Aal
ax, hatchet [cf. also hoe]	tĕmmǎhégan, t'mahégan, tummĕhégan	Axt, Beil
big hatchet	machēēd d'mahégan	gros [Beil]
little ax	tsch'mahéganìs	Beilgen
neck of an ax (or ax handle?)	osétòchkq	[Axt]helm
babble, chatter, gossip, have a chat		plaudern
Don't babble so.	Knisk'tschaǟchsè.	Plauder nicht so.
Don't (pl.) babble so.	[Knisk'tschaǟch]seēku.	Plaudert nicht so.
They are babbling.	Nissktschaǟchsoak.	Sie plaudern.
Why are you (pl.) babbling?	Gaquǟtsch nisskschaǟchsejāku.	Warum plaudert ihr.
Yes, we are chatting.	Káhanne nisskschaǟchsehenà.	Ja wir plaudern.
You are a chatterer, babbler.	Kenanisktschaǟchse.	Du bist ein Plauderer.
He is a chatterer, babbler.	Nanisktschaǟchso.	Er ist ein Plauderer.
back (part of body) [cf. bind the hands behind the back (word for back not in manuscript)]		
bad, evil [see also harm]	machtessò	bös
in evil	matechk	in Bösen
...how bad it is.	...ŏtĕnnè nǎchkĕssēen. [cf. two under see]	...wie bös es ist.
It is bad when...	Mǎchtett...	Das ist bös, wenn...
bad people	–	böse Menschen
It smells bad.	Machtschémǎquàt.	Es riecht bös.
bad things	–	böse Dinge
You bad one	kenáchkse	du böser

36 Schmick's Mahican dictionary

bad [cf. harm]	mằttà [etc.]	
I have said nothing bad.	Astàn nià mátēĕk 'n̈séu.	Ich habe nichts böses gesagt.
He has done nothing bad.	Náhkma astak gaquai anè mátschằĩjéwe.	Er hat nichts böses gethan.
What evil has he done?	Gaquai nahkmà anè mattà nachkáu.	Was hat er übels gethan.
not respected, despised	matanemukséēd	nicht geehrt, verachtet
I ruin.	N'mattschechtǎn. [I-bad-make?]	Ich verderbe.
He (she) is not well.	Mǎttà mǎnn̈ssò.	Er (sie) ist nicht wol.
bad fire	—	schlecht Feuer
You have a bad fire.	Káha kmattenaù assè.	Du hast ein schlecht Feuer.
We have [a] bad fire.	Káhanna k'mattenaù assēhĕnǎů.	Wir haben schlecht Feuer.
bad off (to be), to be in a bad way (in the heart)		schlecht stehen (im Herzen)
I am in a bad way in my heart.	Nmattachksè ntáhak.	Ich stehe schlecht im Herzen.
You are in a bad way in your heart.	K[mattachk]sè ktáhak.	Du stehst [schlecht im Herzen].
He is in a bad way in his heart.	Mattachksò otáhik.	Er steht [schlecht im Herzen].
We are in a bad way in our hearts.	N'mahtachksehenà ntahanánik.	Wir stehen schlecht in unsern Herzen.
You (pl.) are in a bad way in your hearts.	Kmahtachksehemà ktahawáwick.	Ihr steht schlecht in eurem Herzen.
They are in a bad way in their hearts.	Mahtachksoàk otahawǎwuk.	Sie sind schlecht in ihren Herzen.
[cf.:] weak ('bad-hearted'?)	mattàhǎwá(w)u	schwach
badness [see malice]		
bag [see sack]		
baker?	—	Becker [for Bäker?]
band, strap, ribbon [see also under arm]	pequagàn	Band
garter strap	p'ahgĕgǎnápei	Knie[band]
support band, strap, brace, suspenders	machtápei	Trag[band]
swaddling clothes strap, roller strap	tachtonawápei	Windel[band]
waistband, girdle?, apron-string	tahgetschápei	Leib[band], Schürz[band]
straps around the blanket	achpequagenàn, plur[alis] [k or g]	Bänder um die Blanquet
bangle [see bracelet]		
banquet [see love feast]		
baptized ones (all the)	máowe soognepongsetscheek [cf. pour]	alle getaufte
Today we will have a love feast with the baptized ones, who are joyous.	Nonò wáchcamàhk tachtaquèpéhenóók nēĕk soognepongsétscheèk wǎŭnàchtanaméschĕĕk.	Heute werden wir L[iebes]mahl haben mit den getauften, die da vergnügt sind.
bar [see bolt]		
(bark), inner bark	—	Bast
bark [verb]; dog barking	—	Hund bellen
The dog is barking.	Okechgáu ndiáhu.	Der Hund bellet.
barn, shed, granary	—	Scheun[e]
in the barn	tanapachgach'muk	in Scheun[e]
basin [see pan]		
basket	mechtquenótei	Korb
Whose basket is this?	Awǎn nò mechtquenótei.	Wem ist der Korb?
be [Indo-European concept]		sein, seyn

['To be' does not appear in Algonquian, but there may be grammatical, semantic, or verbal elements that approximate to concepts such as 'to be in a place,' ' to be with,' and 'to remain'; note the usage in the following: patient; thirsty; dumb:]

I am patient [have strong heart].	Ntassanetahà.	Ich bin gedultig.
You are patient.	Ktassanetahà.	Du bist gedultig.
He is patient.	Assanetaháu.	Er ist gedultig, stark Herz.
We are patient.	Ntassanetahanà.	Wir sind gedultig.
You (pl.) are patient.	Ktassanetahamà.	Ihr seid gedultig.
They are patient.	Assanetaháwak.	Sie sind gedultig.
I am thirsty.	Ngattósome.	Ich bin durstig.
You are thirsty.	Gattósomè.	Du bist durstig.
He is thirsty.	Gattosomu.	Er ist durstig.
We are thirsty.	Ngattosomechnà.	Wir sind durstig.
You (pl.) are thirsty.	Gattosomechmà.	Ihr seid durstig.

English-Mahican-German 37

English	Mahican	German
They are thirsty.	Gattosomuak.	Sie sind durstig.
I am dumb.	Ntschannéiuwe.	Ich bin dumm.
You are dumb.	Ktschannéiuwe.	Du bist dumm.
He is dumb.	Tschannéiuwe.	dumm
We are dumb.	Ntschanneiwechnà.	Wir sind dumm.
You (*pl.*) are dumb.	Ktschanneiwechmà.	Ihr seid dumm.
They are dumb.	Tschanneiuwéwak.	Sie sind dumm.

[*See also* Pronominal affixes, *two examples of which are as follows:*]

It is mine.	N'tajégan.	Es ist meine. Mein, es ist.
That was mine.	Nágach nià.	Das ist mein gewesen.
⎡I have seen him. [*ms. 369*]	Nià kĕĕp nãŭwãăp. [*cf.* Kià kĕĕp.]	Ich habe ihn gesehen. ⎤
⎢Not I. I am not it.	Astàn nià.	Ich bins nicht. ⎥
⎣You are.	Kià kĕĕp.	Du bist. ⎦
It is not right. [Not it/that.]	Astàn nè.	Es ist nicht recht.
It is right. [That it/that.]	Nàn nè.	Es ist recht.
That is it.	Nè àht. Nè ãăt.	Das ist es. Das ist es.
He was industrious.	Nèpnàhp.	Er war fleissig.

[*The following are not copulative in Mahican but are so used in German and English:*]
[*Subjunctive:*]

... that he may be (or is) sick.	... ŏwénamansohããncùn.	... dass er kranck sey.

[*Imperative:*]

Be still! Be quiet!	Tschè kăpè. [kăpè = sit?]	Sey still.
Be (*pl.*) still.	Tschéĕkpè.	Seyd still.
Be still! / Sit still!	Majà năchpè. / Majánape. [*see* sit]	Sey still. / Siz still.
Don't be thoughtless, or You must not be thoughtless.	Tscheĕn kniskēpēsè.	Sey nicht leichtsinnig. oder Du must nicht leichtsinnig seyn.
Don't be troubled!	Tscheĕn gaquai kschéwahndam.	Sey nicht betrübt.
He has been the same.	Tăătpajohénnau. [é = a *or* o?]	Er ist gleich gewesen.
They are friends with each other.	Ãĭnòkotakeèk.	Sie sind Freunde miteinander.
That is big and important for us.	Kmachchè katàcŏnãnaū.	Das ist uns gross u[nd] wichtig.
We should be thus daily. [Nè = that; ãm = will; kiánau = we]	Nè ãm kiánau tãătĕ pãĭnanàu [come?] wáwochkamákè. [*cf. under* should]	So sollen wir täglich seyn.

[*Cf.* àht *under* be (in a place) *and the following:*]

That is it.	Nè àht. Nè ãăt.	Das ist es. Das ist es.
be (in a place) [*cf.* stay]		
I am [in a place]. [*see* stay]	Ntajè. Ntajeĕn. [*as in* Spommuk ntajè. = → Ich bin droben. = I am up aloft.]
You are	Ktajè.	Du bist. Bistu
He, she, it is (not).	Ajù (sta ... ajéwe); hăjoù (sta ... hăjĕwĕ).	Er ist (nicht).
He always likes to be with the children.	Gŏmmáwe wége ajù awasésik.	Er ist ge[rne?] allezeit bein Kindern.
We are (not).	Ntajehenà (stà ... ntajewehenà).	Wir sind (nicht).
You (*pl.*) are.	Ktajehema.	Seid ihr.
They are (not).	Ájuwak. Ajuwàk. ăjówak (stà ... ajéwek)	Sie sind (nicht).
to be:	—	seyn
He (therefore?) will already (or now) be in New York.	Nonò àht nahà ăjókak N[ew] Yorck.	Er wird schon in New Yorck seyn.
Christian will already (or now) be in Wyoming.	Chr[istian] nonò ãht nãhà ajókak Măchăwoámik.	Chr[istian] wird schon in Wajomick seyn.
I have been, was [in a place].	Noŏm. Nŏm. [*as in* Spommuka noŏm. = → Ich bin droben gewesen. = I was up there.]
You have been, were.	Kŏŏm. Kŏm. [= ?You come from]	Bistu ... gewesen. Du [bist gewesen].
He [*sic*] has been, was.	Kŏŏma. Kŏma. [*sic* both]	Er ist ... gewesen.
We have been, were.	Noŏmhanà. Nŏmhanà.	Wir sind ... gewesen.
You (*pl.*) have been, were.	Koomhamà. Kŏmhamà.	Ihr seid ... gewesen. Ihr seyd [gewesen].
They [*sic*] have been, were.	Koomãăk. Komãk. [*sic* both]	Sie sind ... gewesen.

[*One might expect õŏma, õma, oomãăk, and omãk, but ms. p. (23) clearly shows kŏŏma and koomãăk whereas ms. p. (349) shows kŏm, kŏma, kŏmhamà, and komãk, with these latter k's each covering a g. Was p. (23) an improved copy of p. (349)?*]

Is a horse there?	Nachnióges nhà?	Ist ein Pferd da?
Is a light there?	Wãhs'nanégan n'hà?	Ist ein Licht da?
We are here. We live here.	Pòmájik.	Wir sind hier, wir leben hier.
be present, be with, be by it	—	seyn dabei, seyn mit

38 Schmick's Mahican dictionary

English	Mahican	German
I will be present.	N'wetschechnà.	Ich will dabei seyn.
Have you been with (him, them)? Have you taken part?	Kwetschechnasà.	Bistu dabei gewesen?
He was with us.	Wetschechnǟp.	Er war mit uns.
You were also with Peter.	Kià wăk nò kotschaíjèn Petrussek.	Du warest auch beim Petrus.
You certainly are one of them.	Kià múchtsche wăk kwetscháijìn. [you very also you-with-are]	Gewis, du bist einer davon.
... Joseph would be with Joshua.	... Joseph áu Josuáhik.	... Joseph sey beim Josua.
He likes to go around with the children, or properly He always likes to be with the children.	Gŏmmáwe wége ajù awasésik.	Er geht gerne mit Kindern um. oder *proprië*. Er ist ge[rne?] allezeit bein Kindern.
N. likes to go around with the Indians.	N. wegócháu ananapawechgŏk. [*composed of wége and ajù.]	N. geht gerne mit Ind[ia]nern um. *compos.: von wége u[nd] ajù.
[But cf. Del. *wagáuchĕn*, to walk round about a thing, *Zeisberger's Indian Dictionary*, 1887, p. 224.]		
I always go with God, *i.e.*, I am always thinking about him.	Nian gommáwe ntĕnetáha Pachtamawássek.	Ich gehe immer mit [Gott] um, *i.e.*, ich denke immer [an ihn?].
[see crucify *for further uses of* are ... -ed, was ... -ed, be ... -ed, has been ... -ed *expressed in the Algonquian manner*]		
be with one heart, agree [*see* become (as) one *under* one]		ein Herz seyn *vid[e]* eins seyn [*i.e.*, eins werden?]
beam	—	Balken
beans	t'pachquăn, tpachquaăn	Bohnen
black	nánasgaikè	schwarze
white	wapĕd	weisse
bear	màchq, machquè, machquà, machquò	Bär
bear fat	p'mèh, pòmì	[Bär]fett
bear [*see* bring forth]		
beard	nechquéi	Bart
the hair of the beard?	wechtonajà	(die Haare)
[Mass. *weeshitoon* = [hairy-mouth], beard, *and Mahican (Heckewelder) wichtoneijin* = beard]		
long beard	—	langen [Bart]
He has a long beard.	Wachquanechtonajáu.	Er hat einen langen Bart.
beat [*see* pound; hit; swollen]		
beautiful, pretty (to be)	—	schön seyn
I am beautiful.	Nōnĕsè.	Ich bin schön.
You are beautiful.	K[ōnĕsè].	Du bist [schön].
He is handsome. [She is beautiful.]	Onessò.	Er ist [schön].
We are beautiful.	Non'sehenà.	Wir sind schön.
You (*pl.*) are beautiful.	Kon'sehemà.	Ihr seid [schön].
They are beautiful.	Onessowàk. [Onessoàk?]	Sie sind [schön].
a beautiful child	honesséscho ăwāsēs (ăwāsches)	ein schön Kind
beautiful		
Today is a beautiful day.	Unàchcamáo nóno.	Heute ist ein schöner Tag.
I had a beautiful dream. I dreamt beautifully.	Nò ŏnŏquaàm.	Ich habe schön geträumt.
a beautiful flower [*sic for plural*]	wawunitschischowàn wachawähnschan	eine schöne Blume
a beautiful sermon	Wawunntŏnháu	eine schöne Predig[t]
You are nice. [*see* have good conduct]	Konanachgà.	Du machst es hübsch.
It is proper, fair.	Konenaxè.	Es ist hübsch.
You read beautifully, nicely.	Kăhăgóne kétammen.	Du liesest schön, hübsch.
beautiful weather	Ŏtăkkàn	schön Wetter
beautifully, very well	—	schön (*pulchre*)
You read beautifully.	Kăhăgōnĕ gétammen.	Du liesest schön, hübsch.
You write beautifully.	Kăhăgōnĕ sŏăhēga. [Kosoahega?]	Du schreibest [schön, hübsch].
You work very well.	[Kăhăgōnĕ] ănāchgă.	Du arbeitest [schön, hübsch].
beaver [*English word in manuscript*]	ămùchkq	[Biber]
beaver dam	kupnégan	[Biber]damm
Beaver skin is soaking in the water.	Tămmŏchquèi kamukhà mpēĕk.	*Beaver* Haut weiche ein ins Wasser.
because [*see also* so; so that]	quaăm [= yes?]; otschè	dieweil; darum
Because (*or* as long as) we know.	Quaăm kiánau kwawèchtănānāū.	Dieweil wir wissen.
Because I took snuff.	Snùp ntágushgun otschè.	Darum weil ich Schnupftobak genommen.
because of, for	otschè [*at end of clause*]	darum weil

Because of it. Because of that.	Nè ŏtschè.	Das macht. [*note German idiom:* That makes it.]
become flesh, become man, be incarnated, be embodied		Mensch werden, Fleisch werden
The Savior has therefore become man, or has therefore lived in the world.	Nam Pachtamawáās Táp[anemuc]quàk wātsche óhākkājéwe tanè pomáosetip nànnéttānè ahhkéēk. [n = n *or* k?]	Der Heiland ist darum Mensch worden, oder hat darum in der Welt gelebet.
I am not forgetting that for us he became like a man and died. [*for comparison:*]	Nià astàn wannisséwe, náhk'ma ánènāhxétippĕ hakkánāāk, wāk mbŏŏp.	Ich vergesse es nicht, dass er für uns ist ein Mensch geworden, und gestorben.
Do you believe that the one who came, who made everything, appeared as one of us?	Kŏnsittamennà nò pájakŏp maowe gáquai kescheechtátip ne anènāāxíjàk anènāāxétip. [k̠ = k *or* t?]	Glaubestu dass der, der alles gemacht[,] ist höher kommen als einer von uns.
Therefore we are created to sleep in his arm.	Ni watsche onèhókājàne onàchkeck ngáuweèn.	Wir sind deswegen geschaffen in seinen Arm zu schlafen.
bed	gāchgăwŏjè, kāchgawŏjè, kāchkăwŏjè	Bett
bedstead	gàchgawémuk, kachgawémuk	[Bett]lade, [Bett]stelle
behind the bed	ne áchtāk k̠achgawémuk [k *covers* g]	hintern Bett
under the bed	anámuk [kachgawémuk]	untern [Bett]
bee	amuáu	Biene
little bee	amuáschik	Bienlein
been	—	gewesen
He has been the same. [*translation of* gleich *proper?*]	Taatpajohénnau. [e *might be* a *or* o?] [*cf.* under should]	Er ist gleich gewesen.
I have been ready.	Kekéschanachkáhip. [= 'You have got ready.']	Ich bin fertig gewesen.
He has been inside. [*cf. others under* inside, *i.e.,* in the house]	N'hammachtsch ajù.	Ist er drinne gewesen.
before [*cf.* for]	utschì [= from?]	vor
before his eyes	usketschguk utschì	vor s[einen] Augen
beggar	—	Bettler
beggar, to be a; to be a claimant	—	Heischer seyn
I am a beggar.	Npeschechwà.	Ich bin Heischer.
You are a beggar.	Kpeschechwà.	Du bist [Heischer].
He is a beggar.	Peschechwáu.	Er ist [Heischer].
begin to (want to?) [*see* mawe- *and* mawu- *under* will]		
beginner, in religion	—	Anfänger (des Glaubens)
beginning	—	Anfang
behind	ne áchtāk	hinter
behind the bed(stead)	ne áchtāk k̠achgawémuk	hintern Bett
belief	onìstămawágan	Glauben
believe	—	glauben
There is a difference between 'to believe' and 'to be obedient (or submissive).'		*Differens inter* glauben und gehorsam seyn.
I believe.	Nohnsittammen.	Ich glaube.
You believe.	K[ohnsittammen].	Du glaubest.
He believes.	Ohnsittammen.	Er [glaubt].
We (all) believe.	Kiánok kohnsittammenanok.	Wir glauben.
We (two) believe.	Kianau kohnsittammenánau.	Wir glauben. *Dualis*
You (*pl.*) believe.	Kohnsittammenawà.	Glaubt ihr oder ihr glaubt.
They believe in the Savior.	Ohnsittawawà Pachtama[wa]asnau.	Glauben sie an den Heiland.
Whoever (will) believe him. When someone believes [*fut.*] him.	Awáneetsch ŏnistawáta.	Wer das glaubt.
He believes.	Onístak.	Er glaubt.
When they ask Him (the Savior) with believing hearts. [*see also under* approach]	Ŏnìstăwájăquà ktáhĕnnāāk kmàchmātŭămnēéchĕnà Tápānmŭkāāk. [you]	Wenn sie mit gläubigen Herzen /d[en] Heiland/bitten. /Ihn
You (*pl.*) will not believe it.	Kiáwa astà gohnsíttăwēwāhŏmmà.	Ihr werdets nicht glauben.
Let everyone who will (wants to) believe examine his heart.	Maówe awañ katàu onistawahnta otschemŏnatsch otáha.	Jederman wer da glauben will untersuche s[ein] Herz.
Why is it you (*pl.*) [they?] don't believe in Jesus?	Gaquai watsche astà wáwonistawāwak Jesus.	Warum es nicht an Jesum glaubet.
Do you believe that the one who came, who made everything, appeared as one of us?	Kŏnsittamennà nò pájak̠ŏp maowe gáquai kescheechtátip ne anenāāxíjàk anènāāxétip. [k̠ = k *or* t?]	Glaubestu dass der, der alles gemacht[,] ist höher kommen als einer von uns.

English-Mahican-German   39

40 *Schmick's Mahican dictionary*

Yes, I believe it.	Káhanna nŏhnsittámmen.	Ja ich glaube es.
Do you believe what I have said to you?	Kohnsittawenà anáăptónamenàn?	Glaubestu was ich dir gesagt habe?
Yes, I believe it in my heart that it is true.	Káhanna kohnsittáăn ntáhak tanè nàn nenáju kahanè.	Ja ich glaube es in meinem Herzen; dass es wahr ist.
I do not believe that it is true.	Stà kohnsittáno stannenajéwe.	Ich glaube es nicht, dass es wahr ist.
B[arbara?] believes that God shed (spilled) his blood for her.	B. ohnsittámmen Pachtamawaasnaù op'gachganŏm otenè anawachtéēn sókahanáăp.	B. glaubt, dass Gott s[ein] Blut für sie vergossen.
Yes, I believe that my God spilled his blood for me.	Káhanna nohnsittammen nintenè anawachtéēn n'Pachtamawaas op'gachganom sokahanáăp.	Ja ich glaube, dass Gott s[ein] Blut vor mich vergossen.
We all believe in one God, who is our father.	Niána máowe nohnsēttăwána nà páăschco Pachtamáwăăs, nà watóchiak kiánook.	Wir glauben all an einen Gott, der unser Vater ist.
We belong to (believe in) the Savior.	Kiánau konsittawánau kPachtamawasnau.	Wir gehören dem Heiland an. [*translation?*]
(They) all the believing are in his hand.	Nĕĕk wáhnsettakĕĕk máowe ăjówak nahk'ma onáchgek. [e = e *or* a?]	Alle Gläubigen sind in seiner Hand.
He (the Devil) hates those who believe.	O[schegena]wáwa wáhnsēttăchkè.	Er hasset die Gläubigen.
Help your believers and bless what your portion is, wait for them always with your bloody wages.	Nàchtamawe wáhnsettakwanéĕk, wăk wétahamè gaquai nìk kià áne găttaammawíjáăk, channawèhenana ngommaowe áne p'gachganĕĕth kià kpènhammawágan.	Hilf deinen Gläubigen u[nd] segne was dein Erbtheil ist, warte sie allezeit mit deinen blutigen Verdienst.
bell [*see* sound (*verb*)]	tautaù [= 'ding-dong,' 'tam-tam']	–

[Tautaù *seems to be an onomatopeic word; cf. Nipmuck tau8tau = cloche (= bell)* (*The* Mots loups ..., *G. Day, 1975*).]

belly	–	Bauch
belong, it belongs		gehört (es)
It belongs to me.	Niàn t'páăntammèn.	Es gehört mein [*obsolete genitive*].
It belongs to Thomas.	Thomas t'páăntammèn.	Es gehört dem Thomas.
The gun is my own.	Nŭmpăpéquan tappáăntámmen.	Die Flinte ist mein eigen.
The horse belongs to Joshua.	Josua hŏnăchnăjŏxĕmà.	Das Pferd gehört dem Josua.
We belong to (believe in) the Savior.	Kiánau konsittawánau kPachtamawasnau.	Wir gehören dem Heiland an. [*translation?*]
Whose kettle is this?	Awăn nò nŏtăhósa?	Wem ist der Kessel?
Whose knife is this?	[Awăn] nò otachégan.	[Wem ist] das Messer?
[*cf. also under* mine, it is]		
Whose basket is this?	[Awăn nò] mechtquenótei.	[Wem ist] der Korb?
beloved	–	beliebt
below (there) [*see* down there]		
belt of wampum [*in English*]	ăchquásou	*belt of wampum*
bench [*see* seat]		
benefit of [*see* enjoy]		
benevolent [*see under* good]		
berry, berries	[men]	Beere
blackberry	gaweschemen, *plur[alis]* gaweschemének	Brombeere, Kraz[beere], schwarze [Beere]
huckleberry, bilberry, whortleberry	ménan	Heidel[beere]
raspberry	–	Him[beere]
strawberry	–	Erd[beere]
best [*cf. usage under* good]		
better	Ŏnèttŏŏp ánnowéwe. [good-it-was more]	besser *melius*
Bible or the Holy Book	wănĕhk ŏsŏªhégan	Bibel oder das Heilige Buch
big [*see* great]		
bind	–	binden
bound, obliged [*see* bind!]	[*left untranslated in Schmick's cross-referencing*]	gebunden. *Vide* binden
bind the hands behind the back		Hände auf[de]n Rücken binden
You (they?) have bound his hands behind his back.	Apapáătqua pnawapanè.	Sie haben ihn die Hände auf[de]n Rücken gebunden.
binder	–	Binder
bird [*see under* sing; see]	tschèchtschìs, tschĕĕchtschis	Vogel
bishop	bishop	Bischof

English	Mahican	German
bite		
The flea is biting me.	Papĕĕk nsackamùck.	Der Floh beisst mich.
The fleas are biting me.	Papéquak nsackamuckónau.	Die Flöhe beissen mich.
bite off		
He has bitten off my finger.	Ntemmachtamḗgun ntannahégan. [é or á?]	Er hat mir den Finger abgebissen.
bitter	wĕsăkàn	bitter
bitterness	–	Bitterkeit
black [see beans; cf. brown bread]		
black and blue	mechmenájo	braun und blau [= brown and blue]
blackberry	gaweschemen, plur[alis] gaweschemḗnak	Brombeer
blackbird	–	Amsel
blame [see fault]		
blanket (white blanket)	wāpăssănāi, plur[alis] wāpassānajàn	Blanquet
black blanket	–	schwarze
blue blanket	–	blaue
a heap of blankets	wapassanajan machahndam	ein Haufen Blanquets
my blanket	n'massánai	mein Blanquet
red blanket	–	rothe
striped blanket	–	streifigte
white blanket	wāpăssănāi, plur[alis] wāpassānajàn	weisse
your blanket	k[massánai]	dein
bleed, have a bloody nose	–	Nase (bluten)
My nose is bleeding.	Pagechtanè.	Meine Nase blutet.
You are bleeding from the nose.	K[pagechtanè].	Du [Deine Nase blutet.]
He is bleeding from the nose.	Pagechtanò.	Er [Seine Nase blutet.]
He or it is bleeding.	Pgachganò.	Er blutet.
My nose is bleeding.	[Pgachganò] nachkèwan.	M[eine] Nase blutet.
Your nose is bleeding.	[Pgachganò] kachkèwan.	Deine Nase bl[utet].
bless, consecrate, make sign of cross?, make an incantation? [see also compassion(ate)]		segnen
Whom do you bless? To whom do you show mercy? Whom do you pity?	Awän kaktemaganĕĕdt [or -ĕdt?]?	Wen segnestu? Wess[en] erbarmestu dich?
Have pity [on us?].	Ntĕmácānŏmè.	Erbarme dich.
He blesses, makes sign of cross(?), makes an incantation(?).	Kótangkūūmkŭă. Delaw[are]	Er segne [sic for segnet].
Help your believers and bless what your portion is.	Nàchtamawe wáhnsettakwanĕĕk, wăk wétahamè gaquai nìk kià áne gáttaammawíjaăk.	Hilf deinen Gläubigen u[nd] segne was dein Erbtheil ist.
[May] God bless your [sg. in Mahican] food.	Pachtamáwaas wétahámukquè áne mézĕăn.	Gott segne eure Speise.
He helps along with us.	Wétăhāmākùk.	Er hilft mit uns.
blessed [see blissful]		
blessing [see under good]		
blind	gachgapequáu	blind
blindness of your heart	gachgapequawágan ktahak	Blindheit d[eines] Herzens
blissful, blessed, happy [see also under live]		selig, seelig seyn
You will always be blissful, if you do not leave the Savior.	Kiàtsch kŏnăpātămmĕn tschĕn'kanáhan Pachtamawaās.	Du wirst allezeit selig seyn, wenn du nicht vom Heiland weggehst.
blister [see also bubble]		
blister from working or fire	wăchpĕchquāi	Blase von der Arbeit oder Brand
block, log	pòchkschacháąkq	Block
blood	p'gachgan, p'gachganohm	Blut
in(to) the blood	p'gachganómik, abl[ativus]	in dem [Blut]
He is coughing up blood.	Ochoquénei p'gachganŏ̄.	Er wirft Blut aus.
It isn't bloody or blood.	Astà p'gachganéwe.	Es [ist] nicht blutig oder Blut.
bloodied	ánĕp'gachganeĕk	verwundeten [= wounded]
I have eaten of his wounded (bloodied) body.	Nià pákatschè nahk'ma ánĕp'gachganeĕk óhákkei métsche.	Ich habe von seinem verwundeten Leichnam gegessen.
bloodlet [see comments under Delaware (Lenâpé) words]		
show vein or bloodlet	–	Ader lasszeig
	[The following three sentences are in Delaware:]	
I want to do the bloodletting.	N°gatta pachtsche pommăkè.	Ich will [Aderlassen].

42 *Schmick's Mahican dictionary*

You want to do the bloodletting.	Káttà páchtsche pommăkèh.	Willst du Aderlassen.
You must do the bloodletting.	Kattà páchtsche pommăwè.	Du must Aderlassen.
bloodsucker, leech	—	Blutsauger
bloody	p'gachganĕth, p'gachganĕĕk	blutig
bloody face, when one [is] beaten a lot	p'gachganitschanèquáü	Angesicht, wenn man viel geschlagen.
My spit is bloody.	P'gachganõ nochquénei.	Mein Auswurf ist blutig.
It isn't bloody or blood.	Asta p'gachganéwe.	Es [ist] nicht blutig oder Blut.
blow [*see* wind; east]		
blow a horn, sound a bugle	—	Horn blasen
Did you already blow the horn?	Păkătsche podáha wewĕĕn. [podana?] [horn]	Hastu das Horn schon geblasen?
blow one's nose; snort [*cf.* nose]		
He blows, snorts his nose.	Kăkékwăschăhn.	Er schnaubt die Nase.
Blow your nose.	Kăkékwăschà.	Schnaube die Nase.
blue [*cf. also* black and blue]	onawáju	blau
blush [*see under* redden]		
board, plank	packchàckq [packgàhk *was stricken out*], pákchăkŭ	Brett
boards, trays, platters	páckchăquăn	Bretter
boat [*see* canoe; ship]		
bodice [*see under* breast]		
body [*cf.* self; *see also* become flesh; one, We are one.]	ohákkei [= his body], hakkei, hackay, háckai	Leib; Leichnam [= corpse]
boil, swelling, tumor	pŏmŏwàhs	Beule
boil or cook off fat		
She boiled or cooked off the fat.	Átanèppĕméhaat.	Sie kocht das Fett aus.
boil or cook meat	—	Fleisch kochen
cooked or boiled meat, to boil meat	potaháso wĕjáăs	gekocht Fleisch, Fleisch kochen
Boil meat.	Ānămă ojáăs.	Koche Fleisch.
Today I will cook meat.	Nóno wăchgămăăk ntănămă ojáăs.	Ich will heute Fleisch kochen.
Did you finish cooking meat?	K'tănămòh ojáăs.	Kochstu Fleisch (fertig).
Is the meat ready?	Wĕĕgtà ojáăs?	Ist das Fleisch gaar?
boil over, cook over	—	—
Remove the kettle; it's boiling too much. [*cf. entry at* remove]	Nochpána hoŏs osáme kschĕkămĕscho. [kschĕkămĕ]so.	Rück den Kessel ab, es kocht zu sehr. *idem* [= the same]
It's boiling over.	Paāschĕŭ.	Es kocht über.
It will boil or cook over.	Énĕ păschĕŭ.	Es wird überkochen.
It will boil over soon.	Éne nánäu páschĕŭ.	Es wird gleich überkochen.
It always boils over.	Pàchpāschĕŭ.	Es kocht immer über.
bolt, bar, rail [*which one is correct?*]	n'scheĕmchaknégàn	Riegel
bone	wachgàn	Bein, oder Knochen
book	ŏsŏᵃhégan, osoehégan [*see* inherit], osohégan	Buch
a big book	macháăk ŏsŏᵃhégan	ein grosses Buch
the Holy Book, Bible	wănĕhk ŏsŏᵃhégan	Bibel oder das Heilige Buch
a little book	tschaxẽschāk ŏsŏhégan, tschaxẽschāk ŏsŏᵃhégan	ein kleines Büchelgen
my book	nosoahégan	—
border [*see* edge]		
borer, drill	kwekwágan	ein Bohrer
born [*see* bring forth]		
borrow [*see* lend]		
both	néschewe	beide
both? *or* tired?	neschowe	[*This word was untranslated.*]
bottle	pnàsch [*from German Flasche?*]	Boteille
[*cf. Nipmuck (G. Day, p. 49) plas*ᵉ, *bottle, probably from Dutch fles*]		
bough	ŏttŏhòhn	Ast
bow	sachkenáu	Bogen
bow (head)		
He bowed his head.	Náwăkẽğchnà wénes.	Neigte er das Haupt.
bowl? [*see* pan]		
bowstring	nschĕpan	[Bogen]schnur

box	—	Büchse
bracelet, bangle. Note: The men have only one, but the women have more.	tpenachgápe, *plur[alis]* tpenachgápean	Armspangen. *NB.* Die Männer haben nur eine, die Weiber aber mehrere.
brandy, gin	p'natt'wĕn [*loan word*]	Brandtwein
brave, courageous, spirited	—	beherzt, muthig
bread	tachquòch, taquòch; Del[aware:] achpŏhn [*mod. Del. ahpŚn*]	Brod
brown	nsĕgĕtăhquòch	braun
white	wăpētăhquòch	weiss
my	n'tacchõm	mein
your	g'[tacchõm]	dein
his	otacchomàh	sein
our	n'tacchomnà	unser
your (*pl.*)	g'tacchomwà	eure
their	otacchomawà	ihr
Fetch bread.	Taquachnána.	Hol Brod.
piece of bread	packájis taquoch	Stück Brod
break off, tear off	pàchkĕnĭmmèn	abreissen
breakfast	najapawépĕhn *subst[antivum]*	—
to have breakfast	—	frühstücken
I have breakfast.	Najapawepe.	Ich frühstücke.
You have breakfast.	K[najapawepe].	Du [frühstückest].
He has breakfast.	Najapawépŏŭ.	Er [frühstückt].
We have breakfast.	Nájapàwepéhenà.	Wir
You (*pl.*) have breakfast.	Knajapawepéhemà.	Ihr *etc.*
They have breakfast.	Najapawépoàk.	Sie
Let's have breakfast.	Najapawepetŏŏk.	Lasst uns frühstücken.
breast, chest [*cf.* side]	nachpássei [= my breast]	Brust
her breast, his chest	wachpássei	seine
your breast	ghapássei	deine
in his side	wăchpássei	in [seiner] Seite
in the side	nachpassăk	in d[er] Seite
into the side	wapassăk	in die Seite
neckcloth, breast cloth, bodice, corset	nachpássak ăhănéchek	[Brust]tuch oder Leibgen
The child lies at the breast.	Awăsches kĕnămù wapassajénăk.	Das Kind liegt an der Brust.
bridge, or small wooden bridge	tăjăchquăn	Brücke oder Steg
bright [*see* light]		
brightness [*see* light]		
bring [*see also* fetch; carry; **patăk nè**, p. 155]		
Take me over the hunting ground (district, enclosed area, *etc.*).	Kámik anàhonè.	Bring mich übers Revier.
Bring the pan (basin, bowl).	Konágănŏwáwàn. *or* Konáganes wáwàn.	Bringt die Schüssel.
I'm bringing it back soon.	Ene báschŏă scháwa. [scháwa = at once]	Ich bringe bald wieder.
bring forth, produce, give birth to	—	gebären
I have given birth to a child.	Notajóme.	Ich hab ein Kind geboren.
She has given birth to a child.	Otajomáu.	Sie hat ein Kind geboren.
Mary has brought forth the Savior.	Maria otajoména Pachtamawăăsnau.	Maria hat den Heiland geboren.
When did she give birth to the child?	Tája ŏtajōmōsà?	Wenn hat sie[da]s Kind geboren?
I am born. I was born.	N'mechtappè. Nmechtappè.	Ich bin geboren.
You are (were) born.	K[mechtappè]. G[mechtappè].	Du bist [geboren].
He is (was) born.	Machtáppo. Machtappò.	Er ist [geboren].
We are (were) born.	Nmechtappehenà.	Wir sind geboren.
You (*pl.*) are (were) born.	K[mechtappe]hemà. G[mechtappe]hemà.	Ihr seid [geboren].
They are (were) born.	Machtappuàk.	Sie sind [geboren].
When was John born?	Tája machtappósa Johannes?	Wenn ist Joh[annes] geboren.
Just as the little children are born, so has he been born.	Nĕáne [= just as?] machtappétap awaschees, áhanè [= so?] machtappĕĕd.	Er ist geboren werden, so wie die kleine Kinder.
That you were [he was?]born a man.	Nannoha atane machtappetip na némana.	Dass du geboren bist ein Mensch.
I was born.	Nmachtappéhop. [o͜ = o *or* a?]	Ich bin geboren.
The Savior was born.	Pachtamawăăsnau machtappŏŏp.	Der Heiland ist geboren.

44 Schmick's Mahican dictionary

English	Mahican	German
When were you born?	Tän ănĕquéchque kmĕchtapp'nap?	Wenn bist du geboren?
When were you (pl.) born?	[Tän ănĕquéchque] kmĕchtăppĕhĕmăăp.	Wenn seid ihr geboren?
They were born in Bethlehem.	Bethlehem tanè machtáppuak.	Sie sind in Bethlehem geboren.
Our Savior was born in the stable.	Pachtamawăăsnau tanè machtáppŏŏp kojéganick.	Unser Heiland ist im Stalle geboren.

brook [see creek]

broom	p'nŏmĭs [from English broom]	Besen
what sweeps clean, broom	tschĕchhégan, tschékĕhégan	der rein kehrt
brother (my brother)	netáchgan, netachcan	Bruder
brothers (my), brethren	nétachcanàck	die Brüder
the brothers (your + ?persons?)	getachganenapàh	den Brüdern
brothers R. and G.	wetáchkana (R.) (G.)	die Brüder (R.) und (G.)
the older brother	[netáchgan, netachcan]	der ältere
the oldest brother	gachgajĕd netachgan	der älteste
a single brother, unmarried	gegapau	ein lediger Bruder
the younger brother	[chesem]	der jungere
the youngest brother	tapanmissĕĕd [chesem]	der jüngste

Note: The younger brothers always call the one who is older nétachcan. Each of the younger ones is chesem and plural chésemak. So also the older sisters call each who is younger chesem, plural chésemak. The younger ones call the one who is older mĕĕs, plural mésak.

NB. Die jüngern Brüder nennen immer den der älter ist nétachcan. Jedem der jünger ist chesem, plur. chésemak. So auch die ältern Schwestern nennen jede, die jünger ist chesem, plur. chésemak. Die jüngern nennen die, so älter ist mĕĕs, plur. mésak.

for the sisters and brothers	cheschemushăhk, kétachcanañăhk	Der Br[uder] sagt ...
The Indian brothers and sisters gather together.	... majáwewak anenapaak netachcanenanack, cheismenaak ...	Versammlen sich die Brüder und Schwestern.
Joseph is going with the (his?) brothers.	Josep wăk wetschawà wétáchkanàk.	Joseph geht mit den Brüdern.
Brother says ...	Kténnuk kétachcanau ...	Der Br[uder] sagt ...
brother's wife	nénim	Bruders Frau
brother's child	némat [brother?]	Bruders [Kind]
brother's children, child's children	nèmăchtăk [brother(s)(masc. speaker)?]	Bruders Kinder, Kindes Kinder

[Némat and nèmăchtăk incorrectly glossed by Schmick? See Paul Proulx: Anthropol. Ling., pp. 82-100, spring 1983, § 2.15.]

brotherhood	—	[Brüder]bande

brow [see eyebrows]

brown [Munsee has sense of dark]	sekkàpamuksò	braun
Beaten brown and blue (i.e., black and blue).	Mechmenájo ajenechtahámak.	Braun und blau geschlagen.
brown and blue (black and blue)	mechmenájo	braun und blau
brown bread	nsĕgĕtăhquòch	braun[es Brod]
The horse is brown.	Náhnióges sekkàpamuksò.	Das Pferd ist braun.
something that is brown	sekkàpamukquàt	was braun ist
brown ones, those who are brown	nánăăscăpămŭksétschĕĕk	braune

bubble [see also blister]

bubble that one traps in glasses, also on the water	wŏchpĕchquēi	Blase damit man Gläser zubindt auch aufm Wasser
buck, stag deer	ăchtóhu	Hirsch, Bock-hirsch
buck (male ruminant)	ajápăŭ	Bock
We will sacrifice a buck.	Ajápăŭ kwehegamechnŏŏk.	Wir wollen einen Bock opfern.

buckwheat [see grain]
bud [see flower on trees]
build

I will build a house.	Wékwăchmŏnĕchtà. [house-make]	Ich will ein Hauss bauen.

bunch of grapes [see grapes]

bundle, sheaf	péso [cf. Delaware wiechquepiso, tied round; a bundle; Brinton, 1888]	Bund, Gebinde, Garbe; fasciculum [sic for fasciculus]
one bundle	guttach péso	[Bund]
two bundles	neschach péso	2 Gebind, Garbe
three bundles	nacha péso	3 ———
four bundles	náwa péso	4 ———
little bundle of life [cf. covenant]	p'mawosowagan gnepéso / knepnégan	Bündlein Lebens
burial, funeral, grave	—	Begräbnis

English-Mahican-German 45

burn
  It, the fire, burns.   Păchqūānătĭ.   Es brennt, das Feuer.
  Your heart burns.   Păppăquānăwéĕt ktàh.   Dein Herz brennt.
burn away [*Is the following an idiomatic usage in German?*]
  It is burning away on your hand, foot, or leg; it is shrinking, disappearing.   Káschksò.   Es schwindet, es brennt weg an dein Hand, Fuss, oder Bein.
burning, wood fire, firebrand-fire, conflagration   pòchktschátà   Brand-Feuer, ein Brand
  Put the burning wood together; stoke the fire.   Schaaktanegàh.   Leg die Brände zusammen.
burnt down, flashed   —   abgebrannt
bush   —   Busch
but, however; only   psùck, psuk; ['zero'?]; nŏk? [*see under* learn]   aber, sondern; nur

[*What is the meaning of* psuk *in the following sentence* – only *or* however?]
  We will share it among us (only?).   Niana kdákkennàmāwăchtēnana psuk.   Wir wollens unter uns vertheilen.
  You must look nowhere else but at me.   Tscheén ktackanèn pnamhàn nia psùck pennawe.   Du must nirgends anders hinsehen nur auf mich.
  Take Him not only in your arms, but in your heart.   Nátene nahk'ma tscheén knàchkeck psùck ŏtschè ktáhak ŏtschè. [Take Him not your-arms but from, your-hearts from; *syntax error for* . . . knàchkeck ŏtschè psùck ktáhak ŏtschè?]   Nimm Ihn nicht nur in deine Arme, s[on]d[ern] in dein Herze.
  But I can still say that to you (*pl.*).   Psùkqueék ăm késche kwéchtămăhnhămmà.   Aber doch das kan ich euch sagen.
  Don't put it here, but over there.   Tscheén ktachanăn, ne nónaku.   Sez es nicht hieher, sondern dorthin.
  But you must respect him.   Anuwéwe náhane mosachpéwe. [more must?]   Sondern must ihn hochachten.
butcher [*see* slaughter]
butter   póten [*loan word from Dutch* boter]   Butter
  a churn   —   [Butter]fass
buy   kaufen
  Will you buy that? I will give it to you.   Găttau wăttăwāmĕn[.] Éne gménen.   Wiltu das kaufen[?] Ich will dirs geben.
  I will not buy it.   Aschăn tăttăwāwĕ.   Ich wills nicht kaufen.
  I cannot give it to you. N. is buying it.   Ascha késche menówun[.] N. tattawamokùn.   Ich kan dirs nicht geben. N. kauft es.
  He bought me.   Ntáttawahanăăp.   erkaufte
  He bought me with his blood.   Nahk'ma p'gachganómick utáttawahanăăp. [u *or* n?, *edge shows* u-, he, *but* n-, me?]   Er erkaufte mich mit seinen Blut.
by, at   —   bei   *ad* [= by], *juxta* [= near]
  at the love feast or banquet   tachtaquépuak   beim L[iebes]M[ah]l
  by the wounds of Jesus   neăne pachpaquaik Jesus   bei den Wunden Jesu

cabbage [*see* vegetables]
call, name, be called, be named   —   heissen   *nominari*
  What is he or she called? What's his or her name?   Gaquai ănēwĕsŏ?   Wie heisst er oder sie?
  What's that called? It is used for things not yours.   Gaquai ktēnĕwĕchtămmen?   Wie heisst das?   *De rebus non tuis utitur.*
  What's that or this called? What's that called? or How do you pronounce (express) that?   Gàquai nūktĕnè wéchtamen. Gaquai nùktĕnè wechtamèn.   Wie heist das oder dieses. Wie heist das, oder wie sprichst du das aus.
  My name is John.   Niàn tĕnēwĕsĕ Johannes.   Ich heisse Johannes.
  Your name is John.   Kiak [tĕnēwĕsĕ Johannes].   Du heist [Johannes].
  What is that man's name? What's the man's name?   Gaquai ŏnĕwĕsŏ uwà nēmănă? Gaquai oneweso uwà nemana?   Wie heist der Mann?
  What's the lady's name?   [Gaquai oneweso uwà] p'chanim?   Wie heist die Frau.
  His name is Jacob.   Jacob anéweso.   Er heist Jacob.
  My son has the same name as I do.   Ntajŏm ntáinewesechnà.   Mein Sohn heist, wie ich.
  I am called the same as you.   Ktäinewesehhnaù.   Ich heiss wie du.
  You are called the same as I.   Kteneweseen aneweseà.   Du heisst wie ich.

call, shout [verb]	ŏtschemàhn	rufen
Do you hear someone calling?	Awăn k'pettawà tschēnăŏtik. [cf. sound (verb)]	Hörstu jemand rufen.
(Listen,) someone is calling (crying out).	Awăn tschēnăŏtik.	Horch[,] es schreyt Jemand.
You hear us when we call.	Kpettakonau kiána măchēchsĕăquà.	Du hörst uns, wenn wir rufen.
He called loudly.	Machéchsò ăăptonáu.	Er rief laut.
Cry out. Call out. Scream.	Pāpăgè. [see cry out]	Schreye. Rufe.
to call (to get someone)	—	rufen (einen holen)
Till he calls us to his wounded side. Then we will all truly see Jesus together.	Tăn ánequèchk otschémukquak neáne paquaick wapuchquanik. Ihàn nikkàhtsch kianau máowe kdéttan gnăŭténănaŭ.	Bis er uns in seine verwundte Seite ruft. Da wir Jesu alle zusammen recht sehen werden.
He calls her.	Otschemáwa.	Er ruft sie.
He calls him.	ŏtschēmăŭ	[Er] ruft [ihn].
The bird sings (calls).	Tschenuáu tschĕĕchtschis.	Der Vogel singt.
All (of you [pl.]) sing, or All (of you [pl.]) say. [possible error for They all cry out, sing out?]	Máwe tschenuăăk.	Singt alle, oder sagt alle.
They shouted, called out even more.	Tschénuăăk awăăk.	Sie schrien noch mehr.
Call Esther.	Otschéma Esther.	Ruf die Esther.
Have you called Esther?	Kotschemáu [Esther].	Hastu gerufen [Esther]. [sic]
You (have) called.	Kotschemè.	Hastu gerufen.
Anna is calling you.	Kotschémuk Ánna.	Die A[nna] ruft dich.
They are calling you.	Kotschĕĕmgăk.	Sie rufen dich.
We have called you.	Kotscheĕmnehhenà.	Wir haben dich gerufen.
I am calling him.	Nnattomáu.	Ich rufe ihn.
I am calling you also.	Knattŏmen. [crossed out in manuscript]	Ich [rufe] dich auch.
I am calling you (pl.).	Knattomnechmà.	Ich rufe euch.
I am calling them.	Nattomnawak.	Ich [rufe] sie.
Why are you calling me?	Gaquătsch ntŏmejàn?	Warum rufstu mich?
Why are you calling the man?	[Gaquătsch] ntŏmad na némanáu?	Warum rufstu den Mann?
Why are you calling us?	Gaquătsch ntomejăk?	Warum rufstu uns?
Why are you calling the Indians?	[Gaquătsch] ntomak'nĕĕk anenapáwak?	Warum rufstu die Indianer?
He is calling me.	Nattómuk.	Er ruft mich.
He is calling you.	Knattŏmuk.	Er ruft dich.
N. is calling you; you must come into the little house.	N. knattómuk, naha ahana wekwachmsik.	N. ruft dich, du solst ins kl[eine] Häusgen kommen.
He is calling him or her.	Onattomáwa.	Er [ruft] ihn oder sie.
(The child) is calling his mother.	Onattomáwa okeckà.	Es ruft (das Kind) s[eine] Mutter.
He is calling us.	Knattŏmkónau.	Er ruft uns.
He is calling you (pl.).	[Knattŏm]kówa.	Er ruft euch.
He is calling you both.	Knattomkówa néschewe.	Er ruft euch beide.
can	késche; am [= can, will?]	können
Note: After késche the present always follows.		NB. Nach késche folgt allezeit das *præsens*.
He can.	Késche.	Er kan.
You can work lightly.	M'tschéme ăm k'tannachgà. [soon or easily? + will or can?]	Du kanst leichtlich arbeiten.
He also cannot lie.	Asta ăm ŏăk găggănănăwèhh.	Er kan auch nicht lügen.
No one can tear us away.	Astaăm ŏtsche ktocháun.	Kan uns niemand wegreissen.
[The following have no apparent element of can in Mahican, but note German form:]		
... where they can have peace ...	... atannĕĕtsch anachemĕĕd ...	... wo [sie] können Ruhe haben ...
They cannot go quickly.	Schăschăchĕwŏcháwăk.	Sie können nicht hurtig gehen.
I can do that (I am used to it).	Păchkătschĭn tĕnīntăchtăăn.	Das kan ich thun (ich bins gewohnt).
You can sound the bell.	Taútaù nánămăhà.	Du kanst lauten.
Now the bell can be sounded.	Tápe ăm taútaù nonò knánămăhănăhm. [enough will bell now you-sound-it]	Jezt kan [es] gelautet werden.
candle, candlelight [see also light]	wăhs'nanégan	Licht
candlestick [cf. Natick (Cotton) wequánănetuckonnăuhtuk = candlestick]	was'nanégan ahachtăăk [light ?]	Leuchter
I borrow from you (pl.) your candlestick.	Knattemehenoch'mà was'nanégan ahachtăăk.	Ich lehne euch euren Leuchter.

English-Mahican-German 47

English	Mahican	German
canoe (made of bark?) [*cf.* ship]	ŏtăhágan, otáhacàn	Baddel
captivate, take prisoner	–	gefangen nehmen
The Savior was taken prisoner for us.	Kiánaŭ otschè ne Tapan[emucquak] pehtahanăăp.	Der Heiland ist für uns gefangen worden.
carcass	–	Aas
care for, attend to, provide for	–	sorgen
The Savior always provides for his congregation (church).	Tapan[emucquak] gommáo kachannawechtăhn geméënde.	Der Heiland sorgt vor s[einer] Gemein[d]e.
Let's take care.	Kiánau channaweĕchtatāū.	Lasst uns Sorge tragen.
carry	–	tragen
You can carry [it].	Knajátamen.	Kanstu tragen.
You can carry all [of it].	Mawe n'wéwaschè.	Kanstu alles tragen.
He carried his wood (cross).	Okènnĕmèn nè matòkq.	Er trug sein Creuz.
carry, bring [*see also* bring]	–	führen
Carry [it]; bring [it].	Ăwăttóchănè.	Führe. *Imperat[ivus]*
carve [*see* cut]		
cat [*see under* chase; sit]	póschees, poschesch	Kaz(e)

[*Goddard (in Kraft, H.C.: A Delaware Indian Symposium, Harrisburg, Pa., 1974, p. 156) comments: "Munsee pó:ši:š, cat, Unami pó:š:i:s ... from Dutch poes, dim. poesje, puss (used especially as a call).... The addition of the (originally diminutive) -š or -s would be a straightforward naturalization, but cf. Dutch poessies [little cats]. The reduplicated poes poes or Pus! Pus! ... is the source of Loup p8sp8s, chat (Mots Loups 2, 103). These words cannot come from Proto-Algonquian *pešiwa, Lynx sp[ecies]." But Paul Proulx (pers. comm., 1982) suggests a "contamination." Huden (1962, p. 313) has pussoghk, wildcat (source?—a southern New England word), and Nipmuck Poohookapaug, cat's pond; Massachusett? Poohpoohsaug, cats or wildcats. Compare the following u-forms and e-forms: Narragansett (Williams, 1643) pussoŭgh, wildcat. Mohegan (Prince & Speck, 1904:23) bopoose, cat. Loup (Nipmuck, Day, 1975) p8sp8s, chat; Loup (Abenaki?) pes88is, loup cervier, lynx, and s88is for Abenaki pezois, little cat. Connecticut River? (Judd, 1857, in Trumbull, 1903) pessow, wildcat. Abenaki (Pickering in Trumbull) pes8is, chat; Chippewa (Sag[inaw]) pee shoe, lynx; Chippewa (Mille Lacs, Minn., 1979) bizhiw, lynx; Menominee pah shay ew, lynx. Modern Menominee (1975) pesēw, wildcat, bobcat, lion. Shawnee (Johnston, 1819) peshewa, wildcat, and posetha, cat, and (Denny, 1786, 1859) poosetha, cat; Delaware (Denny, 1785) poosheis, cat. Delaware (NTD, 1982) púšis, cat. Blackfeet (Redhorn, recent) po'osa, cat.*]

English	Mahican	German
catch [*see also* get]		
catch fish	–	Fisch fangen
I will catch fish (*sg.* and *pl.*).	Namăăs (namaássak) kwăhàchkwāmōnè.	Ich will Fische fangen.
Did you catch any fish?	Kpĕtthăăn nămaássak.	Hastu Fische gefangen.
I didn't catch any fish. I haven't caught any fish.	Astam npĕtthăŭ namăăs.	Ich habe nichts [Fisch] gefangen.
Perhaps tomorrow I will catch (some).	Pechtkăăm wápachcă petthà.	Vielleicht werde ich morgen fangen.
We will catch fish.	Namăăs ahátāū.	Wir wollen Fische fangen.
cellar, in the cellar	ahhgeánachguk	im Keller
cemetery	achquandémick	Gottes-acker, Begräbnis-Plaz
certainly	gahŏŭnà, kahouna	freilich
certainly, surely	gahounà, kahoŭnà, múchtsche, kahanántaatsch, kahananfătsch	gewis, gewiss, gewisslich
Certainly I am already married.	Kahounà pakatschè nŏwēwĕ.	Freil[ich] bin ich schon verheirathet.
The Savior is certainly [= very?] kind.	Pachtamawăăs muchtsche onetahawenaxò.	Der Heiland ist gewiss freundlich.
champion [*see* hero]		
chapel, prayerhouse	–	Bethaus
charity [*see* compassion]		
chase (drive, hunt, throw, push) out (away), expel		hinausjagen, nausjagen, wegjagen
Chase out the chickens.	Meuschéha keképsak.	Jag die Hüner naus.
Drive the cows out.	Animmeschéha kójak.	Jag die Kühe naus.
Chase the dog out.	Pachquaschéha ndiáu.	Jag den Hund naus.
Throw (chase) the cat out.	Pachquaitscháha póschees.	Schmeiss die Kaz naus.
I will drive [something] away, chase away, expel.	N'měuschéha.	Ich will wegjagen.
He will chase [it] away.	Meuscheháu.	Er [will wegjagen].
We will chase [it] away.	Meuschehatŏŏk. Meuschehatŏk.	Wir wollen wegjagen.
We (will) chase away.	N'meuschehahenà.	Wir wollen wegjagen. Wir jagen weg.
You (*pl.*) (will) chase away.	K[meuscheha]hemà.	Ihr [wolt wegjagen]. Ihr jagt weg.
They (will) chase away.	Meuscheháwak.	Sie [wollen wegjagen]. Sie [jagen weg].
I hunt (chase) [them, her?], or I will drive them (her?) out.	Nià ntauwatteschehăn.	Ich jage, oder Ich will sie naus treiben.

Drive [it] out.	Awatteschehà.	Treib naus.
He drives [it] out.	[Awattesche]háu.	Er [treibt naus].
We drive [it] out, push out.	[N?]tauwatteschehahanà.	Wir treiben naus.
You (pl.) drive [it] out.	Ktau[wattescheha]hamà.	Ihr [treibt naus].
They drive [it] out.	Awatteschehàwak.	Sie [treiben naus].
[cf.:] I have an inclination (drive) in my heart.	Daūwătāăch anè ndàh.	Ich habe einen Trieb im Herzen.

chastise [see whip (verb)]
chatter [see babble]

cheap, reasonable	—	billig
cheek (my cheek)	nannanò	Backen *gena*
on the cheeks	wánnănōōk tânè	auf den Backen
on his cheeks	kánnanōōk tanè	auf s[einen] B[acken]
on their cheeks	wannànnowowăăk [tanè]	auf ihren
on him [? for on your (pl.) or his cheeks?]	kanànnŏwŏwăăk [tanè]	auf ihn
red cheeks	mammàchgannoáu	rothe [Backen]

chest [see breast]

chestnut	wápeen	Castanie
chew (tobacco or bread)	—	kauen (Tobac oder Brod)
to chew, masticate	Susquachtáwan.	käuen [*German dialect form with* ä]
I chew.	N'susquachtáwan.	Ich käue.
Don't chew.	Tscheēn ksusquachtáwanan.	Käue nicht.
chickens, hens	keképsak [from Dutch kip = chicken]	Hü[h]ner

[*Goddard in* A Delaware Indian Symposium, *1974: Munsee* kì:kí:pas̆ "chicken"; ... *Dutch kip,* -ǝs *is the productive diminutive suffix.* ... *a fully reduplicated form* ... *call to chickens, Dutch* kiep! kiep! ... *Cf. Mahican (M, 1914-1915)* kikipús, chicken; kikípsak, chickens]

child [see under learn]	ăwāschees, awăsches, ăwāsēs, awāses	Kind
children [see under love feast]	awaschesak, awàsésak, ăwāsēsāk	Kinder
I have only one child.	Nuktegehăn.	Ich hab nur 1 Kind.
You have only one child.	Knuktegehàn.	Hastu nur 1 Kind.
He has only one child.	Guttegeháu.	Er hat nur 1 Kind.
We have only one child.	Nuktegehahanà.	Wir haben nur 1 Kind.
You (pl.) have only one child.	Knuktegehamà.	Habt ihr [nur 1 Kind].
They have only one child.	Guttegehawàk.	Sie haben [nur 1 Kind].
He punishes his child.	O[sasam'tscha]háwa otajóma.	Er straft sein Kind.
Do you have children?	Kótăjŏmè?	Hastu Kinder?
How many children do you have?	Kāchwàk kt̆ăjōmāk.	Wieviel Kinder hastu?
When did she bring forth the child?	Tája ŏtajōmōsà?	Wenn hat sie das Kind geboren?
brother's child	némat [brother?]	Bruders [Kind]
brother's children, child's children	nèmăchtăk [brother(s) (masc. speaker)?]	Bruders Kinder, Kindes Kinder

[*Némat and* nèmăchtăk *incorrectly glossed by Schmick? See Paul Proulx:* Anthropol. Ling., *pp. 82-100, spring 1983,* § 2.15.]

chop wood [see also make wood under wood]

I will chop firewood.	Machtăchen nt'omhan.	Ich will Brandholz hacken.
I am chopping wood now.	Nonò machtòkq demmachchăăn. [t *above* demm'hachà. d]	Nun hacke ich Holz.

chopped off
I chopped off my finger.	Tannahégan temmachtáhan.	Ich habe mir einen Finger abgehackt.

chopped up, minced
Have you chopped up the corn?	Kmăătskăhàm.	Hastu den Welschkorn behackt.
When will the corn be chopped up?	Tákahtsch wak móhnskăhàm chásquéme.	Wann wird wi[e]der W[elsch]korn behackt.
Christmas	Xmess [Christmess]	Xstmess

church [see congregation]
cinders [see ashes]
claimant [see beggar]
clarify [see make bright]
clay [see earthen pot]

clean, purify, make clean	—	reinigen oder rein machen
The Savior cleans our hearts [obv.].	Ŏkĕschēchēháwă ktāhănánă Tap[anemucquak].	Der Heiland reinigt unser Herzen.

English	Mahican	German
Our Savior has made our heart clean with his blood.	Pachtamawaasnaù ŏkĕschechtaãn ktáhanau op'gachganom ŏtaŭwáhan.	Unser Heiland hat unser Herzen reine gemacht mit seinem Blute.
They cleaned the room (space).	Nahk'ma kschechàtămŏwà méchcăjŏ.	Sie haben den Raum rein gemacht.
Sweep [it] out. Make [it] clean.	Kscheĕkékà.	Kehr aus, mach rein.
Wash clean.	Ŏkĕschēchpătégān.	Wasche rein.
Wipe (or clean) your nose.	Kscheĕchnè kakéwan.	Wisch deine Nase.
Make the gun clean from rust.	Kscheechnè achquāquănă păchgékăn. [clean of rust the gun]	Mach die Flinte sauber vom Rost.
[cf.:] I'm going to the laundry.	Aăchtahn kschęẹchtecámick wéquamick.	Ich gehe nach[d]en Waschhaus.
what sweeps clean (broom)	tschĕchhégan, tschékĕhégan	der rein kehrt
clear out [see empty out]		
clergyman [see preacher]		
cling to [see hang on]		
close [verb]	—	zumachen claudere
I will close.	N'k'phammen. Nkupphammen.	Ich will zumachen.
Close it.	Kpahè.	Machs zu.
He closes.	O[kupphammen].	Er macht zu.
We close.	Nkupphammenána.	Wir machen zu.
You (pl.) close.	[Kupphamme]náwa.	Ihr machet zu.
They close	O[kupphamme]náwak.	Sie machen zu.
lock up, close up	—	schliessen zu, schlüssen
Lock [it] up. Close [it] up.	Mtscheĕmchakgane.	Schliess zu.
Close up or button(?) up your coat. [?Make up your coat?]	Ŭneĕchtà kpétācăsoŏn.	Mach den [dein?] Rock zu.
cloth	ăhănéchek?	Tuch
neckcloth, breast cloth, etc.	nachpássak ăhănéchek	Brusttuch oder Leibgen
cloud	matàchq̆ [q̆ = qŭ]	Wolcke
coat, frock, (dress?)	petachgasõn	Rock
your coat	kpétācăsóŏn	—
an old coat	machowe petachgasõn	alter Rock
a new coat	uskepétachgásòhn	ein neuer Rock
the one with the white coat	tschachkòchkwáu [see white people]	Eine mit weissen Rock
the ones with the white coats	tschachkòchkwáwak	plur[alis]
cold [see also freeze]	taháo	kalt
Is it cold in the morning (or early)?	Ténăjappáŭ.	Ist es früh kalt?
Yes, it is cold in the morning.	Kahennètténajappáu.	Ja es ist früh kalt.
cold	taháo	kalt
It is cold during the day.	Táhasò.	Es ist kalt am Tage.
It is cold during the evenings.	Ténăkò.	[Es ist kalt] abends.
It is cold in the morning.	Ténăjăppáŭ.	[Es ist kalt] früh.
It is not cold today.	Astà tăhăséwe nono wochgamăk.	Heute ist nicht kalt.
a fresh, cold spring	d'háju t'wachk	eine frische, kalte Quelle
I am cold.	Ntakquachtschè.	Ich bin kalt.
You are cold.	K[takquachtschè].	Du bist [kalt].
He is cold.	Takquachtschóu.	Er ist kalt.
cold [Does -we indicate a negative; thus He is not cold?]	Tăkquăchtschéwe.	kalt
We are cold.	Ntakquachtschehenà.	Wir sind kalt.
You (pl.) are cold.	K[takquachtsche]hemà.	Ihr [seid kalt].
They are cold.	Takquachtschoàk.	Sie sind [kalt].
cold in the head [see headcold]		
collect [see gather; assemble]		
collect wood [see gather wood together]		
color, dye, stain [with red] [verb]	—	färben
I color.	Nmáschechhquè.	Ich färbe.
You color.	K[máschechhquè]. Kmáchgenèn.	Du färbest.
He colors.	Maschéchkŏŭ.	Er [färbt].
We color.	Nmaschèchquehenà.	Wir färben.
You (pl.) color.	K[maschèchquehe]mà.	Ihr [färbet].
They color.	Maschèchgoak.	Sie färben.
You color.	Kmáchgenèn.	Du färbest.
Don't color me.	Tscheen kmachgenĕĕn.	Färbe nicht mich.

Don't put colors on the face.	Tschéĕn maschèchquēhèn.	Mach die Gesicht nicht mit Farben.
He is red colored (tinged, painted?) in the face.	Maschéchgŏ wanammana oskĕtschkŏŏk. [painted]	Er ist roth gefärbt im Gesicht.
comb [verb]	–	kämmen
Comb your hair.	Tschechtschèquaquāsèh.	Kämme dich.
come	–	kommen

When wăk ['also, again'] is placed in front, it means 'to come again,' as Wăk npà. 'I come again.'
Wăk vorgesetzt so heissts widerkommen als Wăk npà. Ich komme wider.

I come (again).	oder [= or] Wăk 1. Npà.	Ich komme.
You come (again).	Wăk 2. Kpà.	Du komst.
He comes (again).	Wăk 3. Páŭ.	Er komt.
We come (again).	oder [= or] Wăk 1. Pahanà.	Wir kommen.
You (pl.) come (again).	[Wăk] 2. Pahawà.	Ihr [kommt].
They come.	– 3. Páwak.	Sie [kommen].
[same:] We come.	N'hàntāhănă.	Wir kommen.
You (pl.) come.	N'ĕhăppajanà.	Ihr kommt.
They come.	Páŭwàk.	Sie kommen.
Many are coming.	Máchche páwak.	Es sind viel gekommen.
Whether Elias is coming.	[Tăn ŭdĕnnè Elias] páu.	Ob Elias kommt.
Whether they are coming.	[Tăn ŭdĕnnè] nahkmáwa pánāwà.	Ob sie kommen.
I am coming back soon.	Enè káăm wăk pà. Ene wak ăm pà.	Ich komme bald wider.
Why are you [is he] coming?	Gaquai waătsch pătip?	Warum kommstu?
He has come. He came.	Pátip.	Er ist gekommen.
Tell me why you are [he is] coming?	Wechtamawèh gaquai wăătsch páăd.	Sag mir, warum du komst.
I hope that when he comes...	Changaap paăd...	Ich hoffe, wenn er kommt...
I know why you are [he is] coming.	Niàn wāwĕchtan wátsche pătip.	Ich weiss, warum du komst.
I am glad that you are coming.	N'tannaména neáne pájan.	Es ist mir lieb, dass du kommest.
Really you still should come to me today.	Múchtschè kahénna kià nono wachkamahk nohàhtsch kpà. Múchtschè kahénna kià nono wachgamăăk ńohaatsch kpà.	Warlich du solst noch heute zu mir kommen.
You come to me.	Nohà patsche.	Du kommst zu mir.
You must come into the little house.	Naha ahana wekwachmsik.	Du solst ins kl[eine] Häusgen kommen.
Think of me when you come to Bethlehem.	Mĕscháhnnĕmà Bethl[ehem] pájănĕ.	Gedenke an mich wenn du nach Bethl[ehem] kommst.
Come here.	Náòwè.	Komm her. (imperat[ivus])
Come here, my dear brother.	Náwe nétachgan ăchwáhnăk.	Komm her m[ein] l[ieber] Bruder.
Come here, my brother; we wish to eat together.	Năwe netáchcana nēschahămátau.	Komm her Bruder wir wollen miteinander essen.
Come (pl.) here, brethren.	Náumǒ̆kq nétachcanak.	Kommt her, Br[üde]r.
Come here. Sit down here.	Náwe tappè.	Komm hieher! Sez dich heran.
Make haste. Come quickly.	Kschócha. Kschoŏchà. [cf. go quickly]	Komm hurtig.
Come quickly to eat.	Kschócha mawépe. Kschóocha mawėpe.	Komm hurtig zu essen.
Come (pl.); let us eat.	Kschochàk mezetŏŏk.	Kommt lasst uns essen.
He is coming back (or again).	Páu tschĕwăk.	Er kommt wider.
He comes alone.	Nquéchtsche ăht páŭ.	Er kommt allein.
He hasn't come yet.	Achquadhà păwe.	Er ist noch nicht kommen.
Isn't Anton coming?	Asch Anton páwè?	Kommt Anton nicht?
When is he to come?	Tája páussa?	Wenn ist er kommen?
Who is coming there?	Awăn nahapáda.	Wer dahin kommt.
We come from Bethlehem.	Nŏmhanè Bethlehem.	Von Bethl[ehem] kommen wir.
We hope we will come to Bethlehem tomorrow.	Ntĕnētāhāh'nà wăpăchgăătsch Bethl[ehem] ntáhănă.	Wir hoffen morgen werden wir nach Bethl[ehem] kommen.
If (when) you (sg., not pl.) come.	N'ĕhăppājanà.	Wenn ihr kommt.
...when you (sg., not pl.) come to Bethlehem.	...n'hăppājănă Bethlehem.	...wenn ihr nach Bethl[ehem] kommt.
I am glad that you came home, or Welcome home.	Netanneména áne wékian pajàn.	Ich freue mich, dass du zu Haus gekommen. oder Willkommen zu Haus.
Where do you (pl.) come from? Where is your homeland?	Thagótschai hamà?	Wo kommt ihr? Wo ist eure Heimath?
Where do you (pl.) come from?	Thakŏmhamà?	Wo kommt ihr her?
Come (pl.).	Páku.	Kommt.
Come (pl.); we will eat. [see also then; begin to; will; eat]	Iha mezetŏŏk. [Iha] mawepetŏŏk. [Iha probably means then rather than come.]	Kommt wir wollen essen.

English-Mahican-German 51

Come (*pl.*) eat.	Năŭmoŏk măŏmétscheek.	Kommt ihr zum Essen.
Let [it?] come to me.	Nohà pachteetsch.	Lasst zu mir kommen.
These *or* they come.	Neēk ŏpájatscheek.	Diese (Sie) kommen.
White people are coming.	Tschachcósak pajatscheek.	Weisse Leute kommen.
Two pairs have come.	Nescheek páksowàk páwak.	2 Paar sind gekommen.
Then came those from Sheko-meko, Nazareth, Bethlehem. [*Shekomeko was 'principal house' of Moravian missions in Dutchess County, New York.*]	Chekomégok ⎫ Názareth ⎬ utschájak páwak. Bethlehem ⎭	Da kommen ⎧ Checomker. ⎨ Nazarether. ⎩ Bethlehem[er?].
The whole family has come—his wife, his daughter[s?], and [his] uncle.	Máwe páwak ahtchwēchteēd. Nák'ma wenajŏma onétschănă, wak wáchĕsă.	Die ganze Familie ist gekommen. Seine Frau, s[eine] Töchter, und Enkel.
Those who come to that place.	Náha pajateetsch.	Die dahin kommen.
When the children come there.	Awasésak nahà pachtéta.	Wenn die Kinder dahin kommen.
[?come + ?; ?only when he comes?]	Pajáza.	[*not translated*]
Do you believe that the one who came, who made everything, appeared as one of us?	Kŏnsittamennà nò pájakŏp maowe gáquai kescheechtátip ne anenăăxíjàk anenăăxétip. [ķ = k *or* t?]	Glaubestu dass der, der alles gemacht[,] ist höher kommen als einer von uns.
Who came there?	Awăn nà pájaat.	Wer kam da.
He came.	Nŏhăpăŭ.	Er kam.
Whether Elias came.	Tăn ŭdĕnnè Elias pàăn.	Ob Elias kam.
Where we arrived.	Pájakàk.	Wo wir hingekommen.
A girl came.	Ăĭnájìck kékăchquáŭ.	Es kam ein Mädgen.
When they arrived there. As they came there.	Nohà pājătéta.	Da ⎫ sie dahin kamen. Da sie hinkamen. Als ⎭
Then they came to Bethlehem.	Ihà náhăpājătéta Beth[lehem].	Da sie nach Bethl[ehem] kamen.
Move (come?) out of my light.	Ktàchcătschŏchquà kámawè nochpajáhxè. [you- ? -you]	Geh mir aus dem Lichten.
They have not come.	Tscheen tachéwe.	Sie sind nicht gekommen.
They have not come; you ought not to cook.	Tscheen tachéwe t'pòchcahăăk.	Du darfst nicht kochen, sie sind nicht gekommen.
The ship of the brothers has arrived or landed [in Manhattan?]. [*see also* ship]	Kétachcanenăăk otàmmachoonwa kschachquamachoŏn mănnăhàtáhănìck ăquòchnáu.	Der Br[üde]r Schiff ist angekommen.

[*For last word* ăquòchnáu *cf. Abenaki Acquehadongonock, place where canoes are slid out of, or into, water, in J.C. Huden:* Indian Place Names of New England, *New York, 1962, Museum of the American Indian; cf. Maliseet əkwítən,*

Come in here.	Ntĕméga.	Komm herein. / 'it floats; canoe.'']
Come (*pl.*) in here.	Ntemégăk'.	Kommt herein.
Come (*pl.*) in here.	Twegăăk.	Kommt herein.
You must not come in here.	Tscheen kănăttămegan.	Du must nicht rein kommen.
I will go to the brook; I will come back soon.	Sébook ntà[,] éne m'tschēmĕmpà.	Ich will zum Bach gehen, ich will bald widerkommen.
Come back soon.	Mĕtschēme páma.	Komm bald wider.
Rain is coming from [in] the east.	[Wapanaăk] otinnăhn.	Von Morgen kommt Regen.

[*For various other words that might contain the meaning* come, *see the short section called "No translation given in German," p. 155*]

come to an end	machtschégáu. *partic[ipium?]*	ausgelaufen
[We come to an end?]	machtschetschoachnáu	[ausgelaufen]
[He comes to an end?]	machtpáchnăŭ	—
come together [*see* assemble]		
comfort, consolation, solace	nauwàchtănămŏwágan	der Trost
comforted, confident, trustful		getrost
We are comforted, confident.	Knannawàchtánemeēchnà.	Wir sind getrost.
command, order	—	Befehl
Communion [*see* love feast]		
companion [*see* ally]		
compassion, charity, mercy (my)	niktemagánometwágan	Barmherzigkeit
with [genuine] compassion	ktĕmàkanemáwak	mit lauter Mitleiden
[*see also* bless]		
compassionate, merciful	—	barmherzig
Yes, that makes him compassionate toward us.	Kahénne déttănè kettemácanemacónaŭ kiánau.	Ja[,] das macht Ihn mitleidig gegen uns.

completely [*part of following or not?*]	–	ganz
Throw yourself completely down.	Anàhaansè.	Wirf dich ganz hin.
completely alone	–	allein ganz
comprehend [*see* understand]		[verstehen]
concerns, as for	aijétscheek	betrifft
conduct [*see* have good conduct]		
confess [*see* reveal]		
confident [*see* comforted]		
confused [*see* astray]		
congregation, church	Geméénde, Geméénde [*German word*]	Gemeine [*for standard Gemeinde*]
conquer [*see* victorious]		
consecrate [*see* bless; compassion]		
consolation [*see* comfort]		
continual, constant, permanent	–	beständig
converse [*see* speak]		
cook [*verb*] [*cf.* roast meat]	–	kochen
in the kitchen	átan t'póchcamik	in der Küche
I cook.	Nátpŏchkà.	Ich koche.
I am cooking meat.	Nàtpochkà ojaash. [*sic* -sh]	Ich koche Fleisch.
Who is cooking?	Awăn nattpochgaăd? Awan nadpochgăd?	Wer kocht?
Are you cooking?	Knattpochgà? G'nattpochgà.	Kochstu.
I am not cooking.	Stà nattpochgàwe.	Ich koche nicht.
Nicodemus is cooking.	Nicod[emus] netepochgáu.	Nicod[emus] kocht.
What are you cooking?	Gaquai ktennatippè? Gaquai gtennatippè [*or*] ktènnatappè.	Was kochstu?
Let's cook.	N't'pochgatŏŏk. Ntpochgatŏk.	Lasst uns kochen.
We will cook.	T'pochgataù.	Wir wollen kochen.
They cook.	N'tepochgáwak.	Sie kochen.
Are you (*pl.*) cooking?	Knattepochgahamà?	Kocht ihr?
We cook.	Nattepochgahanà.	Wir kochen.
I will or must cook.	Gattau n'tĕpochka.	Ich will od[er] muss kochen.
They have not come; you <u>ought</u> not to cook.	Tscheen tachéwe t'pòchcahăăk. [come]	Du darfst nicht kochen, sie sind nicht gekommen.
I have cooked.	N'gesche ntpochgà.	Ich habe gekocht.
I am ready with the cooking.	Nkeschachtippè.	Ich bin fertig mit Kochen.
You are ready with the cooking.	Keschachtippè. Geschachtippè.	Bistu fertig mit Kochen.
He is ready with the cooking.	[Keschach]tippóu.	Er ist fertig [mit Kochen].
We are ready with the cooking.	[Nkeschach]tippehenà.	Wir sind fertig mit Kochen.
You (*pl.*) are ready with cooking.	[Keschach]tippehemà.	Ihr [seid fertig mit Kochen].
Cook meat.	Wiăs anámma. Ănămă ojăăs.	Koch Fleisch. Koche Fleisch.
I will cook meat.	Ojasom ntánnama [*or*] ndannama. Ojásęn ntánnama.	Ich will Fleisch kochen.
I am cooking meat.	Ndánnama ojaash.	Ich koche Fleisch.
You are cooking meat.	Wiăs ktánnama. Wiăs gtannamà.	Kochstu Fleisch.
He (has) cooked meat.	Wiăs anammáu.	Er kocht Fleisch. *perf[ektum]*
Let's cook meat.	[Wiăs] anamatŏk.	Last uns Fl[eisch] kochen.
We will cook meat.	[Wiăs] anamataù.	Wir wollen [Fleisch kochen].
We cook meat.	[Wiăs] ntannamahanà.	Wir kochen Fl[eisch].
You (*pl.*) cook meat.	[Wiăs] k[tannamaha]mà. Wiăs gtannamahamà.	Ihr [kocht Fleisch].
They cook meat.	[Wiăs] anamáwak.	Sie kochen Fl[eisch].
I have cooked meat.	N'tannamà ojăs.	Ich habe Fl[eisch] gekocht.
You have cooked meat.	K[tannama ojăs]. G[tannamà ojăs].	Hastu [Fleisch gekocht].
We have cooked meat.	Nkèsche (n'gesche) anamahanà wiăs.	Wir haben Fleisch gekocht.
The water is boiling.	N'pè otáŭ.	Kocht[da]s Wasser.
It's not yet boiling.	Achquodhà otáu.	Es kocht noch nicht.
Meat is cooking, boiling.	Potaháso wĕjaăs.	Fleisch kocht.
cooked meat, boiled meat; to boil meat	Potaháso wĕjaăs. *it[em]* [= same]	gekocht Fleisch, Fleisch kochen
Cook meat.	Ánămă ojăăs.	Koche Fleisch.
Did you finish cooking meat?	Ktănămòh ojăăs.	Kochstu Fleisch (fertig)?
Is the meat ready?	Weēgtà ojăăs.	Ist[da]s Fleisch gaar.
I will cook meat today.	Nóno wăchgămăăk ntănămă ojăăs.	Ich will heute Fl[eisch] kochen.

English-Mahican-German 53

It's cooking slowly. It's simmering.	Osòh.	Es kocht (gemach).
The kettle hangs over the fire and is cooking. (Delaware)	Ho͞os scheheléuch woak dendéuch. [see under Delaware words]	Der Kessel hängt über Feuer u[nd] kocht. *Dellaw.* [*sic for Delaware*]
cook over [see boil over]		
cooper's wood	quáu	Küfer[baum], Küfer[holz]
		Holz od[er] Baum. Machtòk, oder Machtóqk.
		—— Küfer. quáu.

[*There is a mark over the second* u *in* quáu, *but it is probably not an* n. *The letter in* Küfer *should be* K *because of later* = Knochen. '—— Küfer' *could be untranslated entry separated from* quáu *because of being written smaller and because* quáu *could be plural of* Machtòk; *thus* Machtokquáu *or* Machtokquán?]

cordially [see truly; *also last entry under* heart]	múchtsche káchna [very truly]	herzlich
corn, maize [see also grain]	chasquéme	Welschkorn
corner [see edge]		
correct [see right; true]		
corrupt [see ruin]		
corset [see under breast]		
cost [*verb*]		kosten
I cost the Savior his blood.	Nia ntenawachten Tapan[emucquak] opgachganom.	Ich koste dem Heiland [sein] Blut.
You cost dearly.	Ktenawachtĕ̃n.	Du kostest od[er] kommst theuer zu stehen.
All cost the Savior his blood.	Mawe ckt'nawachtenánau Tapãn'mãgok (Tapan'mukquak) op'gachganõm. [c̲ might be o?]	Alle kosten dem Heiland sein Blut.
We have cost a lot.	Macháne ktenäuchtĕ̃chnau.	Viel haben wir gekostet.
How much does it cost?	Tãn ktennochkãhn.	Wieviel kostets.
It costs me a lot.	Ne machenochkãhn.	Es kostet mich viel
It doesn't cost a lot.	Sta nmachenochkáwun.	Es kostet nicht viel.
cough [*verb*]	—	husten
I cough.	Nochquéna.	Ich huste.
You cough.	K[ochquéna].	Du [hustest].
He coughs.	Ochquenáu.	Er [hustet].
What one spits out when one coughs [phlegm].	Ochoquénei.	Auswurf (das was man auswirft, wenn man hustet)
He is coughing up blood.	Ochoquénei p'gachganõ.	Er wirft Blut aus.
My expectoration is bloody.	P'gachganõ nochquénei.	Mein Auswurf ist blutig.
covenant, league, alliance	anagodwágan [*cf.* anãkótowágàn *and* kne͞epnekan = covenant, *Masthay*, 1980, *from* 1759]	Bund
cover		decken
I will cover my house.	Tãphāsēnãk.	Ich will mein Hauss decken.
Have you covered your house?	Kĕschãchpāhāchkāsò weékma?	Hastu dein Hauss gedecket?
covetous, avaricious	achussò, achwussò *(adject[ivum])* achussowàk, [achwusso]wàk *(plur[alis])*	geizig
I am covetous.	Ntachwussè.	Ich bin geizig.
You are covetous.	Ktachwussè.	Du bist geizig.
avaricious, *i.e.*, one who is always thinking of getting many things.	Gõmmãwe wēsãchgè gãttaù wãchtschāsoãd.	geizig, *i.e.*, der allezeit denket viele Sachen zu krigen.
so miserly that one feels himself proud of nothing.	otachussowehhtawã oháckai.	so karg, dass man sich selbst nichts zu gute thut.
cows	kójak [*loan word; see also* kója *under* fetch]	Kühe

[*Nipmuck (G. Day, p. 49)* k8°i *and* k88i, *cow, probably from Dutch* koe /ku/]

crave [see necessary]		
crawl, creep		kriechen
Crawl here.	Näutschĕksè.	Kriech her.
to crawl in there	ãni̇́ppētscheeksĕjàh	hineinzukriechen
crawl, creep, sneak, slink, move gently, go lightly	—	schleichen (sachte, leise gehen)
He crawls.	Gemocháu.	Er schleicht.
created [see become flesh]		
creator [see under Savior]		

creed, confession	—	Bekenntnis
creek, brook, like the Manahkse [see Monocasy Creek]	séboos [large z covers s; thus zéboos; cf. Zébohk Kidron, Masthay, 1980, p. 32]	Bach; Creek, wie Manahkse [-se covers -es]
little creek	schébohsches [word was stricken out]	little creek [words in English]
to the brook	sébook [not with z-]	zum Bach
creep [see crawl]		
crippled, lame, to be	—	lahm sein
I am crippled.	Nmamatócha.	Ich bin lahm.
You are crippled.	K[mamatócha].	Du [bist lahm].
He is crippled.	Mamatocháu.	Er ist lahm.
We are crippled.	Nmamatochahanà.	Wir sind lahm.
You (pl.) are crippled.	K[mamatochaha]mà.	Ihr [seid lahm].
They are crippled.	Mamatocháwak.	Sie [sind lahm].
cross [see under crucify as verbal form?]	matòkq [= wood, tree]	—
to make the sign of the cross [see bless]		
crown, his crown	Otàpachtóquæpì. [see at Delaware words]	Seine Crone
crucify		creuzigen
As you are crucified.	Neáne schépochquatahásĕàn. Neáne schepòchquatahaseàn.	Wie du gecreuzigt bist.
on the cross	átan schepòchquătāhāssétip	am Creuz
nailed on wood; the one who is crucified	machtóckuk schepochquatahasò.	ans Holz genagelt, der angecreuzigt.
He was crucified.	Schepòchquătāhāssĕĕn.	Er wurde gecreuzigt.
He hung on the cross for my sake, or He was crucified for my sake.	Niàn dennanáchcawagan wăătschè schépochquatahăăssétìp.	Er hing um meinetwillen am Creuz, oder: er wurde um meinetwillen gecreuziget.
That he be (subj.) crucified.	Nè áne schepòchkqtāhāsĕahtsch.	Dass er gecreuzigt werde.
That he has been crucified.	Wătsche schepòchquatahaseēd.	Dass er ist gecreuzigt worden.
We revere the crucified one.	Na schépŏchquătāhăsĕda niána ntānnĕwānĕmána.	Wir ehren den gecreuzigten.
crush [see pound]		
cry, weep	—	weine[n]
Don't cry. Don't weep.	Tscheĕn kmàhn.	Weine nicht.
Don't (pl.) cry.	[Tscheĕn] máhā(kŭ).	Weinet nicht.
Why are you crying?	Gaquatsch kmaăp.	Warum weinestu?
Why are you (pl.) crying?	[Gaquatsch] majákŭ.	Warum weinet ihr?
He went out and cried.	Păquáuchăăn udéttan măhn.	Er ging hinaus und weinte.
He wept for joy.	Scháchannaména.	Er weinte vor Freuden.
cry out, scream, shout, call	—	schreÿen, schreyen
I have cried out. I will cry out.	N'păpaag. [k under third a]	Ich {habe geschrien. / will schreyen.
Cry out. Call. [imperative]	Păpāgè.	Schreye, rufe.
(Listen.) Someone is crying out.	Awân tschēnăŏtik. [awân = someone]	Horch es schreyt Jemand.
They shouted even more.	Tschénuaăk awaăk.	Sie schrien noch mehr.
[see Máwe tschenuaăk under call]		
Don't scream (or cry) so [much].	Kósāmĕnĕs kĕschaachsè.	Schrey nicht so.
cucumber	kumkùmsch, plur. kumkumschàn [from Dutch komkommer (Latin cucumis); Ives Goddard, pers. comm., 1980]	Ajurke [cf. Low German Augurke; German Gurke; Dutch agurkje]
cup, beaker, goblet	—	Becher
cure [see heal; make well]		
curry, dress, prepare, or make the skins soft		Felle weich machen oder zurichten
How soft have you curried (prepared) the skin?	Kahaquegagenĕga?	Wie weich hastu das Fell zugerichtet?
cut [see also under wood]	—	schneiden
I will cut (carve) meat.	Ojásŏn schókschŏn.	Ich will Fleisch schneiden.
to cut (turnips)	—	schneiden (Rüben)
Cut the turnips small. [Dice(?) the turnips.]	Schkuschà paădquăjak.	Schneide die Rüben klein.
I will cut.	Nschukquaschăn.	Ich will schneiden.
You will cut.	Kia schkuscha.	Du [wilst schneiden].

English-Mahican-German 55

Are you cutting turnips?	Kschuckquaschà pääďquăjak.	Schneidestu Rüben.
He is cutting (turnips).	Sguscháu.	Er schneidet [Rüben].
We are cutting (turnips).	Nschukquaschahanà.	Wir [schneiden Rüben].
You (pl.) are cutting (turnips).	K[schukquaschaha]mà.	Ihr [schneidet Rüben].
They are cutting (turnips).	Sguscháwak.	Sie [schneiden Rüben].
to cut (corn or grain)	—	schneiden (Korn)
They are cutting (corn).	Timmesogáwak.	Sie schneiden (Korn).
I am cutting wheat.	N'tummesim manóme.	Ich schneide (Waizen).
You are cutting wheat.	K[tummesim manóme].	Du [schneidest (Waizen)].
I have cut my finger.	Ntemmschim ntannahégan.	Ich habe mich in Finger geschnitten.
I chopped off my finger.	Tannahégan temmachtáhan.	Ich habe mir einen Finger abgehackt.
He has bitten off my finger.	Ntemmachtamę́gun ntannahégan. [é or á?]	Er hat mir den Finger abgebissen.
cutting, circumcision	—	Beschneidung
daily	wáwochcamake, wáwochkamakè	täglich
dam [see beaver dam]		
damage [see harm]		
dappled [see variegated]		
dark (of darkness) [cf. gloomy; unfriendly]		
It got dark.	Pakànmechnátĭ.	Es wurde finster.
darkness	páchgenick	Finsterniss
Mankind loves the darkness more than the light.	Awánetsch achwatachgà páchgenick annuwéwe ne wásaik.	Die Menschen lieben die Finsterniss mehr als das Licht.
daughter(s?) [see family]	onétschănă	Töchter
day	wachkamáo	Tag
two days	neschóaknak [a or o?]	2 Tage
They have gone for four days.	Nawókönàk kà ănìmsópănęęk.	Vor 4 Tagen sind sie gegangen.
Nine days after today is Christmas.	Nóno wachcamàhk nannéwe t'chŏŏknakkekà [Christ]mess.	Heute über 9 Tage ist Xstmess.
beautiful weather	ótăkkàn [= ? + day?]	schön Wetter
Now it is a good day to hunt.	Nono onachkamáo ahánawémik.	Nun ist gut Wetter zu jagen.
Today is a beautiful day.	Unàchcamáo nóno. [= good-day today]	Heute ist ein schöner Tag.
another day, the other day	ktàk wochkamáo	einen (den) andern Tag
When it became day...	Nàn nèn najàppawè. [see early]	Wie es Tag wurde.
dead [see die]		
deaf	—	taub
The Devil stops up (people's ears).	Kpachansò Machtandò.	Der Teufel stopft d[er] Leute Ohren zu.
You (pl.) are deaf.	Kupchahamà.	Ihr seyd taub.
They are deaf.	Kpacháwak.	Sie sind taub.
dear, be dear [see cost (verb)]		theuer zu stehen
death [note usage at die]	oneppuágan [= his death; cf. m'boagän, H]	Tod
He got death. He deserved death.	Opènhämmēn oneppuágan.	Er hat den Tod verdient.
[Note past tense, instead of noun:]		
The Savior has felt, tasted death. The Savior felt how he died.	Pacht[amawáãs]nau otammachtámmen otennè mpennäăp ([or] mbennäăp).	Der Heiland hat den Tod gefühlt, geschmeckt.
debt	tquahogájan [= (that) which you owe]	Schuld
I will pay your debt for you.	Neáne tquahogájan nia pamowähn.	Ich will für dich bezahlen deine Schuld.
[cf. Mass.: oadtuhkau nɷnamontuhquohukquean = pay thy debt (what thou owest)]		
deceit, fraud	kàchkăwémik	Betrug
a deceitful man	păckpàchtschochgăd	ein betrügerischer Mann
declivitous [see sloped]		
deer, stag, male deer [cf. buck]	ăchtóhu, ăchtòh	Hirsch; Bock-hirsch

Delaware words [see next page]

Delaware (Lenâpé) words

[Schmick generally and erroneously used the spelling Dellaware. He marked "Del." by all except wĕlŏmè. These words were checked and commented on in 1980 by Nora Thompson Dean (NTD), a Unami Delaware of Dewey, Oklahoma; her comments appear in double brackets, ⟦ ⟧; ə = ʌ, ə̆ = ə. Symbol x is the velar fricative.]

⟦I have arrived!⟧ ?	Netàn mepæ̀h. [Del. orthography æ]	[untranslated; ms. p. (371)]

⟦This is made emphatic by ta; the translation corresponds to present Delaware Ni ta^mba = I came (emphatic)!⟧

He blesses, makes sign of cross(?), makes an incantation(?).	Kótangkŭŭmkŭ̈ä́. ⟦Affixes do not match translation.⟧	Er segne. [sic for segnet? ms. p. (376)]
I will do the bloodletting. [possibly I want to be bled.]	N°gatta pachtsche pommăkè. ⟦cf. Gátta paxkhamáke = I want to be bled.⟧	Ich will Aderlassen. [ms. p. (1)]
You will do the bloodletting. [possibly Do you want to be bled?]	Káttà páchtsche pommăkèh.	Willst du Aderlassen. [ms. p. (1)]
You must do the bloodletting.	Kàttà páchtsche pommăwè.	Du must Aderlassen. [ms. p. (1)]
bread	achpŏhn ⟦ahpón = bread⟧	Brod [ms. p. (12)]
his crown	otàpachtóquæpì ⟦wtapahtukwépi or topahtukwépi = his crown⟧	Seine Crone [ms. p. (354)]
"fence" [cf. Del. (Brinton): menachkah = fence rail]	mĕénăchkè	Ein Falter [= portcullis; ms. p. (371)]

"Fence," in the specialized perhaps too restricted sense of portcullis (a large vertical grating of iron or wood held by chains over a gateway and lowered to bar entry) [NTD solved Ein Falter by noting that mĕénăchkè resembled Delaware ménaxk = fence, ménxke = He is making a fence, and not memékas = butterfly; thus I could exclude Ein Hälter; the script F resembles the script H, but F is correct. Falter in modern German is either a butterfly or a collapsible or foldable boat (inappropriate meanings), but in Middle High German Falter, valter, valtor, valletor for modern German Falltor, i.e., portcullis, a self-falling vertical gate door, can thus be appropriate for "fence" in Delaware (or perhaps "fort"?).]

fidibus (a paper spill for lighting pipes)	skàssomóăcàn ⟦skəsəmókən = thing used to light a fire; cf. Skə́si = Light it and Skəsəmáí = Light it for me.⟧	fidibus, damit man die Pfeiffen ansteckt. [ms. p. (355)]
bunch of grapes	wĕlŏmè [not marked "Del."]	Weintraube [ms. p. (371)]

[cf. Trumbull's Natick Dictionary, p. 185, weenominneash [wenomis-minneash, vine-fruit], grapes, weenom, a grape, Is. 18,5, and weenomis, a vine.... From waéenu, roundabout(?); cf. New Jersey Delaware jargon "172. virum, grapes," 1684, in Salem Surveys, No. 2, in J. Dyneley Prince: Amer. Anthrop., N.S., 14:518, 1912.] ⟦NTD had no idea what wĕlŏmè is; cf. her wísahkim = grape(s).⟧

gun	pajachkékan ⟦payaxkhíkən⟧	Flinte [ms. p. (378)]
hunting: I am going hunting.	Nĕtanmessè āllaū̄wéwak. [Nĕtanmessè āllaū̄wéĕk.	Ich gehe auf die Jagd. [ms. p. (371)]

⟦Cf. Ni ta naməsi alái = I hunted here and there. The sentences as given do not make good sense; they begin with the form for I (= nĕ-) but end with a form for they (= -wéwak).⟧

The kettle hangs over the fire and is cooking.	Hŏŏs scheheléuch woak dendéuch.	Der Kessel hängt über Feuer u[nd] kocht. [ms. p. (154)]

⟦Another strange sentence. The endings on words are foreign, and it seems to be literally kettle hangs and fire; cf. Álə̆mi wə̆nde na hus shéhălak = The kettle hanging over the fire is beginning to boil.⟧

"Lechchawáchneek." That's what the Munsee town is called.	Lĕchchăwáchnĕĕk ⟦Lɛxaohánɛk⟧	So heist der Mennissinger Town [last word is in English; ms. p. (372)]

[Place name equatable from G.P. Donehoo: A History of the Indian Villages and Place Names in Pennsylvania, 1928: LACKAWANNA. (A river above Pittston entering Susquehanna River) "Christian Seidel and David Zeisberger preached at 'Lechaweke, the Minnissing Town' in October 1755 (Archives, II. 459)." This may have been near or at (1) Adjouquay, Indian village probably on south shore of Lackawanna, near Pittston, (2) Assarughney, Delaware village two miles north of mouth of Lackawanna, near Ransom, and (3) possibly Hazirok, Iroquois village at mouth of Lackawanna. Other forms in Donehoo: "Lachnawanuck.—Scull, map, 1770. Lackawanick.—Rogers (1779) .... Lawahannock.—Howell's map, 1792. Lackawaneck.—Blake (1777). Lackawanna.—Burrowes. Laghawanny.—Hardenburgh. Leghewannunck.—Nukerk. Leighawananeuch.—Gookin." Lĕchchăwáchnĕĕk means (1) forks of the river or fork-stream-at (NTD: if from laxao-) or (2) sand-river-at (NTD: if from lɛkao-), but past authors cite only (1). Exclude Lackawaxen (N.Y.), from Delaware lechau-wiechen, fork of a road, and Lehigh (near Easton, Pa.), from German Lecha, from the variants of Delaware lechauwekink, at the forks.

As for Mennissinger Town, cf. Dutch Minnesinksche Dorpen (G.M. Ascher, 1857, 1960, name 415). Mennissinger is the German ethnic form of Mennissing (= Minisink, N.J., or the entire Munsee area, or the Minnisink, Munsee, Minsi, or Wolf gens or clan of the Munsee tribe, which, in turn, was the Wolf clan of the Delawares), meaning Minsi-at or Munsee-at, i.e., at the place of people of stony country = Min-assin-iu + -ink (Brinton), or perhaps at a place of small stones = Min-assin-ink (Westchester Co., N.Y., Menassink), or where the stones are gathered together = Min-achsin-ink (Menichink, gathering or assembly, less likely, Donehoo); the meaning island-at is impossible because of Minnissingh at Poughkeepsie, N.Y., in 1683, where there is no island, and because the record names of Great Minnisink Island are Menégnock and Menach'hen-ak, which do mean islands and are not cognate with Minnisink, which is the tribal name (see R1); however Goddard (Northeast, 15:237, 1978) states that Brinton is wrong; thus Munsee *mə̆nésənk, ?an archaic word for 'on the island.']

scraper, drawknife, drawshave	lăălhăquákkan ⟦lalhakókən⟧	Schneidmesser [not a chopping or cutting knife; ms. p. (275)]
The sun is shining.	Giischuch olandéuch. ⟦kíšux = sun; Wə̆lánde = The sun is shining brightly.⟧	Die Sonne scheint. [ms. p. (260)]
Turn around. [see turn around]	Kŭlèppĕnè. ⟦Kwə̆lapíhə̆la = Turn around.⟧	Kehr um, oder wende um. [ms. p. (378)]

delicate [see soft]		
delight [see pleasure]		
deluge, flood	chaps	ein Schwall
demand [see necessary]		
deny, retract	—	leugnen
I deny.	Npássoa. *aliud* Ngãdoa.	Ich leugne.
You deny.	K[passo]à. [or] K[gãdoa].	Du [leugnest].
He denies.	Passoáu. Gadowáu.	Er [leugnet].
We (both) will deny it.	— Gadoátau.	Wir wollen es leugnen.
depart (this life), die [see also die]		verscheiden
[cf.:] Stop . . .-ing.	áchque . . .	hör auf . . .
He bowed his head. [and] died.	Náwăkĕ̆chnà wénes. Nàn udàchquènăchăăn.	Neigte er das Haupt. u[nd] verschied.
We depart (this life). We will die.	Achqueètsch náchăjăquà.	Wir verscheiden.
depend on		
You depend on your money; that will not help you.	Kia kotahnsechmà ksehnpattmèn, asta ãm knachtamagöunà.	Du verlässt dich auf dein Geld, das wird dir nicht helfen.
deserve [see earn]		
deserving [see worthy]		
desire [see necessary]		
despise [cf. honor; hate]		
not respected, despised	matanemukséèd	nicht geehrt, verachtet
He despises me.	Nmatánemuk. [crossed through once]	Er verachtet mich.
He despises you.	K[matánemuk].	Er [verachtet] dich. etc.[Er crossed through by error?]
destroy [see ruin]		
devil, Devil, Satan	Machtandò	Teufel
Dice(?) the turnips.[see cut]		
die [see also depart (this life); lay down one's life; death]		sterben
At last he has died.	Wawutăk ŏnèppuwătămĕnaăp.	Auf die lezt ist er gestorben.
He will surely die.	Kahanantătsch m'pò.	Wird gewissl[ich] sterben.
that he died.	wătsche npèck.	Dass er gestorben.
Let him live; I will die for him.	Pmawoseètsch niàn nippen.	Lass ihn leben, ich wil für ihn sterben.
I am dying.	Neppen.	Ich sterbe. [crossed out by error?]
The Savior has died for us.	Pacht[amawaas]nau otschè pennaăp kiánau. [otschè = because?]	Der Heiland ist für uns gestorben.
The Savior has died for us.	Pacht[amawaas] knippowan'kónau.	Der Heiland ist für uns gestorben.
I will die [for you (pl.)?].	Knippowan'nochmătsch.	Ich will [für euch?] sterben.
I will die for you (pl.).	Knippowanochmà.	Ich w[ill] für euch sterben.
He is dead.	Mpŏ̆ŭ.	Er ist tod.
She is dead.	Mpowà. [A sex difference is unexpected.]	Sie *(fœm[ininum])* ist tod.
He doesn't want to die. He is dying unwillingly.	Stà wegampówa. [wega- = willingly; want to]	Er stirbt nicht gerne.
They are dead.	Mpówak.	Sie sind tod.
Does Joshua want to die? Is Joshua dying willingly?	Wega mpŏ Josua.	Stirbt Josua gerne?
Do we die willingly?	Ne wéga npechnà.	Wir sterben gerne?
Do you want to die? Do you die willingly?	Wéga kniìpp.	Stirbstu gerne?
I am dying. or He will die.	Nep.	Ich sterbe. [or] Er wird sterben.
Why do you want to die?	[Gáquătsch] kachtonajàn.	Warum wiltu sterben?
Why do you (pl.) want to die?	Gáquătsch kachtonajăku.	Warum wolt ihr sterben.
Who He will die.	Kattónà.	Wer Er wird sterben. [Note crossed out.]
My father died long ago. [see long]	[Nawachtachgaméqua] noŏch npŏp.	Mein Vater ist schon lange tod.
They have long been dead.	Nawachtà mpoŏp.	Sie sind lange gestorben.
He has long been dead.	[Nawachtà] mpõ.	Er ist lange tod.
Perhaps it is dying.	Pechtschìm mbò.	Vielleicht stirbt es. gern. [crossed out]
He is dead.	Nahk'ma mboŏp. [or] M'boŏp.	Er ist gestorben.
I was dead.	Nià máchtschè m'bépà.	Ich war Tod. [sic for tod?]
diligent [see industrious]		
direct [see show]		
dirty [see filthy]		

58 Schmick's Mahican dictionary

disappear, shrink, burn away	—	—
It's disappearing, shrinking [said of something] on your hand, foot, or leg; it's burning away.	Káschksò.	Es schwindet, es brennt weg an dein Hand, Fuss, oder Bein.
discharge a gun [see shoot a gun]		
disclose [see reveal]		
discourse [see preach]		
disobedient [see also obedient (not)]	papanistàm; [see also eleventh line below]	ungehorsam
[cf.:] obedient	wawunnsettam [-wunn- = good]	gehorsam
I am disobedient.	N'papanistàm.	Ich bin ungehorsam.
He is disobedient.	Pannistàm.	Er ist ungehorsam.
She is disobedient.	Papannsetàm.	Sie ist ungehorsam.
We are disobedient.	Npannesettammechnà.	Wir sind [ungehorsam].
You (pl.) are disobedient.	Gpannsettammechmà.	Ihr seyd [ungehorsam].
They are disobedient.	Pannistamãk.	Sie sind [ungehorsam].
Don't be disobedient.	Tsche pannistamhàn. *imperat[ivus]*	Sey [nicht ungehorsam].
Don't (pl.) be disobedient.	Tsche pannistamháqu.	Seyd nicht ungehorsam.
We will be disobedient.	Pannistammotaù. [dual?]	Wir wollen ungehors[am] seyn.
You are disobedient.	Kěěchtěmměnà.	Du bist ungehorsam.
dissolve [see me]t]		
distant [see far]		
distribute, deliver, spend	—	ausgeben
distribute [see divide]		theilen; vertheilen
district [see enclosed place]		
diverse, of all sorts	—	allerlei
divide, share; distribute, divide, apportion, share		theilen; vertheilen; ausgeben
Distribute [it]. Divide [it].	Tschătschaápnè.	Vertheile.
Divide [it] up. Serve [it] out.	Ákkěnnähè. [Ákkěnnähe]gà.	Theile aus. *idem.* [= same]
You divide [it] up.	Akkennáhămaù kià.	Theile du aus.
We share.	Akkennámăwěnánà.	Wir vertheilen.
You (pl.) must share it among yourselves (pl.).	Akkennámawechteèkq.	Ihr solts unter euch vertheilen.
We will share it among us [only?].	Niana kdákkennàmāwāchtēnana psuk.	Wir wollens unter uns vertheilen.
They divided or distributed it among themselves.	Utschatschaãppěněmmànawawà.	Sie vertheilen ihn unter sich.
do, done [see make]		
do not [see don't for commands; see also under stop]		
doctor	kechkèkaã(ch)waãt	Arzt
[These words were stricken out by Schmick: machmenohanoãd, tachktàn, tachktanò (if not doctor, what meaning then?).]		
dog	ndiáu	Hund
The dog barks.	Okechgáu ndiáhu. [sic -h-]	Der Hund bellet.
don't, do not; don't ... so (much) [cf. stop ...]		
Don't scream or cry so (much).	Kósāměněs kěschaachsè.	Schrey nicht so.
Don't hit.	Tschẽ kpákkămŏwãẵn.	Schlage nicht.
Don't do that. (or Don't do it that way?)	Tschẽ nè ktànnănāchkàhn.	Mach nicht so.
Don't be troubled.	Tschẽn gaquai kschéwahndam.	Sey nicht betrübt.
Don't go in (sg.).	Tschẽẽn haktāān.	Geh nicht nein.
You must not be afraid.	Tschẽẽn kwéschasẽẽn.	Du must dich nicht fürchten.
Don't be afraid.	Tschẽẽn kwaweschasẽẽn.	Fürchte dich nicht.
down [Concept may be present only in German and English in the following:]		
Fall down, or at the <u>feet</u>.	Oseẽdquakajaxèh.	Falle nieder, oder zu Füssen.
You lie down [i.e., to sleep].	K'māugawè. Kmāuŭquà.	Legstu dich nieder.
down there, below (there)	ahhkẽẽk	drunten
I am down here.	[Ahhkẽẽk] ntajè.	Ich bin drunten.
He is down there.	[Ahhkẽẽk] ajù.	Er ist drunten.
Are you down there?	Ahhkẽẽk ktajè?	Bist du drunten?
Are you (pl.) down there?	[Ahhkẽẽk] ktajehemà?	Seyd ihr drunten?
We are not down there.	Stà [ahhkẽẽk] ntajewehenà.	Wir sind nicht drunten.
Are they down there?	Ahhkẽẽk ajuwàk.	Sind sie drunten?
I am going down there (below).	Annàmāquà ntà.	Ich gehe drunten.
I am going down here (when something is steep).	Annàmāākschà nta.	Ich gehe herunter (wenn etwas steil).

English-Mahican-German 59

Go (drive) down there.	Núktĕnè ŏtschè náhthà. *melius* [*Latin* better:] Nónak anàhoossè.	Fahrt dort herunter.
drag, slide, pull along	–	schleifen
He drags him along.	Notatschchanáu.	Er schleift ihn.
drain out [*see* empty out]		
draw near to [*see* approach]		
drawknife, drawshave [*see* scraper]		
dream [*verb*]	–	geträumt [= dreamt]
I have had a beautiful dream.	Nò ŏnŏquaam. [= I well-dreamt; nò = thus *or* I?]	Ich habe schön geträumt.
dress [*see* coat]		
dress skins [*see* curry]		
drill [*see* borer]		
drink [*cf. also* enjoy]	–	trincken
He gave to drink.	Ămmĕnŏhãnãhn.	Er gab zu trincken.
I have already drunk his blood.	Nià pákătschè nò p'gáchganom ménnàhn.	Ich habe sein Blut getruncken.
When N. (he *or* they?) had drunk ...	Na N. págatschè mennáta ...	Da N. getruncken hatten.
[*see* Ihàm no anè mbei, m'nohamè, *and* nohàm awéesmẹek, *p. 155, for possible translations*]		
drive [*noun*] [*see* inclination]		
drive, ride, go, travel	–	fahren
Drive on!	Awatschetschquáwe.	Fahrt zu!
Go (travel) down there.	Núktĕnè ŏtschè náhthà. *melius* [*Latin* better:] Nónak anàhoossè.	Fahrt dort herunter.
Travel this way.	Năŭtàhoossè.	Fahr hierher.
drive out [*see* chase out]		
drowsy [*see* sleepy]		
dry [*adjective*] apples	kàhăăp'néssàk	trocken Äpfel
dry [*verb*], make dry	–	trocken
I make the hide dry.	ĕNsẹnachquăháu chaị.	Ich mache die Haut trocken.
dry, bake, kiln-dry	–	dörren
I want to dry huckleberries.	Ménan nkéeschchasòm.	Ich will Heidelbeere dörren.
duck(s)	[*cf.* Mahican kwitcimo, M, 1914-1915]	Ente(n)
There are many ducks.	Quetschemwechgáu.	Es gibt viel Enten.
Note: If I wish to say, "There are no ducks," *etc.*, then I prefix stà and complete -gáu with -gáwe. For example, Stà quetschemwechgáwe. There are no ducks.		
NB. Wenn ich sagen will: Es gibt keine Enten *etc.* so seze ich vor Stà u[nd] mache aus gáu, gáwe. Z[um] E[xempel]. Stà quetschemwechgáwe. Es gibt keine Enten.		
dumb, stupid	tschannéiuwe	dumm *stupidus*
You are dumb, a fool (it is used for mad).	Kia ktschannéiuwe.	Du bist dumm, ein Narr (wird von toll gebraucht).
I am dumb.	Ntschannéiuwe.	Ich bin [dumm].
We are dumb.	Ntschanneiwechnà.	Wir sind [dumm].
You (*pl.*) are dumb.	K[tschanneiwech]mà.	Ihr seid [dumm].
They are dumb.	Tschanneiuwéwak.	Sie sind [dumm].
dutiful [*see* obedient]		
dwell in [*see* live]		
dye [*see* color]		
each other, one another (*reciprocal in verbs only*)[*see* thereby; the same]	-uto- [*contrast* -tau, *dual first plural imperative,* we two]	einander
They are kissing each other.	Măchgāwụtoàk.	Sie küssen einander.
We don't see each other well.	Kiánau astà knăŭteohénnāū.	Wir sehen wol einander nicht.
so that we may be sensitive to (feel) each other.	nik kiánau kăăm ktammachtamnánāū.	dass wir einander fühlen.
[*see also* speak with]		
They are friends of each other	Ăṁòkotakęek.	Sie sind Freunde miteinander.
[*Note special form of* they two with each other:]		
Joshua is speaking with Joseph.	Josua ahaaptonametoak Josepha.	Josua redet mit Joseph.
We will get water together.	Năspataù. [Let us get water together.]	Wir wollen miteinander Wasser holen.
early, in the morning [*cf.* breakfast]	najáppawe	früh
He has (accordingly) gone early.	Năjăppája animm'sŏŏp.	Er ist früh darnach gegangen.
this morning	nóno najappája [= today early]	heute morgen

Is it cold early (or in the morning)?	Ténăjappáŭ.	Ist es früh kalt?
It is cold in the morning.	Ténăjăppáŭ.	[Es ist kalt] früh.
Yes, it's cold in the morning.	Kahennètténajappáu.	Ja es ist früh kalt.
when it has become day.	Nàn nèn najàppawè.	Wie es Tag wurde.
Tomorrow morning I am going.	Wăpăchkàhtsch nájăppāwe ntănnimsèh.	Morgen früh gehe ich.
earn, deserve, merit [see also wages]		verdienen
I earn.	N'penhámmen.	Ich verdiene.
You earn.	G[penhámmen].	Du verdienst.
He earns.	O[penhámmen].	Er verdient.
We earn.	Npenhamnána.	Wir verdienen.
You (pl.) earn.	[(G)penham]náwa.	Ihr verdienet.
They earn.	[?Openhamnawak?]	Sie verdienen.
He got death. He deserved death. [see failed, missed (Opénhammen. Opàhnnénămèn.)]	Opènhămmĕn oneppuágan.	Er hat den Tod verdient.
We have deserved the punishment.	Kiánau nè knàchmawachtoagan nĕpènhamnána.	Wir haben den Strafe verdient.
ears of corn	—	Aehren
earth [see land]		
earthen pot	ăsusquahŏ̆ [cf. súsoo = clay; Ettwein, 1788]	irdener Topf
east, the east	wăpănaăk [= white (of dawn) - in]	Morgen *oriens*
The wind comes from the east.	Wapanaăk ŏtăcheĕn.	Der Wind kommt von Morgen.
Rain is coming from the east.	[Wapanaăk] otinnắhn.	Von Morgen kommt Regen.
I am going eastward.	[Wapanaăk] ntà.	Ich gehe nach Morgen.
easy, light	—	leicht
That is very easy.	Náhane nĕ nàch nágan. [so? that easy]	Das ist sehr leicht.
You can work lightly. [see soon]	M'tschéme ắm k'tannachgà.	Du kanst leichtl[ich] arbeiten.
You can sleep easily.	[M'tschéme ắm] gawè.	Du kanst leicht schlafen.
eat [see also food; cf. enjoy]	— [z = ts]	essen
I eat.	N'méze.	Ich esse.
You eat.	K'méze.	2. person
He eats.	Mezáu.	3. [person]
We eat.	Mezechnà.	1. *plur[alis]*
You (pl.) eat.	Kmezechmà.	2 *[plur.]*
They eat.	Mézowak.	3 *[plur.]*
I will eat. I want to eat.	Gattáu méze.	Ich will essen.
during eating, or when he had eaten.	Mezéta.	Unterm Essen, oder da er gegessen hatte.
[see p. 155]	Mezechtétahn.	[untranslated]
I have eaten of his wounded (bloodied) body.	Nià pákatschè nahk'ma ánĕp'gachganeĕk óhákkei métsche.	Ich habe von seinem verwundeten Leichnam [= corpse] gegessen.
Come (pl.); we will eat.	Iha mezetŏŏk. [iha = then?, *not* come]	[Kommt, wir wollen essen.]
Come (pl.); we will eat [lunch].	[Iha] mawepetŏŏk.	Kommt wir wollen essen.
At noon we eat vegetables.	Nāwăchquáka eh kmētschĕchnă gónan.	Zu Mittag essen wir Kraut.
What do we have to eat?	Gaquai ene kmezechnŏŏk.	Was haben wir zu essen.
What have you (pl.) eaten at noon?	Gáquaik ĕn kmetschechnŏk naachquăta?	Was habt ihr Mittags gegessen?
Come (pl.); let us eat.	Kschochàk mezetŏŏk.	Kommt lasst uns essen.
Come (pl.) eat.	Năŭmŏŏk măŏmétscheĕk.	Kommt ihr zum Essen.
I have already eaten.	N'machtsche méze. Paggátsche méze.	Ich habe schon gegessen.
Have you [pl. in German but apparently sg. in Mahican] already eaten?	Págatschè kméze. Kmáchtschè. [g has k written above it]	Habt ihr schon gegessen.
Come here, brother; we will eat together.	Nāwe netáchcana nēschahămátau.	Komm her Bruder wir wollen miteinander essen.
We will eat fish.	[Namáăs] mahátāu.	[Wir wollen Fische] essen.
eat lunch, eat the midday meal, dine		Mittag essen
I eat lunch.	Nahaquawépe.	Ich esse Mittag.
You eat lunch.	Knaha[quawépe].	Du [issest Mittag].
He eats lunch.	Nahaquawépo.	Er [isset Mittag].
We eat lunch.	Nahaquawepehenà.	Wir essen Mittag.
You (pl.) eat lunch.	K[nahaquawepehe]mà.	Ihr [esset Mittag].
They eat lunch.	Nahaquawepoàk.	Sie [essen Mittag].
Let us eat lunch.	Nahaquawepetŏŏk.	Lasst uns Mittag essen.
Come (pl.); we will eat [lunch].	[Iha] mawepetŏŏk. [iha = then?]	Kommt wir wollen essen.

English-Mahican-German 61

Come quick to [lunch].	Kschóochà mawḗpe. Kschócha mawépe.	Komm hurtig zum Essen.
eat supper, eat in the evening		essen zu Abend
I eat supper. I eat in the evening.	Nonaquépe.	Ich esse zu Abend.
You eat supper.	Konaquépe.	Du issest [zu Abend].
He eats supper.	Onaquépĕŭ.	Er issest [*sic*] [zu Abend].
We eat supper.	Nonaquepéhena.	Wir essen zu Abend.
You (*pl.*) eat supper.	Konaquepéhema.	Ihr esset [zu Abend].
They eat supper.	Onaquépuak.	Sie essen [zu Abend].
Let us eat supper.	Onaquepetŏŏk.	Lasst uns zu Abend essen.
supper [*written in English*]	onaquépehn	Abendessen
I like to eat it.	N'wēgăchtámmen.	Ich esse es gerne.
You like to eat it.	Kwēgăchtámmĕn.	Issestus gerne.
I have not eaten that for a long time.	Pajachquépogat.	Ich habe das lange nicht gegessen.
Will you eat with us (me?), brother?	Kwĕchpōmĕnăn nétachcan.	Wiltu mitessen Bruder?
[*see* awḗsmeek, *p. 155*]		
eavesdrop [*see* listen]		
edge, border, (corner, ledge?)		Kante
to lay on the edge (*etc.*) [*translation same for second one?*]	Nahnhŏŏn, [*see* Joshua *under* Names] *item* [= also] Aáschawáchkamèn.	auf die Kante legen
eel, eels	máham, mahammáăk	Aal, Aale
egotistic (he is) [*see also* envy]	Issgawanáu.	(Er ist) eigenliebisch.
I am egotistic.	Ntissgawanà.	Ich bin eigenliebisch.
You are egotistic.	K[tissgawanà].	Du bist [eigenliebisch].
We are egotistic.	Ntissgawanáhanà.	Wir [sind eigenliebisch].
You (*pl.*) are egotistic.	K[tissgawaná]hama.	Ihr [seid eigenliebisch].
They are egotistic.	[Issgawanā]wak.	Sie [sind eigenliebisch].
I am not egotistic.	Sta ntisgawanáwe.	Ich bin nicht [eigenliebisch].
You are not egotistic.	[Sta] k[tisgawanáwe].	Du bist nicht [eigenliebisch].
Note: With prefix sta, insert we.	[*In Latin:*] Sta præfixo interponatur we.	
We are not egotistic.	Sta ntisgawanawehanà.	—
You (*pl.*) are not egotistic.	[Sta ktisgawana]wehamà.	—
They are not egotistic.	[Sta isgawana]wéwak.	[–]
eight [*see* Numerals]		
eleven [*see* Numerals]		
else [*see* something else; see]		
embodied [*see* become flesh]		
embrace (?) [*see* neck]		
empty	anacháju	leer
empty out, make empty, drain out [*cf. also* pour]		leer machen oder ausleeren
Empty out.	Anáchen.	Leer aus.
Empty it out.	Schegonè.	Leer es aus.
I empty out.	Nschegonáu.	Ich leere aus.
I have emptied it out.	Nschegonemèn.	Ich hab es ausgeleert.
He has emptied out the sack.	Oschegonemèn tschăchquénōtĕi.	Er hat den Sack ausgeleert.
Let's (both) empty it out.	Schegonemotaù.	Lasts uns ausleeren.
They empty [it] out.	[Schegonemo]náwa. [*stet or delete* o?]	Sie leeren aus.
enclosed place, area, quarter, district, hunting ground	kámik	Revier [*It does not mean river.*]
Take me over the area.	Kámik anàhonè.	Bring mich übers Revier.
I'm passing over.	Kámick tàh. [?district-in I-go?]	Ich gehe über.
[*contrast* plantation, *q.v.*]		
endure [*see* last long]		
enjoy, eat, drink, have the pleasure of or benefit of		geniessen
I eat, drink, enjoy, etc.	Kékachcùn.	Ich geniesse.
The one who enjoys the Savior as his peace . . .	Awánḗetsch Pachtamáwaas pschuk unacotowagan kătăhókuk. natsch.	Wer d[en] Heiland als seinen Frieden geniesset. der.
After ăwáneetsch (who[ever] or which[ever]) follows nàtsch (the one who, that one).		
Auf ăwáneetsch wer; oder welche, folgt nàtsch der oder die.		
enough	—	gnug [*for* genug]
Now it (that?) is enough.	Nàn tápe.	Nun ists gnug.
I have enough.	Niàn nàn tápe.	Ich habe gnug.

Now it can be sounded.	Tápe ăm taútaù nonò knánămắhănắhm. [enough will bell now be sounded]	Jezt kan [es] gelautet werden.
Did you have enough (*i.e.*, food or drink)? Are you satisfied?	N'keēspe.	Bistu satt.
It is enough. [*but cf.* Put the water on]	Sachcakéta.	Es ist gnug.
enter [*see* go in(to) there]		
envious [*see* envy; jealous]		
envy, be envious [*see also* egotistic]	—	neiden, beneiden, neidisch sein
I envy you.	Ktesgawánen.	Ich beneide dich.
You envy me.	Ktesgawáne.	Du beneidest mich.
He is envious.	Esgawanáu.	Er ist neidisch.
Why are you (*pl.*) envious?	Gaquătsch esgawanajăk?	Warum seid ihr neidisch.
He envies me.	Tesgawanòk [*or*] Tesgawangăk.	Er neidet mich.
We envy.	Ntesgawanahanà.	Wir beneiden.
You (*pl.*) envy.	K[tesgawanaha]mà.	Ihr [beneidet].
They envy.	Esgawáwak.	Sie beneiden.
I will not envy you.	Ascha ktesgawanówe.	Ich will dich nicht beneiden.
especially	—	besonders
esteem [*see* honor]		
even more	awăăk	noch mehr
They screamed even more.	Tschénuaăk awăăk.	Sie schrien noch mehr.
even out, make smooth, smoothen	—	eben machen
Joshua makes the way smooth.	Ănăjaháo Josua.	Josua macht den Weg eben.
The way is smooth.	Ánei sachachkáju.	Der Weg ist eben.
You make the way. You have made the way.	Ánei konechtà. [= you-well-made-it?]	Hastu den Weg gemacht.
He can harrow, break up and level (the land).	Kēsché nachàchgāsēgaù.	Er kan egen.
evening, in the evening [*see* sound] [*cf.* I eat supper *under* eat]	onaquéga	Abend *vesperi*
It is cold in the evening.	Ténăkò.	Es ist kalt abends.
evening glow	—	Abendröthe
ever [*see* always]		
everyone, all men, all who	máowe awăn	jederman
everyone	máowe awăn, mawe awăneek	alle Menschen [= all men]
everyone, (all) who(ever)	awánetsch, ăwáneetsch	die Menschen [= the men, the people]
everything	maowenù, máowe gáquäi, máoweetsch	die Welt, (alles)
I will give everything.	Máoweetsch kmēnĕnĕ̆.	Ich will alles geben.
evil [*see* bad; sin]		
examine, search (into) [*see* ask]	otschemŏnatsch [= ?Let him examine?]	untersuche
Let everyone who will (wants to) believe examine his heart.	Maówe awăn katàu onistawahnta otschemŏnatsch otáha.	Jederman wer da glauben will untersuche s[ein] Herz.
exhausted [*see* tired]		
expectoration, that which one casts out when one coughs [phlegm]	ochoquénei	Auswurf (das was man auswurft, wenn man hustet)
expel [*see* chase out]		
experience, learn [*see also* feel]	—	erfahren
You will learn.	Ktenájin.	Du wirst erfahren.
express [*see* pronounce]		
eye [*see also* face]	skétschquan, uskétschùk	Auge
my eye	n'skétschok, *sing.*	*it[em]* [= also, likewise]
eyes	oskétschquan, *plur.*	Augen
my eyes	n'skétschquan, *plur.*	*it[em]*
before his eyes [*see also* face]	usketschguk utschì	vor s[einen] Augen
on(to) the eyes	skeĝtschkunanìk	an den Augen
eyebrows	omàmāwanàch	die Brauen
your [*sg.*] eyebrows	kià kmàmáwàn	deine
his eyebrow(s)	omàmawănà	seine
their(?) eyebrows	omàmāwánăwà	—
eyelids	—	[Augen]lieder

English-Mahican-German 63

face [*see also* friendly; unfriendly; gloomy]	tschanèquáu	Angesicht
bloody face	p'gachganitschanèquáü	[blutiges] Angesicht, wenn jemand viel geschlagen
my face [*see also* eye]	nskétschok	[mein] Gesicht
in his face	oskĕ́tschkŏŏk, oskĕ́tschgok, osketschgok	im Gesicht
fail (of crops); not thrive (?)		
The maize has failed this year.	Stà ntāu̱w̱ăchtówe chasquéme nóno káteek.	Das W[elsch]korn ist heuer nicht gerathen.
failed, missed [*see also* earn *(could this mean* earned, deserved?*)*]		
He has failed or missed. It is used in a good and a bad sense. Also, He has not hit right.	Opénhammen. *item* [= also] Opàhnnénămèn.	Er hat gefehlt, *bonō et malō sensū utitur*. *item* Er hat nicht recht getroffen.
fair, just, right, very nice; ?self-righteous?		selbst gerecht
He thinks of himself: I make it nice (very fair).	Nehenè anètaháu. Nià schaschachkanachcà. [one's self]	Er denkt von sich, ich mache es hübsch (selbst gerecht).
You think of yourself: You are [I am] being very fair (even right).	Nehenè ktenetáha [?nià schaschachkanachcà?]	[Du denkst von dich,] Du bist selbst gerecht.
I think [that] I am being very fair.	Nehenè ntenétaha [nià schaschachkanachcà.]	Ich denke ich bin selbst gerecht.
Let's observe it willingly in our hearts.	Néchene awän aïnachachéĕtsch otáhak.	Lasst uns gerne aufs Herz merken.
fall	neckatachen	fallen
I fall.	Negachtachen.	Ich falle.
You fall.	Knickatachen.	Du fällst.
He falls.	Negechtachĕn.	Er fällt.
We fall.	Negachtachen'hena.	Wir fallen.
You (*pl.*) fall.	[*same as above, but does it end with* -ma?]	—
They fall. They can fall.	Kechtachenaăk.	Sie fallen. Sie können fallen.
He fell.	Mĕĕmschachkáo.	Er fiel.
Don't fall.	Nkechtachenhàn.	Fall nicht.
Don't (*pl.*) fall.	[Nkechtachen]hăku.	Fallt nicht.
I had nearly fallen.	Wăne nĭckătăchĕn.	Bald wär ich gefallen.
He has fallen down (*i.e.*, while fleeing).	Mĕschàchkachtĕeta.	Es ist heruntergefallen neml[ich] im Fliegen.
He is falling down here.	Tpechnáu.	Er fällt herunter.
The kettle has fallen down.	Hŏŏs tpechnáu.	Der Kessel ist runter gefallen.
I have fallen into the water.	Niàṉ gàmquóhennā.	Ich bin ins Wasser gefallen.
You will fall into the water.	Kămŭckque náhàn.	Du wirst ins Wasser fallen.
The knife has fallen into the water.	Chégan gamquechnáu.	Das Messer ist ins Wasser gefallen.
I had nearly fallen into the water.	Wănĕ gāmquĕ́chnà.	Bald wär ich ins Wasser gefallen.
fall (down) at the feet		zu Füssen fallen
Fall down, or at the feet.	Oséĕdquakajaxèh.	Falle nieder, oder zu Füssen.
I fall at your (*sg.*) feet.	Papachgattachnáăn ksédik.	Ich falle zu deinen Füssen.
We fall at your (*sg.*) feet.	Papachgattachnānăn ksédik.	Wir fallen dir zu Füssen.
fall, falling, downfall, accident		
in one's fall	kennhéganek	in seine Falle
You must not grab for me when you fall (in your fall).	Asta ăm kennhogówun kennhéganick kechtăch'mockówu.	Du solt mich mich [*sic*] nicht in deine Falle krigen.
family	ahtchwĕchteĕd	Familie
The whole family has come—his wife, his daughter[?], and [his] uncle.	Máwe páwak ahtchwĕchteĕd. Nák'ma wenajŏma onétschănă, wak wáchĕsă.	Die ganze Familie ist gekommen. Seine Frau, s[eine] Töchter, und Enkel.
famous	—	berühmt
far, distant	—	weit
It is far.	Wachmùk.	Es ist weit. *Longe abest.*
It is not good to go alone far from here.	Tscheèṉ quechtsche wăchnĕmòchăhàn.	Es ist nicht gut allein weit von hier zu gehen.
fast [*see* quick]	—	—
fat		
bear fat	p'mèh, p'omì	[Bär]fett
She boiled or cooked off the fat.	Átanèppĕméhaat.	Sie kocht das Fett aus.

father	–	Vater
my father	nŏŏch	meiner Vater
your father	kócha, kŏŏch	dein Vater
The one who is our father. [or] That is our father.	Nà watóchiak kiánook. [see under believe] [the father our]	Der unser Vater ist.
your (pl.) father	kochwà	eurer Vater
Be (pl.) obedient to your (pl.) father.	Kochwà wawonsittawòchk.	Seid eurem Vater gehorsam.
fault (it is my)	–	Schuld (ich bin)
It is my fault.	Niàn nlenéhan.	Ich bin Schuld.
It is your fault.	K[tenéhan].	Du bist [Schuld].
It is his fault.	Otenehǎn.	Er ist [Schuld].
It is our fault.	Ntenehanánà.	Wir [sind Schuld].
It is your (pl.) fault.	K[tenehana]wà.	Ihr [seid Schuld].
It is their fault.	Otenehanáwa.	Sie [sind Schuld].
... that he has been crucified.	wătsche schepòchquatahaseĕd.	dass er ist gecreuzigt worden.
... that he died.	wătsche npèck.	dass er gestorben.
fearful [see afraid]		
feast [see love feast]		
feel, experience, be sensitive to	amattamen	fühlen
I feel.	Tammatammen.	1. Præsens. Sing.
You feel.	Ktammachtammen.	2.
He feels.	Amáttǎmèn.	3.
We feel.	N'tammatamnánau, ntammachtamhennau.	1. Præsens. Plur.
I wish that I (might) feel, or experience.	Chàn Chàn gǎǎp } ămàttamà.	Ich wünsche dass ich fühle.
I wish that you (might) feel.	[as above] amáttamàn.	Ich wünsche dass du fühlest.
I wish that he (might) feel.	[as above] amáttàck.	Ich wünsche dass er fühlt.
I wish that you (pl.) (might) feel. [you written over we]	[as above] amáttamǎǎkq.	Ich wünsche dass ihr (wir) fühlet (fühlen?).
I wish that they (might) feel.	[as above] amáttamèhteéta.	Ich wünsche dass sie fühlen.
I wish that you may truly experience the Savior's blood, so that we may experience (be sensitive to) each other.	Chànnĕ mámaatsch ne amáttamàn majáwe pgachganŏm Pacht[amawǎǎs] nik kiánau kǎǎm ktammachtamnánaū.	Ich wünsche, dass du d[es] Heilands Blut recht fühlen mögest, dass wir einander fühlen. [for recht cf. trust]
I feel (experience) the Savior.	Pachtamawǎǎs ntammachtammen.	Ich fühle den Heiland.
Do you feel the blood in your heart?	Ktammachtámmen op'gachganŏm ktáhek.	Fühlestu das Blut in deinem Herzen.
Yes, I feel it.	Káhanne n'tammachtammen.	Ja ich fühle es.
I do not feel it.	Sta n'tammǎchtǎmŏwǔn.	Ich fühle es nicht.
Joshua feels.	Josua ŏtǎmmǎchtǎmmĕn.	Josua fühlt.
Do you (pl.) feel?	Ktammachtam'náwa.	Fühlet ihr?
Yes, we feel it in our heart.	Quǎme ntammachtam'nána nĭntǎhǎnǎk.	Wir fühlens in unserm Herzen.
Many feel the blood, etc.	Machǎne otammachtamnáwa, etc.	Viele fühlen das Blut, etc.
I will say to you now why you don't feel, etc.	Nono kwechtammánen gaquai wǎtsch astà ǎmǎttǎmówun (ǎmǎttǎmówŏn), etc.	Ich will dir iezt sagen warum du nicht fühlest, etc.
Even today I still feel warm in my heart.	Nono wachcamǎǎk achschen ntammachtammen ntáhak kástǎǎk.	Auch heute noch fühle ich in meinem Herzen warm.
He feels warm in the heart.	Xschittáwa mámmǎk ndàh.	Er fühlt sich warm im Herzen.
I would like (need?) to feel more of the Savior in my heart.	Niàn tajáhntam annowéwe Pǎchtamáwaas támmachtammen dáhak.	Ich möchte gern mehr fühlen in meinem Herzen von Heiland.
Do you feel the words that you sing in your heart?	Ktammachtammen neĕn aaptonawaganan ǎnèkǎnawójannè ktahàk.	Fühlest du die Worte, die du singest, im Herzen.
The Savior has felt death.	Pacht[amawaas]nau otammachtámmen otennè mpennǎǎp ([or] mbennǎǎp).	Der Heiland hat den Tod gefühlt.
Therefore when (if) someone among us feels that he is sick.	Nè ǔtschè awǎn ǎm kiánau ǎmáttakà, ŏwénamansohǎǎncùn.	Darum wenn jemand unter uns fühlt, dass er kranck sey.
(all) whoever feel, who may feel.	Máowe neĕk ǎmáttakeĕk. [see also help]	(alle) die da fühlen.
Who feels no peace or quiet in his heart.	(Awáneetsch) (Awǎǎn) astà ǎmàttǎmóquà unacotowagan ánǎchémǔachtanamowágàn otáhak.	Wer keinen Frieden oder Ruhe im Herzen fühlet.

English	Mahican	German
fell or hew wood	—	Holz hauen
I will fell or hew wood.	Pèwŏchāckhà.	Ich will Holz hauen.
fence [*see under* Delaware words]		
fetch, go get, bring [*see also* take]		holen
Fetch (go get) the stick.	Nāāde ătoóku.	Hole den Stock.
Fetch water.	Nāāspa.	Hol Wasser.
[?when he fetched water?]	nŏŏspaat [*see p. 155*]	[*untranslated*]
Are you bringing the water here?	Nóctenaspāān.	Holstu Wasser hieher.
I'm taking water there.	Nòn nià ntenaspāān.	Ich hol[e da]s Wasser dort.
We will get water together.	Nāspataù.	Wir wollen miteinander Wasser holen.
You shouldn't bring any water.	Tschēnāāspāhān.	Du solt kein Wasser holen.
Stop getting water.	Ăchquāāspà.	Hör auf Wasser zu holen.
Fetch bread.	Taquachnána.	Hol Brod.
Get bread. The brothers are hungry. They are working.	[Taquachnána.] Nétachcanak gattópuak. Ănăchcătscheék.	Hol Brod. Die Br[üde]r sind hungrig. Sie arbeiten.
I will fetch water.	Mbeì nátĕnīmmēn gattaù. [*see* take]	Ich will Wasser holen.
Fetch water.	Mbeinatem.	Holt Wasser.
Philip is fetching the cows.	Phil[ipp] nātschĕgawáu kója.	Phil[ipp] holt die Kühe.
Get the peels.	Pahwahà.	Hole Rinden.
Take me over the hunting ground (district, enclosed area, *etc.*).	Kámik anàhonè.	Bring mich übers Revier.
Fetch him here.	Nāāthonè.	Hohl ihn herüber.
Please be so good and fetch him here.	Kmachmatuámmen unáje nāāthonè.	Ich bitte dich, sey so gut und hohle ihn herüber.
You must fetch the wood.	Machtáchene ĕ gnatim.	Du must das Holz holen.
When are you getting the wood?	Tákatsch knátim machtachena.	Wenn holstus Holz.
[?He is going to fetch water?]	nochkau mbei [flour water?; *see p. 155*]	[*untranslated*]
few [*see* a little]		
fidibus, a paper spill for lighting pipes [*see under* Delaware words]	skàssomóăcàn *(Delaware)* schekkàssomáchtámak *(Mahican)*	fidibus, damit man die Pfeiffen ansteckt. fidibus
field	—	Acker
fight, war, wage war		fechten, kriegen *bellare* [*Latin*]
He fights or he wages war.	Nahhnowáu.	Er fechtet oder er führt Krieg.
He fights.	Nachnowáu.	Er fechtet.
They are making war.	Nachnowáwak.	Sie kriegen.
fill, fill up [*cf.* full]	—	füllen oder vollmachen
I fill [it] up.	Nōtschŏwŭpāān.	Ich fülle voll.
Fill [it] up.	Otschowupà.	Fülle voll.
He fills him.	Otschowupána.	Er füllet ihn.
Let us fill (the kettle).	Otschowupáta.	Last uns (d[en] Kessel) füllen.
They fill it.	[Otschowu]páwak.	Sie füllen [(d[en] Kessel)].
Let us fill [it].	Kŏtschòwachpátau.	Last uns füllen.
Let us fill [it].	Kŏtschòwachpeékq.	*Idem* [= the same]
We fill him.	Notschowupahanà.	Wir füllen ihn.
You (*pl.*) fill him.	K[otschowupa]hamà.	Ihr [füllet ihn].
I will fill [it] up.	Nià notschòwachtà.	Ich will einfüllen.
full	otschòwachtáu	voll
He fills your heart.	Ŏtschòwachtàhn ktàh.	Er erfüllet dein Herz.
Fill my heart with your blood.	Ŏtschòwachtān ntahak kp'gachganōm.	Füllet mein Herzn mit Blut.
The Savior certainly fills our heart(s) with peace.	Pachtamawans [*sic*] muchtscheétsch ktáhennāāk unàcotowágàn ótschŏwachtāān.	Der Heiland erfüllet gewis unser Herz mit Friede.
Put water (in the kettle) or fill (the kettle).	Kotenippà.	Thu Wasser in Kessel, oder Fülle den Kessel.
I am filling the pipe (*also imperative*).	Newattschósemà.	Ich fülle die Pfeiffe, auch *imperativus*.
He fills up the pipe.	[*Probably should be* Wattscho]semāhn [*or else* Otscho]semāhn.	Er füllet die Pfeiffe.
Fill the pipe.	Utschōōssĕmà.	Stopf die Pfeiffe.
Give me a pipe of tobacco.	Otschosammawè.	Gib mir eine Pfeife Tobac.
fill up, fill in [*see also* pour in]		einfüllen
Fill [it] up.	Pehdhà.	Fülle ein.

English	Mahican	German
I have already filled [it] up.	Nkesche pedhámmen.	Ich habe schon eingefüllt.
I will fill [it] up.	Npēdhámmen.	Ich will einfüllen.
I will fill [it] up.	Nià notschòwachtà.	Ich will einfüllen.
He fills [it] up.	O[pēdhámmen].	Er füllet ein.
He fills [it] with grain.	Pedhammanóme.	Er füllt Korn ein.
He fills [it] with corn.	[Pedham]chasquéme. [stet or delete m?]	[Er füllt] W[elsch]korn ein.
He fills [it] with salt.	Săschuak pēdham. [note m]	Er füllt Salz ein.
filthy, dirty	machtètt	garstig ich bin [= I am filthy.]
I am filthy.	N'mattesése.	Ich bin garstig.
You are filthy.	K[mattesése].	Du bist [garstig].
He is filthy.	Matteséso.	Er ist [garstig].
We are filthy.	Nmattesesehenà.	Wir s[in]d garstig.
You (pl.) are filthy.	K[mattesese]hemà.	Ihr seid [garstig].
They are filthy.	Mattesesoàk.	Sie sind [garstig].
You make it very filthy.	Múchtsche kmáttănăchga.	Du machst es sehr garstig.
finally [see last]		
find, to find	machgámmen, máchcamen, umàchcamèn	finden
to find again	náhapáowe	wieder finden
I find.	N'máchgam.	Ich finde.
You find.	K'[máchgam]. G[máchgam].	Du findest.
He finds.	Machgawáu.	Er findet.
He finds, also to find.	Umàchcamèn. [u = he, him?]	Er findet, item zu finden.
We find nothing, or we haven't found it.	Stà machgamówunána. [see second below]	Wir finden nichts, oder habens nicht gefunden.
You (pl.) find nothing.	Stà kmachgamówun. Stà gmachgamówun.	Findet ihr nichts.
They find nothing.	Sta machgamowunána.	Sie finden nichts.
I cannot find it.	Sta mmachgamóun. [sic, cf. one below]	Ich kans nicht finden.
I have not found it.	Nià astà n'machgamówun.	Ich habs nicht gef[un]den.
I find nothing to it.	Asta nèn niàn dennè machcàmowun.	Ich finde nichts an ihm.
Haven't you (pl.) found it again?	Asch kmachgamowunawa?	Habt ihrs nicht wider gefunden.
I have found it again.	Ne māchgāmmĕn.	Ich habs wider gefunden.
Have you found it?	Kmāchgámmen.	Hastus gefunden?
He has found it.	Omachgammen. [see Umàchcamèn above]	Er hats gefunden.
He has found [us].	Kmàchkăcŏnàhp.	Er hat gefunden.
We have found it.	Nmachgammenána.	Wir [habens gefunden].
You (pl.) have found it.	K[machgamme]náwa.	Ihr [habts gefunden].
They have found it.	O[machgamme]náwa.	Sie [habens gefunden].
I find a knife.	N'máchgam chégan.	Ich finde ein Messer.
What are you finding?	Gaquai kmáchgam?	Was findestu?
He finds a sewing needle.	Machgawáu schăăpnégan.	Er findet ein Nehnadel.
I have not yet found my Savior.	Achquódha nPachtamawăăs nmachgawáwe.	Ich hab den Heiland noch nicht gefunden.
You have found your Savior.	Kpachtamawaasnau kmachgawáu.	Hastu d[en] H[ei]l[an]d gefunden.
You have not found the Savior.	Sta pacht[amawaas(nau?)] kmachgawáwe.	Du hast d[en] Heiland nicht gefunden.
He has found his Savior. [error for literally You (pl.) have found your Savior.]	Kmachgawáwa kpachtamawaasnawà.	Er hat s[einen] Heiland gefunden.
He has not found his(?) Savior.	Sta omachgawáwe [?kpachtamawaasnawà?].	Er hat s[einen] Heiland nicht gefunden.
She has not found.	Stà màchcăwáwè.	Sie hat nicht gefunden.
We have found our Savior.	Nmachgawawunà np[achtamawaas]naù.	Wir haben unsern Heiland gefunden.
We have not found our Savior.	Sta nmachgawawewunà [npachtamawaasnaù].	[Wir haben unsern Heiland] nicht gefunden.
Have you (pl.) found our Savior?	Kmachgawáwa kp[achtamawaas]naù.	Habt ihr unsern Heiland gefunden?
You (pl.) have not found our S.	Sta kmachgawawewà [kpachtamawaasnaù].	Ihr habt [unsern Heiland] nicht gefunden.
They have found him (our Savior).	Omachgawawă kpach[tamawaas]nawa.	Sie haben ihn gefunden.
They have not found him (our S.).	Sta omachgawawewà [kpachtamawaasnawa].	Sie [haben ihn] nicht gefunden.
Whoever loses his life for my sake will find it.	Awăn opomáosowágan ánăchtăăt niàn dennànachkawágan, nàn máchcamen.	Wer sein Leben um meinetwillen verliert, der wirds finden.
finger	ntannahégan [= my finger]	Finger
I have cut my finger.	Ntemmschim ntannahégan.	Ich habe mich in Finger geschnitten.
I chopped off my finger.	Tannahégan temmachtáhan.	Ich habe mir einen Finger abgehackt.
He has bitten off my finger.	Ntemmachtamégun ntannahégan. [é or á?]	Er hat mir den Finger abgebissen.
(as) long as a finger	nà átăn gútta nŏ͞ssà	Wie ein Finger lang

fire	stáŭ, sta	Feuer
He takes fire from the sky (*i.e.*, he ignites it by means of the sun).	Spómmuk ótenìm stáŭ.	Er nimmt Feuer vom Himmel, *i.e.* er zündts d[urch?] die Sonne an.
He sat by the fire.	Hapò schétănăwă stăăk.	Er sass beim Feuer.
his love-fire	achwáhnămamukquàck nístăŭ	sein Liebes-feuer
fidibus [*see under* Delaware words *and also* fidibus]		
light a fire, make fire, kindle, strike fire		Feuer anmachen
Make fire. Strike fire.	Sta ŏnĕchtă̆. [*not:* Don't do it!]	Mach Feuer. Schlag Feuer.
Light a fire. There is no fire.	Podawà. Stà stawéu.	Mach Feuer an. Es ist kein Feuer.
We have (a) bad fire.	Káhanna k'mattenaù assĕhĕnăŭ.	Wir haben schlecht Feuer.
You have a bad fire.	Káha kmattenaù assè.	Du hast ein schlecht Feuer.
I will light a fire.	Npodawà.	Ich will Feuer anmachen.
He lights a fire.	Podawáu.	Er macht Feuer an.
Let's light a fire.	Podawátaù.	Last uns [Feuer anmachen].
Light (*pl.*) the fire.	Podawàqu.	Macht Feuer an.
They are lighting a fire.	Podawáwak.	Sie machen Feuer an.
I will strike fire.	N'sáckhăăn.	Ich will Feuer schlagen.
I will stoke the fire.	Nschaaktanegà.	Ich wills Feuer schieren.
It, the fire, burns.	Păchquānáŭ.	Es brennt, das Feuer.
[*see also* kettle *under* Delaware words]		
fire off [*see* shoot a gun]		
firewood	machtắchen	Brandtiholz, Brandholz
firm [*see also* hard]		
When the ice is firm.	Kpahàn.	Wenn sich das Eis stemmt.
firmly [*see last entry under* hold on (osáma- = very, too much; an intensive)]		
first(?) [*cf.* kscháijajaat, *p. 155*]		
fish [*see also* catch fish]	namăăs; nămắasak, namá'assak *(pl.)*	Fisch
Are you hungry for fish?	Gattope namá'assak.	Bist du hungrig nach Fischen.
There are many fish.	Namăăsechgáŭ.	Es gibt viele Fische.
Note: When I want to say, "There aren't any fish," I prefix stà and complete -gáu with -gáwe, for example, Stà namăăsechgáwe. There aren't any fish.		
NB. Wenn ich sagen will. . . Es gibt keine Fische; so seze ich Stà vor u[nd] mach aus gáu, gáwe, *e.g.* Stà namăăsechgáwe. Es gibt keine Fische.		
[*see also last entry under* great]		
fishhook	wagégan, wakégan	Angel, Fischhaken
fists [*see under* hit]		
five [*see also* Numerals]	nānānè, nánan	fünf
Today it is five years.	Nono wachgamăăk nānānè kahtenà.	Heute ists 5. Jahr.
5 o'clock [*see under* love feast]	nánan tschenuáka	Um 5 Uhr
fixed, settled, certain	—	bestimmt
flatter [*see* have good conduct]		
flax, to winnow flax	pnax- [*English or German loan word*]	Flachs schwingen
I will go winnow flax.	Nmawèschachawachtáha pnáxak.	Ich will Flachs schwingen gehen.
Fleas bite.	—	Flöhe beissen.
The flea is biting me.	Papĕĕk nsackamùck.	Der Floh beisst mich.
The fleas are biting me.	Papéquak nsackamuckónau.	Die Flöhe beissen mich.
flesh [*see* meat; become flesh]		
flint	machnisk	Feuer-stein
Do you have a flint?	Machnisk kachchanè.	Hastu einen Feuer-stein.
flood [*see* deluge]		
flow, melt	—	fliessen
It flowed.	Sŏkănăhp.	Es floss.
It has flowed, or He has let flow.	Sŏkànăkùp.	Es ist geflossen, oder Er hat fliess lassen.
It flowed, ran.	Ksché/kschĕĕch/ná/ă̆. [*on one line and no spaces; are parts interchangeable?*]	Es floss.
A sweet fountain is what flowed from Jesus' side.	T'wàchk wĕgan Tap[anemuc]quàk wapúchquanick wătsche sokachnágup.	Ein süsser Brunn ist was aus Jesu Seite fliesset.
flower	wachawan'schàn	Blume
on maize (corn)	osowáno	Blume oder Blüthe am Welschkorn
on trees	wachawăhn, *plur[alis]* [wachawăh]nàn	Blüthe an Bäumen
a beautiful flower [*sic for plural*]	wawunitschischowàn wachawăhnschan	eine schöne Blume

follow (after)	–	folgen, folgen nach
I follow (after).	Niàn wosochgawà.	Ich folge nach.
You (sg.) follow.	Knosochgawà.	Du [folgest nach].
Who is following?	Awan onosochgawa?	Wer folget nach?
He is going after them.	Náha ŏnōsochgawáwa.	Er gehet nach ihnen.
He follows just the Savior.	Schachagéwe nosochgowáu.	Gerade folgt er nach dem Heiland.
Let's follow.	Nosochgawataù.	Last uns nachfolgen.
We will follow.	Nosochgamóqu.	Wir wollen [nachfolgen].
They follow.	Knosochgawáwa. [k *written above* g]	Sie folgen.
fond [*see under* love]		
food [*cf. next entry*]	mezowagan	Essen
[Did you (sg.?) have food?] [*In German:*] Did you (pl.) have something to eat?	Káchchannè mezowagan.	Habt ihr zu essen gehabt.
food, meal [*cf. above; see also* eat]	mézĕàn [= that which you (sg.) eat; *in next*]	Speise
God bless your (pl.) food. [*see* nochkau mbei, *p. 155*]	Pachtamáwags wétahámukquè áne mézĕàn.	Gott segne eure Speise.
foolishness [*see under* hobble]		
foot, feet	nsēĕd [= my foot]; osétan, osēdan [= his feet]	Fuss, Füsse
My foot hurts me.	Nsēĕd wĕnămăttàm.	Mein Fuss thut mir weh.
Throw yourself at his feet.	Păkkătáchna osédick.	Wirf dich zu seinen Füssen.
They have nailed up his hands and feet.	Ktachquaheganà ktachtahamawáu ŏnàchgĕk, osédik.	Sie haben s[eine] Hände, Füsse angenagelt.
That we thereby kiss his bloody hands and feet.	Nahk'ma p'gachganēĕk onáchgan wăk osétan neén kaām aìkè kmachgáatamnánaan.	Dass wir seine blutigen Hände und Füsse daran küssen.
Warm your feet. [*see* warm] [*cf. Ojibwa* nind abisides *= I warm my feet. (Baraga, 1878)*]	Appĕssēĕd tassè.	Wärme deine Füsse.
Warm your (pl.) feet.	Appessęęk tassęęk. [*see note above*]	Wärmet eure Füsse.
Fall down, or at the feet.	Osēĕdquakajaxèh.	Falle nieder, oder zu Füssen.
I fall at your (sg.) feet.	Papachgattachnáăn ksédik.	Ich falle zu deinen Füssen.
The spots on the hands, feet, and side [*perhaps literally:* Those that spot his hands, his feet, and his side?]	Wēchwēsájŭwăn ŏnáchkăn osēdan, wăk wăchpássei.	Die Maale in Händen, Füssen und Seite
for [*see also* sake]	otsche [= because of?]; kà [?]	für, vor; vor
The Savior was taken prisoner for us.	Kiánau otschè ne Tapan[emucquak] pehtahanàăp.	Der Heiland ist für uns gefangen worden.
for me	nintenè anawachtēĕn [?]	vor (für) mich
I believe that my God spilled his blood for me.	Nohnsittammen nintenè anawachtēĕn n'Pachtamawaas op'gachganom sokahanàăp.	Ich glaube, dass Gott s[ein] Blut vor mich vergossen.
for her	otenè anawachtēĕn [?]	für sie
B. believes that God spilled his blood for her.	B. ohnsittámmen Pachtamawaasnaù op'gachganŏm otenè anawachtēĕn sókahanàăp.	B. glaubt, dass Gott s[ein] Blut für sie vergossen.
They have gone for four days.	Nawókŏnàk kà ănìmsópănęęk.	Vor 4 Tagen sind sie gegangen.
for a long time [*see* long]		
forbidden [*see* restrained]		
forget	–	vergessen
I don't forget it. I won't forget it.	Nià astàn wannisséwe.	Ich vergesse es nicht oder Es kommt mir nicht aus den Sinn.
Don't (pl.) forget it.	Tschēĕn wannisséhaäkq.	... vergesst es nicht.
forsake	–	verlassen
Why have you forsaken me?	Gaquai wátsche ozáñìàn nià.	Warum hast du mich verlassen.
fortune [*see* luck]		
fortunate [*see* lucky]		
fountain [*see* spring]		
four [*see also* Numerals]	náwa, nawè	vier
fourth, quarter	wachpăhm [?]	4tel [viertel]
Take along a fourth [of something] to Bethlehem.	Wachpăhm keninnemamà Bethlehem anè.	Nimm ein 4tel mit nach Bethlehem.

free, set free, release, liberate		los machen, erlösen
He has set me free.	Pamowäänkóǒp.	Er hat mich erlöst.
I have set you free.	Nià kpamowäänkonäăp.	Ich habe dich erlöst.
Jesus said: I have set you free.	Jesus ŏp, nia kpamowánĕkonäăp.	Jesus sagt: Ich habe dich erlöst.
The Savior has set all [us?] nations free.	Maowe kĕnáchănĕkŏnau Pacht[amawäăs] àtchānājăkéssĕjăckŭ. Máowe gĕnáchănĕkónau Tap[anemucquak] ātchānājăgéssĕjăckŭ.	D[er] H[ei]l[an]d hat alle Nationen erlöst.
He has set us free (i.e., let loose with the hands).	Kĕnáchenukkónau. Genáchĕnŭckhănäăp.	Er hat uns erlöst (i.e. mit den Händen losgemacht).
One has set us free.	Pääschco genachnenojagup. genachnenckhanäăp.	Einer hat uns losgemacht.
He, i.e., the Savior, has released me [awáne = all?] from prison.	Pachquachenquakup awáne. Pachquachgenquagup awáne. Pachquachagenùk.	Er hat mich aus dem Gefängniss losgemacht, i.e., der Heiland.
He would (or wanted to) free us.	Unèchnahp pāwŏháǎnà. [one word?]	Er wolte uns frei machen.
Our Savior (Redeemer) has said.	Năchĕnŭckquácku osĕén.	Unser Erlöser hat gesagt.
freeze [see also cold]	—	frieren
It is frozen.	Tăquáttèn.	Es ist erfroren.
[They (inan.)?] are frozen.	Tăquáttĕnà.	[Wir?] sind erfroren.
frozen	kĕnattèn	gefrohren
I'm freezing, it's freezing me, or it has frozen me.	Ntacquatschèh.	Ich friere, es friert mich oder es hat mich gefroren.
(It) freezes you.	K[tacquatschèh].	Friert dich.
It freezes him.	Tacquatschoù.	Es friert ihn.
We are freezing.	Ntacquàtschéhenà.	Wir
You (pl.) are freezing.	K[tacquàtsché]hemà.	Ihr
They are freezing.	Tacquàtschŏwàk.	Sie
fresh [see under spring (fresh cold, salubrious, sweet]		
friend [see also ally]	tēnnāngōmā [see relation, relative]	Freund
The Savior is our best (really good) friend.	Pacht[amawäăs] kachne onájo tēnnāngōmā.	Der Heiland ist unser bester Freund.
Where do your friends stay?	Thà ăjŏwàk tennangómak?	Wo wohnen deine Freunde? proprie Wo bleiben [deine Freunde]?
Who is making the food for the friends?	Awăn onechtăhn mezowagan tennàngomanäăk.	Wer macht Essen vor die Freunde.
They are friends with each other.	Ăïnòkotakęęk.	Sie sind Freunde miteinander.
friends, to have	—	Freunde haben
Do you have many friends?	Măchānāk ktennangomäăk.	Hastu viel Freunde?
I have many friends but none to trust [cf. right].	[Măchānāk] tennangomäăk psùk asta majáwe tennangoma.	Ich habe viel Freunde aber keinen trauen.
friendly, kind (in the face) [cf. also gloomy; unfriendly; face]		
I am friendly, kind.	Nonetáha. [= I-good-heart]	Ich bin freundlich.
You are friendly.	K[onetáha].	Du bist [freundlich].
(He is) friendly, kind.	Onetaháu.	Freundlich (er ist).
We are friendly.	Nonetahahanà.	Wir sind [freundlich].
You (pl.) are friendly.	K[onetaha]hamà.	Ihr seid [freundlich].
They are friendly.	Onetaháwak.	Sie sind [freundlich].
I am friendly (in the face).	Nonetaháwenaxò.	Ich [bin] freundl[ich] (im Gesicht).
We are friendly (in the face).	Nonetahawenaxehenà.	Wir sind freundl[ich] ([im] Gesicht).
[He is] friendly (in the face).	Onetahawenaxò.	[Er ist] freundlich (im Gesicht).
The Savior is certainly [very?] kind.	Pachtamawäăs muchtsche onetahawenaxò.	Der Heiland ist gewiss freundlich.
frivolous [see thoughtless]		
frock [see coat]		
from [see under but; come]	ŏtschè, utschájak	—
frozen [see freeze]		
full [cf. fill]	otschòwachtáu	voll
Take (pl.) [it] full.	Nátĕnimmǭǭk otschòwachtáu.	Nehmet voll.
But when will my (whole) heart become full of my Savior?	Muchtsche ăăm niàn (máowe) dáhak ŏtschòwachtaka năm Pachtamáwäässek. [= very will my (all) my-heart full-become? will Savior-of]	Wenn wird doch mein (ganzes) Herz voll werden von meinen Heiland.
I fill [it] up (full).	Nōtschŏwŭpäăn.	Ich fülle voll.
Fill [it] up (full).	Otschowupà.	Fülle voll.

further, more(?) — weiter
  I have nothing further (or more?) to say.   Astà náha néne gaquai ktennòhōmm̄e-one[?].   Ich habe weiter nichts zu sagen.

gain (*noun*) [*see* wages]
garter strap [*see* band]
gather, gather up, collect [*see also* assemble; *cf*. trust (*verb*)]   sammlen, samlen [*sic for sammeln*]
  He will gather her (them?) up in his arms.   Ōgăttaù onàchkek majawanáwa.   Er will sie samlen in die Arme.
gather together [*see* assemble]
gather wood together, collect wood   Holz zusammentragen
  You must gather it [the wood] together.   Pååschcunōōk knimmăchtánè.   Du must es zusammentragen.
  Gather the wood together.   [Pååschcunōōk] anawachtăk machtachana.   Tragt das Holz zusammen.
  He gathers up the wood.   [Pååschcunōōk] anawachtáu machtachane.   Er trägt das Holz zusammen.
  [Come, (*not in Mah. here*)] we will gather the wood together.   Paaschcunōōk ktenawachtahanà machtáchana.   Kommt, wir wollen das Holz zusammentragen.
  They are gathering up the wood.   [Paaschcunōōk] anawachtáwak [machtachana].   Sie tragen das Holz zusammen.
gaze upon [*see near end of* see]
get, catch, receive, (take)   krigen
  Ask that you (*sg*.) may receive.   Machmatuammè kmischnimmantschè.   Bitte so soltu krigen.
  They should receive.   Omischnimnáwak.   Sie sollen krigen.
  Where Satan cannot catch [anyone].   Nágam Machtandò astà meschinkówe. [where, that, *or* he?]   Wo der Satan nicht krigen kan.
  Who(ever) does not receive(?).   Awãn / Awáneetsch } astà m'schìnmóquà.   Wer nicht krigt.
  He has taken the punishment for us.   Kiánau otschè knachmawachtowágan m̄eschinnemen.   Er hat für uns die Strafe gekrigt.
  When two become one [= agree?], why do they ask that they have to get?   Néschowak ãm paaschkon anè machmatuamnáwak omischnemnáwak. [?what they-ask (is what) they-get?]   Wenn 2 eins werden, warum sie bitten dass sollen sie krigen.
  You must not grab (for) me when you fall (in your fall).   Asta ãm kennhogówun kennhéganick kechtăch'mockówu.   Du solt mich mich [*sic*] nicht in deine Falle krigen.
  what I get   ãhtche ténnema   was ich krige
get confused [*see* astray]
get lost [*see* astray]
get red [*see* redden]
get sick (= vomit) [*see* spit]
get well [*see* well]
ghost [*see* soul]
gift   mēēndowágan   Gabe
  offering (sacrifice) and gift   wehètowágan wak mēēndowágan   das Opfer und Gabe
girdle(?) [*see* band]
girl, maiden   kékăchquáŭ [*cf. Delaware cognates below*]   Mädgen
  A girl came.   Ăĭnájìck kékăchquáŭ.   Es kam ein Mädgen.
[*cf. Delaware (Ettwein, 1788) according to his word order*: ochquetit (a little girl), ochquezitsh (a girl), *wuskochqueu* (a virgin, 'young woman'), *ochqueu* (a woman), *kikochquees* (a woman of years), *chauchschusis* (an old woman)]
give   —   geben, schenken
  I give it to you, or There you have it.   ʼKménen.   Ich gebe dirs, oder, Da hastus.
  Give me.   Méne.   Gib mir.
  Give me, *i.e.*, make a present of it   Méne.   [Gib mir.] *i.e.* Schenke mirs.
  Give [me]. / to me.   Menè.   Gib.
  Give it to me.   Kmenēēn.   Gibstus mir.
  He gives.   Ména.   Er gibt.
  He gives to me.   Mēněkùn.   Er gibt mir.
  He gives you a new heart.   Waskáikè ktahà gménuck.   Er gibt dir ein neu Herz.
  We give it.   Kmenenána.   Wir gebens.
  Let's give.   Menataù. Menátaŭ.   Last uns geben. Lasst uns geben.
  Will you give it to me?   Kméne nenè.   Wilstu mirs geben.
  I will give it to you.   Nmenããn.   Ich will dirs geben.
  I will give it to you at once.   Ene scháwa kmenèn.   Ich will dirs gleich geben.

English	Mahican	German
I will give all that I have.	Máoweetsch kmēněně. Ãhtchek channea.	Ich will alles geben. Was ich habe.
I will give all that I get.	Máoweetsch kmēněně. Ãhtche ténnema.	Ich will alles geben. Was ich krige.
Will you gladly give your heart?	Kwége ménäán nà ktàh.	Wilstu gern dein Herz geben.
We will give it.	Menatṓṓk.	Wir wollen es geben.
He has given him to us.	Kmenekunána.	Er hat ihn uns gegeben.
He has given him to us, or him to you (pl.).	Kmēněkǔnanawàh.	Er hat uns ihn (oder ihn euch) gegeben.
(It) is given to us.	Kméněcǔnánǎǔ.	[Es] ist uns gegeben.
He gave it.	Oménahn.	Er gabs.
Who has given it to you, i.e., sent?	Awãně kmḗḗnkùn. [ò or è?]	Wer hat dirs gegeben, i.e. geschenkt.
Who has given it to you, i.e., lent?	Awãn knattemḗḗchkùn.	Wer hat dirs gegeben, i.e. gelehnt.
Joshua has given it to me.	Josua menekunà.	Josua hat mirs gegeben.
Give me. Note: Always understood in regard to eating.	[N?]Tachamókku.	Gib mir. NB. allezeit von Essen zu verstehen.
Who has given it to you?	Awãn ktachamókku?	Wer hat dirs gegeben?
I will give it to you.	N'tachamáu.	Ich will dirs geben.
I will not give it to you.	Aschãám ntachamáwe.	Ich will dirs nicht geben.
I cannot give it to you.	Ascha késche menówun[.]	Ich kan dirs nicht geben.
Have you given it to him?	Ktachamáu.	Hastus ihm gegeben?
You have given it to someone.	Aschawãn ktachamáu.	Du hasts jemand[em] gegeben.
You must give it to no one.	Tschḗḗn awãn chammáhan.	Du musts niemandem geben.
Give me the hatchet (pickax, hoe).	Nǎǔtschè wǎǎxeehégan. [e or a or delete?]	Gib mir die Hacke.
It has been given to him.	Ménanǎǎp.	Es ist ihm gegeben worden.
Give it to me here.	Nawutenè.	Gib mirs her.
Give it to me here.	Nawutschè.	idem [= the same]

give birth to [see bring forth]
give one's regards [see greet]
glad, be glad, rejoice, be pleased with, delight in — freuen, sich freuen *gaudere*

English	Mahican	German
Yes, I am glad.	Quãme ntannamēne.	Ja, ich freu[e] mich.
I am very glad about that.	Nò wátsche múchtsche ãnnãmmenäjà.	Darüber freue ich mich sehr.
I am glad to see him (your brother) at the love feast (banquet).	N'tannaména áněnáu nahk'ma (ketach[gak?]) tachtaquépǔăk.	Ich freue mich dass ich [ihn] dein Br[ude]r beim L[iebes]m[ahl] sehe.
I am glad that I see the brothers and sisters at the love feast.	Netanneména [e or a?] anenáu kétachcanak, cheismusak tachtaquépuak.	Ich freue mich dass ich die Geschwister beim L[iebes]m[ahl] sehe.
I am glad to see you.	Ntannaména anenawunan.	Ich freue mich, dass ich dich sehe.
I am glad that you are coming.	N'tannaména neáne pájan.	Es ist mir lieb, dass du kommest.
I am glad that you came home, or Welcome home.	Netanneména áne wékian pajàn.	Ich freue mich, dass du zu Haus gekommen. oder Willkommen zu Haus.
I am marvelously happy that I can [give] to you (pl.) my most cordial respects (or greetings).	Nià ndannaména mǎǎschchǎkke, nik nià kiáwa otáhak otschè kwawagṓṓmnochmà.	Ich freue mich erstaunlich, dass ich euch aufs herzlichste Grüssen kan.
We will be glad.	Ãnnǎmménāwátǎmōtṓṓk.	Wir wollen uns freuen.
We will be glad (about it).	Ãnnǎmménāwatǎmōtòòk.	Wir wollen uns (darüber) freuen.
They are glad.	Ánǎmménāchtḗḗt.	Sie freuen sich.
They were glad.	Anǎměchtḗḗt. Ánǎménānāwā.	Sie waren froh.
He wept for joy.	Scháchannaména.	Er weinte vor Freuden.
Now I will say why I am pleased.	Nóno kwechtammánen wãtsche ǒnăchtǎnǎmḗǎ.	Nun will ich sagen warum ich vergnügt bin.
Are you glad in the (your) heart?	Wǎǔnechnǎǔ nà ktàh.	Bist du vergnügt im Herzen.
My heart is glad, pleased, or well.	Niàn dàh wawunàchtanamè.	Mein Herz ist vergnügt, oder wol.
He (she) went with a joyous heart to Bethl[ehem] to work.	Nahǎ ajátǎ káchne onàchtánamowócha odáhak na Bethl[ehem] anachkáwak.	Er (sie) ging mit vergnügten Herzen nach Bethlehem (zu) arbeiten.
Today we will have a love feast with the baptized ones, who are joyous.	Nonò wáchcamàhk tachtaquèpéhenóǒk nḗḗk soognepongsétscheèk wǎǔnàchtanaméschḗḗk.	Heute werden wir L[iebes]mahl haben mit den getauften, die da vergnügt sind.

glitter [see sparkle]
gloomy, morose, sad; dark [cf. dark]; unfriendly [see also unfriendly]

English	Mahican	German
I am unfriendly, etc.	N'machschedtahà.	Ich bin unfreundl[ich].
I am unfriendly, etc.	Nmachschedtahawenaxè.	Ich bin unfreundl[ich].
We have gloomy faces.	Nmachschedtahawenaxehenà.	Wir haben finstre Gesichter.
You (pl.) have gloomy faces.	K[machschedtahawenaxe]hemà.	Ihr [habt finstre Gesichter].
gloomy face	nachxowenaxò	finster Gesicht
I have a gloomy or sad face.	Nachxowenaxè.	Ich hab ein finster Gesicht.

You have a gloomy face.	K[nachxowenaxè].	Du hast [ein finster Gesicht].
We have gloomy faces.	Nachxowenaxehenà.	Wir *etc.*
[he?] to appear gloomy (faced)	Pachgenimménaxò.	Finster (Gesicht) aussehen.
I look sad.	N[pachgenimmé]naxè.	Ich sehe [finster aus].
We look sad.	N[pachgenimmenaxe]henà.	Wir [sehen finster aus].
They look sad.	Pachgenimmenaxoàk.	Sie sehen finster aus.
gnats [*see* mosquitoes]		
go	–	gehen
I am going eastward.	[Wapanaāk] ntà.	Ich gehe nach Morgen.
I am going to the plantation.	Ăkèhatęęk ndà.	Ich gehe auf die Plantage.
I will go.	Tannimsè.	Ich will gehen.
Now I am going.	Nonò tānnĭmsèh.	Nun gehe ich.
Tomorrow morning I am going.	Wăpăchkàhtsch nájăppāwe ntānnimsèh.	Morgen früh gehe ich.
I will go into the sweat-house.	Enimpêēspa.	Ich will in den Schwiz Ofen gehen.
Go!	Anim'sè.	Gehe.
Go ahead.	Animmesè kià schajáu.	Geh du voran.
He goes home. [*sic*]	Ktannimsè. [= You are going.]	Geht er heim.
He has gone.	Anìmsowà. *or* Anìmsóăd.	Er ist gegangen.
[Then too.] Let's go.	Ihà wăk. Animsetau. *idem* [= the same]	Lasst uns gehen.
We will go together, all my brothers.	Anim'sētōŏk máowe netachganak.	Wir wollen alle zusammen gehen.
Go (*pl.*) on, forth.	Animsétau.	Geht fort.
He said, "Go (*pl.*), patrol the earth." And they patrolled (went). *Zechariah 6, 7.*	Nahk'ma ąwà: Nahà ahnà, ănĕmsĕĕkq pámăkĭĕĕck ăhkq, wăk nahk'mawa anìmsowak.	Er sprach: Gehet hin, und ziehet durchs Land! Und sie zogen. *Zack[arias] 6, 7.*
He has (accordingly) gone early.	Năjăppája animm'sōŏp.	Er ist früh darnach gegangen.
They have gone.	Anìm sópănęęk.	Sie s[in]d gegangen.
They have gone for 4 <u>days</u>.	Nawókŏnàk kà ănìmsópănęęk.	Vor 4 Tagen sind sie gegangen.
They have gone.	Anìmsechtétip.	Sie sind gegangen.
They have gone home.	Animsógak.	Sie sind heimgegangen.
[*see also* go home, return home]		
And they patrolled (went).	wăk nahk'mawa anìmsowak.	Und sie zogen. *Zack[arias] 6, 7.*
They shall walk.	Anìmsoak.	Sie wandeln.
From one year they go to another.	Ahànnĕmè katèek áhtkcheetsch anìmsòàk ktákkak. [áhttecheetsch?]	Von einem Jahr zum andern. *N. 710*
I am going.	Pomsè.	Ich gehe.
You go too slowly.	Osame chammawéschè k'pomsè.	Du gehst zu langsam.
You go too slowly.	Kosáme mnónōchà.	Du gehst zu langsam.
You go [too?] slowly.	Kmamm'nonócha.	*idem* [= the same]
You go [too?] slowly.	Kseschachwócha.	*idem*
(Perhaps) he is going (by foot), of one who does not know whether he has a horse.	Pŏmissōŏkăăt.	(Vielleicht) geht er (zu Fuss) wenn man nicht weiss ob er ein Pferd h?[at?].
Go quickly, swiftly.	Kschŏŏchà. Xechenà. Kschechnà.	Gehe hurtig.
You are going too fast.	Kosáme kschŏŏchà. Kosáme kschócha.	Du gehst zu hurtig.
[*see also under* quick; *see also* wegocháu *under* be present]		
Go slowly.	Chammau chăăsche. Chammau chassè.	Geh langsam.
Go & milk the cow. [*Schmick wrote the sentence in English.*]	Ăhănè sēnĕănēgà. ['the cow' *does not appear in Mahican.*]	Geh und melke die Kuh.
He went readily.	Annajin wegè.	Er ging gern.
He (she) went with a joyous heart to Bethlehem to work.	Nahà ajátà káchne onàchtánamowócha odáhak na Bethl[ehem] anachkáwak.	Er (sie) ging mit vergnügten Herzen nach Bethlehem (zu) arbeiten.
He has just gone. [*sic*]	Schĕmà nòómen. [nòómen = I come]	Er ist eben gegangen.
He has <u>just</u> gone there.	Tájachkàm otàhn.	Er ist gerade dorthin gegangen.
He has gone there.	Náha áŭ.	Er ist dorthin gegangen.
They went.	Ne ŏdànāwā.	Sie gingen.
They went.	Áwăk. *item* [= also]	Sie gingen.
He has gone in the house.	Wéquăchmŭk áwu.	Er ist ins Hauss gegangen.
Johanna has gone to Bethlehem.	Johanna Bethlehem áu.	Johanna ist nach Bethlehem gegangen.
He is going to Bethlehem.	Áu Bethlehem.	Er geht nach Bethl[ehem].
He is going to the mill.	Áu tachquaháganick.	Er geht nach d[er] Mühle.
He goes into the cellar.	Áu ahhgeánachguk.	Er geht im Keller.
He goes in the barn (shed, granary).	Áu tanapachgach'muk.	[Er geht] in Scheun.

English	Mahican	German
Didn't you say that Joseph would be (is going) with Joshua?	Asch ktenáwe Joseph áu Josuáhik.	Hast du nicht gesagt Joseph sey beim Josua.
(when 2 or 3 are going)	Ktáhănāu.	(wenn 2 od[er] 3 gehen[)]
(when many go)	Ktahanŏŏk.	(wenn viele gehen)
Tomorrow we (two) will go to Bethlehem.	Wapachgătsch Bethl[ehem] ktáhanau.	Morgen wollen wir (zwei) nach Bethlehem gehen.
He goes quickly (at once) to the Savior and says:	Scháwah ŏmischschātăcăăn Pachtamáwaassèk wak oténnahn.	Er geht geschwind (eilig, gleich) zum Heiland und sagt:

[*see* go in order to (do something)]
go after [*see* follow (after)]

He is going after them.	Náha ŏnōsochgawáwa.	Er gehet nach ihnen.

go along [*see* go with]
go around with [*see under* be present, be with] — umgehen
go away [*see also* go on] — weggehen

You must go away.	Nāhănĕ àh.	Du must weggehen.
Be off with you, you evil one.	[Nāhănĕ àh] kenáchkse.	Scher dich weg, du böser.
... if you do not leave the Savior.	... tschĕen'kanáhan Pachtamawăăs.	... wenn du nicht vom Heiland weggehst.
It is not good to go <u>alone</u> far from here.	Tschĕen quechtsche wáchnĕmòchāhàn.	Es ist nicht gut allein weit von hier zu gehen.

go before, go in front, take the lead, precede — gehen voran

Go ahead.	Animmesè kià schajáu.	Geh du voran.

go get [*see* fetch]
go home, return home — heimgehen oder nach Haus gehen

I will go home.	N'matschĕĕn.	Ich will heimgehen.
Go home.	Matschè.	Gehe heim.

go hunting [*see* hunt]

go in order to (do something)	mawe-, māuwe-, mawu-	—
I will see him.	Ne mawupenawáu.	Ich will ihn sehen.
I am going to spin [yarn].	Nmawè achpéha.	Ich gehe spinnen.
You are going to spin [yarn].	Kmawè [achpéha].	Gehstu spinnen.
Come (*pl.*) [*properly* 'then']; we will eat.	Ihà mawepetŏŏk.	Kommt wir wollen essen.
I will split wood.	Māupāpăchgăchtáham.	Ich will Holz spalten.
I am going (on the side) (*i.e.*, I urinate, I pass natural water).	Māuweschè. [*simply:* urinate-I? I = -è?]	Ich gehe an die Seit. (neml[ich], ich lasse *aquam naturalem*)
go in(to) there	—	gehen hinein
I will go in.	Nhäĕn ntà.	Ich will nein gehen.
Go in there.	Náha áhana. [*cf. below*]	Geh nein.
Go in there.	Nhaà.	Geh nein.
He goes in.	Nhaáu.	Er geht nein.
He has gone there.	Náha áŭ.	Er ist dorthin gegangen.
We go in.	Nhantáhana.	Wir gehen nein.
You (*pl.*) go in.	Nhaktahamà.	Geht ihr nein.
Go (*pl.*) in.	Nhăăgu.	Geht nein.
Go (*pl.*) (away there).	Nahà ahnà. [*cf. above*]	Gehet hin.
They go in.	Nhaáwak.	Sie gehen nein.
Don't go in.	Tschĕĕn haktăăn.	Geh nicht nein.
Don't (*pl.*) go in.	[Tschĕĕn] haktanawà.	Geht nicht nein.
John, go into the house.	(Johannes) wéquăămĕngà. [*Delaware?*]	Joh[annes] geh ins Haus.
... so that the Savior may enter (your hearts).	... Pacht[amawaas] otschinnehà páu.	... dass d[er] Heiland hinein gehe.
I will not go in there (in the ?).	Ascha nattemégawe.	Ich will nicht (in die Ver) [?, Ker?, Ber?] eingehen. [*see ms. p. (81)*]
I will go in there.	Nattemegăăn.	Ich will nein gehen.
Go in.	Ktemégà.	Geh du nein.
He goes in.	Ntemegáu.	Er geht nein.
We will go in.	Ntemegatŏŏk. [= Let's go in.]	Wir wollen nein gehen.
You (*pl.*) go in.	Ntemegáku. [= Go ye in.]	Geht ihr nein.
They go in.	Ntemegáwak.	Sie gehen nein.
I went in yesterday.	Wanaquéga nattemega.	Ich bin gestern nein gegangen.
You did not go in.	Astà knattemégawe.	Du bist nicht nein gegangen.
He did not go in.	[Astà] ntemégawe.	Er ist nicht [nein gegangen].
We did not go in.	[Astà] nattemegawehenà.	Wir sind nicht [nein gegangen].

74 Schmick's Mahican dictionary

English	Mahican	German
You (pl.) did not go in.	[Astà] knatte[megawehe]mà.	Ihr seid nicht [nein gegangen].
They did not go in.	[Astà] ntemegawéwak.	Sie sind nicht [nein gegangen].
You must not go in.	Tscheek knattemégan.	Du solst nicht nein gehen.
He must not go in.	Tschḗn tmegahḗetsch.	Er soll nicht [nein gehen].
You (pl.) must not go in.	Tschḗ knattemeganawà.	Ihr sollt nicht [nein gehen].
You are not going in.	Astà kwétawe.	Du gehst nicht nein.
Go in there. They will say something to you.	Náha áhana. Éne gáquai kténnuk.	Geh nein. Sie wollen dir was sagen.

go lightly [see crawl]
go on, go away — Pannéwà. — Gehe fort.
go out there — — gehen hinaus, gehen aus
  Go out there. — P'haggà. — Geh naus.
  Go (pl.) out there. — P'hagaàhqu. — Geht naus.
  I will go out. — P'hága ntà. — Ich will naus gehen.
  I will go out. — ... éne p'hagan ntãn. — ... ich will naus gehen.
  You go out. — P'hága ktà. — Gehst du naus.
  He goes out. — P'hagäáu. — Er geht naus.
  We will go out. — P'hagaatṍk. — Wir wollen naus gehen.
  You (pl.) go out. — P'hága ktahamà. — Geht ihr naus.
  They go out. — P'hagaáwak. — Sie gehen naus.
  He went out and cried. — Păquáuchããn udéttan mắhn. — Er ging hinaus und weinte.
go over there, go across — — gehen hinüber
  I am going over, passing over [the area?]. — Kámick tàh. — Ich gehe über.
  Go over there. — Kahamuckà. — Geh nüber.
  I am going over the big mountain. — Awàsséwè măchátscho. — Ich gehe über den grossen blauen Berg. [disregard blauen]

go slowly [see slow]
go to
  I am going to the laundry. — Aắchtahn kschẹẹchtecámick wéquamick. — Ich gehe nach[d]en Waschhaus.
go to bed [see lie down]
go to school [see learn]
go with, go along, accompany — — gehen mit
  Will you go along (to hunt)? — Kwétschawè? — Wiltu mit gehen (scil[icet] jagen).
  I will go hunting. — Ntãnnăwè. N'tànnawè. — Ich will jagen gehen.
  He has gone hunting [disregard: without coming home]. — Mawannawèwua. Mawannawéwua. — Er ist jagen gegangen, ohne dass er zu Haus kommt.
  plural: They have gone hunting. — [Mawanna]wéwak. — plur[alis] Sie sind jagen [gegangen].
  Go there; I wish you good luck. — Ăněwè pechtaắm gĕttĕménắk. — Geh du hin, ich wünsche dir gut Glück.
  I go with. I go along. — N'wḗta. — Ich gehe mit.
  Are you going along? — Kwadà? — Gehst du mit?
  Joseph is going along. — Joseph wetáu. — Joseph geht mit.
  Abraham is not going along. — Sta wetáwe Abraham. — Abraham geht nicht mit.
  I will go along. — Kwetschawunèn. — Ich will mitgehen.
  I am going along. — Nia ne wetschawáu. — Ich gehe mit.
  I am not going along. — [Nia] sta [wetscha]wáwe. — Ich gehe nicht mit.
  You are also going along. — Kia wắk kwetschawáu. — Du gehst auch mit.
  You are not going along. — [Kia] ascha [kwetscha]wáwe. — [Du gehst] nicht [mit].
  Is Philip going along? — Kwétschawuk Phil[ipp]. — Geht Phil[ipp] mit?
  He is not going along. — Sta okwetschawawewà. — Er geht nicht mit.
  My brothers are going along. — Niana nétachcanàk owetschawáwa. — Mir Br[üde]r gehen mit.
  We are going along. — Nwetschawawunà. — Wir gehen mit.
  They are going along. — Wetschawawà. — Sie gehen [mit].
  I will go along with you. — Nia ekwetscháwun. [sic e-] — Ich will mit dir gehen.
  Who is going with me? — Awằn nia nŏwétschawùk? — Wer geht mit mir?
  Who is going with you? — Awằn kwétschawùk kià? — Wer geht mit dir?
  Who is going with you (pl.)? — Awằn kwétschắwùkkwḗechmà kiáwa? — Wer geht mit euch.
  Who is going to supper? — Awằn wétschechnáta máchãắk. — Wer zum A[bend]m[ahl] gehet.
  The brothers R. and G. are going to Shamokin over 2 days, and Joseph is going with his brothers. — Wetáchkana (R.) (G.) neschóaknak wétschawà Schắchmàchkẹẹk, Josep wắk wetschawà wétáchkanàk. — Die Br[üde]r (R.) u[nd] (G.) gehen über 2 Tage nach Shomokin, u[nd] Joseph geht mit den Br[üde]rn.

English	Mahican	German
goal [see mark]		
God, Savior, Lord [root meaning pray or help?]	Pachtamáwaas, Pachtamáwaas, Tapanemucquak [for more see Savior]	Gott [abbrev. in script, ms. p (341): ƀ̶ ƀ̶ = Gt], der Heiland (dHld), der Herr
God, the (my) Father	[Pachtamáwaas] Nṏṓch	Gott Vater
God, the Son; Son of God	[Pachtamáwaas] Otaijóma	[Gott] Sohn
God, the Holy Ghost	[Pachtamáwaas] Wáhnsetschè ŏtschìtschachquà	[Gott] Heilger Geist
going to (do something) [see go in order to (do something); mawe-, mawu- under will]		
good	wĕ̄gan	gut; süss [= good]
Rest is sweet, i.e., good.	Anachemewágan wégan.	Die Ruhe ist süss.
It smells good.	Wĕk tschamáquat.	Es riecht gut.
It tastes good.	Nè wēgăchtāmmēn.	Es schmeckt gut.
He is good.	Onáju.	Er ist gut.
Please, be so good and fetch him here.	Kmachmatuámmen unáje nā̰ā̰thonè.	Ich bitte dich, sey so gut und hohle ihn herüber.
The Savior is our best (really good?) friend.	Pacht[amawā́s] kachne onájo tēnnāngōmā̄.	Der Heiland ist unser bester Freund.
in a good place	nŏŭnit	in einen guten Plaz
Are they good?	Wawuntà?	Sind sie gut?
It is not good to come together so late.	Astaù ŏnìttówe mēēchkaù kmajáwenáwa.	Es ist nicht gut so spät zusammen zu kommen.
good children	wáŭnā̌lkĕĕ̌k awàsésak	gute Kinder
in good works	wánechk anè	guten Werken (in)
the good (kind, benevolent) Savior	kahhawanáik Jesus	der gütige Heiland
the good [thing; prob. not goodness], blessing, prosperity	ŭnā̌ĭwágàn	das Gute
My brothers, you must always think about the good Savior.	Netachcanak ng'máowe maamschānòchk wāchwă̆wége Pachpam[āwŏsŏhā̰nŏááad].	Ihr musst allez[eit] an den guten Heiland dencken.
do good, be a benefit		gut thun
It has done you good, the sweating, or in the *péēsbank* or sweathouse.	Konamattāmmen nĕ áne peespājàn. Kōnămă[t]tāmmĕn nĕ ánĕ pĕspājàn.	Hat es dir gut gethan das Schwizzen, oder im *Péēsbank* oder Schwizofen.
good conduct [see have good conduct]		
gossip [see babble]		
grain (or berry, fruit)	-me	—
grain, wheat	manóme	Weizen
maize, corn	chasquéme, chăsquēmĕ̆	Welschkorn
grain, rye, buckwheat	sĕkănōmĕ̆	Korn, Rocken [Roggen], Schwarzkorn
granary [see barn]		
grandmother [see nohàm..., p. 155]		
grapes, in the sense of bunch of grapes, grape cluster [see also comments under Delaware words]	wēlŏmè [probable Delaware word]	Weintraube
grass [cf. mow (grass)]	mēĕchsqŭan	Gras
graveyard	achquandémick	Gottes-acker, Begräbnis-Plaz
gravy, sauce, broth, or soup [see soup]		Brühe oder Suppe
greasy gravy	—	fette [Brühe]
fresh gravy, sweet gravy	—	süsse [Brühe]
great, big, large	—	gros
There is nothing greater (more big).	Astàk gáquai anequèchque m'cháo.	Es ist nichts grössers.
in his great misery	áne mă̆chchè ktĕmă̆kā̄lhattĕĕ̄t	in seinem gro[s]sen Elend
I have great hope.	Niachkĕē̆p mache nachgawosè.	Ich habe grosse Hofnung.
That is big and important for us.	Kmachchè katàcŏnānāu.	Das ist uns gross u[nd] wichtig.
great anger, great rage	máchche nachkessoákan	grosser Zorn
Many are coming.	Máchche páwak.	Es sind viel gekommen.
It is a great matter.	Máchaak.	Es ist eine grosse Sache.
big ax	macheē̆d d'mahégan	gros [Beil]
a big book	machāăk ŏsŏ̆ahégan	ein grosses Buch
big mountain	māchăquăchtschù, măchàttĕ̆nĕŭ	grosser [Berg]
the great water (the ocean?)	máchaak nĕpì, katàch nĕpì	das grosse Wasser
from the old (great?) years	machchowái katènnik	vom Alten
We think big.	Kiánau kmachă̄hntamnánau.	Wir denken gros.

English	Mahican	German
I have a great pain.	Nmămáchāchwăhntam.	Ich habe grossen Schmerz.
My shoes are too big for me.	Mamagáwan măksene.	Meine Schu sind mir zu gros.
a large kind of fish or animal [contrast muskellunge = great pike]	măchmăchèkkēnik	eine grosse Art, von Fischen von Thieren
greet, give one's regards	—	grüssen
I greet. I give my regards.	Nwawagómen. Quawagómen.	Ich grüsse.
Do you greet?	K[wawago]mè. Quawagomè.	Grüssestu?
He greets.	K[wawago]muk. Quawagómak. Wawakŏmmak.	Er grüsset.
We greet.	N'wawagowawunà. Newawagowawunà. N'wāwagōmănă.	Wir grüssen.
You (pl.) greet.	K[wawago]mowà. Quawagomowà.	Grüsset ihr.
I greet him.	N['wawago]máu.	Ich grüsse ihn.
I greet you (pl.).	Nià kwawagŏŏmnochma kiáwa.	Ich grüsse euch.
They send their respects. They send kind regards.	Kwawagòomquăquè. Wawakŏmquăquè.	Sie lassen grüssen.
They most cordially greet. They present many compliments.	Múchtsche káchna kwáwăgŏmuk. Muchtsche káchna kwawagómuck.	Sie grüssen herzlich.
... that I can [give] to you (pl.) my most cordial respects (or greetings).	... nik nià kiáwa otáhak otschè kwawagŏŏmnochmà.	... dass ich euch aufs herzlichste grüssen kan.
My brothers, greet Joseph when you come to Bethlehem.	Nétachcanak n'wawagómau Jos[ep] n'hăppājănă Bethlehem.	Brüder grüsset Joseph wenn ihr nach Bethl[ehem] kommt.
grief [see sadness]		
grits(?), hominy(?), pone(?); potatoes(?) [Warne, p. 177 (33)]	ahpánan [cf. Proto-Algonquian: *wexpenya, tuber, groundnut (Apios); / cf. bread (Delaware)]	Akridges, Akridches [slightly Germanized English word, plural]
grope [see seize]		
ground [see land]		
grow	—	wachsen
Let us grow in your love.	Dănnĕmékenanà achwohndowágan nachpè.	Lass uns in deiner Liebe wachsen.
It is growing.	Késchĕkówa.	Es wächst.
guard, watch [verb and noun]	—	wachen; Wache
the guard, sentinel	achcòhēkà	die Wache
Who is on guard?	Awãn achcòhĕĕkà.	Wer hat die Wache?
Who is on guard?	Awãn achcòhĕğssà.	Wer hat die Wache?
How many are on guard?	Kaãchŏwàck achcòhékātschĕĕk.	Wieviel wachen.
guilt [cf. fault]		
gulp down [see swallow]		
gun; guns	péquan; péquanan pajachkékan (Delaware) [see under Delaware words]	Flinte, sing[ularis]; Flinten, plur[alis] Flinte
my gun	nàn ănĕpéquan	meine Flinte
The gun is my own.	Nŭmpăpéquan tappăăntámmen.	Die Flinte ist mein eigen.
Make the gun clean from rust.	Kschĕĕchnè achquāquănă păchgékăn. [Clean of rust the gun]	Mach die Flinte sauber vom Rost.
[cf. also:] Fire off.	Pāquĕchtà.	Schiesse los.
habit [see accustomed]		
hair [see beard]		
half	passéwe	halb
halfway		Halbe Weg
Now it's halfway.	Nónen nò nánawàt.	Nun ist der Halbe Weg.
Soon it will be halfway.	Pachood knānāwóchachnàu.	Bald ist der Halbe Weg.
hand [including lower arm]		Hand
my hand	n'nachk	meine Hand
in his hand	onáchgek, ŏnàchgĕk	in seiner Hand
their hands	onáchka, onáchgan	[seine] Hände
on the hands	ŏnāchkăn	in Händen
in the [his] arms	onàchkek	in die Arme
My hands hurt.	Wĕnămăttăm náchcan.	Meine Hände thun mir wehe.
on our [incl.] hands	knàchkĕnăăk [see under hang on]	an den Händen
I will warm my hands. [see warm]	Dăppēĕn tschässeĕn onáchcan. [my?]	Ich will meine Hände wärmen.
[cf. bind the hands behind the back]		

English-Mahican-German 77

handsome [see beautiful]		
hang on, cling to	–	hangen, hängen
... we cling to (the Savior's side) ...	... kĕnămméta ...	... wir hangen in ...
The mosquitoes (or gnats) sit and hang onto our eyes and our [incl.] hands.	Pĕkússak nik skęętschkunanik, knàchkĕnäặk wak ŏmischschakanáwa. okénnamēnáwa. sezen hängen	Die *Muskiters* (Mücken) sezen sich an den Augen u[nd] Händen, u[nd] hängen.
The kettle hangs over the fire and is cooking.	[*Delaware:*] Hŏ́ŏs scheheléuch woak dendéuch.	Der Kessel hängt über Feuer u[nd] kocht. *Dellaw.* [*sic for Delaware*]
hang up the kettle [over the fire], put on the kettle		Kessel überhängen
Hang up the kettle. Put the kettle on.	Ãkhóna.	Häng den Kessel über.
Hang the water up. Put the water on.	Akótha npè.	Häng[da]s Wasser über.
I have hung up the kettle. [see also kettle under Delaware words]	Nkeschakhonáu.	Ich habe den Kessel übergehängt.
happen	–	geschehen
It is accomplished, It has happened, or It is done.	Nàn késche ánăchkăhn.	Es ist vollbracht, es ist geschehen, oder es ist gethan.
happy [see blissful; live (twice); lucky(?)]		
hard, firm; stern	assannáju	hart
My (the?) bed is hard.	Assannáju kāchkăwŏjè.	Mein Bett ist hart.
The hands of the white people are hard (stern).	Tschachkósak onáchka assannájuwan.	Der weissen Leute Hände sind hart.
Nail it on hard.	Assannachtáhe ktachquahégan awà.	Nagele es an.
I have remained hard (firm).	Tessanechganachen.	Ich habe hart gelegen.
hard work	Assannáju. [= It is hard.]	schwere, harte [Arbeit]
stubborn work	assannanachgáu	sture [Arbeit]
hero, champion, strong one	áhssănnĕĕ̆t	Held (Starke)
He is patient. He has a strong heart.	Assanetaháu.	Er ist gedultig, stark Herz.
with the powers in heaven	nè ahssannáik wochcamáwenaak (wátschaĭk)	mit den Kräften im Himmel
It's raining hard. [see under lot (much)]		
harm, damage [see also bad]	mātschĕ̌ [not a noun]	Schaden
Take away what causes harm.	Ammáne mātschĕ̌ ăm ănĕchquāk.	Nimm weg was Schaden macht.
harrow [verb]		egen [for eggen]
He can harrow.	Kēsché nachàchgāsēgaù. [Kēsché or Késche?]	Er kan egen.
haste [see hobble; quick]		
hat [see put on a hat]		
hatchet [see ax; hoe]		
hate [verb] [see also despise]	–	hassen
You hate yourself.	Kschegenawà kháckei.	Du hassest dich selbst.
You hate us.	[Kschegena]wehena.	Du hassest uns.
You hate them.	Kschegenawáwak.	[Du hassest] sie.
He hates me.	Nschegenăku.	Er hasset mich.
He hates you also.	Kschegenăk kia wăk.	Er hasset dich auch.
He hates the Christian[s?].	Oschegenawáwa Christian.	[Er hasset] den Xstian.
The Devil hates all of us.	Kschegenakónau máwe Machtandò.	Der Teufel hasset uns alle.
He hates you (pl.).	Kschegenakówa.	Er hasset euch.
He hates those who believe.	O[schegena]wáwa wáhnsĕttăchkè.	Er hasset die Gläubigen.
We hate you.	Kschegenan'henà.	Wir hassen dich.
We hate him (the man).	Nschegenawawuna (nà nemanáu[)].	Wir hassen ihn (den Mann).
We hate you (pl.).	Kschegenanehenà.	Wir hassen euch.
We hate them.	Nschegenawawunà.	Wir hassen sie.
Why do you (pl.) hate me (us?)?	Gaquătsch schegenawojăku.	Warum hasset ihr mich (u[ns?]).
Why do you (pl.) hate poor N.?	[Gaquătsch] schegenawăk kat'maxĕĕ́d N.	Warum hasset ihr den armen N.
Why do you (pl.) hate them?	Gaquătsch schegenawăk?	Warum hasset ihr sie.
Why do they hate me?	[Gaquătsch] schegenawechtĕĕ́d nià?	Warum hassen sie mich.
Why do they hate you?	Gaquătsch schegenáquan?	Warum hassen sie dich.
Why do they hate him[,] Christian?	[Gaquătsch] schegenawaachteed [Chri]stian?	Warum hassen sie ihn Xstian?

Why do they hate us?	Gaquătsch schegenaquăk? [Gaquătsch schegena]quăku?	Warum hassen sie uns?
Why did they hate the Savior?	Gaquătsch schegenawaachtéĕd Tapanemukquahquèh?	Warum haben sie den Heiland gehasset?

haughty [see proud]

have, possess something	–	haben, was besizen
I have.	Nià gáchanĕĕn.	Ich habe.
You have.	K[gácha]nè.	Du hast.
He has.	Channu. Channóu.	Er hat.
We have.	N'gachchanechnà. N'gachchanehennàu. Ngachchanechnàu. Channéqua.	Wir haben. Wir haben.
You (pl.) have.	[K?][Gachchanech]mà.	Ihr [habet].
They have.	Kachànnŏăk.	Sie haben.
I have brothers.	Nià nŏwĕtăchcănĕĕn.	Ich habe Brüder.
You have brothers.	Kià kowe[tachca]nè.	Hastu [Brüder].
I have no brothers.	Stà nowetachcannéu.	Ich habe keine Brüder.
We have brothers.	Niana [nowetachca]nechnà.	Wir haben Brüder.
You (pl.) have brothers.	Kiawa [k?][owetachcanech]mà.	Ihr habt [Brüder].
We are having a love feast.	Tachtaquépĕĕnŏŏk. [Tachtaquépĕĕ]nău.	Wir haben L[iebes]mahl.
Today we are not having a love feast, banquet.	Nónò wáchkamàhk asta ăm tachtaquepéwùn.	Heute haben wir nicht L[iebes]mahl.
Don't you have?	Asch gachchanéu.	Hastu nicht?
I don't have.	Sta gắchchanéwe.	Ich habe nicht.
I don't have.	Sta n'gachchanéwe.	Ich habe nicht.
I have nothing hindering me.	Stàn gachaneu tăchgōgănāpĕ̆. [see delay]	Ich habe kein Happel.
You don't have.	Stak gachchanéwe.	Du hast nicht.
He doesn't have.	Sta gchanéwe.	Er hat nicht.
We don't have.	Stà ngachchanewehenà.	Wir haben nicht.
You (pl.) don't have a knife.	Chegan asch gachchanewehamà.	Ihr habt kein Messer.
They don't have a knife.	Sta asch chegan gchanéwe. [why two negatives: sta + asch?]	Sie haben kein Messer.
Don't you have a broom?	Asch kachchannéwe pnomis. [= broom]	Hastu nicht einen Besen.
[Do you (sg.) have food? (according to Mahican)]	Káchchannè mezowagan.	Habt ihr zu essen gehabt. [= Did you (pl.) have (something) to eat? (according to German)]
Do you have many friends?	Măchānāk ktennangomăăk.	Hastu viel Freunde?
I have many friends but none to trust.	[Măchānāk] tennangomăăk psùk asta majáwe tennangoma.	Ich habe viel Freunde aber keinen trauen.
Keep, retain, remember (namely, the letter or word, verse).	Channawahnta. [contrast wish]	Behalte (scil[icet] die Buchst[abe] oder Wort, Vers).

have good conduct, be nice, be proper; flatter — hübsch machen

You are not being nice.	Kmamachtannachgà.	Du machst es nicht hübsch.
You are nice, well mannered, flattering.	Konanachgà.	Du machst es hübsch.
You are very nice.	Muchtsche konanachgà.	Du machst es sehr hübsch.
It is not fair, proper (a rudeness).	Stà konenaxéwe.	Es ist nicht hübsch (eine Unart).
It is proper, fair.	Konenaxè. [= You look nice.]	Es ist hübsch.
You read beautifully, nicely.	Kăhăgóne kétammen.	Du liesest schön, hübsch.

have to [see must]

he (him), she (her), it [see also Personal pronouns]	nahk'ma, nahkma, náhkĕma, nák'ma [= his, he], uwà- [= he?]; nànè [= him]; nàh [= he]	er, sie, es; ihn
He bought me with his blood.	Nahk'ma p'gachganómick utáttawahanăăp. [u or n?, edge shows u-, he, but n-, me?]	Er erkaufte mich mit seinen Blut.
I am not acquainted with him.	Astàn wawèchtawùn nànè.	Ich kenne ihn nicht.
He writes. [see also the]	Uwà [mamanăăk héga].	Er schreibet.
He has hit (the mark).	Nahkĕma ŏmischschàwà.	Er hat getroffen.

[for she cf. at Mpowà under die and see under disobedient]

head [see also headache]	wénes [= his head; cf. wĩñsus (wĩñsiis?), H]	Haupt [high style in German]
head	t'pà	Kopf [usual word in German]
my head	nĕnes	mein Kopf
The man is the head of his wife.	Nĕmănă ŏwĕhnsehn wĕwa.	Der Mann ist das Haupt s[eine]s Weibes.
headache	–	Kopfschmerzen
My head hurts me.	Nĕnes n'wenamatà.	Mein Kopf thut mir weh.

The head hurts me.	N'sewanà t'pà.	idem [= the same]
I have a headache.	Nsewanadpà.	Ich habe Kopfschmerzen.
You have a headache.	K[sewanadpà].	Hast du [Kopfschmerzen].
He has a headache.	O[sewanad]páu.	Er hat [Kopfschmerzen].
headcold (to have a)	–	Schnuppen haben
I have a cold in the head.	Nsechtanéna.	Ich habe den Schnuppen.
You have a cold in the head.	K[sechtané]na.	Hastu den [Schnuppen].
He has a cold in the head.	Sechtanenáu.	Er hat [den Schnuppen].
heal, cure [see also make well]		heilen
I will heal you.	Nia éne gégahon.	Ich will dich heilen.
Heal me.	Gegahè.	Heile mich.
Heal us.	Gegahenána.	Heile uns.
N. will heal you.	N. gegahŏk tschè.	N. wird dich heilen.
healthful, healthy [see under well; make well; cure; wholesome spring]		
heap, pile	machahndam [?]	Haufen
heap of blankets	wapassanajan machahndam	ein Haufen Blanquets
Did you lay the wood in a woodpile?	Knimmãchtanè machtachanàn.	Hastus Holz auf einen Holz[hau]fen gelegt.
hear, listen, perceive, understand [cf. listen]		hören, vernehmen
I hear. [cf. second series below]	Pettàm.	Ich höre.
You hear.	Kpettàm.	Du hörst.
He hears.	Nahk'ma kpettàm.	Er hört.
We hear.	Niánŏk péttămēchnŏn.	Wir.
You (pl.) hear.	Kiawa kpéttămēchmà.	Ihr.
They hear.	Nahkmawa nptammãhk.	Sie.
I have heard.	Nià mpéttamennãhp.	Ich habe gehört.
I have already heard.	Nià pagatschè mpéttamennãhp.	Ich habe schon lange gehört.
The Savior hears us.	Papacht[amawãắs] kiánau kpettacónau.	Der Heiland höret uns.
Listen, you (sg.).	Péttăwè.	Höre du.
Listen (pl.).	Knístămŏkq.	Höret ihr.
You must listen.	Knístăwè.	Du solst hören.
Give me a favorable hearing. Grant me.	Péttăwēnà.	Erhöre mich.
Grant us a hearing.	Ptauwenanaù.	Erhöre uns.
present tense in another manner:		Aliter Præsens
I hear. [cf. first series above]	Nia mpéttamen.	Ich höre.
You hear.	K[ia] kpéttamen.	Du [hörst].
He hears.	N[ahk'ma] opettamen.	[Er hört.]
We hear.	Niana pettamennána.	– plur[alis]
You (pl.) hear.	[Kiáwa?] k[pettamenna]wa.	–
They hear.	[Nahk'mawa] opettamennawa.	–
They hear it. [see under sheep]	Apetammenáu.	[Sie] hören [es].
perfect tense		Perfect

[Of Schmick's explanation of various ways to use the perfect tense, the following first two words are poorly legible:]
?English? did? + ? or ?i á n? [see long note, pp. 158 and 159] *left didmis*
with dénne or p. suffixed, instead of paggatsche being inserted.
mit dénne od[er] das p. hinten anstatt paggatsche angehängt.

I have heard.	Nia ndénne ptámmen.	Ich habe gehört.
I have heard.	Nią mpettámennãắp.	Ich habe gehört.
You have heard.	Kia k[pettamennããp].	–
He has heard.	N[ahk'ma?] opettamennaap.	–
We have heard.	Niána mpettamennanãắp.	– plur[alis]
You (pl.) have heard.	[Kiáwa?] k[pettamenna]wããp.	–
They have heard.	[Nahk'mawa?] o[pettamenna]wããp.	–
You (pl.) have heard from his mouth what he spoke.	Kpèttawáwà otóhnick otschè ăḿnăăptōnăắt.	Ihr habts aus seinem Munde gehört, was er geredet.
I have heard.	Tennĕsetàm.	Ich habe gehört.
Brother, I have heard (that) you are going to have a love feast.	Nètachcan n'tensettàm achwãhntowepòwãgan kónechtah.	Bruder, ich habe gehört, du wilst ein L[iebes]mahl machen.
Do you hear me?	Kpettăwe.	Hörestu mich.
Yes, I hear you.	Quãme k'pettããn.	Ich höre dich.
I hear that you are speaking.	Kpettãhn ktahaaptona.	Ich höre, dass du redest.

I cannot hear you.	Ascha késche ptánnowe.	Ich kan dich nicht hören.
I want to (will) hear what he says.	Gattaù ptaùwaǔ gaquai mach<u>é</u>ĕt.	Ich will hören was er sagen wird.
Do you hear someone calling?	Awän k'pettawà tschĕnăŏtik.	Hörstu jemand rufen.
You hear us when we call.	Kpettăgŏnǎ kiána măchĕchsĕăquà. Kpettakonau kiána măchĕchsĕăquà.	Du hörst uns, wenn wir rufen.
Are you (pl.) deaf that you don't hear?	Kupchahamà, wăătsch asch ptammowăk.	Seyd ihr taub, dass ihr nicht höret.
All men are deaf and hear not.	Mawe awăneek kpacháwak sta ptămmawewak.	Alle M[en]schen sind taub und hören nicht.
The Devil stops up people's ears so that they don't readily hear.	Kpachansò Machtandò stà wége ptammówe.	Der Teufel stopft d[er] Leute Ohren zu, dass sie nicht gerne hören.
I haven't heard anything about it.	Astàk gaquai păăptamowùn.	Ich habe nichts davon gehört.
letters that are mute (not heard)	kpetonáwan	stumme Buchstaben
The <u>sheep</u> hear my word.	Ne <u>mamaximsàk</u> apetammenáu ntăăptonawágan.	Die Schaafe hören mein Wort.
My sheep hear my voice. [exact translation uncertain]	Nenochtagăk mamaksimsàk onenochtamnáu nawan.	Meine Schaafe hören meine <u>Stimme</u>.
What have you heard [where you come from]?	Gaquai ktăńistămwámàn.	Was hastu gehört wo du herkommst.
What have you (pl.) heard?	Gaquai ktăńistămhámma.	Was habt ihr gehört.
What have the brothers heard?	Gaquai ktăńistăwăwăăk kétachcanenăăk.	Was haben die Br[üde]r gehört.
hearken [see listen]		
heart [see also bad off (in the heart)]		Herz
my heart	dah, niàn dàh, nàn tah [d- is from nt-]	mein Herz
in my heart	dáhak, ntáhak	in meinen Herzen; Ich . . . im Herzen
your heart	ktăh	dein Herz
in your heart	ktáhak	Du . . . im Herzen
What do you have in your heart? How does your heart feel?	Gaquai ktăńétahà.	Was hastu in deinen Herzen. Wie befindestu dich im Herzen.
his heart	otaha	sein Herz
in his heart	otáhik	Er . . . im Herzen
The Savior cleans our hearts [obviative].	Ŏkĕschĕchĕháwă ktăhănănă Tap[ane-mucquak].	Der Heiland reinigt unser Herzen.
Our Savior has made our heart clean.	Pachtamawaasnaù ŏkĕschechtăăn ktáhanau.	Unser Heiland hat unser Herzen reine gemacht.
in our hearts	ntahanánik	in unsern Herzen
your (pl.) hearts	ktáhăwă	eure Herzen
in your (pl.) hearts	ktahawáwick	in eurem Herzen
Their hearts are small. They are small of heart, or meek.	Tsackĕschéssĕwa Tsackĕschéschĕwà } otăhăwà.	Sie s[in]d von Herzen klein oder demüthig.
in their hearts	otahawăwuk	in ihren Herzen
[see also impatient (= small-hearted?); patient (= strong-hearted?); weak (= bad-hearted?)]		
with believing hearts	ŏnìstăwájăquà ktáhĕnnăăk	mit gläubigen Herzen
that I can [give] to you (pl.) my most cordial respects (or greetings).	nik nià kiáwa otáhak otschè kwawagŏŏm-[that I you(pl.) the heart from greet-I-you] nochmà.	dass ich euch aufs herzlichste Grüssen kan.
[see bad off (to be); one (two entries)]		
heaven [see sky]		
help [noun]	nachtamawátŏwágàn	Hilfe, Hülfe
Who needs help?	Awăn ájatachcà nàchtămăwătŏwágan. [or] Awăn ájatachcà nàchtămăwamìck.	Wer hat Hülfe nöthig?
help [verb] [see also end of hope]	—	helfen
I help.	Nachtamăn.	Ich helfe.
You help.	Knachtammawè. Knachtamawè.	Du hilfst.
He helps.	Onachtamawáu.	Er hilft.
He does not help.	Asta náhk'ma onatamówun.	Er hilft nicht.
[Schmick crossed out as an error the German sentence Er ist nicht vergnügt. (= He is not pleased.) Note similarity with Mahican pleased.]		
He helps them.	Nachtamawáu.	Er hilft ihnen.
We help.	Nachtamawahanà.	Wir helfen.
You (pl.) help.	Knachtamawahamà. Gnachtamawahamà.	Ihr helfet.
They help.	Onachtamawáwak.	Sie helfen.

English-Mahican-German 81

English	Mahican	German
Help your believers...	Nàchtamawe wáhnsettakwanêěk...	Hilf deinen Gläubigen...
Help yourself. And us.	Náchtamawà nèchne°wè khákkei. Niána wak.	Hilf derselber. Und uns.
Help me.	Nachtammawè. Nachtamawê.	Hilf mir.
Yes, I will help you. [Ihà = then or yes?; kahane = truly]	Ihà } k'nachtamähn. Kahane	Ja, ich will dir helfen.
We will help.	Nachtamawatôŏk. Nachtamawatŏk.	Wir wollen helfen.
Help (pl.)!	Nachtamawóchqu.	Helfet.
Let's help.	Nachtamawátau. Nachtamawataù.	Lasst uns helfen.
He helps me.	Nachtamăku.	Er hilft mir.
I help him or her. I have helped him.	Nachtamawaú.	Ich helfe ihn oder ihr. Ich habe ihn geholfen.
I will not help you.	Aschà knachtamanówe.	Ich will dir nicht helfen.
Don't help him.	Tschêĕk knachtamawãn.	Hilf ihn nicht.
He will not help me.	Stà ngáttau nachtamagówe.	Er will mir nicht helfen.
We do not help.	Stà nachtamawawunà.	Wir helfen nicht.
You (pl.) do not help.	Asch knachtamawawewà.	Helft ihr nicht
They do not help.	Stà onachtamawawunà.	Sie helfen nicht.
We will not help.	Aschà knachtamawawéunawàk.	Wir wollen nicht helfen.
Don't (pl.) help.	Tschêĕn nachtamawaháku.	Helfet nicht.
He does not help.	Stà nachtamagówe.	Er hilft nicht.
You depend on your money, which will not help you.	Kia kotahnsechmà ksehnpattmèn, asta ăm knachtamagöunà.	Du verlässt dich auf dein Geld, das wird dir nicht helfen.
The Savior will gladly help all those (all of us?) who(ever) feel that they need (his) help.	Pachtamawaas kwége máowe nàchtămăconaù, [n]êĕk amáttakèek, nahkma nachtamawátŏwágàn ájātămããk.	Der Heiland will gern alle helfen, die da fühlen dass sie (seine) Hilfe nöthig haben.
He helps along with us.	Wétăhāmākùk. [see under bless]	Er hilft mit uns.
hens [see chickens]		
herbs [see vegetables]		
here (in this place) [see also stay; cf. there]	nè	hier; alhier
I am sitting here. Here I sit.	Ne ápea.	Hier siz ich.
There she (Anna) sits. [also he]	Nè ápeed. Nà ápeĕd.	Dort sizt sie (Anna). Dort sizt er.
Here we sit.	Ne ápeak. Na ápejak.	Hier sizen wir.
[cf.:] There they sit.	Nêĕk ápetschêĕk.	Dort sizen sie.
[They] are here.	—	hier sind
As for me and all my brothers here, that is our wish.	Nià wàk nohà ăijétscheek máowe [I and here? they are here also what? [concerns?] all] netáchganak ktájahntamnánau. [my brothers, we wish it]	Was mich u[nd] meine Br[üde]r alhier betrifft, so ist unser Verlangen.
around here, around there	Nè átàhn.	Da (Dort) herum
hero, champion, strong one	áhssännêĕt	Held (Starke)
hers [see Pronominal affixes]		
hiccup [verb]	—	[den] Schlucken haben
I have the hiccups.	Ntschachtschap'chăku.	Ich hab[e] den Schlucken.
You have the hiccups.	K[tschachtschap'chăku].	Du
He has the hiccups.	[(O?)Tschachtschap'cha(u or -ku?)] [not written, just a line drawn]	Er
hidden [see safe]		
hide, skin, pelt [see also leather]	chaj, chei	Haut, Fell
I make the hide (or skin) juicy (soft and pliable?).	Dĕnnăknaŭ chaj.	Ich mache die Haut (das Fell) saftig.
I make the hide dry.	ĕNsénachquăháu chaj.	Ich mache die Haut trocken.
Did you remove the hide?	Kĕschĕchpăchēnaŭ?	Hastu die Haut abgezogen?
to skin the stag [I(?) skin the stag.]	n'păchénähn ăchtóhu	den Hirsch abziehen
hill [see under mountain]		
himself [see self]		
hinder, prevent [cf. also hobble]	—	hindern
Do I prevent you?	Knachnechauwonèn.	Hindere ich dich.
Yes, you prevent me.	Quă knachnechauwõne.	Ja, du hinderst mich.

82 Schmick's Mahican dictionary

I have prevented you.	Knachnecháwonen.	Ich habe dich gehindert.
You prevent me. You are hindering me.	Knachnechawóne nia. Knàchnăchăwónè.	Du hinderst mich.
Don't hinder me.	Tschëen knachnechawonën.	Hindere mich nicht.
He hinders me.	Nachnechawónuk.	Er hindert mich.
The white men have hindered us.	Knàchnechauwŏněkónau tschachkósak.	Die weissen Menschen haben uns gehindert.
I have many obstacles.	Nachnechawŏnquane ngáchane.	Ich habe viel Hinderniss.

[*Is* -quane *a plural? If not, perhaps word is in singular.*]

hindered [*see* restrained]
his, her(s) [*see* Pronominal affixes]
    [*One entry showed* nahk'ma *(= he) before its noun; see following:*]

in his name	nahk'ma otenewesowaganick [*see at* sleep]	in Namen sein [sein = his; ≠ to be!]

[*other forms:*]

in his wounded side	neáne paquaick wapuchquanik	in seine verwundte Seite
his blood	nò p'gáchganom	sein Blut

hit, beat, strike [*see also* pound]

Don't hit.	Tschë kpákkămŏwăăn.	Schlage nicht.
Who has hit you, or Who was it who struck you?	Awăn pákkămùck?	Wer hat dich geschlagen, oder wer war es, der dich schlug.
They hit.	Opákkămăwă.	Sie schlugen.
They have hit him.	Opapachgammawăpănè.	Sie haben ihn geschlagen.
They have hit him with fists.	Otajohonawăhn.	Sie haben ihn mit Fäustem geschlagen.
beaten black and blue	Mechmenájo ajenechtahámak.	Braun und blau geschlagen.
It burst in, broke (into pieces).	Păqŭăk. Păquěwăk.	Es schlägt ein.
It struck into the tree.	Păquătămăk măchtōckŭ.	Es hat in einen Baum geschlagen.
Why do you smash with stones?	Gaquai păkkătămhámma.	Warum schmeistu mit Steinen?
Why are you shoving him?	Gaquai watsche pakkàmmat.	Warum stostu ihn?
Why do you strike, push, touch me?	Gaquai watsch kěěchcănnèt.	Warum { stostu / rührstu } [m]ich an?
He (she) has hit me.	Pagatsche pakkamùck.	Er/Sie hat mich geschlagen.

hit the mark [*see under* shoot]
hither, here

Are you bringing the water here?	Nóctenaspăăn. [Nó = here; c = you]	Holstu Wasser hieher.
Drive (come) hither. Drive this way. [*cf. entries under* drive]	Năŭtăhoossè.	Fahr hierher.

hobble (?) [*noun and verb*] [Happel (a hobble?); happeln (to hobble?)]

[Happel *and* happeln *are obsolete dialect words in German.* Happel *means (1)* blundering person, blockhead, lout, *and (2)* rashness, simple-mindedness, foolishness, *but in the sentence* Ich habe kein Happel, *these meanings would be unintelligible and impossible in the following verbal form:* Du must es happeln, *especially because of the presence of* es (= it). *Furthermore,* happeln *means that one's affairs are not going in a proper manner, they are faltering or are being hampered, or there is a problem that just won't go away. The normal form* hapern *means (1) the same as those for* happeln, *(2)* lack *or* be weak in, *and (3)* act rashly. *Both* happeln *and* hapern *(cognates of English* happen) *are of Low and Middle German origin or else from the East Middle German area, since Schmick was born in Königsberg (= Kaliningrad), Prussia. Furthermore, compare the Alsace-Lorraine word* häpple(n), *which means* to walk unsteadily as of toddlers *or* to stumble about as of oldsters; *thus I conjecture that* happeln, *perhaps under English influence, means* to hobble (a horse) *(in* You must hobble it; I have no hobble*) and the ending -*ăpěn *may refer to a cord (thus a 'short-cord'?; see further), but in Delaware a* hobble *means* glikatepi *and modern German is* humpeln *or* fesseln. *In Mahican for the first part, can Mahican* tach(g)- *mean* short *or* together? *Cf. Delaware (Zeisberger in Trumbull)* taquetto, short, *and (Brinton)* thaquetto, short; tangetto, short, small; tachquiwi, together; *cf. also Nipmuck (Day)* taik8as8, court (= short). *For the second part of the word, cf.* act rashly *with Massachusett (Trumbull)* kakenupshont, making great haste, going very swiftly.]

You must hobble(?) it. (?You must not let it get away.)	Tăchgōgănăpěn. [*cf.* impatient]	Du must es happeln.
I have no hobble.	Stàn gachaneu tachgōganăpe. [not I-have-*neg*.-it short? + ? + cord?]	Ich habe kein Happel.
hoe, pickax, hatchet	wăăxeehégan [e *or* a?]	Hacke
hold, keep [*see at* observe]	—	halten
Hold (*pl.*) me.	Kăkáněnè.	Haltet mich.
hold on, hold firmly	—	halten fest
I hold on.	Niàn n'kăkănimměn. [g g *were crossed out*]	Ich halte fest.
You must hold it firmly (the blood-letting bandage)(*e.g.,* if one has done blood-letting and the wound is bound).	Osámapézò. [Osám- = very, too much]	Du must es (die Aderlassbinde) fest halten, (*e.g.* wenn einer Ader gelassen u[nd] die Wunde verbunden ist.)

English	Mahican	German
holes [see wounds]		
holy	wănĕhk [= beautiful?], wáhnsetschè	heilig(e)
Bible or the Holy Book	wănĕhk ŏsŏᵃhégan	Bibel oder das Heilige Buch
God, the Holy Ghost	Pachtamáwaas Wáhnsetschè ŏtschitschachquà	Gott Heilger Geist
the Holy Ghost	Wăh'nssetsche otschitschachquan	der Heil[ige] Geist
hominy [see grits]		
honor, respect [verb] [see also honor, revere, esteem]		ehren *honorare*
Respect me. Honor me.	Macháneme.	Ehre mich.
Respect him.	[Macháne]mà.	Ehre ihn.
He respects me.	Machánemuk.	Er ehret mich.
I revere you as my savior (lord).	Nia kmachánemen muchtsche ánaṳ Tap[ánemuc]quak. [u *not* a]	Ich ehre dich als meinen Heiland.
We (both) will honor the Savior.	Machanemătaù *(Dual[is])* Pacht[amawãās]nau.	Wir wollen den Heiland ehren.
respected man	machanemuksêêd	geehrter Mann
not respected, despised [*q.v.*]	matanemuksêêd	nicht geehrt, verachtet
He despises me.	N~~matánemuk~~. [*crossed through once*]	Er verachtet mich.
He despises you.	K[matánemuk].	~~Er~~ [verachtet] dich. *etc.* [Er *crossed through by error?*]
honor, revere, esteem [*verb*]	—	ehren, hochachten
I honor him.	Nià ntannewanemáu.	Ich ehre ihn.
You (*pl.*) must revere me as your God.	Nia annewaneméẽk kpachtamawasoa n'háckay.	Ihr sollt mich ehren als euren Gott.
Why do you revere the man?	Gaquatsch annowanemájan na némana.	Warum ehrstu den Mann?
He respects or honors me.	Nia ntannewanemócku.	Er ehret mich.
Let us honor Brother Spangenberg.	Annowanematŏŏk kétachcanak Spbg.	Last uns Bruder Spgb [*sic*] ehren.
[On Schmick's ms. pp. (34) and (127) Spgbg, Spbg, Spgb, and Sp represent the surname Spangenberg for Josua Spangenberg.]		
The crucified one we revere.	Na schépŏchquătăhăséda niána ntănnĕwănĕmána.	Wir ehren den Gecreuzigten.
The brothers honor me too much.	Kaha netachcanak nosame annewanemegáãk.	Die Brüder ehren mich zu viel.
But you must respect him.	Anuwéwe náhane mosachpéwe. [more must *or* so?]	Sondern must ihn hochachten.
hope [*verb*]	—	hoffen
I hope.	Ntĕnĕtáha.	Ich hoffe.
I hope she will come.	Ntĕnĕtáha ene páu.	Ich hoffe sie wird kommen.
Hope!	Anetáha.	Hoffe.
Do you hope?	Kt̲enetahà. [e *blotted over* a]	Hoffst du?
He (D.) hopes.	Anetaháu D.	Er hoffet.
We hope.	Ntenetahahanà. Ntĕnĕtāhāh'nà.	Wir hoffen.
You (*pl.*) hope.	K[tenetaha]hamà.	Ihr [hoffet].
They hope.	Anetaháwak.	Sie [hoffen].
I hope Joseph will come today.	Nia ntenetahà nóno éne pau Joseph.	Ich hoffe, Joseph soll heute kommen.
have hope [*cf.* wish that]	—	Hofnung haben
I hope.	Nnachgána.	Ich hoffe.
You hope.	K[nach]ganáu.	Du hoffest.
He hopes.	O[nach]ganà.	Er [hoffet].
We hope.	Knachgananaù.	Wir hoffen.
You (*pl.*) hope.	Kiáwa knachganawà.	Ihr [hoffet].
They hope.	Nĕĕk onachganawàk.	Sie hoffen.
I have great hope.	Niachkéẽp mache nachgawosè.	Ich habe grosse Hofnung.
I have great hope [that] Bathsheba will get well.	Nia nachgawosè machè chàn onammanisseẽd Bathseba.	Ich habe grosse Hofnung Baths[eba] soll gesund werden.
[*translation to match German only:* I hope Spangenberg will help me. I hope, if Sp. comes, he will help you. *See literal translation under the recast sentence below the Mahican.*]	Kahanachganàu Spgbg. changãăp pãăd nachtamakquãăm [*or*] knachtamaquãăm. [*as on ms. p. (127); perhaps sentence should be recast thus:*] Kahanachganàu }Spgbg. pãăd{ nachtamakquãăm [*or*] Changãăp } { knachtamaquãăm.	Ich hoffe Sp. [Spangenberg; *see note under* honor] wird mir helfen. Ich hoffe, wenn Sp. kommt, er wird dir helfen.
[Yes, *or* truly] I hope that } when [Brother?] Spangenberg comes { he will help me, *or* I wish that		he will help you.

hope that [see wish that]
horn [see blow a horn]　　　　　　weweén　　　　　　　　　　　　　　das Horn
horse [the one who carries on his back]　nachnióges, náhnióges, nachnajóges　Pferd
　　[cf. Massachusett nahnaiyeumooadt, a horse, a creature that carries; Delaware (Brinton) nenajunges or (Trumbull) nanayun-
　　ges or (Nora Thompson Dean, 1982) nehənayúngɛs or sometimes nehənaónges, from nayúma, I carry him on my back;
　　Nipmuck (Day) nanai8ghets; contrast Menominee (1975) pǣsekokasiw, one-nail-he-has, and Cree mistatim, big-dog]
　　The horse is my own.　　　　Wăntèi nachnióges tappanemàu.　　Das Pferd ist mein eigen.
　　The horse is brown.　　　　　Náhnióges sekkàpamuksò.　　　　Das Pferd ist braun.
　　The horse was mine.　　　　　Nan nachnajóges nága. [see end of　Das Pferd ist mein gewesen.
　　　　　　　　　　　　　　　　　　Pronominal affixes]
　　How many horses?　　　　　　Kăcha nachnióges?　　　　　　　　Wieviel Pferde?
　　Is a horse there?　　　　　　　Nachnióges nhà?　　　　　　　　　Ist ein Pferd da?
　　This horse belongs to John.　　Johannes hŏnāchnăjŏksĕmà.　　　Dis Pferd gehört Joh[annes].
　　The horse belongs to Joshua.　Josua hŏnāchnăjōxĕmà.　　　　　Das Pferd gehört dem Josua.
　　The horse is ambling along.　　Ounamachnáu [nachnióges].　　　Das Pferd geht den Pass.
hot ashes　　　　　　　　　　　　xep'quachtáu　　　　　　　　　　heisse [Asche]
hothouse for vapor baths [see sweathouse]
hour, o'clock [see also sand]　　　tschenuáka　　　　　　　　　　　Uhr
　　[basic meaning: sound (verb), ring, call; see last entry under sound (verb)]
house　　　　　　　　　　　　　　[weēquachm]　　　　　　　　　　Haus
　　He has gone into the house.　　Wéquăchmŭk áwu.　　　　　　　Er ist ins Hauss gegangen.
　　He has gone into his house.　　Wĕkeed áwu.　　　　　　　　　　Er ist in sein Hauss gegangen.
　　Sleep in the room.　　　　　　Wequamick gawè.　　　　　　　　Schlaf in der Stube.
　　I am glad that you came home,　Netanneména áne wékian pajàn.　Ich freue mich, dass du zu Haus
　　　or Welcome home.　　　　　　　　　　　　　　　　　　　　　gekommen. oder Willkommen zu Haus.
　　No, I have no house.　　　　　Stà weékma ngàchchănéu.　　　　Nein, ich habe kein Hauss.
　new house　　　　　　　　　　　[oskékăn] weékma, uskégăn weĕk'ma　neues Hauss
　in the new house　　　　　　　　oskēkămà weékmă, uskégămà [week'ma]　im neuen Hauss
　　I will build a house.　　　　　Wékwăchmŏnĕchtà.　　　　　　　Ich will ein Hauss bauen.
　　I will cover my house.　　　　Tăphāsēnăk.　　　　　　　　　　Ich will mein Hauss decken.
　　Have you covered your house?　Kĕschăchpāhāchkăsò weékma?　　Hastu dein Hauss gedecket?
　　My wife is at home.　　　　　N'wénajoom wékmachmuk hăjòu.　Meine Frau ist zu Haus.
　　My wife is not at home.　　　 N'wénajoom stà wékmăchmūk hăjĕwe.　Meine Frau ist nicht zu Hauss.
　　My husband is at home.　　　Wáchiă hajòu wékmăchmūk. [sic accents　Mein Mann ist zu Hauss.
　　　　　　　　　　　　　　　　　　and first m; cf. husband]
　　My husband is not at home.　Wáchiă stà hăjĕwĕ wékmăchmūk.　Mein Mann ist nicht zu Hauss.
　　John, go into the house.　　 (Johannes) Wéquaǎměngà.　　　　Joh[annes] geh ins Haus.
　into the little house　　　　　　wekwachmsik　　　　　　　　　　ins kl[eine] Häusgen
how . . . [see also death]　　　　 ŏtēnnè, otennè [?]; ānĕtsch [?; see at teach]　wie . . .
　. . . how bad it is. [see see]　　. . . otennè năchkĕssèhn. [cf. two under see]　. . . wie bös es ist.
how long? [see how long? under　tăn ănĕquèchquè, tăn ănĕquéchque　wie lang?
　when?; see also ready; more]
　How long has he been ready?　[Tăn ănĕquèchquè] okeschanachgaăn.　Wie lang ist er fertig?
how many?　　　　　　　　　　　káchcha, kăcha; kăchwàk, kăăchŏwàck　wieviel
　　　　　　　　　　　　　　　　　kwatscheĭ [= how many!]
　How many arrows do you have?　Káchcha nà képan? [How many those your　Wieviel Pfeile hastu.
　　　　　　　　　　　　　　　　　arrows?]
　How many horses?　　　　　　Kăcha nachnióges?　　　　　　　　Wieviel Pferde?
　How many children do you have?　Kăchwàk ktäjōmăk.　　　　　　 Wieviel Kinder hastu?
　How many are on guard?　　　Kăăchŏwàck achcòhékătscheĕk.　　Wieviel wachen.
　Oh how many white people!　　O kwatscheĭ tschachcósak!　　　　O wieviel weisse Leute.
how much?　　　　　　　　　　　tăn　　　　　　　　　　　　　　　 wieviel
　How much does it cost?　　　　Tăn ktennochkăhn.　　　　　　　　Wieviel kostets.
however [see also but]　　　　　　psùkquèĕk　　　　　　　　　　　　aber doch
huckleberry, bilberry, whortleberry　ménan　　　　　　　　　　　　　Heidel[beere]
hug [see under neck]
humble, meek　　　　　　　　　　　　　　　　　　　　　　　　　　demüthig
　They are small of heart, or meek.　Tsackĕschéschĕwà otāhăwà.　　　Sie sind von Herzen klein oder demüthig.
　　　　　　　　　　　　　　　　　Tsackĕschéssĕwa otāhăwà.
hungry　　　　　　　　　　　　　　—　　　　　　　　　　　　　　　hungrig
　I am hungry.　　　　　　　　　Ngattópe. N'gatópe.　　　　　　　Ich bin hungrig. 1 Sing.
　You are hungry.　　　　　　　　Gatopè. [single -t- prob. incorrect through-　Du bist hungrig.
　　　　　　　　　　　　　　　　　out]

Are you hungry for fish?	Gattope namaássak.	Bist du hungrig nach Fischen.
He is hungry.	Gattópu. Gatópu.	Er ist [hungrig].
We are hungry.	Gattopechnaù. N'gatopech'nà.	Wir s[in]d hungrig.
You (*pl.*) are hungry.	[Gattopech]mà. Gatopechmà.	Ihr seid [hungrig].
They are hungry.	Gattópuak. Gatópuak.	Sie s[in]d [hungrig].
hunt, go hunting [*see also* chase]		jagen gehen
I will go hunting.	N'tànnawè. Ntānnăwè.	Ich will jagen gehen.
He has gone hunting. [maw- = go?]	Mawannawéwua. Mawannawèwua.	Er ist jagen gegangen.
They have gone hunting.	[Mawanna]wéwak.	Sie sind jagen [gegangen].
Now it is a good day [*not* weather] to hunt.	Nono onachkamáo ahánawémik.	Nun ist gut Wetter zu jagen.
I am going hunting. (*Delaware*) [*see comments under* Delaware words]	Nětanmessè āllāūwéwak. [Nětanmessè] āllāūwěěk.	Ich gehe auf die Jagd. *Dell.* [*sic*]
It is time to go hunting.	T'peskāwěchnāŭ āchenāquechk anawěmuk.	Es ist die Zeit jagen zu gehen.
hurt [*verb*], be in pain [*see also* pain]	–	Schmerz haben
I have a great pain.	Nmămáchāchwăhntam.	Ich habe grossen Schmerz.
My hands hurt.	Wěnămăttăm náchcan.	Meine Hände thun mir wehe.
My foot hurts me. [*see also* headache]	Nséěd wěnămăttàm.	Mein Fuss thut mir weh.
hurt oneself by striking, take offense	–	stossen sich
Don't take offense. Don't hurt yourself.	Tschěěk ketaktachenahàn.	Stoss dich nicht.
husband, (my) husband	wāchĭǎ́, wáchĭǎ́	mein Mann
My husband is at home.	Wāchĭǎ́ hajoù wěkmăchmùk. [*sic long marks and first* m; *cf.* house]	Mein Mann ist zu Haus.
My husband is not at home.	[Wāchĭǎ́] sta hăjěwě [wěkmăchmùk].	Mein Mann ist nicht zu Hause.
I (me; my) [*see also* Personal pronouns]	nià, nia, niàn [*for* nià n-?], n-, ne, neáne [= we?; *see* one (Joshua, etc.)]	ich, mich, mein
Why are you asking me?	Gaquai wátsche gutschémohn niákq?	Warum fragstu mich.
Why do they hate me?	[Gaquătsch] schegenawechtéěd nià?	Warum hassen sie mich.
ice [*see* firm]		
if, when [*see also* when; whether]	ăm, ăăm [= will?]; [*verbal suffix*] -kà[?]; psùkquěěk [?; *contrast* but]	wenn
Therefore if (when) someone among us feels that he is sick.	Nè ŭtschè awăn ăm kiánāu ămáttakà, ŏwénamansohăăncùn.	Darum wenn jemand unter uns fühlt, dass er kranck sey.
ill [*see* sick]		
immediately [*see also* as soon as; soon; must]	scháwa, scháwah, schawà, schawăhn	gleich
I will give it to you at once.	Ene scháwa kmenèn.	Ich will dirs gleich geben.
He goes quickly (at once) to the Savior . . .	Scháwah ŏmìschschātăcăăn Pachtamáwaassèk . . .	Er geht geschwind (eilig, gleich) zum Heiland . . .
I am bringing it back at once.	Ene báschŏǎ́ scháwa.	Ich bringe bald wieder.
impatient ('small- or short-hearted'?; pusillanimous?) [*cf.* patient]		ungedultig. klein Herz. (er ist)
He is impatient.	Tăchgētaháu.	Ich bin ungedultig.
I am impatient.	Ntachgetahà.	
You are impatient.	K[tachgetahà].	Du bist [ungedultig].
We are impatient.	[Ntachgeta]hanà.	Wir [sind ungedultig].
You (*pl.*) are impatient.	[Ktachgeta]hamà.	Ihr [seid ungedultig].
They are impatient.	Ktachgetahàwak. [*first* k- *is error?*]	Sie sind [ungedultig].
Remain not in your evil.	Ktaggetaha matechk anè.	Verharre nicht in deinem Bösen.
Don't be impatient.	Tschěěn ktaggetahăăn.	Sey nicht ungedultig.
important		wichtig
That is big and important for us.	Kmachchè katăcŏnānāu.	Das ist uns gross u[nd] wichtig.
improvement, recovery	–	Besserung
in [*cf. also* inside; be (in a place)]	-ik, -ick, tane [*postposition*]	in
in(to) his peace [*cf. under* as]	nè átane ănăchémowáganick	in seine Ruhe
in, into, to [*see under* a, an; as; ask; believe; bring forth; glad; go; honor(?); see(3); tomorrow(?); truly; work]		
inclination [*see also* pleasure]	–	Trieb
I have an inclination (drive) in the heart. [*see* use]	Daūwătăăch anè ndàh.	Ich habe einen Trieb im Herzen.

indeed [*cf.* truly]		
Indians (people)	anenapáwak	die Indianer
Indians	anenápawà [*obv.*], anenapaak, anenápak [*loc.*]	die Indianer
N. likes to go around with the Indians.	N. wegocháu ananapawechgŏ́k.	N. geht gerne mit Ind[ia]nern um.
[Indians?; *see p. 155*]	anapáwechkóók	[*untranslated*]
indicate [*see* show]		
industrious, willing, diligent	Nănippenáu, nahnippenáŭ [= He is industrious.]	*adject[ivum:]* willig, fleissig; fleissig seyn
I am willing, ready, industrious.	Nià nĕchnĭ́ppĕnà.	Ich bin willig, fleissig.
You are willing, industrious.	Knechnĭ́ppenà.	Bistu willig, [fleissig].
He is industrious.	Nach'nănippò.	Er ist [willig, fleissig].
We are industrious.	Nechnepechnà.	Wir sind [willig, fleissig].
You (*pl.*) are industrious.	Knechnepechnà.	Seid ihr [willig, fleissig].
They are industrious.	Năchnĕpŏ̀wàk.	Sie sind [willig, fleissig].
You work diligently.	Anachgà năchnìppĕ̆nămă̆.	Du arbeitest fleissig.
He was industrious.	Nèpnàhp.	Er war fleissig.
Let's be diligent, my brothers.	Kă̆tă̆tĕ̆mŏ́ŏk nĕtă̆chcănăk.	Lasst uns fleissig seyn.
Let's promote (it).	[*? blank or possibly as above?*]	[Lasst uns] fördern.
Let's make haste.	[*? blank or possibly as above?*]	[Lasst uns] fort machen.
infected, by an illness	—	angesteckt (von einer Krankh[eit])
ingenious, artful	—	künstlich
He is ingenious; he can make something.	Tăpă̆năchgáu.	Er ist künstlich, er kan einiges Ding machen.
inherit	—	erben, hinterlassen
I have inherited it from my father.	Nŏŏ́ch nă̆gă̆tă̆chmăgŭ̆nă̆.	Ich habs von meinem Vater geerbt.
I inherited the book from Joseph.	Nagatachmáguna Josep osoehégan.	Ich habe das Buch von Joseph geerbt.
My wife inherits my things, or I bequeath my things to my wife.	Nagatachmawána nwenasŏŏ́m nteẏ́éganan. [ij?]	Meine Frau erbt meine Sachen. oder: Ich hinterlasse meine Sachen me[iner] Frau.
The Savior has bequeathed us his blood as the legacy.	Pachtamawăăs nagatachmaquakùp op'gachganŏ̆m.	Der Heiland hat uns sein Blut zur Erbschaft hinterlassen.
What has your father made over to you, or What have you inherited from him?	Gaquai kócha knackatachmága.	Was hat dir dein Vater vermacht, oder Was hastu von ihm geerbt?
I have inherited nothing.	Stà gáquai nagatachmága.	Ich habe nichts geerbt.
I have inherited <u>the</u> land.	Ne nagatachmága ahhkì.	Ich habe <u>das</u> Land geerbt.
inheritance, portion	gáttaammawĭ́jaăk	Erbtheil
Help your believers and bless what your portion is; wait for them always with your bloody wages.	Nàchtamawe wáhnsettakwanĕĕk, wăk wétahamè gaquai nik kià áne gáttaammawĭ́jăăk, channawèhenana ngommaowe áne p'gachganĕĕth kià kpènhammawágan.	Hilf deinen Gläubigen u[nd] segne was dein Erbtheil ist, warte sie allezeit mit deinen blutigen Verdienst.
inside, within	achtáŭ [*or*] achtáăk	drinne
There is nothing inside.	Stàk gaquai nhachtáwe.	Es ist nichts drinne.
There is a little inside.	Tschachkewesche nhachtáŭ.	Es ist wenig drinne.
It is still inside.	N'haachtáu.	Es ist noch drinne.
What is inside?	Gaquai nechtáu. [*cf.* once]	Was ist drinnen?
Disclose to him all that is in your (*pl.*) hearts.	Máowe mŭchgĕnŭ̆mmăwòk achtáge ktáhawăk.	Offenbaret ihm alles was in euren Herzen ist.
inside, *i.e.*, in the house	—	drinne, *i.e.* im Haus
They are inside.	Nhájuwak.	Sie sind drinnen.
Is he inside?	Nháju?	Ist er drinne.
He is not inside.	Sta nhajéwe.	Er ist nicht drinne.
Are you inside?	Nhaktajè.	Bist du drinne?
I am not inside.	Stà nhantajéwe.	Ich bin nicht drinne.
I am inside.	Nhántajè.	Ich bin drinne.
We are inside.	Nhantajehenà.	Wir sind drinne.
We are not inside.	Stà nhantajewehenà.	Wir [sin]d / ~~Ihr~~ seid nicht drinne.
Are you (*pl.*) inside?	N'haktajehemà.	Seid ihr drinne?
You (*pl.*) are not inside.	Sta haktajehewehemà.	Ihr seid nicht drinne.
They are inside.	Nhájuwak.	Sie sind drinne.
They are not inside.	Sta nhajéwek.	Sie sind nicht drinne.
Have you been inside?	Nhammàchtsch ktajè?	Bist du drinne gewesen.
I have not been inside.	Stà nhammachtsch ntajéwe.	Ich bin nicht drinn gewesen.

Has he been inside?	N'hammachtsch ajù.	Ist er drinne gewesen.
He has [not] been inside.	Stà nhammachtsch ajéwe.	Er ist [nicht] drinn gewesen.
We have been inside.	Nhammachtsch ntajehenà.	Wir sind drinne gewesen.
We have not been inside.	Sta [nhammachtsch] ntajewehenà.	[Wir sind] nicht [drinne gewesen].
Have you (*pl.*) been inside?	Nhammachtsch ktajehemà.	Seid ihr drinne gewesen.
You (*pl.*) have not been inside.	Stà [nhammachtsch] ktajewehemà.	Ihr seid nicht [drinne gewesen].
They have been inside.	Nhammachtsch ájuwak.	Sie sind drinne gewesen.
They have not been inside.	Stà [nhammachtsch] ajéwek.	Sie sind nicht [drinne gewesen].
intention	–	Absicht
interior [*see* internal]		
internal, interior, spiritual	otàwāwĭck	innerlich
into [*see under* in]		
it [*see* he?]	éja, nàn [?], nè [?]	es
No, it lies scattered about.	Stà, éja ptschèssessáchga.	Nein, es liegt zerstreut.
It is not right. [not that/it]	Astàn nè.	Es ist nicht recht.
It is right.	Nàn nè.	Es ist recht.
That is it.	Nè àht.	Das ist es.
its [*see* Pronominal affixes]		

jab [*see* stab]		
jealous, envious	–	eifersüchtig, *jaloux* [French word]
I am jealous, envious.	Nià nkakunána. Nià ngagunána.	Ich bin *jaloux*.
He is jealous, envious.	Kakunanáu. Gagunáu.	Er ist *jaloux*.
joy [*see* pleasure]		
joyous [*see* glad]		
juicy (soft and pliable?)	–	saftig
I make the <u>hide</u> (or <u>skin</u>) juicy (soft and pliable?).	Dĕnnāāknáŭ cha<u>ì</u>.	Ich mache die Haut (das Fell) saftig.
jump, leap, spring	–	springen
I jump.	Nkschechnà. Nxechnà.	Ich springe.
You jump.	Kschechnà. G[xechnà].	Du [springst].
He jumps.	Ksechnáu. Xechnáu.	Er [springt].
We jump.	Ksechnahanà. Xechnahanà.	Wir springen.
You (*pl.*) jump.	[Ksechnaha]mà. [Xechnaha]mà.	Ihr [springt].
They jump.	[Kschechná]wak. [Xech]náwak.	Sie [springen].
Jump quickly.	Kschechnà.	Spring hurtig.
jump (leap, spring) across (over there)	–	hinüberspringen
I will jump across.	Ntäusātscháčken.	Ich will hinüber springen.
just [*see* fair]		
just [*cf.* already]	tájachkàm, schachagéwe	gerade
He has just gone. [*sic*]	Schĕmà nòómen. [nòómen = I come]	Er ist eben gegangen.
He has just gone there.	Tájachkàm otàhn.	Er ist gerade dorthin gegangen.
He follows just the Savior.	Schachagéwe nosochgowáu Pachtĺamawāás].	Gerade folgt er nach dem Heiland.
Tell just us. Just tell us.	Anēnānà niáne.	Sag uns nur.
just alike [*see under* time]		
just as ... so ...	nĕáne ... áhanè ...	so wie
Just as the <u>little children</u> are born, so has he been born.	Nĕáne machtappétap <u>awaschees</u>, áhanè machtappēéd.	Er ist geboren werden, so wie die kleine Kinder.

keep [*see* hold; observe; *cf.* have]		
Keep, retain, remember (namely, the letter or word, verse).	Channawahnta. [*contrast* wish]	Behalte (*scil[icet]* die Buchst[abe] oder Wort, Vers).
keeping, preservation	–	Bewahrung
in your keeping	kàchchannawétowaganick	in deine Bewahrung
kettle [*see also* hang up the kettle (over the fire); kettle *under* Delaware words]	hŏŏs	Kessel
Remove the kettle.	Nochpána hŏŏs.	Rück den Kessel ab.
Whose kettle is this?	Awãn nò nŏtăhósa?	Wem ist der Kessel?
kind [*see under* good]		
kindle [*see under* fire]		
kiss [*verb*]	–	küssen
Kiss me.	Machgáwe. Machgawè.	Küsse mich.

They are kissing each other.	Măchgāwutoàk.	Sie küssen einander.
That we thereby kiss his bloody hands and feet.	Nahk'ma p'gachganeék onáchgan wăk osétan neén kaăm aikè kmachgaátamnánaan.	Dass wir seine blutigen Hände und Füsse daran küssen.
kitchen, in the	átan t'póchcamik	in der Küche
knife	chégan	Messer
my knife [see Pronominal affixes for sentences]	n'tachégan, tăchégan	mein Messer
straight razor [see also scraper under Delaware words]	machmŏŏschmachtámik	Balbier-Messer
knitting needle [see sewing needle]		
knock, knock at, rap, pound [q.v.]	—	klopfen an
Knock; it must (will) be open(ed?).	Pŏpāk'hà éne ktăŭnŏmága.	Klopfe an es soll aufgethan werden.
I will knock.	Pŏpak'hámmen.	Ich will anklopfen.
Have you knocked? Did you knock?	K'popak'hămmen.	Hastu angeklopft.
No, I will not knock.	Stàk staăm n'popak'hammówun.	Nein, ich will nicht anklopfen.
know, be acquainted with [see also know, have knowledge of; understand]	nosse	kennen
I know, am acquainted with.	N'wawehául.	Ich kenne.
You know, etc.	K[wawehául].	Du [kennst].
He knows.	Owawehául.	Er [kennt].
We know.	N'wawehána.	Wir kennen.
We know it. We know.	Kwáwehanánau.	Wir wissen es. Wir wissen.
You (pl.) know.	K[waweha]wà. Kwawehawa.	Ihr [kennt]. Ihr wisset.
They know.	O[wawehá]wak.	Sie [kennen].
They know.	Wawehawa.	Sie wissen.
I don't know.	Stà n'wawehawe.	Ich kenne nicht.
You don't know.	Sta k[wawehawe].	Du [kennst nicht].
He doesn't know.	[Sta] o[wawehawe].	Er [kennt nicht].
We don't know.	Stà newawehaweunà.	Wir kennen nicht.
You (pl.) don't know.	[Sta] kwawehawewà.	Ihr [kennt nicht].
They don't know.	[Sta] wawehawewáu.	Sie [kennen nicht].
I am not acquainted with him.	Astán wáwèchtawùn nà nè.	Ich kenne ihn nicht.
You know me well, or they know me, or they are known to me.	Náwawehóka.	Du kennst mich gut, oder sie kennen mich, oder sie sind bekannt mit mir.
We will (want to?) get to know the Savior.	Wawehataù kattau Tapanmukquak.	Wir wollen den Heiland kennen lernen.
Let's get acquainted.	Wawehatŏŏk.	Last uns kennen lernen.
Do you know the man?	Kwawehául némana.	Kennstu den Mann.
Do you know the woman?	[Kwawehául] p'chánim.	[Kennstu] die Frau.
One who often or many times thinks (knows?) [a personal name]	Nŏŏssawáhněmà.	Einer der oft oder vielmal denkt
(Let us [take]) { (your?) knowledge that / you(?) know or that is known (?) } that we remain in the belief ...	{ kwáweechtowágan / áne wáwěhàk } nàn nè ndàìjeenanà onìstămawágan ...	(lass uns) Erkenntnis zu nehmen dass wir / im Glauben bleiben ...
know, have knowledge of, understand [see also know, be acquainted with; understand]	—	wissen
I know why ...	Niàn wāwěchtan wátsche ...	Ich weiss warum ...
I know where ...	N'wawechtà atanněetsch ...	Ich weiss wo ...
He lets know.	Wáwechtanaăn. Wèchtamawaăn.	Er lässt wissen.
Because or as long as we know.	Quaăm kiánau kwawèchtănănău. [yes?]	Dieweil wir wissen.
We know it. We know.	Kwáwehanánau.	Wir wissen es. Wir wissen.
You (pl.) know.	Kwawehawa. K[waweha]wà.	Ihr wisset. Ihr [kennt].
They know.	Wawehawa.	Sie wissen.
I don't know him.	Astán wáwèchtawùn nà nè. Astán wawèchtawùn nànè.	Ich kenne ihn nicht.
I don't know it.	Astán wāwěchtáwa.	Ich weiss es nicht.

English-Mahican-German 89

Don't you know it?	Àsch kwawèchtawa?	Weistu es nicht.
They don't know it.	Astà wáwechtawanáwa.	Sie wissens nicht.
Don't you (*pl.*) know it?	Asch kwawèchtawanáwà?	Wisst ihrs nicht?
I have not known it. I didn't know it.	Astàn niàn wawèchtawà.	Ich habe es nicht gewust.
They didn't know about it.	Astàn wawèchtawanawà.	Sie habens nicht gewust.
They know what I have said.	Néĕk owáwechtanáwa gaquai nià ãánè tŏhnháijè.	Sie wissen, was ich geredet habe.
knowledge (your?)	kwáweechtowágan	Erkenntnis

lack [*see* delay]
Lackawanna [*see under* Delaware words, "Lechchawáchneek"]
lame [*see* crippled]
lamp [*see* light]

lancet (to have a)	—	Schnepper haben
I don't have my lancet.	Stàn gachanéu tāchtăgămŏăhtámuk.	Ich habe meinen Schnepper nicht.
[My lancet] is not sharp.	Stà gĕgánŏwè.	M[ein] Schnepper ist nicht scharf.
land, earth, ground	ahhkì, ăhkì	Boden, Grund, Land
on the ground	ahhkéĕk	auf Grund

landed [= arrived] [*see under* come; ship]
large [*see* great]
lash [*verb*] [*see* whip (*verb*)]

last	—	lezt
At last (finally, at the end) he died.	Wawutāk ŏnèppuwătāmĕnãáp.	Auf die lezt ist er gestorben.
last year, the other year	ktàk kateèk	vorm Jahr
last long		währen
It will not last long.	Astà ãám schépăkàjēwè.	Es wird nicht lange währen.
late	męchkaù	spät
It is not good [for you (*pl.*)?] to come together so late.	Astaù ŏnìttówe mę́chkaù kmajáwenáwa.	Es ist nicht gut so spät zusammen zu kommen.
laugh	—	lachen
I'm laughing.	N'wawanahntàm. N'wawanãntam.	Ich lache.
Why are you laughing?	Gaquai wătĕnãdămmèn? Gaquai wătschonádammen. Gaqua tnátamen. [*note* Gaqua *has no* -i]	Warum lachstu? Warum lachst du?
I'm not laughing at you.	Stak kwawanenáno.	Ich lach dich nicht aus.
He laughs.	Xr. [= Christian] wawanáhntam.	Er lacht.
We laugh.	N'wawanãhntamhanà.	Wir lachen.
Why are you (*pl.*) laughing?	Gáqua t'natamãqu.	Warum lacht ihr?
They laugh.	Wawanahntamãk.	Sie lachen.
They laugh.	Onãdam.	Sie lachen.
negat[ive]		
Don't laugh.	Tsche wăwănãntammhàn.	Lache nicht.
You are still laughing.	Kwawanantàm.	Du lachst doch.
Aren't you laughing?	Asch kwawanantammówe.	Lachstu nicht?
He isn't laughing.	Stà wawanãntammówe.	Er lacht nicht.
We aren't laughing.	Stà nwawanãntammowuhanà.	Wir l[achen nicht].
You (*pl.*) aren't laughing.	Stà wawunantammowéĕk.	Ihr lacht nicht.
They aren't laughing.	Stà wawanantammawéĕk.	Sie lachen nicht.
Yesterday I laughed a lot.	Wanaquéga muchtsche n'wawanãntam.	Gestern hab ich recht gelacht.
Didn't you (*pl.*) laugh?	Asch kwawanantammowuhanà?	Habt ihr nicht gelacht?

laundry [*see* washhouse]

lay [*see under* edge; put?]	—	legen
Put wood on the fire.	Māttăchàn.	Leg Holz zum Feuer.
Did you lay the wood in a woodpile?	Knimmăchtanè machtachanàn.	Hastus Holz auf einen Holz[hau]fen gelegt.
lay down one's life, die	—	sein Leben lassen
He (has) laid down his life for his congregation (church).	Op'maosowágan nĕ ŭtăchtănáăp Gemĕ́nde.	Er hat s[ein] Leben gelassen vor s[einer] Gemein[d]e.
The Savior has so loved us that he (has) laid down his life [for us].	Pachtamawaas wasáme achwahnuquáqua nannu gnackattumakunánau nè p'mawosowágan.	Der Heiland hat uns so sehr geliebet, dass er s[ein] Leben gelassen hat.

English	Mahican	German
I will lay down my life [for you].	Kia gnackatt<u>e</u>mánen p'mawosowagan. [you]	Ich will mein Leben lassen.
Let him live; I will die for him.	Pmawoseĕtsch niàn nippen.	Lass ihn leben, ich will für ihn sterben.
lazy, indolent	–	faul *piger* [*Latin*]
I am lazy.	Nkechtem'nà.	Ich bin faul.
I am not lazy.	Stà nkechtemm'nàwe.	Ich bin nicht faul.
You are lazy.	Kechtemm'nà.	Du bist [faul].
He is lazy.	Kahtem'náu.	Er ist faul. *piger*
lazy	katemnáu	faul
We are lazy.	Nkechtemm'nahanà.	Wir s[in]d [faul].
You (*pl.*) are lazy.	[Kechtemm'na]hamà.	Ihr seid [faul].
They are lazy.	gKechtemm'náwak.	Sie sind [faul].
lead [*the metal*]	ŏtāchăsèn, w<u>a</u>chtachasèn, taggasèn, otackasèn [-asen = stone]	Bley
leaf [*cf.* sheet of paper]	wanépak, *plur[alis]* wănēpăchquàn	Blatt
maize leaf	onúkquask	Welschkorn[blatt]
a sheet of paper, a leaf	gútta népăchkè	Ein Blatt
one who stays under many leaves	Ănáwèpăkòchq [*see also* Rachel *at* Names]	Die unter viel Blätter bleibt.
league [*see* covenant]		
leap [*see* jump]		
learn [*see also* experience; *cf.* teach]	–	lernen
Will you learn?	Gattaù gagachgĕmgè?	Wiltu lernen?
Will you (*pl.*) learn?	[Gattaù] gagachgemgachmà.	Wolt ihr lernen?
We want to (will) learn (*i.e.*, go to school).	Kianŏk gachgem'gatŏŏk. Kianŏk kachkeēm'gatŏk.	Wir wollen lernen (*i.e.*, in die Schule gehen).
But the children must learn.	Nŏk găgāchgēmgŏsōāk ăwăsēsăk.	Aber die Kinder müssen lernen.
leather [*cf.* hide, skin]	wegagedcheì	Leder
Do you have leather?	Gachanè wegagēĕdcheì.	Hastu Leder.
I haven't any leather.	Sta ngachanéwe wegagedchei.	Ich habe kein Leder.
He doesn't have any leather.	Sta gachanéwe wegagetschè cheija.	Er hat kein Leder.
leave	–	lassen
Don't leave me.	Tscheēn pŏněnéhàn.	Lasst mich nicht.
Let go of him. Leave him alone.	Pŏněna.	Lass ihn los.
ledge [*see* edge]		
left, left-handed	nm'natschéwe	link
I am left-handed.	N'menachtschè.	Ich bin link.
You are left-handed.	K[menachtschè].	Du bist [link].
He is left-handed.	Menatschéu.	Er ist [link].
We are left-handed.	N'menachtschehenà.	Wir sind link.
You (*pl.*) are left-handed.	K[menachtschehe]mà.	Ihr seid [link].
They are left-handed.	Menatschéwak.	Sie sind [link].
on the left side	omenachtschewanìk otakquè	auf der linken Seite.
leg	năchgāchquān [*cf. nkəχkwan*, Swadesh]	Bein
long legs	–	lange Beine
shin, shinbone, tibia	nagáchquan	Schien[bein]
short legs	–	kurze [Beine]
swollen legs	–	geschwollen [Beine]
thick or stocky leg (my?)	n'. păăm [*sic*] *or* nachpăhm	dick [Bein]
your leg	kia gagáchquan	dein [Bein]
lend, borrow *or* borrow, lend	–	leihen oder lehnen oder borgen
I lend to you.	Knattemehenàn.	Ich lehne dir.
I lend my book to Joseph.	Nià nattemeháu Joseph nosoahégan.	Ich lehne dem Joseph mein Buch.
Lend me it.	N'temméhe. N'teméhè.	Leihe oder le[h]ne mirs.
Lend me your scissors.	[N'temméhe] ktackchégan.	Le[h]ne mir deine Schere.
[But?] lend [it] to me.	Pschuk tammēhè.	Borge oder leihe mir.
I borrow from you (*pl.*) your candlestick.	Knattemehenoch'mà was'nanégan ahachtăăk.	Ich lehne euch euren Leuchter.
let	–	lassen, lasst, last, lass
Let it lie there.	Anauunè achtătsch.	Lass das da liegen.
I <u>will</u> let it stay. I <u>will</u> leave it alone.	Anauwéne ănéchen.	Ich wills liegen lassen.

English	Mahican	German
Let him ...	-ĕĕtsch, -ătsch	Lass ihn ...
Let him live.	Pmawosĕĕtsch.	Lass ihn leben.
[contrast let under astray]		
He lets know.	Wáwechtanaã̄n. Wèchtamawaã̄n.	Er lässt wissen.
Let me ...		
I ask him that he will let me look into his pierced side and make my heart bloody.	N'machmátuammàk nahk'ma, nè tákamamukkùp wapuchquanek ne ã̄m wátsche pĕnóchtenĕĕth, wăk nàn dàh ã̄m ánep'gáchganĕĕth.	Ich bitte Ihn, dass er mich wolle in seine d[urch]stochene Seite hineinsehen lassen und mein Herz bebluten.
let see [see at end of see]		
Let us ...	-tau, -taù [we dual]; -tŏŏk, -tŏk [we inclusive]	lasst uns ..., last uns ...
Let's (both) empty it out.	Schegonemotaù.	Lasts uns ausleeren. [Lasts = Last[e]s]
Let's get water together.	Nã̄spataù.	Wir wollen miteinander Wasser holen.
Let's give.	Menátaù.	Lasst uns geben.
Let's help.	Nachtamawátau.	Last uns helfen.
[cf. following two to show first plural ending but different translation:]		
We both will read.	Lesówetaù. [Les- = read, from German]	Wir wollen lesen. Dual[is]
We all will read.	Lesowetŏŏk.	Wir wollen lesen.
Let's get acquainted.	Wawehatŏŏk.	Last uns kennen lernen.
Let's have breakfast.	Najapawepetŏŏk.	Lasst uns frühstücken.
Let's observe it willingly in our hearts.	Néchene awãn äinachachĕĕtsch otáhak. [self who]	Lasst uns nur gerne aufs Herz merken.
Let [it] sound (ring?).	Nánãmãhà taùtaù.	Lass lauten.
Let him loose. Let go of him.	Pónĕna.	Lass ihn los.
lethargic(?) [see sleepy]		
letter [cf. book]	osohégan	Brief
letter (written character)	kpetonáwan	[Buch]stabe
letters that are mute (not heard)	tschechtschenuamegè	stumme Buchstaben
letters that are pronounced [cf. call; sing]		laute Buchstaben
liberate [see free]		
lick	—	lecken
They should lick it.	Nŭchquãtà.	Sie sollens lecken.
lie, tell lies	—	lügen
He also cannot lie.	Asta ã̄m ŏaãk gã̄ggã̄nãnãwèhh.	Er kan auch nicht lügen.
lie (of position)	—	liegen
lies at the breast [see suck]		liegt an der Brust
to lie at the feet	—	zu Füssen liegen
I lie at your feet.	Nià tĕnnĕchăckĕchĕnĕn ksédik.	Ich liege zu deinen Füssen.
Oh Savior, I lie at your feet.	Oi Pacht[amawããs] nià tĕnnĕchăkkechĕnĕn ksédik.	O Heiland, ich liege zu deinen Füssen.
Therefore I lie willingly in the wounds of Jesus.	Ne watsche wege nannãănéchĕnĕ Jesusse papaquaik. [n or m?]	Deswegen liege ich gerne ins Heilandes Wunden.
to lie hard, weak	—	liegen hart, weich
I have stayed firm, hard.	Tessanechganachen.	Ich habe hart gelegen.
I have stayed soft, weak.	Káhă nōtăchgĕchgãnãchĕn.	Ich habe weich gelegen.
I have lain (kept) quiet.	Tschegănĕchĕn.	Ich habe stille gelegen.
to let lie	—	liegen lassen
Let that lie there.	Anauunè achtătsch. [Anauunè = more?]	Lass das da liegen.
I will let it stay. I will leave it alone.	Anauwéne ănéchen.	Ich wills liegen lassen.
lie down, go to bed	—	legen nieder
(You) lie down. Go to sleep.	K'mãügawè. Kmãuŭquà.	Legstu dich nieder.
Go to bed. Go to sleep.	Gawè.	Leg dich schlafen.
Go lie down. Go to bed.	Anàchchakéchè kăuwè.	Leg dich schlafen.
We will go to bed.	Ihà mă̄ŏquãmōtŏk.	Wir wollen uns schlafen legen.
same	Gauwetŏŏk.	idem
Go (pl.) to bed, children.	Gawohnteek ăwãsēsăk.	Legt euch schlafen Kinder.
lie scattered about		zerstreut
It [the wood] lies scattered about.	Éja ptschèssessã̄chga.	Es [das Holz] liegt zerstreut.

life [see also lay down one's life]	p'maosowágan, p'mawosowágan, p°máosowágan	Leben
light [opposite of darkness]	wásaik, wássălk	Licht
It is light [daylight?].	Wássălk.	Es ist Licht.
Mankind loves the darkness more than the light. [cf. Wáchche, p. 155]	Awánetsch achwatachgà páchgenick annuwéwe ne wásaik.	Die Menschen lieben die Finsterniss mehr als das Licht.
light, brightness, candle, candlelight, lamp?, torch? [cf. also candlestick]	wăhs'nanégan	Licht
Is a light there?	Wăhs'nanégan n'hà?	Ist ein Licht da?
I have seen a light here.	Wăhs'nanégan nmachnawẵ.	Ich hab ein Licht hier gesehen.
I will make it bright.	N'wahs'nanemèn. N'waás'nanemèn.	Ich wills helle machen.
Make it bright.	Wăhs'nanè. Waásnanè.	Mache es helle.
He makes it bright.	Ŏwăhs'nanemèn. O['waás'nanemèn].	Er machts helle.
We make it bright.	N'wahs'nanemenána. N['waas'nane]menána.	Wir machens helle.
You (pl.) make it bright.	K[wahs'naneme]náwa. K[waas'naneme]náwa.	Ihr machts [helle].
They make it bright.	O[wahs'naneme]nawàk. O[waas'naneme]náwak.	Sie machens [helle].
The servant puts (snuffs) out the (candle)light.	Ahagenahégaăd otummeschimmen wăhs'nanégan.	Der Diener puzt das Licht.
Move out of my light.	Ktàchcătschŏchquà kámawè nochpajáhxè. [you- ? -you you-go? my? ?]	Geh mir aus dem Lichten.
light(ly) [adjective and adverb] [see easy]		
That is very light [in weight?].	Náhane nĕ nặch nágan.	Das ist sehr leicht.
light a fire [see under fire]		
lightning		
It's lightning.	Wawáchănáhàm.	Es blizt.
like (similar to), as [q.v.]	ánau [?]	wie
They are weak like little children. [see also appear as]	Machtschahawawésuak ánau awásesak.	Sie sind schwach wie kl[eine] Kinder.
like to, would like, readily, willingly	wége, -wége, -wég-	gerne
I like to rest.	Ne wége anachéme. Ne wége tannachéme.	Ich ruhe gerne.
He doesn't want to die. He is dying unwillingly.	Stà wegampówa.	Er stirbt nicht gerne.
Does Joshua want to die? Is Joshua dying willingly?	Wega mpõ Josua.	Stirbt Josua gerne?
Do we die willingly?	Ne wéga npechnà.	Wir sterben gerne?
Do you want to die? Do you die willingly?	Wéga knüpp.	Stirbstu gerne?
I like to eat it.	N'wēgăchtámmen.	Ich esse es gerne.
You like to eat it.	Kwēgŏchtámmĕn.	Issestus gerne.
N. likes to go around with the Indians.	N. wegóchau ananapawechgŏk. [*composed of wége and ajù.]	N. geht gerne mit Ind[ia]nern um. *compos.: von wége u(nd) ajù.
Let us observe it willingly in our hearts.	Néchene awăn äinachachéētsch otáhak. [one's self who]	Lasst uns nur gerne aufs Herz merken.
I would like to feel more of the Savior in my heart.	Niàn tajáhntam annowéwe Pachtamáwaas támmachtammen dáhak.	Ich möchte gern mehr fühlen in meinem Herzen von Heiland.
listen [cf. hear], hearken, overhear	—	horchen
I will listen.	Nkensittawẵn.	Ich will horchen.
Why do you listen?	Gaquatsch knistawojàn?	Warum horchstu.
He listens.	Okensittawáwa.	Er horchet.
We listen.	Nkensittawunà.	Wir horchen.
You (pl.) listen.	K[ensittawa]wà.	Ihr horchet.
They listen to (overhear, eavesdrop on) us.	Kensittakónau.	Sie horchen behorchen uns.
little, small [see also a little]	-s, -sch, -ees, -ēs, -es, -esch [cf. child; creek]	klein(e)
a little book	tschaxēschăk ŏsŏhégan, tschaxĕschăk ŏsŏᵃhégan	ein kleines Büchelgen
little mountain	tschăchgĕschéschĕn wachtschù	kleiner [Berg]
My shoes are too little (small) for me.	Tschatschaxēschne măksĕnĕ. Tschăckĕschĕsan măksen.	Meine Schu sind mir zu klein.
They are small of heart, or meek.	Tsackĕschéssĕwa otăhăwà. Tsackĕschéschĕwà otăhăwà.	Sie s[in]d von Herzen klein oder demüthig.
There is a little inside.	Tschachkewesche nhachtăŭ.	Es ist wenig drinne.

English	Mahican	German
Time is short (little). [see also impatient ('small- or short-hearted'?)]	Tschachquaschéschen majánapowágan.	Die Zeit ist kurz (klein).
live, become alive	–	leben oder lebendig werden
I am or live poor.	[Kat'make] p'máosía.	Ich bin oder lebe arm.
He lives or is blissful (blessed, happy).	Pŏmáoso.	Er lebt, oder ist selig.
He (she) is or lives poor.	Kat'make p'máoseet.	Er/Sie ist/lebt arm.
We live.	Pŏmáŏsēnánău.	[Wir leben.]
You (pl.) live.	[?Pŏmáŏsēna]we. [or] [?Pŏmáŏsēnána]we.	[Ihr lebt.]
They live.	Pŏmaosenáwa.	[Sie leben.]
He lived.	Pŏmáoséŏnăhp.	Er lebte.
where we live, there where we live	átan p'máosémick	wo wir leben, da wo wir leben
So long as I live.	Tăn sàchkăŏsía.	So lang ich lebe.
Let him live.	Pmawoseetsch.	Lass ihn leben.
all the wild ones, or all who live wild	máwe nanáo p'maosétscheek	alle d[ie] Wilde, oder alle die wild leben
He has lived. He lived.	P'mawosoŏp.	Er hat gelebet.
He has revived.	P'máwosòhăăp.	Er hat lebendig gemacht.
He will make us live happily.	Gattaù p'máŏsŏhăănecónau.	Er will uns selig machen.
We are here. We live here.	Pòmájik.	Wir sind hier, wir leben hier.
The Savior has therefore become man, or has therefore lived in the world.	Nam Pachtamawáăs Táp[anemuc]quàk wătsche óhăkkăjéwe tanè pomáosetip nànnéttănè ahhkeĕk. [n or k?]	Der Heiland ist darum Mensch worden, oder hat darum in der Welt gelebet.
live, dwell in	–	wohnen
[that] to(?) live in the new heart.	Nik wáskătkèck tschè ktáhack ŏtájjeen.	In dem neuen Herzen wohnen.
Where do your friends live? Properly, Where do your friends stay?	Thà ăjŏwàk tennangómak?	Wo wohnen deine Freunde? proprie Wo bleiben [deine Freunde]?
living water, springwater	p'măwŏsò mpëi [improper syntax?]	lebendig Wasser, Quellwasser

---

Loan words from European languages in Schmick [see each entry; see also Delaware words and Place names in Schmick]:

Albany, Găstĕnik, [from Dutch kasteel, castle, fort + Mahican -ik, at]

apple, ápenes [see under tree]

bishop, bishop

bottle [pnàsch, from German Flasche?, but cf. Nipmuck (G. Day, p. 49) plas^e, bottle, probably from Dutch fles]

brandy [-wine], p'natt'wĕn

broom, p'nōmĭs

butter, póten [Dutch boter]

cabbage (vegetables), gónan [from German Kohl + Mahican plural -an]

[can; see pitcher]

cat, pussycat, póschees, poschesch [from Dutch poesje /puši/, female cat, kitten (NTD, 1982) + Mahican -s, -sch, little; Goddard (1974) states that "these words cannot come from Proto-Algonquian *pešiwa, Lynx sp[ecies]." Influenced?]

chickens, keképsak [plural reduplicated form of Dutch kip, chicken]

Christmas, Xmess [= Christmess]

congregation, church, Gemẽnde, Geméẽnde [from German Gemeinde]

cows, kójak [cf. Nipmuck (G. Day, p. 49) k8°i and k88i, cow, probably from Dutch koe /ku/; see also stable]

cucumber, kumkùmsch [from Dutch komkommer, from Latin cucumis]

[flask; see bottle]

flax, pnax

money, -mane- [from English; see also silver; cf. Nipmuck (Day, 58; note 456) mannj, money; Abenaki mõni, money, silver]

pay [stem pa-, pajem-, pam- from English]

peach trees, pénĕgĕsàk [see long note at peach trees under tree]

pitcher, kánnisch [from English can? + Mahican -isch, little?]

read [to read = ăchkétă; but additionally, e.g., He reads, Lesówu, thus les-, from German lesen, to read + Mah. -ówu ending]

sheep, mamaksimsàk [from Dutch mekkeren, to bleat?; see sheep]

shirt, my shirt, ntahámed [from hámed, shirt, linen cloth, from Dutch hemd or German Hemd, shirt]

silver, -sehnpatt-, -senpĕtt- [cf. Nipmuck (Day, 1975) sinibat, chinebat, chinibat, money, silver; Munsee šəlpəl, money; wšàlpŏlĕmaš, his small amount of money; from Dutch zilver; silver; cf. zilvergeld, (silver) money (Goddard, 157, in H.C. Kraft: A Delaware Indian Symposium, Harrisburg, 1974, Penn. Hist. Mus. Commission)]

snuff, snùp [from English]

stable? [q.v., from cow]

violin [in Npiŏŏnhaman, I will play the violin; piŏŏn- or piŏn- is likely a corruption of violin; cf. Munsee (Goddard, 1974) păyó:l, violin, from Dutch viool (earlier fiool); but contrast Delaware (Brinton, 1888) achpiquon, flute, fiddle (any musical instrument, Anthony) and unrelated Ojibwa (Baraga, 1878) Nin najabiige, I play on the violin.]

lock [*noun*]	machéganis	Schloss
lock up [*see* close]		
log, block	pòchkschacha̧ąkq	Block
long	–	lang
That is a long word.	Ko̧o̧nnā́ăptónăchkàt.	Das ist ein langes Wort.
the whole day long	kănewachcamắhk, gănŏ́wochgamắk	den ganzen Tag.
For a long time I have seen no maize.	Pajachquénaquat chasquemen.	Ich habe lang kein W[elsch]korn gesehen.
For a long time I have seen no bears.	Pajachquenaxò machquà.	Ich habe lange keinen Bären gesehen.
It is a long time since I have seen you (*sg.*).	Kpaja̧chquenaksè.	Es ist lange, seit ich dich gesehen.
I have not seen them for a long time.	Pajachquenaksoàk.	Ich habe sie lange nicht gesehen.
I have not eaten that for a long time.	Pajachquépogat.	Ich habe das lange nicht gegessen.
They have long since died.	Nawa̧chtà mpŏ́ŏp.	Sie sind lange gestorben.
I have pounded for a long time.	Nawa̧chtà nótschi packhámmen.	Ich habe lange gepocht.
I have not pounded long.	Stà schepachkéwe npópackhămmówun.	Ich habe nicht lange gepocht.
I have known it for a long time.	[–]	Schon lange kan ichs
I have known it for a long time (so do [it]).	Nawachtachgamḗqua.	Ich kan das schon lange (so mach[s?]).
I have not seen my mother for a long time.	Nawachtachgamḗqua astà nanáwe nkĕ́k.	Ich hab meine Mutter lang nicht gesehen.
My father died long ago.	[?Nawachtachgamḗqua?] nŏ́ŏch npŏ́p.	Mein Vater ist schon lange tod.
He has a long beard.	Wachquanechtonajáu.	Er hat einen langen Bart.
So long (as long) as I live.	Tắn sàchkăŏ́sía.	So lang ich lebe.
How long have you (*sg.*) been ready? [*see note under* when?]	Tắn ănĕ́quèchquè keschanachkắắn?	Wie lang bistu fertig?
How long has he been ready?	[Tắn ănĕ́quèchquè] okeschanachgắắn?	Wie lang ist er fertig?
They have long been ready.	Kekeschanachkắ panĕ́ĕk.	Sie sind lange fertig.
long as a finger	nà átắn gútta no̧ŏ́ssà	Wie ein Finger lang
look, view [*noun*]	opènnămèn	Blick
look at, regard, see [*see* see]	–	ansehen, anschauen
The Savior looks at a poor man in his great misery with genuine compassion.	Pachtam[awaas] ŏpĕnàuwāwà kaktĕ́ma̧axétsche áne măchchè ktĕ́mắkắĭhattĕ́ĕt, ktĕ̀màkanemáwak.	D[er] Heiland sieht einen armen Menschen in seinem gro[s]sen Elend mit lauter Mitleiden an.
He looked at it all (all of it).	Nè ŭdèttan máowe náwàhn.	Er sahe das alles an.
He looked at Peter.	Petrussa ŏpènnawáu.	Er sahe Petrus an.
[*see also* let me . . .]		
look at oneself in the mirror, be reflected [*see under* see]		spiegeln sich
look for [*see* seek]		
look like [*see* appear as]		
loose [*cf.* free, set free?]	–	los
Let him loose. Let go of him.	Pónĕna.	Lass ihn los.
It is loose (*i.e.*, the earth or land).	Úskăkájăŭ (ahkì).	Es ist los, locker (*i.e.* die Erde oder Land).
loosen rust [*see* rust]		Rost abmachen
Lord [*see also* God; Savior]	Tapan'mucquak, Tapanemukquak	der Herr
lose	–	verlieren
I have lost.	Ntannachtắn.	Ich habe verlohren.
You have lost.	G[tannachtắn].	Du hast verloren.
He has lost.	Otanachtắn.	Er hat [verloren].
We have lost.	Ntanachtanána.	Wir
You (*pl.*) have lost.	G[tanachta]náma.	Ihr
They have lost.	Otannachtanáwa.	Sie
Don't lose it.	Tschĕ́ ktannachtắn.	Verliers nicht.
Don't (*pl.*) lose it.	Tschĕ́ anechtahăku.	Verliehrts nicht.
Whoever seeks to save his life will lose it.	Awắn op°máosowágan nĕ́ĕchnéowè kwénakà, kakánenik ŏ̀tànắchtắhn.	Wer sein Leben sucht zu erhalten, der wirds verlieren
Whoever loses his life for my sake will find it.	Awắn op°máosowágan ánắchtáắt niàn dennànachkawágan, nàn máchcamen.	Wer sein Leben um meinetwillen verliert, der wirds finden.

lost [see astray]		
lot (much), a lot [cf. much; very; cost]	muchtsche	[viel; recht]
Yesterday I laughed a lot.	Wanaquéga muchtsche n'wawanãntam.	Gestern hab ich recht gelacht.
It's raining a lot.	Machchanahn soognahn.	Es regnet viel.
It's raining hard.	Kschénahn soognahn.	Es regnet stark.
loud, to be loud	măkcheechsè	laut, laut seyn
You are too loud.	Kosáme mamakeéchse.	Du bist zu laut.
very loud	muchtsche [mamakeéchse]	sehr laut
loudly	—	laut
Speak loudly; I cannot hear you.	Mamakeếchse ascha késche ptánnowe.	Rede laut, ich kan dich nicht hören.
Speak loudly.	Mamáăktohnhà. Mamáăktonhà.	Rede laut.
Speak (pl.) loudly.	[Mamáăktohn]hăk. [Mamáăkton]hàk. Mamakeechséqu.	Redet laut.
They speak loudly.	[Mamáăktohn]háwak. [Mamáăkton]háwak. [Mamakeech]sowak.	Sie reden laut.
Don't speak loudly.	Tschĕk kmamaktŏhnhăn. [n written over h] Tschĕk kmamaktŏnhăñn.	Rede nicht laut.
He called loudly.	Machéchsò ằptonáu.	Er rief laut.
He spoke loudly, with a strong voice.	Awà kàchnă macheèchsò. [truly? great- ?]	Er sagte mit gewaltiger Stimme.
love [noun]	achwàhndowágàn, achwohndowágan	Liebe
love [verb] [cf. egotistic]	—	lieben
I love.	N'tachwánen.	Ich liebe.
You love.	Ktachwánen.	Du liebest.
He loves.	Achwanáu. Otachwátamen.	Er liebet.
We love.	Achwanánau.	Wir lieben.
You (pl.) love.	Ktachwanawa.	Ihr liebet.
They love.	Achwanáwan.	Sie lieben.
He loved.	Tachwanăhn.	Er liebte.
He has loved.	Otachwatamóun.	Er hat geliebet.
[Yes] I love you, [my] brother.	Káhà ktachwahnan nétachcan.	Ich habe den Br[uder] lieb.
[Yes] I love you (pl.), [my] brothers.	[Káhà] ktahawahnŏhŏmà netachcanàk.	Ich habe die Brüder lieb.
Don't you need to have love for the Savior?	Àsch ktajátamò Pachtamauus áhnè anàwáhmik.	Verlangstu nicht den Heiland lieb zu haben.
God loves the poor sinner.	Pachtamawaas ach'wahnáu katemaksétsche.	Gott hat die armen Sünder lieb.
He loves us. He is fond of us.	Achwҩáhnĕquáăk.	Er hat uns lieb.
He loves you (pl.).	[Achwҩáhnĕquáăk] kiáwa.	Er hat euch lieb.
How loving he is.	Uténne achwáhnaan.	Wie lieb er hat.
They like us. They are fond of us.	Achwắhnkunque. [n or k?]	Sie haben uns lieb.
We are loved.	Achwąhnquussiàk.	Wir sind geliebet.
But no one must love his wife more than the Savior.	Tschēneēk awăn oténne achwáhnan wĕwa, áne Tapan[emuc]que ăchwáhnăád.	Aber es muss niemand seine Frau mehr lieben als den Heiland.
A man must love his wife as the Savior loves his congregation.	Nemanáu nitschwăk wĕwa ŏtĕnnè channawehăăn Tăpănămŭkquăk ăne channaweĕchtaăd Gemeĕnde.	Ein Mann muss seine Frau lieben, wie der Heiland seine Gemein[d]e.
The Savior loves his congregation [?very much?].	Tap[anamuk]quăk ŏtăchwátămĕn Gemeende.	Der Heiland hat die Gemein[d]e sehr lieb.
The Savior has so loved us that he laid down his life.	Pachtamawaas wasáme achwahnuquáqua nannu gnackattumakunánau nè p'mawosowágan.	Der Heiland hat uns so sehr geliebet, dass er s[ein] Leben gelassen hat.
Why do you love me?	Gaquai wătsch achwánĕăn?	Warum liebstu mich?
I will say why the Savior loves us. [sic no k-]	Nià kwechtammanen ga[quai wáătsch?] achw'ăhnŭquáăkŭ Tap[anemucquak]. Nia wechtammănen ga[quai wătsch?] achwanuquáăkŭ Tap[anamukquak].	Ich will sagen warum uns der Heiland liebt.
The same love must we (both?) also have between ourselves.	Ne achwàhndowágàn kiánau wăk achwàhntetăŭ.	Dieselbe Liebe müssen wir auch unter einander haben.
Mankind loves the darkness more than the light.	Awánetsch achwatachgà páchgenick annuwéwe ne wásaik.	Die Menschen lieben die Finsterniss mehr als das Licht.

English	Mahican	German
love feast, feast, banquet, Communion [cf. Delaware (Brinton) tachquipoagan, feast; cf. love = achwàhndowágàn + -ep'- = ?eat? + noun ending; cf. also Lord's supper (q.v. under supper), tachquachackemahaàn and Tapánemucquak onaquépehn]	táchtaquepuágan, achwahntowep'owãgan	Liebesmahl, L[iebes]mahl, LM
at the love feast	tachtaquépŭăk	beim Liebesmahl
I am glad to see him (your brother) at the love feast (banquet).	N'tannaména áněnăŭ nahk'ma (ketach[gak?]) tachtaquépŭăk.	Ich freue mich dass ich dein Br[ude]r beim L[iebes]m[ahl] sehe.
We are having a love feast.	Tachtaquépĕĕnŏŏk.	Wir haben L[iebes]mahl.
Today we are not having a love feast.	Nònò wáchkamàhk asta ãm tachtaquepéwùn.	Heute haben wir nicht L[iebes]mahl.
Today we will have a love feast (banquet) with the baptized ones, who are joyous.	Nònò wáchcamàhk tachtaquèpéhenŏŏk něěk soognepongsétscheèk wăŭnàchtanaméschĕ̌ĕ̌k.	Heute werden wir L[iebes]mahl haben mit den getauften, die da vergnügt sind.
At 5 o'clock [5 when it rings or calls] the children have a love feast; at 6 o'clock the old ones and all the baptized ones [i.e., Christians] have a love feast.	Nánan tschenuáka awaschesak tachtaquépuak guttáăsch tschenuáka kakatschaíssak wak máowe soognepongsetscheek tachtaquépuak.	Um 5 Uhr haben die Kinder, um 6 die alten u[nd] alle getaufte L[iebes]mahl.
My brother, I have heard you will give or make [made?] a love feast. [see also under hear]	Nétachgan n'tensettàm achwahntowep'owãgan kónechtàh.	Br[uder,] ich habe gehört, du wilt ein L[iebes]mahl geben oder machten.
love-fire, his love-fire	achwáhnămamukquàck nístăŭ	sein Liebes-feuer
low voice [see speak softly under speak]		
luck, fortune, good luck	—	Glück
Go there (i.e., to hunt); I wish you good luck.	Ăněwè pechtáăm gĕttĕménăk. [cf. perhaps]	Geh du hin, ich wünsche dir gut Glück.
lucky, fortunate; happy(?)	—	glücklich
He is lucky.	Ktĕménàkq.	Er ist glücklich.
They are lucky.	Ktĕménakáăk.	Sie sind glücklich.
lunch [see under eat]		
lust, desire	—	Begierde
lust [see pleasure]	—	die Lust
mad [see dumb]		
maiden [see girl]		
maize, corn	chasquéme, chăsquĕ̌mĕ̌, chásquĕ́me, chasquemen	Welschkorn
When will the corn be chopped up?	Tákahtsch wak móhnskăhàm chásquĕ́me.	Wann wird wieder W[elsch]korn behackt.
flower on maize (corn)	osowáno	Blume oder Blüthe am Welschkorn
maize leaf, corn leaf	onúkquask	Welschkorn[blatt]
thin soup of maize	mpejápu	dünne Suppe von Welschkorn
make, do	[? -ănăchga and -echt- suffixes for make?]	machen oder thun
You still cannot do anything.	Kià astà késche dannănàchkăchtăwè.	Du kanst doch nichts thun.
I am not satisfied with you, or it's no use what you do.	Astàn nónătămówun ánănàchcăjàn.	Ich bin nicht zufrieden mit dir, od[er] es taugt nicht was du thust.
The Savior is not satisfied with what you do.	Pacht[amawaas] astà ónătămówun ánanàchcajàn.	Der Heiland ist nicht zufrieden mit den was du thust.
I will build a house.	Wékwăchmŏ̌něchtà. [house + make?]	Ich will ein Hauss bauen.
Don't do [it] that way. Don't make [it] like that.	Tschè nè ktànnănachkàhn.	Mach nicht so.
He does it as he thinks or wills.	Anănăchkaàtsch tãhn ănètahăăt.	Er machts, wie er dencket, oder will.
He has already made [it].	Păggătschĕ ŏtènnanachkăăb.	Er hat gemacht.
It is accomplished, it has happened, or it is done.	Nàn késche ánăchkăhn.	Es ist vollbracht, es ist geschehen, oder es ist gethan.
What evil has he done?	Gaquai nahkmà anè mattà nachkáu. [what he that bad does-he]	Was hat er übels gethan.
... that for us he was made [became like] a man and died.	... náhk'ma ánènăhxétippĕ̌ hakkánáăk, wăk mbŏŏp.	... dass er für uns ist ein Mensch geworden, und gestorben.
I make. I do.	N'onechtăn.	Ich mache.
You make.	Konechtà. Gonechtà.	Du machest.
You will make [it] ... (You are going to have [it] ...) [see under love feast]	kónechtah ... [you-well-make?]	du wilt [es] machen.

English-Mahican-German 97

You make [made] the way [well, smooth].	Ánei konechtà.	Hastu den Weg gemacht.
He makes. He does.	Onechtáu. Onechtáu.[sic]	Er machet.
I have not made or done it.	Stà nonechtáun.	Ich habs nicht gemacht.
	Stà onechtáu(n). [error?]	Ich habs nicht gemacht.
You have not done it.	[Stà] konechtáun. Sta gonechtáu.	Du [hasts nicht gemacht].
He has not done it.	[Stà] onechtáun	Er [hats nicht gemacht].
We make.	Nonechtahanà. N. onechtahanà. [sic]	Wir machen.
You (pl.) make.	Konechtahamà. G. onechtahamà. [sic]	Ihr machet.
They make.	Onechtáwak.	Sie machen.
[see p. 155 at Unèchtawáăk ...]		
Who is making the food for the friends?	Awãn onechtãhn mezowagan tennàngomanáăk.	Wer macht Essen vor die Freunde.
Make me a pair of shoes.	Onechtawè nguttòksenà maksenan.	Mach mir ein Paar Schu.
	Oneĕchtawè nguttò ksenà mãh'ksenan.	Mach mir ein Paar Schue.
Close up or button up your coat (make your coat up).	Ŭneĕchtà kpétăcăsoŏn.	Mach den [for dein?] Rock zu.
You are nice. (You make nice.)	Konanachgà.	Du machst es hübsch.
He has done it willingly.	Nò wége nájìn.	Er hats gern gethan.
He has done it.	Anèhóquanep.	Er hats gethan.
How [is one?] to make it?	Ánăljakquáăm.	Wie es zu machen.
Who has made it?	Awãn õnéhà?	Wer hats gemacht.
I haven't made it yet.	[Achquadhà] nkēschănăchgaŭ.	Ich habs noch nicht gemacht/gethan.
I have done it.	Késchechtãn. Nià késchechtanaáp.	Ich habs gemacht.
You have done it.	Késchechtãn.	2 perf[ectum] idem.
He has done it.	Okeschechtãn.	Er hats gemacht.
No, another (person) has done it.	Stàch, ktàk ogeschechtaan.	Nein, ein ander hats gemacht.
It is done, made.	Keschechtáu.	Es ist gemacht.
We have done [it].	Keschechtahanà.	Wir haben gemacht.
You (pl.) have done [it].	[Keschechta]hamà.	Ihr [habet gemacht].
They have done [it].	[Keschech]táwak.	Sie [haben gemacht].
God has made us.	Pacht[amawaãs] kescheĕchkonáăp.	Gott hat uns gemacht.
God has made me.	[Pachtamawaãs] nkéschehōgŏp.	Gott hat mich gemacht.
God has made you.	[Pachtamawaãs] késchehogoŏp.	Gott hat dich [gemacht].
God has made me.	Pachtamawaãs nkeschehõk.	Gott hat mich gemacht.
God has made you.	[Pachtamawaãs] k[eschehõk].	[Gott hat] dich [gemacht].
God has made him.	[Pachtamawaãs] o[kesche]háwa.	[Gott hat] ihn [gemacht].
God has made us.	[Pachtamawaãs] keschechkónau.	[Gott hat] uns [gemacht].
God has made you (pl.).	[Pachtamawaãs] [keschech]kówa.	[Gott hat] euch [gemacht].
God has made them.	[Pachtamawaãs] okescheháwa.	[Gott hat] sie [gemacht].
God has made everyone [or] everything (the world).	Pachtamawaãs okéschechtánaap maowenù, [or] máowe gáquäi.	Gott hat die Welt (alles) gemacht.
Savior of the world	kékachtátip mawe áněquechkùk ăhkì [he has created, made? all more-on earth]	der Welt Heiland
the Savior of all souls	kékăchquăkùp mawe watschitschàchquajàckq [he has created? all his? souls]	der Heiland aller Seelen
that the one who made everything ...	maowe gáquai kescheechtátip ...	dass der, der alles gemacht ...
make bright, make clear, clarify [see also light]		hell machen
I will make it bright.	N'waás'nanemèn. N'wahs'nanemèn.	Ich wills helle machen.
Make it bright.	Waásnanè. Wãhs'nanè.	Mach es helle.
He makes it bright.	O[waás'nanemèn]. Ŏwãhs'nanemèn.	Er machts helle.
We make it bright.	N['waas'nane]menána. N'wahs'nanemenána.	Wir machen es helle.
You (pl.) make it bright.	K[waas'naneme]náwa. K[wahs'naneme]náwa.	Ihr machts [helle].
They make it bright.	O[waas'naneme]náwak. O[wahs'naneme]nawàk.	Sie machens [helle].

make clean [see clean]
make clear [see make bright]
make over to [see inherit]
make present of [see give me]
make red [see redden]
make sign of cross (?) [see bless]

98 Schmick's Mahican dictionary

make well, make healthy [see also heal, cure]		gesund machen
The Savior will make all mankind (everyone) healthy.	Pacht[amawããs] máowe awan gattau onamackaháãn.	Der Heiland will alle Menschen gesund machen.
Our Savior makes all ill persons well.	Pacht[amawããs] máwe wenamansétsche onamansohána.	Unser Heiland macht alle Krancke gesund.
I will make you healthy.	Kŏnămãnsōhắnĕ ntschè.	Ich will dich gesund machen.
He will make you healthy.	Konamansohánuk tschè. Konamansohánukschè.	Er wird dich gesund machen.
Make me well, or Cure me.	Ŏnămánnissoháne.	Mache mich gesund oder Heile mich.
Make us well. Cure us.	[Ŏnămánnisso]hanenána.	Mache uns gesund. Heile uns.
His wounds and his blood can make healthy, or heal.	Wánamansoháãnquàck áne páquaick wak op'gachganoŏm.	Seine Wunden u[nd] s[ein] Blut kan gesund machen, oder heilen.
so that we could become well or be healed through his wounds.	nikkããtsch kiánau áne páquaick wanamansoháãnquàk.	dass wir durch s[eine] Wunden heil oder gesund werden könnten.
make wood [see under wood]		
malice, spite, naughtiness, badness	măchtschedtāhāwágan	Bosheit
man [see also husband; people]	némana, nemanáu, némanáu, nēmănă; [? tschéscho; see at thin]	Mann, Herr
The man is the head of his wife.	Nēmănă ōwēhnsehn wĕwa.	Der Mann ist das Haupt s[eine]s Weibes.
What is the [that?] man's name?	Gaquai ŏnĕwĕsŏ uwà nēmănă?	Wie heist der Mann?
[He is a] man.	nemanáu	[—]
Manahkse Creek [see Monocasy Creek]		
manifest [see reveal]		
mankind [see Indians; white people; everyone; nations]		
many, a lot, much	macháne, machắne, măchănĕ, măchānāk, machănnta [see below], machchanahn [cf. great]	viel
Oh, I have seen it many times.	Oh măchănĕ nāwáŭ.	O ich habe es vielmal gesehen.
Have you many friends?	Măchānāk ktennangomããk.	Hastu viel Freunde?
many arrows	machănnta wépan [n covers h]	viele Pfeile
Many are coming.	Máchche páwak. [máchche = great (number?)]	Es sind viel gekommen.
It's raining a lot.	Machchanahn soognahn.	Es regnet viel.
There are many	-echgáu.	Es gibt viel(e) ....
There are many fish.	Namããsechgáŭ.	Es gibt viele Fische.
There are many ducks.	Quetschemwechgáu.	Es gibt viel Enten.
The brothers honor me too much.	Kaha netachcanak nosame annewanemegããk.	Die Brüder ehren mich zu viel.
one who often or many times thinks (knows?). [see Judith under Names]	Nŏŏssawáhnemà.	Einer der oft oder vielmal denkt.
mark, the mark, goal, or target at which one shoots [see also under shoot (hit the mark)]	weeshécan [note s + h, not error for sch]	das Merck oder Ziel wornach man schiesset
marks, spots, or moles	—	Maale sehen [= to see marks]
all marks, moles	máowe wechwesáju	alle Marken, Maale
It is (very) good to see the marks.	Muchtsche nawoquátta wēchwēsáju.	Es ist gut zu sehen die Maal.
the spots on the hands, feet, and side	wēchwēsájŭwăn ŏnăchkăn osēdan, wăk wăchpássei	die Maale in Händen, Füssen und Seite
marry; married	—	heirathen; verheirathet
Are you already married?	Kwewè pakatschè	Bistu schon geheirathet?
Certainly, I am already married.	Kahounà pakatschè nŏwĕwĕ.	Freil[ich] bin ich schon verheirathet.
I am already married.	Nŏwĕwĕwechgeĕp.	Ich bin schon verheirathet.
married	wáweepnatiàkq	verheirathet
meal [see food]		
meat, flesh [see also cook meat for usage; roast meat]	wojás, wojās, ojăs, ojããs, wiãs, wĕjăãs, ojààsh; [+ -m?, -n = I] ojasom, ojáson, ojásĕn	Fleisch
I am cooking meat.	Nàtpochkà ojààsh.	Ich koche Fleisch.
I will cut (carve) meat.	Ojáson schókschŏn.	Ich will Fleisch schneiden.
piece of meat	packájis wojás [or wojăs]	[Stück] Fleisch

medicine	nbésohn, béson	Arznei, Arzney

[cf. Delaware (Brinton, 1888) beson ("out of use"), medicine, physic; mbeson (Zeisberger), brandy (spirits, from mbi [= water], Anthony); but Nora Thompson Dean (1982) wrote that bísun is in use for medicine and not brandy or spirits; cf. Nipmuck (Day, 1975) nipisson, medicine]

good medicine	–	gute [Arznei]
bad medicine	–	böse [Arznei]
meek [see humble]		
meet [see assemble]		
meeting [see under assemble]		
melt [see also flow?]	–	schmelzen
It is melting.	Schapasò.	Es schmeltzt.
It is not melting.	Stà schapaséwe.	[Es schmeltzt] nicht.
The butter is melting.	Schapasèch póten.	Die Butter schmelzt.
I have already melted it.	Nkésche schăpōsŏmèn.	Ich habs schon geschmolzen.
I will melt it away, dissolve it.	Nschapásomen.	Ich wills zerschmelzen.
Melt it.	Schapasè.	Schmelz du es.
He is melting lead.	[Schapa]sèm otackasèn.	Er schmelzt Bley.
melt away, dissolve [see melt]		zerschmelzen
men [see people]		
mend [see patch]		
merciful, compassionate	–	barmherzig
mercy [see compassion; bless]		
merit [noun] [see wages]		
merit [verb] [see earn]		
message, news, good news	g'patagonaù, "ahamáwaad. wanechk" [see note at messenger]	Botschaft, gute Botschaft
bad news	–	böse
messenger [see also message]	ahamáwaad. wanechk [one word or two words or alternative words?; does wanechk mean beautiful?]	Bote
milk [verb]; [Schmick wrote in English:] to milk		melken
Go & milk the cow. [Schmick wrote the sentence in English.]	Ăhăně sĕnĕănēgà. ['the cow' does not appear in Mahican.]	Geh und melke die Kuh.
I have milked.	Késche sēnĕănēgă.	Ich habe gemelkt.
mill [cf. nail (noun)]	tachquahágan	Mühle
minced [see chopped up]		
mine [see Pronominal affixes]		
minister [see preacher]		
mirror [see under see]	wapachpĕnāúŭs	Spiegel
Take a look at yourself in the mirror.	Pnawòchk hackai wapachpĕnāúŭs.	Besieh dich im Spiegel.
miserable [see poor]		
miserly [see under covetous]		
misery		
in his great misery	áne măchchè ktĕmăkăíhattēĕt	in seinem gros[s]en Elend
missed [see failed]		
mix [see also touch?]	–	mischen
to mix	kōjămachgenimnà	mischen
I mix.	Nià nojamachgenimnà.	Ich mische.
I mix.	[Nià nojamachgenim]men.	idem [= same]
Mix it.	Kià ōjămāchgĕnè.	Mische es.
mixed. [It is mixed.]	Ojamachgenáso.	vermische
grits [potatoes?] and beans mixed [potatoes? mixed with beans]	ahpánan ojamachgenásoan pachgatsche tpachquăăn [for pachgatsche see already, but cf. păchkătschĭn at accustomed]	Akridches und Bohnen vermischt
moles (on body) [see marks]		
money (also silver)	-mane- [English]; -sehnpatt-, -senpĕtt-	Geld
I have no money.	Ne sta nomanehĕméwe. [Ne sta] nósenpĕttĕmēwĕ.	Ich habe kein Geld.
You depend on your money; that will not help you.	Kia kotahnsechmà ksehnpattmèn, asta ăm knachtamagŏunà.	Du verlässt dich auf dein Geld, das wird dir nicht helfen.

100 Schmick's Mahican dictionary

monkey [?, from Bible], ape (?)	nāchntschōhāgāsch [contrast horse]	Affe [= ape, monkey]
Monocasy Creek [see creek]	–	Creek, wie Manahkse [-se covers -es]

[ms. p. (5)]

[*Equated to the place name from G.P. Donehoo:* A History of the Indian Villages and Place Names in Pennsylvania, 1928: MONOCASY. The name of a creek which enters the Lehigh from the north at Bethlehem, Northampton County. A corruption of Menagassi, or Menakessi, meaning "a stream with several large bends," according to Heckewelder. Reichel says in a note (Ind. Names, 256) that Menagachsink was the name given to the site of Bethlehem by the Delawares. **Manakisy.**–Scull, map, 1759 and 1770. **Manookisy.**–Morris, map, 1848. **Monacasy.**–Evans, map, 1749. **Monocasy.**–Recent maps, State map 1911.]

more [see also under must]	annowéwe, ánnowéwe; ?oténne . . . áne?	mehr
better [good-(it-)was more]	Ŏnèttóŏp ánnowéwe.	besser *melius* [*Latin*]
There is nothing greater [more? big].	Astàk gáquai anequèchque m'cháo. [*cf. entry under* when?]	Es ist nichts grössers.
in the whole world [all more-?-in? land]	mawe ănĕquéchkùk ahki	aufn ganzen Lande
[*cf. further*]		
more than	annuwéwe; ?oténne . . . áne?	mehr als
Mankind loves the darkness more than the light.	Awánetsch achwatachgà páchgenick annuwéwe ne wásaik.	Die Menschen lieben die Finsterniss mehr als das Licht.
But no one must love his wife more than the Savior.	Tschĕnĕĕk awăn oténne achwáhnan wĕ́wa, áne Tapan[emuc]que ăchwáhnăăd.	Aber es muss niemand seine Frau mehr lieben als den Heiland.
[*However, in another example (see under* love*) oténne . . . áne is expressed as* as.]		
morning, in the [see early]		
morose [see gloomy; unfriendly; *cf.* dark]		
mosquitoes	pĕkússak	*Muskiters* [*English*], Mücken
The mosquitoes (or gnats) sit and hang onto the eyes and hands.	Pĕkússak nik skĕĕtschkunanìk, knàchkĕnăăk wak ŏmischschakanáwa. okénnamĕnáwa. sezen hängen	Die *Muskiters* (Mücken) sezen sich an den Augen u[nd] Händen, u[nd] hängen.
mother, my mother	nkĕ́k	Mutter
(The child) is calling his mother.	Onattomáwa okeckà.	Es ruft (das Kind) s[eine] Mutter.
mountain, hill	wachtschù, wachtschóu, wachtschò, machtschóu	Berg
big mountain	māchăquăchtschù, măchàttĕnéŭ	grosser [Berg]
big mountains	–	grosse [Berge]
blue mountains	–	blaue [Berge]
by the mountains over there	–	am Berge hin
high mountains	–	hohe Berge
little mountain	tschăchgĕschéschĕn wachtschù, wachtschòhsch [c *or* o?]	kleiner [Berg], Bergel, *dim.*
on the mountain	–	auf dem [Berge]
on the side of the mountain	–	auf die Seite des Bergs.
the other mountain	ktakkan wachtschò	Der andere Berg.
I am going over the big mountain.	Awàssewè măchátscho.	Ich gehe über den grossen blauen Berg. [*disregard* blauen]
there above, upon the hill	Chăchkóŏk.	Droben. Uppon the Hill [*sic*]
mountainous	–	bergicht
mouth, his mouth	otóhnick	Munde
You (*pl.*) have heard from his mouth what he spoke (said).	Kpèttawáwà otóhnick otschè ănăăptŏnăăt.	Ihr habts aus seinem Munde gehört, was er geredet.
move [see touch]		
move along [see push]		
move gently [see crawl]		
move out of		
Move out of my light.	Ktàchcătschŏchquà kámawè nochpajáhxè. [you- ? -you you-go? my? ?]	Geh mir aus dem Lichten.
mow (grass)	t'măskhămăk [*a conjunct form?*]	Gras mähen
It is time [see time] to mow grass.	Tpescàwechnăŭ ăch'năquĕch t'măskhămăk mĕĕchsqŭan.	Es ist Zeit Gras zu mähen.
It is time to mow wheat.	[Tpescàwechnăŭ ăch'năquĕch t'măskhămăk] manóme.	[Es ist Zeit] Weizen zu mähen.
It is time to mow grain (or rye or buckwheat).	[Tpescàwechnăŭ ăch'năquĕch t'măskhămăk] sĕkănōmĕ́.	[Es ist Zeit] Korn, Rocken, Schwarzkorn [zu mähen].
much [see many]		

English	Mahican	German
must, have to [*probably not present in Mahican verbs here, or mean only* will] [*see also under* speak]		müssen, (sollen)
You must fetch the wood.	Machtáchene ē̆ gnatim.	Du must das Holz holen.
You must go quickly.	Kschocháma.	Du must hurtig gehen.
You (*pl.*) must always think about the good Savior.	Ng'máowe maamschānòchk wāchwāwége Pachpam[āwŏsŏhānŏāăd].	Ihr musst allez[eit] an den guten Heiland dencken.
But you must respect him.	Anuwéwe náhane mosachpéwe. [more must? *or* so?]	Sondern must ihn hochachten.
[*compare:*] That is very easy.	Náhane ně̀ nàch nágan. [so? that easy]	Das ist sehr leicht.
You must go away.	Nāhăně ăh.	Du must weggehen.
N. is calling you; you must come into the little house.	N. knattómuk, naha ahana wekwachmsik.	N. ruft dich, du solst ins kl[eine] Häusgen kommen.
But the children must learn.	Nōk gǎgāchgēmgōsōak ăwāsēsăk.	Aber die Kinder müssen lernen.
When it sounds, you (*pl.*) must come immediately to school.	Tschenuáka tāutāu aaschkě̆ě̆knpè kmajáwě̆ě̆chma.	Wenn gelautet wird, so müsst ihr gleich zur Schule kommen.
But no one must love his wife more than the Savior.	Tschēneěk awān oténne achwáhnan wěwa, áne Tapan[emuc]que ăchwáhnāăd.	Aber es muss niemand seine Frau mehr lieben als den Heiland.
A man must love his wife as the Savior [loves?] his congregation.	Nemanáu nitschwāk wěwa ŏtěnnè channawehāān Tāpănămŭkquāk āne channaweěchtāăd Geméěnde.	Ein Mann muss seine Frau lieben, wie der Heiland seine Gemein[d]e.
One must look to the Savior.	Ainochquatoŏk Pachtamawaasnau áne.	Man muss nach d[em] Heiland gucken.
Knock; it must (= will or soon?) be open(ed?).	Pōpāk'hà éne ktāŭnŏmága.	Klopfe an es soll aufgethan werden.
You must not grab for me when you fall (in your fall).	Asta ām kennhogówun kennhéganick kechtāch'mockówu.	Du solt mich mich [*sic*] nicht in deine Falle krigen.
When two become one [= agree?], why do they ask that they have to get? [*have to not present?*]	Néschowak ām paaschkon anè machmatuamnáwak omischnemnáwak. [?what they-ask (is what) they-get?]	Wenn 2 eins werden, warum sie bitten dass sollen sie krigen.
You (*pl.*) must revere me as your god.	Nia annewaneměěk kpachtamawasoa n'háckay.	Ihr sollt mich ehren als euren Gott.
mute [*explanatory word at* letter (written character)]		
my, mine [*see* Personal pronouns, Pronominal affixes]		
my sake [*see* sake]		
myself, my body [*see also* self]	n'hackai, n'hackay [*etc.*]	mich
nail [*noun*] [*cf.* mill]	ktachquahégan [?]	Nagel
nail [*verb*], nail on	–	nageln (an)
Nail it on hard.	Assannachtáhe ktachquahégan awà. [hard- ?] [nail (*noun*) + awà, *or is it* ktachquahéganawà *as possible verb?*]	Nagele es an.
They have nailed up his hands and feet.	Ktachquaheganà ktachtahamawáu ŏnàchgěk, osédik.	Sie haben s[eine] Hände, Füsse angenagelt.
nailed on wood; the one who is crucified.	machtóckuk schepochquatahasò.	ans Holz genagelt, der angecreuzigt.
name [*noun*]	–	Namen
in his name	nahk'ma otenewesowaganick [*cf.* Delaware (Brinton, 1888) wdellewunsowagan, / name]	in Namen sein [sein = his; ≠ to be!; *see under* sleep]
name [*verb*] [*see* call, name]		

Names—Indian names or Mahican brothers and sisters. Indianische Namen oder Mahic. Geschw[ister]

[*The order of the forms given is as follows. English (actual etymologic meaning), German, Mahican usage, German and English translations*]

[Joshua (Jehovah is salvation)] Josua *alias* Nahnhŏŏn. *item* [= same] Aáschawáchkamèn. Auf die Kante legen. [To lay on the edge (border, corner, ledge).]

[Bathsheba (daughter of the oath)] Bathseba. *al[ias]* Tawàněěm. *i.e.,* sie ist nicht wehrt, dass manche was sagt. [*i.e.,* she is not restrained (hindered, forbidden, protected), which is what many say.]

[Jacob (supplanter)] Jacob. *al.* Māāshàkq. Einer der immer redt. [One who always talks.]

[Rachel (ewe)] Rahel. *al.* Ănáwèpăkòchq. Die unter viel Blätter bleibt. [One who stays under many leaves.]

[Judith (praised)] Judith. Nŏŏssawáhnemà. Einer der oft oder vielmal denkt. [One who often or many times thinks (knows?).]

[Daniel (God's judge)] Daniel. *al.* Maschŏŏt. Einer der getroffen hat. Heisst auch er hat geschossen. [One who has struck (the mark), called also he has shot.]

[Mark (marked)] Marcus. *al.* Pāāptschàck. Scheckicht, bunt. [Pied, piebald, dappled, variegated, colored.]

[Catherine (pure + *diminutive ending*)] Catharina. *al.* Schāwăpéěm. Weich. [Soft, tender, smooth, weak, delicate.]

nations [see under free for sentence]	àtchānājăkéssĕjāckŭ, ātchānājăgéssĕjāckŭ	Nationen
near	—	bei *juxta*
near [*verb*] [*see* approach]		
nearly, almost	**pachŏŏd**	beinahe
necessary; need, require, desire, demand, wish, want, crave [*cf.* will (*noun*); use]		nöthig; verlangen, begehren
It is necessary.	**Ajáhntamă̄hk.** [n *marked for deletion in m.s.*]	Es ist nöthig.
It is necessary that we pray for the sisters and brothers. [*cf. Delaware nachpi,* together with]	**Ajáhtamă̄hk nā́āchpè papachtamawátau cheschemushă̄hk kétachcanană̄hk.**	Es ist nötig, dass wir beten vor die Geschwister.
Don't you need to have love for the Savior?	**Àsch ktajátamò Pachtamauus áhnè anàwáhmik.**	Verlangstu nicht den Heiland lieb zu haben.
Who needs help?	**Awă̄n ájatachcà nàchtă̄mă̄wă̄tŏwágan.** [*or*] **Awă̄n ájatachcà nàchtă̄mă̄wamìck.**	Wer hat Hülfe nöthig?
that they need (his) help.	**nahkma nachtamawátŏwágàn ájātă̄mă̄ă̄k.**	dass sie (seine) Hilfe nöthig haben.
I need or would like . . .	**Niàn tajáhntam.**	Ich verlange, oder ich möchte.
I need or would like more.	[**Niàn tajáhntam**] **annowéwe.**	[Ich verlange, oder ich möchte] mehr.
I want more from the Savior to feel in my heart.	**Niàn tajáhntam annowéwe Pachtamáwaas támmachtámmen dáhak.**	Ich verlange mehr von Heiland im Herzen zu fühlen.
I am looking for or need the pitcher or jug.	**Ntajáhtam kánnisch.**	Ich suche oder verlange den Krug.
Our desire is, or we need.	**Kiánau ktajáhntamnānāu.**	Unser Verlangen ist, oder wir verlangen.
Thus is our wish.	**Ktájahntamnánau.**	So ist unser Verlangen.
neck	**kăchquākachcan** [your neck; *cf. Delaware (Brinton, 1888) ochquekangan*, neck]	Hals
embrace (the neck)	— [*Mahican probably* hug *or* embrace]	um Hals fallen [= to fall on (one's) neck]
I hug you. I fall on your neck (*i.e.,* I embrace [and kiss?] you).	**N'hāmmỹssachgàn kăchquākachcanìck.**	Ich falle dir um Hals.
We embrace [and kiss?] you.	**Missachgajana.** plur[*alis*]	Wir fallen [dir um Hals].
neckcloth [*see under* breast]		
need [*see* necessary; use (*note two meanings there*)]		
needle, sewing needle, knitting needle	**schā̄ăpnégan**	Nehnadel, ein Stricknadel
new	**uske-, oskékā̄n;** [*plural*] **oskēkāwāk**	neu *novus*
My shoes are new.	**Uskájan mā̄hksĕnăn.**	Meine Schu sind neu.
new house	**uskégăn wéék'ma,** [**oskékā̄n**] **weekma**	neues Haus
in the new house	**uskégāmà** [**wéék'ma**], **oskēkāmà weékma**	im neuen Haus
a new dress or coat	**uskepétachgásòhn**	ein neuer Rock
a new earthen pot	**uskáju ăsusquahŏ̄**	ein neuer irdner Topf
What's new?	**Sgāctái nēschămŏ̄?**	Was gibts neues?
He gives you a new heart.	**Waskaíkè ktahà gménuck.**	Er gibt dir ein neu Herz.
to(?) live in the new heart	**Nik wáskākèck tschè ktáhack ŏ̄tájjeen.**	in dem neuen Herzen wohnen
news [*see* message]	[that *or* these?]	
nice [*see* fair; have good conduct]		
night	—	Nacht
in the night	**tpŏchgà**	in der Nacht
this (past) night	**nóno t'pochquéĕk**	vergangne Nacht
When it is night . . .	**t'póchgo**	Wenns Nacht ist . . .
I sleep at night.	**Gawéu nēpáwĕ̄.**	Ich schlaf in der Nacht.
nine	**nannéwe**	9
Nine days after today is Christmas.	**Nóno wachcamàhk nannéwe t'chŏ̄ŏknakkekà Xmess** [= Christmas].	Heute über 9 Tage ist Xstmess.
no [*opposite of* yes]	**stàch**	nein
No, another has done it.	**Stàch, ktàk ogeschechtaan.**	Nein, ein ander hats gemacht.
no [*see* none]		
no one	**tschēĕn awă̄n, tschēnéĕk awă̄n**	niemand
no use [*see* satisfied]		
nod head [*cf.* bow head]		
none, no, not any [*see notes under* duck(s) *and* fish]		kein(e)
I will not have any peace	**Asta ām tácheu ntanachĕ̄me** . . . . [not will (comes-not-it?) I-rest]	Ich will keine Ruhe haben . . . .
noon	—	Mittag
at noon	**naachquăta**	mittags

English	Mahican	German
I eat lunch. [*for more see under* eat]	Nahaquawépe.	Ich esse Mittag.
At noon we eat vegetables.	Nāwăchquáka eh kmētschĕchnắ gónan.	Zu Mittag essen wir Kraut.
nose [*cf. Mah.* wachkiwon (= his nose) *(Heckewelder)*]	—	Nase
my nose	nachkèwan	m[eine] Nase
your nose	kachkèwan, kakéwan	deine Nase
Wipe (*or* clean) your nose. [*see also* bleed; blow one's nose]	Kscheĕ̆chnè kakéwan.	Wisch deine Nase.
not	stà, astà, asch, tschéĕ̆n, tscheĕ́k, tschĕ̆n, tschĕ̆ne, tsche	nicht
will not	aschaă̄m, aschắ, ascham	
bad, evil, [thus] not	mă̆ttà̆ [*see two sentences under* bad]	
Daniel is not well.	Daniel schéwamannissò.	Daniel ist nicht recht gesund.
I will not take it.	Sta ă̄m kennáwe.	Ich wills nicht nehmen.
He did not take it.	Nahk'ma astà onòtĕ̆nimmówùn.	Er nahm es nicht.
They have not come; you ought not to cook.	Tscheen tachéwe t'pòchcahaă̄k.	Du darfst nicht kochen, sie sind nicht gekommen.
I have not eaten that for a long time.	Pajachquépogat. [-achqu- = not?]	Ich habe das lange nicht gegessen.
not any [*see* none]		
not at all	—	keinesweges
I have not thought about it at all.	Kochpenaă̄wat meschātāmoŭ̄n.	Ich habe keinesweges dran gedacht.
not only [*see* but]		
not yet	achquódha, achquódhà, achquadhà	noch nicht
(Isn't Anton coming?	Asch Anton páwè?	Kommt Anton nicht?)
He hasn't come yet.	Achquadhà pă̄we.	Er ist noch nicht kommen.
I haven't made it yet.	[Achquadhà] nkēschănăchgaŭ̆.	Ich habs noch nicht gemacht/gethan.
note [*verb*] [*see* observe]		
nothing	stà gáquai, astàk gáquai	nichts
I have nothing further to say.	Astà náha néne gaquai ktennòhōmme. -one[?]	Ich habe weiter nichts zu sagen.
nothing but, nothing other than	nannipschuk [= that-but?]	nichts als
I will preach nothing but about the blood of the Savior.	Nannipschuk ntenntŏhnhaă̄n Pacht[amawaas]nau op'gachganom.	Ich will nichts als vons Heilands Blut predigen.
now [*cf.* today]	nóno [= now], nóno [= today], nónu, nonò; nàn [= this, that?]	iezt, jezt, jezo, nun
at this time	hannónò [*or read* ạtannónò?; #= h, *not at?*] [*see ms. p. (331)*]	in/zu} dieser Zeit
Now it's halfway.	Nónen nò nánawàt.	Nun ist der Halbe Weg.
Now it [*or that?*] is enough.	Nàn tápe.	Nun ists gnug.
nowhere else	tschéĕ̆n ktackanèn	nirgends anders
Numerals [*see next page*]		
oak [*see* poison oak?]		
obedient, dutiful, submissive (to be) [*cf. also* disobedient]		gehorsam seyn
He was obedient to his parents.	Waŭŏ̄nèstăwápănè. Okeéchschaĭ́mà.	Er war seinen Eltern gehorsam.
I am obedient.	Nwawonistàm. Nià n'wa(w)onistàm.	Ich bin gehorsam.
I am not obedient.	Stà n'waŏnĭstămmóu.	Ich bin nicht gehorsam.
Are you obedient?	Esquaonĭ́stammóu.	Bistu gehorsam?
You are obedient.	Kwàwonistàm. Kwa(w)onistàm.	Du bist [gehorsam].
He is obedient.	Wawunnsettàm. Wawŭ̄nsittàm.	Er ist gehorsam.
[Yes?] he is not obedient.	Kāhă̆ stà waᵒŭ̄nsettammówe.	Er ist nicht gehorsam.
We are obedient.	Nwawonistamhanà.	Wir sind gehorsam.
We are obedient.	Kiánok kwaonistammechnŏ̃k.	Wir s[in]d g[ehorsam].
You (*pl.*) are obedient.	Gwawonistamhamà.	Ihr seid gehorsam.
You (*pl.*) are obedient.	Kiáwa kwaonistammechmà.	Ihr seid gehorsam.
They are obedient.	Wawonsittamă̄k. Wawŭ̄nsittamak.	Sie sind gehorsam.
They are obedient.	Wawonsettă̆màhk. Waunsettă̆màhk.	Sie sind gehorsam.
obedient children	óhnsettamaă̄k awàsésak	gehorsam Kinder
good children	waŭ̆nă̄lkeĕ̆́k awàsésak	gute Kinder
Be obedient to your father.	Kŏ́ŏ̆ch wawonnsittawà.	Sey deinem Vater gehorsam.
Be (*pl.*) obedient to your father.	Kochwà wawonsittawòchk.	Seid eurem Vater gehorsam.

Continued

Numerals [see also at year] [The following list fairly well comprises the corpus of numerals in Mahican sources. Those listed first are by Schmick. 'Sw-e' is an unknown source in Sw; Sw is not fully cited here. For abbreviations see p. 30.]

one ngutte, nguttò, gútta, paaschkon, pááschkun, pa̧a̧schkun, pa̧a̧schco [Sc]; ngwittoh [E]; n-co-tàh, gut-tah [J]; pausquun [W]; (ngut), paaschuk, paaschgu [H1]; gut·e [P]; gutá [M-?]; ngutá [M-AM, -EM, -Me]; gŏ́ta [Sw-R]; gúta·ˈ [Sw-D]; nkwíta [Si]

two nesche, nesc̨ho [c resembles o, ms. p. (377)], neschach [Sc]; neesoh [error for neesch?] [E]; nu-shu, ni-schàh [J]; neesh- [W]; (neschach) [H1]; nethwak [P]; nīsa [M-?]; nīsá [M-AM]; nisá [M-EM]; nisá̧ [M-Me]; ne-sa [Sw-R]; ní·sa [Sw-D]; ní·sa [Si]

three nacha, nechĕk [Sc]; noghhoh [E]; na-hágh, na-cháh [J]; nkha(u)-, naukhh- [W]; (nacha) [H1]; ná́χa [M-?]; naχá [M-AM, -EM]; náχa [M-Me]; náx·a [Sw-R]; ná·xə [Sw-D]; náxa [Si]

four náwa, nawè [Sc]; nauwoh [E]; na-wágh, na-wàh [J]; nawuh- [W]; (náwa) [H1]; nã́wa [M-?, -AM, -Me]; nawá [M-EM]; naó-a [Sw-R]; ná·wə, ná·wa [Sw-D]; náwa [Si]

five nānānè, nánan [Sc]; nunon [E]; no-nun, na-nàn [J]; naunonnu- [W]; (nànànè), nanani [H1]; nốnən [M-?, -AM]; nunán [M-EM]; nyốnən [M-Me]; nó·nən [Sw-R]; nó·nan, nú·nan [Sw-D]; ná·nan [Si]

six guttā́ā́sch [Sc]; ngwittus [E]; n-co-taunsh, ngut-taasch [J]; nquittaus, nquottaus [W]; guttaas̨hu [H1]; gutaⁿs [M-?]; gutəⁿs [M-AM]; gutə́ⁿs [M-EM]; gutɔⁿs [M-Me]; gúdɔus [Sw-R]; gu·tas [Sw-D]; nkwíta·s [Si]

seven tupouwus [E]; tam-pa-waunsh, ta-pau-waasch [J]; taupowwaus [W]; tapawaasch [H1]; tɔⁿpawɔⁿs [M-?]; támpawɔⁿs [M-AM]; tampaɔⁿs [M-EM]; tɔᵐpawɔⁿs [M-Me]; dɔᵐpawɔs [Sw-R]; tə̧pawɑs, tɑpawɑs [Sw-D]; tá·pawa·s [Si]

eight ghusooh [E]; han-shóʻ, chaà-schu [J]; khausoow [W]; chaaschu [H1]; χánsō [M-?, -EM]; nhóⁿsō [M-AM]; hi·ktɑm [Sw-R made error?]; [not given by Sw-D]; xáˑsa [Si]

nine nannéwe [Sc]; nauneeweh [E]; nan-na-wìgh, na-nè-we [J]; nauneweh [W]; nánēwì [M-?]; nānēwi [M-AM]; nā́nīwí [M-EM]; [not given by Sw-R]; há·su·ˈ, há·sɑn [Sw-D hesitant because probable error for eight]; nó·ni·wi [Si]

ten mtannit [E]; n-da-nét, m-tàn-net [J]; donnet, dunnit, dunnet [W]; mdáñat [M-?]; ndañat [M-AM]; ndañat [M-EM]; [not given by Sw-R]; dá·nɪt, tá·nɪt [Sw-D]; mtánit [Si]

eleven n-co-tah-na-caugh, ngùt-ta nkau [J]; gutúⁿkau [M-?]; gutə̧káu̧ (nkwatokaw) [Sw-e.2.20]; nkwíta·nkaw [Si]

twelve néschǎ nǎchkà [1759, Masthay, 1980]; na-shàh-na-caùgh, ni-scha nkau [J]; ní·sa·nkaw [Si]

thirteen naχoχkáu̧ (naχa̧·ka·w) [Sw-e.5.19]

fourteen nau ʷu̧káu̧ (na·wa̧·ka·w) [Sw-e.5.16]

fifteen nonankáu̧ (nya̧·na̧·ka·w) [Sw-e.6.16]

sixteen guta̧sχankán (nkota̧·sχa̧·ka·w) [Sw-e.2.30]

seventeen tu̧paʷu̧sχánkan [Sw-e.10.4]

eighteen χa̧soχánkan [Sw-e.12.6]

nineteen nanewiχánkan (na·ni·wi·χa̧·ka·w) [Sw-e.5.10]

twenty nisínska (ni·si·nska) [Sw-e.6.10,11,12]

thirty nchĕnchkā̆ [1746, Masthay, 1980]; nχe·nska (nχi·nska) [Sw-e.5.20]

forty nawínska (na·wi·nska) [Sw-e.5.17]

fifty no·nínska (nya̧·ni·nska) [Sw-e.6.17]

sixty —

seventy tu̧paʷú̧sχínska [Sw-e.10.5]

eighty χa̧soχínska [Sw-e.12.7]

ninety naníwiχi̧nska (na·ni·wi·χi·nska) [Sw-e.5.12]

one hundred gute̦mdánokana [e̦ = e or a?] [Sw-e.2.50]

one thousand gutá̧tkwaˈᵃ [Sw-e.2.40]

thousands mkhaunuhtquksowuk [W, p. 9, Q. 48, A; probably mkh-, great, or mkhaun-, many (q.v.); for -uhtquk- cf. latter half of Abenaki (Day, 1975) negwedategwa, (one) hundred; -wuk, animate plural (for persons)]

[other numerals in Masthay, 1980: one—páaschko (1759); two—neschóho-, neschŏ̆wàk, néschowàk (1759); three—nachá-, nachchà-, nachà-, nachchó- (1759); five—nanan (1746); nine—nannéwe (1759)]

English-Mahican-German 105

English	Mahican	German
obedient— cont'd		
Be obedient. [contrast believe]	Onistà.	Sey gehorsam. Imperat[ivus]
Be (pl.) obedient.	Onistamŏk.	Seyd gehorsam.
He is obedient to me.	Ŏnĭstăwétà.	Er ist mir gehorsam.
We will be obedient.	Onistamotaù.	Wir wollen gehorsam seyn.
We will not be obedient to the Devil.	Sta onistawawetaù Machtandò.	Wir wollen dem Teufel nicht gehorsam.
observe, keep, perform	—	haltet
and that you (pl.) observe daily.	nik knátămo̊okq wáwochcamake.	u[nd] das haltet ihr tägl[ich.]
observe, note, pay attention [see also attention]		merken oder Achtung geben
Let's observe it willingly in our hearts.	Néchene awằn äinachachéĕtsch otáhak. [self who]	Lasst uns nur gerne aufs Herz merken.
obstacle [see also hinder]		
I have many obstacle(s).	Nachnechawŏ̃nquane ngáchane. [Is -quane a plural? If not, perhaps phrase singular.]	Ich habe viel Hinderniss.
o'clock [see hour; sound (verb); sand]		Uhr
offense [see hurt oneself by striking]		
offer as a sacrifice [see sacrifice]		
offering [see sacrifice]		
often [see also sometimes]		
oh	oi, oh	o
Oh Savior...	Oi Pacht[amawããs]	O Heiland
Oh, I have seen it many times.	Oh măchăně nāwáŭ.	O ich habe es vielmal gesehen.
old	—	alt ætas [= age in Latin]
anciently, of old	—	Alters (vor)
of big ones	machowáju	alt (von gros)
old coat, frock	[machowe] petachgasõn	alter Rock
old friend	—	[alt] (Freund)
How old are you?	—	Wie alt bist du?
of little ones	machowájise[u?]	alt (von klein)
old man	kachtschaì, kachtscháis	alter Mann
the old ones [see under love feast]	kakatschaíssak	die alten
old shoe	[machowe] tschachquáchxen	alte Schuhe [plural]
old shoes	[machowe tschachquachxe]nan. plur[alis]	
old stocking	machowe tschachguttắn	alte Strümpfe [plural]
old stockings	[machowe tschachgutt]anan. plur[alis]	
of things	—	alt (von Sachen)
old woman	wenasóŏs	alte Frau
old woman, with white head	wapáju wénes [= it is white her-head]	[alte Frau] \ mit we[iss]kop[f]
They prosper from the old (great?) years to the new years.	Ŏnămănníssŏ̀ak machchowái katènnik pátsche uskái kátennik.	Sie gedeihen vom Alten bis zum Neuen.
oldest	wawèchtaătschéek, wawèchtăhtschęėk	aeltester
oldest	kakkajòh	ältester it[em] [= same]
oldest brother	gachgajĕd netachgan	der älteste Bruder
omnipotence	—	Allmacht
omnipotent	—	allmächtig
on [note ątannónò? under now]	tanè, e.g.	auf
on the cheeks	wánnănoŏk tânè	auf den Backen
on his cheeks	kánnanoók tanè	auf s[einen] B[acken]
on their cheeks	wannànnowowãắk [tanè]	auf ihren
on him [for on your cheeks?]	kanànnŏwŏwãắk [tanè]	auf ihn
on the whole earth (in the whole world)	mawe ănĕquéchkùk ahkì	aufn ganzen Lande
[see also onto under mosquitoes]		
once	nachtaù [cf. inside]	einmal
one [see also a, an]	ngutte, gútta, nguttò; paaschkon, pããschkun, pąąschkun, pąąschco	eins, ein
Today it is 1 year. Today 1 year ago.	Nono wachgamããk ngutte kahtenà.	Heute ists 1 Jahr.
a word	gúttá àptónachkat	ein Wort
one for you (pl.), one for the wives too.	pããschkun kiáwa, wénajàckq pąąschkun wak.	eine vor euch, u[nd] eine vor die Weiber.

106 *Schmick's Mahican dictionary*

to become (as) one [*i.e.*, to agree]	–	eins werden
When two become one [agree], why do they ask that they have to get?	Nésch°wak ăm paaschkon anè machmatuamnáwak omischnemnáwak. [?what they-ask (is what) they-get?]	Wenn 2 eins werden, warum sie bitten dass sollen sie krigen.
Joshua and I are of one heart [agree].	Josua neáne pããschkŏnŏwăk ntáhănă.	Josua und ich sind ein Herz.
The Savior and I are of one heart [agree].	Pacht[amawãăs] pããschkŏnŏwăk n'táhanããk.	Ich und der Heiland sind 1 Herz.
One ran.	Pąąschco nãhà / áŭ.	Einer lief.
We are one, or we are one body.	Nŏŏchkajĕĕn.	Wir sind eins, oder wir sind ein Leib.
one's own, to be one's own	–	eigen seyn
The gun is my own.	Pequan tappántamen.	Flinte ist mein eigen.
The horse is my own.	Wăntèi nachnióges tappanemàu.	Das Pferd ist mein eigen.
oneself [*see* self]		
only [*see* but]		nur
onward [*see* away]		
open, unlock	–	aufmachen
Open [it].	Tauwéqua.	Schliess auf od[er] mach auf.
I will open.	Ntauwéquammen.	Ich will aufmachen.
You have opened [it].	Ktauwenimmen.	Hastu aufgemacht.
He opens.	Otauwequammen.	Er macht auf.
We will open.	Tauwequamotŏŏk.	Wir wollen aufmachen.
You (*pl.*) have opened.	[Tauwequa]menawà.	Habt ihr aufgemacht.
They open.	Otauwequamenáwa.	Sie machen auf.
The Savior has opened with his blood.	Pacht[amawaas] ktauwequamakunána op'gachganŏm.	Der Heiland hat mit s[einem] Blut aufgemacht.
Open your heart.	Tauwunà ktăh.	Mach dein Herz auf.
The Savior opens his heart.	Pacht[amawaas] otauwunáwa otáha.	Der Heiland macht sein Herz auf.
Open (*pl.*) your hearts so that the Savior may enter.	Tauwuna ktahawăk Pacht[amawaas] otschinnehà páu.	Thut eure Herzen auf dass der Heiland hinein gehe.
open one's heart to [*see* reveal]		
opened	ktăŭnŏmága	aufgethan
or [*see first sentence under* become flesh]	?tanè? [*or* in which *or* therefore *or* on?]	oder
other	ktak	anderer
no other	–	[anderer] kein
no other place	tschĕĕn ktackanèn	nirgends anders
the other mountain	ktakkan wachtschò	der andere Berg
another time	–	andermal
another day, the other day	ktàk wochkamáo	einen andern Tag, den andern Tag
the other year, last year	ktàk katèek	vorm Jahr
They go(?) to another (year).	Anìmsŏàk ktákkak.	. . . zum andern [Jahr].
others (all others)	–	andere (ganz)
ought [*see also under* teach]	–	[dürfen]
They have not come; you ought not to cook.	Tscheen tachéwe t'pòchcahããk. [come] [neg. here?]	Du darfst nicht kochen, sie sind nicht gekommen.
our(s) [*see* Pronominal affixes; *see also under* soul]		
That is our knife.	Niánan ntachegananà.	Das ist unser Messer.
our Lord [*cf.* we]	kiánook Tapănemukquakùk	unser Herrn
That is our father. [*or*] The one who is our father.	Nà watóchiak kiánook. [*see under* believe] [the father our]	Der unser Vater ist.
ourselves [*note similar usage at* self; *see under* the same]		uns [*reflexive*]
outside, beyond, externally	–	ausserhalb
outside, outdoors	p'hágà	draus[s]en
Is the dog outside?	Ndiáu p'hága ajù.	Ist der Hund draus[s]en?
It is not outside.	[Ndiáu] sta [p'hága] ajéwe.	Er ist nicht [draussen].
Are you (*pl.*) outside?	P'hága ktajehemà (gtajehemà).	Seid ihr draus[s]en?
Are they outside? They are outside.	[P'hága] ájuwak.	Sind sie draus[s]en? Sie s[in]d draussen.
They are not outside.	Stà [p'hága] ajéweck (ajewek).	Sie sind nicht draus[s]en.
over there	kámick [*see* enclosed place]	drüben

English	Mahican	German
I have been over there. I come from over there.	Nóŏm kámick.	Ich bin drüben gewesen. [Ich] komme von drüben.
(Do) you come from over there(?). Have you been over there?	Kóŏm kámick.	Komst du von drüben. Bist du drüben gewesen.
I am passing over.	Kámick tàh.	Ich gehe über.
I am going over the hunting ground (district).	Kámick tà.	Ich gehe überm Revier.
overhear [see listen]		
owl; a bird of prey with a flat face	măchŏóksis	Ein Raub-Vogel mit einen platten Gesicht
pain, ache [see also hurt]	wenamattammòwágan	Schmerz
painted [see redden]		
pair	ksenà	Paar
Make me a pair of shoes.	Onéĕchtawè nguttò ksenà mãh'ksenan.	Mach mir ein Paar Schue.
Two pairs have come.	Neschĕek páksowàk páwak.	2 Paar sind gekommen.
pale, wan [cf. white]	wápachkechnàh	blass, bleich
I am pale.	Wapachgechẽn.	Ich bin bleich.
He is pale.	[Wapachgech]náu.	Er ist bleich.
pale face [It or he is pale.]	wăpăchkechnáu	blasses Angesicht
pan	konáganes [= little pan?]	Schüssel
Bring the pan (basin, bowl).	Konágănŏwáwàn. [or] Konáganes wáwàn.	Bringt die Schüssel.
paper [see sheet of paper; cf. leaf]		
pare [see peel]		
parents		
to his parents	okeéchscháĭmà	seinen Eltern
Participles [here in German, not participles but relative clauses; in Mahican, probably conjunct mode]		participia
all those who feel ...	máowe néĕk ămáttakeĕk ...	(alle) die da fühlen ...
who feels no ...	(awáneetsch) astà ămàttămóquà ... (awaắn)	Wer keinen ... fühlet ...
pass over [see under enclosed place]		
"Past" tense, second person	kdettan [?] [properly perfective aspect?; see p. 159]	
"Past" tense, third person	udettan [?]	
He looked at it all.	Nè ŭdèttan máowe náwàhn.	Er sahe das alles an.
Then he thought about the words.	Nè udettàn anètahátamen néĕn ăăptonawáganàn.	Da gedachte er an die Worte.
He went out and cried.	Păquáucháăn udéttan mắhn.	Er ging hinaus und weinte.
patch [noun]	méĕschhágan	Flecke
Don't you have patches to mend a shoe?	Asch kachchanéu méĕschhágan.	Hastu Flecke Schuh zu flicken?
Give me the patch.	Méĕschhágan méne.	Gib mir Flecke.
patch, mend, repair [see also shoes]	—	flicken
I will mend my shoe(s).	Gáttau méĕschhammen máksen. [cf. shoe(s)]	Ich will meine Schuh flicken.
I repair shoes.	N'méĕschhammen.	Ich flicke Schuh.
Fix your shoes.	Kméĕschhámmei.	Flicke deine Schuh.
I will not fix them.	Stà n'méĕschhámmau.	Ich will sie nicht flicken.
I am ready to repair shoes.	Kéĕschchequamè.	Ich bin fertig mit Schuh flicken.
Have you fixed your shoe?	Kĕsche méĕschhammen máksen?	Hastu deine Schuh geflickt?
path [see way]		
patient ("strong-hearted") [cf. impatient]	assannetaháu, mamaquajeu	gedultig [geduldig]
I am [not] patient.	Sta n'mamaquajéwe.	Ich bin [nicht] gedultig.
I am very patient.	Machantassanetahà.	Ich bin sehr gedultig.
He is very patient.	Machãnassanetaháu.	Er ist sehr gedultig.
He is patient. He has a strong heart (will).	Assanetaháu.	Er ist gedultig, stark Herz.
He is patient in good works.	[Assanetaháu] wánechk anè.	Er ist gedultig in guten Werken.
I am patient.	Ntassanetahà.	Ich bin gedultig.
You are patient.	K[tassanetahà].	Du bist gedultig.
We are patient.	N[tassaneta]hanà.	Wir sind gedultig.
You (pl.) are patient.	K[tassanetaha]mà.	Ihr [seid gedultig].
They are patient.	Assanetaháwak.	Sie [sind gedultig].
He has patience.	Chammàwachtánamęetsch.	Er hat Gedult.

pay	[pajem-, pam-]	bezahlen

[cf. Narragansett (Trumbull, 1903, p. 306, from Roger Williams) páum, he pays, "a word newly made from the English: cuppàimish, I will pay you." Cf. Massachusett nuppayum, I pay him; Nipmuck (Day, The Mots loups . . .) kepahamis, Je te paye, I pay you.]

I will pay your debt for you.	Neáne tquahogájan nia pamowă̄hn.	Ich will für dich bezahlen deine Schuld.
I pay.	N'pajemowà.	Ich bezahle.
You pay.	G[pajemowà].	Du [bezahlest].
He pays.	Pajemowáu.	Er bezahlt.
Let us pay.	Pajemowáqu.	Last uns bezahlen.
We pay.	Npajemowahanà.	Wir bezahlen.
You (pl.) pay.	[(G)pajemowa]hawà.	Ihr [bezahlt].
They pay.	[Pajemo]wáwak.	Sie bez[ahlen].
Pay for me.	Pajemowatammawè.	Bezahle für mich.
God has paid us.	Pachtamawasnau pajemowanochgónau.	G[ott] hat uns bezahlt.
God has paid you.	P. [with or without -nau?] gpajemówánok.	G[ott] hat dich bezahlt.
God has paid him.	P. [with or without -nau?] opajemowanawà.	G[ott] hat ihn bezahlt.
pay attention [see observe; attention]		
payer, i.e., the Savior	pamŏ̆ăhnŏquăkùp	Bezahler, i.e. d[er]H[ei]l[an]d
[He] has paid us.	pàmŏ̆áhnkōnă̄áp kianaù.	hat uns bezahlt.
payment	—	Bezahlung
peace, quiet, rest, repose	ănăchémowágan, anachemewágan, anachem'wagan, ánăchémŭachtanamowágàn, unàcotowágàn	Ruhe, Friede
The hero (champion, strong one) whom our Lord calls into his peace.	Nà áhssănnĕĕt nà kiánook Tapă̄nemukquakùk nè átane ănăchémowáganìck ŏtschē̄máŭ.	Der Held (Starke) der unsern Herrn in seine Ruhe ruft.
to rest, repose, or to have rest, peace, quiet	ánachémen	ruhen, oder Ruhe haben
My heart is at peace.	Anachē̄mu nàn tah.	Mein Herz hat Ruhe (Friede).
We are resting also.	Ánăchémĕ̄nánau kianau wă̄k.	Wir ruhen auch.
I know where our souls can have peace by the wounds of Jesus.	N'wawechtà atannĕ̄ĕtsch anachemĕ̄ĕd tschitschachkonanaù neăne pachpaquaik Jesus.	Ich weiss wo unser Se[e]len können Ruhe haben bei den Wunden Jesu.
Have you rested?	K'tannachemè.	Hastu geruhet.
He has rested.	Ánăchémĕ̄nă̄ăp.	Er hat geruhet.
Rest is sweet.	Anachemewágan wégan.	Die Ruhe ist süss.
I like to rest.	Ne wége anachéme. Ne wége tannachéme.	Ich ruhe gerne.
Let's (both) rest.	Ánàchĕ̄mĕ̄taù.	Last uns ruhen. Dual[is]
Rest (you [sg.])!	Anachéme.	Ruhe du.
Now I will rest.	Tanachéme nónu.	Nun will ich ruhen.
I will not have any peace until the Savior gives me peace.	Asta ă̄m tácheu ntanachĕ̄me kschemáneetsch Tap[anemucquak] anachem'wagan menéta.	Ich will keine Ruhe haben bis d[er] Heiland mir Ruhe gibt.
Who feels no peace or quiet in his heart(?). (Awáneetsch) (Awă̄ăn)	astà ă̄màttă̆móquà unacotowagan ánăchémŭachtanamowágan otáhak.	Wer keinen Frieden oder Ruhe im Herzen fühlet.
I will not make myself quiet until I know certainly that the Savior has given me peace. [literally: ? I rest not will so? rests-(it) myself, unless (or perf. + verb + imper.?) I rest, till Savior gives me peace?]	Tanachéme asta ă̄m néhene tanachemohao nháckai, kschemáneetsch ntanachéme, papachtschéwe Tap[anemucquak] anachemohan'oquana.	Ich will mich nicht selber ruhig machen, bis ich gewis weiss, der Heiland hat mir Ruhe gegeben.
The Savior certainly fills our heart(s) with peace.	Pachtamawans [sic] muchtschĕ̄ĕtsch ktáhennă̄ăk unàcotowágàn ótschŏwachtă̄ăn.	D[er] Heiland erfüllet gewis unser Herz mit Friede.
peach [see under tree]		
peel [noun] [see apple skin]		
peel, pare the peel, remove the rind	—	Rinde schälen
to peel, to pare the peel	Pchăckă̆schájahē̄gà.	Rinde schälen
I will remove the rind.	Npachagaschajahegà.	Ich will Rinde schälen.
Get the peels.	Pahwahà.	Hole Rinden.
to peel turnips	—	Rüben schälen

I peel turnips.	Npachaschà paãdquaik.	Ich schäle Rüben.
	Npachaschà paãdquajak.	
You peel turnips.	K[pachaschà paãdquajak].	Du schälest [Rüben].
He peels turnips.	Pachascháu [paãdquaja *(for obviative?)*]	Er schälet [Rüben].
We peel (turnips).	Npachaschahenà.	Wir schälen Rüben.
You (*pl.*) peel (turnips).	K[pachaschahe]mà.	Ihr [schälet Rüben].
They peel (turnips).	Pachascháwak.	Sie [schälen Rüben].

pelt [*see* hide]
people, mankind [*see* Indians; white people; everyone; nations]
perceive [*see* hear; understand]
Perfect tense *or* perfective aspect [*see* "Past" tense *and p. 159*]
perform [*see* observe]

perhaps	péchtkàht, pechtãm, pechtaãd, pechtschìm	vielleicht
perhaps still	pechtkaãtsch	vielleicht doch
Perhaps it is running away.	Pechtãm kemeeksò. [*cf. under* luck]	Vielleicht läuft es weg.
Perhaps tomorrow I will catch (some).	Pechtkaãm wápachcã petthà.	Vielleicht werde ich morgen fangen.
Perhaps our Savior is taking her (the sick person).	Pechtaãd kPachtamawaasnau onátenan.	Vielleicht nimmt sie unser Heiland (die kranke Person).
Perhaps it is dying.	Pechtschìm mbò.	Vielleicht stirbt es.
Perhaps it is still snowing.	Pechtkaãtsch p'chãn.	Vielleicht schneyts doch.

Personal pronouns and some affixes [*see also* each person; *for example*, steal; Pronominal affixes]

I (me)	nià, nia, niàn, n-, niàn n- [*see* I]	ich, mich
you (thou, thee)	kià, kia, k-, g-, kiàtsch	du, dir, dich
he (him), she (her), it [*animate*]	nahk'ma, nahkma, uwa; nànè [him]; o(t)-, w(t)-, w'(t)-	er, sie, (es), ihn, sie, es
we (*exclusive*, both, two, we and not you), us	niána [*see* afraid], niáne [*see* say], niánõk [*see* hear], niánok [*see* We hear.]	wir *(dualis)*, uns
we (*inclusive*, all, we and you), us	kiánau [*see* the same], kiánaũ [*see under* feel; we can say; sick], kiána [*see* hear; teach], kiánok [*see* obedient], kianõk, kiánook [*see* our(s)]	wir, uns
you (*pl.*)	kiáwa, kiawa [*see* hear], kiaua	ihr, euch
they (them)	nahk'mawa, nahkmáwa, nahkmaw [*see* steal]	sie, sie

perspire [*see* sweat]
phlegm [*see* cough]
pickax [*see* hoe]

picture	anénãxian	Bild
piece of bread	packájis taquòch	Stück Brod
piece of meat	packájis wojás, *or* wojãs	[Stück] Fleisch

pierce [*see* stab]
pierced

into his pierced side	nè tákamamukkùp wapuchquanek	in seine d[urch]stochene Seite

pike [*see under* great, a large kind of fish or animal]
pile [*see* heap; woodpile]

pipe	—	Pfeiffe
tube to pipe, pipe to be played	wéknèska	Rohr zu pfeiffen
pipe of <u>stone</u>	mãttássèn	Pfeiffe von Stein
I am filling the pipe. (also imperative)	Nᵉwattschósemà.	Ich fülle die Pfeiffe. auch *imperativus*
Give me a pipe of tobacco.	Otschosammawè.	Gib mir eine Pfeife Tobac.
Fill the pipe.	Utschõõssemà.	Stopf die Pfeiffe.
He fills the pipe. [*entry directly under* Nᵉwattschósemà.]	[*probably should be* Wattscho]semãhn [*or else* Otscho]semãhn.	Er füllet die Pfeiffe.
pitcher [*see sentence under* seek, *Schmick ms. p. (315)*]	kánnisch [*English* can? + *Mah.* -isch, *a diminutive?*]	Krug

pity, show pity [*see* bless; compassion]

place	—	Plaz
in a good place	nõũnit	in einen guten Plaz

place [*verb*] [*see* set (in a place)]

Place names in Schmick [see name or as noted]		
Albany [see Albany]	Mennissinger Town [see under Delaware words]	Nazareth [see under come]
Bethlehem [see under come and elsewhere]	Minisink [see under Delaware words]	New York [see under be (in a place)]
Lackawanna [see under Delaware words, "Lechchawáchneek"]	Minsi [see under Delaware words]	Shamokin [see Shamokin]
Manahkse Creek [see Monocasy]	Monocasy [see Monocasy Creek]	Shekomeko [see under come]
Manhattan(?) [see under ship]	Munsee [see under Delaware words]	Wyoming [see Wyoming]

plagued [see tormented]		
plank [see board]		
plant [verb]	— [cf. ground ahhkì]	pflanzen
I will plant maize.	Chăsquĕ́mĕ̃ tahhkéha.	Ich will W[elsch]korn pflanzen.
It is time to plant maize.	Tĕpesgāwĕchnaū ăhănūckquĕch ăhhkēhāmŭk.	Es ist Zeit W[elsch]korn zu pflanzen.
plantation	akihágan	Plantage
from the plantation	akihágănìck.	von der Plantage
I am going to the plantation.	Ăkèhatẹ̀ẹk ndà.	Ich gehe auf die Plantage.
play	—	spielen
The child is playing.	Awãses ásapo.	Das Kind spielt.
The children are playing.	Awasésak asápuak.	Die Kinder spielen.
play the violin	—	Geige spielen
I will play the violin.	Npiónhaman.[see under Loan words]	Ich wil die Violin spielen.
You play (the violin).	Piŏnhamà.	Spiele du.
He plays (the violin).	Piŏnhamáu.	Er spielt.
We will play (the violin).	[Piŏnha]mataù.	Wir wollen [spielen].
They play (the violin).	[Piŏnha]máwak.	Sie spielen.
pleasant, affable, courteous, quiet, not wild in the face [cf. gloomy face]		leutselig seyn, i.e., still, nicht wild von Angesicht.
I am pleasant (in the face).	Notackénaksè. Notackenaxe.	Ich bin leutselig.
You are pleasant.	K[otackénaksè].	Du bist [leutselig].
He is pleasant.	Otackenaksou. Otackenaxò.	Er ist [leutselig].
We are pleasant.	Notackenaksehenà.	Wir sind leutselig.
You (pl.) are pleasant.	K[otackenaksehe]mà.	Ihr seid [leutselig].
They are pleasant.	Otackenaksòak.	Sie sind [leutselig].
please, or I ask you ...	kmăchmātŭammen	bitte; Ich bitte ...
Please, be so good and fetch him here.	Kmachmatuámmen unáje nā̃gthonè.	Ich bitte dich, sey so gut und hohle ihn herüber.
pleasure, joy, delight, inclination, lust	udannăménāwágàn	die Lust
pleasure (have the) [see enjoy]		
plow	—	pflügen
I plow.	Ntannachkaschegà.	Ich pfluge.
You plow.	K[tannachkaschegà].	Du [pflugst].
He plows for Nathaniel.	An[n]achkaschemawáu N[athanael]. An[n]achkaschegáu N[athanael].	Er pflugt vor Nathanael.
We plow.	Ntannachkaschegahanà.	Wir pflügen.
You (pl.) plow.	K[tannachkaschega]hamà.	Ihr [pflugt].
They plow.	Annachkaschegáwak.	Sie [pflügen].
pocketbook	—	Brief-tasche
point [see show]		
pointed, sharp-pointed [cf. sharp]		spizig
My arrows are not good; they aren't sharp(-pointed).	Stàn népan wawuntoweēn, stà tschachschippajeweēn.	Meine Pfeile sind nicht gut, nicht spizig.
poison (oneself)		
I have poisoned myself (or got infected)(with poison oak).	Ntapskesoók ahapasxowãk.	Ich habe mich vergiftet (mit Giftholz).
poison oak [see poison (oneself) (poison oak stated or implied?)]		Giftholz
pone [see grits]		
poor	măttàhawoóp, ăschókò, kat'maxoóp, kat'makáhnsò, kat'máxo[_] ← [cut off in ms.]	arm pauper [Latin]
poor in the heart	kt'maxoóp	arm am Herzen
poor, miserable, wretched	kaaktemáxia[_]; [kaaktema]xiãg (plur[alis])	arm oder elend; arme, elende

a poor man	kaktĕmaaxétsche	einen armen Menschen
the poor N.	kat'maxéēd N.	den armen N. [*accusative case*]
the poor sinner	katemaksétsche	die armen Sünder
I am or live poor.	[Kat'make] p'máosía.	Ich bin oder lebe arm.
He (she) is or lives poor.	Kat'make p'máoseēt.	Er ist / Sie lebt arm.

portcullis [*see* fence *under* Delaware words]
position [*cf.* place]
possess something [*see* have]
possessions [*see* things]
Possessive affixes [*see* Pronominal affixes]

pot, earthen pot	ăsusquahŏ̆	irdener Topf

potatoes [*see* grits *instead?*]
pound, crush; knock [*q.v.*], rap, beat [*see also* hit] — pochen

I pound [*i.e.*, maize?].	Npòpackuhámmen. [u *or* a *or* '?]	Ich poche.
You pound.	K[pòpackuhámmen].	Du [pochst].
He pounds.	O[pòpackuhámmen?]. [-menau?]	Er [pocht].
We (two) will pound.	Popackhammótau.	Wir wollen pochen *(Dual[is])*.
Why are you (*pl.*) pounding?	Gaquătsch popackhammăku.	Warum pocht ihr?
They pound.	Opopackhammenáwa.	Sie pochen.
I have pounded for a long time.	Nawachtà nótschi packhámmen.	Ich habe lange gepocht.
Have you pounded a long time?	Nawachtà knotschi packuhámmen?	Hastu lange gepocht?
I haven't pounded long.	Stà schepachkéwe npópackhămmówun.	Ich habe nicht lange gepocht.
pour	—	giessen
He poured water.	Mbeì osòknĕmmèn.	Er goss Wasser.

[*cf. also roots for* rain; spill, shed; empty out; baptized ones]

pour in, fill [*see also* fill up]	—	einschenken, eingiessen
He pours in, fills.	Osogaháãn.	Er giesst ein, schenkt ein.
Pour [it] in.	Sogenè.	Schenk ein.
I will pour [it] in.	Nsogenimmen.	Ich will einschenken.
Let us pour [it] in.	Sogenimmotaù.	Lasst uns einschenken.
Pour (*pl.*) [it] in.	[Sogenim]mŏ́qu.	Schenkt ein.
I have already poured [it] in.	Nkesche sogenimmen nhà.	Ich habe schon eingeschenkt.
poverty [*see* misery]	aschoguágan	Armuth
power	—	Kraft
with the powers in heaven	nè ahssannáik wochcamáwenaak (wátschaĩk)	mit den Kräften im Himmel
pray	săchnĕk	beten
I pray.	N'papachtamawãn.	Ich bete.
You pray.	Gpapachtamawà.	Du betest.
He prays.	Opapachtamawáu.	Er betet.
We pray.	N'papachtamwahanà.	Wir beten.
You (*pl.*) pray.	Gpapachtamawahamà.	Ihr betet.
They pray.	Papachtamawàk.	Sie beten.
Let us pray.	Papachtamawatŏk.	Lasst uns beten.
Pray (*pl.*).	Papachtamawáqᵘ.	Betet.
I have prayed.	Kesche npapachtamawãn.	Ich habe gebetet.
You have prayed.	Kesche kpapachtamawà.	Du hast gebetet.
He has prayed.	Kesche papachtamawáu.	Er hat [gebetet].
Note: After kesche the following word is in the present tense.		NB. Nach kesche folgt das Wort *in præsenti*.
how we ought to pray.	ānĕtsch păpāchtămăwájaku.	Wie wir sollen beten.
It is necessary that we pray for the sisters and brothers.	Ajáhtamãhk naăchpè papachtamawátau cheschemushãhk, kétachcanañãhk.	Es ist nötig, dass wir beten vor die Geschwister.

[*cf.* wānāpátamąak, *p. 155*]

preach, discourse, sermonize	—		predigen
I preach.	N'pumm'tŏhnhà. Npummtŏnhà.	Ntenntŏnhãn.	Ich predige.
You preach.	[K?]Pumm'tŏhnhà. [Gpummtŏnhãn.]	KtenntŏnhĂhn. Gtenntŏnhãn.	Predige du. Predige.
He preaches.	Pumm'tŏhnháu. [Pummtŏn]háu.	Annetŏnháu. Annettohnháu.	Er prediget. Er predigt.
We preach.	Pumm'tŏhnhahanà. [Npummtŏn]hahanà.	Ntenntŏnhahanà. N[tenntŏhn]hahanà.	Wir predigen.

You (*pl.*) preach.	[Pumm'tŏhnhaha]mà. Gtenntŏnhahamà. [Gpummtŏn]hahamà. K[tenntŏhn]hahamà.	Ihr [prediget].
They preach.	[Pumm'tŏhn]háwak. Annettohnháwak. [Pummtŏn]háwak. Annettŏnháwak.	Sie [predigen].
a preacher, clergyman, minister	pachpametŏnhäd	ein Prediger
a beautiful sermon	wawunntŏnháu	eine schöne Predig[t]
He preaches about the blood of the Savior.	Annetŏhnháu Pachtamawaasnau op'gachganŏm.	Er predigt vons Heilands Blut.
I will preach nothing but about the blood of the Savior.	Nannipschuk ntenntŏhnhaän Pacht[amawaas]nau op'gachganom.	Ich will nichts als vons Heilands Blut predigen.
He has preached.	Pŏmettŏŏnhaäp.	Er hat geprediget.
I have seen Indians; I have preached to them.	Newajana anenápak pomtohnhamaäk.	Ich habe Ind[ianer] gesehen. Ich habe ihnen gepredigt.
[??Yes, I am happy that Indians are preaching to Indians.??]	Káhanne ntajanaména anamapanà [yes or truly, I-(cf. glad; desire) Indians? (sic m for n?)] anep'mettóhnhamak anenápäk. [preach- -they Indian(s?)]	[*untranslated*]
preacher, clergyman, minister	pachpametŏnhäd	ein Prediger

precede [*see* go before]
prepare skins [*see* curry]
prepared [*see* ready]
present [*see* be present; give]
pretty [*see* beautiful]
prevent [*see* hinder]
prick [*see* stab]
prison [*see under* free *(Mahican noun does not appear there)*]
produce [*see* bring forth]   prompt [*see* quick]

Pronominal affixes

my	n-, nt-	mein
your, thy	k-, kt-, g-, gt-	dein
his, hers, its [animate]	o-, ot-, w-, wt-, w't-, [zero]-; nahk'ma [= he]	sein(e)
our [*see also under* soul; our(s)]	n(t)-...-(na)na; k(t)-...-(na)na	unser
your (*pl.*)	k(t)-...-(a)wa	euer
their	o(t)-...-(a)wa(k), w(t)-...-(a)wa(k)	ihr

[*The following glosses were already written in English by Schmick:*]

It is mine.	N'tajégan.	Es ist meine. Mein, es ist.
It is thine. [It is yours.]	Ne ktajégan.	Das ist deine.
It is his. [*see also* his]	Otajégan. Wtajegana.	Es ist sein.
It is ours.	Ntajegananá. N'tajegananá.	Es ist unser.
It is yours (*pl.*).	Ktajeganawà.	Es ist euer.
[It is] theirs.	O[tajeganawà]. W'[tajeganawà].	Es ist ihre.
The knife was mine.	Nia schajáwe n'tachégan.	Das Messer ist mein gewesen.
[The knife was] thine.	Ktacheganajà.	Das Messer ist dein gewesen.
[The knife was] his.	O[tacheganajà]. Wtacheganaja.	[Das Messer ist] sein [gewesen].
That is our knife.	Niánan ntachegananà.	Das ist unser Messer.
That was mine.	Nágach nià.	Das ist mein gewesen.
[That was] thine.	Wágach kià.	[Das ist] dein [gewesen].
[It was the bishop's. *(correct)*] He was a bishop. [*incorrect*]	Wága Bishop otajégana.	Es ist Bischofs gewesen.
The horse was mine.	Nan nachnajóges nága.	Das Pferd ist mein gewesen.

[*The following two were untranslated or run in with* The horse was mine:]

[?I used to have?]	Ntása	—
[?I have?, ?It is mine?]	Nian ntája.	—
by my creator	näm Pachtamáwaassèk	von meinem Schöpfer

pronounce, express

Pronounce it.	Taquachquewechtàh. [*Does* -wechtàh = say?]	Sprichs aus.
What's that called? or How do you pronounce (express) that?	Gaquai nùktĕnè wechtamèn.	Wie heist das, oder wie sprichst du das aus.

proper [*see* have good conduct]

prosper, thrive [*see also* thrive]	—	gedeihen
They endure and prosper from the old (great?) years to the new years.	Nannò otaijĕnáwa, ónămănníssòak machchowái katènnik pátsche uskái kátennik.	Sie bleiben und gedeihen vom Alten bis zum Neuen. *N. 710*

English-Mahican-German 113

prosperity [*see under* good]		
protect [*see* safe]		
protected [*see* restrained]		
proud, haughty, arrogant	–	hochmüthig
I am proud.	N'machanese.	Ich bin hochmüthig.
You are proud.	K[machanese].	Du bist [hochmüthig].
He is proud.	Machanesò.	Er ist [hochmüthig].
We are proud.	Machanesehenà.	Wir sind hochmüthig.
You (*pl.*) are proud.	K[machanese]chemà.	Ihr seid [hochmüthig].
They are proud.	Machanesowàk.	Sie sind [hochmüthig].
Don't be arrogant (proud).	Tschĕĕk kmachanesenáwe.	Sey nicht hochmüthig.
I am not arrogant.	Sta machanesèwe.	Ich bin nicht hochmüthig.
You are not arrogant.	[Sta] k[machanesèwe].	Du bist [nicht hochmüthig].
provide for [*see* care for]		
pull along [*see* drag]		
puncture [*see* stab]		
punish a child [*see* whip (*verb*)]		strafen ein Kind
punishment [our punishment?]	knachmawachtowágan, knàchmawachtoagan	Strafe
purify [*see* clean]		
purpose	–	Absicht
push, shove	–	schieben
Move (*pl.*) along. Push forward.	Schāquŏnŏmoŏk.	Schiebet fort.
Let's (both) push.	Schaquonomotàu.	Lasst uns schieben *(Dualis)*.
Why are you shoving him?	Gaquai watsche pakkàmmat. [*see* hit]	Warum stostu ihn?
Why do you strike, push, touch me?	Gaquai watsch kĕĕchcănnèt.	Warum { stostu / rührstu } [m]ich an?
push out [*see* chase out]		
pustules (smallpox?)	măchmăchgĕchnāwănān	Blattern
Philip has the pox, pocks, measles (smallpox?).	Philip mămăchgĕchnã̄.	Philip hat die Blattern.
Philip has had the pox (smallpox?).	Philip mamachgechnããp.	Philip hat die Blattern gehabt.
I am afraid of the pox (smallpox?).	Quachŏdam mamachgechnágan.	Ich fürchte mich vor die Blattern.
put [*see also* set (in a place)]		
Throw it away. Put it away.	Attàchpannéwe.	Wirf es weg, oder leg es weg.
Put water in the kettle.	Kotenippà.	Thu Wasser in Kessel, oder Fülle den Kessel.
put on		
put on a hat	–	Hut aufsezzen
They put the thorn hat (crown of thorns) on Him.	Onĕĕchtau anotachosõn méscha.	Sie sezten Ihn den Dornen Hut auf.
Put on the kettle. [*see* hang up the kettle]		
Put on (your) shoes.	Kmàchchăxseme máxxen.	Ziehe Schue an.
Put on the water.	Npe sachgatta. [*cf.* enough]	Sez Wasser zu.
put out (light) [*see* snuff out]		
quarter [*see* fourth]		
quick, fast, swift, prompt	scháwah, aaschkeenpè	geschwind
He goes quickly (at once) to the Savior ...	Scháwah õmischschātăcããn Pachtamáwaassèk ...	Er geht geschwind (eilig, gleich) zum Heiland ...
quick, be quick, nimble	–	hurtig machen
Quick. Be quick.	Gattatáji.	Hurtig. Mach hurtig.
Read quickly.	Gattáte lésowe.	Lies hurtig.
Work quickly.	Gattãātanachkà.	Arbeit hurtig.
Spin quickly [yarns, etc.].	Gattătachpéha.	Spinn hurtig.
Jump or run quickly.	Kschechnà. Xechenà.	Spring oder lauf hurtig.
Run away quickly.	Ánameh kschech'nà.	Lauf hurtig fort.
Sew quickly.	Gattatequagà.	Nähe hurtig.
Wash quickly.	[Gattate] kscheechtága.	Wasch hurtig.
He or she is quick.	Gachgascháju.	Er oder sie ist hurtig.
They are quick.	[Gachgascháj]uwàk.	Sie sind hurtig.
He goes quickly.	Gackeschocháu.	Er geht hurtig.
Make haste. (Come quickly?)	Kschócha.	Komm hurtig. *Make haste.* [*in English*]
Come quickly to eat.	Kschóchà mawĕpe. Kschócha mawépe.	Komm hurtig zum Essen.

Go quickly.	Kschóōchà. Xechenà.	Gehe hurtig.
I cannot go quickly.	Aschān késche kschóchāwĕ.	Ich kan nicht hurtig gehen.
You must go quickly.	Kschocháma.	Du must hurtig gehen.
You are going too quickly.	Kosáme kschócha. Kosáme kschoōchà.	Du gehst zu hurtig.
We are going quickly.	Ngackschochahanà.	Wir gehen hurtig.
We are not going quickly.	Sta ngackschochawuhanà.	Wir gehen nicht hurtig.
Wu is inserted and stà is prefixed.		Wu *(interponitur)* et stà *præponitur.*
You (*pl.*) are going quickly.	[Gackescho]chahamà.	Ihr [geht hurtig].
They are going quickly.	Gackeschocháwak.	Sie [gehen hurtig].
They cannot go quickly.	Schăschāchĕwōcháwāk.	Sie können nicht hurtig gehen.
quicker, swifter	tājàtscheechségo	geschwinder
quiet [*see* peace, pleasant]		
Be quiet. [*see* still]		

rage [*see* anger]
rail [*see* bolt]

rain [*noun does not appear in following sentence:*]		Regen
Rain is coming from the east.	[Wapanaāk] otinnāhn.	Von Morgen kommt Regen.
rain [*verb*]	—	regnen
It's raining.	Sōk'nàhn. Sóganan.	Es regnet.
It's raining a lot.	Machchanahn soognahn.	Es regnet viel.
It's raining hard.	Kschenāhn. Kschénahn soognahn.	Es regnet sehr.
Sometimes it rains; sometimes there is good weather.	Ságechgàu sokanān, sagechgàu móschachquat. [*cf.* sometimes]	Manchmal regnets, manchmal ists gut Wetter.
[*see also* sprinkle; *cf. also* spill, shed]		
rainbow	manákkoon	der Regenbogen
rake [*verb*]	—	rechen
You must rake it together (with a rake).	Kia paaschcunoōk knimmaquamenà.	Du must es zusammen rechen (mit einen Rechen).
rap [*see* knock; pound]		
rapes [*see* turnips]		
rashness [*see note at* hobble]		
razor, straight razor	machmōōschmachtámik	Balbier-Messer
read	[*cf. Del. (Zeis.): achkíndamen,* to read, count]	lesen
to read	ăchkétā	lesen
You read beautifully, nicely.	Kāhăgóne kétammen.	Du liesest schön, hübsch.
[And = further] We will read further.	Wāk ánnĕmăkézētà.	Wir wollen weiter lesen.
[*The German word* lesen, *to read, is used as follows as if it were a Mahican verb:*]		
I read.	N'lesówe.	Ich lese.
Read! [*or perhaps:* You read.]	Lesówe.	Liess.
He reads.	Lesówu.	Er liesst.
We read.	Lesowechnà.	Wir lesen.
You (*pl.*) read.	Klesowechmà.	Ihr leset.
They read.	Lesowàk.	Sie lesen.
We two will read.	Lesówetaù.	Wir wollen lesen *(dual[is]).*
We will read.	Lesowetoōk.	Wir wollen lesen.
Let's read.	Lesówetǭk.	Last uns lesen.
Stop reading!	Áchque lēsówĕkǔ.	Hör auf zu lesen.
readily [*see* like to]		
ready, prepared [*contrast those under* make]		fertig
Are you ready?	Késchănăchkà. Kmattakéhà.	Bistu fertig.
I am ready.	N[késchănăchkà].	Ich bin fertig.
He is ready.	[Keschănăch]káu.	Er ist [fertig].
We are ready.	[N?][keschănăch]kahanà.	Wir sind [fertig].
You (*pl.*) are ready.	[Keschănăch]kahamà.	Ihr seid [fertig].
They are ready.	[Keschănăch]káwak.	Sie sind fertig.
I have been ready.	Kekéschanachkáhip. [k *written* gk]	Ich bin fertig gewesen.
How long [*less likely:* At what time] have you (*sg.*) been ready?	Tān ănĕquèchquè keschanachkāān?	Wie lang bistu fertig?
How long has he been ready?	[Tān ănĕquèchquè] okeschanachgāān.	Wie lang ist er fertig?
How long have you (*pl.*) been ready?	[Tān ănĕquèchquè] keschanachkaṇáwa.	Wie lang seid ihr fertig.

English	Mahican	German
They have long been ready.	Kekeschanachkā panĕĕk.	Sie sind lange fertig.
I think that I will be ready.	Ntenetahà keschanachkāātsch.	Ich denke ich werde fertig.
I think that tomorrow I'll be ready.	[Ntenetahà] wapachgāātsch keschanachkà.	Ich denke morgen werde ich fertig.
I am ready to (can?) sweat.	Nkésche appajuwechnà.	Ich bin fertig mit schwizen.
I am ready to repair shoes.	Kĕĕschchequamè.	Ich bin fertig mit Schuh flicken.
I am ready with the cooking.	Nkeschachtippè.	Ich bin fertig mit Kochen.
You are ready with the cooking.	Keschachtippè. Geschachtippè.	Bistu fertig mit Kochen.
He is ready with the cooking.	[Keschach]tippóu.	Er ist fertig [mit Kochen].
We are ready with cooking.	[Nkeschach]tippehenà.	Wir sind fertig mit Kochen.
You (*pl.*) are ready with cooking.	[Keschach]tippehemà.	Ihr [seid fertig mit Kochen].
Is the meat ready?	Wĕĕgtà ojāās.	Ists Fleisch gaar.

really [*see* truly]
receive [*see* get]

English	Mahican	German
red cheeks	mammàchgannoáu	rothe [Backen]
red sticks, red canes	màchkwèpánăchkwè	Rothe Stöcke
redden, make red, cause to blush	màchkĕnímmèn	Roth machen
to be red	—	Roth seyn
He is red colored (tinged, painted?) in the face.	Maschéchgŏ wanammana oskĕtschkŏŏk. [painted]	Er ist Roth gefärbt im Gesicht.
to blush, to get red, *i.e.*, to be ashamed		Roth werden *i.e.* sich schämen
You are blushing.	K[machktschanné]qua.	Du wirst Roth.
He is blushing.	Māch'k'tschănéquau.	Er wird Roth.
We are blushing.	N[machktschannequa]hanà.	Wir [werden Roth].
You (*pl.*) are blushing.	K[machktschannequa]hamà.	Ihr [werdet Roth].
They are blushing.	[Machktschanne]quáwak.	Sie [werden Roth].
redeemer, our Redeemer, our Savior	Nāchĕnŭckquácku	unser Erlöser

Reflexive verb [*see* among; divide]
regard [*see* look at; see]
relation, relative [*The basic meaning of* familial relative *may appear in Mahican* tēnnāngōmā, friend; *cf.* Nipmuck (Day, *The Mots loups ...) kitelangontemenen,* nous sommes . . . parents (= we are . . . relatives); *Delaware (Brinton) elangomat,* friend, relation (a member of one's family), *elangomellan,* my friend; *and Mass. wuttinnunkumôin,* a kinsman of a female.]
release [*see* free]
remain [*see* stay]

English	Mahican	German
remember [*see also* observe; keep]	—	sich erinnern
I recollect. I remember.	Kmechkŏŏme.	Ich besinne mich. Ich erinnere mich.
Think of (remember) me when you come to Bethlehem.	Mĕscháhnnĕmà Bethl[ehem] pájănĕ. M'schagnnémà Bethlehem pájănĕ.	Gedencke an mich wenn du nach Bethl[ehem] komst.
remove	—	rücken (ab)
remove the hide [*see* hide]		
Remove the kettle; it's cooking too much.	Nochpána hoŏs, osáme kschĕgămēscho. [*cf. entry at* boil over]	Rück den Kessel ab, es kocht zu sehr.
Remove [it] (*i.e.*, from the fire).	Nŏchpápèh. [*or*] Äschápè.	*Imperat[ivus]* Rücke ab (*scil[icet]* vom Feuer).
remove rust [*see* rust]		Rost abmachen

repair [*see* patch]

English	Mahican	German
report (letter)	—	Bericht (Briefe)

repose [*see* peace]
require [*see* necessary]
resemble [*see* appear as]
respect [*see* honor]
rest [*see* peace]

English	Mahican	German
restrained (hindered, forbidden, protected)		wehrt
She is not restrained (*etc.*).	Tawànĕĕm. [*see* Names, Bathsheba]	Sie ist nicht wehrt.
resurrection	—	Auferstehung
He has risen from the dead. He has been resurrected.	Udennè méĭjāzā. [*see* whether, if]	[Er] ist auferstanden.

retain [*see* keep]
retract [*see* deny]
return home [*see* go home]

English	Mahican	German
reveal, manifest, disclose, acknowledge, confess, open one's heart to		offenbahren oder bekennen
To whom have you revealed your heart?	Awān kmūchgĕnŭmmăwānă ktáha.	Wem hastu dein Herz offenbahret.

Who has opened his heart? Who has unbosomed himself?	Awãn nĕũ táha ãne mŭchgĕnaht.	Wer hat s[ein] Herz offenbahrt?
I have not disclosed my heart.	Stà nià ntàh mŭchgĕnãwĕ.	Ich habe mein Herz nicht offenbart.
My brothers, open your (pl.) hearts to the Savior.	Nétăchcănăk mŭchgĕnŭmmăwochk ktáhăwă Tap[anemuc]quak.	Brüder, offenbahret eure Herzen dem Heiland.
Disclose to him all that is in your (pl.) hearts.	Máowe mŭchgĕnŭmmăwòk achtáge ktáhawăk.	Offenbaret ihm alles was in euren Herzen ist.
I confess.	Nia móchgoa.	Ich bekenne.
You confess.	Kia k[móchgoa].	Du [bekennst].
He confesses.	Mochgoáu.	Er [bekennt].
He doesn't confess.	Sta mochgoáwe.	Er bekennt nicht.
[Yes or then?] we will acknowledge it.	Ihà mochgoatŏŏk.	Wir wollens bekennen.
We will not acknowledge it.	Aschăm kmochgoauhanau.	Wir wollens nicht bekennen.
Confess (pl.).	Mochgoáku.	Bekennet.
Don't steal. I will reveal it.	Tschĕĕn kmŏthèn ene kmochgenèn.	Stiehl nicht, ich wills offenbahren.
revere [see honor]		
revive [cf. live]		
He has revived.	P'máwosòhăăp.	Er hat lebendig gemacht.
ribbon [see band]		
rich (to be); rich [adjective]	Pawann'sóu.	Reich seyn. reich
I am rich.	Nia npawánnĕse.	Ich bin reich.
You are rich.	K[pawánnĕse].	Du bist [reich].
He is rich.	Opawannesóu.	Er ist [reich].
We are rich.	Niánau npawann'sehenà.	Wir sind reich.
We [inclusive] are rich.	Kianŏŏk ktschè kpáwannisséhenà.	Wir sind reich.
You (pl.) are rich.	K[pawann'sehe]mà.	Ihr seid [reich].
They are rich.	Pawánnsowak.	Sie sind reich.
ride [see drive]		
ride [on a horse]	—	reiten
I ride.	Ntachapè.	Ich reite.
Where are you riding to?	T'hácta ne tachapè.	Wo reitestu hin?
He rides.	Tachapò.	Er reitet.
We ride.	Ntachapehenà.	Wir reiten.
You (pl.) ride.	K[tachapehe]mà.	Ihr reitet.
They ride.	Tachachpówàk.	Sie reiten.
right, correct	—	recht
It is right.	Nàn nè. [?That (is) that?]	Es ist recht.
It is not right.	Astàn nè. [?Not that?]	Es ist nicht recht.
You are not saying it right.	Stà(k)konechséwe.	Du sagsts nicht recht.
[cf. also recht under wish that]		
rind [see also peel (verb); apple]	p'chakschă	Schaale
ring [verb] [see sound]		
rip [see tear away]		
road [see way]		
roast [verb] meat	—	Fleisch braten
to roast meat	aposasĕĕk ojăăs	Fleisch braten
I will roast meat.	Tăpŏsĕ nojăăs. [= my meat]	Ich will Fleisch braten.
Roast meat.	Ăchpăch ojăăs.	Brate Fleisch.
Let's roast meat.	Achposetaù ojăăs.	Last uns Fleisch braten.
Have you (pl.) roasted the meat?	K'taposeh'm ojăăs.	Habt ihr Fleisch gebraten.
rods	—	Ruthe
with rods	?nepeschàn ăwáhăwăk? [which word?]	mit Ruthen
They have whipped Him with rods.	Ŏsăsămtschăhăwă nepeschàn ăwáhăwăk.	Sie haben Ihn mit Ruthen gepeitscht.
roller strap [see band]		
room		Raum
It is an (open) space.	Méchcăjŏ.	raum (scil[icet] es ist)
Make room.	Mèchcănè.	Mache raum. imperat[ivus]
He makes room.	Nàh ŏmĕmèchcănĕmèn.	Er macht raum.
They have cleaned the room (space).	Nahk'ma kschechàtămŏwă méchcăjŏ.	Sie haben den Raum rein gemacht.
room (in building, i.e., wigwam, house)		Stube
Sleep in the room.	Wequamick gawè.	Schlaf in der Stube.
root out [see under seize]		

English-Mahican-German **117**

ruin, spoil, destroy, corrupt	—	verderben
I ruin.	N'mattschechtãn.	Ich verderbe.
You ruin.	K[mattschechtãn]. G[mattschechtãn].	Du [verderbest].
He ruins.	Omattschechtãn.	Er verderbt.
We ruin.	Nmattschechtananà.	—
You (*pl.*) ruin.	Kmattschechtanawà. [K-?]	—
They ruin.	Omattschechtáwak.	—
run	—	laufen
I run.	Npumm'sè. N'pummsè.	Ich laufe.
You run.	K[pumm'sè]. G[pumm'sè].	Du [läufst].
He runs.	Pummessò.	Er [läuft].
We run.	Pummesehanà.	Wir laufen.
You (*pl.*) run.	[Pummese]hamà.	Ihr [läuft].
They run.	Pummesowàk.	Sie [laufen].
They shall run and not be weary, they shall walk and not be faint. *Isaiah 40, 31*	Pomìssŏàk, ashãm schawàjewéĕk, anìmsoak, asta ãm schéwochsannéweek.	Sie laufen, und werden nicht matt, sie wandeln und werden nicht müde. *Jes[aia] 40, 31.*
Run quickly.	Kschechnà.	Lauf hurtig.
Run away quickly.	Ánameh kschech'nà.	Lauf hurtig fort.
You must not run.	Tschĕn samekschochahan.	Du must nicht laufen.
run after, run away	—	laufen nach, [laufen] weg
to run after someone	Onawanáwa.	einen nachlaufen
[When a Negro has run away,] he has run away.	Kémeexo.	Wenn ein Neger wegläuft, er ist weggelaufen.
Perhaps it is running away.	Pechtãm kemeeksò.	Vielleicht läuftes weg.
Because of that he is running away.	Ni wátsche annahóguk.	Darum läuft er weg.
One ran.	Pa̧a̧schco nãhà / áŭ.	Einer lief.
He cannot let them (her?) run astray.	Sta ãm késche ănĕtãhãwĕ a̧nàu pă̧pamsĕchtéĕtsch.	Er kan sie nicht in der Irre laufen lassen.
run out (*i.e.*, expire) [*see under* sand]		
rust	achquāqŭană [*cf.* Ojibwa (*Baraga*) agwâgwissin, *it is rusty, it is moldy;* Mass. (*Trumbull*) ogquonkquag, *rust*]	Rost
Clean the gun of rust.	Kscheéchnè achquāqŭană păchgékăn.	Mach die Flinte sauber vom Rost.
rye [*see* grain]		
sack, bag	tschăchquénōtēi	Sack
He (has) emptied out the sack.	Oschegonemèn tschăchquénōtēi.	Er hat den Sack ausgeleert.
sacrifice, offering	kwehegamoágan [= your offering], wehètowágan	Opfer, dein Opfer das Opfer
sacrifice [*verb*], offer as a sacrifice		opfern
I sacrifice.	N'wēhĕgāmĕ.	Ich opfere.
You sacrifice.	K[wēhĕgāmĕ].	Opferstu.
He himself has become an offering.	Wĕhètĕnãáp 'nhákkei.	Er ist selbst ein Opfer worden.
They sacrifice.	Wēhētōāk.	Sie opfern.
We will sacrifice.	Kwehegamechnoŏk.	Wir wollen opfern.
What will we offer as a sacrifice?	Gáquai kwehegamechnàu.	Was wollen wir opfern?
We will sacrifice a buck (ram, he-goat).	Ajápăŭ kwehegamechnoŏk.	Wir wollen einen Bock opfern.
Your offering is not good.	Kia kwehegamoágan stà honittówe.	Dein Opfer ist nicht gut.
You have offered yourself.	Kia khackei kwehegamenãáp.	Du hast dich geopfert.
sad, sorrowful [*see also* gloomy; unfriendly]	schewãhndam	betrübt
Why are you sad?	Gaquatsch schewãhndammen.	Warum bist du betrübt.
What is saddening?	S[c]hewahndo[_]. [*cut off in ms.*]	Was betrübtes.
Don't be troubled.	Tschĕn gaquai kschéwahndam.	Sey nicht betrübt.
sadness, sorrow, grief	schewahndamm'wágan	Betrübnis
safe, secure (hidden, secret)		sicher (verborgen)
Take me [us?] to safety. [Hide me? Protect me? Give me asylum?]	Gadhanenána.	Nimm mich in Sicherheit
where I am safe	átăĕ ãm gātăchnēkăjă átăĕ ãm gatachnejan	wo ich sicher bin.

sake
   for my sake | niàn dennanáchcawagan wáätschè [thus + do, make + *noun*] | um meinetwillen
   Whoever loses his life for my sake will find it. | Awãn op°máosowágan ánãchtããt niàn dennànachkawágan, nàn máchcamen. | Wer sein Leben um meinetwillen verliert, der wirds finden.

salt | sãschuak | Salz

salubrious [*see* wholesome spring]

same [*cf.* should; been]
   It is the same. It appears just the same. | Ăne nãquàt. Nánnè ănè naquàt. | Es ist dem gleich. Es sieht ebenso aus.

sand | nãägaù *vel* [=or] nágãū | Sand
   It is 2 o'clock; *i.e.*, the sand has run out twice. | Néschan nágau machtschetschoachnáu. [past - run? it] | Es ist 2 Uhr, *i.e.* der Sand ist 2 mal [he]rausgelaufen.

Satan [*see* Devil]

satisfied | — | zufrieden
   I am not satisfied with you. or It's no use what you do. | Astàn nónãtãmówun ánănàchcăjàn. | Ich bin nicht zufrieden mit dir, od[er] es taugt nicht was du thust.
   The Savior is not satisfied with what you do. | Pacht[amawaas] astà ónãtãmówun ánanàchcajàn. | Der Heiland ist nicht zufrieden mit den was du thust.

satisfied (with food or drink) [*see under* enough]

save, preserve | | erhalten
   Whoever seeks to save his [own?] life will lose it. | Awãn op°máosowágan neẽchnéowè kwénakà, kakánenik ŏtànăchtãhn. | Wer sein Leben sucht zu erhalten, der wirds verlieren.

Savior [*see also* God] | [*basic meaning* pray *or* help?:] Pachtamawããs, Pachtamawããsnau, Pachtamawans [*only once*], Pachtamauus [*once*], Pachtamawasan [*obviative*], Papacht[amawããs]; Tapãn'măgok, Tapanemucquak, Tãpănãmŭkquāk, Tapanemukquahquèh, Tap[anemuc]qua [+ -k?; *see under* suck] | der Heiland, dHld, Gott

   The Savior has therefore become man... | Nam Pachtamawããs Táp[anemuc]quàk wãtsche óhãkkăjéwe... | D[er] H[ei]l[an]d ist darum Mensch worden...
   I think about the Savior all the time. | G'máo maamschan'ma Pãchpămãwõsõhãnõããd. | Ich dencke allezeit an den Heiland.
   Savior of the world | Kékachtátip mawe áněquechkùk ăhkì. [?he-has-created all more(?)-on earth] | Der Welt Heiland
   The Savior of all souls | Kékãchquăkùp [= one who created?] mawe watschitschàchquajàckq. [all souls] | Der Heiland aller Seelen.
   ...by my creator | ...nãm Pachtamáwaassèk | ...von meinem Schöpfer

say, speak, tell [*see also* speak; tell] | | sagen, sprechen
   Do you believe what I have said to you? | Kohnsittawenà anãăptónamenàn? | Glaubestu was ich dir gesagt habe?
   He speaks. [*see* speak] | Udennãăptonan. Udennãăptonãhn. | Er spricht.
   He said... | Nahk'ma awà:... | Er sprach:...
   He spoke loudly (with a strong voice). | Awà kàchnă macheèchsò. [truly?] | Er sagte mit gewaltiger Stimme.
   Jesus says. | Jesus awà. | Jesus spricht.
   Jesus spoke, said. | [Jesus] utenáwa. | [Jesus] sprach.
   Jesus says. | [Jesus] osèn. | [Jesus] spricht.
   Our Redeemer has said... | Năchěnŭckquácku oseẽn... | Unser Erlöser hat gesagt...
   I have said nothing bad. | Astàn nià máteĕk 'n'séu. | Ich habe nichts böses gesagt.
   What are you saying? | Gaquai ksè. | Was sagestu?
   I say thanks. | Ŏnéŏwĕ xè. [= Thanks you say.] | Ich sage Dank.
   We say thanks. | Onéowe xénau. | Wir sagen Dank.
   What do you (*pl.*) say [it is]? | Gaquai kseęchma? | Was deucht euch?
   You are not saying it right. | Stà(k)konechséwe. | Du sagsts nicht recht.
   What has he said? What did he say? | [Gaquai] màchtschõsà. | Was hat er gesagt?
   Say [or tell?] A, *etc.* | Éka A, *etc.* | Sage A. *etc.*
   What he says, that's what he does. | Gaquai étsche nánne ŭttenái. [what he-says that ?] | Was er sagt, thut er auch.
   When (as soon as) he had said that. | Ne máchtsche ne éta. | Als er das gesagt hatte.
   Tell (*pl.*) me what you wish to say. | Kià [Nià?] anèku, gaquai gattaù ẽta. | Sagt mirs was ihr gerne sagen wolt.
   I want to hear what he will say. | Gattaù ptauwãŭ gaquai macheèt. | Ich will hören was er sagen wird.

English	Mahican	German
Tell me.	Kià ănè. [Nià?]	Sage mir.
Say it to me.	Anè.	Sag mirs.
Say (pl.) it to me.	Anĕku.	Sagt mirs.
I want to say something to you.	Gattau gáquai ănèn.	Ich will dir was sagen.
I don't understand what you are saying.	Astà knenochtáno gaquai ánĭăn.	Ich verstehe nicht, was du sagest.
Tell just us. Just tell us.	Anènānà niáne.	Sag uns nur.
If I will tell it to you (pl.).	Nià áăm ănènnáquà.	Wenn ichs euch gleich sage.
I will say it to him.	Êne ndènnahn.	Ich wills ihm sagen.
I say to him.	Nià ntenaù.	Ich sage ihm.
I have said to them.	Nià ntenáwak.	Ich habe ihnen gesagt.
I have said that the Savior is good.	Niàn ntenáwak onáju Pachtamawaasnau.	Ich habe gesagt der Heiland ist gut.
My husband said: Tomorrow we both will go to Bethlehem.	Wáchia ntennùk wapachgătsch Bethl[ehem] ktáhanau.	Mein Mann hat gesagt: morgen wollen wir (zwei) nach Bethlehem gehen.
We have told it to David.	Ntenananà [David].	Wir habens D[avid] gesagt.
You (pl.) have told it to David.	K[tenana]wà [David].	Ihr [habts David gesagt].
Did you tell it to David?	Ktenăhn David?	Hastus David gesagt.
I say to you.	Nià ktēnnèn.	Ich sage dir.
They will say something to you.	Êne gáquai kténnuk.	Sie wollen dir was sagen.
The (your) brother says.	Kténnuk kétachcanau.	Der Br[uder] sagt.
Didn't you say that Joseph would be with Joshua?	Asch ktenáwe Joseph aú Josuáhik.	Hast du nicht gesagt Joseph sey beim Josua.
We will say it to you.	Ktennenána.	Wir wollen dirs sagen.
I have nothing further to say.	Astà náha néne gaquai ktennòhōmme[?].	Ich habe weiter nichts zu sagen.
She didn't say anything. She has said nothing.	Astàk gáquai ktenkówe. / [cf. catch fish]	Sie hat nichts gesagt.
All said [it].	Maowe otènnăwàhn. [ms. p. (370)]	Alle sagten.
He tells me. (also) She (has) said to me.	Niàn tóckun.	Er sagt mir, it[em] sie hat mir gesagt.
He has said it to us.[We have said (delete this sentence?).]	Kt'kónaū.	Er hat zu uns. Wir haben gesagt. [sic]
The brothers talk to us.	Ktehoŏkcunánau kétachcanăŭ ktĕcónau. [incorrect sentence or two sentences?]	Die Br[üde]r sagen zu uns. [sic: zu zuns.]
He is talking with us.	Ktennĕkónānaù.	Er redt mit uns.
... that we can say "Abba" [i.e., that we can call Jesus "Father"].	nik kiánaū Abba ktukkonánaū.	dass wir Abba sagen können.
Jesus said: I have set you free.	Jesus ŏp, nia kpamowánĕkonăăp.	Jesus sagt: Ich habe dich erlöst.
Our Savior (has) said: I will die for you (pl.).	Kt'konăăp kPacht[amawaas]nau knippowanochmà.	Uns[er] Heiland hat gesagt ich w[ill] für euch sterben.
Now I will say why I am pleased.	Nóno kwechtammánen wătsche ŏnăchtănăméă.	Nun will ich sagen warum ich vergnügt bin.
I will now tell you (sg.) why you do not feel.	Nono kwechtammánen gaquai wătsch astà ămăttămówŏn.	Ich will dir iezt sagen warum du nicht fühlest.
I will tell why the Savior loves us.	Nià kwechtammanen ga[quai wăătsch?] ăchw'ăhnŭqŭákŭ Tap[anemucquak]. Nia wechtammānen [sic] ga[quai wătsch?] achwanuquăkŭ Tap[anamukquak].	Ich will sagen warum uns der Heiland liebt.
But I can still say that to you (pl.).	Psùkquéěk ăm késche kwéchtămăhnhămmà.	Aber doch das kan ich euch sagen.
Say it to me.	Wechtammawèh.	Sage mirs.
Tell me why you are [he is] coming.	Wechtammawèh gaquai wăătsch páăd.	Sag mir, warum du kommst.
[see the following under call:]	Máwe tschenuăăk.	Singt alle, oder sagt alle.
scalped	měschòchquanápanéěp	gescalpt
scarce, rare	—	rar (es ist)
Maize is scarce.	Ntaúwat chasquéme.	Das W[elsch]korn ist rar.
It is not scarce.	Stà ntauwattówe.	Es ist nicht rar.
scatter about [see lie scattered about]		
school [see under must]		
scissors [see shears]		
scraper, a drawknife, drawshave	lăălhăquákkan Dell[aware] [sic]	Schneidmesser [not a chopping or cutting knife]
scream [see cry out]		
search [see examine]		

search for [see seek]		
seat, bench	aáchpapémick	Bank
secret [see safe]		
see, look at, regard	—	ansehen, anschauen
see (continuously), look, look at [see also look at]	—	sehen (immer), kucken, gucken
Look!	P'naù.	Siehe.
Look at me.	P'nawè.	Sieh auf mich.
Look (pl.) at me.	P'nawĕku. P'nawĕcku.	Seht auf mich.
You must look nowhere else but at me.	Tscheén ktackanèn pnamhàn nia psùck pennawe.	Du must nirgends anders hinsehen nur auf mich.
I see; I am always looking.	Ntainochquán.	Ich sehe, ich gucke immer.
You see, etc.	K[tainochquán].	Du
He sees, etc.	O[tainoch]quáu.	Er
We see, etc.	Ntainochquanána.	Wir [sehen].
You (pl.) see, etc.	K[tainochqua]náwa.	Ihr
They see, etc.	O[tainoch]quanawak. Otainochquanáwa.	Sie
Why do you always look over there?	Gaquátsch ainochquajàn?	Warum guckst du immer dahin?
One must look to the Savior.	Ainochquatoŏk Pacht[amawaas]nau áne.	Man muss nach dem Heiland gucken.
You are not looking at him.	Stà ktainochquawun'hà.	Du siehst nicht auf ihn.
It is bad when someone looks toward something else. If someone always looks toward something else (as what his heart wishes), he will certainly die.	Máchtett pannewehh [hh shows deletion] awán otáinochquán, awáneetsch gommáwe pannéwe äinochquáda kahanántaatsch m'pò.	Das ist bös, wenn Jemand auf was anders sieht. Wenn jemand allezeit auf was anders sieht (als aufs Herz) wird gewissl[ich] sterben.
I see.	Náwáŭ.	Ich sehe.
You see.	Knáwau.	Du [siehst].
He sees.	Ŏnáwă.	Er sieht.
We see.	Nawahanà.	Wir sehen.
We see you (pl.). [sic]	Nawochnà. [= We see him.]	Wir sehen euch.
You (pl.) see.	K[nawaha]ma [? or] K[nawoch]ma [?]	Ihr [seht, or seht + pronoun?].
They see.	Onáwak.	[Sie]
It is very good to see the marks.	Muchtsche nawoquátta wĕchwēsájŭ.	Es ist gut zu sehen die Maal.
Look at your heart.	P'naù nà ktàh.	Sieh auf dein Herz.
I have seen or looked.	Pennawáu.	Ich habe gesehen.
He looked at Peter.	Petrussa ŏpennawáu.	Er sahe [sic or sahen?] Petrus an.
Look into your heart.	Náwu nà ktàh.	Sieh in dein Herz.
Please (= I ask [you?]), look into your heart.	Kmăchmătŭammĕn náwah nă ktah?	Ich bitte, sieh in dein Herz.
Look (pl.) into your hearts.	Pnăwòchq ktahawăk. Pnăwōchku ktahawăk.	Seht in eure Herzen.
Take a look at yourself in the mirror.	Pnawòchk hackai wapachpĕnăŭūs.	Besieh dich im Spiegel.
The Savior looks into your heart.	Pachtamawaas nawaát ktáhak.	Der Heiland sieht ins Herz.
Look into your heart You will see in your heart how bad it is.	Pnăwù na ktàh, {éne knáwăŭ / ĕnicke náwăŭ} na ktàh otennè năchkĕssĕhn.	Sieh in dein Herz, du wirst sehen in d[einem] Herzen, wie bös es ist.
You (sg.) will see in your heart how bad it is.	Éne knáwăŭ / Enikĕ́ náwăŭ} nà ktàh ŏtĕnnè năchkĕ́ssĕ̌n.	Du wirst sehen in deinem Herzen wie böse es ist.
Our God sees us before his eyes.	K'pacht[amawaas]nau k'nawokónau usketschguk utschi.	Unser Gott sieht uns vor s[einen] Augen.
We (both?) will (or want to?) see. or Let us see.	Pnāūwátāū.	Wir wollen sehen, oder lasst uns sehen.
[My] brothers, look!	Netachcanak pnawéĕk.	Brüder[,?] seht.
What or whom do you (pl.) see?	Awán knăwŏchmà?	Was oder wen seht ihr?
We see a stag.	Áchtòh náwăhăná.	Einen Hirsch sehen wir.
I will also see them (her?).	Tawám pĕnnăwăhn. [I-also-will?]	Ich will sie auch sehen.
Do you also want to see [him]?	Kĭá wăk gattaù p'năwáŭ.	Wiltu auch sehen?
I have already seen [it?]?	Păgăchtschĕ́ kĕ́pnăwáŭ.	Ich habe schon gesehen.
I have seen him. [ms. 369]	Nià keĕp náŭwaáp.	Ich habe ihn gesehen.
Not I. I am not it. [ms. 369]	Astàn nià.	Ich bins nicht.
You are. [ms. 369]	Kià keĕp.	Du bist.

English	Mahican	German
Oh, I have seen it many times.	Oh măchānĕ nāwáŭ.	O ich habe es vielmal gesehen.
I have seen a light here.	Wăhs'nanégan nmachnawă̄.	Ich hab ein Licht hier gesehen.
I see.	Nia námen.	Ich sehe.
You see.	Kià knámen.	Du siehest.
He sees.	Nahk'ma onámen.	Er siehet.
We see.	Niána namenána.	Wir sehen.
You (pl.) see.	Kiáwa knamenáwa.	Ihr sehet.
They see.	Nahk'mawa onamenáwa.	Sie sehen.
I have seen.	Nia namenaăp. *Perfectum*	Ich habe gesehen. *Perfectum*
You have seen.	K[ià] knamenaăp.	2. perf.
He has seen.	N[ahk'ma] onamenaăp.	3. perf.
We have seen.	Niana namenanaăp.	—
You (pl.) have seen.	K[ia]wa knamenawaăp.	—
They have seen.	N[ahk'mawa] onamenawaăp.	—
We don't see each other well.	Kiánau astà knáŭteohénnaū.	Wir sehen wol einander nicht.
Haven't you seen N.? Didn't you see N.?	Àsch knāwáwà (N.).	Hast du nicht (N.) gesehen.
I didn't see.	Astà námŏŭn.	Ich sahe nicht.
I didn't see him.	Stàn námōwè.	Ich sahe ihn nicht.
He looked at it all (all of it).	Nè ŭdèttan máowe náwàhn.	Er sahe das alles an.
When I see Jesus.	Jesus nāmānà.	Wenn ich Jesum sehe.
I see you.	Knáwun.	Ich sehe dich.
Look (pl.) at him.	Knawŏŏk.	Sehet ihn.
Look! (sg.)	Knawè.	Siehe du.
I see him.	Nawáu.	Ich sehe ihn.
I have seen him.	Nawáu.	Ich habe ihn gesehen.
I have not seen him.	Astà nawáwe. [1; see 27; cross-references below:]	— [opposite of Nawáu.]
I don't see you.	Ascha knawunówe.	— [opposite of Knáwun.]
I see myself.	Nawáu nháckai.	Ich sehe mich.
I see you (pl.).	Knawunochmà. [2; see 12]	Ich sehe euch.
I see them.	Náwaumachtsch.	Ich sehe sie.
I don't see you (pl.).	Asta knawuno<u>wu</u>hamà. [3; see 13]	Ich sehe euch nicht.
I don't see them.	Asta nawaweĕk.	Ich sehe sie nicht.
You have seen me.	Kia machtschkenáwe.	Du hast mich gesehen.
You haven't seen me.	Asta [machtschkena]wéwe.	[Du hast mich] nicht [gesehen].
You have seen yourself.	Kháckai knáwa.	Du hast dich gesehen.
You have seen him.	Kia knáwau. Knawáu.	Du [hast] ihn [gesehen]. Hastu [ihn gesehen].
You have not seen him.	Asta [kna]wáwe. [Astà] k[nawa]wè. [4; see 20]	Du [hast] ihn nicht gesehen.
You have seen us.	Kia machtschkenawehenà.	Du hast uns gesehen.
You have seen them.	[Kia machtschkena]wawàk.	Du hast sie [gesehen].
You have not seen us.	Asta knawewuhenà. [5; see 21]	Du hast uns nicht gesehen.
You have not seen them.	[Asta] knawawéwak.	Du [hast] sie [nicht gesehen].
Christian has seen me.	Xstian [= Christian] náwócku.	Xst. hat mich gesehen.
N. has not seen me.	N. asta nawugówe. [6; see 23]	[Xst. (or N.) hat mich] nicht [gesehen].
N. has seen you.	N. k'náwocku. [7; see 24]	Xst. [properly N.] [hat] dich [gesehen].
N. has not seen you.	N. asta knawugówe. [8; see 25]	[N. hat dich] nicht [gesehen].
N. has seen him.	N. onawawà. [9; see 26 and 31]	N. hat ihn gesehen.
N. has not seen him.	[N.] asta onawawewà. [10; see 32]	N. [hat ihn] nicht [gesehen].
Christopher has seen us.	Christoph knawukónau. [11; see 28]	Chr. hat uns gesehen.
N. has not seen us.	N. asta nawugowewunà.	[N. hat uns] nicht [gesehen].
N. has seen you (pl.).	[N.] knawugówa. [cf. 8]	[N.] hat euch gesehen.
N. has not seen you (pl.).	[N.] asta <u>knawugowewà</u>.	[N. hat euch] nicht [gesehen].
We have seen you (sg. & pl.).	Knawunochma. [12; see 2]	Wir haben dich (euch) gesehen.
We have not seen you (sg. & pl.).	Astà knawuno<u>wu</u>hamà. [13; see 3]	[Wir haben dich (euch)] nicht [gesehen].
We have seen him.	Nawawunà. [14; see 29]	[Wir haben] ihn gesehen.
We have not seen him.	Asta nawawewunà. [15; see 16 and 30]	[Wir haben ihn] nicht [gesehen].
We have seen the birds.	Nawa<u>n</u>anà tschèchtschìs. [n covers h]	Wir haben sie (Vögel) gesehen.
We have not seen them.	Astà nawawewunà. [16; see 15 and 30]	[Wir haben sie] nicht [gesehen].
Have you (pl.) seen me?	Knawechmà.	Habt ihr mich gesehen?
?You (pl.) haven't seen me. [*the meaning* We haven't seen you (sg.) *would not follow pattern*]	Astà knawewè. [17; cf. 18 and 20]	[(Habt ihr mich)] nicht gesehen. [*at beginning the words* Wir haben dich *were correctly crossed out by Schmick*]

You (*pl.*) have seen him.	Kiawà knawawà. [*18; cf. 17 and 20*]	Habt ihr [ihn] gesehen.
You (*pl.*) have seen Joseph.	Knawahamà Joseph. [*19; cf. 22*]	Habt ihr den Joseph gesehen.
You (*pl.*) haven't seen [him].	Astà knawawè. [*20; cf. 4, 17, and 18*]	[Habt ihr (ihn)] nicht [gesehen].
You (*pl.*) have seen us.	Knawechenamàchtsch.	Habt ihr uns gesehen.
You (*pl.*) haven't seen us.	Asta knawewuhenà. [*21; see 5*]	[Habt ihr uns] nicht [gesehen].
Have you (*pl.*) seen them?	Knawahemà? [*22; cf. 19*]	Habt ihr sie gesehen?
Haven't you (*pl.*) seen them?	Asch k'nawawewà?	[Habt ihr sie] nicht [gesehen]?
They have seen me.	Nawugŏk.	Sie haben mich gesehen.
They haven't seen me.	Asta nawukówe. [k *covers* g] [*23; see 6*]	[Sie haben mich] nicht [gesehen].
They have seen you.	Knawòcku. [*24; see 7*]	Sie haben dich [gesehen].
They haven't seen you.	Asta knawukówe. [*25; see 8*]	[Sie haben dich] nicht [gesehen].
They have seen him.	Onawawà. Onáwawa. [*26; see 9 and 31*]	Sie haben ihn gesehen.
They haven't seen him.	Astà nawáwe. [*27; see 1*]	[Sie haben ihn] nicht [gesehen].
They have seen us.	Knawucónau. [*28; see 11*]	Sie haben uns gesehen.
They haven't seen us.	Astà nawukowenà.	[Sie haben uns] nicht [gesehen].
They have seen you (*pl.*). [*sic*]	Nawawunà. [= We see him.] [*29; see 14*]	Sie haben euch [gesehen].
They haven't seen you (*pl.*). [*sic*]	Asta nawawewunà. [*30; see 15 and 16*] [We don't see him.]	[Sie haben euch] nicht [gesehen].
They have seen them.	Onawawà. [*31; see 9 and 26*]	Sie haben sie gesehen.
They haven't seen them.	Astà onawawewà. [*32; see 10*]	[Sie haben sie] nicht [gesehen].
I will see Christian.	Ne mawunáwau Xstian.	Ich will den Xste͜ [= Christian] sehen.
I will see you.	Kmawupenãn.	Ich will dich sehen.
I will not see you.	Ascha kpennanõw.	Ich will dich nicht sehen.
You will see me.	Kmawupenawè.	Wiltu mich sehen.
You will not see me. [?]	Ascha kpennawéwe.	[Wiltu mich nicht sehen.] [*untranslated*]
I will (want to) see him.	Ngattaù pnawáu.	Ich will ihn sehen.
I will see him.	Ne maw̥upenawáu.	Ich will ihn sehen.
I will see you (*pl.*).	K'pennanahama.	Ich will euch sehen.
I will not see you (*pl.*).	Aschà kpennanowuhamà.	[Ich will euch] nicht [sehen].
I will see the sisters.	Npennawáwak ne chésemak.	Ich will die Schwestern sehen.
I will not see them.	Aschan pennawáwek.	[Ich will (sie)] nicht [sehen].
I will not see him.	Ascham pennawawe.	Ich will ihn nicht sehen.
I will not see [all?] them. [*Contrast previous sentence* Ne maw̥upenawáu.]	Astà ngattaù mawe pennawawe.	Ich will ihnen nicht sehen.
[He] looks at [him].	... ŏpĕnaùwāwà ...	[Er] sieht [ihn] an.
Look in the mirror.	P'naù pachpenawùs.	Sieh im Spiegel.
I look in the mirror.	Npachpenawussè.	Ich sehe im Spiegel.
He looks in the mirror.	Pachwenawussò. [*sic first* w *for* p?]	Er sieht im Spiegel.
We look in the mirror.	Pachpenawussehenà.	Wir sehen im Spiegel.
You (*pl.*) look in the mirror.	K[pachpenawussehe]mà.	Ihr seht [im Spiegel].
They look in the mirror.	Pachpenawussoàk.	Sie sehn [*sic*] [im Spiegel].
I have looked in the mirror the whole day long [the long-day].	Kănewachcamãhk npachpenawussè.	Ich hab den ganzen Tag im Spiegel gesehen.
Let's look in the mirror.	Pachpenawussetŏŏk.	Lasst uns im Spiegel sehen.
We (both) will look in the mirror.	[Pachpenawus]sétaù. *Dualis*	Wir wollen im Spiegel sehen.
The whole day long [long-day] you look at yourself [he looks at himself?].	Gănŏwochgamãk ăpănnāwā̆wă̆ ohàckai.	Du besiehst dich den ganzen Tag.
For a long time I have seen no maize.	Pajachquénaquat chasquemen.	Ich habe lang kein W[elsch]korn gesehen.
For a long time I have seen no bears. Note: It is used of living animals or men.	Pajachquenaxò machquà.	Ich habe lange keinen Bären gesehen. NB. wird von lebenden Thieren oder Menschen gebraucht.
It is long since I have seen you.	Kpaja͜chquenaksè.	Es ist lange, seit ich dich gesehen [*sic*]
I have not seen them for a long time.	Pajachquenaksoàk.	Ich habe sie lange nicht gesehen.
I am glad to see you.	Ntannaména anenaw̥unan.	Ich freue mich, dass ich dich sehe.
I am glad to see you (*pl.*).	[Ntannaména] anenaw̥unãku.	Ich freue mich, dass ich euch sehe.
so that we will all see each other.	Nikkàhtsch kiánau máowe kdéttan, gnaŭténānaù.	Damit werden wir uns alle sehen.
Then we will all truly see Jesus together.	Ihàn nikkàhtsch kianau máowe kdéttan gnaŭténānaù.	Da wir Jesu alle zusammen recht sehen werden.
We don't see each other well.	Kiánau astà knaŭteohénnaū.	Wir sehen wol einander nicht.

English	Mahican	German
to see or let see, let gaze upon	—	sehen oder schauen lassen
I ask Him that he (will) let me look into his pierced side and make my heart bloody.	N'machmátuammàk nahk'ma, nè tákamamukkùp wapuchquanek ne áām wátsche pĕnóchteneéth, wăk nàn dàh áăm ánep'gáchganeéth.	Ich bitte Ihn, dass er mich wolle in seine d[urch]stochene Seite hineinsehen lassen u[nd] mein Herz bebluten.
seek, search for, look for	—	suchen
What are you looking for?	Gaquaik quênam? [-k = you?]	Was suchest du?
I'm looking for David.	N'quénăwáu David.	Ich suche David.
I'm looking for or need the pitcher.	Ntajáhtam kánnisch.	Ich suche oder verlange den Krug.
You are looking for the ax.	Kwénam t'mahégan.	Du suchst die Axt.
We are looking for the horse(s).	Kwenawunà nachnióges [sg.].	Wir suchen die Pferde [pl.].
What are you (pl.) looking for?	Gaquajà kwenamechmà.	Was sucht ihr?
I'm looking. I'm seeking.	Nkwenamèn.	Ich suche.
I'm looking for the Savior.	Nquenawáu Pachtamawaas.	Ich suche d[en] Heiland.
I'm not looking for him.	Sta quenawáwe.	[no translation]
The Savior is looking for you.	Quenăku Pach[tamawaas]nau.	Der Heiland sucht dich.
He isn't looking for you.	Stà quenakówe.	[no translation]
Whoever seeks to save his life will lose it.	Awãn op°máosowágan neĕchnéowè kwénakà, kakánenik ŏtànăchtăhn.	Wer sein Leben sucht zu erhalten, der wirds verlieren.
The Savior is looking for us.	Quenacónau kPach[tamawaasnau].	Der Heiland sucht uns.
He is not looking for us.	Sta quenacowenaù.	[(Er) sucht uns] nicht.
The Savior is looking for them, the Indians.	KPacht[amawaas]nau oquenawawà anenápawà.	Der Heiland sucht sie die Indianer.
He is not looking for them.	Sta oquenawawewà.	[(Er) sucht sie] nicht.
The Savior is looking for me.	Pacht[amawaas] nquénakŭ.	Der Heiland sucht mich.
He is not looking for me.	Sta quenacówe.	[(Er) sucht mich] nicht.
You seek the [our] Savior.	Kwenàu kPach[tamawaas]naù.	Du suchst d[en] Heiland.
You don't seek him.	Sta quenawáwe.	[Du suchst (ihn)] nicht.
We are searching.	Nquenawahanà.	Wir suchen.
You (pl.) are looking for the Savior.	Quenawòchkŭ P[achtamawaas].	Ihr sucht d[en] Heiland.
They are looking for the Savior.	Quenawáwak [P(achtamawaas)].	Sie suchen [den Heiland].
If you (pl.) search for the Savior, then you will find him.	Quenàu kP[achtamawaas]nau kmachcawăŭtschi.	Suchet d[en] Heiland, so werdet ihr ihn finden.
seem		
What does it seem to you? What do you think?	Gaquai kseêchma? [What do you (pl.) say (about it)?]	Was deucht euch?
seem(s) [see also appear as]		
So it seems.	Anè nãquàk.	Es sieht so aus.
It appears just the same.	Ăne nãquàt. Nánnè ănè naquàt.	Es sieht ebenso aus.
to appear sad (faced)	pachgenimménaxò	finster (Gesicht) aussehen
I look sad.	Npachgenimménaxè.	Ich sehe finster aus.
seize, grab; grope?, touch?	—	kroppen
I seize, grab, etc.	Nmachgahachquà. Nià machcàhachquà.	Ich kroppe.
You also seize.	Kià wak kmachcàhachquà.	Kropfstu auch.
He grabs, i.e., roots out bushes.	Machgahachquáu.	Er kroppet, i.e. rottet Sträuche aus.
The brothers seize.	Machcàhachquáăk nétachcanenanak.	Die Brüder kroppen.
[see also grab under get]		
self (body, q.v.)	-hakkei, -hackay, -hackei, -hackai; nehenè, néhene, néchene, nèchne°wè, neĕchnéowè	sich, selber, selbst
myself	nháckai, [etc.]	mich, mich selber
yourself	k'hackei, [etc.]	dich, dich selbst
oneself, himself, herself	ohákkei, oháckai, [etc.]	sich selbst, sich
He himself has become an offering.	Wĕhètĕnáăp 'nhákkei.	Er ist selbst ein Opfer worden.
I will not make myself quiet.	Asta ãm néhene tanachemohao nháckai.	Ich will mich nicht selber ruhig machen.
He thinks of himself: "I make it nice (i.e., I am being fair)."	Nehenè anètaháu. Nià schaschachkanachcà.	Er denkt von sich, ich mache es hübsch (selbst gerecht).
[see also fair; help; let; like to; lose; observe; peace; seek; think]		
sentinel [see guard]		
sermon [cf. preach]	—	Predig[t]
a beautiful sermon	wawunntõnháu [a verb in the third person]	eine schöne Predig[t]
servant, attendant	ahagenahégăăd	der Diener

servant, vassal, a menial	—	Knecht
the servants of the Savior	Pachtamawaasnàu otannachgágana	des Heilandes Knechte
his servants	otènnanáchcanàhn [na *crossed out for* otènnáchcanàhn; *cf.* Delaware (Brinton) *allogagan*, servant]	seine Knechte
serve	—	dienen
I serve.	Ntahagenahéga.	Ich diene.
You serve.	K[tahagenahéga]. G[tahagenahéga].	Du [dienst].
He serves (or in the perfect tense).	Ackenahegáu. Hackenahegáu.	Er [dienet]. od[er] *perfect[um]*
We serve.	N'tackenahegahanà. T'hackenahegahanà.	Wir [dienen].
You (*pl.*) serve.	K't'hackenahegahamà. Nt'ackenahegahamà.	Ihr [dienet].
They serve.	Hackenahegáwak. /[↑ *sic* n]/	Sie [dienen].
Let us serve.	Ackenahegatóŏk. Ackenahegatŏk.	Last uns dienen.
(May you [*pl.*]) serve.	Ackenahegáăk. Ackenahegák.	Dienet ihr.
We will serve [*or in perfect tense*].	Ackenahegátau.	Wir wollen dienen.
I have served yesterday.	Wanaquega ntackenahéga.	Ich habe gestern gedienet.
You have served.	Tackanahegà.	Hast du gedienet.
I serve the Devil.	Ntackenahamawa Machtando.	Ich diene dem Teufel.
You serve the Devil.	K[tackenahamawa Machtando].	Du dienest [dem Teufel].
He serves the Devil.	Ackenahamawáu [Machtando *(or in obv.?)*].	Er dienet [dem Teufel].
We serve the Devil.	Ntackenahamawahanà [Machtando].	Wir dienen [dem Teufel].
You (*pl.*) serve the Devil.	K[tackenahamawaha]mà [Machtando].	Ihr dienet [dem Teufel].
They serve the Devil.	Ackenahamawáwak [Machtando *(in obv.?)*].	Sie dienen.
Don't serve the Devil.	Tschéĕk tackenahamawáăn Machtando.	Diene dem Teufel nicht.
Don't (*pl.*) serve the Devil.	[Tschéĕk tackenahama]wanewà [Machtando].	Dienet [dem Teufel nicht].
Christian serves the Savior.	Chr[istian] ackenahamawáu oPachtamawása.	Chr[istian] dienet dem Heiland.
You serve the meat.	Kojásom ktackenahamawà.	Du dienest dem Fleisch.
You follow the way of sin.	Kmatschaiwagan [ktackenahamawà].	Du dienest der Sünde.
and we will serve (from the heart ...	wăk nè ăm áne ănàchkāchtána ...	dass wir ... und dienen von Herzen ...
set (in a place), place, put	—	sezen, sezzen
Should I place or set it here?	Nèn tachañăn.	Soll ichs daher stellen oder sezen.
Set it on the ground.	Achtà ahhkeĕk.	Sez es auf Grund.
[*cf.:*] Sit on the ground.	Mattapè ahhkeĕk.	Sez dich aufn Grund.
Don't put it here, but over there.	Tscheĕn ktachañăn, ne nónaku.	Sez es nicht hieher, sondern dorthin.
Behind the bed.	Ne áchtăk kachgawémuk.	hintern Bett.
Throw it away. Put it away.	Attàchpannéwe.	Wirf es weg, oder leg es weg.
seven [*see* Numerals]		
sew	—	nähen
Sew quickly.	Kattatequagà. Gattatequagà.	Nähe hurtig.
sewan (wampum)		Seewand
arm band of sewan	anápe	[Arm-]band von Seewand
String the sewan.	Nabhà.	Fädele den Seewanden.
belt of wampum [*written in English*]	ăchquásou	—
sewing needle, knitting needle	schăăpnégan	Nehnadel, ein Stricknadel
shall [*see* will; *see also under* speak]	[*often uncertainty in translating from German*	sollen; *cf.* must]
I have great hope [that] Bathsheba will get well.	Nia nachgawosè machè chàn [I hope - I great hope] onammanisseĕd Bathseba. [get-well-*conjunct*]	Ich habe grosse Hofnung Baths[eba] soll gesund werden.
Shall I place or set it here?	Nèn tachañăn.	Soll ichs daher stellen oder sezen.
Shamokin [= Sunbury, Pa.]	Schăchmàchkeĕk [= to or in Shamokin]	nach Shomokin

[*Shamokin was at the forks of the Susquehanna River; distinguish present Shamokin, 17 miles east on Shamokin Creek, and named in 1867. Meaning* eel-place-at *or* crayfish-place-at? *Gerard (1896) has* Shûmokenk, *where horns, or antlers, are plenty (Delaware* wschummo, *archaic for* horn; wiaki, plenty, *or cf.* machquigen, plenty of bears; -enk, at); Reichel (1870) has place of chiefs or rulers (sakima, chief), probably incorrect; Heckewelder is incorrect about place where guns are straightened (Donehoo, 1928), but his Schahamokink, place of eels, may be correct. Nora Thompson Dean (1982) wrote: "This is one place where I used to hear the old people talk about," and insisted that it is from Sahamóking, crayfish-place, from šhamwis, crayfish, which Pentland (pers. comm., 1985) reconstructs as "Proto-Algonquian *ahšākēwa, crayfish, lobster (which should give Unami xa·ke··). It appears to be from (pseudo-)Proto-Algonquian *ahsāhk- with diminutive consonant symbolism, or from ps-PA šahk-. There are other complications; the Unami word seems to demand *ahšāhk- plus a suffix (not fish, -amēk-)." In addition, NTD notes that eel is šóxamskw, from šóxe, it is slippery, slick, and -mekw, fish; cf. Brinton: schachamek, eel; Anthony's annotation to w'schachamek, straight fish: "or a slippery fish, eel"; NTD excludes straight fish because that would be šaxáhkamskw; thus a choice: eel-place or crayfish-place.*]

share [see divide]		
sharp [cf. pointed]	gégan	scharf
Sharp is my knife.	Gégan tachégan.	Mein Messer ist scharf.
It is not sharp.	Stà gĕgănōwè.	[Es] ist nicht scharf.
to sharpen	gĕĕkhégan	schärfen
Have you sharpened my knife?	Gĕĕkhămmăwèh tăchégan.	Hastu mein Messer scharf gemacht?
Tomorrow I will sharpen my knife.	Wapachgătsch ngĕĕkhammen tachégan.	Morgen will ich[da]s Messer scharf machen.
she [see he; **Mpowà** under die; disobedient]		
sheaf [see bundle]		
shears, scissors	ktackchégan [= your shears]	deine Scheere
Lend me your shears.	[N'temméhe] ktackchégan.	Le[h]ne mir deine Scheere.
shed [see barn]		
shed [verb] [see spill]		
sheep (pl.)	mamaksimsàk	Schaafe

[cf. Delaware (Brinton) mekis, memekis, sheep (memekis, imitative of bleating, Anthony); Nipmuck (Day) mamakis — note 675: "a loan word from Mahikan (Frank T. Siebert . . . 1971)." It is probably a loan word from Delaware, but Nora Thompson Dean notes the Dutch word mekkeren, to bleat, and mekkert, he bleats; if so, Nipmuck, Mahican, and Delaware forms may be from Dutch.]

The sheep hear my word.	Ne mamaximsàk apetammenáu ntăăptonawágan.	Die Schaafe hören mein Wort.
My sheep hear my voice. [exact translation uncertain]	Nenochtagăk [=me-hear-they] mamaksimsàk onenochtamnáu nawan. [he hears/they hear him? + what I say?]	Meine Schaafe hören meine Stimme.
No man shall tear my sheep away from my hand.	Sta ăm mamaksimsà ótsche ktōchănáwan náchkek.	Niemand soll meine Schaafe aus meiner Hand wegreissen.
All souls (are) his sheep.	Máowe waadtschachquétsche ŏmămăksimmà.	Alle Seelen sind seine Schaafe.
sheet of paper [cf. leaf]	népăchkè	Blatt Papier
a sheet	gútta népăchkè	ein Blatt
Shekomeko [stress on penultimate syllable preferable; great village (R1), big house, or principal house of Moravian missions in Dutchess County, N.Y.]		
those from Shekomeko	Checomégok utschájak [see under come]	—
shinbone [see leg]		
shine	—	scheinen
The sun is shining.	Giischuch olandéuch. [see under Delaware words]	Die Sonne scheint. Dellaw[are] [sic]
ship, boat [made of wood?; cf. canoe]	—	Schiff
The ship of the brothers has arrived [in Manhattan?]. [Which underlined is properly ship, or both—one in verb, one in noun?]	Kétachcanenăăk otàmmachoonwa kschachquamachoōn mănnăhàtáhănìck ăquòchnáu. [brothers they-ship-(go) + ship Manhattan(?)-at landed-it]	Der Br[üde]r Schiff ist angekommen.

[cf. modern Mahican (M., 1914) mɐxón, canoe (made of wood, dugout?); Nipmuck (Day, The Mots loups . . . , 1975) amis8l, canot de bois; and Natick mushoon, mishoon, boat (of wood)]

shirt	[-hámed, from Dutch hemd or German Hemd; cf. Mah. Hámet, linen cloth (Masthay, 1980, p. 37, from 1759]	Hemde waschen [= to wash a shirt]
Wash my shirt.	Kschĕĕchta ntahámed.	Wasche mein Hemd.
Give (Put) your (pl.) shirts (in the wash).	Ktahámedowan náwutennemook.	Gebt eure Hemde in die Wäsche.
Give it [to me to put] in the wash [we wash it].	Nawutenè kescheechtananà.	Gibs in die Wäsche.
shoe(s) [see also patch (verb)]	máksen, măksen, măksĕnĕ, máxxen	Schu, Schue, Shuh
shoe [little or short moccasin?]	tschachquáchxen	[Schuh]
shoes	[tschachquachxe]nan, plur[alis]	Schuhe
The shoes are torn.	Pºquèechnāō măxxen.	Die Schu sind zerrissen.
I want to mend my shoes.	Gáttau mĕschhamen máksen. [cf. patch]	Ich will meine Schu flicken.
My shoes are too big for me.	Mamagáwan măksene.	Meine Schu sind mir zu gros.
My shoes are too small for me.	Tschatschaxĕschne măksĕnĕ. Tschăckĕschĕsan măksen.	Meine Schu sind mir zu klein.
My shoes are new.	Uskájan măhksĕnăn.	Meine Schu sind neu.
I repair shoes.	N'mĕschhămmen.	Ich flicke Schu.

126 *Schmick's Mahican dictionary*

Fix your shoes.	Mĕschhámmei.	Flicke deine Schu.
I will not fix them.	Stà n'mĕschhámmau.	Ich will sie nicht flicken.
I am ready to repair shoes.	Kĕschequamè.	Ich bin fertig mit Schu flicken.
Make me a pair of shoes.	Onechtawè nguttòksenà maksenan.	Mach mir ein Paar Schu.
	Onĕĕchtawè nguttò ksenà mãh'ksenan.	Mach mir ein Paar Schue.
Put on (your [*sg.*]) shoes.	Kmàchchaxŏéme máxxen.	Ziehe Schue an.
old shoe	machowe tschachquáchxen [*sg.*]	alte Schuhe [*pl.*]
shoot	–	schiessen
I shoot. I am shooting.	Niàmpáquè.	Ich schiesse.
I shoot.	Np'mà.	Ich schiesse.
You shoot.	K[p'mà].	Du [schiessest.]
He shoots.	Op'máw.	Er [schiesst.]
We will shoot.	P'matŏŏk.	Wir wollen schiessen.
Let's (both) shoot.	P'mataù.	Lasst uns [schiessen]. *(Dualis)*
Why are you (*pl.*) shooting?	Gaquatsch p'mãk?	Warum schiesst ihr?
He hits (the) things (by shooting).	Udàinimschawàh.	Er trift die Sache.
I didn't shoot anything.	Stàn nĕmĕscháu.	Ich habe nichts geschossen.
You did hit (the mark).	Kmìschcháwà.	Hast du getroffen.
He (has) shot (a stag).	Mĕscháŭ.	Er hat einen Hirsch geschossen.
He (has) hit (the mark).	Náhkĕma ŏmìschschàwà.	Er hat getroffen.
They (have) hit (the mark).	[Náhkĕmawa ŏmìschschàwà.	Sie haben getroffen.
One who has struck (the mark), called also He has shot.	Maschŏŏt. [=] *Daniel* [*as personal name*]	Einer der getroffen hat. Heisst auch er hat geschossen.
I (have) hit it, namely, on the mark.	Mĕschótamen.	Ich habe getroffen, *scil[icet]* ins Ziel.
He (has) hit the mark.	Ōmĕschótamen.	Er hat ins (nach) Ziel getroffen.
He has (*or* did) not hit it, or He has shot past it, or missed.	Asta ōmĕschótamówe.	Er hat nicht getroffen *v[el]* Er hat vorbeigeschossen.
The mark, goal, or target, at which one shoots	weeshécan [*note* s + h, *not error for* sch]	Das Merck oder Ziel wornach man schiesset.
Who is shooting?	Awàn nàpáqueĕt.	Wer schiesst.
Who has shot?	Awan kpãquánà.	Wer hat geschossen.
to shoot a gun, discharge a gun Fire off. Fire. Shoot.	– Pãquĕchtà.	Flinte losschiessen Schiesse los.
short [*see also* little]	–	kurz (oder klein)
Time is short (little).	Tschachquaschéschen majánapowágan.	Die Zeit ist kurz (klein).
a short word [*contrast* long word *under* long; *see also under* word]	tschachquaăp tschŏnãchgãtschò	ein kurzes Wort
[*see* tschachkochquà *and* tschachquachaju, *p. 155*]		
should [*often sense not present in Mahican, but in German*]		sollen
You shouldn't bring any water.	Tschēnããspãhãn	Du solt kein Wasser holen.
We should be thus daily.	Nè ãm kiánau tããtĕ pãĩnanaù wáwochka- [that will we be, *etc.*] / mákè.	So sollen wir täglich seyn.
shoulder	ntennemágan	Achsel
shout [*see* cry out; call]		
shove [*see* push]		
show, indicate, direct, point		[weisen]
He (she) pointed with the hand.	Ánàham onàchk.	Er (sie) wiess mit der Hand.
Show me.	ĕMpènnãmèn.	Weise mir.
show mercy or pity [*see* bless; compassion]		
shrink [*see* disappear]		
sick [*see also* spit]	–	krank
Therefore when someone among us feels that he is sick.	Nè ŭtschè awãn ãm kiánãu ãmáttakà, ŏwénamansohããncùn.	Darum wenn jemand unter uns fühlt, dass er kranck sey.
All are sick in the heart.	Máwe awãn wénamánsoak otáhawãk.	Alle sind krank am Herzen.
all the sick ones	máwe wenamansétsche	alle Kranke
I will visit the sick man.	N'gechganãhn nemanáu wenamanseĕd.	Ich will den kranken Mann besuchen.
I have seen the sick one.	Nià nawáu wenamanseĕd.	Ich habe den kranken gesehen.
You have seen the sick one.	Kià knawáu k[wenamanseĕd]. [*sic*]	Hastu den kranken [gesehen].
You (*pl.*) have seen the sick one.	[Kia]wa knawawà [wenamanseĕd].	Habt ihr [den Kranken gesehen].
[Yes?] Dry apples don't make one sick.	Kàhããp'néssàk astà mémachpĕŭnããk.	Trocken Äpfel machen einem nicht kranck.

English-Mahican-German 127

English	Mahican	German
side [*see also* breast]	wapuchquanek	Seite
in his wounded side [? in the wounds of his side?]	neáne paquaick wapuchquanik	in seine verwundte Seite
in his pierced side	nè tákamamukkùp wapuchquanek	in seine d[urch]stochene Seite
They pierced him in his side with a spear.	Aschawachkhéganà tachkamáăp wapóchquanik.	Sie haben ihn mit einem Spiess gestochen.
A sweet fountain is what flowed from Jesus' side.	T'wàchk wĕgan Tap[anemuc]quàk wapúchquanick wătsche sokachnágup.	Ein süsser Brunn ist was aus Jesu Seite fliesset.
in the (his) side	néa wapuchquanìk	in der Seite
in the (his) side	wachpassei	in [der] Seite
They (have) stabbed him in his side.	Otakkamáwak wapassăk.	Sie haben ihn in die Seite gestochen.
If we all cling to his (the Savior's) side, . . .	Nĕtschăwăn măwe nachpassăk kĕnămméta, . . .	Wenn wir in d[er] Heilands Seite hangen, . . .
on the left side [*delete* side?]	omenachtschewanìk otakquè	auf der linken Seite
sifter [*see* ashes, ash sifter]		
silver [*see* money, depend on, help]	-sehnpatt-, -senpĕtt- [*from Dutch?; see* Loan words]	
similar to [*see* like]		
simmering; it's cooking slowly, it's simmering.	Osòh.	Es kocht (gemach).
sin, evil, the doing of evil, way of sin	matschaiwagan	Sünde
You serve the (your) way of sin.	Kmatschaiwagan ktackenahamawà.	Du dienest der Sünde.
sin [*verb*]	—	sündigen
I sin.	Nmátschai.	Ich sündige.
You sin.	G[mátschai].	Du [sündige]st.
He sins.	Matschaju.	Er [sündige]t.
We sin.	Nmatschaihanà.	Wir sündigen.
You (*pl.*) sin.	G[matschai]hamà.	Ihr [sündige]t.
They sin.	Matschajuwàk.	Sie sündigen.
I have sinned.	N'matschaihòp.	Ich habe gesündiget.
You have sinned.	G[matschaihòp].	Du [hast gesündiget].
He has sinned.	Matschaijŏp.	Er [hat gesündiget].
We have sinned.	Matschaihennăăp.	Wir haben [gesündiget].
You (*pl.*) have sinned.	Gmatschaihammŏp.	Ihr [habt gesündiget].
since [*see* as]		
sing	—	singen
I sing.	Nachgochemà.	Ich singe.
You sing.	K[nachgochemà].	Du singest.
He sings.	Onachgochemáu.	Er singet.
We sing.	Nachgochemahanà.	Wir singen.
You (*pl.*) sing.	K[nachgochemaha]wà. Gnachgochemahawà.	Ihr singet.
They sing.	Onachgochemáwak. Nachgochemáwak.	Sie singen.
Sing!	(K)nachgochemà. Nachgòmămà.	Singe.
Joseph sings.	Jos[eph] nachgochemáu.	Jos[eph] singt.
Let's both sing.	Nachgochematáū.	[Lasst uns singen.] *Dual[is]*
Let's all sing.	Nachgochematook máowe.	Lasst uns alle singen.
Let's sing.	Nachcòmātŏŏk.	Lasst uns singen.
Sing (*pl.*)!	Nachgochemáku. Nachgochemáqu.	Singet.
They sing.	Nachgochemáwak.	Sie singen.
They have not yet sung.	Achquódhà nnachgochmawĕĕk. Achquodho nachgochmawĕĕk.	Sie haben noch nicht gesungen.
Let's sing an Indian verse.	Ananapawĕk ganáwetŏk.	Lasst uns ein Indianer Versel singen.
Do you feel the words that you sing in [your] heart?	Ktammachtammen nĕĕn aaptonawaganan ănèkănawójannè ktahàk.	Fühlest du die Worte, die du singest, im Herzen.
The bird sings (calls).	Tschenuáu tschĕĕchtschis.	Der Vogel singt.
All (of you [*pl.*]) sing, or All (of you [*pl.*]) say. [*2nd p. pl. imperative; cf.* call, shout]	Máwe tschenuaăk.	Singt alle, oder sagt alle.
single, unmarried		ledig seyn
I am single.	Nià ngēgăpáwe.	Ich bin ledig.
Are you single?	Gegapawè.	Bist du ledig?
Are you (*pl.*) unmarried people?	Gegapawechmà.	Seyd ihr ledige Leute.
They are unmarried people.	Gegapawàk.	Sie sind ledige Leute.
a single, unmarried (man)	gegapau	ein lediger Bruder [= an unmarried brother]

sister [see also under brother]
  younger sister | chesem
  younger sisters | chésemak | die jüngern Schwestern
  older sister | mēēs
  older sisters | mésak | die ältern Schwestern
  the sisters | cheismenaak | die Schwestern
  for the sisters | cheschemushāhk, cheismusak | vor die Geschwister [sisters *here only*]
sit | — | sezen, sezzen; sizzen
  Sit down. Sit still. | Matachpè. | Sez dich, sez still.
  Be still! | Tschè kăpè. | Sey still.
  Be still (*pl.*)! | Tschēēkpè. | Seyd still.
  Be still! / Sit still! | Majà năchpè. Majánapè. | Sey still. Siz still.
  Sit down. Take a seat. | Mattappè. | Sez dich.
  Sit down here. | Tappè. | Sez dich heran.
  Sit on the ground. | Mattapè ahhkeēk. | Sez dich aufn Grund.
  <u>Sit</u> by the fire. | (X)schétanà <u>wapè</u>. [be hot] | Sez dich beim (zum) Feuer.
  I will take a seat. | Happétau. | Ich will mich sezen.
  Sit by me or together with me. | Néschapetaù. | Sez dich mit mir, oder [Sez dich] mit mir zusammen.
  Come, sit down. | Năwe mătăchpè. | Komm sez dich nieder.
  You are (now?) sitting in a good | Nónu mătăchpè nŏŭnit. | Du sizest in einen guten Plaz.
  He sat by the fire. / place. | Hapò schétănāwă stăăk. | Er sass beim Feuer.
  I will (now?) sit in the wounds [of the Savior]. | Nono n'táppe paquaik. | Ich will in den W[un]den sizen.
  The (female?) cat is sitting under [the table (*not in Mahican*)]. | Anámuk poschesch achpóu. [underneath cat sits-she] | Die Kaze sizt untern Tisch.
  Why are you sitting? | Gaquătsch nmăttăchpējàn. | Warum sizestu?
  Here I sit. I'm sitting here. | Ne ápea. | Hier siz ich.
  There (here?) he sits. | Nà ápeēd. | Dort sizt er.
  There she (Anna) sits. | Nè ápeed. | Dort sizt sie (Anna).
  There we sit. Here we sit. | Na ápejak. Ne ápeak. | Da sizen wir. Hier sizen wir.
  Let's sit. | Átăpétŏŏk. | Lasst uns sizzen.
  Where are you (*pl.*) sitting? | Tăn ktăppēnāwă? | Wo sizt ihr?
  There they sit. | Neĕk ápetscheĕk. | Da sizen sie. Dort sizen sie.
  I have already sat. [cf. under until] | Nkeschemàchtsch nmattapè. | Ich habe schon gesessen.
  I am <u>tired</u> of sitting. | Neschéwa kapè. | Ich bin müde zu sizzen.
  [they] sit on [*poss.* alight on?] | ŏmìschschakanáwa. [see mosquitoes] | sezen sich an
situation [*cf.* place]
six | guttaăsch | sechs
  6 o'clock [see under love feast] | guttaăsch tschenuáka [when it rings 6?] | sechs Uhr
skin [*noun and verb*] [*see* hide; apple skin]
skunk [*for* Biss-kaz = biting cat? *cf. Piss Katze*, pol-cat (*sic*), Delaware (Zeisberger, 1887) *sschkaăk*; no Schmick Mahican word]
sky, heaven [*see also* up there] | — | Himmel
  in the sky, in heaven | wochcamáwenaak | im Himmel
slaughter, butcher [*verbs*] | t'mequachsáu | schlachten
sleep [*verb*] [*see also* bed] | — | schlafen
  I sleep. | N'gawè. Ngawè. | Ich schlafe.
  You sleep. | Kawè. Gawè. | Du [schläfst].
  Go to bed. Go to sleep. | Kăuwè. Gawè. | Leg dich schlafen. Geh schlafen.
  Go lie down. Go to bed. | Anàchchakéchè kăuwè. | Leg dich schlafen.
  Have you slept already? Did you sleep already? | Gawè pagatschè. | Hastu geschlafen.
  Sleep in the room (wigwam?). | Wequamick gawè. | Schlaf in der Stube.
  He is sleeping. He sleeps. | Gauwéu. Gawéu. | Er [schläft].
  She sleeps. | Gawéwa. | Sie schläft.
  Thus we sleep in his name. | Nò gauweenanau nahk'ma otenewesowaganick. | So schlafen wir in Namen sein.
  They sleep. They are sleeping. | Gawéwak. | Sie schlafen.
  Have you slept well? (Did . . . sleep) | Konamansè anagáwoja. | Hastu wol geschlafen.
  Have you slept well? | [Kŏne] kawè. Góne gawè. Gŏne gawè. | Hastu [wol geschlafen].
  Have you rested well? | Góne gawè. | Hastu wol geruht.
  Have you (*pl.*) slept well? | Kŏne kaweĕchmà? Gŏne gaweĕchmà. | Habt ihr wol geschlafen.

Have you (*pl.*) rested well?	Góne găwĕĕchmà.	Habt ihr wol geruhet.
Sleep (*pl.*) well.	Gŏnè gaweémaak.	Schlaft wol.
I cannot sleep well at night.	Stà ngésche gawéu kŏne tpŏchgà.	Ich kan nicht schlafen in der Nacht.
I sleep at night.	Gawéu nĕpáwĕ.	Ich schlaf in der Nacht.
When it is night, I will go to sleep.	Ngawĕhn t'póchgo.	Wenns Nacht ist, will ich schlafen gehen.
Did you sleep this (past) night?	K'gāwĕ nóno t'pochquĕĕk?	Hastu vergangne Nacht geschlafen?
You lie down. Lie down. Go to sleep. [*see also* lie down]	Kmäŭgawè. Kmaüuquà.	Legstu dich nieder.
We will go to bed.	Ihà măŏquămŏtŏk.	Wir wollen uns schlafen legen.
(the same)	Gauwetŏk.	*idem*
Therefore we are created to sleep in his arm.	Ni watsche onèhókăjàne onàchkeck ngáuweèn.	Wir sind deswegen geschaffen in seinen Arm zu schlafen.
Go (*pl.*) to bed, children.	Găwŏhntĕk ăwāsĕsàk.	Legt euch schlafen Kinder.
They are sleeping.	Nahk'mawa gauwenawa.	Sie schlafen.
Are the brothers in bed?	Kĕschĕchgăwŏntŏăk ketachcanenăăk?	Sind die Br[üde]r zu Bette.
sleepy, drowsy; lethargic(?)	—	schläfrig seyn
I am sleepy.	N'gāgăŭkcheĕn. Gagawokcheĕn.	Ich bin schläfrig.
He is sleepy.	Gagauuquacheĕn.	Er ist schläfrig.
slide along [*see* drag]		
slink [*see* crawl]		
sloped (it is), declivitous	nămáju	abhängigt
slow	—	langsam
Go slowly.	Chammau chassè. Chammau chăăsche.	Geh langsam.
You are going too slowly.	Osame chammawéschè k'pomsè.	Du gehst zu langsam.
He is slow.	Sasche pachgáju.	Er ist langsam.
They are slow.	[Sasche pachgá]juwak.	Sie sind langsam.
I go slowly.	N'mammenonóchà.	Ich gehe langsam.
You go slowly.	K[mammenonóchà].	Du gehest [langsam].
He goes slowly.	Mammenonocháu.	Er gehet [langsam].
We go slowly.	N'mammenonochahanà.	Wir gehen [langsam].
You (*pl.*) go slowly.	K[mammenonochaha]mà.	Ihr gehet [langsam].
They go slowly.	Mammenonocháwak.	Sie gehen [langsam].
Go slowly.	M'nonochamà.	Geh langsam.
Go (*pl.*) slowly.	Mnonochamăku.	Geht [langsam].
We will go slowly.	[Mnono]chátaù.	Wir wollen langsam gehen.
Let's go slowly.	[Mnono]chatŏk.	Lasst uns [langsam gehen].
You go too slowly.	Kosáme mnónŏchà.	Du gehst zu langsam.
same [?You go slowly. *repetit.*]	Kmamm'nonócha. [*see previous tenth one*]	*idem*
same [?You go slowly.]	Kseschachwócha. [*cf. preceding one*]	*idem*
small [*see* little; a little]		
smash [*see* hit]		
smell	nĕmĕnnátămèn	riechen
It smells good.	Wĕk tschamáquat.	Es riecht gut.
It smells good (namely, the gunpowder).	Weĕktschàmmakwàt. [m̄ *for* mm?] [*cf. Massachusett Weetimungquot.* It smells sweetly.]	Es riecht gut (neml[ich] das Pulver).
It smells bad.	Machtschémăquàt.	Es riecht bös.
It stinks or smells evil.	Mättschàmmakwat. [m̄ *for* mm?] [*cf. Mass. Matchemungquot.* It smells badly.]	Es stinkt, oder riecht übel.
smoking	—	Rauch
It is smoking, or it is smoke.	Xschàchtăŭ.	Es raucht, oder es ist Rauch.
smooth [*see* smoothen; soft]		
smoothen [*see* even out]		
sneak [*see* crawl]		
sneeze [*verb*]	—	niesen
I sneeze.	Ntágusk. [same] Ntaksáme.	Ich niese.
You sneeze.	K[tágusk].	Du niesest.
He sneezes.	Átusk. *it[em]* [= same] Aksámu.	Er [nieset].
Why are you sneezing?	Gaquai wătsch águshkun?	Warum niesestu?
Because I took snuff.	Snùp ntágushgun otschè. [sh = *which:* s + h, *or* sch (= š)?]	Darum weil ich Schnupftobak genommen.
snort [*see* blow one's nose]		

snow [*verb*]	–	schneien, schneÿen, schneyen
It will snow soon.	Pachŏd pĕchããn.	Es wird bald schneÿen.
I believe (think) it will snow today [*delete* today].	N'tenetahà éne p'chãn. [I-think will snow]	Ich glaube es wird heute schneÿen.
I think it will not snow.	[N'tenetahà] aschã p'chanówe.	[Ich glaube es wird] nicht schneyen.
Perhaps it's still snowing.	Pechtkããtsch p'chãn.	Vielleicht schneyts doch.
It is not much snow.	Astan mapĕchããnnaowe.	Es ist nicht viel Schnee.
There is not much snow (namely, this winter).	Astan mĕcháchtãwè.	Es ist nicht viel Schnee (diesen Winter, neml[ich]).
It's snowing hard.	Kschŭchpóu.	Es schneyt sehr.
snuff [*noun*]	snùp [*from English*]	Schnupftobak
snuff out, put out (light)	–	puzen
Snuff out the (candle)light, or cut the light.	Tŭmmeschè wãhs'nanégan.	Puze das Licht oder Schneide [das Licht].
I will snuff it out.	Ntŭmmeschímmen.	Ich wills puzen.
I can't put it out; you put it out.	Ascha nkésche tummeschemówun, kia tummeschè.	Ich kans nicht puzen; puze du es.
The servant puts out the (candle)light.	Ahagenahégããd otummeschimmen wãhs'nanégan.	Der Diener puzt das Licht.
so [+ *adjective*]		so
I am so afraid.	[N?]weschasoõpkà, [*a different function?*]	Ich bin so fürchtsam.
So (as) long as I live.	Tãn sàchkãósía.	so lang ich lebe.
so much, so very much	wasáme	so sehr
[He] has so much loved us, that...	... wasáme achwahnuquáqua nannu ...	[Er] hat uns so sehr geliebet, dass ...
so [much]; too much(?)	-ósãmĕnĕs	so
Don't scream or cry so [much].	Kósãmĕnĕs kĕschaachsè.	Schrey nicht so.
so, thus, then [*see also* because; so that; that; **náhane** *under* must; **néhene** *under* peace *and* self?]	nò; nè [?], nĕáne [?], ŭtschi [?], anè [?]	so; weil?
We should be thus daily.	Nè ãm kiánau tããtĕ pãïnanaù [that? will we be, *etc.*] wáwochkamákè.	So sollen wir täglich seyn.
So it seems.	Anè nãquàk.	Es sieht so aus.
He has so spoken with me.	Tennããptonamũkkùn.	Er hat mit mir so geredt.
Thus we sleep ...	Nò gauweenanau ...	So schlafen wir ...
Just as the little children are born, so has he been born.	Nĕáne machtappétap awaschees, áhanè wie [= just as] so [= so] machtappĕĕd.	Er ist geboren werden, so wie die kleine Kinder.
so long as [*see under* long]		
so that, then	nikkàhtsch, nikkããtsch; ŭtschi [?]	damit, da, dass; so
so that we could become well or be healed through his wounds.	nikkããtsch kiánau áne páquaick wanamansohããnquàk.	dass wir durch s[eine] Wunden heil oder gesund werden könnten.
Then we <u>will</u> all truly see Jesus together. *or* So that we <u>will</u> all see each other.	(Ihàn) nikkàhtsch kiánau máowe <u>kdéttan</u>, gnãŭténãnaù.	Da wir Jesu alle zusammen recht sehen werden. [*or*] Damit werden wir uns alle sehen.
[If] you (*pl.*) search for the Savior, then you (*pl.*) will find him. *or* Search (*pl.*) for the Savior so that you will find him.	Quenaù kP[achtamawaas]nau kmachcawãŭtschi.	Suchet d[en] Heiland, so werdet ihr ihn finden.
soak	–	einweichen
Beaver skin is soaking in the water.	Tãmmõchquèi kamukhà mpĕĕk.	*Beaver* Haut weiche ein ins Wasser.
soft, tender, smooth, delicate, weak [*see* weak]		weich
soft, tender, *etc.*	Schãwăpĕĕm. [*see* Names, Catherine]	weich
I have stayed <u>soft</u>. [*cf.* lie (hard)]	Káha nõtăchgĕchgănãchĕn. [káha =?]	Ich habe weich gelegen.
How soft have you curried (prepared) the skin?	Kahaquegagenĕga?	Wie weich hastu das Fell zugerichtet?
soft and pliable [*see* juicy]		
soften skins [*see* curry]		
softly, in a low voice		leise
They are speaking <u>softly</u>.	Gĕĕmtonháwak. [*for more, see at* speak]	Sie reden leise.
solace [*see* comfort]		
someone, somebody, anyone	awãn; aschawãn [= no (matter) who]	jemand
if someone always	awáneetsch gommáwe	wenn jemand allezeit
something	gáquai	etwas

English-Mahican-German 131

something else [*see also* see]	pannewe	was anders
sometimes, often	—	manchmal
Sometimes it rains; sometimes there is good weather.	Sāsechgaù sóganan, [-s-!] sāsĕchgaù móschachquat.	Manchmal regnets, manchmal ists gut Wetter.
Sometimes it rains; sometimes there is good weather.	Ságechgaù sokanãn, sagechgaù móschachquat. [-g-!]	Manchmal regnets, manchmal ists gut Wetter.
sometimes here, sometimes there	—	bisweilen hier bisw[eilen] dort
son	otaijóma [= his son; his possession?; *cf.* things]	Sohn
my son	ntajōm	mein Sohn
soon, after a little while [*cf.* immediately]	éne, ene, ẽn [*see under* write]	bald, über ein Weilchen
Soon it will be halfway.	Pachood knānāwóchachnaù.	Bald ist der Halbe Weg.
It will snow soon.	Pachŏd pᵉchãán.	Es wird bald schneyen.
Come again soon. Come back soon.	Metscheme páma. [*cf. Delaware (Brinton) metschimi,* soon, presently]	Komm bald wider.
You can work lightly.	M'tschéme ãm k'tannachgà.	Du kanst leichtlich arbeiten.
sorrow [*see* sadness]		
sorrowful [*see* sad]		
sort, kind, species, race	—	Art, Gattung
soul, ghost	ŏtschìtschaquà, otschitschachquan	Seele, Geist
all souls	maowe waadtschachquétsche	alle Seelen
many souls	utschitschàchquénããk	viele Seelen
the Savior of all souls	Kékāchquăkùp mawe watschitschàchquajàckq	der Heiland aller Seelen
our souls	otschitschachcunána	unsre Seelen
our souls	tschitschachkonanaù	unser Selen [*sic*]
soul's work	annachgawágan otschitschachk<u>wéwe</u>	Seelen[-arbeit]
sound, ring [*verb*] [*see* bell]	—	lauten [*poss. not* läuten = to ring, to toll]
You sound [a bell].	Tautaù mamatahà.	Laute du.
I will sound.	Nià nmamatahãn.	Ich will lauten.
He will sound.	Omamatahaú.	Er [will lauten].
We will sound.	Nmamatahanána.	Wir wollen lauten.
You (*pl.*) will sound.	K[mamatahana]ma.	Ihr [wollt lauten].
They will sound.	Omamatahawak.	Sie [wollen lauten].
It (bell) sounds (rings).	Tautaù tschenuaú. [tschenuaú = it calls]	Es lautet.
It has sounded (rung).	Paggatschè tschenuáu.	Es hat gelautet.
Soon when it gets to be evening, it (the bell) sounds (rings). . . . [*or* As soon as it is sounded toward evening, . . .]	schétà Éne tãppăchchétà tautautschenuaú . . .	So bald gegen Abend gelautet wird, . . .
Let the bell sound (ring?).	Nánāmāhà taútaù.	Lass lauten.
You can sound the bell.	Taútaù nánāmāhà.	Du kanst lauten.
It is time to ring the bell for the meeting.	Tautau nanamaha kmajàwēēchnaù.	Es ist Zeit zur Versammlung zu lauten [*sic for* läuten?].
Now the bell can be sounded.	Tápe [= enough] ãm taútaù nonò knánāmáhānãhm.	Jezt kan [es] gelautet werden.
Now it is time to sound [it].	Nono tepìskăwēchnaú knánāmáhānãhm.	Jezo ist Zeit zu lauten.
When the bell sounds (rings?), . . .	Tschenuáka tāūtāū . . .	Wenn gelautet wird, . . .
letters that are pronounced (sounded)	tschecht<u>schenuam</u>egè	laute Buchstaben
at 5 o'clock . . . at 6 o'clock [when it rings 5 . . . when it rings 6]. . . .	Nánan tschenuáka . . . guttããsch tschenuáka . . .	Um 5 Uhr . . . um 6 . . .
sound a bugle [*see* blow a horn]		
soup	—	Suppe
thin soup, water-gruel	mpejapuwẽw [water + *PA *-āpō-* = fluid?]	dünne Suppe, Wasser Suppe
thin soup of maize	mpejápu	dünne Suppe von Welschkorn
source [*see* spring]		
space [*see* room]		
sparkle, emit sparks, glitter, twinkle	nowàsécŏsócùn	funckeln
speak, talk, converse [*cf.* say]	—	reden
I speak.	Nia ntãắptonà. Nià netaaptonà.	Ich rede.
You speak. Do you speak?	K[tãắptonà]. Ktắptonà.	Du redest. Redest du?

He speaks.	Aãptonáu. Ãptonáu.	Er [redet].
He speaks.	Udennaãptonan. Udennaãptonãhn.	Er spricht.
We speak.	Taãptonachnà. Taãptonahanà. Tãptonachnà. Tãptonahanà.	Wir reden.
You (pl.) speak.	K[taãptonaha]mà. [K tãptona]hamà.	Ihr [redet].
They speak.	Aãptonáwak. Aaptonáwàk.	Sie [reden].
They should speak. [but see below]	Ahãaptonáwak.	Sie sollen reden.
I hear that you are speaking.	Kpettãhn ktahaaptona.	Ich höre, dass du redest.
I have spoken.	Ntahaãptona.	Ich habe geredt.
You have spoken.	K[tahaãptona].	Du hast [geredt].
He has spoken. [sic]	Ahaaptonawunà. [= ?He has not spoken.]	Er hat [geredt].
We have spoken.	Tahaaptonahanà.	Wir haben [geredt].
You (pl.) have spoken.	K[tahaaptonaha]mà.	Ihr habt [geredt].
They have spoken. [see above]	Ahaãptonáwak.	Sie haben [geredt].
Tomorrow I will speak.	Wapachgãtsch ntahaãptonà.	Morgen will ich reden.
Tomorrow you will (have to, must) speak.	[Wapachgãtsch] k[tahaãptonà].	Morgen solstu reden.
Tomorrow he will (has to, must) speak.	[Wapachgãtsch] ahaaptonáu.	[Morgen] soll er [reden].
Tomorrow we will speak.	[Wapachgãtsch] ntahaaptonahanà.	[Morgen] wollen wir reden.
He has so spoken with me.	Tennaãptonamükkùn.	Er hat mit mir so geredt.
Do you believe what I have said to you?	Kohnsittawenà anaãptónamenàn?	Glaubestu was ich dir gesagt habe?
You (pl.) have heard from his mouth what he spoke (said).	Kpèttawáwà otóhnick otschè ãlnaãptōnaãt.	Ihr habts aus seinem Munde gehört, was er geredet.
[?You (pl.) / He speak(s) to him?]	Udaãptónama. [delayed imperative?]	[no translation]
[?They/you (pl.) have spoken? or ?You (pl.) speak?; see p. 155]	Udennaaptonamawa.	[no translation]
When he says to me only "fetch something."	Aãptónāzā.	Wenn er mir nur hol etwas gesagt hätte.
That is a long word.	Koõnnaãptónãchkàt.	Das ist ein langes Wort.
a short word	tschachquaãp tschõnãchgãtschò	ein kurzes Wort
a word	gúttà aptónachkat	ein Wort
two words	nescha aptónachkat	2 Wörter
Speak loudly; I cannot hear you.	Mamakeẽchse ascha késche ptánnowe.	Rede laut, ich kan dich nicht hören.
Speak loudly.	Mamaãktohnhà. Mamaãktonhà.	Rede laut.
Speak (pl.) loudly.	[Mamaãktohn]hãk. [Mamaãkton]hàk. Mamakeechséqu.	Redet [laut].
They speak loudly.	[Mamaãktohn]háwak. [Mamaãkton]háwak. [Mamakeech]sowak.	Sie reden [laut].
Don't speak loudly.	Tschẽk kmamaktõhnhãn. Tschẽk kmamaktõnhãņn. [n covers h]	Rede nicht laut.
He called loudly.	Machéchsò aãptonáu.	Er rief laut.
He spoke loudly, with a strong voice.	Awà kàchnã macheèchsò. [truly?]	Er sagte mit gewaltiger Stimme.
They know what I have said.	Neẽk owáwechtanáwa gaquai nià aãnè tõhnháijè.	Sie wissen, was ich geredet habe.
We (both) will speak softly.	[Geẽmton]hataù.	Wir wollen leise reden.
Speak (pl.) softly.	[Geẽmton]hákŭ.	Redet leise.
They are speaking softly.	Geẽmtonháwak. [see below]	Sie reden leise.
I will speak softly.	Ngeẽmtonhãn.	Ich will leise reden.
I have spoken softly.	[Ngeẽmton]hamàchtsch.	Ich habe leise geredt.
You have spoken softly.	Keemtonhamàchtsch.	Hastu [leise geredt].
He has spoken softly.	Keemtonháu.	Er hat [leise geredt].
They have spoken softly.	[Keemton]háwak. [see above]	Sie haben [leise geredt].
Why don't you speak softly?	Gaquãtsch asch geẽmtonhawàku?	Warum redest du nicht leise?
Who has spoken?	Awãn ahaãptonaãt?	Wer hat geredt?
One who always talks.	Mãashàkq. [personal name]	Einer der immer redt.
speak with, converse with	—	reden mit, reden miteinander
Tomorrow we will speak with each other.	Wãpãchgãtsch ktahaaptonamatéhena.	Morgen wollen wir miteinander reden.

English	Mahican	German
They speak with each other.	Ahaaptonametoàk.	Sie reden miteinander.
Will you speak with me soon?	Ene ktahaaptonamè?	Wiltu bald mit mir reden?
I will speak with Christian.	[Ene] Xstian ntahaaptonahanà.	Ich will mit Xst[ian] reden.
Joshua is speaking with Joseph.	Josua ahaaptonametoak Josepha.	Josua redet mit Joseph.
Will you (*pl.*) talk with each other [*a request?*]; I will go out.	Ktahaaptonamettehenà éne p'hagan ntān.	Wolt ihr miteinander reden, ich will naus gehen.
spear, with a spear	aschawachkhéganà	mit einem Spiess
spill, shed [*cf.* rain]	–	[vergiessen]
He has spilled, shed.	Sókahanáăp. Sokahatŏŏp. Sokahanăhp. Sokahatŏhp.	Er hat vergossen.
spin, whirl around (yarn, *etc.*)	–	spinnen
I spin.	Nia tachpéha.	Ich spinne.
You spin.	K[tachpe]hà.	Du [spinnest].
He or she spins.	Achpéhăŭ.	Er od[er] sie spinnet.
We spin.	Ntachpehananà. [n *covers* h]	Wir [spinnen].
You (*pl.*) spin.	K[tachpehana]mà. [n *covers* h]	Ihr [spinnet].
They spin.	Achpeháwak.	Sie [spinnen].
You <u>stop</u> spinning!	Ktachquachpéha.	Hörstu auf zu spinnen.

[*In ms.* Ktach<u>quach</u>péha, *but if underlining is to show prohibitive, it should properly be at first part:* K<u>tachqu</u>achpéha.]

Stop spinning!	Achquachpéha.	Hör auf zu spinnen.
Don't stop spinning!	Tscheĕg tăchquăchpéhan.	Hör nicht auf zu spinnen.
Spin quickly!	Gattătachpéha.	Spinn hurtig.
I'm <u>going to</u> (<u>will</u> [*see* see]) spin.	N<u>mawè</u> achpéha.	Ich gehe spinnen.
You are going to spin.	Kmawè [achpéha].	Gehstu spinnen.
spiritual [*see* internal]		
spit [*verb*], vomit, get sick [*cf. also* expectoration, cough]		speÿen (vomiren); anspeien [=spit upon]
I got very sick, *i.e.*, at sea.	Nia muchtsche nsúsque.	Ich habe mich sehr gebrochen, *i.e.* auf der See.
He vomits, spits.	Sukquéu.	Er speyet.
They vomit, spit, get sick.	Sukquéwak.	Sie vomiren, speyen, brechen sich.
I spit him in the face.	Nsisgomáu [osketschgok].	Ich spey ihm ins Gesicht.
He spits me in the face.	Nsisgómuk osketschgok.	Er speyt mir ins Gesicht.
You must not spit at the old (man).	Tscheéen ksisgomān ka<u>ch</u>tscháis.	Du must den alten (Mann) nicht ins Gesicht speyen. [*disregard* ins Gesicht]
They spat in the Savior's face.	Ŏsissĕgŏmáwa Pachtamawásan oskĕtschgok.	Sie haben dem Heiland ins Gesicht gespeyt.
split [*see* tear away]		
split open	–	aufgerissen, [aufge]schlizt
split wood	–	Holz spalten
I will split wood.	Māūpāpăchgăchtáham.	Ich will Holz spalten.
spoil [*see* ruin]		
spots [*see* marks]		
spread about [*see* lie scattered about]		
spring, source, fountain	–	Quelle
a spring, a fountain	t'wàchk	eine Quelle, Brunn
a fresh cold spring	d'háju t'wàchk	eine frische, kalte Quelle
salubrious spring	honammanissò t'wàchk	gesund [Brunn]
good source, sweet spring	t'wàchk wĕgan	gute Quelle, süsser Brunn
living water: springwater	p'māwosò mpëi [*improper syntax?*]	lebendig Wasser: Quellwasser
A sweet fountain is what flowed from Jesus' side.	T'wàchk wĕgan Tap[anemuc]quàk wapúchquanick wātsche sokachnágup.	Ein süsser Brunn ist was aus Jesu Seite fliesset.
spring [*verb*] [*see* jump]		
springwater [*see* living water *under* spring]		
sprinkle		
He has sprinkled me with water.	N'sŏŏgnetaàk.	Er hat mich mit Wasser begossen.
Don't sprinkle him.	Ktscheĕn sŏŏgnĕtăwĕĕn.	Begiess ihn nicht.
stab, pierce, prick, stick, jab, puncture, sting		stechen
I prick(ed?) myself.	Nian gottau on'mawáo. [gottau, *not* gattau]	Ich steche mich.
They (have) stabbed him.	Ktaù on'mawáo.	Sie haben ihn gestochen.
I stab (him?).	Ntakkamáu.	Ich steche.
I stab you.	Ktakkamèn.	Ich steche dich.
You stab.	Tachkamà.	Stich du.
[Yes,] prick me [*or*] stab me.	Quá takkamechgà.	Stich mich.

You're jabbing me.	Ktakkamè.	Du stichst mich.
He has stabbed himself.	Ntakkamócku.	Er hat sich gestochen.
He stabbed.	Otackkamáwa.	Er stach.
We stab.	Takkamaunà.	Wir stechen.
You (pl.) stab.	[Takkamau]wa.	Ihr [stechet].
They stab.	Otakkamáwak.	Sie [stechen].
They (have) stabbed him in the side.	[Otakkamáwak] wapassãk.	Sie haben ihn in die Seite gestochen.
They (have) pierced him in his side with a spear.	Aschawachkhéganà tachkamáãp wapóchquanik. [or it pierced him?]	Sie haben ihn mit einem Spiess gestochen.
stable, in the stable	kojégan, kojéganick [cf. cows]	Stalle, im Stalle [see under bring forth]

stag [see deer]
stain [see color]
stand — stehen. *Plura vid[e]* aufstehen [= For more, see aufstehen (*entry not given*).]

I have stood still.	Tscheganachksè.	Ich bin stille gestanden.

stay, remain [see also Rachel under Names; lie] — bleiben

I will stay here. [cf. be (in a place)]	Nannentajéēn.	Ich will hier bleiben.
Stay here.	Nánne ajè. Nannáje.	Bleib hier.
He stays here.	Nànn otajéēn.	Er bleibt hier.
[He is staying, (whereas)] They are going (when one is asked where he or she is).	Ŭtáĭjéēn.	Sie gehen (wenn von jemand gefragt wird wo er [sie] ist).
We will stay here.	[Nànn] ajétau.	Wir wollen hier bleiben.
Stay (pl.) here.	[Nànn] ajẽqu.	Bleibt hier.
You (pl.) stay here.	[Nànn] gtajenawà.	Bleibt ihr hier.
Where do your friends stay? [in a sense: Where do they live?]	Thà ăjŏwàk tennangómak?	Wo wohnen deine Freunde? *proprië* Wo bleiben [deine Freunde]?
When we remain by ...	ăjéēta	Wenn wir bleiben in ...
They endure and prosper from the old (great?) years to the new years.	Nannò otaĭjēnáwa, ónămănníssŏak machchowái katènnik pátsche uskái kátennik.	Sie bleiben und gedeihen vom Alten bis zum Neuen. N. 710
... that we remain in the belief.	... nàn nè ndaĭjeenanà onìstămawágan.	... dass wir im Glauben bleiben.
Remain not in your evil. [see impatient]	Ktaggetaha matechk anè. [you-small-heart(?)(impatient) evil in]	Verharre nicht in deinem Bösen.

steal

I steal.	Nia ngmoŏt.	Ich stehle.
You steal.	Kia k'moŏt.	Du stiehlst.
He steals.	[N]ahkma kmoŏt.	[no translation]
[?Who steals? or ?He steals that?]	[?] anè kmoŏt? [Awanè?]	[no translation]
We steal	Kianau kmoŏthénnāū.	Wir
You (pl.) steal.	Ki[awa kmoŏt]hamna.	Ihr
They steal.	Nahkmaw kmoŏtáãk.	Sie
Don't steal. I will reveal it.	Tschéēn kmoŏthèn ene kmochgenèn.	Stiehl nicht, ich wills offenbahren.

stern [see hard]

stick [noun]	ătóoku	Stock
red sticks, red canes	măchkwèpánăchkwè.	rothe Stöcke

stick [verb] [see stab]
still [see yet; quiet; pleasant; achschen under feel]

I have lain, or kept, quiet.	Tschegănēchēn.	Ich habe stille gelegen.
If you (pl.) don't keep still ...	Asch tschēkapewaqua ...	Wenn ihr nicht still seid ...
Be still.	Tschè kăpè. Tschéēkpè.	Sey still. Seyd still.
Be still. Sit still.	Majà năchpè. Majánapè.	Sey still. Siz still.
Sit still. Sit down.	Matachpè. [= Sit down.]	Sez still, sez dich.

sting [see stab]
stink, smell (have a bad odor) — stincken

It stinks.	Machtschémaquàt. Mãttschàm̃akwat. [m̃ = m or mm?] [cf. Massachusett *Matchemungquot*, It smells badly.]	Es stinckt.

stir up [see touch]

stocking; stockings	tschachguttãn; [tschachgutt]anan *plur[alis]*	[Strumpf]; Strümpfe
old stocking	machowe tschachguttãn [*singular*]	alte Strümpfe [*plural*]

stoke the fire [*cf. entries under* fire]		
Put the burning wood together, stoke the fire, stir up the fire.	Schaaktanegàh.	Leg die Brände zusammen. Schiers [schüre das] Feuer.
I will stoke the fire.	Nschaaktegà.	Ich wills Feuer schieren.
He will stoke the fire.	[Schaaktane]gáu.	Er [wills Feuer schieren].
Let's stoke the fire.	[Schaaktane]gataù.	Lasst uns [Feuer schieren].
They stoke it.	Schaaktanegáwak.	Sie schierens.
stone [*see* pipe of stone]		
stop [*cf.* depart (this life)]	–	hör auf
Stop getting water.	Ắchquǎǎspà.	Hör auf Wasser zu holen.
[achqu- = *a prohibitive*]		
Stop reading.	Ắchque lēsówěkǔ.	Hör auf zu lesen.
Stop spinning.	Achquachpéha. [*see note under* spin]	Hör auf zu spinnen.
Don't stop spinning [yarn, *etc.*].	Tschēēg tǎchquǎchpéhan.	Hör nicht auf zu spinnen.
stop up [*see also* deaf]	–	stopft zu
The Devil stops up [people's ears] so that they don't readily hear.	Kpachansò Machtandò stà wége ptammówe.	Der Teufel stopft d[er] Leute Ohren zu, dass sie nicht gerne hören.
strangle, suffocate with a cord	ktschèchquapéso	erdrosseln, ersticken mit einem Strick
strap [*see* band]		
strike [*see* hit; swollen]		
strike fire [*see under* fire]		
Make fire, strike fire.	Sta ǒněchtǎ.	Mach Feuer, Schlag Feuer.
I will strike fire.	N'sáckhǎǎn.	Ich will Feuer schlagen.
string [*cf.* bowstring]		
String the sewan (wampum).	Nabhà.	Fädele den Seewanden.
arm band of sewan	anápe	[Arm-]band von Seewand
strong [*see* hard; hero]		
strong voice, with a [*see* loud]		
stupid [*see* dumb]		
submissive [*see* obedient]		
suck	–	saugen
to suck	nōnǒsò	saugen
I suck.	Nià nōnǒsè.	Ich sauge.
I will suck the blood of the Savior.	Nià nōnǒsè Tap[anemuc]qua op'gachganǒm. [*sic for* Tap[anemuc]quak?]	Ich will des Heilandes Blut saugen.
The child lies at the breast.	Awǎsches kěnǎmù wapassajénǎk.	Das Kind liegt an der Brust.
The child is sucking.	Awǎses nonóso.	Das Kind säuget.
Soon will Elizabeth suckle it, *i.e.*, the child.	Ene onochnáwa Elisab[eth].	Bald wird es Elis[abeth] träncken, *i.e.* das Kind.
suckle, give to suck [*see* suck]		
suffocate with a cord [*see* strangle]		
sun [*no Mahican word given; see under* Delaware words]		
superficial person [*see* delay]		
supper [*see also* eat supper]	onaquépehn	*Supper* [*in English*], Abendessen
Lord's supper	Tapánemucquak onaquépehn [*ms. p. (39), but on ms. p. (1) note order:*] onaquépehn Tapánemucquak oder [= or] tachquachackemahaàn [*cf.* love feast]	*Lords Supper* [*sic in English*], des He[r]rn Abendmahl [*ms. p. (39)*]; Abendmahl des H[errn] [*less likely:* H[eilands], *ms. p. (1)*]
Who is going to supper?	Awǎn wétschechnáta máchǎǎk. [*ms. p. (82)*]	Wer zum A[bend]m[ahl] gehet.
support, assistance	–	Beistand
support or keep a company	–	Bande halten
surely [*see* certainly]		
suspenders [*see* band]		
swaddling clothes strap [*see* band]		
swallow, gulp or drink down	–	schlucken (hinter)
Swallow [it] down.	Kussēchtà.	Schluck hinter.
I swallow.	Nkussechtǎhn.	Ich schlucke.
I (have) already swallowed [it].	Pagatschè nkussechtǎhn.	Ich habe es hintergeschluckt.
He swallows.	Okussechtǎhn.	Er schluckt.
The dog already swallowed it up.	Apagatschè kussechtǎhn ndiáu.	Der Hund hats schon verschluckt.
swear, vow	–	schwören
I swear.	Nià nmammachtóa.	Ich schwöre.

Why do you swear?	Gáquai wáätsch mamattowájan?	Warum schwörstu?
Don't swear.	Tscheén kmammattowãn.	Schwör nicht.
Don't (*pl.*) swear. [The k is affixed at the end of instead of before the word.]	[Tscheén] mammattoahāk. [The k is affixed at the end of instead of before the word.]	Schwöret nicht. Das k wird hinten angehängt anstatt vor de[m] Wort zu sezen.
He swears, or has sworn.	Mammattoáu.	Er schwöret, oder hat geschworen.
They swear.	Mammattoãk.	Sie schwören.
sweat, perspire	—	schwizzen, schwizen
I sweat.	Ntappajuwechnà.	Ich schwizze.
You sweat.	K[tappajuwechnà]. G[tappajuwechnà].	Du schwizzest.
He sweats.	Appajuwechnáu.	Er schwizzet.
We sweat.	Ntappajuwechnahanà.	Wir schwizzen.
You (*pl.*) sweat.	K[tappajuwechnaha]mà. G[tappajuwech]nahamà.	Ihr [schwizzet].
They sweat.	Appajuwechnáwak.	Sie schwizzen.
They sweat.	Kappajuwechnah'noõk. [*sic* K- *for* Kt-] Gtappajuwechnah'nõk.	Sie schwizzen.
I am ready to sweat. I sweat readily.	Nkésche appajuwechnà.	Ich bin fertig mit schwizen.
Didn't you [go] sweat yesterday?	Onáqua asch ktappajuwechnà.	Hastu gestern nicht geschwizt.
I (have) heard you sweated yesterday.	Tennĕsetàm káchani ktappajowechnà onáqua.	Ich habe gehört, du hast gestern geschwizt.
He has sweated blood.	Nàn ne uttäinappajuwechnáãn p'gachganõm.	Er hat geschwizzet Blut.
I should also sweat.	Nia wãk n'gattawechpeióha.	Ich solte auch schwizen.
sweathouse	[peésbank *or* peésbäácàn *(Mah.)*; see below]	Schwizofen [Schwitzbad]

[*For* peésbank, *cf. Narragansett* pésuponck = 'hot house' for vapor baths, *but is* peésbank *a loan word from a language of southern New England? See the following.*]

It has done you good, the sweating, or in the peésbank or sweathouse.	Kõnămã[t]tãmmĕn nĕ ánĕ pēspājàn (peespājàn).	Hat es dir gut gethan das Schwizzen, oder im Peésbank oder Schwizofen.
Today I will also go into the sweathouse.	Nono wachgamãk enimpeéspa.	Ich will heute auch in den Schwiz Ofen gehen.
I want the brethren to make themselves a sweathouse.	Chánn'mámaatsch nétachcanàck peésbäácàn.	Ich wünsche die Br[üde]r machen sich Peesbank.
sweep out, sweep clean [*cf.* clean (*verb*)]		kehren aus
Anna, sweep out the house.	Anna tscheékhà weéquachm.	Anna kehr[da]s Hauss aus.
Yes, I will soon sweep it out.	Quã ntscheékhammen éne.	Ja, ich wills bald auskehren.
Did you sweep it out [already]?	Késche tscheékhammĕn.	Hastus ausgekehrt.
I haven't yet swept it out.	Achquódha ntscheékhamówun.	Ich habs noch nicht ausgek[ehrt].
I am not sweeping [it] out.	Aschã ntscheékhamówun.	Ich mag nicht auskehren.
Sweep [it] out. Make [it] clean.	Kscheékékà.	Kehr aus, mach rein.
He is sweeping it clean.	Õtscheékhammen.	Er kehrt aus.
We are sweeping [it] out.	N[tscheekhamná]na.	Wir [kehren aus].
Sweep (*pl.*) [it] out.	Tscheékhammoõk.	Kehret aus.
They are sweeping [it] out.	Otscheekhamnáwa.	Sie kehren aus.
Is it swept out? [*or* ?It is . . .]	Késche tscheekhasò.	Ists ausgekehrt.
It's not yet swept out.	Achquódha tscheékhaséwe.	Es ist noch nicht ausgekehrt.
what sweeps clean, broom	tschĕchhégan, tschékĕhégan	der rein kehrt
sweetness (your sweetness?)	kónãĩwágan, ktànnãĩwágan	Süssigkeit
swelling, tumor, boil	pŏmŏwàhs	Beule
swift [*see* quick]		
swim	—	schwimmen
to swim	as'wehhn	schwimmen
I swim.	Niàn tás'wehhn.	Ich schwimme.
Have you swum? Did you swim?	Knĕchtãwè as'wehhn?	Hastu schwimmen? [*sic*]
Let's (both?) swim.	Sawehtaù.	Last uns schwimmen.
swollen		geschwollen
My hand is swollen.	N'nàchk n'mãckwēsĕn. [*or*] [N'nachk n'mãckwē]se.	Meine Hand ist geschwollen.
the same		*idem*
My face is swollen.	Nskétschok [n'mãckwēsĕn].	[Mein] Gesicht [ist geschwollen].
You are swollen.	Kmakwése.	Du bist geschwollen.
He or she is swollen.	Omakweséĕn.	Er oder sie ist geschwollen.
We are swollen.	Nmakwesehenà.	Wir [sind geschwollen].

You (pl.) are swollen.	K[makwesehe]mà.	Ihr [seid geschwollen].
They are struck or beaten.	Machkwesoàk.	Sie sind geschlagen.

[*Apparently* struck *is an aspect to show what happened before the* swollen *state, since* machkwe- *in* Machkwesoàk *is the same as* makwe- *for* swollen. *All glosses here are on ms. p. (87).*]

sympathy [*see* compassion]

take, fetch [*see also* fetch; get; accept]		
to take or fetch	nátenimmen	nehmen oder holen
Take what you like.	Nátĕnĕ nettaän wātĕnímmàn.	Nimm was du wilt.
Take Him not only in your arms, but [also] in your heart.	Nátene nahk'ma tscheēn knàchkeck psùck ŏtschè ktáhak ŏtschè. [*poor syntax?; see* but]	Nimm Ihn nicht nur in deine Arme, s[on]d[ern] in dein Herze.
You take.	Knātĕním.	Du nimmst.
He takes fire from the sky (*i.e.*, he ignites it by means of the sun).	Spómmuk ótenìm stáŭ.	Er nimmt Feuer vom Himmel, *i.e.*, er zündts d[urch?] die Sonne an.
Perhaps our Savior is taking her (the sick person).	Pechtáăd kPachtamawaasnau onátenan.	Vielleicht nimmt sie unser Heiland (die kranke Person).
I will soon take [it].	Éne nátenan.	Ich will bald nehmen.
Why are you taking it?	Gaquătsch natenájan.	Warum nimstus?
Philip has taken it.	Philip onátenan.	Phil[ipp] hats genommen.
I will not take it.	Sta ăm kennáwe.	Ich wills nicht nehmen.
Take along a fourth [of something] to Bethlehem.	Wachpăhm keninnemamà Bethlehem anè.	Nimm ein 4tel [= Viertel] mit nach Bethlehem.
Take.	Keninnè.	Nimm.
Take us into your keeping (preservation).	Nátenenána nik kàchchannawétowaganik.	Nimm uns in deine Bewahrung.
I will fetch water.	Mbeì nátĕnímmēn gattău. [*see* fetch]	Ich will Wasser holen.
He didn't take it.	Nahk'ma astà onòtĕnimmówùn.	Er nahm es nicht.
Fetch water.	Mbeinatem.	Holt Wasser.
Take (*pl.*) [it] full.	Nátĕnímmǫ̋ǫ̋k otschòwachtáu.	Nehmet voll.
If (whether) he takes him.	Udennè nĕ́ĕchnàan.	Ob er ihn nimmt.
take away, take off	—	nehmen (weg), nehmen (ab)
Take away what causes harm.	Ammáne mātschĕ ăm ănĕchquāk.	Nimm weg was Schaden macht.
Take [it, him] away.	Ăwănóchkq.	Nehmt hin.
Take me to safety (Protect me? Give me asylum?).	Gadhanenána.	Nimm mich in Sicherheit.
take (the) lead [*see* go before]		
take off [*see* take away]		
take offense [*see* hurt oneself by striking]		
take part (in) [*see* be present]		
take prisoner [*see* captivate]		
take punishment	—	Strafe krigen
He has taken the punishment for us.	Kiánau otschè knachmawachtowágan mĕschinnemen.	Er hat für uns die Strafe gekrigt.
taken upward	—	aufgenommen (in die Höhe)
talk [*see* speak]		
target [*see* mark]		
taste (good or bad) [*verb*]	—	schmecken
It tastes good.	Nè wĕgăchtāmmēn.	Es schmeckt gut.
so that we may taste the sweetness in the heart	nè ăm wátsche wégachtama {kónăĭwágan / ktànnăĭwágan} nᵉⁿdáhak	so dass wir die Süssigkeit im Herzen schmecken
The Savior has felt, tasted death. [*Mahican word:* felt]	Pacht[amawaas]nau otammachtámmen otennè mbennáăp.	Der Heiland hat den Tod gefühlt, geschmeckt.
taste food, try food	—	kosten Speise
Try it. Taste it.	Ktāttăchgà.	Versuche es, koste es.
teach [*cf.* learn]	—	lehren
I will teach you.	Gachgachg'hammánĕn.	Ich will dich lehren.
I will teach you.	Nià gagachgémen.	Ich will dich lehren.
I will teach you.	Nia ĕn gagachkhammăn.	Ich will dich lehren.
I will teach them.	[Nia] enen [gagachkham]máwăk.	Ich will sie lehren.
I will not teach you.	Ascha gagachkhammanóu.	Ich will dich nicht lehren.
I am teaching you (*pl.*).	Nià gagachgemnochmà.	Ich lehre euch.
I will teach children.	Māwĕgăgachgēmà ăwāsēsāk.	Ich will Kinder lehren.

138 *Schmick's Mahican dictionary*

But the children must learn.	Nŏk găgāchgēmgōsōāk ăwāsēsāk.	Aber die Kinder müssen lernen.
Teach me, brother.	Gachgachg'hămmawè netachgan.	Lehre mich, Bruder.
Teach me.	Gachgéme.	Lehre mich.
I am thankful that you have taught me.	Onéowe něāně găchgāchg'hămmāwějàn.	Ich danke, dass du mich gelehret hast.
The Holy Ghost teaches us how we ought to pray.	Wăh'nssetsche otschitschachquan kiána gagachkhammakona, ănětsch păpăchtămăwájaku.	Der Heil[ige] Geist lehrt uns wie wir beten sollen.
The Savior teaches us.	Kpachtamawaas gagachgemkónau.	Der Heiland lehret uns.
We teach.	Kàchcămăcónau.	Wir lehren.
teaching, gospel, doctrine?	paachwechcawatowágan	— [*see* NO TRANSLATION]
tear [*see* torn]		
tear away, rip away, split	—	reissen
No man shall tear my sheep away from my hand.	Sta ăm mamaksimsà ótsche ktōchănáwan náchkek.	Niemand soll meine Schaafe aus meiner Hand wegreissen.
If we all cling to (remain by) the [Savior's] side, no one can (will) tear us away.	Nětschăwăn măwe nachpassăk kěnămméta (ăĭjěěta) astaăm ótsche ktocháun.	Wenn wir in d[er] Heilands Seite hangen/bleiben, so kan uns niemand wegreissen.
tear off [*see* break off]		
tell [*see also* say]	—	erzehlen
Tell [it] quickly. Go ahead and tell it.	Animmachkése.	Erzehle fort.
I will tell you something.	Nià éne gáquai ntagétam.	Ich will dir [et]was erzehlen.
ten [*see* Numerals]		
tender [*see* soft]		
thank, to say thanks		Dank sagen
I thank … [*see under* teach]	Onéowe. [*Edwards, 1788, wneeweh,* I	Ich danke.
I say thanks.	Ŏnéŏwě xè. / thank you]	Ich sage Dank.
We say thanks.	Onéowe xénau.	Wir sagen Dank.

[*Mahican* ŏnéŏwě, *Shawnee (E. Denny, 1786 [1859]) neeaway, thank, and Delaware (Zeisberger's Indian Dict., 1887) uleèwe,* I thank you, *may be cognate to Abenaki (Day,* The Mots loups, *1975) 8li'8in, 8li8ini, je te remercie—cf. his note 460: "Abenaki oliwni* thank you, *literally that is good," but the Algonquian words* ŏnéŏwě, *neeaway, and uleèwe may have a connection with the Iroquoian variants of Seneca nyaweh,* thank you *(contrast Mohawk tekŭnŭwaratū, je te remercie [Day, 1975, from R. Wright]; contrast also Algonquian Nipmuck [Day, 1975, p. 64] n88a8ang8man, je le remercie,* I thank him*). Some other forms of interest: Menominee (Miner, 1975) wæwænen,* thank you, *or (Bloomfield, 1976) wɛwɛnen, in the proper way, acceptably,* thank you; *Delaware (Zeisberger, 1887) genamel,* I thank thee, *anischik,* I thank you; *(NTD) wanɪši,* thank you; *Nipmuck (Day, p. 61) tabatěksian, je te remercie,* I thank you; *Narragansett (1643) taûbotne,* thank you; *Shinnecock (Harrington, 1902) tabutnī́,* thank you; *Derby, Conn. (Quinnipiac; Orcutt, 1882) arumshemocke,* thank you *(perhaps compare Quinnipiac [1658, p. 55] werranjemokauweten,* gospel, *or Pequot [Noyes in Stonington, to 1679] ashmeconca(?),* how do you do*), but Derby tuputney,* you are welcome; *and Ojibwa (Nichols and Nyholm, 1979) miigwech,* thanks.]

that, it [*see also under* easy; our(s)]	nè	das
That is it.	Nè àht.	Das ist es.
Don't do that [*or* that way?].	Tschè nè ktànnănāchkàhn.	Mach nicht so.

that [*relative pronoun; Mahican word usually unexpressed; German* dass; *English often unexpressed or infinitive*]

I am glad to see you.	Ntannaména anenawunan.	Ich freue mich, dass ich dich sehe.
when someone among us feels that he is sick.	awăn ăm kiánāu ămáttakà, ŏwénamansohăăncùn.	wenn jemand unter uns fühlt, dass er kranck sey.
that he be crucified.	nè áne schepòchkqtāhāsěahtsch.	dass er gecreuzigt werde.
I am thankful that you have taught me.	Onéowe něāně găchgāchg'hămmāwějàn.	Ich danke, dass du mich gelehret hast.
that we can say Abba [= father].	nik kiánāu Abba ktukkonánāu.	dass wir Abba sagen können.
that you were born a man.	nannoha atane machtappetip na némana.	dass du geboren bist ein Mensch.
that or who(ever) feel that they need (his) help.	něěk amáttakeèk, nahkma nachtamawátŏwágàn ájătămăăk.	die da fühlen dass sie (seine) Hilfe nöthig haben.
I believe … that it is true.	Kohnsittāăn … nàn nenáju kahanè.	Ich glaube es …, dass es wahr ist.
I do not believe that it is true.	Stà kohnsittáno stan nenajéwe.	Ich glaube es nicht, dass es wahr ist.
Are you (*pl.*) deaf that you do not hear?	Kupchahamà, wăătsch asch ptammowăk.	Seyd ihr taub, dass ihr nicht höret.
that he has been crucified.	wătsche schepòchquatahasěěd.	dass er ist gecreuzigt worden.
[*cf.*] Disclose to him all that (what) is in your (*pl.*) hearts.	Máowe mūchgěnümmăwòk achtáge ktáhawăk.	Offenbaret ihm alles was in euren Herzen ist.

English-Mahican-German 139

the [*see also under* our(s)]	nà [=that?, in(to)?]; uwà [= he]	der, die, das
in the world	nànnéttänè ahhkéĕk [n *or* k?]	in der Welt
the hero whom our Lord calls ...	nà áhssännéĕt nà kiánook Tapãnemukquakùk ... ŏtschēmáǔ.	der Held der unser Herrn ... ruft.
What is that (the) man's name?	Gaquai ŏnēwĕsŏ uwà nēmănã?	Wie heist der Mann?
the same	ne	derselbe, dieselbe, dasselbe
The same (that?) love must we also have among ourselves.	Ne achwàhndowágàn kiánau wãk achwàhntetāū.	Dieselbe Liebe müssen wir auch unter einander haben.
with that or, *i.e.*, with the same thing.	néttakãm.	Damit oder *i.e.* mit demselben oder derselben Sache.
their	o(t)- ... -wa	ihre
their(s) [*see* Pronominal affixes]		
It is theirs.	O[tajeganawà]. W'[tajeganawà].	Es ist ihre.
then [*see also* so that]	iha, ihà	da
there	nà	da
there [*cf. also* here; thither]	nè, nà, nòn	dort, da
Here I sit. [*same as* there]	Ne ápea.	Hier siz ich.
There he (she) sits.	Nè ápeed. Nà ápéĕd.	Dort sizt sie.(Anna). Dort sizt er.
There we sit. Here we sit.	Na ápejak. Ne ápeak.	Da sizen wir. Hier sizen wir.
There they sit.	Néĕk ápetschéĕk.	Dort sizen sie. Da sizen sie.
thereabouts	nè átàhn	da herum, dort herum
I am taking water there.	Nòn nià ntenaspãăn.	Ich hol[e da]s Wasser dort.
but over there	ne nónaku	sondern dorthin
Go (travel) down there.	Núktěnè ŏtschè náhthà. *melius* [=better] Nónak anàhoòssè.	Fahr dort herunter. Fahr dort herunter.
He has just gone (over) there.	Tájachkàm otàhn.	Er ist gerade dorthin gegangen.
He has gone (over) there.	Náha áǔ.	Er ist dorthin gegangen.
there is [a lot of?], there are [many?]	-echgau	es gibt ...
There are many ducks [*q.v.*].	Quetschemwechgáu.	Es gibt viel Enten.
There are many fish.	Namãăsechgáǔ.	Es gibt viele Fische.
There aren't any fish. [*see* fish]	Stà namãăsechgáwe.	Es gibt keine Fische.
thereby [?? *or* each other??]	kaãm áikè [*which word or neither?*] [will?] [*see* new, *last two entries; cf.* will *(noun)*]	daran
That we thereby kiss his bloody hands and feet.	Nahk'ma p'gachganéĕk onáchgan wãk osétan neén kaãm áikè kmachgáatamnánaan.	Dass wir seine blutigen Hände und Füsse daran küssen.
[*cf.:*] so that we may be sensitive to (feel) each other.	nik kiánau kaãm ktammachtamnánāū.	dass wir einander fühlen.
therefore, for that reason, hence	nò wátsche, ni wátsche, nè ǔtschè, ne watsche, nò wãătsche, otschè [*at end of clause*]	darum oder deswegen, daher
Therefore when someone among us feels that he is sick.	Nè ǔtschè awãn ãm kiánāu ãmáttakà, ŏwénamansohãăncùn.	Darum wenn jemand unter uns fühlt, dass er kranck sey.
Because of it (that).	Nè ŏtschè.	Das macht.
Because I took snuff.	Snùp ntágushgun otschè.	Darum weil ich Schnupftobak genommen.
therefore, *or* in the?	nànnéttänè [*see below*]	
The Savior has therefore become man, or has therefore lived in the world.	Nam Pachtamawãăs Táp[anemuc]quàk wãtsche óhãkkäjéwe tanè pomáosetip nànnéttänè ahhkéĕk.	Der Heiland ist darum Mensch worden, oder hat darum in der Welt gelebet.
these, those, those who	néĕk [*see under* approach]	diese; die
they [*see also* Personal pronouns]	nahk'mawa, nahkmáwa, [náhkĕ̃mawa [*see under* shoot]	sie
thick		
It is too thick.	Osámick opákka.	Es ist zu dick.
thin, slender	tschãchgáchu	dünn
thin gentleman or man	tschãchgãchu tschéscho	dünn H[er]r oder Mann
slender (tree)	[tschãchgãchu] quattischò	dünn (Baum)
[*Could this word be related to* thin *and possibly mean* You are thin or short?]	tschachkochquà	[*no translation*]

thin soup, water-gruel	mpejapuwêw	dünne Suppe, Wasser Suppe
thin soup of maize	mpejápu	dünne Suppe von Welschkorn
a little thin	machachŭquattschischò	ein wenig dünn
thine [see Pronominal affixes]		
things [cf. son]	nteỹéganan [= my things, my possessions]	meine Sachen
My wife inherits my things, or I bequeath my things to my wife.	Nagatachmawána nwenasőŏm nteỹéganan. [ỹ or ij?]	Meine Frau erbt meine Sachen. oder: Ich hinterlasse meine Sachen me[iner] Frau.
It is a great [matter].	Máchaak.	Es ist eine grosse Sache.
with that or, i.e., with the same thing	néttakâm	damit od[er] i.e. mit demselben od[er] derselben Sache.
[cf. also under covetous]		
think		denken, dencken
I think. I believe.	Ntenètáha.	Ich denke, ich glaube.
You think.	gK[tenètáha].	Denkstu.
He thinks.	O[teneta]hắán. O[teneta]háu. Anètaháu.	Er denket.
We think.	N[teneta]hahanà.	Wir denken.
You (pl.) think.	K[teneta]hahamà. Anètahāwằ.	Ihr [denket].
They think.	Anetaháwak. [Anètahā]wàk.	Sie denken.
I (have) thought.	Netenetáha.	Ich habe gedacht.
I have not thought.	Sta netenetaháwe.	Ich habe nicht gedacht.
You (have) thought.	Gtenetáha.	Du [hast gedacht].
He (has) thought.	Anetaháu.	Er [hat gedacht].
We (have) thought.	Netenetahanà.	—
You (pl.) (have) thought.	G[tenetaha]mà.	—
They (have) thought.	Anetaháwak.	—
Then he thought about the words.	Nè udettàn anètahátamen nèến ăăptonawáganàn.	Da dachte er an die Worte.
They think. [?When they think?]	Anètahámachtéta.	Sie denken.
I thought that he wasn't to return.	Ntenètahà ascha páwe.	Ich habs gedacht er kommt nicht wieder.
I think [that] I am being very fair.	Nehenè ntenétaha nià schaschachkanachcà.	Ich denke ich bin selbst gerecht.
Christian thought that Christ [? or Christopher?] will soon come.	[Chri]stian anètaháu C[hrist?] ene páu.	Xstian hat gedacht C[hristus?] werde bald kommen.
Think, or You think (about it).	Anètaheetà.	Denke oder du solt (dran) denken.
I have not thought about it at all.	Kochpenăăwat meschātămőŭn.	Ich habe keinesweges dran gedacht.
You (sg.) must think about it.	Máămschātămĕmănĕ.	Du must dran denken.
I think about the Savior all the time.	G'máo maamschan'ma Pāchpămāwŏsŏhānŏáăd.	Ich dencke allezeit an den Heiland.
Have you (sg.) always thought about the Savior?	G'omáo kmaamschanaù Pachp[ămāwŏsŏhānŏáăd].	Hastu allezeit am Heiland gedacht.
My brothers, you must always think about the good Savior.	Netachcanak ng'máowe maamschānòchk wăchwăwége Pachpam[āwŏsŏhānŏáăd].	Ihr musst allez[eit] an den guten Heiland dencken.
You (pl.) should think. Let us think.	Anètahámatőŏk.	Ihr sollt dencken. Lasst uns denken.
Think of (remember) me when you come to Bethlehem.	Mĕscháhnnĕmà Bethl[ehem] pájănĕ. M'schạ̄nnémà Bethlehem pájănĕ.	Gedencke an mich wenn du nach Bethl[ehem] komst.
We think big.	Kiánau kmacháhntamnánau.	Wir denken gros.
One who often or many times thinks (knows?).	Nőőssawáhnĕmà. [see Judith under Names]	Einer der oft oder vielmal denkt.
Avaricious, i.e., one who is always thinking of getting many things.	Gōmmāwe wēsăchgè găttaù wăchtschāsŏắd.	Geizig, i.e., der allezeit denket viele Sachen zu krigen.
thirst	găttŏsŏmŏwágàn	der Durst
thirsty, to be thirsty	—	durstig seyn
I am thirsty.	Ngattósome. N'gatósome.	Ich bin durstig.
You are thirsty.	Gattósomè. Gatosomè.	Du bist [durstig].
He is thirsty.	Gattosomu. Gatósomu.	Er ist [durstig].
He(?) is thirsty also.	Gattosomo wak.	—
that we may (will?) always thirst after you.	nè ắm áne gommaowe gattósomo nè nánăắk. [we-you(sg.) ending?]	dass wir . . . dürsten stets nach dir.
We are thirsty.	Ngattosomechnà. Gatosomechnà.	Wir sind durstig.
You (pl.) are thirsty.	Gattosomechmà. Gatosomechmà.	Ihr [seid durstig].
They are thirsty.	Gattosomuak. Gatosomuak.	Sie [sind durstig].
this [cf. today; this year]	nò	dies(er)

English-Mahican-German 141

thither, there, to there	ne [?] [= there, here; *not usually expressed separately in Mahican?*]	hin
Where are you riding to?	T'hácta ne tachapè.	Wo reitestu hin?
Where are you going to?	Thâǎk tàh.	Wo gehstu hin?
thorn hat [*cf.* sack]	[anota- = hat *or* sack?; -choson = thorn?]	Dornen Hut
They put the thorn hat (crown of thorns) on Him.	Onēēchtau anotachosōn méscha. [*cf. M, 1914:* oχōθón = hat]	Sie sezten Ihn den Dornen Hut auf.
those [*see* these]		
thou [*see* you (*sg.*)]		
thoughtless, frivolous		leichtsinnig
John is thoughtless, frivolous.	Joh[annes] képēschò.	Johannes ist leichtsinnig.
Don't be thoughtless, or You must not be thoughtless.	Tschēēn knìskēpēsè.	Sey nicht leichtsinnig, oder Du must nicht leichtsinnig seyn.
three [*see* Numerals]	nacha, nechěk	drei
thrive, turn out well [*cf.* prosper]	–	gerathen (wol)
The other year (last year) the maize turned out well (thrived).	Ktàk kateèk négena chasquéme.	Vorm Jahr ist das Welschkorn gut gerathen.
[*cf.:*] The maize has failed this year.	Stà ntāūwǎchtówe chasquéme nóno káteek.	Das W[elsch]korn ist heuer nicht gerathen.
through, throughout?	pámǎk'íēěck [?]	durch[da]s
Patrol (*pl.*) (go through or over) the land, . . .	Ănĕmseēkq pámǎk'íēěck āhkq, . . .	und ziehet durchs Land!
throw	–	wirf [*imperative*]
Throw it away, or Put it away.	Attàchpannéwe.	Wirf es weg, oder leg es weg.
Throw yourself at his feet.	Pǎkkǎtáchna osédick.	Wirf dich zu seinen Füssen.
Throw yourself completely down.	Anàhaạnsè.	Wirf dich ganz hin.
throw out [*see also* chase out]		
thus [*see* therefore; so]	?	also
Because of it (that). Thus.	Nè ŏtschè.	Das macht. [*note German manner:* That makes (it).]
thy [*see* Pronominal affixes]		
till [*see* until]		
time [*see also* until *(any sense of time?)*]	majánapowágan	Zeit
at this time	hannónò [*or read* ațannónò?; ḫ = h, *not* at?]	in zu} dieser Zeit [*see ms. p. (331)*]
It is time to ring the bell for the meeting. [*see* gather]	Tautau nanamaha kmajàweēchnaù. [bell ring? gather - we *(incl.)*]	Es ist Zeit zur Versammlung zu lauten [*sic for* läuten?].
Now it is time to sound [it].	Nonò tepìskǎwēchnáǔ knánāmǎhǎnǎhm.	Jezo ist Zeit zu lauten.
It is time to go hunting.	T'peskāwēchnāǔ āchenāquechk anawěmuk.	Es ist die Zeit jagen zu gehen.
It is time to mow grass.	Tpescàwechnāǔ āch'nǎquēch t'māskhǎmǎk mēēchsqŭan.	Es ist Zeit Gras zu mähen.

[*cf. Delaware (Brinton, 1888)* tpisgauwihhilleu, tpisquihilleu, *the time is at hand, from* tpisgauwi, *just alike, even, and* tpisqui, *just alike, even, just so, opposite, and cf.* āchenāquechk *with Delaware* elikhikqui *and* juke likhiqui, *at this time, from* likhikqui, *now, about this time, as soon as; as, so as; also* ehelikhique, *at which time; cf. Nipmuck (Day, 1975)* ten l8k8i, tagatch al8k8i, ten lak8i, tech l8k8i, *when; cf. Natick* tou anúckquaque, *how much? how big?*]

timid [*see* afraid]		
tinged [*see* redden]		
tired, exhausted (to be)	–	müde seyn
[*Schmick wrote the following three in English:*]		
I am tired.	Nia n'schewochsannè.	Ich bin müde.
Art thou tired?	Kschewochsannè.	Bistu müde?
I am not tired.	Sta nschewochsannéwe.	Ich bin nicht müde.
I am tired of sitting.	Neschéwa kapè.	Ich bin müde zu sizzen.
?both *or* I'm tired (or weak)??	neschowe	[*no translation*]
They shall run and not be weary, they shall walk and not be faint. *Isaiah 40, 31*	Pomìssŏàk, ashām schawàjewēěk, anìmsoak, asta ām schéwochsannéweẹk.	Sie laufen, und werden nicht matt, sie wandeln und werden nicht müde. *Jes[aia] 40, 31.*
to, at	[átan, -k, -uk]	am ad
to [*see also* until; *cf.* into; in]	-ik [*and variants*]; áne, anè [*coming after the noun*]	nach
One must look to the Savior.	Ainochquatoŏk Pachtamawaasnau áne.	Man muss nach d[em] Heiland gucken.
Take along a fourth to Bethlehem. [*see also under* work]	Wachpǎhm keninnemamà Bethlehem anè.	Nimm ein 4tel [= Viertel] mit nach Bethlehem.

142 Schmick's Mahican dictionary

I am going to the laundry.	Aǟchtahn kschḛḛchtecámick wéquamick.	Ich gehe nach[d]en Waschhaus.
that we may (will?) always thirst after you.	nè ǟm áne gommaowe gattósomo nè nánaǟk. [we-you(sg.) ending?]	dass wir . . . dürsten stets nach dir.
to me	nohà [?]	zu mir
You come to me.	Nohà patsche.	Du kommst zu mir.
Let [it?] come to me.	Nohà pachteḛtsch.	Lasst zu mir kommen.
Really you should still come to me today.	Nohàhtsch kpa.	Warlich du solst noch heute zu mir kommen.
[but cf. nŏhā and náha:]		
He came.	Nŏhāpáǔ.	Er kam.
When they arrived there.⎫ As they came there.⎭	Nohà pājătéta.	Da⎫ sie dahin kamen. Da sie hinkamen. Als⎭
to that place, thither	náha, nohà	dahin
Who is coming there?	Awǟn nahapáda.	Wer dahin kommt.
tobacco [not given, but see pipe]		Tobac
today [cf. sky]	nóno, nono wachgamǟk, nónò wáchkamàhk, nóno wāchgǟmaǟk	heute
this morning	nóno najappája	heute morgen
Today is a beautiful day.	Unàchcamáo nóno.	Heute ist ein schöner Tag.
together	–	beisammen
together with another	–	[beisammen] einander
together [see gather wood together]	paǟschcunoŏk [unit or one + in?(-k)]	zusammen [see also rake]
Sit by me or together with me.	Néschapetaù.	Sez dich mit mir, oder [Sez dich] mit mir zusammen.
Come here, brother; we will eat together.	Nǟwe netáchcana nēschahǎmátau.	Kom her Bruder wir wollen miteinander essen.
toll [verb] [see sound]		
tomorrow	wápachcǎ, wǎpǎchgaǟtsch, wapachgǎtsch	Morgen cras [Latin]
Tomorrow we will work again.	Wāpǎchgà wǎk tǎnnǎchkāch°naù.	Morgen wollen wir wider arbeiten.
Tomorrow morning I am going.	Wǎpǎchkàhtsch nájǎppāwe ntānnimsèh.	Morgen früh gehe ich.
Perhaps tomorrow I will catch [some].	Pechtkaǟm wápachcǎ petthà.	Vielleicht werde ich morgen fangen.
tomorrow morning	wapachgatsh na wachquága	Morgen Vormittag
too, too much	osáme, osámick	zu
You're going too slow.	Osame chammawéschè k'pomsè.	Du gehst zu langsam.
It is too thick.	Osámick opákka.	Es ist zu dick.
You must hold it firmly (the blood-letting bandage) (e.g., if one has done blood-letting and the wound is bound).	Osámapézò.	Du must es (die Aderlassbinde) fest halten (e.g. wenn einer Ader gelassen u[nd] die Wunde verbunden ist.)
You're going too quickly.	Kosáme kschócha. Kosáme kschoŏchà. [cf. so much]	Du gehst zu hurtig.
The brothers honor me too much.	Kaha netachcanak nosame annewanemegaǟk. [kaha = yes?]	Die Brüder ehren mich zu viel.
[see also boil over]		
torch [see light]		
tormented, vexed, worried, plagued		geplagt.
That one is tormented.	Nà ăwátah.	Der ist geplagt.
torn	–	zerrissen
The shoes are torn.	P°queḛchnāō mǟxxen.	Die Schu sind zerrissen.
They are torn.	Kpòqueechtà.	Sind zerrissen.
torn up, split open	–	aufgerissen
touch, move [see also seize?]		rühren
to touch, (to mix?)	ŭkùttanimmèn	anrühren
to stir up	–	umrühren
Stir [it] up.	Ójākà.	Rühre um. Imperat[ivus]
toward us		
Yes, that makes Him compassionate toward us.	Kahénne déttǎnè kettemácanemacónaǔ kiánau.	Ja das macht Ihn mitleidig gegen uns.
travel [see drive]		
trays [see boards]		
tree	(properly) wǎstàchquaǟm	Baum (proprie) wǎstàchquaǟm
in a tree	mǎchtōckŭ	in einen Baum

English-Mahican-German   143

English	Mahican	German
apple tree [see also apple]	ápĕnĕssáchkq [cf. Unquachog, 1791: applesanck]	Apfel[baum]
apple tree (also) [could it be sheep + apple	schèpáăchpenès [schepáăchpene]ssàchq[u-_?], plur[alis] [cut off in ms.]	Apfel[baum] iterum —
big tree	machatscháchq	grosser Baum
birch tree	—	Birken[baum]
cooper's wood	quáu [see note at cooper's wood]	Küferbaum, Küferholz
fallen tree	—	umgefallener Baum
fallen because of death	—	todgehackter [Baum]
garden tree	—	Garten[baum]
hewn down	—	umgehackter [Baum]
[elder tree?]	—	Holer [Holder? = elder?] [baum]
little tree	—	kleiner [Baum]
peach trees	pénĕgĕsàk	Pfirschbäume

[from Jersey Dutch (Ives Goddard, 1981) /piˑrkes/, peach, or through Delaware (Brinton, 1888) pilkisch from probably Jersey Dutch; cf. Moraviantown Delaware (Goddard 1965-70, 1981) píˑlkəš, píˑlăkəš (not through German by metathesis of Pfirs(i)ch, peach) from Latin persica, the Persian apple or tree-fruit; contrast Unquachog, 1791, peachesanck, peach tree, from English]

English	Mahican	German
slender [small, short?] tree	[tschăchgāchu] quattischò	dünn (Baum)
standing tree	—	stehender [Baum]
tree of life	—	Baum des Lebens
wild tree	—	wilder [Baum]
wood	machtòk, machtóqk, machtòkq	Holz, Baum
triumph [see victorious]		
true, correct	nenáju	wahr
Yes, I believe it in my heart that it is true[, yes].	Káhanna kohnsittaăn ntáhak tanè nàn nenáju kahanè.	Ja ich glaube es in meinem Herzen; dass es wahr ist.
I don't believe that it is true.	Stà kohnsittáno stannenajéwe.	Ich glaube es nicht, dass es wahr ist.
truly	múchtschè kahénna	warlich, wa[h]rlich
truly, indeed	káhanna [= yes]; káchna [= truly?]; kachne [= truly?]	wirklich
Yes, I believe it.	Káhanna nŏhnsittámmen.	Ja ich glaube es.
They most cordially greet.	Múchtsche káchna kwáwăgŏmuck. [very truly?]	Sie grüssen herzlich.
The Savior is our best friend.	Pacht[amawáăs] kachne onájo tēnnāngōmā. [truly good-he-is]	Der Heiland ist unser bester Freund.
He (she) went with a joyous heart to Bethlehem to work. [see truly (majáwe?) under wish that] [cf. káchani under sweat] [see kachnáăt, p. 155]	Nahà ajátà káchne onàchtánamowócha odáhak na Bethl[ehem] anachkáwak.	Er (sie) ging mit vergnügten Herzen nach Bethlehem (zu) arbeiten.
trust [verb] [cf. gather; assemble]	majáwe [?]	trauen
I have many friends but none to trust.	Măchānāk tennangomáăk psùk asta majáwe tennangoma.	Ich habe viel Freunde aber keinen trauen.
[cf. truly:] I wish that you may truly experience the Savior's blood.	Chànnè mámaatsch ne amáttamàn majáwe pgachganŏm.	Ich wünsche dass du d[es] Heilands blut recht fühlen mögest.
trustful [see comforted]		
try it [see taste food]		
tumor, swelling, boil	pŏmŏwàhs	Beule
turn around, turn over		kehr um, wende um
Turn around.	Kŭnèppĕnè. (Mahic[an]) Kŭlèppĕnè. (Del[aware]) [see under Delaware words]	Kehr um, oder wende um.
He turned around, or over.	Nahk'ma udennikuneppĕĕn.	Er wandte sich um.
turn out well [see thrive, prosper]		
turn over [see turn around]		
turnips, rapes	páădquăjak, páădquaik	Rüben
I peel turnips.	Npachaschà páădquaik. Npachaschà páădquajak.	Ich schäle Rüben.
Cut the turnips small. [Dice(?) the turnips.]	Schkuschà páădquăjak. [for more, see peel; cut]	Schneide die Rüben klein.

144 Schmick's Mahican dictionary

twelve [see Numerals]		
twice	níssanè [ms. p. (11)], néschan	zweimal bis [Latin]
It is 2 o'clock; i.e., the sand has run out twice.	Néschan nágau machtschetschoachnáu.	Es ist 2 Uhr, i.e. der Sand ist 2mal [he]rausgelaufen.
twinkle [see sparkle]		
two [see also Numerals]	nesche; neschach [see bundle]	2 [= zwei]
Today it is 2 years.	Nono wachgamáäk nesche kahtenà.	Heute ists 2 Jahr.
two days	neschóaknak	2 Tage
Two pairs have come.	Neschéěk páksowàk páwak.	2 Paar sind gekommen.
two persons	néschºwak	2 [Personen]
two words	[nescha] aptónachkat [c resembles o]	2 Wörter [ms. p. (377)]
uncle [see family]	wáchěsă [his(?) uncle]	Enkel
under [perhaps see also down there]	anámuk	unter; runter [for herunter]
under the bed(stead)	anámuk [kachgawémuk]	untern [Bett]
The [female?] cat is sitting under [the table, not given].	Anámuk poschesch achpóu. [underneath cat sits-she]	Die Kaze sizt untern Tisch.
understand, comprehend [see also hear; know (wissen)]		[verstehen]
I don't understand you.	Asta knenóchtănò.	Ich verstehe dich nicht.
I don't understand it.	Astà kněnòchtănò.	Ich verstehe es nicht.
I don't understand what you are saying.	Astà knenochtáno gaquai áníăn.	Ich verstehe nicht, was du sagest.
unfriendly, unkind; gloomy [see also gloomy]		unfreundlich; finster
I am unfriendly.	N'machschedtahà.	Ich bin unfreundl[ich].
You are unfriendly.	K[machschedtahà].	Du bist [unfreundlich].
He is unfriendly.	Machschedtaháu.	Er ist [unfreundlich].
another way:	aliud [sense of face not present?; perhaps bad-heart?]	
I am unfriendly.	Nmachschedtahawenaxè.	Ich bin unfreundl[ich].
You are unfriendly.	K[machschedtahawenaxè].	Du bist [unfreundlich].
He is unfriendly.	Machschedtahawenaxò.	Er ist [unfreundlich].
We have gloomy faces.	Nmachschedtahawenaxehenà.	Wir haben finstre Gesichter.
You (pl.) have gloomy faces.	K[machschedtahawenaxe]hemà.	Ihr [habt finstre Gesichter].
[for more, see gloomy]		
unless, except	[kscheméneetsch? for bis?; see until]	
unlock [see open]		
unmarried [see single]		
until, till [see also to; cf. also already sat under sit]	nahà pátsche	bis
to (until) the new years	pátsche uskái kátennik	bis zum Neuen
... till he calls us.	... tăn ánequèchk otschémukquak. [see under when]	... bis er uns ruft.
I will not have any peace until the Savior gives me peace.	Asta ăm tácheu ntanachěme kscheméneetsch [not will (comes-not-it?) I-rest unless?] Tap[anemucquak] anachem'wagan menéta. [-éta = when]	Ich will keine Ruhe haben bis der Heiland mir Ruhe gibt.
... until I know certainly that the Savior has given me peace [q.v.].	... kscheméneetsch ntanachéme, [unless? I rest] papachtschéwe Tap[anemucquak] [redupl. of until? or certainly?] anachemohan'oquana.	... bis ich gewis weiss, der Heiland hat mir Ruhe gegeben.
unusual, uncommon, extraordinary	—	ausserlich
unwillingly [see under like to]		
up there, high up there, there above	spommuck, spommuk, spommuka	droben
upon the hill	chăchkóŏk	droben Uppon the Hill [sic]
I am up here.	Spommuk ntaje.	Ich bin droben.
Are you up there?	[Spommuk] ktajè.	Bistu droben.
Are you (pl.) up there?	[Spommuk] ktajehemà.	Seid ihr droben.
Yes, I am up here (upstairs).	Quăă ntajéěn.	Ja ich bin hoben.
Yes, we are up here.	[Quăă] ntajehenà.	Ja wir sind [hoben].
Is he up there?	Spommuk ajù.	Ist er droben.
He is not up there.	Sta [spommuk] ajéwe.	Er ist nicht [droben].
They are up there.	[Spommuk] ájuwak.	Sie sind [droben].
They are not up there.	[Sta spommuk] ajéwek.	Sie s[in]d nicht [droben].

I have been up there.	Spommuka nŏŏm.	Ich bin droben gewesen.
You have been up there.	[Spommuka] kŏŏm.	Bistu [droben gewesen].
He has been up there.	[Spommuka] kŏŏma.	Er ist [droben gewesen].
We have been up there.	[Spommuka] nŏŏmhanà.	Wir sind [droben gewesen].
You (*pl.*) have been up there.	[Spommuka] koomhamà.	Ihr seid [droben gewesen].
They have been up there.	[Spommuka] koomáăk.	Sie sind [droben gewesen].
He takes fire from the sky (*i.e.*, he ignites it by means of the sun).	Spómmuk ótenìm stáŭ.	Er nimmt Feuer vom Himmel, *i.e.*, er zündts d[urch?] die Sonne an.
upwards	ăchgŏttámu, ăchgŏttáju, ăchgŏttáwè	aufwärts

urinate
- I am going (on the side)(*i.e.*, I urinate, I pass natural water). — Maūweschè. [= I (am going to?) urinate.] — Ich gehe an die Seit. (neml[ich], ich lasse *aquam naturalem*)
- I have made myself somewhat light (*i.e.*, when water is passed). — Dăăppenà kawáhăsè. [?I loose, release?; *cf.* Mass. *ompeneau*, he loosens (him)] — Ich habe mir etwas leicht gemacht (*i.e.*, wenn Wasser gelassen).

us [*see* we]

use
- of no use [*see* satisfied]
- Now we will not need (*or* use) any more witness(es). — Nóno ăăm astà wăk dăwăháu kákkēnōnōwágàn. — Nun brauchen wir nicht mehr Zeugen.
- I have an inclination (drive) in the heart. [*or* I have a need in the heart.] — Daŭwătăăch anè ndàh. — Ich habe einen Trieb im Herzen.

variegated, colored, piebald, dappled	Păăptschàck [*see also* Marcus *under* Names]	bunt oder scheckicht
vegetables, herbs, cabbage	gónan [German *Kohl*, cabbage + *Mah. pl.*]	Kraut
vein	—	Ader
bandage for veins	—	Aderbinde
show vein or bloodlet [*see* bloodlet]	—	Ader lasszeig
very [*see* lot (much); many]	múchtsche; machăn, machane [*cf.* great]	sehr
I am very glad about that.	Nò wátsche múchtsche ănnămmenăjà.	Darüber freue ich mich sehr.
[*see also* osáma- *under* hold on; too]		
[*cf.*:] That is very easy.	Náhane nĕ nàch nágan. [so? + that + ? + easy]	Das ist sehr leicht.

very well [*see* beautifully]
vexed [*see* tormented]

victorious (to be), triumph, conquer		gesiegen
He has triumphed, won.	Opmuchgawăăn. Opmuchgawăn.	Er hat gesieget.
I will conquer you.	Kp'muchganen ene.	Ich will dich überwinden.
view, look [*nouns*]	opènnămèn	Blick
violin, to play the violin	—	Geige spielen
I will play the violin.	Npiŏŏnhaman.	Ich wil die Violin spielen.
[*see others under* play; Loan words]		
visit	—	Besuch
I will visit him.	N'gechgañăhn.	Ich will [ihn] besuchen.
at the visit	nè átan ótăwĕchtĕĕt	bei dem Besuch
Why don't you visit me?	Gaquatsches ŏtawănéwàn.	Warum besuchst du mich nicht.
They are visiting.	Otàwŏwàk.	Sie besuchen.

[*The initial German words seem to be illogical; so note translation:*]
- [He is staying, (whereas)] They are going (when one is asked where he or she is). — Ŭtáñĕĕn. — Sie gehen (wenn von jemand gefragt wird wo er (sie) ist).
- [He is visiting, (whereas)] They are [there already?]. (Perhaps he is visiting) when someone asks, "Where is your father?" He is visiting R. — Otáŏŏkăăt. — Sie s[in]d. (vielleicht besucht er) wenn mir je[ma]nd fragt, wo ist dein Vater? D[en] R. er besucht.

voice — [?nawan = what I say?] — Stimme
- My sheep hear my voice. [*exact Mahican translation uncertain*] — Nenochtagăk mamaksimsàk onenochtamnáu nawan. — Meine Schaafe hören meine Stimme.
- He spoke with a strong voice (loudly). — Awà kàchnă macheèchsò. [he-speaks truly big-voice?] — Er sagte mit gewaltiger Stimme.

vomit [*see* spit (*verb*)]
vow [*see* swear]

146 *Schmick's Mahican dictionary*

wages, gain; merit [*see sentence at* believe]	kpènhammawágan [= your wages; *see* earn; wait for]	deinen Verdienst
waistband [*see* band]		
wait for [*cf.* wish]		[warten]
... wait for them always with your bloody wages.	... channawèhenana ngommaowe áne p'gachganèéth kià kpènhammawágan.	... warte sie allezeit mir deinen blutigen Verdienst.
walk [*see* go]		
They shall walk. *Isaiah 40, 31*	Anìmsoak.	Sie wandeln. *Jes[aia] 40, 31*
wampum [*see* sewan; belt of wampum]		
wan [*see* pale]		
want [*see* necessary]		
want to [*see* will; like to]	gattau; wega-; mawe-, mawu- [?] [= begin to, go in order to do]	
war [*see also* fight]	ktajótŏăwákan	Krieg
war [*verb*] [*see* fight]		
warm [*adjective*]	–	warm
Even today I still feel warm in my heart.	Nono wachcamăăk achschen [= even?] ntammachtammen ntáhak kástăăk. [warm?]	Auch heute noch fühle ich in meinen Herzen warm.
He feels warm in the heart.	Xschittáwa mámmăk ndàh.	Er fühlt sich warm im Herzen.
[*cf.:*] Sit by the fire.	(X)schétanà wapè. [hot-be + ? sit]	Sez dich beim (zum) Feuer.
warm weather	kschenàtáu	warm Wetter
warm [*verb*] [*cf. also* assè *under* fire]	–	wärmen
I will warm myself.	Niàn dappsè.	Ich will mich wärmen.
Warm!	Appessè.	Wärme.
Warm (*pl.*)!	Appessèk.	Wärmet.
It's very warm to me.	Dàp tschassè.	Es ist mir sehr warm.
I will warm my hands.	Dăppeèn tschăssèen onáchcan.	Ich will meine Hände wärmen.
Warm your hands.	Appeèn tschassè _____.	Wärme deine Hände.
Warm your (*pl.*) hands.	Appeèn tschassèek _____.	Wärmet eure Hände.
Warm your feet. [*see* foot]	Appessèed tassè _____.	Wärme deine Füsse.
Warm your (*pl.*) feet.	Appessèed tassèek _____.	Wärmet eure Füsse.

[*In the preceding Mahican sentences note the bound verbal form for* hands *or* feet *(cf. Mass.* wunnutch, *his hand; Ojibwa (Baraga)* nind abinindjisodis, *I warm my hands;* nind abisides, *I warm my feet) and note the redundant free form (*onáchcan*), below which only ruled lines for the respective nouns were drawn for each sentence.*]

wash [*see also* clean; laundry]	–	waschen
Wash my shirt.	Kscheéchta ntahámed.	Wasche mein Hemd.
Give it [to us to put] in the wash [we wash it?].	Nawutenè kescheechtananà.	Gibs in die Wäsche.
Wash clean.	Ŏkĕschēchpătégān.	Wasche rein.
washhouse, laundry	kschęęchtecámick wéquam- [*from below*]	Waschhaus
I'm going to the laundry.	Ăăchtahn kschęęchtecámick wéquamick.	Ich gehe nach[d]en Waschhaus.
watch [*see* guard]		
water [*cf.* medicine]	mbeì, mpëï, n'bè, npè, nĕpì, n'pè	Wasser
in the water	mbéčk	in Wasser
Fetch water.	Náăspa.	Hol Wasser.
We will get water together.	Năspataù. [=Let us get water together.]	Wir wollen miteinander Wasser holen.
I will fetch water.	Mbeì nátĕnimmēn gattaù.	Ich will Wasser holen.
living water: springwater	P'măwŏsò mpëï. [*improper syntax?*]	lebendig Wasser: Quellwasser
thin soup, water-gruel	mpejapuwèw	dünne Suppe, Wasser Suppe
thin soup of maize	mpejápu	dünne Suppe von Welschkorn
[*see p. 155*]	Ihàm no anè mbei.	[*no translation*]
[*see p. 155*] [He is going to fetch water. ?]	Nochkau mbei.	[*no translation*]
[*see also four entries under* fall]		
way, path, road	ánei	Weg
You make the way.	Ánei konechtà.	Hastu den Weg gemacht.
The way is smooth.	Ánei sachachkáju.	Der Weg ist eben.
Joshua makes the way smooth.	Ănăjaháo Josua.	Josua macht den Weg eben.
Now it's halfway.	Nónen nò nánawàt.	Nun ist der Halbe Weg.
Soon it will be halfway.	Pachood knănāwóchachnaù.	Bald ist der Halbe Weg.

English-Mahican-German 147

we [see also Personal pronouns; Let us . . . ; rich]		
we (exclusive, both, two, we and not you), us	niána [see afraid; see], niáne [see say], niánŏk [see hear], niánok [see we hear]	wir (dualis), uns
Ask (pl.) us.	Niána kutschemonemääk.	Frage uns.
We hear. [ms. p. (102)]	Niánŏk péttămēchnŏn.	Wir [hören].
We (both) will honor the Savior. [cf. also read]	Machanemátaù (Dual[is]) Pacht[amawaas]nau.	Wir wollen den Heiland ehren.
We will chase [s.th.] away.	Meuschehatŏŏk. Meuschehatŏk. [cf. also go; sing]	Wir wollen wegjagen.
we (inclusive, all, we and you), us	kiánau [see the same; belong; necessary; thereby], kiánaū [see under feel; we can say; sick], kiána [see hear; teach], kiánok [see obedient], kianŏk, kiánook [see our(s)], kianŏŏk [see rich]	wir, uns
My husband said: Tomorrow we (two) will go to Bethlehem.	Wáchia ntennùk wapachgátsch Bethl[ehem] ktáhanau.	Mein Mann hat gesagt: morgen wollen wir (zwei) nach Bethlehem gehen.
The Savior died for us.	Pacht[amawaas]nau otschè pennááp kiánau.	D[er]H[ei]l[an]d ist für uns gestorben.
You hear us when we call.	Kpettāgŏnā́ kiána machēchséáquà.	Du hörst uns wenn wir rufen.
We don't see each other well.	Kiánau astà knáŭteohénnaū.	Wir sehen wol einander nicht.
[for affixes:]		
He asks us.	Okutschemŏŏnkónau. [cf. also make (made)]	Er fragt uns.
[see make well]	-nána	
[? see hope]	-nanaù, -hanà, -h'nà	
He whips us.	N[ahkma] ksasamtschahokhana.	Er peitscht uns.
We stab.	Takkamaunà.	Wir stechen.
[see know]	-nánau, -nānaū	
[see reveal]	k-. . . -ennau, or -anau	
We read.	Lesowechnà.	Wir lesen.
[see sacrifice]	k-. . . -chnook, k-. . . -chnaù	
[see so that]	kiánau . . . -quàk	
[see pray]	-jaku	
[see read for three types]		
[see see for many suffixes]		
look like us [see become man]	ánènāhxétippĕ [?]	für uns ist [ein Mensch] geworden
weak (to be) [contrast soft]	—	schwach seyn
They are weak like little children.	Machtschahawawésuak ánau awásesak.	Sie sind schwach wie kl[eine] Kinder.
weak ('bad-hearted'?)	mattàhăwá(w)u	schwach
wear a hat [perhaps see put on a hat]		
weary [see tired]		
weather	—	Wetter
Sometimes there is good weather.	Sāsĕchgàu móschachquat.	Manchmal ists gut Wetter.
beautiful weather	ótăkkàn	schön Wetter
warm weather	kschenàtáu	warm Wetter
Now it is good weather (a good day) to hunt.	Nono onachkamáo ahánawémik.	Nun ist gut Wetter zu jagen.
weep [see cry]		
well [adverb for good]	kŏne, góne, gŏnè [you + well]	wol
Have you slept well?	Kŏne kawè. Góne gawè.	Hastu wol geschlafen.
Sleep (pl.) well.	Gŏnè gaweémaak.	Schlaft wol.
Have you slept well?	Konamansè anagáwoja.	Hastu wol geschlafen.
You make the way [smooth]. You have made the way [smooth].	Ánei konechtà. [= you-well-made-it?]	Hastu den Weg gemacht.
well, healthy, wholesome [see wholesome spring; see also make healthy]		
Daniel is not well.	Daniel schéwamannissò.	Daniel ist nicht recht gesund.
I have great hope (that) Bathsheba will get well.	Nia nachgawosè machè chàn onammanisséêd Bathseba.	Ich habe grosse Hofnung Baths[eba] soll gesund werden.
But when will my (whole) heart become well by my creator?	Múchtsche áám niàn (máowe) dáhak otschòwachtaka nám Pachtamáwagssèk.	Wenn wird doch mein (ganzes) Herz wol werden von meinem Schöpfer.
He (she) is not well.	Máttà mănnìssò.	Er (sie) ist nicht wol.
[cf. also well under glad]		

west [noun?]	tachgamããk	Abend	occidens
what [interrogative and relative pron.]	gaquai, gaquaik, gaquajà; ắhtche(k), [etc.]	was	
What's his or her name?	Gaquai ănĕwĕsŏ?	Wie heisst er oder sie?	
What are you looking for?	Gaquaik quĕnam? [-k = you?]	Was suchest du?	
What are you (pl.) looking for?	Gaquajà kwenamechmà.	Was sucht ihr?	
Take what you like.	Nátĕnĕ nettáăn wătĕnĭmmàn.	Nimm was du wilt.	
Disclose to him all that (what) is in [see inside] your (pl.) hearts.	Máowe müchgĕnümmắwòk achtáge ktáhawắk.	Offenbaret ihm alles was in euren Herzen ist.	
I will give all (of) what I have.	Máoweetsch kmēnĕnĕ. Ãhtchek chánnea.	Ich will alles geben. Was ich habe.	
I will give all (of) what I get.	Máoweetsch kmēnĕnĕ. Ãhtche ténnema.	Ich will alles geben. Was ich krige.	
[see also when? (how long, at what time?)]			
[cf. also was (= what) under here]			
wheat, grain [see also grain]	manóme	Weizen	
when?	tája, tắn, tákatsch, tákahtsch wak	wann? wenn?	
When was John born?	Tája machtappósa Johannes?	Wenn ist Joh[annes] geboren.	
When did she bear the child?	Tája ŏtajōmōsà?	Wenn hat sie das Kind geboren?	
how long? at what time? when? [cf. entry under more; ready]	tắn ănĕquèchquè [cf. Delaware (Brinton) Ta likhikqui, at what time?]	wie lang? [= how long?]	
How long has he been ready?	[Tắn ănĕquèchquè] okeschanachgáăn.	Wie lang ist er fertig?	
When (at what time) were you born?	Tắn ănĕquéchque kmēchtapp'nap?	Wenn bist du geboren?	
When are you getting the wood?	Tákatsch knátim machtachena.	Wenn holstu[da]s Holz?	
when [cf. if]	[verb +] -eta, -ka	wann, wenn	
When (then) N. [they?] had drunk, during eating, or when (then) he had eaten	Na N. págatschè mennáta, mezéta	Da N. getruncken hatten, unterm Essen oder da er gegessen hatte	
Then they came to Bethlehem, when we all	Ihà náhāpājātétà Beth[lehem], nĕtschắwắn mắwe	Da sie nach Bethl[ehem] kamen, wenn wir	
(But) when will my (whole) heart become full of my Savior?	Muchtsche ắắm niàn (máowe) dáhak ŏtschòwachtaka nắm Pachtamáwắắssèk. [cf. sentence under well]	Wenn wird doch mein (ganzes) Herz voll werden von meinen Heiland.	
When (as soon as) he said that . . .	Ne máchtsche ne éta.	Als er das gesagt hatte.	
where?	tắn, nettáăn; t'hácta, thắk; ihà [?]	wo?	
Where are you (pl.) sitting?	Tắn ktắppēnãwắ?	Wo sizt ihr?	
Where is your wig?	Kmĕschòchquắgàn nettáăn.	Wo ist deine Paruque.	
Where are you riding to?	T'hácta ne tachapè.	Wo reitestu hin?	
Where are you going to?	Thắk tàh.	Wo gehstu hin?	
Where do you (pl.) come from? Where is your (pl.) homeland?	Thagótschai hamà?	Wo kommt ihr? Wo ist eure Heimath?	
Where do you (pl.) come from?	Thakŏmhamà?	Wo kommt ihr her?	
Where do your friends stay?	Thà äjŏwàk tennangómak?	Wo bleiben [deine Freunde]?	
where [relative pronoun]	átan, átắnĕ, atannēĕtsch; nágam [?!]	wo	
where we live.	átan p'máosémick.	wo wir leben.	
where I am safe.	átắnĕ ắm gãtắchnēkắjắ. átắnĕ ắm gatachnejan.	wo ich sicher bin.	
I know where our souls can have peace by the wounds of Jesus.	N'wawechtà atannēĕtsch anachemēĕd tschitschachkonanàu neắne pachpaquaik Jesus.	Ich weiss wo unser Selen können Ruhe haben bei den Wunden Jesu.	
where Satan cannot catch [anyone].	nágam Machtandò astà meschinkówe. [?that (not present) + -m→M-]	wo der Satan nicht krigen kan.	
whether, if	ŭdĕnnè	ob	
If (whether) he takes him.	Udĕnnè nĕchnaan.	Ob er ihn nimmt.	
Whether Elias came.	Tắn ŭdĕnnè Elias páăn.	Ob Elias kam.	
Whether Elias is coming.	[Tắn ŭdĕnnè Elias] páu.	Ob Elias kommt.	
Whether they are coming.	[Tắn ŭdĕnnè] nahkmáwa pánāwà.	Ob sie kommen.	
[If?] he has risen from the dead. [If?] he has been resurrected.	Udĕnnè méljāzā.	[Er] ist auferstanden.	
whip, lash, punish, chastise	—	peitschen oder strafen	
I whip him.	N'sasắmtschaháu.	Ich peitsche ihn.	
I punish him. I give him the rod.	Nsasamtscháhau.	Ich strafe es [= a child]. Ich geb ihm die Ruthe.	
I whip you.	Ksasắm'tschahoŏn.	Ich [peitsche] dich.	
I whip myself.	Nháckai nsasắmtscháha.	Ich [peitsche] mich.	
I whip them.	Nsasắm'tschaháwak.	Ich [peitsche] sie.	

English-Mahican-German 149

I will whip you (*pl.*), if you (*pl.*) don't keep quiet.	Ene ksasămtschahon'hamà, asch tschēkapewaqua.	Ich will euch peitschen, wenn ihr nicht still seid.
Why are you whipping me?	Gaquătsch sasam'tscháhajan?	Warum peitschstu mich?
Punish him. Give him the rod.	Sasamĕtscháha.	Strafe es. Gib ihm die Ruthe.
Whip him.	Sasam'tschahòchk.	Peitsche ihn.
Have you whipped him? [Did . . . ?]	Késche ksasam'tschaháu?	Hastu ihn gepeitscht.
You are punishing us too much.	Kōsămĕ sasam'tschahehenà.	Du peitschest ihn [*delete* ihn] uns zu sehr.
You are punishing them too much.	Kōsămĕ sasam'tschaháwak.	Du peitschest sie zu sehr.
He whips me.	Sasam'tschahè.	Er peitscht mich.
Why does he whip you?	Gaquătsch sasam'tschahóquan.	Warum peitscht er dich.
He whips us.	N[ahkma] ksasamtschahokhana.	Er peitscht uns.
He whips you (*pl.*).	[Nahkma] [ksasamtschahok]hamà.	[Er peitscht] euch.
He whips them.	[Nahkma] sasam'tschaháwa.	Er peitscht sie.
He punishes his child.	O[sasam'tscha]háwa otajóma.	Er straft sein Kind.
We punish him.	Nsasamtschahana. [*ms. p. (314) possibly with* Nsasamtschahaŭna.]	Wir strafen ihn.
You (*pl.*) punish him.	K[sasamtscha]háŭwà.	Ihr [straft ihn].
They have whipped Him with rods.	Ŏsăsămtschāhāwă nepeschàn ăwáhāwăk.	Sie haben Ihn mit Ruthen gepeitscht.
whirl around (yarn, *etc.*) [*see* spin]		
white (it is) [*cf.* pale]	wapáju	—
old woman, with white head	wapáju wénes [white-it-is his/her-head]	[alte Frau] \ mit we[iss]kop[f]
white blanket [*cf.* blanket]	wāpăssănāi	weisse Blanquet
white bread	wăpĕtăhquòch	weiss [Brod]
white beans	wapĕd [*thus or* wapĕd + tpachquaăn?]	weisse [Bohnen]
white people	tschachkósak	die weissen Leute
the one with the white coat	tschachkòchkwáu	Eine mit weissen Rock
the ones with the white coats	tschachkochkwáwak	plur[alis]
Oh how many white people!	O kwatschĕr̆ tschachcósak!	O wieviel weisse Leute.
White people are coming.	Tschachcósak pajatschéĕk.	Weisse Leute kommen.
who, who?	awăn, awănò [?]	wer
who(ever) . . . , that one . . .	awáneĕtsch . . . , nàtsch . . .	—
After ăwáneetsch, 'who' or 'which,' follows nàtsch, 'the one who, that one.' Auf ăwáneetsch wer, oder welche, folgt nàtsch der oder die.		
The one who enjoys the Savior as his peace (that one) . . .	Awáneĕtsch Pachtamáwaas pschuk unacotowagan kătăhókuk, nàtsch	Wer d[en] Heiland als seinen Frieden geniesset, der
Who has given it to you?	Awăn ktachamókku?	Wer hat dirs gegeben?
Who has given (presented) it to you?	Awănò [awănĕ?] kmeĕnkùn?	Wer hat dirs gegeben, *i.e.*, geschenkt.
If we (all) cling to the (Savior's) side.	Nĕtschăwăn măwe nachpassăk kĕnămméta. [whoever? all]	Wenn wir in d[er] Heilands Seite hangen.
whole [*see also* all]	mawe, máwe, maowe, máowe, máᵒwe	ganz
on the whole earth, in the whole world, in all the world	mawe ănĕquéchkùk ahki	aufn ganzen Lande
the whole day long [*see under* long]		
wholesome spring or fountain	honammanissò t'wachk	gesund [Brunn]
whom [*direct object; see* who]	awăn	wem
why? [*interrogative*]	gaquai wătsch, gaquai watsche, gaquătsch, gaquatsch, gaquatsches	warum
why [*relative pronoun*]	gaquai waătsch, wătsche	warum
Why are you afraid?	Gaquătsch kchàt?	Warum fürchtestu dich?
Why are you crying?	Gaquatsch kmăăp.	Warum weinestu?
Why doesn't one believe in Jesus?	Gaquai watsche astà wáwonistawăwak Jesus.	Warum es nicht an Jesum glaubet.
I will now say to you why you don't feel, *etc.*	Nono kwechtammánen gaquai wătsch astà ămăttănămówun, *etc.*	Ich will dir iezt sagen warum du nicht fühlest, *etc.*
Why don't you visit me?	Gaquatsches ŏtawănéwàn.	Warum besuchst du mich nicht.
Now I will say why I am pleased.	Nóno kwechtammánen wătsche ŏnăchtănămĕă.	Nun will ich sagen warum ich vergnügt bin.
wife [*see* woman]		
wig (your)	[(k)mĕschòchquăgàn]	Paruque
Where is your wig?	Kmĕschòchquăgàn nettăăn.	Wo ist deine Paruque.
wild [*noun, adj., adv.*]	nanáo	Wilde, wild
all the wild ones, or all who live wild	Máwe nanáo p'maosétscheek.	alle d[ie] Wilde, oder alle die wild leben.

150 *Schmick's Mahican dictionary*

will [*noun*] [*cf.* necessary]	–	Will(en)
That you can do (experience) after his will.	Né áne ájatakkáãm kténnajin. Nè áne áãm ájatak kténnajin.	Dass du nach seinem Willen thun kanst.
will, shall [*future*] [*see also* shall; must; like to; speak]	áãm, aãm; éne [= soon]; tschè; gattau; késche [= can?]; [*zero*]; mawe-, mawu- [*see* go in order to]; [*see also under* Delaware words]	werden [= will, become], wollen [= will, wish to, want to]
(But) when will my (whole) heart become full of my Savior?	Muchtsche áãm niàn (máowe) dáhak ŏtschòwachtaka nãm Pachtamáwáãssèk. [*cf. sentence under* well]	Wenn wird doch mein (ganzes) Herz voll werden von meinen Heiland.
I will not take it.	Sta áãm kennáwe.	Ich wills nicht nehmen.
I will soon take [it].	Éne nátenan.	Ich will bald nehmen.
I believe (think) it will snow today.	N'tenetahà éne p'chãn.	Ich glaube [*for* denke] es wird heute schneÿen.
I will conquer you.	Kp'muchganen ene.	Ich will dich überwinden.
I will soon write.	Ãhschkechnpè en mãmãnahkhégã.	Ich will bald schreiben.
I will teach you.	Nià gagachgémen.	Ich will dich lehren.
I will teach you.	Nia en gagachkhammãn.	Ich will dich lehren.
I will teach them.	Nia enen gagachkhammáwãk.	Ich will sie lehren.
N. will heal you.	N. gegahŏk tschè.	N. wird dich heilen.
I will make you healthy.	Konamansoháne ntschè.	Ich will dich gesund machen.
He will make you healthy.	Konamansohánuk tschè.	Er wird dich gesund machen.
I think I will be ready.	Ntenetahà keschanachkáãtsch.	Ich denke ich werde fertig.
He will surely die.	Kahanantãtsch m'pò.	Wird gewissl[ich] sterben.
The Savior will make all mankind (everyone) healthy.	Pacht[amawáãs] máowe awan gattau onamackaháãn. [wants to]	Der Heiland will alle Menschen gesund machen.
I will fetch water.	Mbèi nátĕnĭmmēn gattãu.	Ich will Wasser holen.
I will mend my shoes.	Gáttau meëschhammen máksen.	Ich will meine Schuh flicken.
We will (want to) get to know the Savior.	Wawehataù kattau Tapanmukquak.	Wir wollen den Heiland kennen lernen.
We two will read.	Lesówetaù.	Wir wollen lesen *(Dual[is])*.
We will read.	Lesowetoŏk.	Wir wollen lesen.
I will eat. [want to]	Gattáu méze.	Ich will essen.
He will gather her (them?) up in his arms.	Ŏgãttaù onàchkek majawanáwa.	Er will sie samlen in die Arme.
It will snow soon.	Pachŏd pĕchaãn.	Es wird bald schneyen.
I will dry huckleberries.	Ménan nkeëschchasòm.	Ich will Heidelbeere dörren.
You will learn (or experience).	Ktenájin. [*see* will (*noun*)]	Du wirst erfahren.
Come (*pl.*) [*properly* then]; we will eat.	Iha mezetoŏk. [*see* Let us]	Kommt wir wollen essen.
Come (*pl.*) [*properly* then]; we will eat.	Iha mawepetoŏk.	Kommt wir wollen essen.
[Then] we will acknowledge it.	Ihà mochgoatoŏk.	Wir wollens bekennen.
We will not acknowledge it.	Aschãm kmochgoauhanau. ennau.	Wir wollens nicht bekennen.
I will not fix them.	Stà n'meëschhámmau.	Ich will sie nicht flicken.
We will serve.	Ackenahegátau.	Wir wollen dienen.
We will be glad.	Annamménawatamotoŏk.	Wir wollen uns freuen.
I have great hope [that] Bathsheba will get well.	Nia nachgawosè machè chàn onammanisseĕd Bathseba.	Ich habe grosse Hofnung Baths[eba] soll gesund werden.
I will see him. [*for more, see* go in order to (do something)]	Ne ma<u>w</u>upenawáu.	Ich will ihn sehen.
willing [*see* industrious]		
willingly [*see* observe; fair; like to]		
win [*see also* won *under* victorious]	–	gewinnen
He has won our souls.	Ogauhowána otschitschachcunána.	Er hat gewonnen unsre Seelen.
wind [*noun*] [*see also* east]		Wind
The wind comes from the east.	Wapanáãk ŏtăcheēn.	Der Wind kommt von Morgen.

[*Cf. Mass.* waban, *wind, and Narragansett* waúpi, *wind, but here* wapanáãk *seems to mean* east-in *or* white (of dawn)-in *and might not be connected with* wind; *thus* ŏtăcheēn *perhaps basically means* to blow *or else* to come, *q.v.; cf. also Delaware (Brinton)* kschachan, *the wind blows hard.*]

winnow [*see* flax]
Wipe your nose. [*see* clean]

English-Mahican-German 151

English	Mahican	German
wish [see luck, necessary]	—	
wish that, hope that		wünschen dass
I wish that ...	Chàn ..., Chàn gáǎp ..., Chànně ...	Ich wünsche dass ...
I wish that I could feel.	Chàn ămàttamà. Chàn gáǎp ămàttamà.	Ich wünsche dass ich fühle.
I have great hope [that] Bathsheba will get well.	Nia nachgawosè machè chàn onammanisseēd Bathseba.	Ich habe grosse Hofnung Baths[eba] soll gesund werden.
I hope that when Sp[angenberg] comes, he will help you.	Kahanachganàu Spgbg. changáǎp pǎǎd nachtamakquáǎm [or] knachtamaquáǎm. [for more see at hope]	Ich hoffe, wenn Sp. kommt, er wird dir helfen.
I wish that you may truly experience the [Savior's] blood.	Chànně mámaatsch ne amáttamàn majáwe pgachganǒm.	Ich wünsche dass du d[es] Heilands blut recht fühlen mögest.
I want the brethren to make themselves a sweathouse.	Chánn'mámaatsch nétachcanàck peęsbǎǎcàn.	Ich wünsche die Br[üde]r machen sich Peesbank.
with [see also be present]	ŭtschè, wátschaǐk [?], -ik	mit
with the powers in heaven	nè ahssannáik wochcamáwenaak (wátschaǐk) [the powers-with? heaven-in with]	mit den Kräften im Himmel
He always likes to be with the children.	Gǒmmáwe wége ajù awasésik.	Er ist ge[rne?] allezeit bein Kindern.
with believing hearts	onìstawájaquà ktáhennǎǐk ŭtschè	mit gläubigem Herzen
with his blood	op'gachganom ǒtaŭwáhan	mit seinem Blute
[see go with: Is root -wet- or -wetsch-?]		
[see speak with]		
with each other [see each other]		
with that or, i.e., with the same thing	néttakǎm	damit oder i.e. mit demselben oder derselben Sache.
within [see inside]		
witness	kákkēnōnōwágàn	Zeugen [plural]
Now we will not need (use) any more witness[es].	Nóno aǎm astà wǎk dāwǎháu kákkēnōnōwágàn.	Nun brauchen wir nicht mehr Zeugen.
woman, wife	p'chánim	Frau
old woman	wenasóǒs	alte Frau
brother's wife	nénim	Bruders Frau
my wife	nwenasóǒm, n'wénajoom	meine Frau
My wife inherits my things, or I bequeath my things to my wife.	Nagatachmawána nwenasóǒm nteyéganan. [y or ij?]	Meine Frau erbt meine Sachen, oder: Ich hinterlasse meine Sachen me[iner] Frau.
My wife is at home.	N'wénajoom wékmachmuk hǎjoù.	Meine Frau ist zu Haus.
one for you (pl.) and one for the wives.	pǎǎschkun kiáwa, wénajàckq pagschkun wak.	eine vor euch, u[nd] eine vor die Weiber.
his wife	wěwa, nák'ma wenajǒma [see family]	seine Frau
But no one must love his wife more than the Savior.	Tschēněěk awǎn oténne achwáhnan wěwa, áne Tapan[emuc]que ǎchwáhnǎǎd.	Aber es muss niemand seine Frau mehr lieben als den Heiland.
wood	machtock, machtòkq, machtǎchen, machtáchena, machtáchana [-a = ?]	Holz
cooper's wood	quáu [see note at cooper's wood]	Küfer[baum], Küfer[holz]
split wood, chop wood, put wood on [fire]		Holz spalten, hauen, anlegen
I will split wood.	Māūpāpǎchgǎchtáham.	Ich will Holz spalten.
I will fell or hew wood.	Pèwǒchǎckhà.	Ich will Holz hauen.
I will chop firewood.	Machtǎchen nt'omhan.	Ich will Brandholz hacken.
I make (cut) wood. (Note: One can place machtáchena after all these words.)	Tǎttāmǎchtáhom [machtáchena].	Ich mache Holz. NB. Machtáchena kan man hinter alle diese worte sezen.
Cut wood.	Tattamachtáhe {machtáchena].	Mache Holz.
You are cutting wood.	Ktattamachtáhom [machtáchena].	Machstu [Holz.]
He cuts wood.	Tattamachtáhom [machtáchena].	Er macht Holz.
Yes, we are cutting wood.	Quǎ! Ntattamachtahamechnà.	Ja, wir machen Holz.
We will cut wood.	Tattamachtah'mótau [machtáchena].	Wir wollen Holz machen.
We will cut wood.	Ktattamachtahamechnǒǒk [machtáchena].	Wir wollen Holz machen.
Are you (pl.) cutting wood?	K[tattamachtahamech]mà [machtáchena].	Macht ihr Holz?
They are cutting wood.	Tattamachtahamǎk machtáchena.	Sie machen Holz.
Did you lay the wood in a woodpile?	Knimmǎchtanè machtachanàn.	Hastu[da]s Holz auf einen Holz[hau]fen gelegt.
No, it lies scattered about.	Stà, éja ptschèssessǎchga.	Nein, es liegt zerstreut.

gather wood together, collect wood			Holz zusammentragen
You must gather it [the wood] together.	Pããschcunóõk knimmãchtánè.		Du must es zusammentragen.
Gather the wood together.	[Paaschcunóõk] anawachtãk machtachana.		Tragt das Holz zusammen.
He gathers up the wood.	[Pããschcunóõk] anawachtáu machtachane.		Er trägt das Holz zusammen.
[Come; *not in Mahican here*] we will gather the wood together.	Paaschcunóõk ktenawachtahanà machtáchana.		Kommt, wir wollen das Holz zusammentragen.
They are gathering up the wood.	[Paaschcunóõk] anawachtáwak [machtachana].		Sie tragen das Holz zusammen.
fetch wood	—		Holz holen
You must fetch the wood.	Machtáchene ẽ gnatim.		Du must das Holz holen.
When are you getting the wood?	Tákatsch knátim machtachena.		Wenn holstu[da]s Holz?
Put wood on the fire.	Mãttãchàn.		Leg Holz zum Feuer.
woodpile, in a	machtachanàn		auf einen Holz[hau]fen
word	ntaãptonawágan [= my word]		mein Wort
words	ãáptonawáganàn		Worte
Then he thought about the words.	Nè udettàn anètahátamen neẽn ãaptonawáganàn.		Da gedachte er an die Worte.
a word	gúttã aptónachkat		ein Wort
two words	[nescha] aptónachkat [c *resembles* o]		2 Wörter [*ms. p. (377)*]
That is a long word.	Kõõnnããptónãchkàt.		Das ist ein langes Wort.
a short word	tschachquaãp tschõnãchgãtschò		ein kurzes Wort
work [*noun*]	ánachgátã, ãnàchgãwãgàn		Arbeit
hard work	ãssannáju [= it-is-hard]		schwere, harte [Arbeit]
soul's work	annachgawágan otschitschachkwéwe		Seelen[-arbeit]
stubborn work	assannanachgáu		sture [Arbeit]
He is patient in good works.	Assanetaháu wánechk anè.		Er ist gedultig in guten Werken.
work [*verb*]			arbeiten
Work quickly.	Gattaãtanachkà.		Arbeit hurtig.
You work diligently.	Anachgà nãchnippẽnãmã.		Du arbeitest fleissig.
You work very well.	[Kãhãgõnè] ãnachgã.		Du arbeitest [schön, hübsch].
You can work lightly.	M'tschéme ãm k'tannachgà.		Du kanst leichtl[ich] arbeiten.
Tomorrow we will work again.	Wãpãchgã wãk tãnnãchkach°naù.		Morgen wollen wir wider arbeiten.
They are working.	Ãnãchcãtscheẽk.		Sie arbeiten.
He has worked.	Nè nánnachkàat.		Er hat gearbeitet.
He has worked for me.	Anè ãnàchkachtawétip.		Er hat vor mich gearbeitet.
He (she) went with joyous heart(s) to Bethlehem to work.	Nahà ajátà káchne onàchtánamowócha odáhak na Bethl[ehem] anachkáwak		Er (sie) ging mit vergnügten Herzen nach Bethlehem (zu) arbeiten.
You still cannot do anything.	Kià astà késche dannãnàchkãchtãwè.		Du kanst doch nichts thun.
world	—		Welt
the world (all) [*see under* make]	maowenù [= everyone, 'all-who'], máowe gáquaï [= everything, 'all-what']		die Welt (alles)
in the world, on the earth	nànnéttãnè ahhkeẽk [therefore? *or* in? earth-on]		darum in der Welt
in this world, on this earth	nannò ahkeẽk		in diese Welt
Savior of the world	kékachtátip mawe ánẽquechkùk ãhkì [created, made? all more(?)-on earth]		der Welt Heiland
worried [*see* tormented]			
worthy, be worthy, be deserving			—
because I am not worthy (unworthy, undeserving) of the Savior.	Quaãm nià astàn ktenquechquagewùn Pachtamáusnau.		Weil ich ein unwürdiger d[es] Heilands bin. [= an unworthy one of the Savior]
would (wanted to)	—		wolte
He would (or wanted to) free us.	Unèchnahp pãwõhããnà. [*sic or* pp, / *one word?*]		Er wolte uns frei machen.
would like [*see* like to]			
wounded [*see* bloodied; *see also under* side]			
wounds [*perhaps properly* holes?]	—		Wunden
My heart is by the wounds of the Savior.	Nià n dàh nàn nè Pachtamáwããs paquaik.		Mein Herz ist bei den Wunden d[es] Heilandes.
Therefore the Savior (has) let himself be struck so that we could become well or be healed through his wounds.	Pachtamawaas nò wããtsche pãpãquatahasétip, nikkããtsch kiánau áne páquaick wanamansohããnquàk.		D[er] Heiland hat sich darum Wunden schlagen lassen, dass wir durch s[eine] Wunden heil oder gesund werden könnten.

by the wounds of Jesus	neâne pachpaquaik Jesus.	bei den Wunden Jesu.
with his (or the) wounds	ánepapáquaik	mit s[einen] Wunden
Therefore I lie willingly in the wounds of Jesus.	Ne watsche wege nannǎǎnéchĕnè Jesusse papaquaik. [n or m?]	Deswegen liege ich gerne ins Heilandes Wunden.
wretched [see poor]		
write [cf. book; does root mean to paint?]		schreiben
I write.	Nōsŏǎhéga.	Ich schreibe.
You write.	Kosoahega.	Du [schreibe]st.
You write beautifully.	Kǎhǎgōnĕ sŏǎhēga.	Du schreibest [schön, hübsch].
He writes.	Sohégǎu.	Er [schreibe]t.
We write.	Nosoahegahanà.	Wir schreiben.
You (pl.) write.	K[osoahegaha]mà.	Ihr [schreibe]t.
They write.	Sohegǎǎk.	Sie [schreibe]n.
Write!	Osoahegà. *imperat[ivus]*	Schreibe du.
What are you writing?	Gaquai kosoahàm?	Was schreibstu?
another way:		*aliud*
I write.	Mǎmǎnǎǎk héga.	Ich schreibe.
You write.	K[mǎmǎnǎǎk héga].	Du [schreibe]st.
He writes.	Uwà [mamanǎǎk héga]. [uwà = he; cf. next]	Er [schreibe]t.
She writes.	Mamanaakhéga. [no sign of gender]	Sie schreibet.
We write.	Mamanahkhegáhanà.	Wir schreiben? [sic]
You (pl.) write.	K[mamanahkhegá]hamà.	Ihr schreibet.
They write.	Mamanahk hégaak. [k covers g]	Sie [schreiben].
I will soon write.	Ǎhschkechnpè ĕn māmānahkhégǎ.	Ich will bald schreiben.
I will now write down something for you.	Nóno gáquai kmamanackhanánahamà. [n is all right, but could be m]	Ich wil euch iezt was anschreiben.
Wyoming [= Wilkes-Barre, Pa.]	Mǎchǎwoámik [= big-field-at]	Wayomick

[Mǎchǎwoámik, *i.e.*, Wyoming, *was the principal settlement of Shawnees and Mahicans at Wilkes-Barre, not the present Wyoming a few miles north of Wilkes-Barre; cf. Delaware M'cheuwómink = upon the great plain,* but contrast R1 (p. 175): *Machawameck (= great fishing place), presently Black Rock, in south part of Athens, N. Y.*]

Christian is already (will already be) in Wyoming.	Chr[istian] nonò ǎht nāhà ajókak Mǎchǎwoámik.	Chr[istian] wird schon in Wayomick seyn.
yawn	—	jähnen [*dialect for gähnen*]
I yawn.	Ntǎpchawǎk.	Ich jähne.
You yawn.	K[tǎpchawǎk].	Du jähnest.
He yawns.	Ǎpchawáku.	Er jähnet.
year	káteek, katĕĕk, kahtenà	Jahr
this year	nóno káteek	heuer
a year ago, last year	ktàk katĕĕk [= other year]	vorm Jahr
[see also go, From one year (*etc.*).]		
Today it is 1 year. Today 1 year ago.	Nono wachgamǎǎk ngutte kahtenà.	Heute ist[e]s 1 Jahr.
Today it is 2 years.	[Nono wachgamǎǎk] nesche kahtenà.	Heute ists 2 Jahr.
Today it is 3 years.	[Nono wachgamǎǎk] nechĕk kahtenà.	Heute ists 3 Jahr.
Today it is 4 years.	[Nono wachgamǎǎk] nawè [kahtenà].	Heute ists 4. Jahr.
Today it is 5 years.	[Nono wachgamǎǎk] nānānè [kahtenà].	[Heute ists] 5. Jahr.
yes	quǎ, quǎǎ, quǎǎm [*see* worthy], quǎme; káhanne, káhanna, kahane [= truly]; kahénne [= truly?]; iha, ihà, ihàn [= then (*or* truly?) = recht]; ?kǎhǎ, káhà [= ? all right, yes, *or with* ich habe (= I have)?]	ja
Yes, I will soon sweep it clean.	Quǎ ntscheĕkhammen éne.	Ja, ich wills bald auskehren.
Yes, I will help you.	Ihà } k'nachtamǎhn. Kahane	Ja, ich will dir helfen.
Yes, it's cold in the morning.	Kahennètténajappáu.	Ja es ist früh kalt.
yesterday	wanaquéga, onáqua	gestern
Didn't you (have a) sweat yesterday?	Onáqua asch ktappajuwechnà.	Hastu gestern nicht geschwizt.
yet, still [see also not yet]	—	noch
Even today I still feel warm in my heart.	Nono wachcamǎǎk achschen [= even *or* still?] ntammachtammen ntáhak kástǎǎk. [warm?]	Auch heute noch fühle ich in meinen Herzen warm.

154 *Schmick's Mahican dictionary*

It is still inside. [*untranslated:* still]	N'haachtáu.	Es ist noch drinne.
They screamed even more. They called even more.	Tschénuaãk awaãk.	Sie schrien noch mehr.
you (*sg.*), thou	kià, kia, kĭă; k-, kt-, g-, gt-; kiàtsch	du
You will always be blissful, (if) . . .	Kiàtsch kōnăpătămměn, . . .	Du wirst allezeit selig seyn, wenn . . .
you (*pl.*) [*see also* Personal pronouns]	kiáwa, kiawa, kiaua	ihr, euch
You (*pl.*) hope.	Kiáwa knachganawà.	Ihr [hoffet].
[*see also* know (*both types*) *for others*]		
young		
the youngest brother	tapanmisseẽd netachgan	der jüngste Bruder
younger, youngest [*see* brother]		
your, yours (*sg. and pl.*) [*see* Pronominal affixes]		
your(s) (*sg.*)	k-, kĕ-, ket-	dein
That is yours.	Ne ktajégan.	Das ist deine.
your(s) (*pl.*)	k- . . . -oa, k- . . . -awa	euer, eure
You (*pl.*) must reverence me as your God.	Nia annewaneměẽk kpachtamawasoa n'háckay.	Ihr sollt mich ehren als euren Gott.
It is yours (*pl.*).	Ktajeganawà.	Es ist euer.
yourself [*see* self]		

LONG SENTENCES OR RELATED TEXTS THAT WERE SPLIT UP FOR DICTIONARY EXAMPLES

1. Let us grow in your love and take knowledge that we remain in the belief and serve from the heart so that we may taste the sweetness in our hearts and always thirst after you.

    Dănněměkenanà achwohndowágan nachpè, { kwáweechtowágan / áne wáwĕhàk } nàn nè ndaijeenanà, onìstãmawágan, wăk nè ãm áne ănàchkăchtána nè ãm wátsche wégachtama { kónălwágan / ktànnălwágan } n^endáhak nè ãm áne gommaowe gattósomo nè nánaãk.

    Lass uns in deiner Liebe wachsen und Erkenntniss zu nehmen dass wir im Glauben bleiben, und dienen im (?von?) Herzen so, dass wir die Süssigkeit im Herzen schmecken und dürsten stets nach dir.

2. Help your believers and bless what your portion is, wait for them always with your bloody wages (gain, merit).

    Nàchtamawe wáhnsettakwaneẽk, wăk wétahamè gaquai nìk kià áne gáttaammawĭjaãk, channawèhenana ngommaowe áne p'gachganeẽth kià kpènhammawágan.

    Hilf deinen Gläubigen u[nd] segne was dein Erbtheil ist, warte sie allezeit mit deinen blutigen Verdienst.

3a. He said, "Go (*pl.*), patrol (go about) the earth." And they patrolled (went).
b. From one year they go to another.
c. They shall run and not be weary, they shall walk and not be faint.
d. They endured and prospered from the old (great?) years to the new years.

    Nahk'ma áwà: Nahà ahnà, ănĕmseẽkq pámăkĭeẽck ãhkq, wăk nahk'mawa anìmsowak.
    Ahànněmè kateèk áhtkcheetsch [*or* ?áhttecheetsch?] anìmsŏàk ktákkak.
    Pomìssŏàk, ashãm schawàjeweẽk, anìmsoak, asta ãm schéwochsannéweẹk.
    Nannò otaìjēnáwa, ónămănnìssŏàk machchowái katènnik pátsche uskái kátennik.
    Er sprach: Gehet hin, und ziehet durchs Land! Und sie zogen. *Zack[arias] 6, 7.*
    Von einem Jahr zum andern. *N. 710.*
    Sie laufen, und werden nicht matt, sie wandeln und werden nicht müde. *Jes[aia] 40, 31.*
    Sie bleiben und gedeihen vom Alten bis zum Neuen. *N. 710.*

4. Soon when it gets to be evening, it sounds (rings); then the [Indian] brothers (and) sisters gather together, [*or:*] As soon as it is sounded toward evening, our [Indian] brothers (and) sisters gather together, and that[*] you (*pl.*) observe (*or* hold) daily; don't forget it. [*In the German text there was a w or v; thus error for v[ergesst] crossed out?; sense could also have been* 'mass' *or* 'meeting.']

    schétà
    Éne tăppăchchétà   tautautschenuáŭ nitsch tanè majáwewak anenapaak netachcanenanack, cheismenaak, nik knátămoòkq wáwochcamake, tscheẽn wannisséhaãkq.

    So bald gegen Abend gelautet wird, so versammlen sich die Br[üde]r u[nd] Schw[estern] u[nd] das [*] haltet ihr tägl[ich,] vergesst es nicht.

5. The Savior looks at a poor man in his great misery with genuine compassion.
Yes, that makes him compassionate toward us.
   Pachtam[awaas] ŏpĕnàuwāwà kaktĕmạaxétsche áne măchchè ktĕmăkăĭhattĕĕt, ktĕmàkanemáwak.
   Kahénne déttăne kettemácanemacónaụ kiánau.
   D[er] Heiland sieht einen armen Menschen in seinem gros[s]en Elend mit lauter Mitleiden an.
   Ja das macht Ihn mitleidig gegen uns.

6. *Manuscript p. (369) has four conversational lines, a sequence that does not occur in the rest of the manuscript [see also at see].*
   a. I have seen him.   **Nià kĕĕp náŭwăăp.**   Ich habe ihn gesehen.
   b. Not I. I am not it.   **Astan nià.**   Ich bins nicht.
   c. You are.   **Kià kĕĕp.**   Du bist.
   d. You certainly are one of them. **Kià múchtsche wăk kwetscháijìn.** Gewis, du bist einer davon.

NO TRANSLATION GIVEN IN GERMAN

[*I have tried to compensate for the lack of translations by indicating some possible or general meanings and by consulting Emily Johnson (E.J.) of Thamesville, Ontario, in April 1981, who as a fluent Munsee speaker in her seventies brought forth further possible meanings consistent with her Delaware dialect or language, which was a neighboring language to Mahican.*]

Original order of words:

[*These are on ms. pp. (374) and (375); several others are scattered throughout manuscript.*]

Pajáza.	tschachquachaju	udennăăptonan	Er spricht.	[He speaks.]
kscháijajaat	nochkau mbei	wáchche		
nŏŏspaat	tschachkochquà	kachnăăt		
ihàm no anè mbei	wānāpátamạak	. . .		
mezechtétahn	udennaaptonamawa			
udăăptónama	gattosomo wak	pānnăkékăck [see p. 159 for order in text]		
neschowe	patăk nè			
m'nohamè	nohàm awĕĕsmẹek			

Alphabetical order of words with speculative translation:

Anapáwechkŏŏk. [*cf.* Indians = anenapáwak?; *cf. Munsee* anapawexkuɛ = Indian(?)(woman?), *given by E.J., 1981; but cf. Mahican* pānnéwĕ ánāpŏwèchkănàht = misleading (everyone), *Masthay, 1980, p. 35.*]
ihàm no anè mbei [?then drink the? water (= mbei); ihàm = then?] [*cf. untranslated* m'nohamè (?drink? + ?) *and untranslated* nohàm awĕĕsmẹek (?drink + eat? *or better* ?My grandmother has eaten?, *as in Munsee, E.J., 1981; cf. Mahican [E]* nohhum = my grandmother) [no anè = in it?]
kachnăăt [*see truly* kachn- *under* truly; ?when he is . . . -ing?; ?when he is coming? *as in Munsee, E.J.*]
kscháijajaat [?old man?; ?(someone) went first? *as in Munsee, E.J.;* ?first = kschai-?]
mezechtétahn [mez- = eat; ?when (?he was, they were?) eating it?; *cf.* mĕzĕĕchtĕtà = when (*or* after) they were eating, *Masthay, 1980, p. 29;* ?he makes food?]
m'nohamè [?drink? + ?]
neschowe [?both *or* I'm tired (*or* weak)?; *cf.* tired]
Netàn mepàeh. [æ *usually is characteristic of Delaware in Schmick;* I have arrived! *(This is made emphatic by* -ta-*); translated as a Delaware sentence corresponding to present Del.* Ni ta^mba *by Nora Thompson Dean (Dewey, Oklahoma, 1980)*]
nochkau mbei [mbei = water; ?he is going to fetch water? *as in Munsee, E.J., but cf. Mahican* nochkăŏ = flour, meal, *Masthay, 1980, p. 38*]
nŏŏspaat [?(when?) he fetched water?; *also agreed to by E.J.*]
Pajáza. [?come + ?; ?only when he comes?; ?someone is coming? *as in Munsee, E.J.; cf.* Ăăptónāzā *under* speak]
pānnăkékăck [*cf.* go on; see; -ăck = at, in?; ?he came here? *as in Munsee, E.J.; see p. 159*]
patăk nè [?brought it to me? *as in Munsee, E.J.*]
tschachkochquà [*see next*]
tschachquachaju [-aju = it is, he is; *cf.* short; thin; *contrast* mill; soul]
udăăptónama [*see next and* speak]
udennaaptonamawa [*see* speak; ?they speak for a long time? *as in Munsee, E.J.;* or ?they speak of?; *cf. Delaware (Brinton)* wundaptonen = to speak of; *or* ?they should speak?]
Unèchtawăăk, astà ăăm wáchnemick kdèttan unèchtanáwa. [*ms. p. (334)*]
[they are doing it?, not will (can) (*noun*)-in? (?*past tense*?) he does it]
wáchche [*cf.* husband, *but unlikely; cf. Delaware (Brinton)* wachejeu = light, bright; *or* it is daylight = waxɛu, *in Munsee, E.J.*]
wānāpátamạak [? + ?prayed? *as in Munsee, E.J.*]

156 Schmick's Mahican dictionary

Untranslated "biblical" exhortative text on ms. p. (366) [Ives Goddard, 1980, helped on a few words below. See facing page.]

Nànò Tapan'mukquàk awa: [thus Lord saith: / *or* Thus (= verily) saith the Lord:]
natsch késchechtátip, wăk   [the one who made / ?the one who made (you?) is also the one who helps?]
nè onach'tamawaăn.   [so? (that?) he-has-helped]

                                                                                *[You(*pl.*) loves-he <u>not</u> / ?you

tscheen kwéschaseēn   Kiáwų^{a?} ktachwăăk tscheēn   [Do (*sg.*)(*or* You must) not be afraid.]   who love? / ?when you love?]
nia anàchcagàn Jacob.   usàijakechnáu.   [I am the servant Jacob]   [?<u>misery-makes-he</u>? / ?<u>Don't</u> be]
woăk wahnsettak   wéschaseēn.   [and he who believes]   [afraid (?he-is-afraid?).]

Oi kténne pomáosétscheēk   [oh (?you should be as?) those who live]
neek wahnsettakeēk   [(those) those who believe]
awáneetsch onistaweta   [if anyone believes (*or* ?is obedient to him?)]
woăk amáttaka Tap[an'mukquak]   [and (if he) feels the Savior's]
paachwechcawatowágan,   [teaching (gospel?),]
natsch ạsta ⁿ weschasewe.   [that one is not afraid of]
Machtando, matschaiwagan otsche.   [the Devil (Satan), because of (from, on account of) sin (evil, doing of evil).]
/dastannowaganik Jesus opgachganomik m'schinmèn . assannáik/   [in (*noun,* ?deliverance?) in the blood of Jesus (one) lies
                                                                                 or thinks(?) strong (*or* is strong?)]
Muchtsched anachemen unochtǫ̊^{a?}nomowe pmaoso,   [very much to rest helps(?) one to live,]
psuck awăn ăăm asch wawochcamake amáttamaquà   [but whoever of you (*pl.*) who will not daily feel]
Tap[an'mukquak] paachwechcawatowagan   [the Savior's teaching (gospel?)]
neáne pachpaquaik,   [by (in) his wounds,]
asta ăm pmaséwe,   [not will live,]
asta ăm anachemewe.   [not will rest.]
muchtscheed gommáowe wéschaso.   [very much always he is (will be) afraid.]

---

*[*The following are other ways one could read the three lines:*]
  [You(*pl.*) loves-he / ?you who love? / ?when you love? <u>not</u>]   [?He-loves-you(*pl.*).]
  [?miserable-makes-he?]   [?He <u>doesn't</u> make one miserable?]
  [?he-is-afraid?]   [?<u>Don't</u> be afraid? *or* ?He is <u>not</u> afraid?]
                                     [?He-loves-you(*pl.*) <u>not</u>.]
                                       [?He makes one miserable, he afflicts one?]
                                       [?He-is-afraid?]

SCHMICK MANUSCRIPT PAGE (366)

[see far]
tschëen quechtsche wetsch — es ist nicht gut allein
nemochahan. — mit zu gehen.

[see facing page]
Nàno tapanimukquak awa:
natsch keschechtatip, wäx
nè onachtamawaan

torheen wweschaseen   Kiawu ktachwaan Yeteen
nia anachcagan Jacob. usaijakechnen.
wäx wahtsettak   weschaseen.

Oi ktenne pomáosetscheen
neek wahnsettakeen
awanetsch onistaweta
awun amáttama sap.
paachoseechoawatowagan.
natsch astu"weschaseen.
Machtando, matschaiyaya
trpha. muchtschid ahache- das tannowaganik sepus opgachqapomin
neu, pmaoso,   unarhpnomowe   mschinnem. arsatnaik
pfuer. awan gan asth wawoch.
tamaxe amáttamaqua
sap. paachosechoawatowagan
ceà ne packpaguein, asta am
pmaseue, asta am penachemera.
muchtschid gomawut weschaso

158 Schmick's Mahican dictionary

SCHMICK MANUSCRIPT PAGE (102) (the hardest page to transcribe)

hear *hörren:*

Praesens. Sing.
1. Pettäm ich hör
2. kpettäm du hörst
3. nahǐma kpettäm er hört

Praes. Plur.
1. Niánōx pettämechaōn
2. kiawa kpettämechma
3. nahxmawa nptammākk

Perfectum. *hören, vorvorher.*
Nia mpettamennähp. ich habe gehört 1. Nétachcan n'tensettam
Nia pagatsché mpettamen- achwahntowepwagan kó-
nahp. ich habe schon lange gehört. nechtah. Bruder ich habe
Papacht- kianau kpettagonau. gehört, du willst nun lassen
ofter hört muss.
                                Kupchahama, wäätsch ach
                                ptammouäk.

Imperat.
Pettawè. höre du.   kpettawè hörstu nun
knistämōx. höret ihr.   huäme kpettaän ich höre dich.
knistäwè! du sollst hören.   etwan kpettawa tochenaotik
                                  kpettagoga hiana machechseagua
Pettäwenà — — —
Ptauwenanau — — —   *[see facing page]*

Awe awangen upachawak sta
ptammouwak
aliti Praesens. nia ndónna ptame Perfect
                    men.
nia mpettamen. ich höre   nia mpettamennähp
k-kpéttamen — du —   kia-k
n-opettamen — —   n- opettamennaap.

plur.   **plur.**
niana pettamennara   niana mpettamennanäap.
— — k — — — wa.   k — — — wäap.
— — opettamennawa.   o — — — wäap.

kwochanso Machtando stä wege
ptammowe - - - - -

Original manuscript p.(375) part concerning p̄ānnăkékăck (see page 155):

[handwritten manuscript excerpt]   [see Savior]

                                                                     [see glad]

p̄ānnăkékăck   [untranslated]
[*Although the root meaning may be* come, *another possibility is the Mahican plural of English* pancake. *This explanation is attractive because of Nipmuck (Day, The* Mots loups . . .*) paneg8g. (pl.) -gak, crespes (espece de patisserie), and Gordon Day states that paneg8g is a "loan from English pancake," but my explanation is just conjectural.*]

← *Problem on ms. p. (102); see facing page (and under* hear*):*

[*Superficially the first and second words appear to be* "Engl. didne." *On examining the microfilm by microscope, I found that the edge of Schmick's ms. p. (102) shows faint marks above and after didne causing me to see wishfully* Engl[isch] didnot *or* didnŏt *(past tense in the negative), but since the fourth word,* dénne, *is made certain by the nearby clearly written* Nia ndénne ptámmen *(*I have heard*), the second word,* diáne *(probably Mahican, not English), appears to contain two letters that by microscope look like either á or preferably* d, *with this d matching Schmick's handwritten d's elsewhere (* *and* *). Furthermore, if didne were to be read* áiáne, *this form would have vowels and accents that combined do not appear in his manuscript; thus it may be either* diáne *or* didne, *but the -dn- would be an un-Mahican consonant pair, and even* diáne *is unattested in Moravian Mahican elsewhere. Could it be* did nur *(= only), or* did noch *(= besides)? They both make sense with either* Engl. *or* Legt. *It is neither* kiána, *nor* niána. *The second upper dot may be the period ending the previous sentence.*

The first word could be Engl. *for English; in addition,* Legt *(plural imperative for* Put *or* Place*) is a strikingly strong possibility, but it still clashes with the verb* angehängt. *The third letter is definitely* g, *but exclude* Ergl. *or* Ergk., *unless the ending* ɭ *is an abbreviation mark, possibly for* Erg[änze], *supply, add. Exclude also* bez[üglich], *respecting;* beyl[eg], *add, attribute;* begl[eitte], *accompany;* eig[entlich], *properly;* vgl. *for* vergleiche, *compare; and* lez[tlich], *finally.* T.L. Markey (1981) *suggested that it is Latin* leg[it], *one reads, but I doubt that; nor is it* legātur, *it should be read.*

The third word is mit *(= with), not* auch *(= also), because there is no descender as expected for German script* h.

All told for Mahican here and throughout the manuscript, the probable "perfective-aspect" forms are (1) diáne? *(unattested elsewhere),* (2) dénne, (3) *-p in* -ăăp *and* -ăhp, (4) pag(g)atsche *(= already),* (5) machtsche *(= after, past, done, already; see under* eat*),* (6) kesche *(not to be confused with that for* can*; see under* patch*;* hide, skin, pelt*;* sit, already sat*;* sleep, last entry*), and* (7) *see also* Past tense.]

MAHICAN-ENGLISH GLOSSARY AND INDEX

SYMBOLS AND USAGE

Order: **bold**, 'roman serif' / [roman serif *(notes: italic serif; other glosses: italic sans serif)*], that is:
  Mahican word or phrase *(with occasional notes)*, 'full or partial English translation' *(find Mahican word at or under these main or subordinate 'English words')* / [glossed also in English-Mahican section *(with occasional notes and sometimes with other glosses)*]
To refer to the English-Mahican section, use the primary or secondary words in the English translation.
No capitalization; words treated as isolated items, except names.
Schmick's x is ks, but other sources using Greek chi (χ) or x indicate velar fricative ch, alphabetized under ch; thus χ, x, and ch are mixed.
— = Deleted gloss in revision.
(?) = Uncertain meaning.
( ) = Pronoun or word affects meaning or is alternative translation.
[ ] = Pronoun not in German replaces noun, or supplementary or added words, often not in Mahican-English section, or not in Schmick.
\ \ = Conjectural or highly uncertain reading (cf. **áiáne, diáne, didne**). But / / = on one line, divided word or interchangeable parts? (cf. **ksché**).
(2), (3), etc. = Number of times lexical item occurs under entry in English-Mahican section.
Alph. = 'Alphabetical order of words with speculative translation' under section called 'NO TRANSLATION GIVEN IN GERMAN.'
cf. = compare   pl. = plural
obv. = obviative   rel. pron. = relative pronoun (who, where, that, etc.)
Orig. = 'Original order of words' (see Alph.)   sg. = singular

THE GLOSSARY AND INDEX

aáchpapémick 'seat, bench'
ăchtahn 'I am going to' / [clean, to, washhouse]
ăm 'will' / [ask, full, last long, let, say, see *(at end)*, use, well, when, will *(noun)*, will, witness; No Translation (Alph. *at* Unĕchtawǎǎk; Untranslated "biblical" text)]
ăm 'can' / [will *(noun)*]
ăne tŏhnhaije '[what] I have said' / [know, speak]
-ăăptónăchkat / [long, speak, word]
ăptónau 'he called' / [loudly]
ăăptonáu 'he speaks' *(2)*
-ăăptonawágan 'word' / [sheep]
ăăptonawáganăn, aaptonawaganan 'words' / [feel, "Past" tense, sing, think]
ăăptonáwak, aaptonáwăk 'they speak'
ăăptónăzá 'when he says to me only "fetch something"' (? 'when he speaks to me only to get something' ?) / [speak; No Translation (Alph. *at* pajáza)]
-ăp tschŏnăchgătschò 'word' / [short, speak]
Aáschawáchkamĕn 'lay on edge' / [edge, Names]
aaschkĕĕknpè ('immediately' or 'school' ?) / [assemble, must]
aaschkĕĕnpè 'quick, fast'
-ăăspähän / [fetch, should]
ăăt '(that) is (it)' / [be *(2)*]
Abba ("Father") / [say, that]
Abraham / [go with]
-achchannawétowagan- 'keeping, preservation' / [take]
achcòhĕĕka '[who] is on guard?'
achcòhĕĕssa '[who] is on guard?'
achcòhĕka 'guard, sentinel'
achcòhĕkatschĕĕk '(they) are on guard' / [how many]
ăchenăquechk '...time to...' / [hunt]
ăchgŏttáju, ăchgŏttámu, ăchgŏttáwe 'upwards'
ăchkĕtá 'to read' / [Loan words]
ăch'năquech '...time to...' / [mow, time]
ăchpach 'roast (it)!'
achpéha, -achpéha 'to spin [yarn]' / [go in order to, quick]
achpéhäu 'she spins'
achpeháwak 'they spin'
achpequagenăn 'straps around blanket' / [band]
achpŏhn 'bread' / [Delaware]
achposetau 'let's roast (it)'
achpóu 'she sits'
-achu- 'not' /
ăchquăăspă 'stop getting water, don't fetch water'
achquachpéha 'stop spinning!'
achquadhà 'not yet' / [come, make]
achquandémick 'cemetery, graveyard'
achquăquănă 'rust' / [clean, gun]
ăchquăsou 'belt of wampum' / [sewan]
áchque 'don't, stop ... -ing' / [depart, read]
achqueètsch ['stop + will'] / [depart this life]
achquodhà, achquódha, achquódhà 'not yet' / [cook, find, sing, sweep out *(2)*]

achquodho 'not yet' / [sing]
achschen 'still (= even?), yet' / [feel, warm]
achtá 'set it [there]'
achtăăk 'inside, within'
achtáge '(that) is in' / [inside, reveal, that, what]
achtăk (*or* ne áchtak) ('behind') / [set]
-ăchtámmen 'eat'
-ăchtammen, -ăchtámmĕn 'taste' / [good, like to]
achtătsch 'let lie' ?/ [lie (of position)]
achtáŭ 'inside, within'
ăchtòh 'deer, stag' / [see]
ăchtŏhu 'deer, buck, stag deer' / [hide]
achussò, '[he is] covetous, avaricious'
achussowăk '[they are] covetous, avaricious'
ăchwáhnăăd ('one who loves him' ?] / [love, more than, must, woman]
achwáhnagan '[how] loving he is' / [love]
ăchwáhnăk 'dear' / [come]
achwáhnămamukquăck ('love + ?') / [fire, love-fire]
achwáhnan '(he) must love (her)' / [more than, must, woman]
ach'wahnáu 'he loves him'
achwáhndowágăn 'love' *(noun)* / [love *(verb)*, the same]
achwǎhnkunque 'they like us' / [love]
achwǎhnquussiăk 'we are loved' / [love]
achwahntetáu 'we have love between ourselves [for each other]' / [love, the same]
achwǎhntowep'owagan, achwahntowep'owăgan 'love feast, Communion' *(2)* / [hear]
achw'ăhnŭquăku '(why) he loves us'
achwahnuquáqua 'he loved us' /[lay down one's life, so]
achwanănau 'we love'
achwanáu 'he loves'
achwanáwan 'they love'
achwanĕcăn [why] do you love me?'
achwanuquăkŭ, achw'ăhnŭquăkŭ '[why] he loves us' / [say]
achwatachgà '(he) loves (it)' / [darkness, light, more than]
achwoǎhnĕquaăk 'he loves us'
achwohndowágan 'love' / [grow; Long Sentences, 1]
achwóonkunque 'they like us' / [love]
achwussò '[he is] covetous, avaricious'
[achwusso]wăk '[they are] covetous, avaricious'
-ăck ['at, in'?; '*plural*'?] / [No Translation (Alph. *at* păănăkékáck)]
ackenahamawáu 'he serves (him)' *(2)*
\ **ackenahamawáwak** 'they serve (him)'
ackenahegăăk '(may you [*pl.*]) serve'
ackenahegăk '(may you [*pl.*]) serve'
ackenahegátau 'we will serve, we have served' / [will]
ackenahegatŏk 'let us serve'
ackenahegatŏĕk 'let us serve'
ackenahegáu 'he serves, he has served'
águshkun '[why] are you sneezing?'

ăh 'go away' [*imperative?*] / [away, must]
ahăăptonăăt '(who) has spoken?' / [speak]
ahaaptonametoak 'he is speaking with him (they are speaking to each other)' / [each other]
ahaaptonametoăk 'they speak with each other'
ahaaptonáu 'he will (has to, must) speak'
ahăăptonáwak 'they should speak, they have spoken'
ahaaptonawună 'he has [not?] spoken' / [speak]
ahachtăăk [*see* candlestick] / [lend]
ahagenahégăăd 'servant' / [light, snuff out]
ahamáwaad. wanechk 'message'
ahana '(you must) come' (?) / [call, must]
áhana 'go in(to) there
ahánawémik 'to hunt, for hunting' / [day, weather]
áhanè 'so' / [bring forth, just as]
áhanè 'go!' / [milk *(verb)*; *cf.* náhane]
ăhănĕchek 'cloth' (?) / [breast, neckcloth]
ahănnĕmè ? / [go; Long Sentences, 3b]
ăhănŭckquech ? / [plant]
ahapasxowăk (? 'with poison oak' ?) / [poison (oneself)]
ahátău 'we will catch (fish)'
ahhgeánachguk 'in(to) the cellar' / [go]
ahhkĕĕk 'down there, on the ground, in the world, on the earth' / [become flesh, land, live, set, sit, the, therefore, world]
ăhhkĕhámŭk 'to plant it'
ahhki 'land' / [inherit, plant]
ăhki, ahki 'earth, land' / [loose, make, more, on, Savior, whole, world]
ǎhkq 'earth, land' / [go, through; Long Sentences, 3a]
ahnă 'go!' [*imperative plural*] / [go in(to) there; Long Sentences, 3a]
áhne 'for' (?) / [love, necessary]
ahpánan 'grits(?), hominy(?), pone(?); (potatoes?!)' / [mix]
ăhschkechnpè ('soon' ?) / [will, write]
ahssannáik 'with the powers' / [hard]
áhssănnĕĕt 'hero, champion, strong one' / [hard, peace, the]
ăht '(that) is (it)' / [be *(2)*, be (in a place), it]
ăht 'he is at or in' / [alone, be (in a place), come, Wyoming]
ăhtche (? rel. pron.: 'that, what') / [get, give]
ăhtchek (? rel. pron.: 'that *(plural)*, those, what') / [give]
ahtchwĕchtĕĕd 'family' / [come]
áhtkcheetsch 'from' (?) / [go; Long Sentences, 3b]
ăhttecheetsch(?) 'from' (?) / [go; Long Sentences, \ áiáne ? ? / [hear]\   ces, 3b]
ăijéta 'when we remain by' / [stay, tear away]
ăijétscheek 'as for, concerns' / [here]
aikè 'thereby' (?) / [foot, kiss]
-áin-, -ain- (? 'thus, in that way') / [as, call (name), see, sweat]
-áin- (? 'thus, in that way') / [heard, heart]
ăinăptŏnăăt 'what he spoke' / [hear, mouth, speak]
ăinachachĕĕtsch 'let's observe it' / [let, like to]

161

aínájick 'she came' /[come, girl]
ainochquáada 'if (he) looks toward (it)' / [see]
ainochquaján '[why] do you always look over there?' / [see]
ainochquatoŏk 'one must look to him' / [must, see, to]
aínokotakęęk 'they are friends with each other' / [be, each other, friends]
ajáhntamāhk 'it is necessary'
ajáhtamāhk 'it is necessary' / [pray]
ajápaǔ 'buck' / [sacrifice]
ajátà 'he went' / [glad, go, truly, work]
ajatchcà 'who needs it' / [help, necessary]
ájatak 'after his will' (?) / [will (noun)]
ájatakkaām [for ájatak áám?] 'after his will' (?) / [will (noun)]
ájátamaāk 'that they need it' / [help, necessary, that]
ajè 'stay!'
ajenechtahámak 'beaten, hit' / [brown]
ajèqu 'stay [pl.] (here)!'
ajétau 'we will stay (here)'
ajéwe 'he has not been (inside), it [anim.] is not there, he is not there' / [be (in a place), outside, up there]
ajéweck, ajéwek, ajewek 'they have not been (there), they are not (there)' / [be (in a place), outside, up there]
ajókak, ajókak 'he is already in or at' / [be (in a place), Wyoming]
ájówak, ajówàk 'they are in, they stay' / [be in a place), believe, friend, live (dwell in), where]
ajù 'he has been (inside), it [anim.] is there; is he there?' / [be (in a place), been, down there, go around, inside, like to, outside, up there, with]
-aju / [No Translation (Alph. at tschachquachaju)]
ájuwak, ajuwàk 'they have been (inside); are they (there)?' / [be (in a place), down there, outside, up there]
äkèhatęęk 'to the plantation' / [go]
akihágan 'plantation'
akihágánick 'from the plantation'
äkhóna 'hang up the kettle'
akkennáhämaù 'you divide [it] up'
ákkěnnähè 'divide [it] up!'
[ákkěnnähe]gà 'divide [it] up!'
akkennámawechteèkq 'you must divide (share) it among yourselves' / [among]
akkennámáwěnánà 'we divide, share'
akótha 'hang (the water) up'
aksámu 'he sneezes'
Albany / [Place names]
ällāuwéěk, ällāuwéwak '(they?) hunt' / [Delaware]
àm, am 'will, shall' / [astray, be, but, can, come, depend on, enough, fall (noun) (must?), feel (when?), get (when?), harm, have (present tense?), love feast (present tense?), money, must (2), none, not, one, peace, run, safe (present tense), say (ääm), self, serve, sheep, sick, take, take away (present tense?), tear away, thirsty, tired, until, where (present tense?); No Translation (Untranslated "biblical" text)]
äm 'can, may' / [but, easy, enough, lie (tell lies), say, soon, sound, taste, thirsty, to, work (verb); Long Sentences, 1 (3)]
äm 'can' and 'will' mixed / [astray, but, easy, harm]
äm 'if(?), should (?) (= will?)' / [be, should, so]
äm 'must (= will)' / [fall (noun), get]
äm (ääm) 'when (? will)' / [feel, sick, that, therefore]
-amachóŏn ('canoe') / [come, ship]
amáttack 'that he feel'
ämáttakà 'when one feels' / [if, sick, that, therefore]
amáttaka (? 'one who feels, if he feels' ?) / [No Translation (Untranslated "biblical" text)]
ämáttakěěk, amáttakeèk 'those who feel' / [feel, help, Participles, that]
ämáttamà 'that I (could) feel' / [wish that]
amáttamaākq 'that you [pl.] feel'

amáttamàn 'that you feel (2), experience' / [trust, wish that]
amáttamaquà '[who will not feel]' / [No Translation (Untranslated "biblical" text)]
amáttamèhteéta 'that they feel'
amáttamen 'feel, experience'
amáttämèn 'he feels'
ämáttämóquá 'one who feels not' / [feel, Participles, peace]
ämáttämówŏn '[why] you don't feel' / [say]
ämáttämówun '[why] you don't feel' / [why]
ammáne 'take away' / [harm]
ämměnŏhänähn 'he gave to drink' / [drink]
amuáschik 'bee (little)'
amuáu 'bee'
ämùchkq 'beaver'
anäáptónamenàn 'what I have said to you' / [believe, say, speak]
anacháju '[it is] empty'
anàchcagàn [? 'servant'] / [No Translation (Untranslated "biblical" text)]
ánáchcátschéěk 'they are working' / [fetch]
anàchchakéchè 'go lie down' / [lie down, sleep]
anachéme '(I) rest; rest! [sg.]' / [like to, peace]
anachemeéd 'where they have peace' / [can, peace, where]
ánachémen 'to rest, to have peace' /[peace; No Translation (Untranslated "biblical" text)]
ánáchéměnäáp 'he has rested' / [peace]
ánáchéměnánau 'we are resting' / [peace]
ánáchémětau 'let's (both) rest' / [peace]
anachemewágan 'peace, quiet, rest' / [good]
anachemewe ('he-not-rest') / [No Translation (Untranslated "biblical" text)]
anachemohan'oquana 'that he has given me peace' / [peace, until]
ánáchémowágan 'peace, quiet'
ánáchémowáganick 'in his peace'
anachému 'it is at peace'
ánáchémüachtanamowágàn 'peace, quiet' / [feel]
anachem'wagan 'peace, quiet' / [until]
anáchen 'empty out'
ánàchgä, anachgà 'you work' / [beautifully, industrious]
-änáchga 'make, do'
ánachgátä 'work [noun]'
änàchgäwägan 'work [noun]'
-anachkà, -änáchkà 'work' / [quick, ready]
-anachkään / [long, ready]
ánáchkáchtána '... we will serve' / [Long Sentences, 1]
ánàchkachtawétip 'he has worked for me' / [glad, go, truly]
ánáchkähn 'happen, make'
anachkawak '[she went] to work' / [glad, go, truly]
ánáchtäät 'one who loses it' / [find, sake]
-anachtän / [lose]
anagáwoja 'sleep [in conjunct?]' / [well]
anagodwágan 'covenant, league, alliance'
anáhągnse 'throw yourself completely down'
ánàham 'he pointed with (it)' / [show]
anàhonè 'bring (take)(me [over it])' / [enclosed place, fetch]
anähoǫssè 'go (drive) down (there)!' / [down there, drive, there]
ánäíjakquaäm 'how [is one?] to make it' / [make]
änäjaháo '(he) evens (it) out' / [even out, way]
[anàkótowágàn 'covenant']
ánämä 'cook (it)!'
ánämä 'cook (boil) (it)!'
-anamahanà '(we) cooked'
anamapanà ? / [preach]
anamatau 'we cook (it)'
anamatŏk 'let's cook (it)'
anamáwak 'they cook'
anàměchtéět 'they were glad'
ánameh 'away' / [quick, run]
ánäměnänäwä 'they were glad'
anámma 'cook (it)!'
anammáu 'he has cooked (it)'
ánämménáchtéět 'they are glad'
-änämòh / [boil or cook meat, cook]
anámuk 'under' / [bed, sit]
ánänàchcäjàn, ánanàchcajàn 'what you do' / ↑

↓ [make (2), satisfied]
anánáchkaätsch 'he does it...' / [make]
ananapawechgŏk 'with the Indians' / [go around, like to]
ananapawěk (? 'in Indian' ?; 'an Indian verse') / [sing]
ananeges 'ants'
anapáwechkoǒk / [Indians?; No Translation (Alph.)]
anápe 'arm band of sewan' / [sewan, string the sewan]
[ánäpōwèchkănàht, see No Translation at Anapáwechkoǒk]
ănaù [? 'as, like' ?] / [astray, run]
ánau, ánau 'as(?), like (similar to)' / [honor, weak]
anauunè ? / [let, lie (of position)]
anauwéne ? / [let, lie (of position)]
anawachtäk 'gather (the wood) together!' / [wood]
anawachtáu 'he gathers up' / [wood]
anawachtáwak 'they are gathering (it) up' / [wood]
anawachtěěn 'for' (?) (2) / [believe]
anàwähmik 'to have love for' / [necessary]
anawěmuk 'to go hunting' / [time]
Ánáwèpäkòchq 'one who stays under many leaves' / [leaf, Names]
ǎnè, anè 'tell me, say it to me'
anè 'in' / [chase out, good, impatient, inclination, patient, stay, use, work]
anè 'to (there?)' / [fourth, take]
anè 'that' / [bad, make (that?)]
anè 'than' or 'that' (?) / [must]
anè ['why?, what?, that which?, thus?'] / [ask, get, one]
anè, änè, äne 'so, thus' / [seem(s), work (for me?)]
anè [no translation] / [steal, water, work (for me?); No Translation (Original order and Alph. at ihäm)]
áne 'that [rel.], therein(?)' / [come, crucify, food, glad, house]
áne 'the, those, (in his? or through his?)' / [make well (2), so that, wounds]
áne 'the, (with) that' / [believe (2), bless, inheritance (2), wait for; Long Sentences, 1]
áně, áne 'the, in the(?)' [part of ně áne] / [good, sweat]
áne 'in, in the, in that(?)' / [great, know, look at, misery, will (noun); Long Sentences, 5]
áne 'to' / [see, to]
áne ('than' and 'to') / [must (2)]
áne 'than(?), as(?)' / [love, more than, woman]
áne ('thus?, in?') / [serve]
áne ('the?, thus?') / [thirsty; Long Sentences, 1 (second half)]
ǎne 'as' / [love, must]
ǎne ? / [reveal]
anè näquàk 'so it seems'
äne näquàt, änè naquàt 'it is the same, it appears the same' / [seem(s)]
änéchen (? 'let it stay' ?) / [let, lie (of position)]
änéchquäk 'what causes...' / [harm, take away]
anechtaháku 'don't [pl.] lose it'
anèhóquanep 'he has done it' / [make]
ánei, anei 'way, path' / [even out, make, well]
änèkänawójanne '[those] that you sing' / [feel]
anèku 'tell [pl.] me, say [pl.] it to me'
äněmsěěkq 'patrol [pl.]!' / [go, through; Long Sentences, 3a]
änèn 'that I say it to you'
anenäáxétip ['(he) appeared as'] / [appear as, as, become flesh, believe, come]
anenäáxiják 'looks like (we) look' / [appear as, as, become flesh, believe, come]
ánènähxétippě ['(he) became like a'] / [become flesh, make, we (for us)]
anènäná 'tell just (us)!' / [just, say]
anenapąąk 'people, Indians' / [assemble, brother; Long Sentences, 4]
anenápak 'Indians' / [preach]
anenápawà 'Indians' / [seek]
anenápawak 'Indians' / [call; No Translation (Alph. at Anapáwechkoǒk)]
ánènáu, anenáu '(that I) see (him/them)' / [glad]

anenawunáku 'to see you [pl.], (that I see you [pl.])'
anenawunan 'to see you (? that I see you ?)' / [glad, that]
anénaxian 'picture'
ănènnáquà 'if I tell it to you [pl.]' / [say]
ánepapáquaik 'with his wounds' / [acquainted with]
ănĕpéquan 'my gun'
ánĕp'gachganĕĕk 'bloodied' / [eat]
ánep'gáchganeĕth 'bloody' / [let, see (at end)]
ánequèchk ? / [call (shout), until]
ănĕquéchkùk, ănĕquechkùk (? 'more-in, more-on' ?) / [make, more, on, Savior, whole, world]
anequèchque, ănĕquèchquè, ănĕquéchque 'more' / [great, how long, long, ready]
anetáha 'hope!'
ănètaháãt 'as he thinks or wills' / [make]
anètahámachtéta '[? when ?] they think'
anètahámatóōk 'you [pl.] should think; let us think'
anètahátamen 'he thought about (them, inan.)' / [("Past" tense, think, word]
anetaháu, anètaháu 'he hopes, he thinks; he (has) thought' (2) / [self]
anètahāwā 'you [pl.] think'
anetaháwak 'they hope'
anetaháwak, [anetahā]wàk 'they think; they (have) thought'
ănĕtāhāwĕ 'he (can)not let them (her) ...' / [astray, run]
anètaheetá 'you think about it'
ănĕtsch (? 'how' ?) / [how, pray, teach]
ănĕwè 'go there (go now)!' / [go with, luck]
aneweseà 'call, name' / [as]
ănĕwĕsŏ, anéweso '[what] is he called?, [what] is his (her) name?' / [call, what]
ánĩan 'what you are saying' / [say, understand]
animmachkése 'tell [it] quickly!'
animmeschéha 'chase (drive them) out'
animmesè 'go!' / [go before]
animm'sóŏp 'he has gone, he went' / [go, early]
anim'sè 'go!'
animsechtétip 'they have gone, they went'
animsetau 'let's go'
animsétau 'go [pl.] on, go forth'
anim'sètóŏk 'we will go'
anìmsóăd 'he has gone'
animsoak, animsŏak 'they shall walk, they go' / [go, other, run, tired; Long Sentences, 3b, 3c]
animsógak 'they have gone home'
anim sópănĕĕk 'they have gone' / [go]
ănìmsópănĕek 'they have gone' / [day, for, go]
animsowà 'he has gone'
animsowak 'they patrolled' / [go; Long Sentences, 3a]
ănĩppĕtscheeksĕjàh 'crawl in there'
Anna, Anna / [call, sweep out]
annachgawágan 'work' [noun] / [soul]
an[n]achkaschegau 'he plows for him'
annachkaschegawak 'they plow'
an[n]achkaschemawáu 'he plows for him'
-annachtăn / [lose]
annahóguk 'that he is running away'
annajin 'he went' / [go]
annàmăãkschà 'down there (when steep)'
annàmăquà 'down there'
ănnămmenájà 'I am glad' / [about that, very]
ănnămménāwátămótóōk 'we will be glad'
ănnămménāwatămŏtoōk, annamménawatamotóōk 'we will be glad (about it)' / [will]
-annawe- 'hunt' / [go with]
ánnĕmăkézētà 'we will read (further)'
annetŏhnháu 'he preaches about it'
annetŏnháu 'he preaches'
annettohnháu 'he preaches'
annettŏhnháwak 'they preach'
annettŏnháwak 'they preach'
annewanemeĕĕk 'you must revere (reverence) me' / [honor, must, your(s)]
annewanemegăăk 'they honor me' / [many, too]
annowanemájan 'that you revere him' / [honor]
annowanematóōk 'let us honor him'

ánnowéwe, annowéwe 'more' / [better, feel, like to, necessary]
annuwéwe 'more, more than' / [darkness, light, love]
anotachosŏn 'thorn hat' / [put on]
Anton 'Anthony' /[come, not yet]
anuwéwe 'more' / [but, honor, must]
apagatschè 'already' / [swallow]
ăpánnāwāwă 'you look at yourself (he looks at himself?)' / [see]
apapăãtqua 'bind the hands behind the back' (?)
ăpchawáku 'he yawns'
ápea 'I sit, I am sitting' / [here, there]
ápeak 'we sit' / [here, there]
ápĕĕd, ápeed 'she sits' / [here, there]
ápejak 'we sit' / [here, there]
ápenes, ápĕnĕs 'apple' / [Loan words]
ápĕnĕsak 'apple tree'
ápĕnĕssáchkq 'apple tree' / [tree]
apenessàchquăăm 'apple tree'
-apéso ('tie one with a cord') / [strangle (with a cord)]
apetammenáu (2) 'they hear it' / [sheep]
ápetschĕĕk 'they sit' / [here, there]
-apézò / [hold on, too]
-ăp'nèssàk 'apples' / [dry, sick]
aposaseĕk 'to roast'
appajuwechnà '(I) ... to sweat' / [ready]
appajuwechnáu 'he sweats'
appajuwechnáwak 'they sweat'
appĕĕn tschassè 'warm your hands!'
appĕĕn tschassĕĕk 'warm your [pl.] hands!'
appessè 'warm!'
appĕssĕĕd tassè, appesseed tassè 'warm your feet!' / [foot, warm]
appesseed tassĕĕk 'warm your [pl.] feet!' / [foot, warm]
appessĕĕk 'warm [pl.]!'
aptónachkat 'word(s)' / [one, speak, two]
ăptonáu 'he speaks'
-ăp tschŏpăchgătschò 'word' / [short, speak]
-ápu ['fluid' ?] / [soup, thin, water]
-apuwĕw 'it is fluid' ?] / [soup, thin, water]
ăquòchnáu '(ship) arrived or landed' / [come, ship]
ásapo 'he is playing'
asápuak 'they are playing'
asch, àsch, -àsch 'not, not yet (?), (not again?)' / [afraid (-àsch ta-), come, find, go, have (4), hear, help, know, laugh, love, necessary, patch (noun) ('yet' ?), say ('didn't'), see (2), speak, still, sweat, that, whip, yesterday; No Translation (Untranslated "biblical" text)]
ascha, aschà 'not' / [buy, envy, go in(to) there, go with, hear, help (2), loudly, see (4), snuff out, speak, teach ('will not'), think]
aschā 'will not' / [not, snow, sweep out]
aschāām 'will not (not-will)' / [give, not]
aschām, ascham 'will not' / [not, reveal; cf. also run]
ascham 'not-will-I' (?) / [see]
aschăn, aschan 'not I' / [buy, quick, see]
ăschápe 'remove [it] (from the fire)'
aschawachkhéganà 'spear, with a spear' / [side, stab]
aschawăn 'someone (anyone?), [no (matter) who]' / [give]
aschk ('don't' ?) / [ashamed]
aschoguágan 'poverty'
ăschókò 'poor'
-àsch ta(n) 'not' / [afraid]
ashām 'shall not' / [run, tired; Long Sentences, 3c]
-ăssănāi 'blanket' / [white]
assanetaháu 'he is patient, he has a strong heart' / [be, hard, work]
assanetaháwak 'they are patient' / [be]
assannachtáhe 'nail it on hard'
assannáik ('strong + ?') / [No Translation (Untranslated "biblical" text)]
assannáju '(it is) hard' / [work]
assannájuwan 'they are hard'
assannanachgáu 'stubborn work' / [hard]
assè [see also tassè] 'fire' / [bad fire]

assĕhĕnău / [bad fire, fire]
-ássèn 'stone' / [pipe of stone]
astà, asta 'not, don't' / [apple, attention, believe, blood, bloody, can, cold, depend on, each other, fall, feel (2), find, friends, further, get, go in(to) there, have, help, know, last long, lie (tell lies), long, love feast, make, money, none, nothing, Participles, peace, run, satisfied, say, see, self, shoot, sick, take, tired, trust, understand, until, use, we (incl.), where, why, witness, work; Long Sentences, 3c; No Translation (Untranslated "biblical" text [2])]
astà ăăm 'not will' / [No Translation (Alph. at Unèchtawăăk)]
astaăm, asta ăm 'not-can, cannot; not-will, will not' / [depend on, have, help, lie (tell lies), love feast, money, must, none, peace, run, self, tear away, tired, until, use (ăăm astà), witness (ăăm astà); No Translation (Untranslated "biblical" text)]
astak 'not' / [bad]
astak gaquai, astăk gáquai 'nothing, not anything' / [bad, great, hear, more, say]
astam 'not, didn't' / [catch fish]
astàn, astan 'not, not-I, not it' / [afraid, bad, be, become flesh, forget, he, it, know, make, right, satisfied, say, see, snow, worthy; Long Sentences, 6]
astaⁿ 'not' / [No Translation (Untranslated "biblical" text)]
astaù 'not' / [assemble, good, late]
ăsusquahŏ 'pot, earthen pot' / [new]
as'wehhn 'to swim'
átàhn 'around' / [here, there]
átan 'at, in, on; to; where ...' / [cook, crucify, kitchen, live]
átăn [? 'in, at' ?] / [a, an, as, finger, long]
atane [? 'in, at' ?] / [a, an, bring forth, that]
átane 'in' / [peace]
átănĕ (? 'wherein, in that' ?), 'where' / [safe]
átanĕppéméhaat 'she boiled or cooked off fat' / [fat]
atannĕĕtsch 'where (can)' / [can, know, peace]
atannónò 'now, at this time' / [on, time]
ătăpétóōk 'let's sit'
-átau 'let us (excl.]...' / [properly -tau]
-atau 'each other' / [properly -tau]
ătchānájăgéssĕjăckŭ, ătchānājákéssĕjăckŭ 'nations' / [free]
-atŏk 'let us [excl.]...' / [properly -tŏk]
-atoōk 'let us [incl.]...' / [properly -toōk]
ătooku 'a stick' / [fell]
-atsch 'will' / [accept]
-ătsch 'let him'
attăchpannéwe 'throw it away, put it away!' / [set]
átusk 'he sneezes'
áŭ 'he has gone, he is going' / [a, an, go, go in(to) there, one, run, there]
áu ('he would be with him') / [be present, say]
-áu 'he goes' / [go out there]
-äusătschăcken [see jump across]
áwà, awà, awa 'he said, he spoke, he says, he saith' / [go, loudly, say, speak, voice; Long Sentences, 3a; No Translation (Untranslated "biblical" text)]
awà ? / [hard, nail]
awăăk 'even more' / [call (shout), cry out, yet]
awăăn 'who' / [feel, Participles, peace]
ăwăhwăk ('with rods' ?) / [rods, whip]
áwak 'they went' / [go]
-áwak 'they go' / [go out there]
awăn, awan, awàn 'who, whom; whose; someone, whoever; to whom' / [basket, belong, bless, call (shout), come, cook, cry out, fair, feel, find, follow, friend, get, give, go with, guard, hear ('someone'), help, hit, if, lose, love, make, make well, more than, must, necessary, no one, observe, reveal ('to whom'), sake, save, see (1st: 'someone'; 2nd: 'whom'), seek, shoot (awàn), sick, speak, supper, that, therefore ('someone'), to that place, whom, will, woman]
awàn ['whoever' ?] / [let, like to; No Translation (Untranslated "biblical" text)]
awăn 'who (all the people)'
awáne 'all [= ? (all) whoever]' / [free]

awānè (awānò ?) 'who' / [give]
[awanè ?] ? / [steal]
awāneek '(all the people)'
awāneetsch, awāneētsch, ăwáneetsch 'everyone, whoever, who[ever]' / [believe, enjoy, feel, get, Participles, peace, see, someone; No Translation (Untranslated "biblical" text)]
awánetsch 'everyone, mankind, all whoever' / [darkness, light, love, more]
awānò (awānè ?) 'who' / [give]
ăwănóchkq 'take [it, him] away!'
ăwāschees, awaschees 'child' / [bring forth, just as, so]
awāshes, awāsches 'child' / [assemble, suck]
ăwāsches, awāsches 'child' / [beautiful, breast]
awaschesak 'children' / [love feast]
ăwāsēs, awāses 'child' / [beautiful, play, suck]
awàsésak, awasésak, ăwāsēsāk, awásesak 'children' / [come, good, learn, lie down, like (similar to), must, obedient, play, sleep, teach, weak]
awasésik 'with the children' / [be (in a place), go around]
awàsséwè 'I am going over' / [go over there, mountain]
ăwátah '(that one is) tormented'
awatschetschquáwe 'drive on!'
awatteschehà 'chase [it] out, drive [it] out!'
[awatteschehá]háu 'he chases [it] out, he drives [it] out'
awatteschehawak 'they chase [it] out, they drive [it] out'
ăwăttóchāne 'carry [it], bring [it]!'
awēesmęęk / [No Translation (Original order of words and Alph. at ihàm)]
áwu 'he has gone' / [go, house]

báschoā 'I'm bringing it back' / [immediately]
Bathseba 'Bathsheba' / [hope, Names, well, will, wish that]
béson 'medicine'
Bethlehem, Bethl[ehem] 'Bethlehem, Pa.' / [bring forth, come, fourth, glad, go, greet, remember, say, take, think, to, truly, we, when (if), work]
bishop 'bishop' / [Loan words, Pronominal affixes]

-cà / [help, necessary]
Catharina / [Names]
chāāsche 'go (slowly)' / [slow]
[chaa-schu (J), chaaschu (H1) 'eight' / [Numerals]]
chăchkoók 'there above, upon the hill, up there' / [mountain, up there]
chaj 'a hide, skin, pelt' / [dry, juicy]
chammahan 'must give'
chammau 'slowly' / [go]
chammàwachtánameętsch 'he has patience'
chammawéschè 'slowly' / [go, too]
chàn 'I wish that ...' / [feel, hope, shall, well, will]
chàn gāāp 'I wish that ..., I hope ...' / [come, feel]
changaap, changāāp 'I wish that ..., I hope ...' / [come, feel]
channawahnta 'keep, retain, remember [it]!' / [have]
channawēēchtaād '(he [one who] loves (it)' / [as, must]
channawēēchtataū 'let's take care' / [care for]
channawehaān 'he must love her' / [as, must]
channawèhenana n- 'wait for them' / [believe, inheritance; Long Sentences, 2]
chànnē mámaatsch 'I wish that ...' / [feel, trust]
chánnea 'that I have' / [give, what]
channéqua 'we have'
chánn'mámaatsch 'I want [them] to, I wish that ...' / [sweathouse]
channóu 'he has'
channu 'he has'
[xánsō (M-?, -EM) 'eight' / [Numerals]]
chaps 'deluge, flood'
[xá-sa (Si) 'eight' / [Numerals]]
[xǫsoxánkan (Sw-e) 'eighteen' / [Numerals]]

[xǫsoxínska (Sw-e) 'eighty' / [Numerals]]
chāsquéme, chasquéme, chāsquémě 'corn, maize' / [chopped up, fail, fill up, plant, scarce, thrive]
chasquemen 'corn, maize' / [long, see]
chassè 'go (slowly)' / [slow]
Checomégok 'from Shekomeko'
chégan, chegan 'knife' / [fall, find, have]
chel 'hide, skin, pelt'
-chei [see leather]
cheija ('skin') / [leather]
cheismenąąk 'our sisters, the sisters' / [brother; Long Sentences, 4]
cheismusak 'for the sisters' / [glad]
Chekomégok 'Shekomeko' / [come]
cheschemushāhk 'for the sisters' / [brother, necessary, pray]
chesem 'younger brother, younger sister'
chésemak 'younger brothers, younger sisters' / [see]
-choson 'thorn' (?) / [thorn hat]
C[hrist ?] / [think]
Christian, [Chri]stian, Chr[istian], Xstian / [hate, see (2), serve, speak with, think, Wyoming]
[Christ]mess 'Christmas' / [day, nine]
Christoph 'Christopher' / [see]
-chtammen 'taste' / [good, like to]
-ck opákka 'it is thick' / [too]
ckt'nawachtenánau '(they/we?) cost'
-ctenaspāān 'you bring water' / [hither]

dāāpenà (? 'release' ?) / [urinate]
dàh, dah 'heart, my heart' / [acquainted with, glad, let, see (at end), wounds]
dáhak '(in) my heart' / [feel, full, like to, necessary, well, when, will]
Daniel / [Names, not, well (healthy)]
[dá·nɪt (Sw-D) 'ten' / [Numerals]]
dannănachkāchtāwe '(you can)not do (it)' / [make, work]
dănněmékenanà 'let us grow...' / [Long Sentences, 1]
dāppeēn tschāsseęn 'I will warm (them)' / [hand]
dappsè 'I will warm myself'
dáp tschassè 'it's very warm to me'
dastannowaganik (? 'in deliverance') / [No Translation (Untranslated "biblical" text)]
daūwătāāch 'I have an inclination (a drive)' / [chaæ out, use]
David / [say, seek]
dāwāháu '(I, we?) use (need)' / [witness]
ḑemmachchāān 'I chop wood'
demm'hachà 'I chop wood'
dendéuch [? 'fire' or 'cook' (Del.)] / [cook, Delaware, hang on]
dĕnnāāknaú 'I make it juicy (soft and pliable)' / [hide (noun)]
dennanáchcawagan, dennànachkawágan 'my sake' / [crucify, find, lose]
dennè / [find]
dénne ? / [hear]
déttănè ('? + in' ?) / [compassionate, toward us; Long Sentences, 5b]
d'háju 'fresh, cold' / [spring]
\ diáne ? ? / [hear]\ didne ? ? / [hear]\
d'mahégan 'ax' / [great]
[dǫ́mpəwǫs (Sw-R) 'seven' / [Numerals]]
[donnet (W) 'ten' / [Numerals]]
-dpa 'head' / [headache]
[dunnet, dunnitt (W) 'ten' / [Numerals]]

ē ? / [fetch, must, wood]
-echgáu, -echgaū 'there are many, there is (a lot of)' / [duck(s), fish, many]
-echt- 'make, do [with it?]'
-eèchsò / [say, voice]
-ees 'little, small'
-ēetsch 'let him'
eh / [eat, noon]
éja (? 'it') / [lie scattered about, wood]
éja ptschèssessāchga 'it lies scattered about' [it, wood]
éka 'say [imperative sg.], tell (?)'
ékà [imperative?] / [sweep out]

ekwetscháwun 'I will go along with you' / [go with]
Elias / [come, whether]
Elisab[eth] / [suck]
ĕmpènnamēn 'show me!'
ēn 'I' (?) / [ask]
ēn ? / [eat]
ēn 'soon' / [will, write]
ēn 'will' / [teach]
éně, éne, enè, ene 'will, soon; at once' /[ask, boil over, bring, buy, come (3), eat, give, go in(to) there, go out there, heal, hope (2), immediately, knock ('must, will'), must, reveal, say (2), see (2), snow, sound, speak with, steal, suck, sweep out, take, tell, think, victorious (after verb), whip, yes; Long Sentences, 4]
enen 'will-I' / [teach]
ēnicke [for éne k-] 'will-you, soon-you' / [see]
enikē [for éne k-] 'will-you, soon-you' / [see]
enimpēēspa 'I will go into the sweathouse'
-enn(i)- 'so' / [speak, turn around]
-enotei 'sack'
ēnsénachquāháu 'I make it dry' / [hide (noun)]
-épe 'eat' / [noon]
-equagà (?) 'sew' / [quick]
-ēs, -es 'little, small'
-esch 'little, small'
esgawanajāāk '[why] are you [pl.] envious?' / [envy]
esgawanàu 'he is envious' / [envy]
esgawáwak 'they envy'
esquaonīstammóu 'are you obedient?'
Esther / [call]
éta 'when he had said (it)' / [as soon as, say, when]
ēta 'what you (wish to) say' / [say]
-éta [see -ta] 'until, when'
étsche '(what) he says'
-étsche ' ... ones' / [sick]

g- 'you' / [Personal pronouns, Pronominal affixes]
gachanè 'do you have (it)?' / [leather]
gáchanēēn 'I have'
gachaneu, gachanéu 'I don't have, I have no' / [lancet, hobble]
gachanéwe 'he doesn't have any' / [leather]
[gachchanech]mà 'you [pl.] have'
gachchanéu 'you don't have'
gāchchanéwe, gachchanéwe 'I (you) don't have'
gachchanewehamà 'you [pl.] don't have (it)'
gāchchānněwātāāch 'he is not paying attention' / [attention]
gachgachg'hammánēn 'I will teach you'
gachgachg'hammawè 'teach me!'
gāchgachg'hammāwējàn 'that you have taught me' / [teach, that]
gachgajēd 'oldest' / [brother]
gachgapequáu '[he is] blind'
gachgapequawágan 'blindness'
gachgascháju 'he is quick'
[gachgaschá]juwàk 'they are quick'
gàchgawémuk 'bedstead'
gāchgāwǒjè 'bed'
gachgéme 'teach me!'
gachgem'gatōōk 'we will learn'
[gackescho]chahamà 'you [pl.] are going quickly' / [quick]
gackeschocháu 'he goes quickly' / [quick]
gackeschocháwak 'they are going quickly' / [quick]
gadhanenána 'take me (us?) to safety' / [safe, take away]
gadoátau 'we deny'
gadowáu 'he denies'
-gāgachgēmà / [teach]
gagachgémen 'I will teach you' / [will]
gagachgemgachmà '(will) you [pl.] learn?'
gagachgēmge '(will) you learn?'
gāgachgēmgōsōāk 'they (must) learn' / [must, teach]
gagachgemkónau '(he) teaches us'
gagachgemnochmà 'I am teaching you [pl.]'
gagachkhammakona '(he) teaches us'
gagachkhammān 'I (will) teach you' / [will]
gagachkhammanóu 'I will not teach you'
gagachkhammáwāk 'I will teach them'

gagáchquan 'your leg'
gagauuquacheĕn 'he is sleepy'
gagawokchĕĕn 'I am sleepy, drowsy'
gággănānāwèhh 'he (can)not lie (tell a lie)' / [can]
gagunáu 'he is jealous, envious'
gahóŭnà, gahounà 'certainly, surely'
gămquĕchnà 'I had [nearly] fallen into the water'
gamquechnáu '(it) has fallen into the water'
-gàmquóhēnnā 'I have fallen into the water'
ganáwetŏk 'let's sing (it)'
gănŏwochgamăk 'the whole day long' / [see]
gaqua, gáqua 'what, why' / [laugh (2)]
gaquai, gáquai, gàquai, gáquäi 'what; something; why' / [as, ask, bad, be, become flesh, believe, bless, call, cook, don't ('anything'?), eat, find, further, go in(to) there, great, hear, heart, hit ('why'), inherit, inheritance (rel. pronoun), inside, know, laugh ('why'), make, man, more, nothing, pronounce, sacrifice, sad ('anything'), say (12), seem, speak, tell, the, understand, write (2); Long Sentences, 2]
gaquai nik '... what (rel. pronoun)' / [inheritance; Long Sentences, 2]
gaquai wăătsch, ga[quai wăătsch?], gáquai wăătsch 'why' / [come, love, say, swear]
gaquai wătsch, gaquai watsch 'why' / [feel, hit, love, push, say, sneeze]
gaquai wátsche, gaquai watsche 'why' / [ask, believe, forsake, hit, I, push]
gáquaik, gaquaik 'what' / [eat, seek]
gaquajà 'what (oblique or obv.)' / [seek]
gáquătsch, gaquătsch, gaquatsch 'why' / [afraid, babble, call (shout), cry, envy, hate, honor, I, listen, pound, sad, see, shoot, sit, speak, take, whip]
gaquatsches 'why' / [visit]
Gästenik 'Albany' / [Loan words]
gatachnejan '[where] I am safe' / [where]
gătăchnĕkājă '[where] I am safe' / [where]
gatopechmà 'you [pl.] are hungry'
gatópu 'he is hungry'
gatópuak 'they are hungry'
gatopè 'you are hungry'
gatosomè 'you are thirsty'
gatosomechmà 'you [pl.] are thirsty'
gatosomechnà 'we are thirsty'
gatósomu 'he is thirsty'
gatosomuak 'they are thirsty'
gáttaammawijăăk 'inheritance, portion' / [believe, bless; Long Sentences, 2]
gattătanachkà 'work quickly' / [quick]
gattătachpéha 'spin quickly' / [quick]
gattatáji 'quick, be quick!'
gattáte 'quick, quickly'
gattatequagá 'sew quickly'
găttau, găttaŭ, gattáu, gattaù, gattau, gattăau, gáttau, -gáttau 'want to, will' / [buy, cook, covetous, eat, fetch, gather, hear, help, learn, live, make well, patch, say (3), see, shoe(s), take (note syntax), think, water]
gattope 'you are hungry' / [fish]
[gattopech]mà 'you [pl.] are hungry'
gattopechnau 'we are hungry'
gáttŏpu 'he is hungry'
gattópuak 'they are hungry' / [fetch]
gattósomè 'you are thirsty' / [be]
gattosomechmà 'you [pl.] are thirsty' / [be]
gattósomo '[he is / we are?] thirsty' / [to; Long Sentences, 1]
gattosomo ['he (?) is thirsty'] / [No Translation (Original order of words)]
gáttŏsŏmŏwăgăn 'thirst'
gattosomu 'he is thirsty' / [be]
gattosomuak 'they are thirsty' / [be]
gauweenanau 'we sleep [in him]' / [so]
auwenawa 'they are sleeping'
gauwetŏk 'we will go to bed' / [sleep]
gauwetŏŏk 'we will go to bed (sleep)' / [lie down]
iuwéu 'he is sleeping, he sleeps'
gawè 'go to sleep!, you sleep (6), you rest' / [easy, lie down, room, well]
gawĕchmà 'have you [pl.] slept?'
găwēĕchmà 'have you [pl.] rested' / [sleep]

gaweémaak 'sleep [pl.]!' / [well]
gaweschemen 'blackberry' / [berry]
gaweschemĕnak 'blackberries' / [berry]
gawéu '(I) don't sleep'
gawéu 'I sleep'
gawéu 'he is sleeping, he sleeps'
gawéwa 'she sleeps'
gawéwak 'they sleep, they are sleeping'
gawohnteek 'go [pl.] to bed' / [lie down]
găwŏhntĕk 'go [pl.] to bed' / [sleep]
gchanéwe (2) 'he doesn't have, they don't have'
gēĕkhămmăwèh 'have you (did you) sharpen (it)?'
gĕĕkhégan 'to sharpen'
[gēĕm]tonhákŭ 'speak [pl.] softly'
[gēĕmton]hataù 'we (both) will speak softly'
gēĕmtonháwak 'they are speaking softly'
gēĕmtonhawàku '[why] don't you speak softly?'
gegahè 'heal me!'
gegahenána 'heal us!'
gegahŏk 'he (will) heal you' / [will]
gégahon 'I will heal you'
gégan 'sharp'
gĕgánŏwè 'it is not sharp' / [lancet]
gegapau 'a single, unmarried (man), single brother' / [brother, man]
gegapawàk 'they are unmarried people' / [single]
gegapawè 'are you single?'
gegapawechmà 'are you [pl.] unmarried people?' / [single]
Gemēĕnde, Gemeeende, gemēĕnde, Gemĕnde 'congregation, church' / [as, care for, lay down one's life, Loan words, love, must]
gemocháu 'he crawls'
gēnăchănĕkónau 'he has set [us?] free' / [free]
genáchĕnŭckhănaù 'he has set us free' / [free]
genachnenckhanăăp 'he has set us free' / [free]
genachnenojagup 'he has set us free' / [free]
geschachtippè 'you are ready with the cooking, you are finished cooking' / [cook]
-gesche '(already) have' / [cook]
getachganenapàh 'brothers'
gétammen '[you] read' / [beautiful, beautifully]
gĕttĕmĕnăk 'good luck' (?) / [go with, luck]
ghapássei 'your breast, chest'
[ghusooh (E) 'eight' / [Numerals]]
giischuch [Del.] 'sun' / [Delaware, shine]
gkechtemm'náwak 'they are lazy'
g[máchgam] 'you find'
gmachgamównu 'you [pl., sg.?] don't find [it]' / [find]
g'máo 'always' / [Savior, think]
g[mátschai] 'you sin'
g[matschai]hamà 'you [pl.] sin'
gmatschaihammŏp 'you [pl.] have sinned'
g[matschaihòp] 'you have sinned'
g[mattschechtăn] 'you ruin'
gmechannsè 'you are ashamed'
g[mechannse]hemà 'you [pl.] are ashamed'
g[mechtappè] 'you were born' / [bring forth]
g[mechtappe]hemà 'you [pl.] were born' / [bring forth]
gménen 'I (will) give it to you' / [buy]
gménuck 'he gives it to you' / [new]
gnachgochemahawà 'you [pl.] sing'
gnachtamawahamà 'you [pl.] help'
gnackattemánen 'I will lay down (my life)' / [lay down one's life]
gnackattumakunánau 'he laid down (his life) [for us]' / [lay down one's life, love]
gnatim '(you) fetch, get (it)' / [must, wood]
g'nattpochgà 'are you cooking?'
gnăŭtĕnănaù 'we will see each other' / [call (shout), see (2), so that]
gnepéso 'bundle'
gnótenuck 'he (will) accept you'
gohnsíttăwĕwăhŏmmà 'you [pl.] will not believe it'
g'omáo 'always'
gommáo 'always' / [care for]
gommáowĕ, gommaowe, -gommaowe 'always' / [believe, thirsty, to; Long Sentences,

↓ 1, 2; No Translation (Untranslated "biblical" text)]
gŏmmáwe, gŏmmăwe, gommáwe 'always' / [be (in a place), covetous, go around (2), see, someone, think, with]
gónan 'vegetables, cabbage' / [eat, Loan words, noon]
góne, gŏne, gŏnè 'have you ... well?, you ... well, well' / [sleep]
gonechtà 'you make'
g. onechtamà 'you [pl.] make'
gonechtáu 'you have not done it' / [make]
[goŏta (Sw-R) 'one' / [Numerals]]
gottau on'mawáo 'I prick(ed?) myself' / [stab]
g[pajemowà] 'you pay'
[(g)pajemowa]hawà 'you [pl.] pay'
gpajemowánok 'he has paid for you' / [pay]
gpannsettammechmà 'you [pl.] are disobedient'
gpapachtamawà 'you pray'
gpapachtamawahamà 'you [pl.] pray'
g'patagonàu 'message' (?)
g[penhámmen] 'you earn'
[(g)penham]náwa 'you earn'
g[pumm'sè] 'you run'
[gpummtŏn]hahamà 'you [pl.] preach'
[gpummtŏnhăn] 'you preach'
gt- 'you, your' / [Pronominal affixes]
g'[tacchŏm] 'your bread'
g'tacchomwà 'your [pl.] bread'
-g tăchquăchpéhan 'don't stop spinning!'
g[tahagenahéga] 'you serve'
gtajehemà 'are you [pl.] there [outside]?' / [outside]
gtajenawà 'you [pl.] stay (here)'
g[tanachta]náma 'you [pl.] have lost' / [lose]
g[tannachtăn] 'you have lost' / [lose]
gtannamà, g[tannamà] 'you cook (it)'
gtannamahamà 'you [pl.] cook (it)'
g[tappajuwechnà] 'you sweat'
g[tappajuwech]nahamà 'you [pl.] sweat'
gtappajuwechnah'nŏk 'they sweat'
gtenetáha '(you (have) thought' / [think]
g[tenetahal]mà 'you [pl.] (have) thought' / [think]
gtennatippè '[what] are you cooking?'
gtenntŏnhahamà 'you [pl.] preach'
gtenntŏnhăn 'you preach'
[gúdqus (Sw-R) 'six' / [Numerals]]
[gutá (M-?) 'one' / [Numerals]]
[gúta·· (Sw-D) 'one' / [Numerals]]
[gutakáu (Sw-e) 'eleven' / [Numerals]]
[gu·tas (Sw-D) 'six' / [Numerals]]
[gutasxankán (Sw-e) 'sixteen' / [Numerals]]
[gutătkwa·ˀ (Sw-e) 'one thousand' / [Numerals]]
[gut·e (P) 'one' / [Numerals]]
[gutemdánokana [e or a?] (Sw-e) 'one hundred' / [Numerals]]
[gutaⁿs (M-?) 'six' / [Numerals]]
gutschémohn '[why] are you asking me?' / [I]
gútta 'a, an, one' / [as, finger, leaf, long, Numerals, sheet of paper, speak]
gúttá áptónokkat 'a word' / [one, speak]
guttăăsch 'six' / [love feast, Numerals, sound]
[guttaaṣhu (H1) 'six' / [Numerals]]
guttach 'one' / [bundle]
guttegeháu 'he has only one child'
guttegehawàk 'they have only one child'
[gutúⁿkau (M-?) 'eleven' / [Numerals]]
gwawonistamhamà 'you [pl.] are obedient'
g[xechnà] 'you jump'

-hăăk 'ought not' / [come, cook]
-hăăkq 'don't (you, pl.)' / [forget; Long Sentences, 4]
háckai 'body'
hackai, -hackai '(your)self' / [mirror, see]
hackay, -hackay 'body' / [self]
-hackei 'body' / [self]
hackenahegáu 'he serves, he has served'
hackenahegáwak 'they serve'
hăjĕwĕ, hăjĕwe, hăjéwĕ, hăjĕwĕ 'he/she is not there' / [be (in a place), house, husband]
hăjoù, hajou 'he/she is there' / [be (in a place), house, husband, woman]
-hākkĭjéwe / [become flesh, live, Savior]
hakkánăăk 'body' / [become flesh, make]

hakkei, -hakkei 'body' / [self]
haktáān 'don't go in!' / [don't, go in(to) there]
haktajehewehemà 'you [pl.] are not inside'
haktanawà 'don't [pl.] go in!' / [go in(to) there]
hamà [see thagótschai hamà, thakōmhamà]
-hámed 'shirt' / [Loan words, wash] [hamet 'linen cloth' (Masthay 1980, 1759) / [shirt]]
-hanà 'we' / [Pronominal affixes]
hannónò 'now, at this time' / [time]
[han-shó (J) 'eight' / [Numerals]]
hapò 'he sat' / [fire, sit]
happétau 'I will take a seat' / [sit]
[há·san (Sw-D) 'nine' [error for 'eight'?] / [Numerals]]
[há·su·' (Sw-D) 'nine' [error for 'eight'?] / [Numerals]]
héga [ending to 'write'] / [he]
hégaak [ending to 'write'] / [write]
[hi·ktan (error?; Sw-R) 'eight' / [Numerals]]
-h'nà 'we' / [Pronominal affixes]
-hōmà [see ktahawahnŏhōmà]
hŏnāchnājŏksĕmà, hŏnāchnājŏxĕmà 'horse belongs to him'
honammanissò 'wholesome, salubrious, healthful' / [spring]
honesséscho 'beautiful'
honittówe 'it is not good' / [sacrifice]
hōŏs 'kettle' / [boil over, cook, Delaware words, fall, hang on, remove]

-ick 'in, into'
ihà, iha 'then, yes (?), come (?)' / [come (2), eat, friend, go, go in order to, help, lie down, reveal, sleep, when ('then'), will, yes]
ihàm no anè mbei / [drink, water; No Translation (Orig. and Alph.)]
ihàn 'then' / [call (shout), see, so that, yes]
-ik 'in, into; to; with (?)'
-isch 'little (?)' / [pitcher]
[issgawana]wéwak 'they are not egotistic'
issgawanáu 'he is egotistic'
[issgawanà]wak 'they are egotistic'

Jacob / [call, Names; No Translation (Untranslated "biblical" text)]
-jaku 'we' / [Pronominal affixes]
Jesu 'Jesus' / [approach]
Jesus 'Jesus' / [believe, by, free, good, peace, say (4), see, where, why, wounds; No Translation (Untranslated "biblical" text)]
Jesusse 'of Jesus' / [lie (of position), wounds]
Johanna / [go]
Johannes, Joh[annes] 'John' / [bring forth, call, go in(to) there, horse, house, thoughtless, when]
Joseph, Josep, Jos[eph] 'Joseph' / [be present, brother, each other, go, go with (2), greet, hope, inherit, lend, say, see, sing]
Josepha 'Joseph' [obviative] / [speak with]
Josua 'Joshua' / [belong, die, each other, even out, feel, give, go, horse, like to, Names, one, speak with, way]
Josuáhik 'with Joshua' / [be present, say]
Judith / [Names]

k- 'you, your, thy' / [Personal pronouns, Pronominal affixes]
-k 'to, at; plural; inverse]
k-...-anau 'we' / [Pronominal affixes]
k-...-(a)wa 'your(s) [pl.]' / [Pronominal affixes]
k-...-chnaù 'we' / [Pronominal affixes]
k-...-chnook 'we' / [Pronominal affixes]
k-...-ennau 'we' / [Pronominal affixes]
k-...-(na)na 'our [incl.]' / [Pronominal affixes]
k-...-oa 'your(s) [pl.]' / [cf. kpachtamawasoa]
kà ? / [day, for, go]
-kà 'if, when (?)' / [feel, sick, so, that, therefore, well (healthy)]
-kà [imperative?] / [sweep out, touch]
kāāchòwàck 'how many' / [guard]
kaaktemáxia[_] 'poor, miserable, wretched'
[kaaktema]xiāg [pl.] poor, miserable, wretched'

kāām, kaām 'will (?), may be (?), may' / [come, each other, feel, foot (like subjunctive?), kiss, thereby (2)]
kaām áikè 'thereby (?), each other (?)'
kācha 'how many' / [horse]
káchani [? 'truly'] / [sweat]
kachannawechtāhn 'he provides for (it)' / [care for]
kachànnŏàk 'they have'
kàchămăcónau 'we teach'
káchcha 'how many' / [arrows]
kachchanè 'do you have?' / [flint]
kachchanéu 'don't you have (it/them)?' / [patch (noun)]
kàchchannawétowaganik 'in(to) your keeping'
káchchannè 'do you have?' / [food, have]
kachchannéwe 'you don't have it'
kachgawémuk 'bed (behind)' / [set, under]
kāchgawŏjè 'bed'
kàchkăwémik 'deceit, fraud'
kāchkāwŏjè 'bed' / [hard]
kachkēēm'gatŏk 'we will learn'
kachkèwan 'your nose'
kachna, kàchnā, káchna 'truly' / [cordially, greet, loudly, say, speak, voice]
kachnāāt / [No Translation (Orig. and Alph.)]
káchne, kachne 'very, truly, really (?)' / [friend, glad, go, good, work]
kāchquākachcan 'neck'
kāchquākachcanìck 'on your neck'
kachtonajāku '[why] do you [pl.] want to die?'
kachtonajàn '[why] do you want to die?'
kachtschai 'old man'
kachtscháis 'old man (little?)' / [spit]
kāchwàk 'how many' / [child]
káha, kaha, káhā, káhà, kāhā ('yes' ?) / [bad fire, fire, honor, lie (of position), love, many, obedient, soft, too, yes]
kàhāāp'néssak / [apple, dry, sick]
kāhāgóne 'beautiful, beautifully' / [read]
kāhāgŏnĕ 'beautifully' / [have good conduct, work, write]
kahamuckà 'go over there'
kahanachganau 'yes, I hope that ...' / [wish that]
kahanántaatsch, kahanantātsch 'certainly, surely' / [die, see, will]
kahanè, kahane (? 'truly, yes, indeed, very, certainly' ?) / [believe, help, that, true, yes]
káhanna 'yes' / [bad fire, believe, fire, true, truly]
káhanne 'yes' / [babble, feel, preach]
kahaquegageněga 'how soft did you curry the skin?' / [curry, soft]
kahénna 'truly' / [come]
kahéne 'yes' / [compassionate, toward us; Long Sentences, 5b]
kahennétténajappáu 'yes, it's cold in the morning' / [cold, early, yes]
kahhawanaìk 'the good (kind, benevolent) [one]'
kahoūnà, kahounà, kahouna 'certainly, surely' / [marry]
kahtem'náu 'he is lazy'
kahtenà 'year' / [five, one, two]
kākánĕnĕ 'hold [pl.] me!'
kakánenik [? 'that one' ?] / [lose, save, seek]
kakatschāìssak 'the old ones' / [love feast]
kākékwāschà 'blow your nose!' / [blow one's nose]
kākékwāschāhn 'he blows (snorts) his nose' / [blow one's nose]
kakéwan 'your nose' / [clean]
kakkajòh 'oldest'
kákkĕnōnōwágàn 'witness' / [use]
kaktĕmaaxétsche 'poor man' / [look at; Long Sentences, 5a]
kaktemaganēēdt '[whom] do you bless?'
kakunanáu 'he is jealous, envious'
kámawè ? / [come, light, move out of]
kámick 'enclosed place-in, over there' / [go
kámik 'enclosed place, area, hunting ground' / [bring, fetch]
kāmŭckque 'into the water' / [fall]
kamukhá 'it is soaking' / [beaver]
-'kanáhan 'leave (not)' / [blissful, go away]

kanànnŏwŏwāāk '(your?) cheeks' / [on]
kănāttămēgan 'you must not come in here'
kānewachcamāhnk 'the whole day long' / [see]
kánnanŏŏk '(your or his?) cheeks' / [on]
kánnisch 'pitcher' / [Loan words, necessary, seek]
kāpè 'be still; still, quiet(?)' / [be, sit]
kapè '(I am) sitting, of sitting' / [sit, tired]
kappajuwechnah'nŏŏk [sic k- for kt-] 'they sweat'
káschksò 'burn away (?), disappear (?)'
kástāāk 'warm' / [Albany, feel, yet]
katàch 'great'
katàcŏnānāū 'it is (important) for us' / [be, great]
kātāhókuk 'enjoys (?)' / [who]
kātātĕmŏŏk 'let's be diligent, industrious'
katàu 'want to, will' / [believe, examine]
káteek, katèek 'year' / [fail, go, last, other, thrive; Long Sentences, 3b]
katemaksétsche 'the poor sinner' / [love]
katemnáu '[he is] lazy'
katènnik, kàtennik 'from years, to years' / [great, old, prosper, stay, until; Long Sentences, 3d]
kat'makáhnsò '[he is] poor'
kat'make 'poor' / [live]
kat'maxēēd 'the poor one' / [hate]
kat'máxo[_] '[he is] poor'
kat'maxŏŏp '[he became?] poor in the heart'
kātschĕnáu 'accustomed'
káttà, kattà 'want to, must' / [bloodlet, Delaware]
kattatequagà 'quickly-sew, sew quickly'
kattau 'want to, will' / [know]
kattónà 'he will die'
kāuwè 'go to sleep!' / [lie down]
kawāhāsè ['? + I'] / [urinate]
kawè 'you sleep' (2) / [well]
kawēēchmà 'have you [pl.] slept?' / [sleep]
kcháhan 'you must not be afraid'
kchàt '[why] are you afraid?' / [why]
kdákkennàmāwāchtĕnana 'we will divide, share it among us' / [among, but]
kdéttan, kdettan, kdèttan / [call (shout), "Past" tense, see (2), so that; No Translation (Alph. at Unèchtawāāk)]
kĕ- 'your(s)'
kechkèkaà(ch)wāāt 'doctor'
kechtachenāāk 'they fall'
kechtāch'mockówu 'when you fall' / [get, must]
kechtemm'nà 'you are lazy'
[kechtemm'na]hamà 'you [pl.] are lazy'
kēēchcānnèt '[why] do you strike, push me?' / [hit]
kēēchtĕmmĕnà 'you are disobedient'
-keèk 'those who' / [feel, help, Participles]
keemtonhamàchtsch 'you have spoken softly' / [speak]
keemtonháu 'he has spoken softly' / [speak]
[keemton]háwak 'they have spoken softly' / [speak]
kēēp [kēē- or kĕ- + -pnaw-?] / [be, see (2); Long Sentences, 6a, 6c]
-kēēschchasòm 'want to dry them' / [will]
kēēschchequamè 'I am ready to repair (shoes)' / [patch]
kékachcùn 'I enjoy, etc.'
kékāchquāākùp (? 'he has created' ?; 'Savior') / [make, Savior, soul]
kékāchquātĭ 'girl, maiden' / [come]
kékachtátip (? 'one who created' ?) / [make, Savior, world]
keképsak 'chickens, hens' / [chase out, Loan words]
kekéschanachkáhip 'I have been ready' / [been]
kekeschanachkā panĕĕk 'they have long been ready' / [long]
kemeeksò 'it is running away' / [perhaps]
kémeexo 'he has run away'
kĕnāchnĕkŏnau 'he has set [us?] free' / [free]
kĕnáchenukkónau 'he has set us free' / [free]
kenáchkse 'you bad one' / [go away]
kĕnămmèta 'if we cling to (it)' / [hang on, side, tear away, who]
kĕnāmù '(he) lies at (it)' / [breast, suck]

kenanisktschaāchse 'you are a chatterer, babbler' / [babble]
kĕnattèn 'frozen' / [freeze]
keninnè 'take!'
keninnemamà 'take (it) along' / [fourth, to]
-kénnamēnáwa 'hang on'
kennáwe '(I will) not take it' / [not, will]
kennhéganek 'in one's fall' / [get]
kennhéganick 'in your fall' / [must]
kennhogówun 'you must not grab (for) me' / [fall, get, must]
kensittakónau 'they listen to us'
k[ensittawa]wà 'you [pl.] listen'
kĕpan 'arrows' / [how many]
képèschò 'he is thoughtless, frivolous'
kĕpnăwaŭ 'I have seen [it?]'
kĕschaachsè '[you] scream' / [cry out, don't, so]
kĕschăchpāhāchkăsò 'cover (already covered?), you have covered it' / [house]
keschachtippè 'you are ready with cooking, you have finished cooking' / [cook]
[keschach]tippehemà 'you [pl.] are ready with cooking' / [cook]
[keschach]tippóu 'he is ready with the cooking' / [cook]
-keschanachgāăn 'been ready' / [how long]
-kĕschănăchgāŭ '[I] haven't made it' / [make, not yet]
késchănăchkà, keschanachkà 'are you ready?, that I'll be ready'
keschanachkăăn '[how long] have you been ready?' / [long]
keschanachkāătsch 'that I will be ready' / [will]
[keschănăch]kahamà 'you [pl.] are ready'
keschanachkanawa '[how long] have you [pl.] been ready?'
[keschănăch]káu 'he is ready'
[keschănăch]káwak 'they are ready'
késche, kĕsché 'can' / [astray, but, buy, even out, harrow, hear (note and below note), loudly, make (first one), quick, run, say, speak, sweat (?) will, work]
késche, kĕsche, kesche 'already (done)' / [happen, make (second one), milk, patch, pray, sweat (?), sweep out (2), whip]
kĕschĕchgăwŏntŏăk 'are they in bed? [already-?-sleep + ? + -they]' / [sleep]
keschechkónau 'he has made us' / [make]
[keschech]kówa 'he has made you [pl.]' / [make]
kĕschĕchpăchĕnăŭ 'did you remove the hide?'
-keschecht- 'clean'
[keschechta]hamà 'you [pl.] have done [it]' / [make]
keschechtahanà 'we have done [it]' / [make]
késchechtăn 'I have done it, you have done it' / [make]
késchechtanăăp 'I have done it' / [make]
késchechtatip '(? 'one who made' ?) / [No Translation (Untranslated "biblical" text)]
keschechtáu 'it is done, made' / [make]
[keschech]tăwak 'they have done [it]' / [make]
keschĕĕchkonăăp 'he has made us' / [make]
kescheechtananà '[? 'we wash it' ?] / [shirt, wash]
keschechtátip 'one who made it' / [appear as, as, become flesh, believe, come, make]
késchehogoŏp 'he has made you' / [make]
k[eschehŏk] 'he has made you' / [make]
kĕschĕkówa 'it is growing'
kĕschequamè 'I am ready to repair shoes'
ket- 'your(s)'
kétachcanak 'brothers' / [glad, honor]
kétachcananăhk 'for the brothers' / [brother, necessary, pray]
kétachcanau '(our) brother' / [say]
kétachcanău 'the (our) brothers' / [say]
kétachcanenăăk, ketachcanenăăk '(our) brothers' / [come, hear, ship, sleep]
(ketach[gak?]) 'your brother' / [glad, love feast]
ketachgenanak '(our) brothers' / [ask]
ketaktachenahàn 'don't take offense, don't hurt yourself'
kétammen '[you] read' / [beautiful, beautifully, have good conduct]
kettemácanemacónaŭ 'it makes Him compassionate, merciful toward us' / [toward us; ↑

↓ Long Sentences, 5b]
-kewesche 'a little, few'
k[gácha]nè 'you have'
[k?][gachchanech]mà 'you [pl.] have'
k[gădoa] 'you deny'
k'gāwĕ 'did you sleep?'
kháckai 'yourself' / [see]
kháckei, khackei, k'hackei 'yourself' / [hate, sacrifice, self]
khákkei 'yourself' / [help]
[khausoow (W)] 'eight' / [Numerals]]
kià, kia 'you [sg.], your' / [afraid, be, be present, believe, bless, come, cut, depend on, divide (kià after verb), dumb, eyebrows, go, go before, go with, hate, have, help, inheritance, lay down one's life (nia?), leg, make, mix, money, Personal pronouns, Pronominal affixes, rake, reveal, sacrifice, say, see, seize, sick, snuff out, steal, wait for, work; Long Sentences, 2 (2), 6c, 6d]
kiă 'you' / [see]
kiak [= kia k-] 'you, your' / [call]
kiána 'us, we' / [call (shout), hear, Personal pronouns, teach, we (incl.)]
kiánau, kianau, kiánaŭ, kiánāŭ, kiánāu 'we [incl.]' / [be, because, believe, belong, call (shout), captivate (kiánaŭ), care for, compassionate ('us'), each other, earn, feel (kiánāu, kiánāu), for, great, if, know, love, make well, necessary, peace, Personal pronouns, say, see (4), should, sick (kiánāu), so, so that, steal, that (kiánāu, kiánāu), the same, thereby, think, wounds]
kiánau '(for) us, toward us' / [die, get, hear, payer, take punishment, toward us, we (incl.); Long Sentences, 5b]
kiánāu 'among us' / [feel, that, therefore]
kiánok, kianŏk 'we (all)' / [believe, learn, obedient, Personal pronouns]
kianŏŏk 'we [incl.]' / [rich]
kiánook 'our; we' / [believe, father, peace, Personal pronouns, the]
kiàtsch 'you will' / [blissful, Personal pronouns]
kiáwa, kiawa, kiawà, [kia]wa, ki[awa] 'you [pl.]' / [believe, glad, go with, greet (2), have, hear, heart, hope, love, obedient, one, Personal pronouns, see (also kiawà), sick, steal, woman]
kiáwa, [or kiáwų?] ? / [No Translation (Untranslated "biblical" text)]
klesowechmà 'you [pl.] read'
kmaăp '[why] are you crying?' / [why]
kmāătskăhàm 'have you chopped (it) up?'
kmachāhntamnánau 'we think big' / [great]
kmachánemen 'I revere you' / [honor]
k[machanese] 'you are proud'
k[machanese]chemà 'you [pl.] are proud'
kmachanesenáwe 'don't be arrogant, proud'
k[machaneséwe] 'you are not arrogant, proud'
kmachcàhachquà 'you seize'
kmachcawăŭtschi '(then) you will find him' / [seek, so that]
kmăchchăxseme [s or o?] 'put on (your shoes)' / [shoe(s)]
kmachchè '(our)-big, our-great ...' / [be, important]
kmachgaátamnánaan 'that we kiss (them)' / [foot, thereby]
k'[máchgam], máchgam 'you find' (2)
kmăchgámmen 'have you found it?, did you find it?' / [find]
k[machgamme]náwa 'you [pl.] have found it' / [find]
kmachgamówun 'you [pl.] don't find'
kmachgamowunawa 'you [pl.] don't find it'
kmachgawáu 'you have found him' / [find]
kmachgawáwa 'you [pl.] have found him' (2) / [find]
kmachgawáwe 'you have not found him' / [find]
kmachgawawewà 'you [pl.] have not found him' / [find]
kmachgeneēn 'don't color me' / [color, dye]
kmáchgenen 'you color, dye'

kmàchkăcŏnàhp 'he has found [us]' / [find]
k[machktschanné]qua 'you are blushing' / [redden]
k[machktschannequa]hamà 'you [pl.] are blushing' / [redden]
kmăchmătŭammĕn, kmachmatuámmen 'I ask you ..., please' / [ask (request of), fetch, good, see]
kmăchmătŭămneēchĕnà '[when] they ask (him [sic for you])' / [believe]
k[machschedtahà] 'you are unfriendly'
k[machschedtahawenaxè] 'you are unfriendly'
k[machschedtahawenaxe]hemà 'you [pl.] have gloomy faces' / [unfriendly]
kmáchtschè 'you-already' / [eat]
kmàhn '(don't) cry, weep!'
kmahtachksehemà 'you are in a bad way' / [bad off]
kmajáwĕĕchma 'you [pl.] must assemble' / [must]
kmajawĕĕchnaŭ '[we] assemble' / [sound, time]
kmajawéh'naŭ 'we assemble'
kmajawenáwa '[you (pl.?)] assemble' / [good, late]
kmakwése 'you are swollen'
k[makwesehe]mà 'you [pl.] are swollen'
kmamachtannachga 'you are not being nice' / [have good conduct]
kmamaktŏhnhăn 'don't speak loudly!'
kmamaktŏnhănn 'don't speak loudly!'
k[mămănăăk héga] 'you write'
kmamanockhaņanahamà [n or m?] 'I will write (it) down for you'
k[mamanahkhegá]hamà 'you [pl.] write'
k[mamatahana]ma 'you [pl.] will sound, ring'
k[mamatócha] 'you are crippled'
k[mamatochaha]ma 'you [pl.] are crippled'
kmàmáwàn 'your [sg.] eyebrows'
kmammattowăn 'don't swear!'
k[mammenonóchà] 'you go slowly'
k[mammenonochaha]ma 'you [pl.] go slowly'
kmamm'nonócha 'you go too slowly [repetitively]'
k[máschechhquè] 'you color, dye'
k[maschèchquehe]mà 'you [pl.] color, dye'
k[massánai] 'your blanket'
k[maténmuk] 'he despises you' / [honor]
kmatschaiwagan '[your] sin' / [serve]
k[mattachk]se 'I am in a bad way' / [bad off]
kmattakéhà 'are you ready?'
k[mattănăchga 'you make it filthy'
kmattenaù, k'mattenaù / [bad fire, fire]
k[mattesése] 'you are filthy'
k[mattesese]hemà 'you [pl.] are filthy'
k[mattschechtăn] 'you ruin'
kmattschechtanawà 'you [pl.] ruin'
k'māŭgawè, k'maŭgawè 'lie down, go to sleep' / [down]
kmaŭuquà, kmaüuquà 'lie down, go to sleep' / [down]
kmawè 'you are going to' / [go in order to, spin]
kmawupenăn 'I will see you'
kmawupenawè 'you will see me'
k[mechannsewe]hamà 'you [pl.] aren't ashamed'
k[mĕchănsè] 'you are ashamed'
k[mechansehe]ma 'you [pl.] are ashamed'
kmechànséu 'you aren't ashamed'
kmechkŏŏme 'I remember'
k[mechtappè] 'you were born' / [bring forth]
k[mechtappe]hemà 'you [pl.] were born' / [bring forth]
kmĕchtăppĕhĕmăăp '[when] were you [pl.] born?' / [bring forth]
kmĕchtapp'nap '[when] were you born?' / [bring forth, when]
kmeēnkun 'he has given (gave, sent) it to you' / [give, who]
kmeēschhámmei 'fix (your shoes)' / [patch]
k[menachtschè] 'you are left-handed'
k[menachtschehe]mà 'you [pl.] are left-handed'
kméne 'you give it to me'
kmĕnĕcŭnánaŭ '(it) is given to us'
kmeneēn 'give it to me'
kmenekunána 'he has given it to us'
kmĕnĕkŭnanawàh 'he gave him to us/you [pl.]' / [give]

kménen, kmenèn 'I give it to you' / [immediately]
kmenenána 'we give it'
kměněně 'I will give (it)' / [everything, what]
kměschòchquágàn 'your wig' / [where]
kmětschěchnǎ 'we eat' / [noon]
kmetschechnōk '[what] have you eaten?'
k[meuscheha]hemà 'you [pl.] chase out'
k'méze 'you eat' (2)
kmezechmà 'you [pl.] eat'
kmezechnōōk '[what] do we have to eat?'
kmischnimmantschè 'that you may receive' / [ask, get]
kmischscháwà 'you hit [the mark]'
kmochgenèn 'I (will) reveal it' / [steal]
k[móchgoa] 'you confess' / [reveal]
kmochgoauhanau 'we will not acknowledge it' / [reveal]
kmochgoauhennau 'we will not acknowledge it' / [reveal]
k'mǒōt, kmǒōt 'you steal, he steals'
kmǒōtǎǎk 'they steal'
[kmǒōt]hamna 'you [pl.] steal'
kmǒōthénnāū 'we steal'
kmǒthèn 'don't steal' / [reveal]
kmūchgěnǎǎk '[to whom] have you revealed it?'
knachgananaù 'we hope'
k[nach]ganáu 'you hope'
knachganawà 'you [pl.] hope' / [you]
k[nachgochemà] 'you sing'
(k)nachgochemà 'sing!'
k[nachgochemaha]wà 'you [pl.] sing'
knàchkeck 'in your arms' / [but, take]
knàchkěnǎǎk 'on our (incl.) hands' / [hang on, mosquitoes]
knàchmawachtoagan, knachmawachtowágan '[our?] punishment' / [earn, get, take punishment]
knàchnǎchǎwóně 'you prevent me' / [hinder]
knachnechauwóne, knachnechauwóne 'you prevent me' / [hinder]
knàchnechauwóněkónau 'they hindered us' / [hinder]
knachnechauwonèn 'do I prevent you?' / [hinder]
knachnecháwonen 'I have prevented you' / [hinder]
knachnechawonēn 'don't hinder me'
knachtamagöunà '(it) will not help you' / [depend on, money]
k'nachtamǎhn 'I will help you' / [yes]
knachtamanówe 'I will not help you'
knachtamanquǎǎm 'he will help you' / [hope, wish that]
knachtamawahamà 'you [pl.] help'
knachtamawǎn 'don't help him'
knachtamawawéunawàk 'we will not help'
knachtamawawewà 'you [pl.] do not help'
knachtamawè 'you help?'
knachtammawè 'you help'
k[nachxowenaxè] 'you have a gloomy face'
knackatachmága 'you inherited it from him'
knaha[quawépe] 'you eat lunch'
k[nahaquawepehe]mà 'you eat lunch'
k[najapawepe] 'you have breakfast'
knajapawepéhemà 'you [pl.] have breakfast'
knajátamen 'you can carry [it]'
-knak, -knakkekà 'day' / [go with, nine, two]
knámen 'you see'
knamenaǎp 'you have seen'
knamenáwa 'you [pl.] see'
knamenawǎǎp 'you [pl.] have seen'
knǎnǎmǎhǎnǎhm '(we) can sound (the bell)' (2) / [can, enough, time]
knǎnǎwóchachnau 'it will be halfway' / [soon, way]
knannawàchtánemēēchnà 'we are comforted, confident'
knátǎmǒokq 'that you observe (it)' / [Long Sentences, 4]
knǎtěnǐm 'you take'
knátim 'you are getting it' / [fetch, get, when, wood]
knattemēēchkùn '[who] has given (lent) it to you?' / [give]
knattemégan 'you must not go in(to) there'

knattemeganawà 'you [pl.] must not go in' / [go in(to) there]
knattemégawe 'you did not go in' / [go in(to) there]
knatte[megawehe]mà 'you [pl.] did not go in' / [go in(to) there]
knattemehenàn 'I lend to you'
knattemehenoch'mà 'I borrow (it) from you [pl.], or you [pl.] lend (it) to me' / [candlestick]
knattepochgahamà 'are you [pl.] cooking?'
knattōmen-[crossed out] 'I am calling you also'
knattōmkónau 'he is calling us'
[knattōm]kówa, knattomkówa 'he is calling you [pl.]'
knattomnechmà 'I am calling you [pl.]'
knattōmuk, knattómuk 'he is calling you' / [must]
knattpochgà 'are you cooking?'
knaūteohénnāū 'we don't see each other well' / [each other, see (2), we (incl.)]
knáwa 'you have seen (yourself)'
knawahamà 'you [pl.] have seen (him)'
k[nawaha]ma(?) 'you [pl.] see'
knawahemà 'have you [pl.] seen them?'
knáwau, knǎwǎǔ, knawáu 'you see, you will see, you have seen him' (5) / [sick]
knawawà 'you [pl.] have seen him' / [sick]
knǎwáwà 'didn't you see (him)?'
[kna]wáwe, k[nawa]wè 'you have not seen him'
knawawè 'you [pl.] haven't seen (him)'
k'nawawewà 'haven't you [pl.] seen them?'
knawawéwak 'you have not seen them'
knawè 'look! [sg.]'
knawechenamáchtsch 'you [pl.] have seen us'
knawechmà 'have you [pl.] seen me?, did you [pl.] see me'
knawewè 'you [pl.] haven't seen me'
knawewuhenà 'you have not seen us, you [pl.] haven't seen us'
k[nawoch]ma(?), 'you [pl.] see'
knǎwǒchmà '[whom] do you see?'
k'náwocku 'he has seen you'
knawòcku 'they have seen you'
k'nawokónau 'he sees us'
knawǒōk 'look [sg.] at him' / [see]
knawucónau 'they have seen us, they saw us'
knawugówa 'he has seen you [pl.]'
knawugówe 'he has not seen you'
knawugowewà 'he has not seen you [pl.]'
knawukónau 'he has seen us'
knawukówe 'they haven't seen you'
knáwun 'I see you'
knawunochmà 'I see you [pl.]'
knawunochmà 'we have seen you [sg. and pl.]'
knawunówe 'I don't see you'
knawunowuhamà 'I don't see you [pl.]'
knawunowuhamà 'we have not seen you [sg. and pl.]'
knechnepechnà 'you [pl.] are industrious'
knechnippenà 'you are willing, industrious'
knèchtǎwè 'have you ..., did you ...?' / [swim]
[knēēpnekan 'covenant']
knenóchtǎnò 'I don't understand you'
kněnòchtǎnò, knenochtáno 'I don't understand it' / [say]
knepnégan 'bundle'
knickatachen 'you fall'
kniipp 'you die' / [like to]
knimmǎchtánè, knimmǎchtanè 'gather wood; did you lay wood in a pile?' / [heap, lay, wood]
knimmaquamenà 'you must rake it together'
knippowan'kónau 'he died for us'
knippowan'nochmǎtsch 'I will die [for you (pl.)?]'
knippowanochmà 'I will die for you [pl.]' / [say]
kniskēpēsè 'don't be thoughtless, you must not be thoughtless' / [be]
knisk'tschǎǎchsè 'don't babble so'
[knisk'tschǎǎch]seēku 'don't [pl.] babble so'
knistǎmǒkq 'listen [pl.]' / [hear]
knistǎwè 'you must listen' / [hear]
knistawojàn '[why] do you listen?'
knosochgawà 'you follow'
knosochgawáwa 'they follow'

knotschi packuhámmen 'you have pounded (for a long time)'
knuktegehahamà 'you [pl.] have only one child'
knuktegehàn 'you have only one child'
kócha 'your father' / [inherit]
kochpenāāwat 'not at all' (?) / [think]
k[ochquéna] 'you cough'
kochwà 'your [pl.] father' / [obedient]
kohnsittǎǎn 'I believe it (that) ...' / [that, true]
k[ohnsittammen] 'you believe'
kohnsittammenánau 'we (two) believe'
kohnsittammenanok 'we (all) believe'
kohnsittammenawà 'you [pl.] believe'
kohnsittáno 'I do not believe (it)' / [that, true]
kohnsittawenà 'do you believe (it)?' / [say, speak]
kója [sg.?] 'cows'
kójak 'cows' / [chase out, Loan words]
kójǎmachgenimnà 'to mix [= you mix?]'
kojásom 'the (your) meat [obv.]' / [serve]
kojégan 'stable'
kojéganick 'in the stable' / [bring forth, Loan words (cf. cows)]
kǒm 'you have been, you were [there]' ('you come from') / [be (in a place)]
kǒma 'he has been, he was [there]' / [be (in a place)]
komǎk 'they have been, they were [there]' / [be (in a place)]
kǒmhamà 'you [pl.] have been, you were [there]' / [be (in a place)]
konáganes wáwàn 'bring the pan'
konágǎnǒwáwàn 'bring the pan'
kónǎlwágan '(your?) sweetness' / [taste; Long Sentences, 1]
-kǒnàk kà 'day' / [go]
konamansè 'did you ... well?' ['how are you?': cf. present Stockbridge-Munsee newsletter name: Quina-montha?] / [sleep, well]
kǒnǎmǎnsǒhǎnē ntschè, konamansoháne ntschè 'I will make you healthy' / [make well, will]
konamansohánuk tschè 'he will make you healthy' / [make well, will]
konamansohánukschè 'he will make you healthy' / [make well]
konamattǎmmen, kǒnǎmǎ[t]tǎmměn 'it has done you good' / [good, sweathouse]
konanachgà 'you are nice' / [beautiful, have good conduct, make]
kǒnǎpǎtǎmměn '[you are] blissful' / [you]
konaquépe 'you eat supper'
konaquepéhema 'you [pl.] eat supper'
kǒne 'have you ... well?, did you ... well?, well' / [sleep (3)]
konechsèwe 'you are not saying it right'
konechta (? 'you made it well' ?) / [even out, way]
konechtà 'you make' (2) / [well]
kónechtah, kónechtǎh 'you are going to have it, you will give or make it' / [hear, love feast, make]
konechtahamà 'you [pl.] make'
konechtáun 'you have not done it' / [make]
konenaxè 'it is proper, fair' ('you look nice') / [beautiful, have good conduct]
konenaxéwe 'it is not fair, proper' / [have good conduct]
k[ǒněsè] 'you are beautiful'
k[onetáha] 'you are friendly, kind'
k[onetaha]hamà 'you [pl.] are friendly, kind'
kon'sehemà 'you [pl.] are beautiful'
kǒnsittammenà 'do you believe that ...?' / [appear as, as, become flesh, come]
konsittawánau 'belong to(?), believe(?)'
kǒōch 'your father' / [obedient]
kǒōm 'you have been (were) [there]' ('you come from') / [be (in a place), over there, up there]
kǒōma 'he has been, he was [there]' / [be (in a place), up there]
koomǎǎk 'they have been, they were [there]' / [be (in a place), up there]
koomhamà 'you [pl.] have been, you [pl.] were [there]' / [be (in a place), up there]
kǒǒnnǎǎptónǎchkàt 'that is a long word' / [speak]
-k opákka 'it is thick' / [too]

kosáme, kōsǎmě 'you-too (much)' / [go, loud, quick, slow, too, whip (kōsǎmě)]
kosáme mnónōchà 'you go too slowly'
kósāměněs 'you-so-much, you-too-much' / [cry out, don't, so]
kosoahàm '[what] are you writing?'
kosoahega 'you write' / [beautifully]
k[osoahegaha]mà 'you [pl.] write'
k[otackénaksè] 'you are pleasant'
k[otackenaksehe]mà 'you [pl.] are pleasant'
kotahnsechmà 'you depend on (it)' / [help, money]
kótǎjǒmě 'do you have children?' / [child]
kótangkǔǔmkǔǎ [Del.] 'he blesses' / [Delaware]
kotenippà 'fill or put water in (the kettle)'
kotscheěmnehhenà 'we have called you'
kotschemáu 'have you called (her)?, did you call (her)?'
kotschemè 'you (have) called'
kotschēmgāk 'they are calling you'
kotschémuk '(she) is calling you'
kotschaíjèn 'you were with (him)' / [be present]
kŏtschòwachpátau 'let us fill [it]'
kŏtschòwachpeěkq 'let us fill [it]'
k[otschowupa]hamà 'you [pl.] fill him'
kowe[tachca]nè 'you have brothers'
[k?][owetachcanech]mà 'you [pl.] have brothers'
kpà, kpa 'you come' / [to me]
kpachansò 'he stops up' / [deaf, hear]
k[pachaschà] 'you peel them'
k[pachaschahe]mà 'you [pl.] peel them'
kpacháwak 'they are deaf' / [hear]
k[pachpenawussehe]mà 'you [pl.] look in the mirror'
kpachtamawaas '(our?) Savior' / [teach]
kp[achtamawaas]naù, kpachtamawaasnau, kPacht[amawaas]nau, kPach[tamawaas]nàù, kP[achtamawaas]nau 'your Savior' / [afraid, find, perhaps, say, see (K'pacht[amawaas]nau 'our God'), seek, so that, take (kPachtamawaasnau 'our Savior')]
kpach[tamawaas]nawa, kpachtamawaasnawà 'your [pl.] Savior' / [afraid, find]
kPachtamawasnau 'our Savior' / [believe, belong]
kpachtamawasoa 'as your God' / [honor, must, your(s)]
k[pagechtanè] 'you are bleeding (from the nose)'
kpahàn 'when the ice is firm' / [firm]
kpahè 'close it!'
kpajachquenaksè 'it is a long time since I have seen you' / [long, see]
kpákkǎmǒwǎǎn 'don't hit'
kpamowǎǎnkonǎǎp 'I have set you free' / [free]
kpamowánčkonǎǎp 'I have set you free' / [free, say]
kpapachtamawà 'you have prayed'
kpǎquánà '[who] has shot?' / [shoot]
k[passo]à 'you deny'
k[pawánněse] 'you are rich'
kpáwannisséhenà 'we are rich'
k[pawann'sehe]mà 'you [pl.] are rich'
kpènhammawágan 'your wages' / [believe, inheritance; Long Sentences, 2]
k'pennanahama 'I will see you [pl.]'
kpennanǒw 'I will not see you'
kpennanowuhamà 'I will not see you [pl.]'
kpennawéve 'you will not see me' (?, untranslated)
kpeschechwà 'beggar'
kpétācǎsoōn 'your coat' / [close, make]
kpetonáwan 'letters that are mute (not heard)' / [hear]
k'pettǎǎn 'I hear you'
kpettacónau 'he hears us'
kpettāgǒnǎ 'you hear us' / [we (incl.)]
kpettǎǎn 'I hear that you ...' / [speak]
kpettakonau 'you hear us' / [call (shout)]
kpettàm 'you hear'
kpettàm (? 'he hears you')
kpéttǎměchmà 'you [pl.] hear'
kpéttamen 'you hear'

k[pettamennǎǎp] 'you have heard'
k[pettamenna]wa 'you [pl.] hear'
k[pettamenna]wǎǎp 'you [pl.] have heard'
k'pettawà 'do you hear (him)?' / [call (shout)]
kpèttawáwà 'you [pl.] have heard' / [mouth, speak]
kpèttǎwe 'do you hear me?'
kpětthǎǎn 'did you catch [fish]?'
kp'gachganǒm 'your blood' / [fill]
k[p'mà] 'you shoot'
kp'muchganen 'I (will) conquer you' / [victorious, will]
k'pomsè 'you go, you are going' / [slow, too]
k[pòpackuhámmen] 'you pound'
k'popak'hämmen 'did you knock?'
kpòqueechtà 'they are torn'
k[pumm'sè] 'you run'
[k?]pumm'tōhnhà 'you preach'
-k quěnam '[what] are you looking for?' / [seek, what]
ksasam'tschaháu 'have you whipped him?'
k[sasamtscha]hǎǔwà 'you [pl.] punish him' / [whip]
[ksasamtschahok]hamà 'he whips you [pl.]'
ksasamtschahokhana 'he whips us' / [we (affixes)]
ksasǎmtschahon'hamà 'I whip you [pl.]'
ksasǎm'tschahoǒn 'I whip you'
ksch- [see below for words with the various meanings of] hard, rough, quickly]
kschachquamachoǒn '(? great ?) ship' / [come]
kschǎijajaat [? 'first' ?] / [No Translation (Orig. and Alph.)]
ksché/kschéěch/ná/ǎ 'it flowed, ran'
kschechàtǎmǒwà 'they have cleaned (it)' / [room]
kschech'nà, kschechnà 'run, go quickly' / [away, go]
kschechnà, kschech'nà 'you jump; jump quickly, run quickly' / [quick]
-/kschéěch/ná/ǎ 'flow'
kschéěchne, kscheechnè 'clean (it)!, wipe (it, nose)!' / [gun, nose, rust, wipe]
kschéěchta 'wash (it)!' / [shirt]
kscheechtága 'wash!' / [quick]
kschegěchtecámick wéquamick 'to the laundry (house)' / [clean, go to, to, washhouse]
kschěěkéká 'sweep (it) out clean' / [clean]
kschegǎměscho 'it's cooking (too much)' / [remove; cf. also at boil over]
kschegenak 'he hates you'
kschegenakónau 'he hates us'
kschegenakówa 'he hates you [pl.]'
kschegenanehenà 'we hate you [pl.]'
kschegenan'henà 'we hate you'
kschegenawà 'you hate (yourself)'
kschegenawáwak 'you hate them'
[kschegena]wehena 'you hate us'
kschěkǎméscho 'it's boiling over' [see also kschegǎměscho]
[kschěkǎmé]so 'it's boiling over'
kschemáneetsch 'until' (2) / [peace (2), unless]
kschénahn, kschenǎhn 'hard (of raining)' / [lot, rain]
kschenatáu 'warm weather'
kschéwahndam 'don't be troubled' / [be, don't, sad]
kschewochsannè 'art thou tired?'
kschócha 'come quickly, go fast, make haste' / [come, eat lunch, go, quick (2), too]
kschochàk 'come [pl.]' / [eat]
kschocháma 'you must go quickly'
kschóchǎwě '(I can)not go quickly' / [quick]
kschoǒchà, kschócchà 'come quickly, go quickly, make haste' / [eat lunch, go, quick (3), too]
kschǔchpóu 'it's snowing hard'
kschuckquaschà 'you are cutting (them)'
k[schukquaschaha]mà 'you [pl.] are cutting (them)'
ksè 'you say'
[ksechnaha]mà 'you [pl.] jump'
ksechnahanà 'we jump'
ksechnáu 'he jumps'
[ksechná]wak 'they jump'
k[sechtané]na 'you have a headcold'

ksédik 'at your feet' / [fall down at the feet, foot, lie]
ksegěchma '[what] does it seem to you [pl.]?, [what] do you say [about it]?' / [say, seem]
ksehnpattmèn 'money' / [depend on, help]
ksenà 'pair (of shoes)' / [a, an, make; see nguttòkseschachwócha 'you go [too?] slowly' \\ ksenà]
k[sewanadpà] 'you have a headache'
ksisgomǎn 'you must not spit at (him)'
ksusquachtáwanan 'don't chew'
kt- 'you, your, thy' / [Pronominal affixes]
k(t)-...-(a)wa 'your [pl.]' / [Pronominal affixes]
k(t)-...-(na)na 'our [incl.]' / [Pronominal affixes]
ktà 'you go' / [go out there]
k[tǎǎptonà] 'you speak, do you speak?'
k[tǎǎptonaha]mà 'you [pl.] speak'
ktachamáu (2) 'you have given it to him (for eating)' / [give]
ktachamókku '[who] has given it to you?' / [who]
ktachanǎn 'don't put (it here)' / [but, set]
k[tachapehe]mà 'you [pl.] ride'
ktàchcǎtschǒchquà 'move out of' (?) / [come]
ktacheganajà 'the knife was thine' / [Pronominal affixes]
k[tachgetahà] 'you are impatient'
[ktachgeta]hamà 'you [pl.] are impatient'
ktachgetahawak 'they are impatient'
k[tachpe]hà 'you spin'
k[tachpehana]mà [n covers h] 'you [pl.] spin'
ktachquachpéha 'you stop spinning'
ktachquahégan 'nail' / [hard]
ktachquaheganà 'nails' (?) / [foot]
ktachtahamawáu 'they have nailed (him?) up' / [foot]
ktachwǎǎk ? / [No Translation (Untranslated "biblical" text)]
ktachwahnan 'I love you'
ktachwanawa 'you [pl.] love'
ktachwánen 'you love'
ktachwussè 'you are covetous'
ktackanèn 'else, other place' / [but, nowhere else, other, see]
ktackchégan 'your shears, scissors' / [lend]
ktackenahamawa 'you serve (him)'
ktackenahamawà 'you serve (it)' / [sin]
k[tackenahama]mà 'you [pl.] serve (him)'
k[tacquatschèh] '(it) freezes you'
k[tacquatsché]hema 'you [pl.] are freezing'
ktaggetaha 'remain not' / [impatient, stay]
ktaggetahǎǎn 'don't be impatient'
k[tágusk] 'you sneeze'
ktàh, ktǎh 'your heart' / [ask, burn, fill, give, glad, open, see (6)]
-k tǎh 'you go, you are going to' / [thither, where]
ktahà, ktáha 'your heart' / [give, new, reveal]
ktahaaptona '(that) you are speaking' / [hear]
k[tahǎǎptona] 'you have spoken, you spoke'
k[tahǎǎptonà] 'you will (have to, must) speak'
k[tahaaptonaha]mà 'you [pl.] have spoken' / [speak]
ktahaaptonamatéhena 'we will speak with each ktahaaptonamè '(will) you speak with'
ktahaaptonamettehena 'will you [pl.] talk with each other?'
ktáhack 'in the heart' / [live (dwell in), new]
k[tahagenahéga] 'you serve'
ktáhak, ktahǎk, ktahak 'in(to) your heart' / [bad off, blindness, feel, see, sing, take]
ktahamà 'you [pl.] go' / [go out there]
ktahámedowan 'your [pl.] shirts'
ktǎhǎnǎnà 'our hearts [obviative]' / [clean]
ktáhanau 'our heart' / [clean]
ktáhanau 'we (two) will go' / [say, we (two!)]
ktǎhǎnǎu '(when 2 or 3 are going)' / [go]
ktahanǒǒk '(when many go)' / [go]
ktáhawa, ktǎhǎwǎ 'your hearts' / [ask, reveal]
ktahawahnǒhǒma 'I love you [pl.]'
ktahawǎk, ktahawǎk 'in your [pl.] hearts, your hearts' / [inside, open, reveal, see, that, what]
ktahawáwick 'in your hearts' / [bad off]
ktǎhek 'in your heart' / [feel]
ktǎhennǎǎk, ktáhennǎǎk 'with hearts' / [ask, believe, fill, peace]
ktáhennǎǎk 'hearts' / [approach, with]

ktáhennáǎk 'our heart(s)' / [fill]
ktáǐnétahà '[what] do you have in your heart? (how do you feel?)' / [heart]
ktäinewesehhnaù 'I am called the same as you' / [as, call (name)]
ktáǐnistämhámma '[what] have you [pl.] heard?'
ktáǐnistämwámàn '[what] have you heard?'
ktáǐnistäwáwáǎk '[what] have they heard?'
ktainochquán 'you see'
k[tainochqua]náwa 'you [pl.] see'
ktainochquawun'hà 'you are not looking at him' / [see]
ktájahntamnánau 'we wish it' / [here]
ktajáhntamnänäu 'we need' / [necessary]
ktajátamò '(don't) you need to' / [love, necessary]
ktajè 'you have been (inside); are you there?' / [be (in a place), down there, inside, up there]
ktajégan '(it) is thine' / [Pronominal affixes, your(s)]
ktajeganawà 'it is yours [pl.]' / [Pronominal affixes]
ktajehemà 'have you [pl.] been inside?; are you [pl.] there [outside]?' / [be (in a place), down there, outside, up there]
ktajewehemà 'you [pl.] have not been (inside)'
ktájómǎk 'your children' / [how many]
ktajótóǎwákan 'war'
ktak, ktak 'another, other, another person' / [day, last, make, no, thrive]
ktákkak 'to another' / [go, other; Long Sentences, 3b]
ktakkamè 'you're jabbing me' / [stab]
ktakkamèn 'I stab you'
ktakkan 'other' / [mountain]
k[takquachtschè] 'you are cold'
k[takquachtsche]hemà 'you [pl.] are cold'
ktammachtámmen, ktammachtammen 'you feel' /(3) / [sing]
ktammachtamnánau 'sensitive to (feel) each other, we feel, experience' / [thereby]
ktammachtam'náwa 'you [pl.] feel'
k'tǎnǎmòh, ktǎnǎmòh 'did you finish cooking (it)?' / [boil or cook meat, cook]
ktanetahá [see ktenetahá]
k'tannachemè 'have you rested?, did you rest?' / [peace]
k'tannachgà 'you work' / [can, easy, soon]
k[tannachkaschegà] 'you plow'
k[tannachkaschega]hamà 'you [pl.] plow'
ktannachtǎn '[don't] lose it; [you have lost]' / [lose]
ktǎnnǎǐwágan '(your?) sweetness' / [taste; Long Sentences, 1]
ktánnama 'you cook'
k[tannamaha]mà 'you [pl.] cook'
ktannǎnǎchkǎhn 'don't do (it) that way, don't do that' / [make, that]
ktannimsè 'he goes home' [sic for 'you are going']
k[táǐpchawǎk] 'you yawn'
k'taposeh'm 'have you [pl.] roasted it?'
ktappajuwechnà 'you sweated, [? you have (taken) a sweat]
k[tappajuwechnà], ktappajuwechnà 'you sweat; you have (taken) a sweat' (?) / [yesterday]
k[tappajuwechnaha]mà 'you [pl.] sweat'
ktǎppēnǎwà '[where] are you sitting?' / [where]
ktáptonà 'you speak, do you speak?'
[ktáptona]hamà 'you [pl.] speak'
ktassanetahà, k[tassanetahà] 'you are patient' / [be]
ktassanetahamà, k[tassanetaha]mà 'you [pl.] are patient' / [be]
ktǎttǎchgà 'try it, taste it'
k[tattamachtahamech]mà 'are you [pl.] cutting wood?' / [wood]
ktattamachtahamechnǒǒk 'we will cut wood'
ktattamachtáhom 'you are cutting wood'
ktǎünǒmága 'it will be opened' / [knock, must, opened]
ktaù on'mawáo 'they stabbed him'
ktau[wattescheha]hamà 'you [pl.] drive [it] ↑ out' / [chase out]
ktauwenimmen 'you have opened [it]'
ktauwequamakunána 'he has opened (us?) with it'
ktěcónau 'they talk (say) to us' / [say]
ktehoōkcunánau 'they talk to us, they say to us' / [say]
ktěmǎkǎlhatteět 'misery' / [great, look at; Long Sentences, 5a]
ktěmǎkanemáwak 'with compassion' [verb?] / [look at; Long Sentences, 5a]
ktemégà 'go in!' / [go in(to) there]
ktěménakǎǎk 'they are lucky, fortunate'
ktěménákq 'he is lucky, fortunate'
ktenǎhn 'did you tell it to him?' / [say]
ktenájin 'you will learn, experience' / [will]
k[tenana]wà 'you [pl.] have told it to him' / [say]
ktenäuchtěchnau 'we cost'
ktenawachtahanà 'we will gather (wood) together' / [wood]
ktenawachtěn 'you cost dearly'
ktenáwe 'didn't you say (it)?' / [go]
k[tenéhan] 'your fault'
k[tenahana]wà 'your [pl.] fault'
[ktenetáha] 'you think, you (have) thought' [for gk[tenètáha] and gtenetáha]
ktenetahá 'do you hope?'
k[tenetaha]wà 'you [pl.] hope'
k[teneta]hahamà 'you [pl.] think'
ktěněwěchtámmen '[what] is that called?'
-k těněwěsě 'your name is ...' / [call, name]
kteneweseen 'you are called (as I am)' / [as, call (name)]
ktenkówe 'she didn't say (it)'
kténnajin '[that] you can do after (like?)' / [will (noun)]
ktennangomǎǎk '(your) friends' / [have, many]
ktennangómen 'ally'
ktěnnatappè '[what] are you cooking?'
ktennatippè '[what] are you cooking?'
ktěnne (? 'how, you-how') / [No Translation (Untranslated "biblical" text)]
ktennēkōnǎnaù 'he is talking with us' / [say]
kténnèn 'I say to you'
ktennenána 'we will say it to you'
ktennochkǎhn '[how much] does it cost?' / [how much]
ktennōhōmme 'I have no(thing) to say' / [further, nothing]
ktennòhōmone [?] [see ktennòhōmme]
k[tenntóhn]hahamà 'you [pl.] preach'
ktenntōhnhǎhn 'you preach'
kténnuk 'they (will) say it to you, he says (it to you)' / [brother, go in(to) there]
ktenquechquagewùn 'I am not worthy of (him)'
k[tesgawanaha]mà 'you [pl.] envy'
ktesgawáne 'you envy me'
ktesgawánen 'I envy you'
ktesgawanówe 'I will not envy you'
k't'hackenahegahamà 'you [pl.] serve'
k[tisgawánawe] 'you are not egotistic'
[ktisgawana]wehamà 'you [pl.] are not egotistic'
k[tissgawanà] 'you are egotistic'
k[tissgawaná]hama 'you [pl.] are egotistic'
kt'konǎǎp 'he had said' / [say]
kt'kónaū 'he (has) said it to us; we have said (?)' / [say]
kt'maxóōp 'poor in the heart'
-kt'nawachtenánau '(we/they?) cost'
ktōchǎnáwan (? 'he shall not tear them away') / [sheep, tear away]
ktocháun '(he) will not tear us away' / [can, tear away]
k[tschachtschap'chǎku] 'you have the hiccups'
k[tschannéiuwe 'you are dumb' / [be]
k[tschanneiwech]mà 'you [pl.] are dumb' / [be]
ktschè ? / [rich]
ktschěchquapéso 'strangle, suffocate with a cord'
ktscheěn 'don't-you' / [sprinkle]
ktukkonánaū 'that we (can) say (it)' / [that]
k[tummesim] 'you cut (are cutting) (it)'
küleppěně [Del.] 'turn around!' / [Delaware]

kumkùmsch 'cucumber' / [Loan words]
kumkumschàn 'cucumbers' / [Loan words]
künèppěně 'turn around!'
kupchahamà 'you [pl.] are deaf' / [hear, that]
kupnégan 'beaver dam' / [dam]
[kupphamme]náwa 'you [pl.] close'
kussěchtà 'swallow [it] down [or up]'
kussechtǎhn 'he swallowed it up'
kutschemóna 'ask (them/it)' (2)
kutschemonamà 'ask him'
kutschemonáu 'I will ask him'
kutschemonáwa 'he asks them'
kutschemonemà 'ask me'
kutschemonemǎǎk 'ask [pl.] us' / [we]
kutschemonén 'I ask'
kutschemonòchk '(they) ask'
-kutschemónuk [see n'kutschemónuk under ask]
kutschemóōnkówa 'he asks you [pl.]'
k[waas'naneme]náwa 'you [pl.] make it bright' / [light]
kwachaan 'don't be afraid'
kwachanawà 'don't [pl.] be afraid'
kwacháu 'you are afraid of (him)'
kwachawà 'you [pl.] are afraid of (him)'
kwacheàn '[why] are you afraid of me?'
kwacheěn 'don't be afraid of me'
kwachódam 'I am afraid'
kwachóōn 'I am afraid of you'
kwadà 'are you going along?' / [go with]
kwǎhàchkwǎmòně 'I will catch them [fish]'
k[wahs'naneme]náwa 'you [pl.] make it bright' / [light]
kwaonistammechmà 'you [pl.] are obedient'
kwaonistammechnǒk 'we are obedient'
kwatschěǐ 'how many!' / [white people]
k[wawago]mè 'do you greet?'
k[wawago]mowà 'you [pl.] greet'
kwawǎgōmuk, kwawagōmuck 'they greet' / [truly]
k[wawago]muk 'he greets'
kwawagōōmnochma, kwawagōōmnochmà 'I greet you [pl.]' / [glad, heart]
kwawagoomquǎqué 'they send their respects' / [greet]
kwawanantàm 'you are still laughing'
kwawanantammówe 'aren't you laughing?'
kwawanantammowuhanà 'didn't you [pl.] laugh?'
kwawanenáno 'I am not laughing at you'
kwawěchtǎnǎhau 'we know' / [because]
kwawěchtawa 'don't you know it?'
kwawèchtawanáwà 'don't you [pl.] know it?'
kwáweechtowágan 'knowledge' / [know; Long Sentences, 1]
kwáwehanánau 'we know it, we know'
kwawehau 'do you know him?'
k[waweháu] 'you know'
kwawehawá, k[waweha]wà 'you [pl.] know'
k[wawehawe] 'you don't know'
kwawehawewà 'you [pl.] don't know'
kwaweschaseěn 'don't be afraid'
kwàwonistàm, kwa(w)onistàm 'you are obedient'
kwěchpōměnǎn 'will you eat with us (me?)'
kwěchtǎmǎhnhámmà 'I (can) say (it) to you [pl.]' / [but]
kwechtammánen, kwechtammanen 'I will say (it) to you, I will say (it), I will tell [it to] you' / [feel, glad, love, say, why]
kwěgǎchtammèn 'you like to eat it'
kwége 'you-gladly' / [give, help]
k[wěhěgǎmě] 'you sacrifice'
kwehegamechnau 'we will offer it as a sacrifice' / [sacrifice]
kwehegamechnoōk 'we will sacrifice' (2) / [buck]
kwehegamenǎǎp 'you have offered (yourself)' / [sacrifice]
kwehegamoágan '(your) sacrifice, offering'
kwekwágan 'borer, drill'
kwénaka '(whoever) seeks' / [lose, save]
kwénam 'you are looking for (it)' / [seek]
k[wenamanseěd] [sic] '(your) sick one'
kwenamechmà '[what] are you [pl.] looking for?' / [seek, what]
kwenàu 'you seek (him)'
kwenawawuná 'we are looking for them [anim.]' / [seek]

kwéschasè[?] 'are you afraid?'
kwéschaseechmà 'you [pl.] are afraid'
kwéschaseēn 'you must not be afraid, don't be afraid' / [don't; No Translation (Untranslated "biblical" text)]
kwétawe 'you are not going in' / [go in(to) there]
kwetscháijin 'you are one of them' / [be present; Long Sentences, 6d]
kwetschawáu 'you are going along' / [go with]
[kwetscha]wáwe 'you are not going along' / [go with]
kwétschawè 'will you go along [to hunt]?' / [go with]
kwétschawùk 'he is going with you' / [go with]
kwétschawuk 'is he going along?' / [go with]
kwétschăwùkkweēchmà 'he is going with you [pl.]' / [go with]
kwetschawunèn 'I will go along' / [go with]
kwetschechnasà 'have you been with (him, them)?' / [be present]
kwewè 'are you married?'
[kwitcimo 'duck']

lăŭhāquákkan [Del.] 'scraper, drawknife, drawshave' / [Delaware] ('Lackawanna') / [Delaware, Place names]
Lěchchăwáchneek 'Lechaweke' / [Delaware]
lesowàk [German-Mahican] 'they read'
lésowe 'read!' / [quick]
lesowechnà 'we read' / [we (affixes)]
lēsōwěkŭ '(stop) reading!'
lesówetaù 'we both will read' / [let, will]
lesowetook, lésowetŏŏk 'we will read, let's read' / [let, will]
lesówu 'he reads' / [Loan words]

ma- 'much'(?) / [snow]
maamschan'ma 'I think about (him)' / [Savior]
maamschănochk 'you [pl.] must think about (him)' / [good]
măamschătămĕmănè 'you [sg.] must think about it'
mǎaschchākke 'astonishingly, marvelously' / [glad]
Măăshàkq 'one who always talks' / [Names, speak]
-mǎatskǎham 'chopped up'
máchaak 'it is a great [matter]; great' (2) / [great, things]
machāāk 'big, great' / [book]
máchāāk (? 'supper' ?) / [go with, supper]
machachŭquattschischò 'thin, a little thin' / [a little, few]
-máchāchwǎhntam '[I] have a great pain' / [great, hurt]
machahndam 'heap' / [blanket]
-machǎhntamnánau '[we] think big' / [great, think]
machǎn 'very'
măchanāk 'many' / [friends, have, trust]
machănassanetaháu 'he is very patient'
macháne, machǎne, măchǎne 'a lot, many, much, many times' / [cost, feel, oh, see]
machane 'very'
[mačhane]mà 'respect him!' / [honor]
machanemătaù 'we (both) will honor him' / [we]
macháneme 'honor me, respect me'
machánemuk 'he respects me' / [honor]
machanemukseēd 'respected man' / [honor]
machanesehenà 'we are proud'
machaneséwe 'I am not arrogant, proud'
machanesò 'he is proud'
machanesowǎk 'they are proud'
machǎnnta 'many' / [arrows]
machantassanetahà 'I am very patient'
māchăquăchtschù 'big mountain' / [great]
machatscháchq 'big tree'
măchátscho 'big mountain' / [go over there]
măchăttěněŭ 'big mountain' / [great]
Măchăwoámik 'Wyoming, Pa.' / [be (in a place)]
machcàhachquà 'I seize, grab'
machcàhachquāāk 'they seize'
máchcamen 'find (2); (he) will find it' / [lose, sake]

machcàmowun 'I find not'
màchcǎwáwè 'she has not found' / [find]
machchanahn 'a lot, lot, many, much' / [rain]
máchche, mǎchchè 'great, many' / [anger, come, look at, misery; Long Sentences, 5a]
machchowái 'old (great?)' / [prosper, stay; Long Sentences, 3d]
machè, mache 'great' / [hope (2), shall, well, will, wish that]
māchēchseǎquà, māchēchseǎquà 'when we call' / [call (shout), hear, we (incl.)]
machéchsò 'loudly [by voice]' / [call (shout), speak]
macheēchsò 'with a strong voice, loudly' / [say, speak]
macheēd 'big, great' / [ax]
macheēt 'what he (will) say' / [hear]
machéganis 'lock' (noun)
machenochkǎhn '(it) cost me a lot'
machgahachquáu 'he grabs, roots them out' / [seize]
machgámmen, mǎchgămmen 'find' / [again]
mǎchgǎmmĕn 'I found it'
machgamówunána 'we find (nothing), we haven't found it'
machgamowunána 'they don't find' [sic?]
machgawáu 'he finds' (2)
machgáwe, machgawè 'kiss me'
mǎchgǎwutoàk 'they are kissing each other' / [each other]
màchkěnímmen 'redden, make red, cause to blush'
mǎch"k'tschǎnéquau 'he is blushing' / [redden]
[machktschanne]quáwak 'they are blushing' / [redden]
mǎchkwèpánǎchkwè 'red sticks, red canes'
machkwesoàk 'they are struck or beaten'
mǎchmǎchèkkěnik 'great (fish or animal?)'
mǎchmǎchgěchnǎwǎnǎn 'pustules (smallpox?)'
machmatuammě 'ask...!' / [get]
machmàtŭǎmnǎhkwà 'I will ask you [pl.]'
machmatuamnáwak 'they ask (it?)' / [get, must, one]
machmenohanóǎd [word stricken out; see at doctor]
machmōŏschmachtámik 'razor, straight razor' / [knife]
machnisk 'flint'
[mǝχón 'canoe' (M, 1914) / [ship]]
mǎchǫoksis 'owl'
-machoōn ('canoe') / [come, ship]
machowájise[u?] 'old (of little ones)'
machowáju 'old (of big ones)'
machowe 'old' / [coat, shoe, stocking]
màchq 'bear'
machquà 'bear' / [long, see]
machquè 'bear'
machquò 'bear'
machschedtaháu 'he is unfriendly'
machschedtahawenaxò 'he is unfriendly'
macht- 'bad, evil'
machtáchana, machtachana 'wood' / [gather wood together]
machtachanǎn 'wood [pl.?]; (in a) woodpile' / [heap, lay]
machtachane 'wood' / [gather wood together]
machtǎchen 'firewood, wood' / [chop wood]
machtáchena, machtachena 'wood' / [fetch, when]
machtáchene 'wood' / [fetch, must]
Machtandò, Machtando 'Devil' / [deaf, get, hate, hear, obedient, serve, stop up, where; No Translation (Untranslated "biblical" text)]
machtápei 'support band' / [band]
machtappeēd 'he has been born' / [bring forth, just as, so]
machtappétap '[just as] they are born' / [bring forth, just as, so]
machtappetip '(that you were [he was]) born' / [a, an, bring forth, that]
machtáppo, machtappò 'he is (was) born' / [bring forth]
machtappōōp, machtappŏŏp '(he) was born' / [bring forth]

machtappósa '[when] was he born?' / [bring forth, when]
machtappuàk, machtáppuak 'they were born' / [bring forth]
machtessò 'bad'
machtètt, mǎchtett 'it is bad when ...; [I am] filthy, dirty' / [see]
machtock 'wood'
mǎchtōcku 'in a tree' / [hit]
machtóckuk 'on wood' / [crucify, nail]
machtòk 'wood' / [tree]
machtòkq 'wood' / [chop wood, tree]
machtóǫk 'wood' / [tree]
machtpǎchnǎŭ ['(he?/we?) come to an end']
-mǎchtsch ('already') / [sit]
machtschahawawésuak 'they are weak (like children)' / [like (similar to)]
máchtsche 'when, as soon as (= after?)' / [say]
machtschè, máchtschè, -machtsche ('already, past, completed, finished') / [afternoon, die, eat, hear (note)]
mǎchtschedtǎhǎwǎgan 'malice, badness'
machtschégáu 'it(?) comes to an end'
machtschémǎquat, machtschémǎquat 'it smells bad, it stinks'
machtschetschoachnáu ['(it?/we?) come to an end, it has run out' / [sand, twice]
[machtschkena]wawàk 'you have seen (saw) them]
machtschkenáwe 'you have seen (saw) me'
machtschkenawehenà 'you have seen (saw) us'
[machtschkena]wewe 'you haven't seen me, you didn't see me'
màchtschōsà '[what] did he say?'
machtschóu 'mountain, hill'
-mǎckweseēn 'swollen'
máhā(kŭ) 'don't [pl.] cry'
máham 'eel'
mahammǎǎk 'eels'
mahátau 'we will eat'
mǎh"ksenan, mǎhksenǎn 'shoes' / [a, an, make, new, pair]
mǎhn '(don't) cry, weep; he cried' / [go out there, "Past" tense]
mahtachksoàk 'they are bad off, in a bad way'
majà [? 'still'] / [be, sit, still]
majahanátau 'we [both] will meet (together)' / [assemble]
majákŭ '[why] are you [pl.] crying?'
majánapè 'be still, sit still!' / [be, sit]
majánapowágan 'time' / [little, short]
majáowenánau 'we are coming together, assembling' / [assemble]
majáowenáwa '(they) are assembling'
majawánáwa 'he gathers her/them' / [will]
majáwe 'truly, true, right; trust(?)' / [feel, friends, have, wish that]
-majàweechnaù [? 'for us to assemble'] / [assemble, sound, time]
majáwewak 'they gather (them) together' / [assemble, brother; Long Sentences, 4]
mǎkcheechsè 'loud [in voice]'
mǎkōōs 'awl'
máksen, mǎksen 'shoe' / [little, patch, will]
maksenan 'shoes' / [make]
mǎkseně, mǎksene 'shoes' / [little]
mamǎǎktohnhà 'speak loudly!'
[mamǎǎktohn]hǎk 'speak [pl.] loudly!'
[mamǎǎktohn]hǎwak 'they speak loudly'
mamǎǎktonhà 'speak loudly!'
[mamǎǎkton]hàk 'speak [pl.] loudly!'
[mamǎǎkton]hǎwak 'they speak loudly'
mámaatsch [? 'wish' ?] / [feel, trust, with that]
-mǎmáchǎchwǎhntam '[I] have a great pain' / [hurt]
mǎmǎchgěchnǎ 'he has the pox, pustules'
mamachgechnǎǎp 'he has had the pox, pustules'
mamachgechnágan 'pustules (pox, smallpox?)'
mamagáwan 'they are too big for me' / [great, shoe(s)]
mamakeēchse 'loud [in voice]'
mamakēēchse 'speak loudly!'
mamakeechséqu 'speak [pl.] loudly!'
[mamakeech]sowak 'they speak loudly'
mamaksimsà 'sheep [obviative plural]' / [tear away]

mamaksimsàk 'sheep [pl.]' / [hear, Loan words, voice]
mamanaakhéga 'she writes' uwa [mamanāāk héga] 'he writes' / [he]
mămănaāk héga 'I write'
mămănahkhéga 'I will write' / [will]
mamanahk hégaak 'they write'
mamanahkhegáhanà 'we write'
mamaquajeu 'patient'
mamatahá 'you sound (a bell), ring'
mamatocháu 'he is crippled'
mamatocháwak 'they are crippled'
mamattowájan '[why] do you swear?'
mamaximsàk 'sheep [pl.]' / [hear, Loan words]
mammàchgannoáu 'red cheeks'
mámmăk 'he feels [mentally]'
mammattoahǎk 'don't [pl.] swear'
mammattoāk 'they swear'
mammattoáu 'he swears, he has sworn'
mammenonocháu 'he goes slowly'
mammenonocháwak 'they go slowly'
Manahkse 'Monocasy Creek' / [Place names]
manákkoon 'rainbow' ('Manhattan') / [Place names, ship]
-mane- 'money' / [Loan words]
männăhàtăhănick (?'Manhattan') / [come, ship]
mǎnnìsso 'he (she) is well' / [bad]
manóme 'wheat, grain' / [cut, mow]
-manóme 'grain' / [fill up]
măŏmétscheek '[come you (pl.) to] eat!' / [come]
maŏquamŏtŏk 'we will go to bed' / [lie down, sleep]
máowe, maowe, máowe or máowe, maówe [aó for áo] 'all, whole' / [baptized ones, become flesh, believe (2) (maòwe), call (shout), examine (maówe), feel, free, full, go, help, here, inside, look at, love feast, marks, Participles, "Past" tense, reveal, say, see, sheep, sing, so that, soul, that, well, what, when, will]
máowe awăn, maówe awăn [aó for áo or áo] 'everyone, all the people, all men, all who' / [believe, make well, will; examine (maówe awăn)]
máowe gáquai, maowe gáquai 'everything' / [appear as, as, become flesh, believe, come, make (2), world]
máoweetsch 'all-will, everything' / [give, what]
maowenù 'everything (everyone?)' / [make, world]
mapěchăănaowe 'it is not much snow'
Marcus / [Names]
Maria 'Mary' / [bring forth]
maschéchkŏu 'he colors, dyes'
maschéchgŏ 'he is red colored, red dyed' / [color, dye, redden]
maschèchgoak 'they color red, dye red'
maschèchquěhèn 'don't put red color, red dye on (it, the face)'
Maschŏŏt 'one who has struck (the mark)' / [Names, shoot]
-massánai 'blanket'
mătăchpè, matachpè 'sit down!' / [still]
matàchq 'cloud'
matanemukséēd 'bad, despised, not respected' / [honor]
matechk 'in bad, evil' / [impatient, stay]
máteek 'bad [+ verb]' / [say]
matòkq 'cross, wood (cross)'
matschaihennăap 'we have sinned'
mátschajewe '... (that) is bad'
matschaijŏp 'he has sinned'
matschaiwagan, -matschaiwagan 'sin, evil, the doing of evil' / [serve; No Translation (Untranslated "biblical" text)]
matschaju 'he sins'
matschajuwàk 'they sin'
matschè 'go home!'
mǎtschě 'harm' [preverb?]' / [take away]
mătta, mattà 'bad; not' / [make, not, well (not)]
mattăchàn 'put wood on the fire' / [lay]
mattachksò 'he has bad off, in a bad way'
mattăhăwá(w)u 'weak (bad-hearted?)' / [bad off]
măttàhawŏŏp 'poor'

mattapè 'sit [there]!' / [set]
mattappè 'sit down!'
māttássèn 'pipe of stone'
matteséso 'he is filthy'
mattesesoàk 'they are filthy'
māttschămakwat 'it stinks, smells'
māttschàmmakwat 'it stinks or smells evil'
māū- 'go in order to' / [split wood, urinate]
-māūgawè, -māūgawè 'go to sleep, lie down' / [down]
māūpăpāchgăchtáham 'I will split wood' / [go in order to, wood]
-māūūquà 'lie down, go to sleep' / [down, sleep]
māūweschè 'I am going to urinate, I urinate' / [go in order to]
[mawanna]wéwak 'they have gone hunting' / [go with]
mawannawèwua, mawannawéwua 'he has gone hunting' / [go with]
-mawè- 'will go' / [flax, spin]
mawe- 'begin to, go in order to (do something), going to (do something); want to' / [cf. at eat lunch, spin, will]
máwe, mawe, māwe 'all, whole' / [call (shout), carry, come, cost, family, hate, live, make, make well, more, on, Savior, say, sick, side (māwe), sing, soul, tear away, when, who, wild]
mawe ánĕquechkùk ăhkì, mawe ănĕquéchkùk ahkì 'world' / [more, on, Savior, whole]
máwe awān 'all' / [sick]
mawe awāneek 'everyone, all the people, all men, all who' / [hear]
mawe pennawawe '(I) will not see them, or (I will) not see all of them' ?
māwěgăgāchgěmà 'I will teach (them)'; ? 'I am going to, I want to, I am about to teach them' ?
mawépe, mawěpe 'come to eat!' / [come, eat lunch, quick]
mawe pennawawe [see under mawe]
mawepetŏŏk 'we will eat' / [go in order to]
mawu- 'begin to, go in order to (do something), going to (do something); want to'
mawunáwau '(I) will see (him)'
mawupenawáu '(I) will see him' / [will]
máxxen, mǎxxen 'shoes' / [put on, torn]
mbáp'maín '(it) is acquainted with (them (inan.)')
mbeek 'in the water'
mbei, mbei 'water' / [fetch (2), pour, take, will; No Translation (Orig. and Alph. at ihàm and at nochkau)]
mbeinatem 'fetch water!' / [take]
mbennaăp 'he died' / [death, feel, taste]
m'bépà '(I was) dead' / [die]
mbò 'it is dying' / [die, perhaps]
[m'boagăn 'death']
mbŏŏp, m'bŏŏp 'he is dead' / [become flesh, die, make]
m'cháo 'great' / [more]
[mdánot (M-?) 'ten' / [Numerals]]
-me 'grain, berry'
měchachtăwè 'there is not much snow'
mechanissò 'he (she) is ashamed'
[mechan]nesewewàk 'they aren't ashamed'
mechannesowàk 'they are ashamed'
mechannsè 'I am ashamed'
mechannsehenà 'we are ashamed'
mechannsewehenà 'we aren't ashamed'
mechann'sewewàk 'they aren't ashamed'
mechannsò 'he (she) is ashamed'
mechansehenà 'we are ashamed'
mechanséwe 'she isn't ashamed'
mechansò 'he (she) is ashamed'
mechansówak 'they are ashamed'
méchăjŏ, méchsăjŏ 'it is an (open) space; room (open space)' / [clean]
mèchcànè 'make room!'
mechmenájo '[it is] black and blue' / [brown, hit]
mechtquenótei 'basket' / [belong]
meechkaù 'late (?)' / [assemble, good, late]
měechsquan 'grass' / [mow, time]
měemschachkáo 'he fell' / [fall]

meěnăchkè "fence," ('portcullis'?), ('fence rail'?) / [Delaware]
meěndowágan 'gift'
mees 'older sister' / [brother]
meěschhágan 'patch' [noun]
meěschhammen 'I mend it' / [patch (2), will]
méljăză 'he has been resurrected'
mémachpéunăăk 'they don't make [one] sick' / [apple]
men 'berry'
ména 'he gives'
ménăān 'will (you) give (it)?'
ménan 'huckleberries' / [berry, dry, will]
ménanāăp 'it has been given to him'
menataù, menátău 'let's give'
menatŏŏk 'we will give it'
menatschéu 'he is left-handed'
menatschéwak 'they are left-handed'
méne (2) 'give me (make a present of it to me)' / [patch (noun)]
menè 'give!'
měněkùn 'he gives it to me'
menekunà 'he has given it to me'
menéta '(until) he gives (it) to me' / [peace, until]
ménnăhn 'I have drunk (it)' / [drink]
mennáta 'when he had drunk' / [drink, when] (Mennissinger Town 'Minisink' / [Delaware, Place names])
menówun 'I (can)not give it to you' / [buy]
mepǽh / [Delaware; No Translation (Alph. at Netàn)]
mésak 'older sisters' / [brother]
méscha ? / [put on, thorn hat]
měschàchkachteěta 'he has fallen down (while fleeing)'
měscháhnněmà 'think of me' / [come, remember]
meschătămŏun 'I have not thought about it' / [not, think]
měscháu 'he shot (it)'
měschhamen 'I will mend them' / [shoe(s)]
měschhammei 'fix your shoes'
meschinkówe '[where] he (can)not catch (get) (him)' / [get, where]
měschinnemen 'he has taken it' / [get, take punishment]
-měschòchquágàn 'wig' / [where]
měschòchquanápaneěp 'scalped'
měschótamen 'I (have) hit it, namely, on the mark' / [shoot]
métsche 'I have eaten of (it)' / [bloodied]
mětschéme 'again, back' / [come]
metscheme 'soon'
meuschéha 'chase (them) out'
meuschehatŏk 'we will chase (it) away' / [chase out, we]
meuschehatŏŏk 'we will chase (it) away' / [chase out, we]
meuscheháu 'he will chase (it) away'
meuscheháwak 'they will chase away'
mezáu 'he eats'
méze '[I have] eaten (?); I (will) eat' / [already, will]
mézeăn 'food (what you eat)' / [bless]
mezechnà 'we eat'
mezechtétahn [? 'eat' ?] / [No Translation (Orig. and Alph.)]
[mězeěchtětà 'when (after) they were eating' / [see No Translation (Alph. at mezechtétahn)]
mezéta '(when) he had eaten' / [eat, when]
mezetŏŏk 'we will eat' (2)
mezowagan 'food' / [friend, have, make]
mézowak 'they eat' ('Minisink, Minnisink) / [Delaware, Place names] ('Minsi') / [Delaware, Place names]
-mischaschakanáwa 'sit on' / [hang on]
missachgajana 'we embrace you' / [neck]
[mkhaunuhtquksowuk (W) 'thousands' / [Numerals]
mmachgamóun [sic m-] 'I cannot find it'
m'nohamè ? / [drink; No Translation (Orig. and Alph. at ihàm)]
mnónŏchà '[you] go slowly'
m'nonochamà 'go slowly!'
mnonochamăku 'go [pl.] slowly!'

Mahican-English 173

[mnono]chátaù 'we will go slowly'
[mnono]chatŏk 'let's go slowly'
móchgoa 'I confess' / [reveal]
mochgoáku 'confess [pl.]!' / [reveal]
mochgoatŏŏk 'we will acknowledge it' / [reveal, will]
mochgoáu 'he confesses' / [reveal]
mochgoáwe 'he doesn't confess' / [reveal]
móhnskăhăm '[when will it be] chopped up?' / [maize]
('Monocasy Creek') / [Place names]
mosachpéwe '[you] honor, respect him' / [but, must]
móschachquat 'there is good weather' / [rain, sometimes]
mpĕĕk 'in the water' / [beaver, soak]
mpëi 'water' / [living water, spring]
mpejápu 'thin soup of maize' / [maize, water]
mpejapuwêw 'thin soup, water-gruel' / [water]
mpennăăp 'he died' / [death, feel]
ĕmpènnămĕn 'show me'
mpéttamen 'I hear'
mpéttamennăăp 'I have heard'
mpéttamennăhp (2) 'I have heard'
mpettamennanăăp 'we have heard'
'm'pò 'he (will) die' / [see, will]
mpŏ 'he has been dead' / [like to]
mpoŏp 'they died' / [long]
mpóu 'he is dead' / [die]
mpowà 'she is dead' / [die]
-mpówa 'to die' / [like to]
mpówak 'they are dead'
m'schaănnéma 'think of me' / [remember]
m'schínmen [? 'one lies in or thinks'?] / [No Translation (Untranslated "biblical" text)]
m'schinmóquà '(who) does not receive' / [get]
[mtánit (Si) 'ten' / [Numerals]]
[m-tăn-net (J) 'ten' / [Numerals]]
[mtannit (E) 'ten' / [Numerals]]
mtscheĕmchakgane 'close [it] up, lock [it] up'
m'tschéme 'easily(?), lightly(?), soon(?)' / [can, easy, work]
m'tschēmēmpà 'I will come back'
mŭchgĕnaht '(who) has revealed it?'
mŭchgĕnăwĕ 'I have not revealed (disclosed) it'
mŭchgĕnŭmmăwochk 'open [pl.] (them) to (him)' / [reveal]
mŭchgĕnŭmmăwŏk 'reveal (disclose) (it/them) to (him)' / [inside, that, what]
múchtsche, muchtsche 'a lot, lot, certainly, very, surely, most' / [about that, be present, filthy, friendly, full, glad, greet, have good conduct, honor, laugh, loud, marks, see, spit, well (note usage), when, will; Long Sentences, 6d]
múchtsche káchna, muchtsche káchna 'very truly, cordially' / [heart, greet, truly]
múchtschè kahénna 'very certainly (?), truly' / [come]
muchtscheed, muchtscheed (? 'very much' ?) / [No Translation (Untranslated "biblical" text)]
muchtschĕĕtsch 'certainly' / [fill, peace]
('Munsee') / [Delaware, Place names]

-n, n- 'my' / [acquainted with, Personal pronouns, Pronominal affixes]
n-...-(na)na 'our [excl.]' / [Pronominal affixes]
nà, na 'in, into, to' / [a, an, as, ask, believe, bring forth, glad, go, honor(?), see (3: 'at,' 1; 'into,' 1; 'in,' 1), tomorrow(?), truly, work ('to, into')]
nă 'into' (?) / [ask, see]
nà, na 'the, that; that one, that one who(m)' / [a, an, believe ('in' or 'the' + 'that who'?), bring forth, call ('the'), come ('that one who'), crucify ('the' or 'in the'?), drink ('the'), father ('the one who'), give ('the'?), glad ('in' or 'the'?), hate ('the'), honor (2: 'the' or 'in the'?), our(s) ('the one who'), peace ('the, that'?), the, tomorrow ('in' or 'the'?), tormented ('that one'), when ('the'?)]
nà 'those' / [arrows, how many]
nà 'that-in' / [a, an, as, finger, long]

nà, na 'there, here' / [sit]
nà ... nà ... 'the (... one) who(m) (or that), the (... one) that ..., that (one) ... that ..., in that (one) ... who ...?' / [believe, peace]
na- [see under be (That was mine.)]
-/ná/ă̄ ? / [[flow]
nà nè, nàne '(with him' (?) / [know]
na wachquaga '(the or in?) morning'(?) / [tomorrow]
năăchpè (? 'together with' ?) / [necessary, pray]
naachquàta 'at noon' / [eat]
năăchquatà 'afternoon'
năăde 'fetch (it)!'
năăgaù 'sand'
năăspa 'fetch water!'
-năăspăhăn 'don't bring water' / [fetch, should]
năăthonè, năăthonè 'fetch him here!' / [good, please]
nabhà 'string the sewan!'
nàch nágan 'easy' / [must, very]
nacha 'three' / [bundle, Numerals]
[(nacha) (H1) 'three' / [Numerals]]
[nachá-, nachà- (1759) 'three' / [at end of Numerals]]
[naxá (M-AM, M-EM), náxa (M-Me), náxə (Si), náx·a (Sw-R) 'three' / [Numerals]]
nachàchgăsĕgaù 'he (can) harrow' / [even out]
[na-cháh (J) 'three' / [Numerals]]
náchăjăquà 'we will die' / [depart this life]
[(naxa·ka·w) (Sw-e) 'thirteen' / [Numerals]]
náchcan 'my hands' / [hurt]
[nachchà- (1759) 'three' / [at end of Numerals]]
[nachchd- (1759) 'three' / [at end of Numerals]]
nachcomātŏŏk 'let's sing'
[nd·xə (Sw-D) 'three' / [Numerals]]
năchĕnŭckquácku 'redeemer, our Savior' / [free, say]
năchgăchquăn 'leg'
-nachganáu 'I hope'
nachgawosè 'I hope' / [great, shall, well, will, wish that]
nachgochemá 'I sing'
nachgochemahaná 'we sing'
nachgochemáku 'sing [pl.]!'
nachgochemáqu 'sing [pl.]!'
nachgochematáu 'let's both sing'
nachgochematook 'let's sing'
nachgochemáu 'he sings'
nachgochemáwak 'they sing'
nachgochmaweĕk 'they have not (yet) sung' / [sing]
nachgòmămă 'sing!'
nachkáu ['he does it' ?] / [bad, make]
náchkek 'from my hand' / [sheep, tear away]
năchkĕsseĕn '(how) bad it is' / [see]
năchkĕssèhn '(how) bad it is' / [how, see]
nachkessoákan 'anger' / [great]
nachkèwan 'my nose'
nàch nágan 'easy, light' / [must, very]
nachnajóges 'horse' / [Pronominal affixes]
nach'nănippò 'he is industrious'
nachnechawónquane 'obstacle(s)' / [hinder]
nachnechawónuk 'he hinders me'
năchnĕpŏwăk 'they are industrious'
nachnióges 'horse' / [ambles along, be in a place, how many, one's own, seek]
năchnippĕnămă 'industrious(ly), diligent(ly)' / [work]
nachnowáu 'he fights'
nachnowáwak 'they fight'
năchntschŏhăgăsch 'monkey'(?), 'ape'(?)
[naxoxkáu (Sw-e) 'thirteen' / [Numerals]]
nachpăhm 'thick leg' / [leg]
nachpassăk 'in (my, our?, his?) side' / [breast, chest, side, tear away (the sentence), who]
nachpássak ăhănéchek 'neckcloth, breast cloth' / [breast, cloth]
nachpássei 'my breast, chest'
năchpè, nachpè 'still (be still, sit still!)' / [be, grow, sit; Long Sentences, 1]
năchtămăconàu 'he helps us'
nachtamagówe (2) 'he does not help (me)'
nachtamakquăăm 'he will help you' / [hope, ↑

↓ wish that]
nachtamăku 'he helps me'
nachtamăn 'I help'
náchtamawà 'help [yourself/us]!'
nachtamawaháku 'don't [pl.] help!'
nachtammawahaná 'we help'
nàchtămăwamìck 'help(-in?)' / [necessary]
nachtamawátau, nachtamawataù 'let's help'
nachtamawatŏŏk 'we will help'
nachtamawatŏŏk 'we will help'
nachtamawátŏwágan, nàchtămăwătŏwágan 'help [noun]' / [necessary, that]
nachtamawáu 'I (have) help(ed) him'
nachtamawáu 'he helps them'
nachtammawawuná 'we do not help'
nàchtamawe, nachtamawe 'help (them)!' / [believe, bless, inheritance; Long Sentences, 2]
nachtamawĕ 'help me!'
nachtamawóchqu 'help [pl.]!'
nachtammawĕ 'help me!'
nachtàu 'once'
nachxowenaxè 'I have a gloomy or sad face'
nachxowenaxehená 'we have gloomy faces'
nachxowenaxò '[he has a ?] gloomy face'
nadpochgăd '[who] is cooking?'
nága 'that [not present]' / [horse, Pronominal affixes]
nágach nià 'that was mine' / [be, Pronom. aff.]
nagáchquan 'shin(bone), tibia' / [leg]
nágam (? 'where [rel. pron.?]'; 'he'; 'that'?) / [get]
nágan ? / [easy, light, must, very]
nagatachmága 'I have inherited it'
năgătăchmăgŭnă, nagatachmáguna 'I have inherited it'
nagatachmaquakùp 'he has bequeathed it to us' / [inherit]
nagatachmawána 'I bequeath them' / [inherit, things, woman]
nágaū, nágau 'sand' / [twice]
năh 'he' / [room]
nahà 'be (in a place) (?); come or go (there)' / [glad, go (2), go in(to) there, truly, until, work; Long Sentences, 3a]
náha 'come there, go after (?), over there (?); to that place, thither' / [come, follow, further, go, go in(to) there, nothing [good example of usage], say, there]
năhà 'one ran' / [a, an; one, run]
nàhà ? / [be (in a place), Wyoming]
naha ahana '[you] must come [into]' / [call]
nahà ahnà 'go [pl.] (away there)!' / [go in(to) there; Long Sentences, 3a]
nahà pátsche 'until, till'
[na-hágh (J) 'three' / [Numerals]]
náhàn 'you will fall into (it)'
nāhănĕ 'must' (?) / [away, go away]
náhane 'must (?), so (?)' / [but, easy, honor, very]
nahapáda '[who] is coming there?' / [to that place]
náhăpājătétă '(then) they came to ...' / [come, when]
náhapáowe 'to find again' / [again]
nahà pátsche 'until, till'
nahaquawépe 'I eat lunch' / [noon]
nahaquawepehená 'we eat lunch'
nahaquawepetŏŏk 'let's eat lunch'
nahaquawépo 'he eats lunch'
nahaquawepoàk 'they eat lunch'
nahhnowáu 'he fights'
náhkĕma 'he, she, him, her' / [shoot]
[náhkĕ]mawa 'they' / [shoot]
nahk'ma, náhk'ma 'he, his, him' / [ask, become flesh, believe, bloodied, but, buy, die, eat, foot, glad ('him), go, hear, help, his, kiss ('his'), let ('him'), love feast, make, name, not, Personal pronouns, Pronominal affixes, room, say, see (also at end: 'him'), sleep ('his'), take ('Him, he'), thereby ('his'), turn around; Long Sentences, 3a]
náhkma, nahkmà, [n]ahkma, n[ahkma] 'he' / [bad, make, Personal pronouns, steal, we (affixes), whip]
nahkma, nahk'ma [sic] 'they' / [afraid, clean, help, necessary, that]
nahk'maatsch 'he will' / [accept]

nahkmaw 'they' / [Personal pronouns, steal]
nahkmáwa, nahk'mawa, nahkmawa 'they' / [come, go, hear, Personal pronouns, see, sleep, whether; Long Sentences, 3a]
Nahnhŏŏn 'lay on edge' ? / [edge, Names]
náhnióges 'horse' / [brown]
nahnippenáŭ 'he is industrious'
náhthà ['go down there'] / [down there, drive, there]
najapawepe 'I have breakfast'
nájapàwepéhenà 'we have breakfast'
najapawépĕhn 'breakfast'
najapawepetŏŏk 'let's have breakfast' / [let]
najapawépoàk 'they have breakfast'
najapawépoŭ 'he has breakfast'
nǎjáppája, najappája 'early' / [go, today]
-najappáu ('it - in the morning') / [cold, early, yes]
najáppawè, najáppawe, nájáppāwe 'become day, early, in the morning, morning' / [as, go, tomorrow]
nájin 'he has done (it)' / [make]
nák'ma 'his' / [come, family, woman]
nam 'the'; ? 'my' ? / [become flesh, live, Savior]
năm 'my'; ? 'the' ? / [Pronominal affixes, Savior, well, when, will]
namáăs 'fish' / [catch fish, eat]
namăăsechgáŭ 'there are many fish' / [there is]
namăăsechgáwe 'there aren't any fish' / [there is]
namaássak, nămaássak 'fish [pl.]' / [catch fish, hungry]
nămáju '[it is] sloped'
nămănà 'when I see (him)'
namen 'I see'
namenáăp 'I have seen'
namcnána 'we see'
namenanăăp 'we have seen'
námŏŭn 'I didn't see'
námŏwè 'I didn't see him'
nàn 'it, that (?); this (?)' / [be, believe ('that' or 'it'?), enough ('it, that'), find ('then' or 'that one'?), happen ('it'), lose ('that one'?), make ('it'), now ('it, that'?), sake ('that one'?), see (at end) ('the' or 'my'?), stay ('that, rel.'), sweat ('that' or 'he'?), that ('it'?), true ('that, it'?); Long Sentences, 1 ('that, rel.')]
nan 'the (that of mine?)' / [horse, Pronominal affixes]
nàn [= nà -n?] 'my, mine, (that of mine?)' / [gun, heart ('the' or 'my'?), let ('the' or 'my'?), peace, see (at end) ('the' or 'my'?)]
nàn 'as (?), when (?), then (?)' / [day, depart, early, find ('then' or 'that one'?), lose ('then' or 'that one'?), sake ('then' or 'that one'?)]
nàn nè 'that + it/that' (?); 'it is right'; 'that-in' (?) / [acquainted with, be, know, right, stay, wounds; Long Sentences, 1 ('that')]
nàn ne (see above) / [sweat, wounds]
nàn nèn (? 'as, when it') / [cf. at day, early]
-nána 'we' / [Pronominal affixes]
-nánăăk / [thirsty, to; Long Sentences, 1]
nánăăscápămŭksétschĕĕk 'brown ones'
nánămăhà 'you can sound (the bell), let (it) sound' / [can, let, sound]
nanamaha 'to ring (the bell)' / [assemble, sound, time]
nánan 'five' / [love feast, Numerals, sound]
[**nanan** (1746) 'five' / [at end of Numerals]
[**na-nàn** (J), ná-nan (Si) 'five' / [Numerals]]
nănăne 'five' / [Numerals, year]
[(**nànànè**) (H1) 'five' / [Numerals]]
[**nanani** (H1) 'five' / [Numerals]]
nanáo 'wild' / [live]
nánasgaikè 'beans, black beans'
nánàu (concept of 'over'?) / [boil over]
-nanaù, -nánau, -nănăŭ 'we' / [Pronominal affixes]
nánawàt '(it is) halfway' / [now, way]
nanáwe 'I have not seen her' / [long]
-nănawóchachnàu '[it will be] halfway' / [way]

nànè 'him' / [he, know (second), Personal pronouns]
[**na-nè-we** (J) 'nine' / [Numerals]]
[**nánēwì** (M-?), **nānēwi** (M-AM) 'nine' / [Numerals]]
[**nanewixánkan** (Sw-e) 'nineteen' / [Numerals]]
nānippenáu 'he is industrious'
nanisktschaáchso 'he is a chatterer, babbler' / [babble]
[(**Ina·ni·wi·xa·ka·w**) (Sw-e) 'nineteen' / [Numerals]]
[**naníwixinska** (na·ni·wi·xi·nska) (Sw-e) 'ninety' / [Numerals]]
nànn 'here' / [stay]
nannăănéchĕnĕ 'I lie in (them)' / [wounds]
nánnachkăat 'he has worked'
nannáje 'stay here!'
nannanó 'my cheek'
[**nan-na-wìgh** (J) 'nine' / [Numerals]]
nánnè ('it, that' ?); 'just the same' / [same, seem(s)]
nánne 'that' / [say]
nanne-, nánne 'here' / [stay]
nàn nè, nàn ne [see under **nàn**]
nannentajéĕn 'I will stay here'
nànnéttănè [n or k?] (? 'in that, that-in' ?) / [become flesh, live, the, therefore, world]
nannéwe 'nine' / [day, Numerals]
[**nannéwe** (1759) 'nine' / [at end of Numerals]]
nannipschuk 'nothing but' / [preach]
nannó 'they' (?)('those here' ?); 'this' / [prosper, stay, world; Long Sentences, 3d]
nannoha 'that' / [a, an, bring forth]
nannu 'that' (rel. pronoun?) / [lay down one's life, love, so]
nànó ('thus' ?) / [No Translation (Untranslated "biblical" text)]
[**nao-ə** (Sw-R) 'four' / [Numerals]]
náówè 'come here!'
nàpáquĕĕt '(who) is shooting?'
nàquak 'it seems' / [so]
nàquàt, naquàt 'it appears (so)' / [same, seem(s)]
[**na-shàh-na-càugh** (J) 'twelve' / [Numerals]]
năspataù 'let us get (fetch) water together' / [each other, let us ...]
-natem 'fetch (it)!' / [take]
natenájan '[why] are you taking it?'
nátenan 'I (will) take [it]' / [will]
nátene, nátĕnĕ 'take (it, him)!' / [but, what]
nátenenána 'take us [into it]!'
nátĕnĭmmĕn, nátĕnĭmmēn 'I (will) fetch (it)' / [take, water, will]
nátenimmen 'to take or fetch'
nátĕnĭmmŏŏk 'take [pl.] [it] full'
N[athanael] 'Nathaniel' / [plow]
nátpŏchkà, nàtpochkà 'I cook, I am cooking' / [meat]
natsch, nàtsch 'the one who, that one' / [enjoy, who(ever); No Translation (Untranslated "biblical" text [2])]
nātschĕgaváu '(he) is fetching (them)'
nattemèga 'I went in' / [go in(to) there]
nattemegáăn 'I will go in there'
nattemègawe 'I will not go in(to) there'
nattemegawehenà 'we did not go in' / [go in(to) there]
nattemeháu 'I lend it to him'
nattepochgahanà 'we cook'
nattomnawak 'I am calling them'
nattómuk 'he is calling me'
nattpochgăăd '[who] is cooking?'
nattpochgáwe 'I am not cooking'
[**naukhh-** (W) 'three' / [Numerals]]
náumŏkq 'come [pl.] here!'
năŭmŏŏk 'come [pl.]!' / [eat]
[**nauneeweh** (E) 'nine' / [Numerals]]
[**nauneweh** (W) 'nine' / [Numerals]]
[**naunonnu-** (W) 'five' / [Numerals]]
năŭtàhqósse 'drive hither; travel this way' / [hither]
năŭtschè 'give me it'
năutschĕksè 'crawl here!'
náŭwaăp [for -p náŭwaăp?] 'I have seen him' / [be; Long Sentences, 6a]

nauwàchtănămŏwágan 'comfort, consolation'
[**nauwoh** (E) 'four' / [Numerals]]
[**nayᵂykáy** (Sw-e) 'fourteen' / [Numerals]]
náwa 'four' / [bundle, Numerals]
[(**Ináwa**) (H1), nāwa (M-?, -AM, -Me), ná·wa (Sw-D), náwa (Si), nawá (M-EM) 'four' / [Numerals]]
nawaăt '[he is one who?)] looks into (it)' / [see]
na wachquaga '(in or the?) morning' (?) / [tomorrow]
nāwăchquáka 'at noon' / [eat]
nawachquega 'afternoon'
nawachtà 'long (since), long time' / [die, pound]
nawachtachgaméqua 'for a long time, long ago' / [die, long (3)]
[**na-wágh** (J) 'four' / [Numerals]]
náwah 'look into (it)!' / [ask, see]
[**na-wàh** (J) 'four' / [Numerals]]
nawahana 'we see'
náwăhănă 'we see (it, anim.)'
náwàhn 'he looked at it' / ["Past" tense, see]
[(**Ina·wa·ka·w**) (Sw-e) 'fourteen' / [Numerals]]
náwăkĕĕchnà 'he bowed [his head]' / [depart]
nawan (? 'what I say' ?; 'voice') / [hear, sheep]
nawananà 'we have seen them'
náwaŭ 'I have seen it' / [many, oh]
nawáu (3) 'I see him, I have seen him, I see (myself)' / [sick]
náwaŭ 'I see; I have seen it'
náwaŭ [for -k náwaŭ] 'you will see' (2)
náwaumachtsch 'I see them'
nawáwe 'I have not seen him'
nawáwe 'they haven't seen him'
nawawèĕk 'I don't see them'
náwawehóka 'they know me well; they know me; they are known to me'
nawawewunà (3) 'we have not seen him/them'
nawawewunà 'they haven't seen you [pl.]'
nawawunà 'we have seen him'
nawawunà 'they have seen you [pl.]'
náwe, năwe, năwe 'come here!' / [eat, sit, together]
nawè 'four' / [Numerals, year]
[**ná·wa** (Sw-D) 'four' / [Numerals]]
[**nawínska** (na·wi·nska) (Sw-e) 'forty' / [Numerals]]
nawochnà 'we see you [pl.]' [sic: 'we see him']
náwócku 'he has seen me'
nawókŏnàk kà 'four days' / [for, go]
nawoquátta '(it's good) to see (them)' / [marks]
náwu 'look (into it)' / [see]
nawugŏk 'they have seen me'
nawugówe 'he has not seen me'
nawugowewunà 'he has not seen us'
[**nawuh-** (W) 'four' / [Numerals]]
nawukówe 'they haven't seen me'
nawukowenà 'they haven't seen us'
nawutenĕ 'give it to me here' / [shirt, wash]
náwutennemook (? 'you [pl.] give me (them, inan.)' ?) / [shirt]
nawutschĕ 'give it to me here'
Názareth / [come, Place names]
n'bè 'water'
nbésohn 'medicine'
[**nchĕnchkă** (1746) 'thirty' / [Numerals]]
[**nxe·nska** (Sw-e) 'thirty' / [Numerals]]
[**(nxi·nska)** (Sw-e) 'thirty' / [Numerals]]
[**(n-co-tàh** (J) 'one' / [Numerals]]
[**n-co-tah-na-caugh** (J) 'eleven' / [Numerals]]
[**n-co-taunsh** (J) 'six' / [Numerals]]
ndà 'I go, I am going' / [plantation]
ndàh, -n dăh 'my heart' / [chase out, feel ('his heart'?), inclination, use, wounds]
ndaljeenanà 'we remain' / [know, stay; Long Sentences, 1]
[**n-da-nét** (J) 'ten' / [Numerals]]
ndánnama, ndannama 'I cook'
ndannaména 'I am happy' / [glad]
-n dappsè 'I will warm myself'
[**ndənət** (M-EM), **ndənət** (M-AM) 'ten' / [Numerals]]
ndénnahn 'I (will) say it to him'
-n dennanáchcawagan 'my sake' / [crucify]
ndénne ('I-so'... ?) / [hear]
-n dennè machcàmowun 'I find nothing [to it]'
ndiáhu 'dog' / [bark]

Mahican-English 175

ndiáu 'dog' / [chase out, outside, swallow]
ne 'I' (?) / [go in order to, inherit, like to, money?, peace, see *(mid, after 32) (2)*, will]
ne 'it, that, the' / [again, appear as, as, as soon as, become flesh, believe, but, captivate, come, cost, darkness, die, feel, find, for, go, hear, let, lie (of position), light, love, money?, more than, Pronominal affixes, say, see *(2)*, set *(2)*, sheep ('the'), that, when, wish that, your(s); No Translation (Orig. and Alph. *at* patăk)]
nè 'it, that, the; he (?); thus' / [acquainted with ('it' ?), ask ('that he' ?), be (many), because of [that] ('thus' ?), carry ('the'), crucify ('that he' ?), earn ('the'), good ('it'), hard ('the'), it (right), know (2: 'him, 'that we'), lay down one's life ('his' = 'the'), let ('that'), look at ('it' *or* 'he' ?), love ('his' *or* 'the' ?), make ('that way'), "Past" tense ('he' *or* 'it' ?), peace ('it, his' ?), pierced ('the' ?), power ('the'), right ('that, it' ?), serve ('it, we' ?), should ('thus'), sick ('it'), side ('the' ?), so, stay ('we'), taste ('it'), think ('then, he' ?), to ('it, we' ?), visit ('it' ?), will *(noun)* (né = 'that'), with ('the')]
nè '(so) that' / [taste, thirsty; Long Sentences, 1 *(5)*]
né 'that *(rel. pronoun)*' / [will *(noun)*]
nè, ne 'here, there; thither' / [sit, stay (?), visit (?)]
nè 'then' (?) / [think, word]
ne 'the same' / [love]
nè ? / [work, wounds]
ne ? / [ride, sweat]
nè 'him (= that one?)' / [know]
nè ? / [No Translation (Untranslated "biblical" text)]
nĕ 'that (?), he (?)' / [easy, lay down one's life, must, sweathouse, to, very]
ne 'I' / [see, will]
ne- 'we' (?) / [inherit]
ne áăm wátsche 'so that will' (?) / [let]
ne áchtăk [*or* neáchtăk?] 'behind' / [bed, set]
nè áht 'that is it'
nè ăm áne (? 'that ... may' ?) / [thirsty, to; Long Sentences, 1]
nè ăm wátsche 'so that ... may' / [taste; Long Sentences, 1]
nè áne, né áne [*see* neane] 'that ...' / [crucify, will]
nĕ ánĕ, nĕ áne 'the, in the' (?) / [good, sweathouse]
nè átähn 'around here, around there, thereabouts' / [here, there]
nè átan 'at, at the' / [visit]
nè átane 'in, into (it?)' / [peace]
ne máchgämmĕn 'I found it again'
ne mawunáwau 'I will see (him)'
ne mawupenawáu 'I will see him'
ne nónaku ('[but] over there') / [set, there]
nĕ ŏtschè 'because of it (that)' / [therefore, thus]
nè ŭdèttàn 'of it' (?), nè udettàn 'then he' (?) / [look at, think, word]
nè ŭtschè 'therefore, for that (reason)' / [feel, if, sick]
ne watsche 'therefore, for that (reason)' / [lie (of position), wounds]
ne ... wátsche ('so that' ?), nè ... wátsche 'so that' / [let, taste]
néa 'the' / [side]
[neáchtăk *for*] ne áchtăk 'behind' / [bed, set]
neáne [*see* nè áne] 'as, the (?), his (?), that *(rel. pron.)*, what (= that which)' / [call (shout), come, crucify, debt, glad, his, pay, side]
neáne ('by, in') / [No Translation (Untranslated "biblical" text)]
neáne 'we (?), I (?)' / [I, one (Joshua, *etc.*)]
nĕáne [*see* nĕ áne] 'just as' (?) / [bring forth, so]
nĕáne̊ 'that *(rel. pronoun)*' / [teach]
neáne ... áhanè ... 'just as ... so ...'
neáne (? 'therein, in there' ?); 'by' / [peace, where, wounds]

[*náχa (M-?)* 'three' / [Numerals]]
nechĕk 'three' / [Numerals, year]
néchene (? 'oneself') / [fair, let, like to, observe, self]
nèchneᵒwè (? 'oneself') / [help, self]
nechnepechnà 'we are industrious'
nĕchnĭppĕnà 'I am willing, industrious'
nechquéi 'beard'
nechtáu 'it is inside'
-nĕchtăwè ? / [swim]
neckatachen 'to fall'
nĕchnąąn '[if] he takes him' / [whether]
neechneowè (? 'oneself') / [lose, seek, self]
neēk, neek 'these, those, those (who), they' / [approach, baptized ones, believe, come, feel, glad, help, hope, know, love feast, speak, that; No Translation (Untranslated "biblical" text)]
neēk 'there' / [here, Participles, sit]
neēn 'the [*pl.*?]' / [feel, "Past" tense, sing, think, word]
neén 'that' (?) / [foot, kiss, thereby]
neén kaām áike 'thereby' (?)
[*neesh- (W)* 'two' / [Numerals]]
[*neesoh* [*neesch?*] *(E)* 'two' / [Numerals]]
negachtachen 'I fall'
negachtachen'hena 'we fall'
negechtachĕn 'he falls'
négena 'it turned out well, it thrived'
n'chăppajaną 'you [*sg.*] come'
n'chăppajaną 'if (when) you [*sg., not pl.*] come'
nehene (? 'oneself') / [fair, self, think]
néhene (? 'oneself') / [peace, self]
nèmăchtăk 'brother's children, child's children' / [child] [*See* Paul Proulx: Mahican social organization and the Middle Atlantic Algonquian cultural climax, *Anthropol. Ling.*, pp. 82-100, Spring, 1983, §2.15, *for discussion of incorrect glossing; properly* 'brother(s) *(masc. speaker)*.']
némana, nĕmănă, nemana 'man' / [a, an, bring forth, call, head, honor, know, that, the]
nemanáu, némanáu 'man, [he is a] man' / [as, call, hate, love, must, sick]
némat 'brother's child' / [child] [*See* nèmăchtăk *for note on incorrect glossing; properly* 'brother.']
nĕmĕnnátămèn 'smell [*verb, sense of reception*]'
nĕmĕscháu 'I didn't shoot (it)'
nèn 'it' (?) / [day, early, find]
nèn [nè + -n?] 'it + I' (?) / [serve, shall]
ne nagatachmága 'I have inherited (it)'
nenajewe, -nenajéwe 'it is not true' / [believe, that]
nenáju '(it is) true' / [believe, that]
nè nanaăk ['we-you [*sg.*]' ending?] / [thirsty, to; Long Sentences, 1]
nᵉⁿdáhak 'in [our] heart' / [taste; Long Sentences, 1]
nenè ('it' ?) / [give]
néne gaquai ['something' ?] / [further, nothing, say]
nēnes 'my head' / [headache]
néním 'brother's wife' / [woman]
nenochtagăk ('me-hear-they' ?) / [hear, sheep, voice]
nep 'I am dying' / [die]
népăchkè ('sheet of paper' ?), 'leaf' / [a, an]
népan '(my) arrows' / [pointed]
nĕpáwĕ 'at night' / [sleep]
nĕpènhamnána ['we earn, deserve], we have deserved (it)'
nepeschàn ăwáhăwăk 'with rods' / [whip]
nĕpì 'water' / [great]
nèpnàhp 'he was industrious' / [be]
neppen 'I am dying' / [die]
[*ne-sa (Sw-R)* 'two' / [Numerals]]
nescha- 'two' / [speak, word]
neschach 'two' / [bundle, Numerals]
[(*neschach*) *(H1)* 'two' / [Numerals]]
neschahămatau 'we will eat together' / [come]
nĕschămŏ̆ ? / [new, what]
néschan '2 (o'clock); twice' / [sand]
[*neschă năchkà (1759)* 'twelve' / [Numerals]]

néschapetaù 'sit by me or together with me'
nesche 'two' / [Numerals, year]
neschĕĕk 'two' / [come, pair]
neschéwa 'I am tired of ...-ing'
neschéwa kapè 'I am tired of sitting'
néschewe 'both' / [call (shout)]
nescho 'two' / [Numerals]
neschóąknak 'two days' / [go with]
[*neschŏ̆ho- (1759)* 'two' / [at end of Numerals]]
néschᵒwak '[they are two], two persons' / [get, must, one, two]
[*neschŏ̆wàk, néschowàk (1759)* 'two' / [at end *of* Numerals]]
neschowe [? 'both' *or* 'tired' ?] / [No Translation (Orig. *and* Alph.)]
netaaptonà 'I speak'
nétachcan, nètachcan, netachcan 'my brother' / [eat, hear, love]
netáchcana 'my brother' / [come, eat, together]
nétachcanàck 'my brothers' / [sweathouse, wish that]
netachcanak, nétachcanàk, netachcanak, nĕtăchcănăk, netachcanàk, nĕtăchcănăk 'my brothers, brethren' / [come, fetch, go with, good, greet, honor *(second)*, industrious, love, many, reveal, see, think]
netachcanenanack 'our brothers' / [brother; Long Sentences, 4]
nétachcanenanak ('the (our?) brothers' / [seize]
netáchgan, nétachgan, netachgan 'my brother (older brother)' / [come, love feast, oldest, teach, youngest]
netáchganak, netachganak 'my brothers' / [go, here]
netàn mepèeh [? 'I have arrived' ?] / [Delaware; No Translation (Alph.)]
nĕtanmessè 'I am going ...' (?) / [Delaware, hunt]
netanneména 'I am glad' / [come, house]
netenetáha 'I (have) thought' / [think]
netenetahaná 'we (have) thought' / [think]
netenetaháwe 'I have not thought' / [think]
netepochgáu '(he) is cooking'
[*nethwak (P)* 'two' / [Numerals]]
nĕtschăwăn măwe ['if (when) we all' (= 'if everyone' ?)] / [side, tear away, when, who]
nettaăn 'where; (what[ever]?)' / [take, what]
néttakăm 'with that or, *i.e.*, with the same thing' / [the same, things]
neŭ taha '(the?) his heart' / [reveal]
N[ew] Yorck 'New York' / [be (in a place), Place names]
newajana 'I have seen them, I saw them' / [preach]
nᵉwattschósemà 'I am filling the pipe; fill the pipe'
newawagowawunà 'we greet'
newawchaweunà 'we don't know'
ne wetschawáu 'I am going along' / [go with]
N[ew] Yorck [*see under* N[ew]]
ngáchane 'I have' / [hinder, obstacle]
-n gachaneu, -n gachanéu 'I don't have, I have no' / [lancet, hobble]
ngachanéwe 'I haven't any' / [leather]
n'gachchanechnà 'we have'
ngachchanechnàu 'we have'
n'gachchanehennàu 'we have'
ngăchchănéu 'I have no' / [house]
n'gachchanéwe 'I don't have'
ngachchanewehenà 'we don't have'
ngackschochahanà 'we are going quickly' / [quick]
ngackschochawuhanà 'we are not going quickly' / [quick]
ngádoa 'I deny'
-n [gagachkham]máwăk 'I will teach them'
n'găgălkchēēn 'I am sleepy, drowsy'
ngagunána 'I am jealous, envious'
-n gamquóhĕnnă 'I have fallen into water'
n'gatópe 'I am hungry'
n'gatopech'nà 'we are hungry'
n'gatósome 'I am thirsty'
nᵒgatta [*Delaware*] 'I want to' / [bloodlet, Delaware]
ngattaù 'I will (want to)' / [*see (2)*]
ngáttau 'he will (want to)' / [help]
n'gattawechpeióha 'I should sweat'
ngattópe 'I am hungry'

ngattósome 'I am thirsty' / [be]
ngattosomechnà 'we are thirsty' / [be]
ngáuweèn '[we] to sleep [in]' / [become flesh]
n'gawè, ngawè 'I sleep'
ngawëhn 'I will go to sleep'
n'gechganǎhn 'I will visit him' / [sick]
ngéëkhammen 'I (will) sharpen (it)'
[ngeëmton]hamàchtsch 'I have spoken softly' / [speak]
ngeëmtonhǎn 'I will speak softly'
ngēgǎpáwe 'I am single'
n'gesche 'I or we (already) have ...,' / [cook (2)]
ngésche 'I cannot ...' / [sleep]
ng'máowe 'always' / [good, must, think]
ngmóót 'I steal'
ngommaowe 'always' / [believe, inheritance, wait for; Long Sentences, 2]
[ngut] (H1) 'one' / [Numerals]
ngutá (M-ÁM, -EM, -Me) 'one' / [Numerals]
ngutəⁿs (M-AM) 'six' / [Numerals]
[ngutəⁿs (M-EM), ngutəⁿs (M-Me) 'six' / [Numerals]]
[ngut-tsaasch (J) 'six' / [Numerals]]
[ngùt-ta nkaw (J) 'eleven' / [Numerals]]
ngutte 'a, an, one' / [Numerals]
nguttò 'a, an, one' / [make, Numerals, pair, shoe(s)]
nguttòksenà [ms. p. (282)], nguttò ksenà [ms. p. (223)] 'a pair (of shoes)' / [make, pair, shoe(s)]
[ngwittoh (E) 'one' / [Numerals]]
[ngwittus (E) 'six' / [Numerals]]
nhà, n'hà 'is (it, anim. and inanim.) there?' / [be (in a place), horse, light, pour in]
nhaá 'go in(to) there!'
n'haachtáu 'it is still inside' / [yet]
nháágu 'go [pl.] in!' / [go in(to) there]
nhaáu 'he goes in' / [go in(to) there]
nhaáwak 'they go in' / [go in(to) there]
nhachtáǔ 'it is inside' / [a little, few, little]
nhachtáwe 'it is not inside'
n'hackai, nháckai 'myself, my body' / [peace, see, self (2), whip]
n'háckay 'myself, me' / [honor, must, your(s)]
nhäën 'in' / [go in(to) there]
nhajéwe 'he is not inside'
nhajéwek 'they are not inside'
nháju 'is he inside?'
nhájuwak (2) 'they are inside'
nhákkei 'himself' [sic] / [sacrifice]
nhákkei 'himself' [-n + hákkei, for 'myself'?) / [self]
nhaktahamà 'you [pl.] go in' / [go in(to) there]
nhaktajè 'are you inside?'
n'haktajehemà 'are you [pl.] inside?'
n'hammachtsch, nhammàchtsch 'inside' / [been]
n'hǎmmíssachgàn 'I hug or embrace you' / [neck]
n'hǎntǎhǎnǎ 'we come'
nhantáhana 'we go in' / [go in(to) there]
nhántajè 'I am inside'
nhantajehenà 'we are inside'
nhantajéwe 'I am not inside'
nhantajewehenà 'we are not inside'
n'hǎppäjǎnǎ 'when you [pl.] come' / [greet]
[nhǝⁿsǝ (M-AM) 'eight' / [Numerals]]
ni ('that' ?) / [become flesh, run after, therefore]
ni wátsche, ni watsche 'because of that, therefore' / [run away, sleep]
nià, nia 'I (me, my)' / [ask, bad, be, become flesh, bloodied, but, chase out, cost, debt, die, drink, eat, fair, fetch, fill, fill up, find, forget, free, glad, go with, greet, hate, have, heal, hear, heart, honor, hope, industrious, jealous, know, lend, lie (of position), love, make, mix, must, obedient, pay, Personal pronouns, Pronominal affixes, reveal, rich, say, see, seize, self, shall, sick, single, sound, speak, spin, spit, steal, suck, swear, sweat, teach, tell, there, think, tired, will, wish that, worthy, your(s); Long Sentences, 6a, 6b; No Translation (Untranslated "bibli- ↓ cal" text)]

nià, nia 'me' / [forsake, here, I, well]
niachkéép 'I have' / [great, hope]
niakq 'me' / [ask, I]
niàmpáquè 'I shoot, I am shooting'
niàn [= nià n-], nian, nian n- 'my, I' / [acquainted with, belong, call, come, crucify, die, enough, fault, feel, find (2), follow, full, glad, go around, heart, hold on, know (2), lay down one's life, like to, lose, necessary, Personal pronouns, Pronominal affixes, sake, say, stab, swim, warm, well, when, will, wounds]
niana 'my, (our?)' / [go with]
niána 'we' / [afraid, ask, believe, crucify, hear, honor, Personal pronouns, see]
niána 'us' / [help, we]
niana 'we' / [among, but, divide, have, hear, see]
niánan 'that' / [our(s), Pronominal affixes]
niánau 'we (both, excl.)' / [rich]
niáne 'us' (?) or 'in that' (?) / [just, Personal pronouns, say, we]
niàn gàmquóhēnnǎ 'I have fallen (fell) into the water'
niánǒk, niánok 'we (excl.)' / [hear, Personal pronouns]
niàn tajáhntam 'I would like (need?) to' / [feel, necessary]
niàsch tàn [= nia aschta n-] 'I am not' / [afraid]
nickátáchēn 'I had fallen'
Nicod[emus] / [cook]
nik, nik 'what, that (?), so that; and that; in it (?)' / [believe, bless, each other, feel, glad, greet, hang on, heart, inheritance, live (dwell in), mosquitoes, new, observe, say, take (? 'in it' ?), that, thereby; Long Sentences, 2, 4]
nikkǎǎtsch 'so that ..., then' / [make well, wounds]
nikkàhtsch 'so that ..., then' / [call (shout), see (2)]
niktemagánometwágan 'compassion, charity, mercy'
nīntǎhǎnǎk 'in our heart' / [feel]
nintenè 'for me' / [believe, for]
nippen 'I will die' / [lay down one's life]
[nīsa (M-?), nīsá (M-AM), nisá (M-EM), nī·sa (Sw-D, Si), nisá (M-Me) 'two' / [Numerals]]
[nī·sa·nkaw (Si) 'twelve' / [Numerals]]
[ni·schàh (J) 'two' / [Numerals]]
[ni·scha nkaw (J) 'twelve' / [Numerals]]
[nisínska (ni·si·nska) (Sw-e) 'twenty' / [Numerals]]
-niskēpēsè ? / [thoughtless]
nisquán 'arm'
níssanè 'twice'
nisskschǎǎchsejǎku '[why] are you babbling?'
nisskschǎǎchsehenà 'we are chatting' / [babble]
nissktschǎǎchsoak 'they are babbling (chatting)'
nístǎǔ 'fire' / [love-fire]
nitsch tanè 'then (?), so (?), (that-in ?)' / [assemble; Long Sentences, 4]
nitschwǎk ('as (?), as also (?), that also (?)') / [as, love, must]
ni watsche 'therefore' / [become flesh]
n'kakánimmēn 'I hold on'
nkakunána 'I am jealous, envious'
[nkechtachen]hǎku 'don't [pl.] fall'
nkechtachenhàn 'don't fall'
nkechtemm'nahanà 'we are lazy'
nkechtemm'náwe 'I am not lazy'
nkechtem'nà 'I am lazy'
nkēëschchasòm 'I dry (them)' / [will]
n'kéëspe 'enough'
nkěk 'my mother' / [long]
nkensittawǎn 'I will listen' / [like to]
nkensittawunà 'we listen'
nkeschachtippè 'I am ready with the cooking, I got the cooking ready, the cooking is done' / [cook, ready]
[nkeschach]tippehenà 'we are ready with cooking' / [cook, ready]
↑ nkeschakhonáu 'I (have) hung up the kettle'

nkēschǎnǎchgǎǔ 'I haven't made it yet' / [make, not yet]
n[késchǎnǎchkà] 'I am ready'
[n?][keschǎnǎch]kahanà 'we are ready'
nkésche, nkesche 'I already (have)' / [fill up, melt, pour in]
nkésche 'I am ready to ...' / [sweat]
nkésche 'I can' / [snuff out]
nkèsche 'we already (have)' / [cook]
nkéschehōgōp 'he has made me' / [make]
nkeschehōk 'he has made me' / [make]
nkeschemàchtsch 'I have already sat' / [sit]
[nkha(u)- (W) 'three' / [Numerals]]
[(nkotạ·sxạ·ka·w) (Sw-e) 'sixteen' / [Numerals]]
n'k'phammen 'I will close'
nkschechnà 'I jump'
nkupphammen 'I will close'
nkupphammenána 'we close'
nkussechtǎhn 'I swallow' (2)
nkutschemonáu 'I will ask (it)'
n'kutschemónuk 'he asks me'
nkwachahanà 'we are afraid of (him)'
nkwacháu 'I am afraid of (him)'
nkwacháwe 'I am not afraid'
nkwachaweunà 'we are not afraid'
[(nkwatokaw) (Sw-e) 'eleven' / [Numerals]]
nkwenamèn 'I am looking, I am seeking'
[nkwíta (Si) 'one' / [Numerals]]
[nkwíta·nkaw (Si) 'eleven' / [Numerals]]
[nkwíta·s (Si) 'six' / [Numerals]]
n'lesówe 'I read'
n'machanese 'I am proud'
nmachenochkáwun 'it doesn't cost a lot'
nmachgahachquà 'I seize, grab'
n'máchgam 'I find' (2)
nmachgammenána 'we have found it' / [find]
n'machgamówun 'I have not found it'
nmachgawáwe 'I have not found him' / [find]
nmachgawawewunà 'we have not found him' / [find]
nmachgawawunà 'we have found him' / [find]
n[machktschannequa]hanà 'we are blushing' / [redden]
n'machmátuammàk 'I ask him' / [let, see]
nmachnawǎ 'I saw (have seen) it here' / [light, see]
n'machschedtahà 'I am unfriendly' / [gloomy]
nmachschedtahawenaxè 'I am unfriendly' / [gloomy]
nmachschedtahawenaxehenà 'we have gloomy faces' / [unfriendly]
nmachtappèhop 'I was born' / [bring forth]
n'machtsche 'I already' / [eat]
n'mǎckwēse 'it is swollen [on me]'
n'mǎckwēsēn 'it is swollen [on me]'
n'mahtachksehenà 'we are bad off [mentally], we are in a bad way'
nmakwesehenà 'we are swollen'
nmǎmǎchǎchwǎhntam 'I have a great pain' / [hurt]
n'mamaquajéwe 'I am not patient'
nmamatahǎn 'I will sound, ring'
nmamatahanána 'we will sound, ring'
nmamatócha 'I am crippled'
nmamatochahanà 'we are crippled'
nmammachtóa 'I swear'
n'mammenonóchà 'I go slowly'
n'mammenonochahanà 'we go slowly'
nmáschechhquè 'I color, dye'
nmaschèchquehenà 'we color, dye'
n'massánai 'my blanket'
nmaténǝmuk 'he despises me' / [honor]
nmátschai 'I sin'
nmatschaihanà 'we sin'
n'matschaihòp 'I have sinned'
n'matschēēn 'I will go home'
nmattachksè 'I am bad off [mentally], I am in a bad way'
nmǎttǎchpējan '[why] are you sitting?'
nmattapè 'I have already sat, I'm already sitting' / [already, fill up, sit]
n'mattesése 'I am filthy'
nmattesesehenà 'we are filthy'
n'mattschechtǎn 'I ruin' / [bad]
nmattschechtananà 'we ruin'

nmawè 'I am going to' / [go in order to, spin]
nmawèschachawachtáha 'I will go winnow' / [flax]
n'méchănsè 'I am ashamed'
n'mechtappè, nmechtappè 'I am (was) born' / [bring forth]
nmechtappehenà 'we were born' / [bring forth]
n'mééschhámmau 'I will not fix (it)' / [patch]
n'mééschhammen 'I repair (shoes)' / [patch]
nmenáăn 'I will give it to you'
n'menachtschè 'I am left-handed'
n'menachtschehenà 'we are left-handed'
n'méschhámmau 'I will not fix them'
n'méschhămmen 'I repair (shoes)'
n'méuschéha 'I will chase, drive [it] away' / [chase out]
n'meuschehaenà 'we will chase away, out'
n'méze 'I eat'
nm'natschéwe 'left, left-handed'
nnachgána 'I hope'
nnachgochmawéĕk 'they have not (yet) sung' / [sing]
n'náchk, n'nachk 'my hand' / [swollen]
nnattomáu 'I am calling him'
nò 'his' (?) / [his]
nò [see nò wátsche] 'that' / [appear as, as, basket, be present, beautiful, become flesh, believe, belong, come, drink, halfway, make, now, therefore, way]
nò 'this'
nò 'so, thus' / [sleep]
no ? / [water]
nò 'I + ...' (?) / [beautiful, dream]
no anè ? / [No Translation (Orig. and Alph. at ihàm)]
nò wăătsche 'therefore, for that (reason)' / [wounds]
nò wátsche 'about that, therefore, for that (reason)' / [glad, therefore, very]
[nochkőő (Büttner in Masthay, 1980) 'flour, meal' / [No Translation (Alph. at nochkau)]]
nochkau ? / [fetch, water; No Translation (Orig. and Alph.)]
nochpajáhxè ? / [come, light, move out of]
nochpána 'remove (it)' / [boil over, keep]
nŏchpápèh 'remove [it] (from the fire)'
nochquéna 'I cough'
nochquénei 'my spit, my expectoration' / [bloody, cough]
nóctenaspăăn 'are you bringing water here?' / [fetch, hither]
[noghhoh (E) 'three' / [Numerals]]
nohà 'as'; 'let'(?) / [come (3), here]
nohà 'to me; to that place, thither'
nohaatsch 'should' (?) / [come]
nohàhtsch (? 'should';'should ... still ... to me' ?) / [come, to me]
nohàm ? / [drink; No Translation (Orig. and Alph. at ihàm)]
nŏhàpăŭ 'he came' / [come, to me]
[nohhum (E) 'my grandmother' / [see No Translation (Alph. at ihàm)]]
nohnsēttăwána 'we believe in (him)'
nohnsittammen, nŏhnsittámmen 'I believe it' / [for, truly]
nojăăs 'my meat' / [roast]
[nojamachgenim]men 'I mix'
nojamachgenimnà 'I mix'
nŏk 'but' (?) / [learn, must, teach]
nŏm 'I have been, was [there]' / [be (in a place)]
nomanehĕmĕwe 'I have no money'
nŏmhanà 'we have been, were [there]' / [be (in a place)]
nŏmhanè 'we come from'
nòn 'there' / [fetch]
nónak 'over there' / [down there, drive, there]
nónaku '(but) over there' (?) / [but, set, there]
[nŏ·nən (Sw-D) 'five' / [Numerals]]
[nonankáy (Sw-e) 'fifteen' / [Numerals]]
nonaquépe 'I eat supper, I eat in the evening'
nonaquepéhena 'we eat supper'
nónătămówun 'I am not satisfied with (it)' / [make]

nonechtahanà 'we make'
n. onechtahanà [sic] 'we make'
n'onechtăn 'I make, I do'
nonechtáun 'I have not made or done it'
[nŏnən (M-?, -AM) 'five' / [Numerals]]
nónen nò 'now it's ...' / [halfway, way]
nŏnĕsè 'I am beautiful'
nonetáha '(I-good-heart?), I am friendly, kind'
nonetahahanà 'we are friendly'
nonetahawenaxehenà 'we are friendly (in the face)'
nonetaháwenaxò 'I am friendly (in the face)'
[no·nínska (Sw-e) 'fifty' / [Numerals]]
[nŏ·ni·wi (Si) 'nine' / [Numerals]]
nóno 'today' / [beautiful, cold]
nóno, nonò, nono 'now, this; today' / [ask, baptized ones, be (in a place)', boil or cook meat, can, chop wood, day, early, enough, fail, feel, glad, go, hope ('today'), hunt, say, sit, sound, thrive, time, use, warm, weather, why, witness, write, Wyoming]
nóno káteek 'this year' / [fail, thrive]
nóno najappája 'this morning' / [today]
nono onachkamáo 'now good-day, today good-day' / [hunt]
nóno t'pochquéĕk 'this (past) night' / [sleep]
nono wachcamáăk 'today' / [feel, warm, yet]
nonò wáchcamàhk, nóno wachcamàhk 'today' / [baptized ones, day, glad, nine]
nóno wăchgămăăk, nono wachgamăăk 'today' / [boil or cook meat, come, cook, five, one, two, year]
nono wachgamăk 'today' / [sweat]
nónò wáchkamàhk, nono wachkamahk 'today' / [come, have, love feast]
nono wochgamăk 'today' / [cold]
[nŏ·nən (Sw-R) 'five' / [Numerals]]
nŏnŏsè 'I suck'
nŏnŏsò 'to suck'
nonóso '(he) is sucking'
non'sehenà 'we are beautiful'
nónu 'now' / [peace, sit]
[no-nun (J) 'five' / [Numerals]]
nŏŏch 'my father' / [die, God, inherit, long]
nŏŏchkajéĕn 'we are one' / [one]
nooktàhăăchtaaptonamăăk 'is that the way you are answering?' / [answer]
nŏŏm 'I have been, was [there]' / [be (in a place), over there, up there]
nŏŏmen 'he has gone' [sic for 'I come'] / [go, just]
nŏŏmhanà 'we have been, were [there]' / [be (in a place), up there]
nŏŏspaat ? / [fetch?; No Translation (Orig. and Alph.)]
nŏŏssà ('finger' ?) / [a, an, as, long]
Nŏŏssawáhnĕmà 'one who often or many times thinks (knows?)' / [know, many, Names, think]
nosame 'I-too much' / [honor, many, too]
nósenpĕttĕmĕwĕ 'I have no money'
nŏsŏáhĕga 'I write'
nosoahegahanà 'we write'
nosoahégan 'my book' / [lend]
nosochgamóqu 'we will follow'
nosochgawataù 'let's follow'
nosochgowáu 'he follows him' / [just]
nosse 'to know, be acquainted with'
nŏtăchgĕchgănáchĕn 'I have stayed soft, weak' / [lie (of position)]
notackénakse 'I am pleasant (in the face)'
notackenaksehenà 'we are pleasant'
notackenaxe 'I am pleasant'
nŏtăhósa 'kettle' / [belong]
notajóme 'I have given birth to a child' / [bring forth]
notatschchanáu 'he drags him along'
-notei 'sack'
-nótenuck [see gnótenuck 'he (will) accept you']
nótschi packhámmen 'I have pounded [for a long time]' / [long]
notschŏwachtà 'I will fill [it] up' (2)
nŏtschŏwŭpăăn 'I fill [it] up (full)'
notschowupahanà 'we fill him'
nŏŭnit 'in a good place' / [sit]
nowàsécŏsócun 'to sparkle, glitter'

[nowetachca]nechnà 'we have brothers'
nŏwĕtăchcănéĕn 'I have brothers'
nowetachcannéu 'I have no brothers'
nŏwĕtschawùk 'he is going with me' / [go with]
nŏwĕwĕ 'I am married' / [certainly]
nŏwĕwĕwechgeĕp 'I am already married'
npà, npa 'I come' / [again]
n. păăm [sic] 'thick leg' / [leg]
npachagaschajahegà 'I will remove the rind' / [peel]
npachaschà 'I peel (them)' / [turnips]
npachaschahenà 'we peel (them)'
n'păchénăhn 'to [I?] skin (it)' / [hide]
n[pachgenimmé]naxè 'I look sad' / [gloomy, seem(s)]
n[pachgenimmenaxe]henà 'we look sad' / [gloomy]
npachpenawussè 'I look in the mirror' / [see (2)]
n'Pachtamawaas, nPachtamawăăs 'my God' / [believe, find, or]
np[achtamawaas]naù 'our Savior' / [afraid, find]
n'pajemowà 'I pay'
npajemowahanà 'we pay'
npannesettammechnà 'we are disobedient'
n'păpaag 'I have cried out, I will cry out'
n'papachtamawăn 'I pray' (2)
n'papachtamwahanà 'we pray'
n'papanistàm 'I am disobedient'
npássoa 'I deny'
npawánnĕse 'I am rich'
npawann'sehenà 'we are rich'
n'pè, npè, npe 'water' / [cook, hang up the kettle, put on]
npechnà 'we die' / [like to]
npèck '[that] he died' / [fault]
npĕdhámmen 'I will fill [it] up'
n'penhámmen 'I earn'
npenhamnána 'we earn'
npennawáwak 'I will see them'
-n pennawáwek 'I will not see them'
npeschechwà 'beggar'
npĕtthăŭ 'I didn't catch [fish], I haven't caught any [fish]'
npiŏŏnhaman 'I will play the violin' / [Loan words]
np'mà 'I shoot'
npodawà 'I will light a fire' / [fire]
npŏp 'he died' / [long]
npópackhămmówun 'I have not pounded' / [long]
npòpackuhámmen 'I pound'
nptammăhk [sic n- for k- or for 'me'?] 'they hear'
npumm'sè, n'pummsè 'I run'
n'pumm'tŏhnhà 'I preach'
npummtŏhnà 'I preach'
[npummtŏn]hahanà 'we preach'
nquéchtsche, -n quechtsche 'alone' / [come, far, go away]
nquénakù '(he) is looking for me' / [seek]
nquenawahaná 'we are searching' / [seek]
nquenawáu, n'quénăwáu 'I am looking for (him)' / [seek]
[nquittaus (W) 'six' / [Numerals]]
[nquottaus (W) 'six' / [Numerals]]
nsackamùck 'it bites me'
nsackamuckónau 'they bite me'
n'sáckhăăn 'I will strike fire'
nsasămtscháha 'I whip (myself)'
nsasamtschahana 'we punish him' / [whip]
nsasamtschaháu, n'sasămtschaháu 'I punish him, I give him the rod, I whip him'
[? nsasamtschahaŭna ? 'we punish him' / [whip]]
nsasăm'tschaháwak 'I whip them'
nschaaktanegà 'I will stoke the fire' / [fire]
nschapásomen 'I will melt it away'
n'schĕĕmchaknégàn 'bolt, bar, rail'
nschegenăku 'he hates me'
nschegenawawuna 'we hate him'
nschegenawawunà 'we hate them'
nschegonáu 'I empty out'
nschegonemèn 'I have emptied it out'
nschĕpan 'bowstring'
n'schewochsannè 'I am tired'
nschewochsannéwe 'I am not tired'
? -n schókschŏn 'I will cut (it) [cut with a knife]'

nschukquaschahanà 'we are cutting (them)'
nschukquaschän 'I (will) cut'
nsechtanéna 'I have a headcold'
nsēēd 'my foot' / [hurt]
nsĕgĕtähquòch 'brown bread'
ēnsĕnachquăhau 'I dry (it), I make (it) dry'
n'sèu 'I have not said it' / [bad, say]
n'sewanà 'it hurts me' / [headache]
nsewanadpà 'I have a headache'
nsisgomáu 'I spit at him'
nsisgómuk 'he spits at me'
n'skétschok, nskétschok 'my eye, my face' / [swollen]
n'sketschquan 'my eyes'
nsogenimmen 'I will pour [it] in'
n'soŏgnetaàk 'he (has) sprinkled me with water'
n'susquachtáwan 'I chew'
nsúsque 'I got sick, i.e., at sea' / [spit]
nt- 'my, I' / [Pronominal affixes]
n(t)-...-(na)na 'our (excl.)' / [Pronominal affixes]
ntà, nta, ntà' 'I go' / [come, down there, east, go in(to) there, go out there]
ntaaptonà 'I speak'
ntaaptonawágan 'my word' / [hear, sheep]
n'tacchōm 'my bread'
n'tacchomnà 'our bread'
n'tachamáu 'I will give it to you (for eating)'
ntachamáwe 'I don't give it to you (for eating)'
[n?]tachamókku 'give me (for eating)'
-n tachanän '(should/shall) I place it here?' / [set, shall]
ntachapè 'I ride'
ntachapehenà 'we ride'
n'tachégan 'my knife' / [Pronominal affixes]
ntacheganà 'our knife' / [Pronominal affixes]
ntachgetahà 'I am impatient'
[ntachgeta]hanà 'we are impatient'
ntachpehananà [n covers h] 'we spin'
n'tachwánen 'I love'
ntachwussè 'I am covetous'
ntackenahamawa 'I serve (him)'
ntackenahamawahanà 'we serve (him)'
ntackenahéga 'I have served'
nt'ackenahegahamà [sic first n] 'you [pl.] serve'
n'tackenahegahanà 'we serve'
ntacquatschèh 'I'm freezing, it's freezing me, it has frozen me' / [freeze]
ntacquàtschéhenà 'we are freezing'
ntagétam 'I will tell (it) to you'
ntágushgun '(because) I sneeze [it?]' / [because, snuff, therefore]
ntágusk 'I sneeze'
ntàh, ntah 'my heart' / [ask, reveal]
ntahaaptona 'I have spoken'
ntahaaptonà 'I will speak'
ntahaaptonà 'I will speak with (him)'
ntahaaptonahanà 'we will speak'
ntahagenahéga 'I serve'
ntáhak, ntahak 'in my heart' / [bad off, believe, feel, fill, true, warm, yet]
ntahámed 'my shirt' / [Loan words, wash]
ntáhänä 'we will come'
ntáhänà 'our heart' (?) / [one]
n'táhanääk 'of our heart(s)' (?) / [one]
ntahanánik 'in our hearts' / [bad off]
ntäinewesechnà '(he) has the same name as I' / [as, call (name)]
ntainochquän 'I see, I am always looking'
ntainochquanána 'we see'
ntája (? 'I have' ?) / [Pronominal affixes]
ntajáhtam 'I'm looking for or need (it)' / [necessary, seek]
-n tajáhntam 'I would like (need?) to' / [feel, like to]
ntajanaména (? 'I am happy [that]' ?) / [preach]
ntaje, ntajè 'I am [in a place]' / [be (in a place), down there, up there]
ntajeēn, -ntajeēn 'I am [in a place], I am (up) here' / [be (in a place), stay, up there]
n'tajégan 'mine' / [be, Pronominal affixes]

ntajegananà, n'tajegananà 'it is ours' / [Pronominal affixes]
ntajehenà 'we have been (inside), we are (up) here' / [be (in a place), up there]
ntajéwe 'I have not been (inside)'
ntajewehenà 'we have not been (inside)' / [be (in a place, not), down there]
ntajōm 'my son' / [as, call]
ntakkamáu 'I cook' / [him?)'
ntakkamócku 'he (has) stabbed himself'
ntakquachtschè 'I am cold'
ntakquachtschehenà 'we are cold'
ntaksáme 'I sneeze'
ntammachtamhennau 'we feel'
ntammachtammen, n'tammachtammen 'I feel (3) / [warm, yet]
ntammachtam'nana 'we feel'
n'tammächtämōwŭn 'I don't feel'
n'tammatamnánau 'we feel'
ntän 'I will go' / [go out there, speak with]
ntanachéme, ntanachéme 'I have peace, I rest' / [none, until (2)]
ntănămä 'I cook' / [boil or cook meat]
ntannachkaschegà 'I plow'
ntannachkaschegahanà 'we plow'
ntannachtän 'I have lost' / [lose]
ntannahégan 'my finger' / [bite off, cut]
ntannama 'I cook'
n'tannamà 'I have cooked'
ntannamahanà 'we cook'
n'tannaména, ntannaména 'I am glad (to)' / [come, love feast, see, that]
ntannaméhe 'I am glad'
ntännäwè, n'tànnawè 'I will go hunting' / [go with]
ntännēwänĕmána 'we revere' / [crucify, honor]
ntannewanemáu 'I honor him'
ntannewanemócku 'he respects or honors me'
ntännimsèh 'I go, I am going' / [early, tomorrow]
ntäpchawäk 'I yawn'
ntappajuwechnà 'I sweat'
ntappajuwechnahanà 'we sweat'
n'táppe 'I sit (in)'
ntapskesoōk 'I have poisoned myself' / [poison (oneself)]
ntása (? 'I used to have'?) / [Pronominal affixes]
ntassanetahà 'I am patient' / [be]
ntassanetahanà, n[tassaneta]hanà 'we are patient' / [be]
ntattamachtahamechnà 'we are cutting wood'
ntáttawahanäāp 'he bought me' / [buy]
-n tättäwawĕ 'I will not buy it'
ntäusätschäcken 'I will jump across'
ntaŭywächtówe ? / [fail, thrive]
ntaúwat '(it) is scarce, rare'
[n?]tauwatteschehahanà 'we drive, push [it] out' / [chase out]
ntauwatteschehän 'I will chase them out, I hunt (them)' / [chase out]
ntauwattówe 'it is not scarce'
ntauwéquammen 'I will open'
[nteijéganan?] nteyéganan 'my things, my possessions' / [inherit, woman]
ntěmácănŏme 'have pity [on us?]' / [bless]
ntěméga 'come in here!'
ntemégak' 'come [pl.] in here!'
ntemegéha 'go ye in' / [go in(to) there]
ntemegatoōk 'let's go in' / [go in(to) there]
ntemegáu 'he goes in' / [go in(to) there]
ntemegáwak 'they go in' / [go in(to) there]
ntemégawe 'he did not go in' / [go in(to) there]
ntemegawéwak 'they did not go in' / [go in(to) there]
n'teméhe 'lend me it'
ntemmachtamégun 'he has bitten (it, my finger) off' / [bite off, cut, finger]
n'temméhe 'lend me it' / [shears]
ntemmschim 'I have cut (it, my finger)' / [finger]
ntenananà 'we (have) told it to him' / [say]
ntenaspään 'I am taking water there' / [fetch, there]

ntenaù 'I say to him'
ntenawachten 'I cost'
ntenáwak 'I have said to them' (2)
ntenéhan 'my fault'
ntenehanánà 'our fault'
ntenĕtahà, ntenĕtáha, ntĕnĕtáha, ntĕnĕtáha, ntenetahà, n'tenetahà 'I think (2), 'I hope' / [go around, ready, snow, will]
ntenetahà 'I thought ...' / [think]
n'tenetahà 'I believe' [for 'think'] / [will]
ntenetahahanà 'we hope'
n[teneta]hahanà 'we think'
ntĕnĕtăhăh'nà 'we hope' / [come]
-n tĕnĕwĕsĕ 'my name is ...' / [call (name)]
-n tĕnntăchtăän 'I can do that, I am used to it' / [accustomed]
ntennemágan 'shoulder'
ntenntŏhnhaän 'I will preach it' / [nothing but]
n[tenntŏhn]hahanà 'we preach'
ntenntŏnhahanà 'we preach'
ntenntŏnhän 'I preach'
ntennùk 'he said [to me]' / [say, we]
n'tensettàm 'I have heard' / [love feast]
n'tepochgáwak 'they cook'
n'tĕpochka 'I cook'
ntesgawanahanà 'we envy'
nteyéganan [nteijéganan?] 'my things, my possessions' / [inherit, woman]
ntisgawanáwe 'I am not egotistic'
ntisgawanawehanà 'we are not egotistic'
ntissgawanà 'I am egotistic'
ntissgawanähanà 'we are egotistic'
-n tòckun 'he tells me, she said to me' / [say]
ntŏmad '[why] are you calling (him)?'
ntomak'neĕk '[why] are you calling (them)?'
ntomejäk '[why] are you calling us?'
ntŏmejän '[why] are you calling me?'
nt'omhan 'I (will) chop (it)' / [wood]
ntpochgà 'I (have) cooked'
ntpochgatŏk 'let's cook'
n't'pochgatoōk 'let's cook'
ntschachtschap'chäku 'I have the hiccups'
ntschannéiuwe 'I am dumb' / [be]
ntschanneiwechnà 'we are dumb' / [be]
ntschè '(I?)-will' / [make well]
ntscheĕkhammen 'I (will) sweep it out' / [yes]
n[tscheekhamná]na 'we are sweeping [it] out'
ntscheĕkhamówun 'I didn't sweep it out, I am not sweeping [it] out'
ntŭmmeschímmen 'I will snuff it out'
n'tummesin 'I cut'
nŭchquäta 'they should lick it'
nuktegehahanà 'we have only one child' / [child]
nuktegehän 'I have only one child' / [child]
núktĕnĕ 'down there' / [drive, there]
núktĕnĕ wéchtamèn, núktĕnĕ wechtamèn '[what] is that called?, how do you pronounce that?' / [call (name), pronounce; cf. down there]
nŭmpäpéquan 'gun' / [belong]
[nŏ·nan (Sw-D)] 'five' / [Numerals]
[nunón (M-EM)] 'five' / [Numerals]
[nunon (E)] 'five' / [Numerals]
[nu-shu (J)] 'two' / [Numerals]
n'waás'nanemèn 'I will make it bright' / [light]
n['waas'nane]menána 'we make it bright' / [light]
n'wahs'nanemèn 'I will make it bright' / [light]
n'wahs'nanemenána 'we make it bright' / [light]
n'waŏnístähmóu 'I am not obedient'
n'wawagŏmäu 'we greet'
n'wawagómau 'you [pl.] [for we?] greet him'
n['wawago]máu 'I greet him'
nwawagŏmen 'I greet'
n'wawagowawunà 'we greet'
n'wawanahntàm 'I'm laughing'
n'wawanähntamhanà 'we laugh'
n'wawanäntam 'I'm laughing (2), I laughed' / [lot]
nwawanäntammowuhanà 'we aren't laughing'
n'wawechtà 'I know' / [peace, where]
-n wäwĕchtan 'I know'
-n wäwĕchtáwa 'I don't know it'
-n wawèchtawà 'I didn't know it'
-n wawèchtawùn, n' wäwechtawùn 'I am not acquainted with him' / [he, know]
n'wawehána 'we know'

n'waweháu 'I know, am acquainted with'
n'wawehawe 'I don't know'
nwawonistàm, n'wa(w)onistàm 'I am obedient'
nwawonistamhanà 'we are obedient'
n'wēgáchtámmen 'I like to eat it'
n'wĕhĕgămĕ 'I sacrifice'
n'wénajoom 'my wife' / [house, woman]
n'wenamatà 'it hurts me' / [headache]
nwenasōōm 'my wife' / [inherit, things, woman]
n'wéschasè 'I am afraid'
n'weschaséhĕĕnà 'we are afraid'
-n wéschasewahannà 'we are not afraid'
ⁿweschasewe (? 'he / I? + afraid + not' ?) / [No Translation (Untranslated "biblical" text)]
[n?]weschasoōpkà 'I am so afraid' / [so]
n'wĕtà 'I go with'
nwetschawawunà 'we are going along' / [go with]
n'wetschechnà 'I will be present' / [be present]
n'wéwaschè 'you (can) carry (it)'
nxechnà 'I jump'
[(nya·na·ka·w) (Sw-e) 'fifteen' / [Numerals]]
[(nya·ni·nska) (Sw-e) 'fifty' / [Numerals]]
[nyŏnən (M-Me) 'five' / [Numerals]]

o 'oh' / [how many, white people]
o- 'he, his' / [Personal pronouns, Pronominal affixes]
o-...-(a)wa(k) 'their' / [Pronominal affixes]
ŏáăk 'also' / [can, lie (tell lies)]
-ócha, -óchà 'go' / [come, quick, slow]
ochoquénei 'cough, expectoration' / [blood]
ochoquénei 'phlegm; he coughs up' / [cough]
ochquenáu 'he coughs'
odáhak 'with (her) heart' / [glad, go, truly, work]
ŏdànăwă 'they went' / [go]
ŏgáttaù 'he will (wants to) ...' / [gather]
ogauhowána 'he has won (them)' / [win]
ogeschechtaan 'he has done it' / [make, no]
oh 'oh' / [many, see]
oháckai 'himself' / [covetous, see, self]
óhăkkăjewe 'he has become man [= body], he was incarnated' / [become flesh, live, Savior]
óhákkei 'body' / [bloodied, eat, self]
óhnsettamăăk 'obedient (ones)'
ohnsittámmen, ohnsittammen 'he believes' / [for]
ohnsittawawà 'they believe in (him)'
oi 'oh' / [lie (of position); No Translation (Untranslated "biblical" text)]
ojáăs 'meat' / [boil or cook meat, cook, ready, roast]
ojáash [sic -sh], ojaash 'meat' / [cook (2)]
ójăkà 'stir [it] up' / [touch]
ojamachgenáso '[it is] mixed'
ojamachgenásoan 'mixed [with]'
ójămăchgĕnĕ 'mix it'
ojăs 'meat' / [cook]
ojáșęn 'meat + I' / [cook]
ojasom 'meat + I?' / [cook]
-ojásom 'meat' / [serve]
ojáson [= ojasom + n-?] 'meat + I' / [cut]
okechgáu '(it) is barking'
okecká 'his mother' / [call]
okeéchschálmă 'to his parents' / [obedient]
okénnamĕnăwa 'they hang on' / [mosquitoes]
okènnĕmen 'he carried (it)'
okensittawăwa 'he listens'
okeschanachgáăn '[how long] has he been ready?' / [how long, long, when]
ŏkĕschĕchĕhăwă 'he cleans them' / [heart]
ŏkĕschĕchpătégán 'wash clean!'
ŏkĕschechtăn '(he) has made (them) clean' / [heart]
okeschechtán 'he has done it' / [make]
okéschechtánaap 'he has made (him/them)' / [make]
o[kesche]háwa, okescheháwa 'he has made him/them' / [make]

-òksenà, -ò ksenà [see nguttòksenà]
o[kupphammen] 'he closes'
o[kupphamme]náwak 'they close'
okussechtăhn 'he swallows'
okutschemonáwa 'he asks him'
o[kutsche]mōōnkónau 'he asks us' / [we (incl.)]
okwachawa 'he is afraid (of him)'
okwacháwa 'they are afraid'
okwacháwe 'he is not afraid'
okwachawewă 'they are not afraid'
okwetschawawewă 'he is not going along' / [go with]
olandéuch [Del.] '(it) is shining' / [Delaware]
omachgammen 'he has found it' / [find]
o[machgamme]náwa 'they have found it' / [find]
omachgawawă 'they have found him' / [find]
omachgawáwe 'he has not found him' / [find]
omachgawawewà 'they have not found him' / [find]
omakweséĕn 'he or she is swollen'
ŏmămăksimmă 'his sheep'
omamatahául 'he will sound, ring'
omamatahawak 'they will sound, ring'
omàmăwanăch 'eyebrows'
omàmăwănă 'his eyebrow(s)'
omàmăwánăwà 'their(?) eyebrows'
omattschechtăn 'he ruins'
omattschechtáwak 'they ruin'
ŏmĕmĕchcănĕmĕn 'he makes room'
omenachtschewanik 'on the left side'
oménahn 'he gave it' / [give]
ōmĕschótamen 'he (has) hit the mark' / [shoot]
ōmĕschótamówe 'he did not hit it, he shot past it' / [shoot]
omischnemnáwak 'they get' / [ask, must, one]
omischnimnáwak 'they should receive' / [get]
ŏmischschakanáwa 'they sit on' / [hang on, mosquitoes]
ŏmischschătăcăăn 'he goes quickly' / [go, immediately]
ŏmischschăwà 'he has hit (the mark)' / [he, shoot]
onáchcan 'hands [his or mine?]' / [warm]
onáchgan 'his hands, their hands' / [foot, kiss, thereby]
o[nach]ganà 'he hopes'
onachganawàk 'they hope'
ŏnăchgĕk 'in his hand' / [foot, nail]
onáchgek 'in his hands' / [believe]
onachgochemáu 'he sings'
onachgochemáwak 'they sing'
onàchk 'his hand' / [show]
onáchka 'their hands' / [hard]
onachkamáo 'a good day' / [hunt, weather]
ŏnăchkăn 'his hands' / [foot, marks]
onàchkeck 'in his arm' / [become flesh, sleep]
onàchkek 'in his hands, in his arms' / [arm, gather, will]
onach'tamawaan [? 'that he has helped' ?] / [No Translation (Untranslated "biblical" text)]
onachtamawáu 'he helps'
onachtamawáwak 'they help'
onachtamawawunà 'they do not help'
ŏnăchtănăméă '[why] I am pleased' / [glad, say, why]
onàchtánamowócha 'joyous' / [glad, go, truly, work]
onádam 'they laugh'
onáham '(these [who?]) approach (him)'
-onălwágan 'sweetness' / [taste]
onájo '[he is] good' (adj.) / [friend, truly]
onáju 'he is good' / [say]
onamackahăăn 'he (will) make (them) healthy' / [make well, will]
ónămănníssŏăk 'they prosper' / [old, stay; Long Sentences, 3d]
ŏnămánnissoháne 'make me well, cure me' / [make well]
[ŏnămánnisso]hanenána 'make us well, cure us' / [make well]
onamansohána 'he makes them well' / [make well]
onámen 'he sees'
onamenăăp 'he has seen'

onamenáwa 'they see'
onamenawăăp 'they have seen'
onammanissĕĕd 'that she will get well' / [hope, shall, will, wish that]
onáqua 'yesterday' / [sweat (2)]
onaquéga 'evening'
onaquépehn 'supper' / [love feast]
onaquepetōōk 'let us eat supper'
onaquépĕŭ 'he eats supper'
onaquépuak 'they eat supper'
onatamówun 'he does not help'
ónătămówun 'he is not satisfied with (it)' / [make]
onátenan 'he is taking her, he has taken it' / [perhaps]
onattomáwa 'he is calling him/her' / [mother]
ŏnáwă 'he sees'
onawáju '[it is] blue'
onáwak 'they see'
onawanáwa 'to run after someone'
onawawà 'he has seen him'
onawawà, onáwawa 'they have seen him/them'
onawawewă 'he has not seen him'
onawawewă 'they haven't seen them'
-onechséwe / [right, say]
ŏnĕchtă 'make (it)' / [fire, strike fire]
-ōnĕchtă 'make' / [build, house]
onechtăhn 'he makes (it, food)' / [friend, make]
onechtáu, onechtăŭ 'he makes, he does'
onechtáun 'he has not done it' / [make]
onechtáu(n) (?) 'I have not made or done it' / [make]
onechtáwak 'they make'
onechtawè 'make (it) for me!' / [shoe(s)]
ŏnĕechonămówe 'you are not paying attention'
onĕĕchtau 'they put it on him' / [put on, thorn hat]
onĕĕchtawĕ 'make (it) for me!' / [pair, shoe(s)]
onĕekchannawatamōōk 'pay [pl.] attention'
ŏnĕhà '[who] has made it?' / [make]
onĕhókăjăne 'we are created' / [become flesh, sleep]
onĕnchăsè 'pay attention!'
onenochtamnáu [? 'they/he-hears-it' ?] / [hear, sheep, voice]
onéowe, ŏnéŏwĕ, onéowe 'I am thankful, I thank' / [say, teach]
oneppuágan 'death'
ŏnĕppuwătămĕnăăp 'he died' / [last]
onessò 'she is beautiful, he is handsome'
onessoàk (?) 'they are beautiful'
onessowàk [onessoàk?] 'they are beautiful'
onetaháu 'he is friendly, kind'
onetaháwak 'they are friendly'
onetahawenaxò 'kind, good-hearted, [he is] friendly (in the face)' / [certainly]
onétschănă 'daughter[s?]' / [come, family]
ŏnèttŏŏp 'better' / [? good-it-was] / [good?]
ŏnĕwĕsŏ, oneweso '[what] is his name?, [what] is he called?' / [call (name), man, the]
onistà 'be obedient!'
onístak 'he believes'
onistămăwágan 'belief' / [know, stay; Long Sentences, 1]
onistamŏk 'be [pl.] obedient!'
onistawahnta '[who will] believe' / [examine]
ŏnistăwájăquà 'believing' (adj.) / [ask, believe, heart]
onistawàjaquà 'believing' / [approach, with]
ŏnistawáta '[whoever] believes (him)'
onistawawetaù 'we will not be obedient to him'
ŏnistăwétà 'he is obedient to me'
onistaweta [? 'who believes in or is obedient to him' ?] / [No Translation (Untranslated "biblical" text)]
ŏnìttówe 'it is not good' / [assemble, late]
on'mawáo '[they] stabbed him, [I] pricked myself' / [stab]
onochnáwa 'she (will) suckle it'
ŏnŏquăam '(I had a) beautiful dream' / [beautiful]
onosochgawa '[who] is following?'
ŏnŏsochgawáwa 'he follows them' / [go after]
onòtĕnimmŏwùn 'he did not take it'
onúkquask 'maize leaf' / [leaf]

ŏp 'he said' / [free, say]
oPachtamawása '[his] Savior' / [serve]
opàhnnénǎmèn 'he has failed, [he has deserved it]' / [earn]
ŏpájätscheek 'they come'
opajemowanawà 'he has paid him' / [pay]
opákka [probably for -ck + opákka; cf. Del. kopachkan, thick] '(it is) thick' / [too]
opákkǎmǎwǎ 'they hit'
opapachgammawǎpǎnè 'they have hit him'
opapachtamawáu 'he prays'
opawannesóu 'he is rich'
o[pĕ̄dhámmen] 'he fills [it] up'
ŏpĕ̄nàuwǎwà '(he) looks at (him)' / [Long Sentences, 5a]
opènhámmen, o[penhámmen] 'he deserved (it), he earns' / [death]
openhammen 'he has failed, missed; he has not hit right' / [earn]
[? openhamnawak ?] 'they earn'
opènnǎmèn 'look, view' (noun)
ŏpènnawáu 'he looked at him' / [see]
opettamen 'he hears'
opettamennaap 'he has heard'
opettamennawa 'they hear'
o[pettamenna]wǎǎp 'they have heard'
op'gachganŏm, op'gachganom, opgachganom 'blood, his blood' / [believe, clean, cost (2), feel, for, inherit, nothing but, open, preach, suck, with]
opgachganomik 'in his blood' / [No Translation (Untranslated "biblical" text)]
op'gachganŏŏm 'his blood' / [make well]
op'maosowágan 'his life' / [lay down one's life]
op'máw 'he shoots'
opmuchgawǎǎn, opmuchgawǎn 'he is victorious, he has triumphed, won'
op°máosowágan 'his life' / [find, lose, sake, save, seek]
opopackhammenáwa 'they pound'
o[pòpackųhámmen?] 'he pounds'
oquenawawà '(he) is looking for them' / [seek]
oquenawawewà 'he is not looking for them' / [seek]
osáma- 'very, too much' / [firmly, hold on]
osámapézò 'you must hold it firmly' / [hold on, too]
osáme, osame 'too, too much' / [boil over, go, remove, slow]
-osame 'too, too much' / [honor, loud, many, quick]
-ósǎmĕ̄nĕ̄s 'so much, too much (?)' / [cry out, don't, so]
osámick [-ck with thick] 'too (much)' / [thick]
ŏsǎsǎmtschǎhǎwǎ 'they (have) whipped him' / [child]
o[sasam'tscha]háwa 'he punishes (him)' / [whip]
oschegenawáwa 'he (they?) hates him, he hates them (?)'
o[schegena]wáwa 'he hates them' / [believe]
oschegonemèn 'he has emptied (it) out' / [empty out, sack]
oseedan 'his feet' / [marks]
osédick 'at his feet' / [foot, nail, throw]
osédik 'his feet'
oseedquakajaxèh 'fall down (at the feet)!' / [down, fall (down), foot]
oseen 'he said(?), he has said' / [free, say]
osen 'he says'
osétan 'his feet' / [kiss, thereby]
osétòchkǫ 'neck of an ax' / [ax]
o[sewanad]páu 'he has a headache'
ŏsǐssĕ̄gŏmǎwa 'they spat (at him)' / [spit]
oskekǎmǎ '(in the) new' / [house]
oskékǎn 'new' / [house]
oskekǎwǎk 'new ones'
osketschgok, osketschgok 'in his face' / [spit]
osketschkóŏk 'in/on his face, in the face' / [color, redden]
osketschquan 'eyes'
osoahegà 'write!'
ŏsŏahégan 'book' / [Bible, great, holy]
osoehégan 'book' / [inherit]
osogahǎǎn 'he pours in, fills'

osŏh 'it's cooking slowly, it's simmering'
osóhegan, ŏsŏ́hégan 'book'
osohégan 'letter'
osŏknĕ̄mmèn 'he poured it'
osowáno 'flower on maize'
o(t)- 'he, his' / [Personal pronouns, Pronominal affixes]
o(t)-...-(a)wa(k) 'their' / [Pronominal affixes]
otacchomǎh 'his bread'
otacchomawà 'their bread'
ŏtǎchǎsèn 'lead [the metal]'
ŏtǎcheen [? 'the wind comes from (or blows?)] / [east, wind (see note)]
otachégan 'knife' / [belong]
o[tacheganajà] 'the knife was his' / [Pronominal affixes]
otachussowehhtawǎ́ 'covetous (so miserly that one feels ... proud of nothing)'
otachwátamen 'he loves'
ŏtǎchwátǎmèn 'he loves it'
otachwatamóun 'he has loved'
otacaksèn 'lead [the metal]' / [melt]
otackenaksoak 'they are pleasant'
otackenaksou 'he is pleasant'
otackenaxŏ 'he is pleasant'
otackkamáwa 'he stabbed'
otáha 'his heart' / [believe, examine, open]
otáhacàn 'canoe'
ŏtǎhágan 'canoe'
otáhak 'in his heart, from heart' / [fair, feel, greet, let ('in our hearts'), glad, like to, observe, peace]
otǎhǎwà 'their hearts' / [humble, little]
otáhawǎk 'in the heart' / [sick]
otahawǎwuk 'in their hearts' / [bad off]
otáhik 'in his heart' / [bad off]
otàhn 'he has gone there' / [go, just, there]
-otahnse- 'depend on'
ŏtǎjjeen 'to(?) live in' / [live (dwell in), new]
otaijenáwa 'they endure' / [prosper, stay; Long Sentences, 3d]
otaijóma 'the son' / [God]
otǎinochquǎn '[when] one looks toward it' / [see]
otainochquanáwa 'they see'
o[tainoch]quanawak 'they see'
o[tainoch]quáu 'he sees'
otajĕ̄en 'he stays (here)'
otajégan 'it is his' / [Pronominal affixes]
otajégana 'it was his, he was a ...' / [Pronominal affixes]
o[tajeganawà] '(it is) theirs' / [Pronominal affixes]
otajohonawǎhn 'they (have) hit him with fists'
otajóma 'child' / [whip]
otajomáu 'she has given birth to a child' / [bring forth]
otajoména 'she has brought him forth, she has given birth to him' / [bring forth]
ŏtajŏmŏsà '[when] did she give birth to (it)?' / [bring forth, child, when]
otakkamáwak 'they stab, they stabbed him' / [side]
ótǎkkàn 'beautiful weather' / [day, weather]
otakquè 'on the (side)' / [left, side]
otàmmachoonwa (? 'they-ship-[go]' ?) / [come, ship]
ŏtǎmmǎchtǎmmĕ̄n, otammachtámmen 'he feels, felt' / [death, taste]
otammachtamnáwa 'they feel'
ŏtànǎchtǎhn 'he will lose it' / [lose, save, seek]
otanachtǎn 'he has lost' / [lose]
otannachgágana 'servants'
otannachtanáwa 'they have lost' / [lose]
otáŏŏkǎǎt '[He is visiting, (whereas)] They are [there already?].'; thus 'he is visiting (him)' / [visit]
otàpachtóquæpì [Del.] 'his crown' / [Delaware]
otáu̇, otáu '(it) is boiling' / [cook]
-otaù 'let us ...' (excl.)
ŏtǎu̇wáhan ['with'?] / [clean, with]
otauwequamenáwa 'they open'
otauwequammen 'he opens'
otauwunáwa 'he opens it'

ŏtawǎnéwàn '[why] don't you visit me?' / [why]
otàwǎwǐck 'internal, spiritual'
ŏtǎwĕ̄chtęę̆t (? 'when one is visiting' ?), 'at the visit' / [at, visit]
otàwŏ̆wàk 'they are visiting'
otenè 'for her' / [believe]
otenehǎn 'his fault'
otenehanáwa 'their fault'
o[teneta]hǎǎn 'he thinks'
o[teneta]háu 'he thinks'
otenewesowaganick 'in his name' / [his, name, sleep]
óteni̇m 'he takes (it) from (it)' / [fire, up there]
ŏtĕ̄nin +? ['he-thus- + ?'] / [accustomed]
otènnáchcanàhn 'his servants'
otènnahn 'he says' / [go]
otènnanáchcanàhn [see otènnáchcanàhn]
ŏtènnanachkǎǎb 'he has made (it)' / [make]
otènnǎwàhn '(they) said (it)' / [say]
ŏtĕ̄nnè, otennè 'as, how' / [death, feel, must, taste]
ŏtĕ̄nnè, otennè (?), oténne, ŏtĕ̄nnè 'how; (so much, that much)' / [bad, love (2), more than, must, see]
? oténne ... áne 'more, more than' / [must, woman]
otinnǎhn 'it is coming' / [come, east, rain]
otŏ́hnick '(from) his mouth' / [hear, speak]
ótsche 'away, away from' / [can, sheep, tear away]
otschè, otsche 'because, because of, for, from, therefore' / [captivate, die, get, glad, greet, hear, heart, mouth, sneeze, speak, take punishment, we (see for split usage); No Translation (Untranslated "biblical" text)]
ŏtschè 'because of, from' / [but, down there, drive, take, there, therefore, thus]
ŏtscheekhammen 'he is sweeping it clean'
otscheekhamnáwa 'they are sweeping [it] out'
otschéma 'call (her)!'
ŏtschemàhn 'to call, shout' ['shout' German usage probably not applicable here]
ŏtschemǎú 'he calls him' / [peace, the]
otschemáwa 'he calls her'
otschemónatsch 'examine (ask)!' [? 'let him examine' ?] / [believe]
otschémukquak '[till] he calls us' / [call (shout), until]
-ótschi [preverbal 'from'] / [long]
otschinnehà 'so that he may enter' / [go in(to) there, open]
otschitschachcunána 'our souls' / [win]
otschitschachkwéwe 'soul's' / [work]
ŏtschitschachquà 'soul, ghost' / [God, holy]
otschitschachquan 'soul, ghost' / [holy, teach]
otschosammawè 'give me a pipe of tobacco' / [fill, pipe]
[otscho]semàhn (?) 'he fills it' / [pipe]
ŏtschŏwachtǎǎn '(he) fills (them with it)' / [peace]
ŏtschŏwachtàhn 'he fills it'
otschòwachtaka 'when will (it) become full' / [full, well, when, will]
ŏtschòwachtǎn 'he fills (it)'
otschòwachtáu '[it is] full' / [fill, take]
otschowupǎ 'fill [it] up (full)'
otschowupána 'he fills him'
otschowupáta 'let us fill (it)'
[otschowu]páwak 'they fill it'
ŏttŏhŏhn 'bough'
otummeschimmen 'he puts (snuffs) out' / [light; cf. also cut, snuff out]
ounamachnáu '(it) is ambling along, (it) ambles along' / [horse]
o[waás'nanemèn] 'he makes it bright' / [light]
o[waas'naneme]náwak 'they make it bright' / [light]
ŏwǎ́hs'nanemèn 'he makes it bright' / [light]
o[wahs'naneme]nawàk 'they make it bright' / [light]
owáwechtanáwa 'they know (it)' / [speak]
owawecháwa 'he knows'
o[wawehá]wak 'they know'
o[wawehawe] 'he doesn't know'
ŏwēhnsehn 'he is the head of her' / [he, man]
ŏwénamansohǎǎncùn '(that) he is sick' / [be, ↑

Mahican-English 181

↓ feel, if, that, therefore]
owetschawáwa 'they are going along' / [go with]
ozánîan '(that) you have forsaken me'

pà 'I come'
pa- 'pay' / [Loan words]
paachwechcawatowágan ['teaching, gospel, doctrine'?] / [No Translation (Untranslated "biblical" text (2))]
páád '(when) he comes, (that) you are (he is) coming' / [hope, say, wish that]
páádquaik, páádquájak, páádquajak 'turnips' / [cut, peel]
-páám ('thick or stocky leg')
páán '(whether he) came' / [come, whether]
pááptamowùn 'I haven't heard it'
Pááptschàck 'pied, piebald, dappled, variegated' / [Names]
paáschco, páaschco 'a, an, one' / [believe, free, Numerals, run]
páaschcunóók, paaschcunóók 'together' / [gather, rake, wood]
paáschéú 'it's boiling over'
[paaschgu (H1) 'one' / [Numerals]]
[páaschko (1759) 'one' / [at end of Numerals]]
paaschkon 'one' / [get, must, Numerals]
páaschkónówak '(we/they?) are of one ...' / [one]
páaschkun, paáschkun 'one' / [Numerals, woman]
[paaschuk (H1) 'one' / [Numerals]]
pachascháu 'he peels them'
pachaschawak 'they peel them'
pachgáju ? / [slow]
[pachgá]juwak ? / [slow]
páchgékán 'gun' / [clean, rust]
páchgenick 'darkness' / [light, love, more than]
pachgenimménaxò '[he?] to appear gloomy (faced)' / [seem(s)]
pachgenimmenaxoàk 'they look sad' / [gloomy]
páchkátschîn [for páchktàtschî (= 'already') + -n (= 'I')?] / [accustomed, can, mix]
páchkénîmmen 'to break off, tear off'
pachóód 'soon' / [snow, will]
pachóód, pachood 'almost, nearly, soon' / [halfway, way]
Páchpámáwóshánóáád, Pachpam[áwóshánó-áád] 'Savior' / [good, must, think]
pachpametónhád 'preacher, clergyman, minister' / [preach]
pachpaquaik 'wounds' / [by, peace, where; No Translation (Untranslated "biblical" text)]
pàchpáschéú 'it (always) boils over'
pachpenawùs 'mirror' (?) / [see]
pachpenawussehenà 'we look in the mirror' / [see]
[pachpenawus]sétaù 'we (both) will look in the mirror'
pachpenawussetóók 'let's look in the mirror'
pachpenawussoàk 'they look in the mirror'
pachquachagenùk 'he has released (me from prison)' / [free]
pachquachenquakup, pachquachgenquagup 'he has released (me?)(from prison)' / [free]
pachquaitscháha 'chase (it) out'
páchquánáú 'it (fire) burns' / [fire]
pachquaschéha 'chase (it) out'
Pachtamáusnau 'of the Savior' / [worthy]
Pachtamauus 'Savior' / [love, necessary]
Pachtamáwáás, Pachtamáwáas, Pachtamáwaas, Pachtamawaás, Pachtamawaas, Páchtamáwaas 'God, Savior, Lord' / [believe, bless, blissful, certainly, die, enjoy, feel (3), food, free, friend, friendly, go away, go in(to) there, good, help, holy, inherit, just, lay down one's life, lie (of position), like to, live, look at, love, make, make well, necessary, oh, one, open, satisfied, see, seek, truly, who, will, wounds; Long Sentences, 5a]

Pachtamawáás Táp[anemuc]quàk 'Savior' / [become flesh, live]
Pachtamawaasnau, Pachtama[wa]asnau, Pachtamawaasnaù, Pachtamawáásnau, Pacht[amawaas]nau '(our) Savior, God' / [believe (2), bring forth, clean, death, die, feel, find, for, heart, honor, must, nothing but, perhaps, preach, say, see, seek, servant, taste, to, we (2)]
Pachtamáwáássèk, Pachtamáwaássèk, Pachtamáwaassèk [respectively:] 'of (my) Savior, by (my) creator', to the Savior' / [full, Pronominal affixes, quickly, well, will]
Pachtamawaassèk, Pachtamáwáássèk, Pachtamáwaassèk 'to the Savior' / [go, immediately, well, when]
Pachtamawans [sic] 'Savior' / [fill, peace]
-Pachtamawása 'Savior' (obv.) / [serve]
Pachtamawasan 'Savior('s)' (obv.) / [spit]
Pachtamawásnau 'God' / [pay]
Pachtamawássek 'about God, with God' / [go around]
pachteétsch 'let [it?] come (to me)' / [to me]
pachtéta 'when they come'
pachtsche pommákè 'to bloodlet' / [Delaware]
páchtsche pommákèh 'to bloodlet' / [Delaware]
páchtsche pommáwè '(must) bloodlet' / [Delaware]
pachwenawussò [sic for p?] 'he looks in the mirror' / [see]
packájis 'piece' / [bread, meat]
packchàckq 'board, plank'
páckcháquán 'boards'
packhámmen '[to] pound' / [long]
páckpáchtschochgád 'a deceitful man'
-páda / [come, to that place]
págáchtschè 'already' / [see]
pagátsche, págátsche, pagatschè, pagatsche 'already' / [drink, eat, hear, hit, sleep, swallow, when]
pagechtanè '(my nose) is bleeding'
pagechtanò 'he is bleeding (from the nose)'
paggátsche, pággátschè, paggatschè, paggatsche 'already' / [eat, hear (note), make, sound]
pahanà 'we come'
pahawà 'you come'
p'ahgégánápei 'garter strap' / [band]
pahwahà 'get the peels!' / [fetch]
páînanáu ? / [be, should, so]
pájaat 'who came' / [come]
pajachkékan [Del.] 'gun' / [Delaware]
pajachquenaksoàk 'I have not seen them for a long time' / [long, see]
pajachquénaquat 'for a long time I have seen no [inan.]' / [long, see]
pajachquenaxò 'for a long time I have seen no [anim.]' / [long, see]
pajachquépogat 'I have not eaten that for a long time' / [eat, long, not]
pájakàk 'where we arrived' / [come]
pájakóp [k or t?] 'the one who came' / [appear as, as, become flesh, believe]
pájan, pajàn 'that you come' / [glad, house]
pájáné 'when you come to ...' / [remember, think]
pajateétsch 'those who come'
pájatéta 'as they came, when they arrived' / [as, come, to me]
pájatóp [t or k?] 'the one who came' / [appear as, as, become flesh, believe]
pajatscheék 'they are coming' / [come, white people]
pajáza ? / [come; No Translation (Orig. and Alph.)]
pajem- 'pay' / [Loan words]
pajemowanochgónau 'he has paid for us' / [pay]
pajemowáqu 'let us pay'
pajemowatammawè 'pay for me'
pajemowáu 'he pays'
[pajemo]wáwak 'they pay'
pakànmechnáú 'it got dark'
pakatschè, pákatschè, pákátschè 'already' / [afternoon, bloodied, certainly, drink, eat, marry]
pákátsche 'already' / [blow a horn]
pákchákú 'board, plank'

pakkàmmat '[why] are you shoving (pushing) him?' / [hit]
pakkamùck 'he has hit me'
pákkámùck '[who] has hit you?'
pákkátáchna 'throw yourself at [feet]!' / [foot]
pákkátámhámma 'you smash with it' / [hit]
pákkátámkóóp 'he has set me free' / [free]
páksowak 'pairs' / [come, two]
páku 'come [pl.]!'
pam- 'pay' / [Loan words]
páma 'come (sg.)!' / [again, soon]
pámákieéck (?) 'through, throughout' / [go; Long Sentences, 3a]
pàmóáhnkónááp '[he] has paid us' / [payer]
pamóáhnóquákup 'payer (the Savior)'
pamowaánkóóp 'he has set me free' / [free]
pamowáhn 'I will pay it' / [debt]
-pamowánéckonááp / [free]
pánáwà '(whether) they come' / [whether]
panéék [an ending?] / [long, ready]
pánnákékáck ? / [No Translation (Orig. and Alph. and at end with partial copy of ms. p. (375)), p. 159]
pannéwà 'go on, go away!'
pannéwe 'something else' / [see]
-pannewe 'away' / [set]
[pánnéwé ánápówéchkánàht 'misleading (everyone)' / [see No Translation (Alph. at Anapáwechkóók)]]
pannewehh [for deletion] 'something else' / [see]
pannistàm 'he is disobedient'
pannistamák 'they are disobedient'
pannistamhàn 'don't be disobedient'
pannistamháqu 'don't [pl.] be disobedient'
pannistammotaù 'we will be disobedient'
-pápáchgáchtáham 'split wood' / [go in order to]
papachgattachnáán 'I fall (down) at (your feet)' / [fall down at the feet, foot]
papachgattachnánán 'we fall (down) at (your [pl.] feet)'
Papacht[amawáás] 'Savior' / [hear]
pápáchtámáwájaku '[how] we ought to pray' / [teach]
papachtamawàk 'they pray'
papachtamawáqu 'pray [pl.]!'
papachtamawátau 'we pray for them' / [necessary]
papachtamawatók 'let us pray'
papachtamawáu 'he pray(s/ed)'
papachtschéwe [? 'certainly'??] / [peace, until]
pápáge 'cry out, call out!' / [call (shout)]
pápamsèchteétsch (? 'let go astray, get lost, get confused'?) / [astray, run]
papanistàm 'disobedient'
papannsetàm 'she is disobedient'
pápaquaik 'in the woods' / [lie (of position)]
pápáquatahasétip 'he let himself be struck' / [wounds]
papéék 'flea' / [bite]
papéquak 'fleas'
páppáquánáwéét '(it, your heart) burns'
paquaick, páquaick 'wounded, his wounds' / [call (shout), his, make well, side, so that]
paquaik 'in the wounds' / [sit]
páqüak 'it broke (into pieces)' / [hit]
pá quátámák 'it struck into it' / [hit]
pá quáuchaán 'he went out' / [cry, go out there, "Past" tense]
-páquè '(I) shoot'
páquéchtá 'fire off, fire, shoot' / [gun, shoot a gun]
páquewák 'it broke (into pieces)' / [hit]
páschéú, páschéú 'it (will) boil over, cook over'
passéwe 'half'
passoáu 'he denies'
paták nè ? / [bring; No Translation (Orig. and Alph.)]
pátip 'he come, he came'
pátip '[why] are you (is he) coming?, [why] you are (he is) coming' / [come (2)]
patsche, pátsche 'you come; to?; until' / [old, prosper, stay, to me; Long Sentences, 3d]
páú, páu 'he comes (4), he/she (will) come' / [again, alone, go in(to) there, hope (2), open, think, whether]
-páú 'he came' / [to me]
[pausquun (W) 'one' / [Numerals]]

páussa '[when] is he to come?'
páwak 'they have come, they are coming' (5) / [family, great, many, pair, two]
páüwăk 'they come'
pawann'sóu 'to be rich, [he is] rich'
pawánnsowak 'they are rich'
páwe, páwè 'he hasn't come' / [not yet]
páwe 'he was not to return (come)' / [think]
pāwŏháánà [single word or last half of word?] / [free, would]
pchăckăschājăhēga 'to peel, pare'
p'chakschā 'rind' / [apple]
p'chăn 'it is snowing, it will snow' / [perhaps, will]
p'chanim, p'chánim 'woman, lady' / [call, know]
p'chanŏwe 'it will not snow'
pĕchăân 'it will snow' / [soon]
pechtáăd 'perhaps' / [take]
pechtáăm ['perhaps will be' ?] / [go with, luck]
pechtăm 'perhaps' / [run after]
pechtkáăm 'perhaps' / [catch fish, tomorrow]
pechtkáătsch 'perhaps still' / [snow]
péchtkăht 'perhaps'
pechtschìm 'perhaps' / [die]
pĕdham, pedham- 'he fills [it]' / [fill up]
pedhammanóme 'he fills [it] with grain'
pedhámmen 'fill up, [I have already] filled [it] up'
peesbáăcan 'sweathouse' / [wish that]
peesbank [see note] 'sweathouse' / [wish that]
peespájàn 'sweating (?), sweathouse' / [good]
pehdhà 'fill [it] up'
pehtahanáăp '(he) was taken captive, he was taken prisoner' / [captivate, for]
pĕkússak 'mosquitoes (gnats)' / [hang on]
pénĕgĕsàk 'peach trees' / [Loan words, tree]
-pènhammawágan 'wages' / [believe, inheritance; Long Sentences, 2]
pennáăp 'he died' / [we]
pĕnnăwăhn 'I will see them (her?)'
pennawáu 'I have seen or looked [at him?]' / [see]
pennawawe '(I will) not see him/them'
pennawáwek '(I) will not see them'
pennawe ['look' ?] / [but, see]
pĕnóchtenéeth 'let me look into' / [see (at end)]
pequagàn 'band'
péquan, péquanan 'gun, guns' / [one's own]
peschechwáu '[he is a] beggar'
péso 'bundle, sheaf'
pēspājàn 'sweating (?), sweathouse' / [good]
-petácasóon 'coat' / [close, make]
-petáchgásòhn 'dress or coat' / [new]
petachgasŏn 'coat' / [old]
Petrussa '(at) Peter' / [look at, see]
Petrussek 'Peter' / [be (present)]
pettàm 'I hear'
pettămĕchnŏn 'we hear' / [we]
pettamennána 'we hear'
péttăwè 'listen [you, sg.]' / [hear]
péttăwènà 'grant me a hearing' / [hear]
pettkà 'I will catch [fish]' / [perhaps, tomorrow]
pèwŏchăckhà 'I will fell or hew wood'
p'gachgan 'blood'
p'gachganéek 'bloody' / [foot, kiss, thereby]
p'gachganéeth 'bloody' / [believe, inheritance, wait for; Long Sentences, 2]
p'gachganĕth 'bloody'
p'gachganéwe 'it isn't bloody, it isn't blood' / [blood]
p'gachganitschaneqúaúi 'bloody face'
pgachganò 'he (it) is bleeding'
p'gachganŏ 'blood' / [bloody, cough]
p'gachganohm 'blood' [plus -ohm, appropriate to possessed nouns but a personal prefix is lacking]
p'gachganŏm, p'gáchganom, p'gachganom 'blood' [plus -om; see above] / [drink, feel, his, sweat, trust, wish that]
p'gachganómick 'with his blood' / [buy, he]
p'gachganómik 'in(to) the blood'
p'haga 'outside, outdoors; go out there' (3)

p'hagaàhqu 'go [pl.] out there'
p'hagaatóok 'we will go out' / [go out there]
p'hagáău 'he goes out'
p'hagaáwak 'they go out' / [go out there]
p'hagan '[I will go] out' / [go out there, speak with]
p'haggá 'go out there!'
Phil[ipp], Philip / [fetch, go with, pustules, take]
pióon- 'violin' / [Loan words, play]
piŏnhamà 'you play (the violin)'
[piŏnh]amataù 'we will play (the violin)'
piŏnhamáu 'he plays (the violin)'
[piŏnha]máwak 'they play (the violin)'
-pióon- 'violin' / [Loan words, play]
p'măk '[why] are you [pl.] shooting?'
p'máoséet 'he lives ...' / [poor]
p'máosémick 'where we live'
p'maosétscheek 'those who live' / [wild]
p'máosia 'I live ...' / [poor]
pmaoso ('he lives, to live' ?) / [No Translation (Untranslated "biblical" text)]
p'máŏsŏhááneconau 'he (will) make us live'
p'maosowágan 'life'
pmasewe [? 'lives-not-he' ?] / [No Translation (Untranslated "biblical" text)]
p'mataù 'let's (both) shoot'
p'matŏok 'we will shoot'
pmawoseëtsch 'let him live' / [die, lay down one's life]
p'măwŏsò 'living' (adj.) / [spring, water]
p'máwosòhááp 'he has revived' / [live]
p'mawosóop 'he has lived, he lived'
p'mawosowágan, p'mawosowagan 'life' / [bundle, lay down one's life, love]
p'mèh 'fat' / [bear fat]
pnamhàn '(you must) look (not elsewhere)' / [but, see]
pnàsch 'bottle' / [Loan words]
p'natt'wĕn 'brandy' / [Loan words]
p'naù, p'naù 'look!' / [see (3)]
-p naúwaăp 'I have seen him, I saw him'
pnaúwátaú 'we (both?) will see, let us see'
pnawapanè '(you / they?) have bound (his hands) [behind his back]' / [bind the hands behind the back]
p'năwáú '[do you want to] see [him]?'
pnawáu '[I will] see him'
p'nawè 'look at me' / [see]
pnaweëk 'look [pl.]!' / [see]
p'nawèku, p'nawĕckŭ 'look [pl.] at me' / [see]
pnawòchk 'take a look at (it)' / [mirror, see]
pnăwŏchku 'look [pl.] (into them)' / [see]
pnăwŏchq 'look [pl.] (into them)' / [see]
pnăwù 'look (into it)!' / [see]
pnax- 'flax' / [Loan words]
pnáxak 'anim. pl. or in the flax'?
p'nŏmìs, pnomis 'broom' / [have, Loan words]
pòchkschachaàkq 'block, log'
pòchktschátá 'burning, wood fire, firewood, etc.'
podáha weweën '(did) you blow the horn?'
[podana ?] weweën [see podáha weweën] / [blow a horn]
podawà 'light a fire!' / [fire]
podawàqu 'light [pl.] the fire!' / [fire]
podawátaù 'let's light a fire' / [fire]
podawáu 'he lights a fire' / [fire]
podawáwak 'they light a fire'
pòmájik 'we live here, we are here' / [be (in a place)]
pŏmáŏsénánăù 'we live'
[? pŏmáŏsĕnána]we [perhaps delete -na-?] 'you [pl.] live'
pŏmaosenáwa 'they live'
[? pŏmáŏsĕna]we 'you [pl.] live'
pŏmáŏséŏnăhp 'he lived'
pomáosetip 'he has lived' / [become flesh]
pomáosétscheëk ('those who live') / [No Translation (Untranslated "biblical" text)]
pŏmáoso 'he lives (happy)'
p°máosowágan 'life'
pŏmettŏonhááp 'he has preached'
pŏmi, p°mi 'fat' / [bear fat]
pomissŏak 'they shall run' / [tired; Long Sentences, 3c]

pŏmissóokáăt 'one who goes by foot' / [go]
pommăkè [Del.] 'to bloodlet' / [Delaware]
pommăkèh [Del.] 'to bloodlet' / [Delaware]
pommăwè [Del.] '(must) bloodlet' / [Delaware]
pŏmŏwàhs 'boil, swelling, tumor'
pomsè 'I am going'
pomtohnhamáák 'I have preached to them'
pŏněna 'let go of him, leave him alone' / [leave, let, loose]
pŏněnéhàn 'don't leave me'
popackhammáku '[why] are you [pl.] pounding?'
popackhammótau 'we (two) will pound'
-pŏpackhămmŏwun '(I) have not pounded' / [long, pound]
pŏpăk'hà 'knock!' / [must]
pŏpak'hámmen 'I will knock'
p°queęchnăŏ '(they [it?]) are torn' / [shoe(s)]
póschees 'cat' / [chase out, Loan words]
poschesch 'cat' / [Loan words, sit, under]
potaháso '(it) is cooking, boiling; cooked, boiled (adj.)' / [boil or cook meat]
póten 'butter' / [Loan words, melt]
p'queęchnăŏ [see p°queęchnăŏ]
p'queì 'ashes, punk'
pschuk 'but'(?) / [enjoy, lend, who]
psuck, psuck 'but' / [see, take; No Translation (Untranslated "biblical" text)]
psùk, psuk 'but, only' / [among, divide, friends, have, trust]
psùkqueëk 'but, however; if (?)' / [say]
ptămmawewak 'they don't hear'
ptammowăk '[that] you don't hear' / [that]
ptammówe 'they don't hear' / [stop up]
ptánnowe 'I (can)not hear you' / [loudly, speak]
ptauwăk 'I (want to) hear (it)' / [say]
ptauwenanaù 'grant us a hearing' / [hear]
ptschèssessáchga 'it lies scattered about' / [it, wood]
puckqueüw 'ashes, punk'
pùkqueü 'ashes, punk'
[pummese]hamà 'you [pl.] run'
pummesehanà 'we run'
pummesowàk 'they run'
pummessò 'he runs'
[pumm'tŏhnhaha]mà 'you [pl.] preach'
pumm'tŏhnhahaná 'we preach'
pumm'tŏhnháu 'he preaches'
[pumm'tŏhnh]áwak 'they preach'
[pummtŏn]háu 'he preaches'
[pummtŏn]háwak 'they preach'

quă 'yes' / [hinder, sweep out, wood]
quà 'yes' (?) / [stab]
quáă 'yes' / [up there]
quáăm 'because (?), yes (?)' / [know (second), worthy]
quachŏdam 'I am afraid of it' / [pustules]
-quagà (?) 'sew' / [quick]
-quăk 'we' / [Pronominal affixes]
-quakajaxèh 'fall down at' / [down, foot]
quăme 'yes' / [feel, glad, hear]
quattischò 'tree' / [thin]
-quattschischò [cf. 'tree'?] / [thin]
quáu 'cooper's wood' [= ?] / [tree, wood]
quawagomè 'do you greet?'
quawagómen 'I greet'
quawagomowà 'you [pl.] greet'
quawagómuk 'he greets'
-quechtsche 'alone' / [far, go away]
quenacónau 'he is looking for us' / [seek]
quenacowe [see quenakówe] 'he is not looking for me' / [seek]
quenacowenaù 'he is not looking for us' / [seek]
quenakówe [see quenacówe] 'he isn't looking for you' / [seek]
quenăku 'he is looking for you' / [seek]
quĕnam '[what] are you looking for?' / [seek, what]
quenaù '(if) you [pl.] search for (him)' / [seek, so that]
quenawáwak 'they are looking for (him)' / [seek]
quenawáwe 'I'm not looking for him, you don't seek him' / [seek]
quenawòchkŭ 'you [pl.] are looking for (him)' / [seek]
quetschemwechgáu 'there are many ducks' / ↑

Mahican-English 183

↓ [there is]
quetschemwechgáwe 'there are no ducks'

Rahel 'Rahel, Rachel' / [Names]

-s 'little, small'
sachachkáju 'it is smooth' / [even out, way]
sachcakéta 'enough'
sachgatta 'put on (the water)!'
sàchkiǒsia '(as) I live' / [long, so]
sachkenáu 'bow [to shoot arrows with]'
sǎchněk 'to pray' / [accustomed]
-sackamùck '(it) is biting [me]' / [fleas]
-sackamuckónau '(they) are biting [me]' / [fleas]
-sáckhǎǎn '[I] will strike fire' / [fire]
ságechgàu, sagechgàu [cf. säsěchgàu] 'sometimes' / [rain]
samekschochahan 'you must not run'
-sǎnǎi 'blanket' / [white]
sasamětscháha 'whip him, punish him, give him the rod'
sasam'tscháhajan '[why] are you whipping me?'
sasam'tscháhawa 'he whips them'
sasam'tschahàwak '(you) are punishing them' / [whip]
sasam'tschahè 'he whips me'
sasam'tschahehenà '(you) are punishing us' / [whip]
sasam'tschahòchk 'whip him'
sasam'tschahóquan '[why] does he whip you?'
sasche pachgáju 'he is slow'
săschuak 'with salt' / [fill up]
săsěchgàu, säsechgàu [cf. ságechgàu] 'sometimes' / [weather]
sawehtaù 'let's (both?) swim'
-sch 'little, small'
-schaaktanegǎ 'stoke the fire' / [fire]
schaaktanegàh 'stoke fire' / [burning]
[schaaktane]gataù 'let's stoke the fire'
[schaaktane]gáu 'he will stoke the fire'
schaaktanegàwak 'they stoke it'
schǎǎpnégan 'sewing needle, knitting needle' / [find]
schachagéwe 'just; straight (?)' / [follow]
scháchannaména 'he wept for joy' / [cry]
-schachawachtǎka '[I] ... winnow [it]' / [flax]
Schǎchmàchkek 'to Shamokin' / [go with]
schajáu 'ahead' (?) / [go, go before]
schajáwe ? / [Pronominal affixes]
schapasè 'melt it'
schapasèch 'it (butter) is melting'
[schapa]sèm 'he is melting (it)'
schapaséwe 'it is not melting'
schapasò 'it is melting'
schǎpōsǒměn '(I) melted it'
schǎquonǒmǒōk 'push [pl.] forward, move [pl.] along!'
schaquonomotaù 'let's (both) push'
schǎschǎchěwǒcháwǎk 'they cannot go quickly' / [can, quick]
schaschachkanachcà 'I am being fair (I make right or straight??)' / [self, think]
scháwa 'at once, immediately' / [bring]
schawà, scháwa 'as soon as, at once' / [give]
scháwah 'as soon as, at once, immediately, quick(ly), fast' / [go]
schawǎhn 'as soon as, immediately'
schawajewéěk 'they (will) not be weary' / [run, tired; Long Sentences, 3c]
Schǎwǎpěěm 'soft, tender, weak' / [Names]
-schè 'will' / [make well]
schébohsches [word stricken out] 'little creek'
schechtégan 'ash sifter'
-scheěmchaknégan 'bolt, bar, rail'
schegenaquǎk 'they hate us'
[schegena]quǎku 'they hate us'
schegenáquan 'they hate you'
schegenawaachtěěd, schegenawaachteed 'they hate him'
schegenawǎk (2) 'you [pl.] hate him (them)' / [I]
schegenawechtěěd 'they hate me' / [I]
schegenawojǎku 'you [pl.] hate me (us?)'
schegonè 'empty it out'
[schegonemo]náwa 'they empty [it] out'
schegonemotaù 'let's (both) empty it out' / [let]

-schéha / [chase out]
scheheléuch [Del.] ['beginning to boil'] / [cook, Delaware, hang on]
schekkàssomáchtámak 'fidibus' [see English-Mahican section]
schěmà 'just'(?) / [go]
schèpǎǎchpenès 'apple tree' / [tree]
[schepǎǎchpene]ssàchq[u-_?] 'apple trees' / [tree]
schepachkéwe 'long [of time]' / [long, pound]
schepǎkàjěwè 'it will not last long'
schepòchkqtǎhǎšěahtsch '(that he) be crucified' / [that]
schépochquatahǎǎssétip 'he was crucified'
schepòchquatahaseàn, schepòchquatahásěǎn '(as (since)) you are crucified' / [as]
schépòchquǎtǎhǎséda '(the) crucified one' / [honor]
schepòchquatahaséěd '[that] he has been crucified' / [fault, that]
schepòchquatahasò 'one who is crucified' / [nail]
schepòchquǎtǎhǎsséěn 'he was crucified'
schepòchquǎtǎhǎssétip 'the cross' / [crucify]
-schétanǎ 'warm, by the fire' / [sit, warm]
schétǎnǎwǎ ('by the fire') / [fire, sit]
-schéwa 'tired of' / [sit]
schewǎhndam 'sad, sorrowful'
schewǎhndammen '[why] are you sad?'
schewahndamm'wágan 'sadness, sorrow, grief'
s[c]hewahndo[_] 'what is saddening?'
schéwamannissǒ '(he) is not well'
-schewochsannè 'I am / you are tired'
schéwochsannéwęęk 'they (shall) not be faint' / [run, tired; Long Sentences, 3c]
-schik 'little' / [bee]
schkuschà, schkuscha 'cut (them) small' / [turnips]
schókschǒn 'I will cut (carve) [meat]' / [meat]
sébook 'to the brook, creek' / [come]
séboos 'creek, brook'
sechtanenáu 'he has a headcold'
-sehnpatt- 'silver, money' / [depend, help, Loan w.]
sěkǎnǒmě 'grain, rye, buckwheat' / [mow]
sekkàpamukquàt 'brown, s.th. that is brown'
sekkàpamuksò '(it) is brown' / [horse]
sěněǎnégà 'milk (it)!' / [go]
-senpětt- 'silver, money' / [Loan words]
-sewanà '(my) head hurts (me)' / [headache]
sgǎctái ? / [new, what]
sguscháu 'he is cutting (turnips)'
sguscháwak 'they are cutting (turnips)' ('Shamokin') / [Place names]
('Shekomeko') / [come, Place names]
-sisgomáu 'to spit'
-skǎhǎn 'chopped up, maize'
sǒk'nǎhn 'it's raining'
soognahn 'it's raining' / [lot, many]
soognepongsétscheěk, soognepongs·tscheek 'baptized ones' / [glad, love feast (2)]
sǒǒgnětǎwěen 'don't sprinkle him' \\ wish that
Spgbg '(Josua?) Spangenberg' / [honor, hope,

spommuck, spómmuk, spommuk 'sky; up there' / [be (in a place), fire, take]
spommuka [see spommuck]
sskéwesche 'a little, few'
sta 'fire' / [strike fire]
sta, stà 'not' / [arrows, ashamed, astray, be (in a place), believe, cook, cost, die, down there, ducks, egotistic, fail, feel, find, growth, have, have good conduct, hear, help, house, husband, inside, it, know, lancet, laugh, lazy, leather, like to, long, make, melt, mix, obedient, outside, patch, patient, pointed, pound, proud, quick, reveal, right, run, sacrifice, scarce, see, seek, sharp, sheep, shoe(s), sleep, stop up, take, tear away, that, there is, think, thrive, tired, true, up there, will, wood]
stà gáquai 'nothing' / [inherit]
stǎǎk 'by the fire, at the fire' / [sit]
stàch 'no' / [make]
stak, stà(k) 'not-you' / [have, laugh, right, say]
stàk gaquai 'nothing' / [inside]
stǎn 'not'; 'not-I, not-my' / [arrows, cost (sta n-), delay (sta n-), lancet, pointed, see, shoot, that]
stannenajéwe 'it is not true' / [believe, that]
stǎǔ 'fire' / [take, up there]
stawéu 'there is no fire'
sukquéu 'he vomits, spits' / [sick]
sukquéwak 'they vomit, spit, get sick'
[súsoo (Ettwein, 1788) 'clay' / [earthen pot]
susquachtáwan 'to chew'
-súsque 'get sick (vomit)' / [spit]

tà 'I go' / [over there]
-ta ('when, conjunct') / [as, come, glad, go (went), go with, hang on, noon, peace, read, supper, tear away, think (2); cf. tormented (awǎtah); truly, until, who]
tǎǎptonachna 'we speak'
tǎǎptonahanà 'we speak'
tǎǎtě [see next entry]
tǎǎtě pǎǐnanau 'same' (?) / [be, should, so]
taǎtpajohěnnau 'same' / [be, been]
-tacchǒm 'bread'
tachachpówǎk 'they ride'
tachamǒkku 'give to me (for eating)'
tachanǎn '(should/shall) I place it here?' / [serve, shall]
tachapè '[to where] are you riding?' / [thither, where]
tachapò 'he rides'
tǎchégan, tachégan 'my knife' / [sharp]
tácheu [cf. tachěwe] ['comes-not-it' ?] / [none, peace, until]
tachéwe (2) 'they have not come' / [cook, not, ought]
tachgamǎǎk 'west'
tǎchgětaháu 'he is impatient' / [hobble]
tǎchgǒgǎnǎpě 'hobble' (?) / [have]
tǎchgǒgǎnǎpěn 'hobble' (?)
tachkamà 'you stab'
tachkamǎǎp 'they [it?] pierced him' / [side, stab]
tachktàn, tachktanǒ [both stricken out] [see at doctor]
tachpéha 'I spin'
tachquachackemahàan 'Lord's supper' / [love feast, supper]
tǎchquǎchpehan 'don't stop spinning!'
tachquahágan 'mill' (noun)
tachquahágánick 'to the mill' / [go]
tachquǒch 'bread'
tǎchtǎgāmǒǎhtámuk '(my?) lancet'
[tachtaquépěě]nǎu 'we are having a love feast; [? there is (he has?) a love feast]' / [have]
tachtaquépěěnǒǒk 'we are having a love feast' / [have]
tachtaquépéhenǒǒk 'love feast' / [baptized ones, glad]
tachtaquepéwùn 'we are not having a love feast' / [have]
táchtaquepuágan 'love feast, feast, banquet; Communion (?)'
tachtaquepuak, tachtaquépǔǎk 'at the love feast (banquet)' (4) / [by, glad]
tachtonawápei 'swaddling clothes strap' / [band]
tachwanǎhn 'he loved'

tackanahegà 'you have served'
tackenahamawáãn 'don't serve (him)'
[tackenahama]wanewà 'don't [pl.] serve (him)'
tacquàtschŏwăk 'they are freezing'
taggasèn 'lead [the metal]'
tah, -tah 'heart' / [peace]
tăh 'I go' / [enclosed place, go over there, over there]
tàh [for -k tàh] 'you go' / [thither, where]
táha '(his) heart' / [reveal]
tahaaptonahanà 'we have spoken' / [speak]
taháo '[it is] cold'
tăhăséwe 'it is not cold [of weather]'
tăhasò 'it is cold during the day' / [cold]
tahgetschápei 'waistband' / [band]
tahhkéha 'I will plant it'
tăhn [cf. tăn] 'as' (?) / [make]
-tăhquŏch 'bread' / [white]
tája 'when' / [bring forth (2), child, come]
tájachkàm 'just' / [go, there]
tajăchquăn 'bridge'
tajăhntam 'I would like (need?) to' / [feel, like to, necessary]
tăjatscheechsègo 'quicker, swifter'
-tajom 'son' / [as, bring forth]
tákahtsch wak 'when [+ also?]' / [chopped up, maize]
tákamamukkùp 'pierced' [verb as adj.] / [let, see, side]
tákatsch 'when' / [fetch, wood]
takkamaunà 'we stab' / [we (affixes)]
[takkamau]wa 'you [pl.] stab'
takkamechgà 'stab me, prick me'
tăkquăchtschéwe '[he is (not?)] cold'
takquachtschoàk 'they are cold'
takquachtschóu 'he is cold'
támmachtammen, támmachtámmen 'to feel' / [like to, necessary]
tammatammen 'I feel'
tamměhè 'lend [it] to me'
tăm̆mŏchquèi 'beaver skin' / [soak]
[tampaoⁿs (M-EM) 'seven' / [Numerals]]
[tam-pa-waunsh (J) 'seven' / [Numerals]]
tăn 'not-I' / [afraid]
tăn 'how much' / [cost]
tăn 'so long as, as long as' / [live, long, so]
tăn 'when'
tăn 'where' / [sit]
tăn ănequèchk 'till, until' / [call (shout)]
tăn ănéquéchque, tăn ănéquèchquè 'when, how long, at what time(?)' / [bring forth, long, ready]
tăn ŭdènnè 'whether' / [come]
tanachéme 'I rest' / [peace (2)]
tanachemohao 'I will not make (myself) quiet' / [peace, self]
tanapachgach'muk 'in the barn' / [go]
tanè, tăne 'on, in; then(?)' / [assemble, become flesh, believe, bring forth, cheek, live, true ('in')]
tane 'in'
tanè 'or(?); in(?)' / [Long Sentences, 4]
[tá·nzt (Sw-D) 'ten' / [Numerals]]
tannachéme 'I rest' / [like to, peace]
tănnăchkächºnaù 'we will work' / [tomorrow]
tannahégan '(my) finger' / [chopped off, cut]
tannimsè 'I will go'
tănnŭ̆msèh 'I go'
tăpănăchgáu 'he is ingenious, he can make something'
Tăpănămŭkquăk, Tap[anamuk]quak 'Savior' / [as, love, must, say]
Tap[anemuc]qua [sic or missing final -k?] 'Savior' / [suck]
Táp[anemuc]quàk, Tap[anemuc]quàk, Tapan[emucquak], Tap[anemucquak], Tapánemucquak, Tap[anemuc]quàk 'Savior, Lord, God' / [become flesh, captivate, care for, clean, cost, flow, for, free, heart, honor, live, love feast, peace, reveal, say, side, spring, supper, until]
Tapan[emuc]que 'Savior' / [love, more than, must, woman]
Tapanemukquahquèh 'Savior' / [hate]
Tapanemukquak 'Lord, Savior'
Tapănemukquaquùk '(our) Lord' / [our(s), ↑ peace, the]
Tapăn'măgok 'Savior' / [cost]
tapanmisséěd 'youngest' / [brother]
Tăpănmŭkăăk 'Lord, Savior' / [ask, believe]
Tapan'mukquak, Tapanmukquak 'Savior, Lord' / [cost, know, will; No Translation (Untranslated "biblical" text (3))]
[ta-pau-waasch (J) 'seven' / [Numerals]]
[tapawaasch (H1) 'seven' / [Numerals]]
[ta·pawa·s (Si), tapawas (Sw-D), tapawas (Sw-D) 'seven' / [Numerals]]
tápe 'enough' / [can, now, sound]
tăphăsěnăk 'I will cover (it, my house)' / [house]
tăpŏsě 'I will roast it'
tappăăntămmen 'it belongs to me, it is my own' / [gun]
tăppăchcheschéta (perh. tăppăchchéta) 'when it gets to be evening, toward evening' / [sound; Long Sentences, 4]
tăppăchchéta 'when it gets to be evening, toward evening' / [sound; Long Sentences, 4]
tappanemàu 'it [anim.] is my own' / [hope, one's own]
tappántamen 'it [inan.] is my own' / [one's own]
tappè 'sit down (here)!' / [come]
tăptonachnà 'we speak'
tăptonahanà 'we speak'
taquachnána 'fetch bread!'
taquachquewechtăh 'pronounce it!'
tăquáttèn 'it is frozen' / [freeze]
tăquáttěnă '[they (inan.)?; not we?] are frozen' / [freeze]
taquòch, taquoch 'bread' / [piece]
tassè [see also assè] / [foot, warm]
tasseek / [foot, warm]
tás'wehhn 'I swim'
tattamachtahamăk 'they are cutting wood'
tattamachtáhe 'cut wood!'
tattamachtah'mótau 'we will cut wood'
tăttămăchtáhom 'I cut wood'
tattamachtáhom 'he cuts wood'
tattawamokùn '(he) is buying it'
tăttăwăwě '(I) will not buy it'
-tau 'let us'
[taupowwaus (W) 'seven' / [Numerals]]
tautaù, taútaù, taútaù, taūtaū, tautau '["dingdong," "tom-tom"], bell; sound [verb]' (?) / [can, enough, let, time]
taūtaū, tautau 'bell' / [assemble, must, sounds (verb)]
tautautschenuáů '(the bell) sounds (rings)'
tauwéqua 'open [it]'
[tauwequa]menawà 'you [pl.] have opened'
tauwequamotóok 'we will open'
tauwunà [sg.], tauwuna [pl.] 'open [it]'
tawăm '(I-also-will' ?) / [see]
Tawăneěm 'she is not restrained' / [Names]
t'chŏŏknakkekà '(beyond? + day), day' / [nine]
temmachchaăn 'I am chopping (wood)'
temmachtáhom 'I chopped (it, my finger) off' / [cut, finger]
těmmăhégan 'ax'
[tampawoⁿs (M-AM) 'seven' / [Numerals]]
ténăjappáů, tenăjăppáů 'it is cold in the morning' / [cold, early]
ténăko 'it is cold during the evenings' / [cold, evening]
těněwěsě '(my /your) name is ...' / [call (name)]
teníntăchtăăn '(I am) accustomed to it, (I) can do that, (I am) used to it'
tennăăptonamũkkùn 'he has so spoken with me' / [so, speak]
těnnăngŏmă, tennangoma 'friend' / [good, have, relation, truly, trust]
tennangomăăk 'friends' / [have, trust]
tennangómak '(your) friends' / [live (dwell in), stay, where]
tennàngomanăăk 'for the friends' / [make]
těnněchăckěchěněn, těnněchăkkechěněn 'I lie at (them, your feet)'
ténnema '[what] I get' / [give, what]
tennemaganégan 'arm'
tenněsetăm 'I have heard' / [sweat]
těpesgăwěchnăů ăhănŭckquěch 'it is time to ...' / [plant]
tepiskăwěchnáů 'it is time to ...' / [sound]
tesgawangăk 'he envies me'
tesgawanŏk 'he envies me'
tessanechganachen 'I have remained hard' / [lie (of position)]
thà 'where' / [friend, live (dwell in), stay]
thăăk [for thăăk + k-, or thăă- + k-(you)?] 'where to?' / [thither]
t'hackenahegahanà 'we serve'
t'hácta 'where'
t'hácta ne 'where to' / [ride, thither]
thagótschai hamà 'where do you come from?'
thakŏmhamà 'where do you come from?'
Thomas / [belong]
timmesogáwak 'they cut (corn)'
t'mahégan 'ax' / [seek]
t'măskhămăk 'to mow (grass)' / [time]
tmegahéětsch 'he must not go in' / [go in(to) there]
t'mequachsáu 'to slaughter, to butcher'
t'natamăqu '[why] are you [pl.] laughing?'
tnátamen '[why] are you laughing?'
tóckun [-n tóckun?] 'he tells me, she said to me' / [say]
tŏhnnháijè '[what I] have said' / [know, speak]
[toⁿpawoⁿs (M-?, M-Me) 'seven' / [Numerals]]
-tŏk, -tŏŏk 'let us [inclusive]'
t'pà 'head' / [headache]
t'păăntammen 'it belongs to ...'
tpachquaăn 'beans' / [mix, white]
t'pachquăn 'beans'
tpechnáu 'he falls (is falling) down'
tpenachgápe 'bracelet' / [arm]
tpenachgápean 'bracelets' / [arm]
tpescăwechnăů ăch'năquech 'it is time to ...' / [mow]
t'peskăwěchnăů ăchenăquechk 'it is time to ...' / [hunt]
t'pòchcahăăk 'you ought not to cook' / [come, not, ought]
t'póchcamik 'in the kitchen' / [cook]
tpŏchgà 'in the night, at night' / [sleep]
t'pochgataù 'we will cook'
t'póchgo 'when it is night ...' / [sleep]
t'pochqueěk 'night + on(?)' / [sleep]
tquahogájan 'debt (that which you owe)' / [pay]
tsackěschéschěwà 'they are small, little' / [heart, humble]
tsackěschéssěwa 'they are small, little' / [heart, humble]
-tsch 'will; (possibly third person imperative)' / [accept]
tschachcósak 'white people' (2) / [come, how many]
tschăchgáchu, tschăchgáchu 'thin, slender' / [tree]
tschăchgěschéschěn 'little' / [mountain]
tschachguttăn 'stocking' / [old]
[tschachgutt]anan 'stockings' / [old]
tschachkewesche 'a little, few' / [inside, little]
tschachkŏchkwáu 'the one with the white coat' / [coat, white people]
tschachkŏchkwáwak 'the ones with the white coats' / [coat, white people]
tschachkochquà ? / [short, thin; No Translation (Orig. and Alph.)]
tschachkósak 'white people, white men' / [hard, hinder]
tschachquaăp [Is ăp part of word?] 'short' / [speak, word]
tschachquachaju ? / [short; No Translation (Orig. and Alph.)]
tschachquáchxen '(short or little?) shoe' (2) / [old]
[tschachquachxe]nan '(short or little) shoes' / [old]
tschachquaschéschen 'it is short' / [little]
tschăchquénótei 'sack, bag'
tschachschippajeweěn 'they are not sharp(-pointed), pointed' / [arrows]
-tschachtschap'chaku 'hiccup' (verb)
tschăckěschěsan '(they are) too little, small for me' / [shoe(s)]
-tschămakwat 'it smells' / [stink]
tschamáquat 'it smells' / [good]
-tschàmmakwàt, -tschàmmakwat 'it smells'
tschanèquáu 'face'

tschannéiuwe 'dumb' / [be]
tschanneiuwéwak 'they are dumb' / [be]
tschassè 'warm' (2)
tschasseèk / [warm]
-tschässeen 'warm' / [hand]
tschätschaápnè 'divide [it]'
tschatschaxĕschne '(they are) too little (for me)' / [little, shoe(s)]
tschaxĕschhăk 'little' (adj.) / [book]
tsche, tschè, tschē 'not, don't (be)' / [afraid, be, disobedient, go in(to) there, hit, laugh, lose, make, that]
tschē 'will' (?) / [heal, make well]
tschè ? / [live (dwell in), new]
tschè [imperative?] / [sit, still]
tschē- 'not, don't' / [should]
-tsche '... ones' / [sick, ?until?]
tschĕchhégan 'broom, what sweeps clean' / [clean, sweep out]
tschechtschenuamegè 'letters that are pronounced' / [sound]
tschèchtschis 'bird' / [see]
tschēēchtschis 'bird' / [call, sing]
tschēēg 'don't' / [spin, stop]
tschēēk 'not, don't' / [afraid, go in(to) there, help, hurt oneself ..., proud, serve]
tschēēkhà 'sweep out [the house]!'
tschēēkhammén 'did you sweep it out?'
tschēēkhammóōk 'sweep [pl.] [it] out'
tschēēkhasēwe 'it's not swept out' / [sweep]
tscheekhasò 'it is swept out' / [sweep]
tschēēkpè 'be still [pl.]!' / [be, sit]
tschēēn, tscheen, -tschēēn 'not, don't, must not, no' / [afraid, be, but, chew, color, come, cook, cry, forget, give, go in(to) there, help, hinder, impatient, leave, other ('no'), ought, reveal, serve, spit, sprinkle (ktschēēn), steal, swear, take, thoughtless; Long Sentences, 4; No Translation (Untranslated "biblical" text (2))]
tscheèn 'not' / [alone]
tschēēn awān 'no one'
tschēēn ktackanèn 'nowhere else' / [see]
tscheèn quechtsche 'alone, not alone' / [far, go away]
tscheganachksè 'I (have) stood still' / [stand]
tschegānĕchēn 'I have lain (kept) quiet' / [lie (of position), still]
tschehtschèquaquăsēh 'comb your hair!'
tschēk 'don't' / [loudly, speak]
tschĕkapewaqua 'if you [pl.] don't keep still' / [still, whip]
tschékĕhégan 'broom, what sweeps clean' / [clean, sweep out]
-tschémăquàt, -tschémaquàt 'it smells' / [bad, stink]
tschēn, tschēn- 'don't, not; must not' / [be, blissful, go away, run, sad, should]
tschēnăăpăhān 'you shouldn't bring any water' / [fetch, should]
tschēnăōtik 'someone calling; call (shout), cry out, sound' / [hear]
tschēne 'not, don't be' / [afraid]
tschēnēēk awān 'no one' / [love, more than, must, woman]
tschēn'kanáhan '[if] you do not leave (him)' / [blissful]
tschenuăk, tschenuăăk 'call, cry out, shout, scream; you [pl.] sing, you [pl.] say, they called' / [even more, say, sing, yet]
tschenuáka 'when it sounds [verb] (3), o'clock, hour' / [assemble, five, love feast, must, six]
tschenuáu 'it calls, sounds, rings; it has sounded' / [sing]
tschéscho 'man' (?) / [thin]
tschēwăk 'again' / [come]
-tschi 'will' / [seek]
tschitschachkonanau 'our souls' / [peace, where]
tsch'mahéganis 'ax (little)'
tschŏnáchgätschò ['word'] / [short, speak, word]
tummĕhégan 'ax'
tŭmmeschè, tummeschè 'snuff [it] out, cut [it]; put it out'

tŭmmeschemówun '(I can't) put it out' / [snuff out]
[typaʷysxánkan (Sw-e) 'seventeen' / [Numerals]]
[typaʷúsxínska (Sw-e) 'seventy' / [Numerals]]
[tupouwus (E) 'seven' / [Numerals]]
t'wachk, t'wachk 'spring, fountain' / [cold, flow, side, wholesome]
twegāāk 'come [pl.] in here!'

udăăptónama ['speak' ?] / [No Translation (Orig. and Alph.)]
udàchquènăchăān 'he died, departed (this life)'
udàinimschawàh 'he hits (the) things (by shooting)'
udannămĕnăwăgán 'pleasure, joy, delight'
udennăăptonāhn 'he speaks' / [say]
udennaaptonamawa / [see speak; No Translation (Orig. and Alph.)]
udennăăptonan 'he speaks' / [say; No Translation (Orig.)]
ŭdĕnnè, udennè ['he-that much- (?); whether, if'] / [come, resurrection, take]
udennè méljāzā '(if?) he has been resurrected' / [whether]
udennikuneppēēn 'he turned around, or over'
udéttan, udettàn, ŭdèttan ['then (?); of it (?)'] / [cry, go out there, look at, "Past" tense (3), see (ŭdèttan 'of [it]' ?), think, word ('then he' ?)]
-uk 'to, at; inverse'
ŭkŭttanimmèn 'to touch, (to mix?)'
umàchcamèn (2) 'he finds, to find'
unàchcamáo 'beautiful day' / [today]
unăcotowágàn, unacotowagan 'peace (3), quiet' / [enjoy, feel, fill, who]
ŭnălwágan 'the good'
unáje 'be good!' / [fetch, please]
unèchnahp pāwŏhăănà 'he wanted to free us' / [would]
unèchtanáwa [? 'he does it' ?] / [No Translation (Alph. at Unèchtawāāk)]
unèchtawāāk ? / [make; No Translation (Alph.)]
ŭneĕchtà 'close [it] up, button(?) [it] up; (well-make-it ?)' / [make]
unochtonomowe, unochtonomowe (? 'it helps one' ?) / [No Translation (Untranslated "biblical" text)]
usàijakechnáu [? 'misery-makes-he' ?] / [No Translation (Untranslated "biblical" text)]
uskái 'new' / [old, prosper, stay, years, until; Long Sentences, 3d]
uskájan 'they are new' / [shoe(s)]
uskáju '[it is] new'
úskăkájăŭ 'it is loose'
uske- 'new'
uskégămà '(in the) new' / [house]
uskégān 'new [house]' / [house]
uskepétachgásohn 'a new dress or coat' / [new]
usketschguk 'his eyes' / [before, see]
uskétschuk 'eye'
ŭtăchtănăăp 'he laid down (his life)' / [lay down one's life]
-ŭ taha '(his?) heart' / [reveal]
ŭtăljēēn (? 'they are going' ? ['he is staying' ?]) / [stay, visit]
ytáttawahanăăp 'he bought me [by means of it]' / [buy, he]
utenáwa 'he spoke, he said' / [say]
uténne 'how ...' / [love]
-uto- 'each other'
utschájak 'those from' / [come, from, Shekomeko]
utschatschăăppĕnĕmmànawawà 'they divided it among themselves' / [among]
ŭtsche 'with, for' / [approach, if, sick, therefore]
utschì 'before (from ?)' / [eye, see]
ŭtschi ? / [so(?), so that(?)]
utschitschàchquénăāk 'many souls'
utschōōssĕmà 'fill the pipe!'
uttäinappajuwechnăān 'he has sweated (it, blood)'
ŭttenái 'what he does' / [say]
uwà 'that (the), he' / [call, man, Personal ↑

↓ pronouns, the, write]
uwà- 'he' (?) / [? write]

w-, w'- 'he, his' / [Personal pronouns, Pronominal affixes]
w-...-(a)wa(k) 'their' / [Pronominal affixes]
-wa [verb final implying 'she, her'?; see mpowà and otschemáwa]
waadtschachquétsche 'souls' / [sheep]
waăsnanè 'make it bright' / [light]
wăătsch 'that (= because, why)' / [hear, love, say, swear, why]
wăătschè, wăătsche 'for' / [crucify, sake, wounds]
wăăxeehégan 'hatchet (pickax, hoe)' / [give]
wachawāhn 'flower on trees'
[wachawāh]nàn [plural of above]
wachawāhnschan 'flower[s?]' / [beautiful]
wachawan'schān 'flower'
wachcamāāk ('day') / [yet]
wáchcamàhk, wachcamahk 'day [whether today or any other day]' / [baptized ones, nine]
-wachcamāhk 'day' / [long, whole?]
wáchche ? / [No Translation (Orig. and Alph.)]
wáchĕsă '[his?] uncle' / [come, family]
wăchgămāāk, wachgamāāk ('today, day') / [boil or cook meat, come, year]
wăchgămāk '(to)day' / [cook]
wachgàn 'bone'
wăchīā, wáchīă, wáchia 'my husband' / [house, say, we]
wáchcamàhk, wachkamahk ('today') / [come, have, love feast]
wachkamáo 'day'
wachmùk 'far'
wáchnemick [? 'far'? + ?] / [No Translation (Alph. at Unèchtawāāk)]
wăchnĕmòchahān 'to go far from' / [go away]
wachpāhm 'fourth, quarter' (?) / [take, to]
wachpássei, wachpassei 'her breast, his chest, in the side'
wăchpassei 'in his side, on his side' / [breast, chest, foot, marks]
wăchpĕchquăi 'blister (from working or fire)'
wachquaga 'morning' (?) / [tomorrow]
wachquanechtonajáu 'beard' / [long]
wachtachasèn 'lead [the metal]'
wăchtschăsoăd 'one who is (? thinking of getting?) things' / [covetous, think]
wachtschò 'mountain, hill' / [other]
wachtschòhsch 'little mountain'
wachtschóu 'mountain, hill'
wachtschù 'mountain, hill' / [little]
wăchwăwége 'good' (adj.) / [must, think]
wăga 'that [not present]' / [Pronominal affixes]
wágach kià 'that was thine' / [Pronominal affixes]
wagégan 'fishhook'
wăhnsetschè 'holy' / [God, ghost]
wăhnsettăchkè 'those who believe' / [believe, hate]
wahnsettak [? 'he who believes' ?] / [No Translation (Untranslated "biblical" text)]
wăhnsettakēēk, wahnsettakēēk 'the believing ones, those who believe' / [believe; No Translation (Untranslated "biblical" text)]
wăhnsettakwanēēk 'believers' / [believe, bless, help, inheritance; Long Sentences, 2]
wāh'nssetsche 'holy' / [teach]
wāhs'nanè 'make it bright' / [light]
wāhs'nanégan 'candle, light, brightness' / [be (in a place), see, snuff out]
wāk, wăk, wak 'and, also, again, too; further; any more' [cf. awāāk] / [assemble, be present, become flesh, believe, bless, brother, chopped up, come (10), family, foot (2), gift, go (3), go with (2), hang on, hate, help, here, inheritance, kiss, let, love, love feast, make, make well, marks, mosquitoes, one, peace, read ('further'), see, seize, serve, sweat, the same, thereby, thirsty, tomorrow, use ('any more'), witness, woman, work; Long Sentences (4); No Translation (Orig. at gattosomo; Untranslated "biblical" text)]
wak [untranslated after tákahtsch, perhaps ↑

↓ 'also'?] / [chopped up, maize]
wakégan 'fishhook'
wánamansohááⁿquàck 'they [inan.] can make healthy' / [make well]
wanamansoháánquàk 'that we could become well through (them, inan.)' / [make well, so that, wounds]
wanammana 'painted' [contrast maschéchgŏ] / [color, redden]
wănāpátamąak ? / [pray; No Translation (Orig. and Alph.)]
wanaquéga, wanaquega 'yesterday' / [go in(to) there, laugh, lot, serve]
wănĕ, wăne 'nearly' / [fall]
wánechk 'good (works)' / [patient, work]
wanechk 'beautiful' (?) / [message]
wănĕhk 'beautiful' (?) / [Bible, book, holy]
wănēpáchquàn 'leaf' (plural)
wanépak 'leaf'
wannánnowowááⁿk 'their cheeks' / [on]
wánnăno͞ok 'cheeks' / [on]
wannisséhãákq 'don't [pl.] forget it' / [Long Sentences, 4]
wannisséwe '(I) won't forget (it)' / [become flesh]
wăntèi ? / [horse, one's own]
waˢûnsettammówe 'he is not obedient'
wápachcă 'tomorrow' / [catch fish, perhaps]
wăpăchgà 'tomorrow' / [work]
wăpăchgáătsch, wapachgăătsch 'tomorrow (-will?)' / [come, ready]
wapachgátsch, wăpăchgătsch 'tomorrow (-will?)' / [go, say, sharp, speak, speak with (wăpăchgătsch), we]
wapachgatsh 'tomorrow'
wapachgechĕn 'I am pale'
[wapachgech]náu 'he is pale'
wăpăchkahtsch 'tomorrow' / [early, go]
wăpachkechnàh 'pale, wan'
wăpăchkechnáŭ 'pale face [he is pale]'
wapachpĕnáŭŭs 'mirror' / [see]
wapáju ['it is white'] / [old]
wăpănăăk, wapanăăk 'in (from) the east, (white [of dawn] -in)' / [come, go, rain, wind]
wapassajénăk 'at the breast' / [suck]
wapassăk 'in(to) the side' / [breast, chest, stab]
wăpăssănăi 'white blanket'
wăpassănajàn, wapassanajan '[white] blankets' / [heap]
wapè 'sit [by it]!' / [warm]
wapĕd 'beans, white beans'
wápeen 'chestnut'
wăpētăhquòch 'bread, white bread'
wapóchquanik 'in his side' / [stab]
wapuchquanek 'into his side' / [let, pierced, see]
wapúchquanick 'from his side' / [flow, spring]
wapuchquanik '(in)to his side' / [call (shout), his]
wásaik '(the) light' / [darkness, love, more than]
wasáme 'so (much), so very much' / [lay down one's life, love]
waskáikè 'new' (adj.) / [give]
wăskăikèck tschè '(in the) new' / [live (dwell in), new]
was'nanégan ahachtááⁿk 'candlestick' / [lend]
wássăik '(the) light'
wăstàchquăăm 'tree'
wătĕnăd̆mmèn '[why] are you laughing?'
wătĕnimmàn ['what one takes' ?] / [take, what]
watóchiak 'father' / [believe, our]
wătsch, watsch ('why') / [feel, hit, love, push, say, sneeze]
wátschăik [? 'with' ?] / [hard, power]
wátsche, wătsche, watsche 'why' / [ask, become flesh, come, glad, know, let, lie (of position), push, run after, say, see (at end), sleep, spring, wounds]
wátsche ['because of, about (that)'] / [about that, very]
wătsche 'therefore, that [rel. pronoun], from, why [rel. pronoun]' / [become flesh, crucify, die, fault, flow ('from' ?), ↑

↓ live, Savior, side ('from')]
watschitschàchquajàckq 'souls' / [make, Savior]
wătschonádammen '[why] are you laughing?'
wăttăwămĕn '[do you want to] buy (it)?'
[wattscho]semăhn (?) 'he fills it' / [pipe]
wăŭnăchtanaméschcęk 'joyous' / [baptized ones, glad, love feast]
wăŭnăikĕĕk 'good' (plural) / [obedient]
wăŭnechnáŭ '(it, your heart) is glad'
waunsettămăhk 'they are obedient'
wăŭŏnèstăwápănè 'he was obedient to them'
wawáchánáham 'it's lightning'
wawakŏmmak 'he greets'
wawakŏmquăkquè 'they send their respects' / [greet]
wăwan [see bring] / [pan]
wawanáhntam 'he laughs'
wawanahntamăk 'they laugh'
wawanantammawĕĕk 'they aren't laughing'
wăwănăntammhàn 'don't laugh'
wawanăntammówe 'he isn't laughing'
wawèchtăătschèek 'oldest'
wawèchtăhtschęęk 'oldest'
wăwĕchtan [or -n wăwĕchtan] 'I know' / [come]
wăwechtanăăn 'he lets know'
wăwĕchtáwa '(I) don't know it'
wawĕchtawà '(I) didn't know it'
wăwechtawanáwa 'they don't know it'
wawèchtawanawà 'they didn't know about it'
wawèchtawùn, wăwèchtawùn '(I am) not acquainted with him' / [he, know]
wáweepnatiàkq 'married'
wăwĕhàk (? 'know') / [know; Long Sentences, 1]
wawehataù 'we get to know him' / [will]
wawehato͞ok 'let's get acquainted' / [know]
wawehăwa 'they know'
wawehawewáu 'they don't know'
wáwochcamake, wawochcamake 'daily' / [observe; Long Sentences, 4; No Translation (Untranslated "biblical" text)]
wăwochkamăkè 'daily' / [be, should, so]
wăwonistawăwak '[why] doesn't one (don't they) believe in him?' / [why]
wawonnsittawà 'be obedient to him!'
wawonsettămăhk 'they are obedient'
wawonsittamăk 'they are obedient'
wawonsittawòchk 'be [pl.] obedient to him/them' / [father]
wawunàchtanamè '(it, my heart) is glad'
wawunantammowĕĕk 'you [pl.] aren't laughing'
wawunitschischowàn 'beautiful' (adj.) / [flower]
wawunnsettam, wawunnsettàm 'obedient, he is obedient' / [disobedient]
wawunntŏnháu 'beautiful sermon' / [preach, sermon]
wawûnsittam 'he is obedient'
wawŭnsittamak 'they are obedient'
wawuntà 'are they good?' / [arrows]
wawuntowĕĕn '(they, my arrows) are not good' / [arrows, pointed]
wawutăk 'at last' (?) / [die, last]
-we 'not' [negative ending on verbs] / [ducks, egotistic, fish, forget]
-wechtàh ['say' ?] / [pronounce]
wèchtamawăăn 'he lets know'
wechtamawèh 'tell me (it)!' / [come]
wéchtamen, wechtamèn '[what's] it called?, [how do you] pronounce (it)?' / [call, pronounce]
wechtammănen 'I will say (it)' / [love]
wechtammawèh 'say it to me'
wechtonajà 'beard, beard hair'
wĕchwĕsăju, wechwesáju 'marks, spots' / [see]
wĕchwĕsăjŭwăn 'the spots (on body), marks' / [foot]
wĕĕgtà 'is (it, the meat) ready?' / [boil or cook meat, cook]
weékma, weékma, weekma, weékmă, wĕĕk'ma 'house' / [cover, new]
weĕktschàmmakwàt 'it smells good'
weĕquachm 'house' / [sweep out]

weęshécan [s + h] 'mark, goal, target' / [shoot]
-wĕg- 'like to'
wĕga, wega 'want to, willingly' / [die, like to]
wĕgachtama 'that we (may) taste (it)' / [Long Sentences, 1]
wĕgăchtămmĕn 'it tastes good'
-wĕgăchtámmen, -wĕgăchtámmĕn 'like to eat it'
wegagedchei, wegagedchei 'leather'
wegagĕĕdchei 'leather'
wegagetschè cheija 'leather'
wegampówa 'he doesn't want to die' / [die, like to]
wĕgan, wégan '(it) is sweet, good' / [flow, peace, side, spring]
wége, wegè, wege 'like, like to; readily, willingly' / [be (in a place), go, go around, hear, lie (of position), make, peace, stop up, with, wounds]
-wége 'gladly, like to' / [give, think]
wegocháu 'he likes to go around with (them)' / [be present, go, Indians, like to]
wĕhètĕnăăp 'he has become an offering' / [sacrifice, self]
wĕhetŏăk 'they sacrifice'
wehetowágan 'offering (sacrifice)' / [gift]
wĕjaăs 'meat' / [boil or cook meat, cook]
wĕk 'good' / [smell]
wĕkeed 'into his house'
wékian 'home, house' / [come, glad]
wékmăchmŭk, wĕkmăchmùk, wékmachmuk 'at home' / [house, husband, woman]
wéknèska 'pipe (to be played)'
wékwăchmŏnĕchtà 'I will build a house' / [make]
wekwachmsik 'into the little house' / [call, come, must]
welŏmè 'bunch of grapes, grapes' / [Delaware]
wénajàckq 'for the wives' / [one, woman]
wenajŏma 'his wife' / [come, family, woman]
-wénajoom 'wife' / [house, woman]
wenamansĕĕd 'the sick (one)'
wenamansétsche 'the sick ones, ill persons' / [make well]
wénamánsoak 'they are sick'
-wénamansoh- 'sick' / [feel]
-wenamatà '(it, my head) hurts (me)' / [headache]
wĕnămăttàm 'it hurts me'
wĕnămăttăm 'they hurt' / [hand]
wenamattammòwágan 'pain, ache'
-wenaso͞om [see nwenaso͞om]
wenaso͞os 'old woman' / [woman]
wénes 'his (her) head' / [bow (head), old, white]
wépan 'arrows' / [many]
wéquăăménga 'go into the house!' / [go in(to) there, house] [Delaware word?]
wéquăchmŭk 'into the house' / [go]
wéquamick, wequamick 'to the house, in the room' / [clean, go to, laundry, room, sleep, to, washhouse]
wĕsăchgè (?"thinking or getting' ?) / [covetous, think]
wĕsăkàn 'bitter'
wéschasè [for -n wéschasè] '(I) am afraid'
-wéschasè '(I am / you are) afraid'
wéschasĕĕn [? 'afraid' + ?] / [No Translation (Untranslated "biblical" text)]
wéschăséhàn 'you must not be afraid, timid, fearful'
weschasewe ['he is not afraid'] / [No Translation (Untranslated "biblical" text)]
weschasò, wéschasò, wéschaso 'he is afraid' / [No Translation (Untranslated "biblical" text)]
(n?)weschasoŏpkà 'I am so afraid' / [so]
wéschasowàk 'they are afraid'
-wesowagan- 'name' / [his, sleep]
-wĕta 'go with'
wetáchkana 'brothers' / [go with]
wetáchkanàk 'his brothers' / [go with]
wĕtăhămăkùk 'he helps along with us' / [bless]
wétahamè 'bless (it)!' / [believe, bless, inheritance; Long Sentences, 2]
wĕtahámukquè '[may] (he) bless (it)' / [food]
wetaú 'he is going along' / [go with]
wetáwe 'he is not going along' / [go with]
wétschăwà, wetschawà 'they are going (to- ↑

↓ gether) [to]' / [go with, brother]
wetschawáu '(I am) going along' / [go with]
wetschawawà 'they are going along' / [go with]
[wetscha]wáwe 'I am not going along' / [go with]
wetschechnáäp 'he was with us' / [be present]
wétschechnáta máchääk '[who] is going to supper?' / [go with, supper]
wéwa, wéwa 'his wife' / [as, he, love, man, more than, must, woman]
-wewè 'marry'
weweēn [see podáha weweēn] 'horn'
wiäs 'meat' / [cook]
[wihsus [or wihsiis?] (H) 'his head']
woak [Del.] 'and' / [cook, Delaware (kettle), hang on]
woäk [Mah.] 'and' / [No Translation (Untranslated "biblical" text (2))]
wochcamáwenaak 'in heaven, in the sky' / [hard, power, with]
-wochgamäk 'day' / [long]
wochganépuk 'ashes, hard ashes'
wochkamáo 'day [today or any day]' / [another, other]
wŏchpĕchquēi 'bubble'
wojás, wojäs 'meat' / [piece]
wosochgawà 'I follow'
w(t)-, w'(t)- 'he, his' / [Personal pronouns, Pronominal affixes]
w(t)-...-(a)wa(k) 'their' / [Pronominal affixes]
wtacheganaja 'the knife was his' / [Pronominal affixes]
wtajegana 'it is his' / [Pronominal affixes]
w'[tajeganawà] '(it is) theirs' / [Pronominal affixes]
('Wyoming') / [Place names]

x₁ x [see ch, but Schmick x is ks]
xè 'I say' [sic for 'you say'] / [thank]
xechenà 'go quickly, jump or run quickly' / [quick (2)]
[xechnaha]mà 'you [pl.] jump'
xechnahanà 'we jump'
xechnáu 'he jumps'
[xech]náwak 'they jump'
xénau 'we say' / [thank]
xep'quachtáu 'ashes, hot ashes'
Xmess [Christmess] 'Christmas' / [day, Loan words, nine]
Xr. 'Christian' / [laugh]
xschàchtäü 'it is smoking, it is smoke'
(x)schétanà ('warm, by the fire') / [sit, warm]
(x)schetanà wapè 'sit by the fire!' / [sit, warm]
xschittáwa '[he feels] warm [in his heart]' / [feel]
Xstian 'Christian' / [ask, see (2), speak with, think]

zébǫǫs [see sébǫǫs] 'creek, brook'

With Fig. 2 on p. 7:

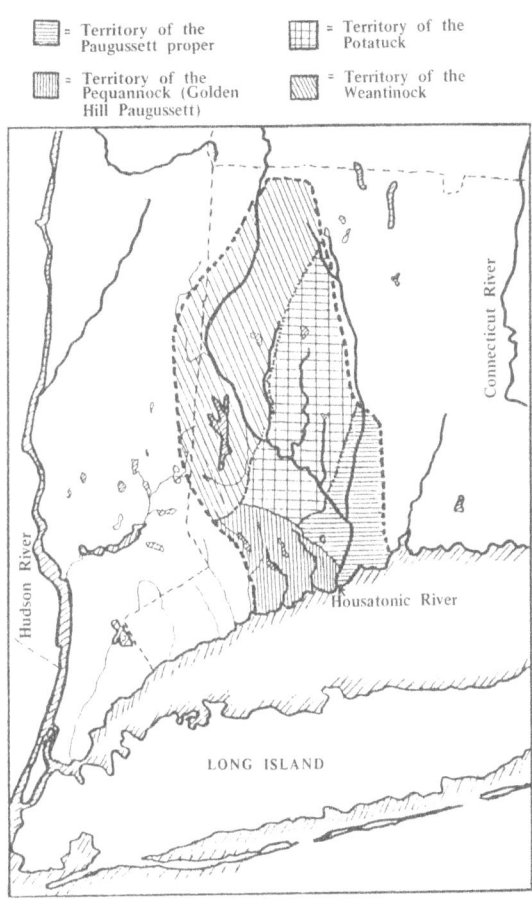

Fig. 4. The four Paugussett tribes and their territories about 1630 A.D. (From the well-researched book by Franz L. Wojciechowski: *The Paugussett Tribes*, Nijmegen, 1985, Catholic University of Nijmegen, Department of Cultural and Social Anthropology, Thomas van Aquinostraat 1, Postbus 9108, 6500 HK Nijmegen, The Netherlands.)

𓏺 𓈖 𓃯 𓄿 𓂧 𓏭𓏭 𓈖 𓏥 𓀀𓁐 𓈇𓏥

Decorative word "Mahican" made up in several obscure languages
28 Montagnais syllabics: *Mahiganiouetch*
28 Cherokee: *Mahikani*
156 Ogham alphabet: *Mahikan*
156 Old Germanic runes: *Mahikansk*
160 Chinese ideographs (Mandarin): *Măhēīk'ĕn-yŭwén;*
    (Cantonese): *Mă hak háng-uĕ mân* = 'Mahican language'
187 Maya hieroglyph: *Ma'ikcaan*
188 Egyptian hieroglyphs: *Re en Mahikan-iu (nation, man-woman, plural, land)* = 'language of Mahican-s'

www.ingramcontent.com/pod-product-compliance
Lightning Source LLC
Chambersburg PA
CBHW080735300426
44114CB00019B/2598